Contents

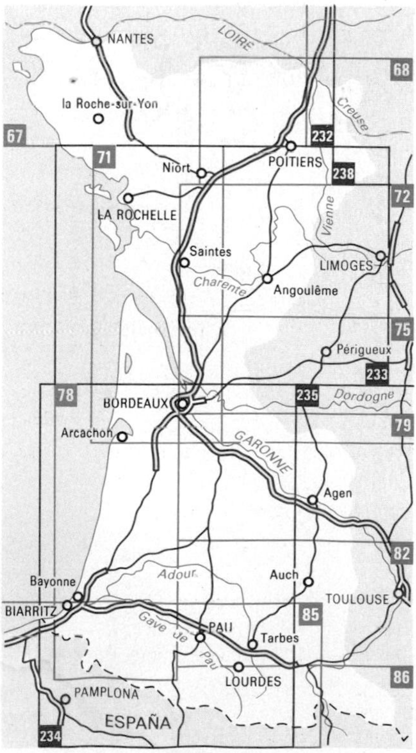

*The **Michelin maps** which accompany this guide are :*

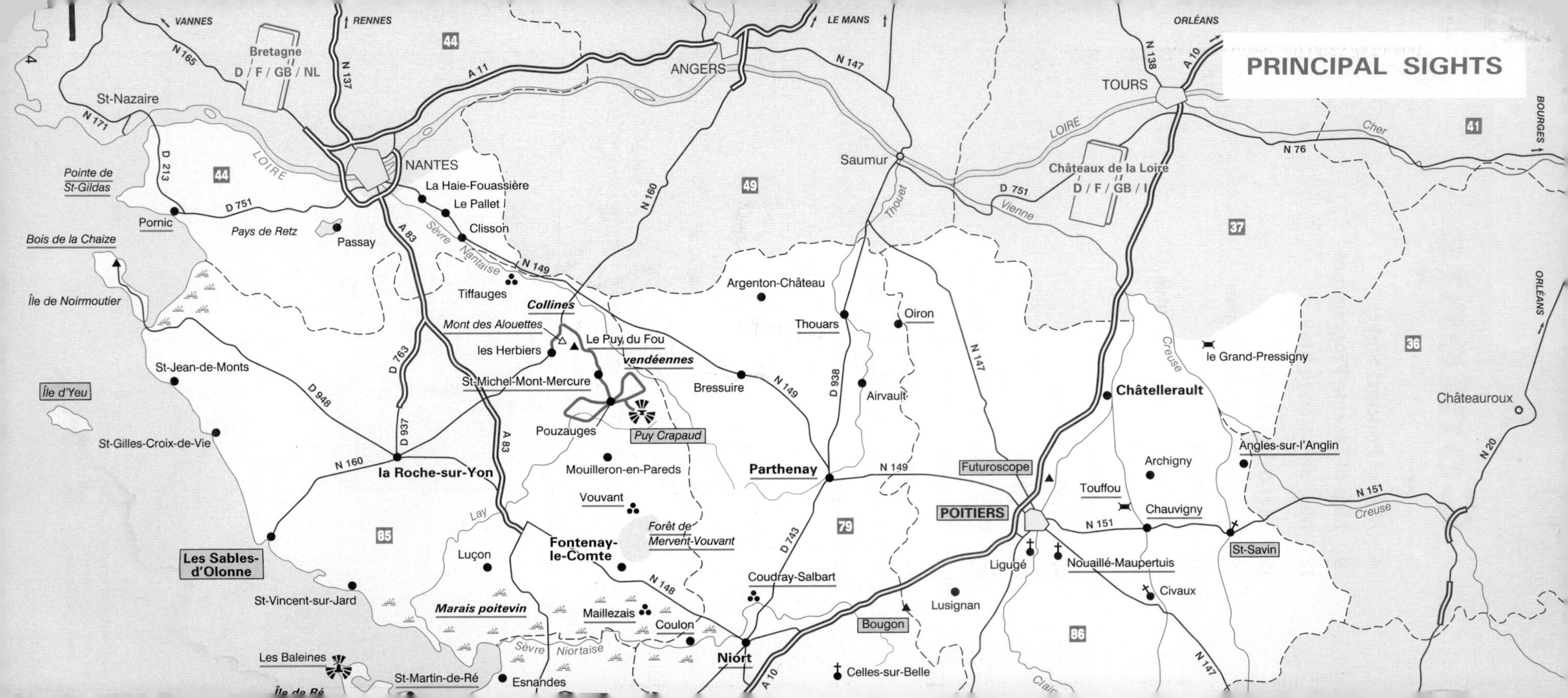

PRINCIPAL SIGHTS
4
VANNES
RENNES
LE MANS
ORLÉANS
BOURGES
Bretagne D / F / GB / NL
Châteaux de la Loire D / F / GB / I
N 165
N 171
N 137
A 11
N 147
N 138
A 10
N 76
D 213
D 751
A 83
N 149
N 160
D 763
D 937
D 948
D 938
D 743
N 148
N 151
N 20
44
49
37
41
36
85
79
86
St-Nazaire
Pointe de St-Gildas
Pornic
Bois de la Chaize
Île de Noirmoutier
Île d'Yeu
Pays de Retz
Passay
NANTES
La Haie-Fouassière
Le Pallet
Clisson
Sèvre Nantaise
LOIRE
ANGERS
Saumur
TOURS
Cher
Vienne
Thouet
Tiffauges
Collines
Mont des Alouettes
Le Puy du Fou
vendéennes
les Herbiers
St-Michel-Mont-Mercure
Pouzauges
Puy Crapaud
Bressuire
Argenton-Château
Thouars
Oiron
Airvault
Parthenay
St-Jean-de-Monts
St-Gilles-Croix-de-Vie
la Roche-sur-Yon
Mouilleron-en-Pareds
Vouvant
Forêt de Mervent-Vouvant
Fontenay-le-Comte
Lay
Luçon
Les Sables-d'Olonne
St-Vincent-sur-Jard
Marais poitevin
Maillezais
Coulon
Sèvre Niortaise
Niort
Coudray-Salbart
Les Baleines
Île de Ré
St-Martin-de-Ré
Esnandes
Bougon
Lusignan
Celles-sur-Belle
Futuroscope
POITIERS
Ligugé
Nouaillé-Maupertuis
Civaux
Clain
Châtellerault
Creuse
le Grand-Pressigny
Archigny
Touffou
Chauvigny
St-Savin
Angles-sur-l'Anglin
Châteauroux

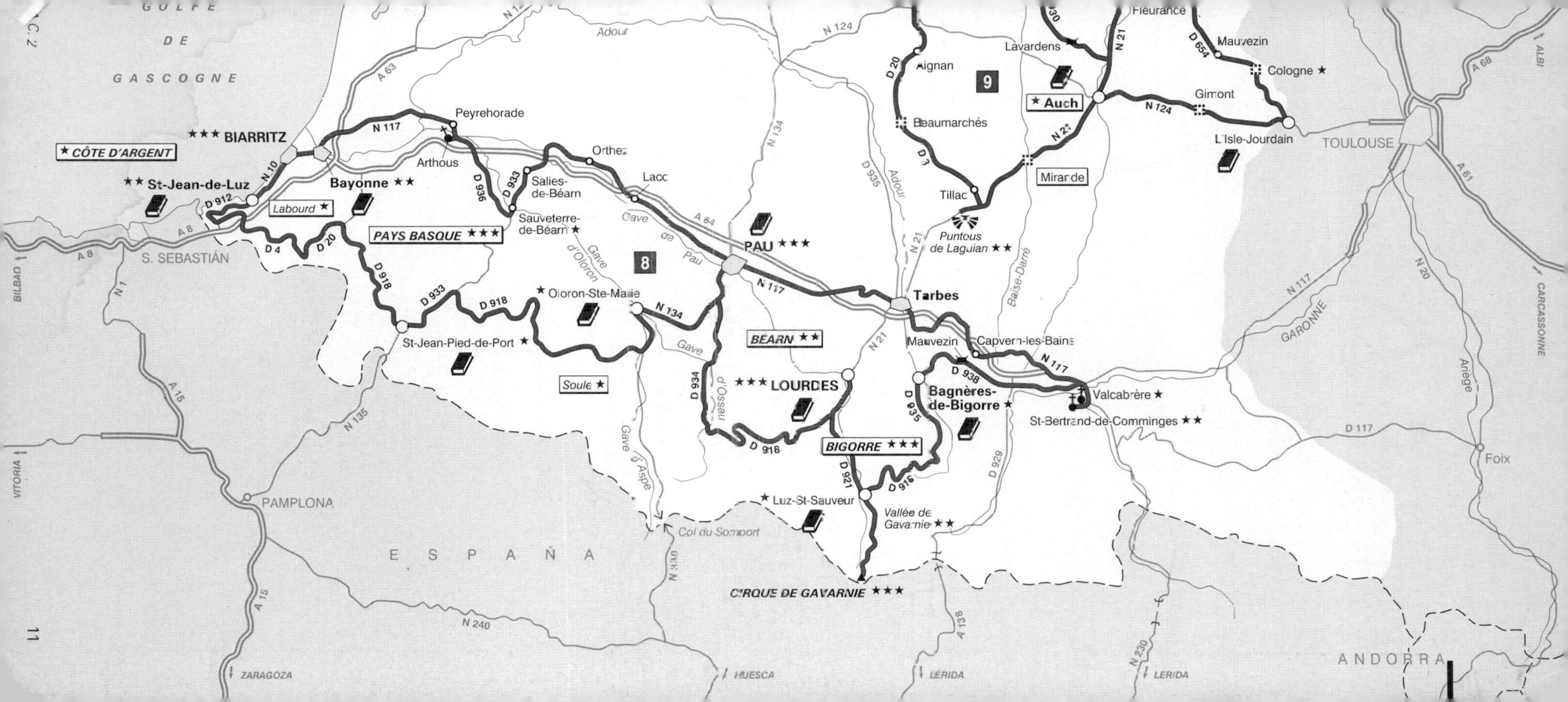
GOLFE DE GASCOGNE
★ CÔTE D'ARGENT
★★★ BIARRITZ
★★ St-Jean-de-Luz
Bayonne ★★
Labourd ★
PAYS BASQUE ★★★
Peyrehorade
Arthous
Orthez
Salies-de-Béarn
Sauveterre-de-Béarn ★
Lacq
PAU ★★★
Tarbes
Oloron-Ste-Marie
St-Jean-Pied-de-Port ★
Soule ★
BÉARN ★★
★★★ LOURDES
BIGORRE ★★★
Bagnères-de-Bigorre ★
Mauvezin
Capvern-les-Bains
Valcabrère ★
St-Bertrand-de-Comminges ★★
Luz-St-Sauveur ★
Vallée de Gavarnie ★★
CIRQUE DE GAVARNIE ★★★
Col du Somport
Puntous de Laguian ★★
Tillac
Mirande
Beaumarchés
Aignan
Lavardens
★ Auch
Fleurance
Mauvezin
Cologne ★
Gimont
L'Isle-Jourdain
TOULOUSE
Foix
Ariège
GARONNE
Adour
Gave de Pau
Gave d'Oloron
Gave d'Ossau
Gave d'Aspe
Baïse-Darré
ESPAÑA
ANDORRA
S. SEBASTIÁN
PAMPLONA
BILBAO
VITORIA
ZARAGOZA
HUESCA
LÉRIDA
ALBI
CARCASSONNE
A 8
A 15
A 63
A 64
A 61
A 68
A 138
N 1
N 10
N 117
N 124
N 134
N 135
N 21
N 20
N 240
N 330
N 230
D 912
D 4
D 20
D 918
D 933
D 936
D 934
D 921
D 916
D 935
D 938
D 929
D 117
D 654
D 3
8
9
A.C. 2

PLACES TO STAY

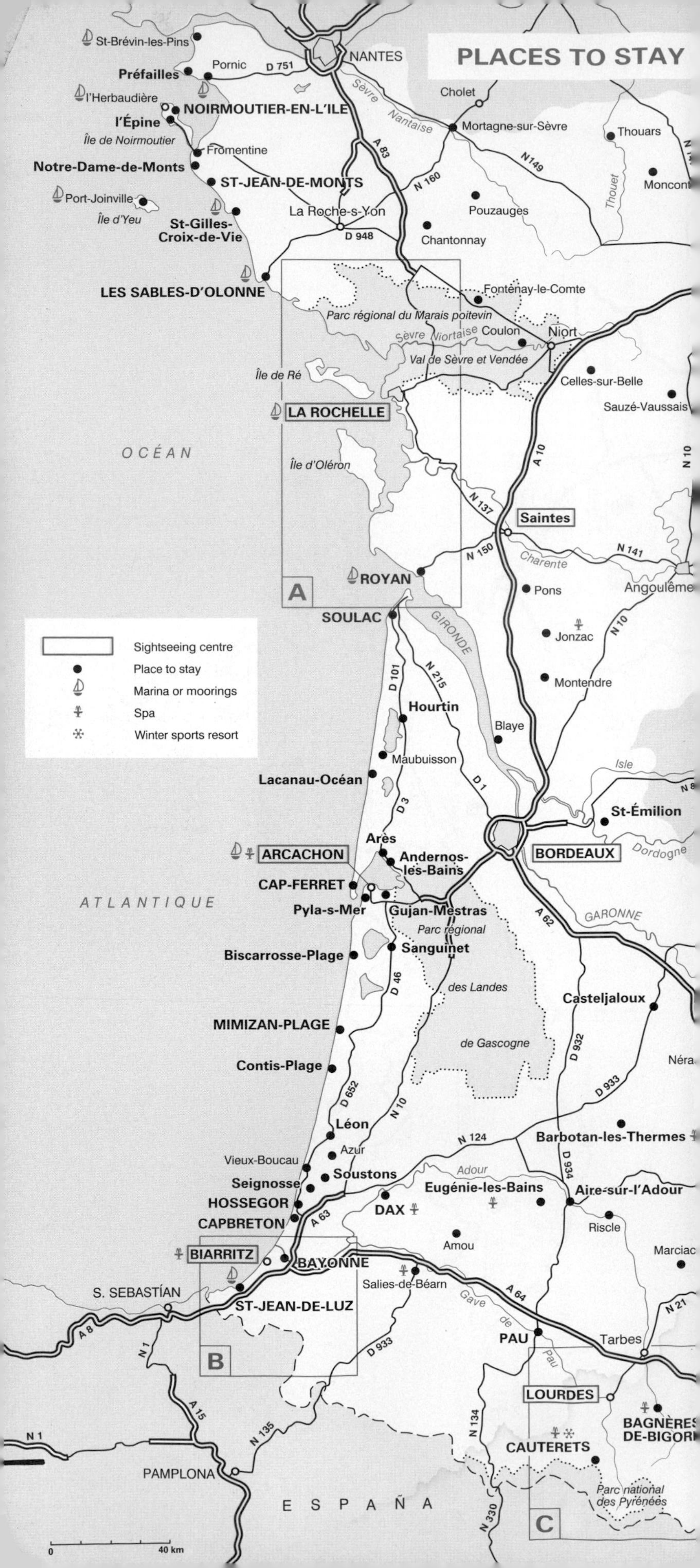

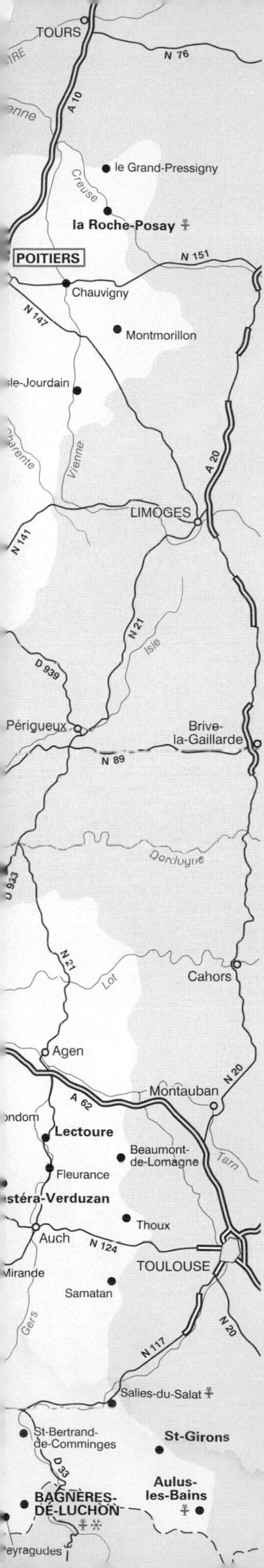
TOURS
N 76
A 10
Creuse
le Grand-Pressigny
la Roche-Posay
POITIERS
N 151
Chauvigny
N 147
Montmorillon
Vienne
LIMOGES
A 20
N 141
N 21
Isle
D 939
Périgueux
Brive-la-Gaillarde
N 89
Dordogne
D 933
N 21
Lot
Cahors
Agen
N 20
Montauban
A 62
Lectoure
Beaumont-de-Lomagne
Tarn
Fleurance
Thoux
Auch
N 124
TOULOUSE
Mirande
Samatan
Gers
N 117
N 20
Salies-du-Salat
St-Bertrand-de-Comminges
St-Girons
D 33
BAGNÈRES-DE-LUCHON
Aulus-les-Bains

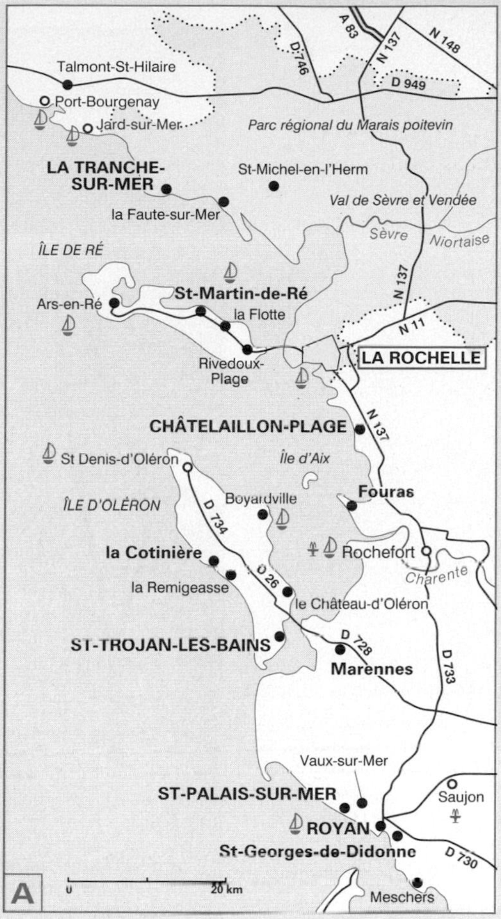
A 83
N 137
N 148
D 746
D 949
Talmont-St-Hilaire
Port-Bourgenay
Jard-sur-Mer
Parc régional du Marais poitevin
LA TRANCHE-SUR-MER
St-Michel-en-l'Herm
la Faute-sur-Mer
Val de Sèvre et Vendée
Sèvre
Niortaise
ÎLE DE RÉ
St-Martin-de-Ré
Ars-en-Ré
la Flotte
N 137
N 11
Rivedoux-Plage
LA ROCHELLE
CHÂTELAILLON-PLAGE
N 137
St Denis-d'Oléron
Île d'Aix
ÎLE D'OLÉRON
Boyardville
Fouras
D 734
la Cotinière
Rochefort
Charente
la Remigeasse
D 26
le Château-d'Oléron
ST-TROJAN-LES-BAINS
D 728
Marennes
D 733
Vaux-sur-Mer
ST-PALAIS-SUR-MER
Saujon
ROYAN
St-Georges-de-Didonne
D 730
0
20 km
Meschers
A

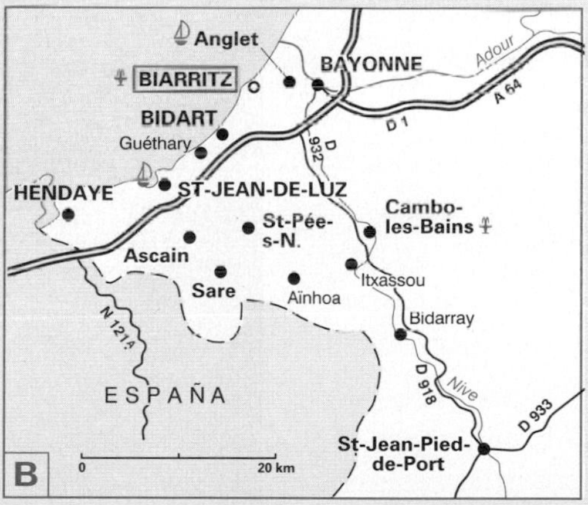
Anglet
BAYONNE
Adour
BIARRITZ
A 64
BIDART
D 932
D 1
Guéthary
HENDAYE
ST-JEAN-DE-LUZ
Cambo-les-Bains
St-Pée-s-N.
Ascain
Sare
Aïnhoa
Itxassou
Bidarray
N 121 A
D 918
Nive
ESPAÑA
D 933
St-Jean-Pied-de-Port
0
20 km
B

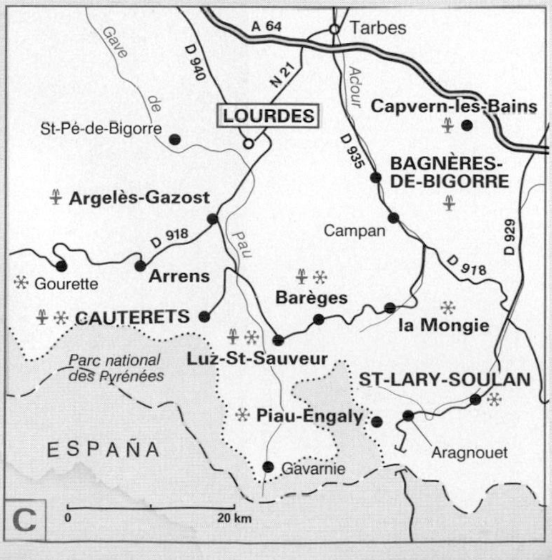
A 64
Tarbes
Gave
de
D 940
N 21
Adour
Capvern-les-Bains
LOURDES
St-Pé-de-Bigorre
D 935
BAGNÈRES-DE-BIGORRE
Argelès-Gazost
D 929
D 918
Pau
Campan
D 918
Gourette
Arrens
Barèges
CAUTERETS
la Mongie
Parc national des Pyrénées
Luz-St-Sauveur
ST-LARY-SOULAN
Piau-Engaly
ESPAÑA
Aragnouet
Gavarnie
0
20 km
C

The Gavarnie Cirque.

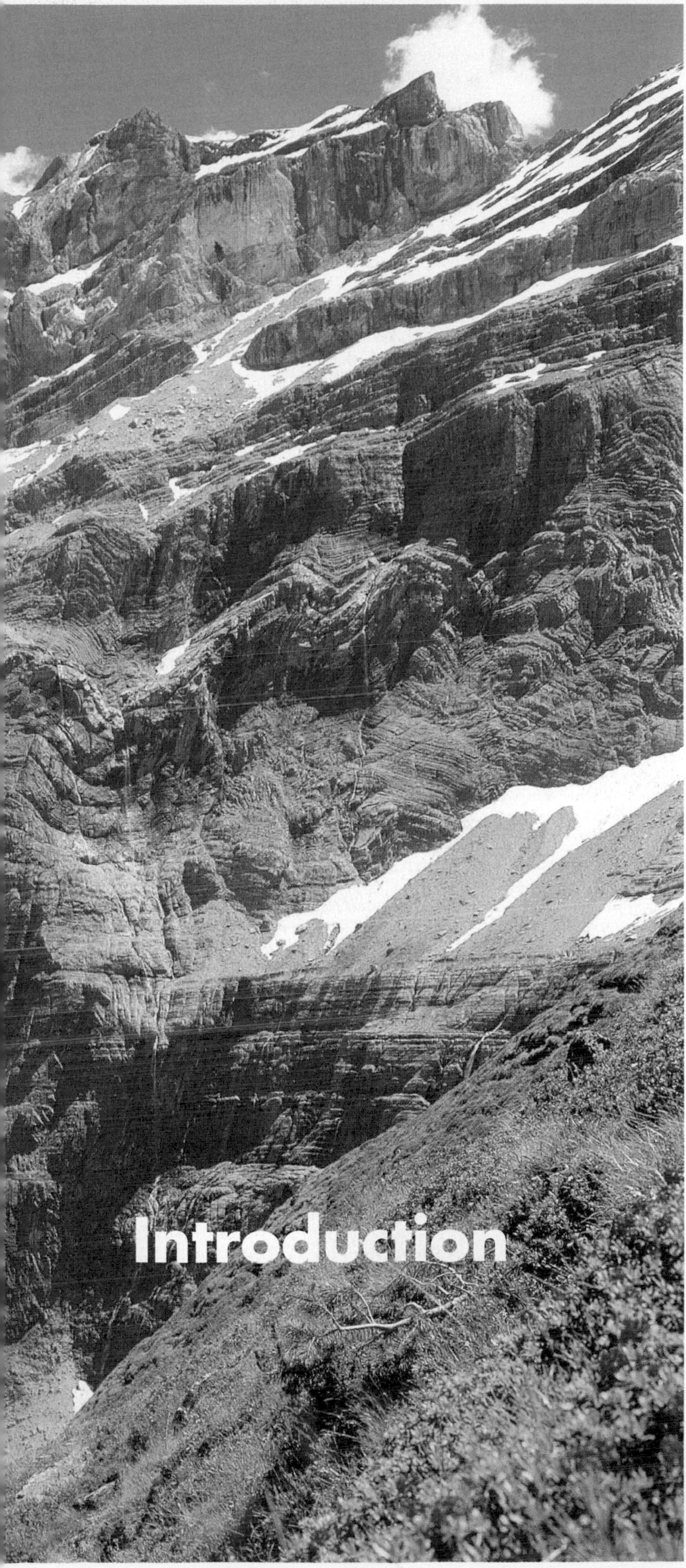

Introduction

J. Jolfre/IMAGES PHOTOTÈQUE

DESCRIPTION OF THE REGION

This guide describes the regions, bordering the Atlantic Coast, which lie between the estuary of the River Loire, to the north, and the barrier of the Pyrenees to the south.

POITOU

This large and ancient province centred on the town of Poitiers incorporates the Pays de Retz, Vendée and the Marais Poitevin (the Poitou marshlands).

The plain – The limestone plateau between the ancient massifs of the **Vendée** (which are the southern extremity of the Armorican peninsula on which Brittany sits) and Limousin (the region east of Angoulême) describes a crescent stretching from Loudun to Luçon. Almost denuded of trees and gashed with deep valleys, the plain seems to roll away to infinity, its succession of fields, meadows and moors scarcely interrupted by the occasional village.
Certain nuances however are discernible : in the north the plain is actually part of Touraine (the region around Tours); from Thouars to Châtellerault there are outcrops of local chalk, carpeted with thin patches of cultivation and moorland cropped by sheep. Here and there deposits of sand occur, and fields of asparagus can be seen in the middle of pinewoods. On the exposed hillsides bordering the Thouet and Vienne rivers, the scattered wine-growers' houses are built of tufa (a hard crystalline chalk with a high mica content). The areas around Chauvigny and Montmorillon (on the Poitou borders), composed of sands and clay, were once a region of infertile heaths or **"brandes".** In certain areas this heathland still subsists, supporting flocks of sheep and goats (the goat's cheese of Chauvigny is well known). In other places, where the heath has been cleared, Charollais or Limousin bullocks are raised. Flocks of *"pirons"* (a variety of goose raised for its skin and *duvet* or down) wander near the farms. West of Clain, continuing as far as Melle and St-Maixent, the Jurassic limestone, lacerated by valleys, has decomposed on the surface into what is locally called **"terre de groie"** (a compound soil part clay, part gravel, part lime, of proverbial fertility – especially for cereals and fodder plants such as clover and alfalfa).

Le Bocage – The areas of the Vendée and the **Gâtine** ("wasteland") de Parthenay, south and west of the Thouet River, have many features in common. This is the region known as *le bocage* – an empire of lush meadows bordered by hedgerows of hawthorn or broom, with sunken lanes leading to smallholdings and farms half-hidden in leafy copses. The breeding of cattle fattened for beef takes pride of place in this patchwork of small fields where the speckled brown Parthenay bullocks graze. The area is dotted with apple orchards and the occasional field of fodder plants grown to feed the cattle. A chain of low, rounded hills forms the backbone of this productive agricultural area, and these are known as *Les Collines Vendéennes* (the Hills of the Vendée).

Marshlands and coast – The marsh (Marais) area extends from the schists of the **Pays de Retz** to the limestone cliffs of the **Aunis** – an ancient region centered on La Rochelle. Between these cliffs, which mark the limit of the prehistoric Bay of Biscay (or Golfe de Gascogne as it is known in France), and the sea, salt-marshes transformed into oyster farms glitter in the sun, sheep and cattle graze in the water-meadows, early fruit and vegetables ripen on the alluvial soil and wild duck paddle the canals beneath over-hanging hedgerows alive with smaller birds. The marshland, formed from debris accumulated by rivers and ancient ocean currents, lies sheltered behind the coastal dunes; rocky islets from an earlier epoch thrust through here and there, and that ancient coastline defines the area's inner limit. From north to south the route passes successively through the Breton-Vendée marshland, which includes the marshes of Monts, the marshes of Olonne and of Talmont and the famous **Marais Poitevin,** the Poitou marshlands.
Huge beaches of fine sand lie along the foot of the dunes and on the offshore bars; between Noirmoutier and the mainland, on either side of the causeway known as the Passage du Gois, enormous stretches of mud-flat are exposed at low tide. Noirmoutier itself and the more southerly Ile d'Yeu (isle of Yeu) provide yet more contrast : the one flat, peaceful and gentle, the other rocky and savage on its western coast.

Port du Bec, Vendée.

CHARENTES

The region known as the Charentes comprises the two *départements* of Charente and Charente-Maritime, separated by the green and placid valley of the River Charente, which themselves embrace the ancient provinces of **Angoumois** (the Angoulême region), **Aunis** *(see above)* and **Saintonge** (the region around Saintes).
Charente itself, abutting the foothills of the Massif Central, divides into four natural geographic areas : to the west the wine country of Cognac, at the centre the cereal-growing Angoumois, in the northeast the Confolentais with its plateaux, and to the south the Montmorélien, a hilly landscape of mixed farming.
Charente-Maritime, facing the Atlantic, presents a coastline of rocks and dunes and sandy beaches, with a rural interior of forests and plains.

Vineyards – The heart of the Charentes beats in the town of Cognac, the capital of that chalky **"champagne"** area (the soil is similar to that in the Champagne region, east of Paris) bordering the south bank of the river, which nourishes the fruit from which the world-famous spirit bearing the name of the town is distilled.

The Plain – The limestone plateau which extends from Angoulême to La Rochelle provides a slightly monotonous landscape, only rarely cut by valleys (such as that of the Boutonne), dotted with small towns and an occasional whitewashed hamlet. As in Poitou, the Jurassic bedrock is cloaked with a reddish *terre de groie (see above)* or a fertile alluvium on which cornfields take second place to "artificial" meadows of clover and alfalfa or fields of sugar-beet grown as fodder.

Coast – The Charentais coast is slightly unusual because, especially towards its centre, alluvial deposits from the Charente and the Seudre rivers have combined with marine currents to form an area of marshland not unlike that in Poitou. Most of this swampy land has been either reclaimed as **polders** (low-lying lands protected by dykes) on which crops are grown, or transformed – especially near Marennes – into shallow basins in which mussels and oysters are farmed. The distance the tide goes out varies from 2 to 5km – 1 to 3 miles.
Not far offshore, the low-lying and sandy islands of Oléron and Ré, scattered with pretty white houses, define the outer limit of an inner sea – the **Mer de Pertuis,** so-called because the only way its waters can reach the open sea is via one or other of the straits *(pertuis)* dividing these isles from the mainland.

BORDELAIS

The region known as Le Bordelais, at the heart of the ancient province of **Guyenne** (Aquitaine), centres on the confluence of the Garonne and Dordogne rivers. This transitional area between the limestone plains of Charentes to the north and the vast sandy expanse of the Landes to the south is drained by the Garonne and its tributaries towards the zone of subsidence around the estuary.
Agriculture here is dominated by the cultivation of vines.

Gironde estuary – The Gironde is the name given to the great estuarial stretch of water lying between the Garonne-Dordogne convergence and the sea. It is a modest reminder of the marine reaches which covered the Aquitaine basin long ago in the Tertiary era.
The northern bank of the estuary is bordered by limestone hills known as the Côtes de Bourg and Côtes de Blaye. On the south bank, where the land on the whole is lower, similar limestone formations have been eroded and then covered by gravels, producing the topsoil in which the famous vines of the Médoc flourish.
Covering the limestone bedrock of the Gironde are deposits washed down by the two great rivers; these deposits, stirred by the action of the tides, have determined the formation of marshes, which are separated from the running water by an alluvial belt, the **"palus".**
Some of the marshland has been transformed, in the Dutch manner, into polders *(see above)* where meadows now lie; the rest remains the province of hunters and waterfowl. Artichokes are grown on the *palus,* and certain vines which produce a "Palus Wine".
Over the centuries the movement of the water has created a number of elongated islands as well as sandbanks which are revealed at low tide.

Médoc – This world-famous wine-producing area is divided into three separate zones: the region of viticulture proper, a zone of coastal forest, and the *palus (see above)* which punctuates the limestone bluffs of St-Estèphe and Pauillac. Fine red wines come from the first zone : north of St-Seurin-de-Cadourne these are produced mainly by local cooperatives and sold under the simple overall description of "Médoc"; to the south, from St-Seurin to Blanquefort, lies the district meriting the more distinguished "Haut-Médoc" appellation.

LANDES

The word *Landes* (moors) still conjures up a vision of the more desolate aspect of this part of the coast which existed prior to the 19C, when a remarkable project of arboreal husbandry transformed the area into a huge pine forest.

Coast and dunes – The Landes sit on an enormous plain, roughly triangular in shape, covering an area of 14 000km^2 – 5 400 sq miles. The side of the triangle runs down the 230km – 143 miles of coast from the Gironde estuary to the mouth of the Adour, and turns eastwards from the two points to meet at the triangle's apex 100km – 62 miles inland.
This ruler-straight shoreline, known as the **Côte d'Argent** (Silver Coast), is essentially one vast beach on which the sea deposits sand at an annual rate of 15 to 18m^3 per metre of coast – 20 to 24 cu yds per yard of coast. The sand – especially in those reaches of the strand only reached by the highest equinoctial tides – is then dried and blown inland by the west wind, where it accumulates in dunes. Until the last century these dunes then moved away from the sea at a speed varying between 10 and 27 metres – 32 and 88 feet per year. Today, fixed in position by the plantation of shrubs, grasses and forest trees, the dunes form a continuous but static coastal belt 5km – 3 miles wide. The strip is the longest – and highest – series of dunes in Europe.

Lakes, lagoons and the plain – Most of the watercourses in the region find themselves blocked by the dune barrier, the one exception being the Leyre (known also as the Eyre in its lower reaches) which finds its way directly to the sea via Arcachon Lagoon. Elsewhere the streams have formed lakes, the surfaces of which are 15 to 18m – 50 to 60ft above sea level. Most of these lakes intercommunicate; their waters force a passage through to the ocean with difficulty, via turbulent "currents" popular with water-sports enthusiasts; the Huchet and Contis Currents are typical examples.

The lakes and currents are well stocked with fish (trout, tench, carp, eel etc) but the huge areas of water involved make these coastal lakes and lagoons particularly suitable for the use of large-scale boating equipment (for instance at Bombannes, *qv*).
Sands distributed over the inner areas of the Landes originally formed part of material gouged from the Pyrenees by Quaternary era glaciers; they exist now as a layer of brown sandstone, no more than 50cm – 20in thick, known as the **alios.** This bed inhibits the percolation of water and blocks the extension of roots, and this, combined with the poor drainage of the plains because of their negligible slopes, adds to the dampness of the region and the sterility of its soils. Until the middle of the 19C this inner zone was no more than an unhealthy stretch of moorland, transformed into a swamp when the rains came, and supporting only a scanty shepherd population which went about on stilts. Even the sheep were raised more for their manure than for their meat or wool.

Wayward river – Over the centuries the course of the **River Adour** and its outlet to the sea has been altered by the region's shifting sands. Documents reveal that in AD 907 the river left Capbreton to carve a route to the sea via Vieux-Boucau-Port-d'Albret; in 1164 it again channelled a new path, this time near Bayonne, but later returned to Capbreton. A terrible storm in the 14C blocked the river's way and so it once again flowed to Port-d'Albret. Meanwhile, the port at Bayonne was being engulfed by sand. In 1569 Charles IX insisted that the river should be given a fixed estuary, which saved the harbour at Bayonne : nine years later a channel leading through 2km – $1\frac{1}{4}$ miles of dunes beyond Bayonne was opened, and the port at Boucau-Neuf was created.

Consolidation of the dunes – As early as the Middle Ages it was known that "mobile" sand dunes could be fixed by the use of maritime pines or plants with spreading roots. A number of experiments were made in the Landes but it was **Nicolas Brémontier** (1738-1809), an engineer from the Roads and Bridges Department, who perfected the process and started the gigantic task here in 1788. First he constructed a dyke designed to check the movement of the sand at its starting point, then, about 70m – 230ft from the high-water mark, he planted a palisade of stakes against which the sand could pile up. Adding to the height of the palisade as the accumulated sand rose higher, he formed eventually an artificial "coastal dune" 10 to 12m – 33 to 39ft high, which acted as a barrier. He fixed the surface sand by sowing **marram grass,** a variety of grass with a thick network of rapidly spreading roots. He then turned his attention to the problem of the inland dunes.
Brémontier mixed the seeds of maritime pines with gorse and broom seeds, sowing them beneath brushwood which temporarily held back the sand. After four years the broom had grown into bushes nearly 2.5m – 7ft high. These sheltered the slower-growing pines, which eventually outgrew the bushes, and, as they died and rotted, provided fertilizer for the young trees. By 1867 the work was almost complete : 3 000ha – 7 500 acres of coastal dunes were carpeted with marram grass and 80 000ha – 198 000 acres of inland dunes were planted with pine trees.

Cleaning up the interior – At the beginning of the 19C the inner part of the Landes area was still a fever-swamp unfit for cultivation; it was badly drained and resisted all attempts to establish an agricultural presence. Under the Second Empire, however, an engineer named **Chambrelent** found the answer : he systematically broke up the unfertile layer of *alios (see above)* and then drew up a scheme of drainage, clearance and re-afforestation. The results justified the large-scale planting of maritime pines, cork-oaks and ilex trees : the Landes *département* soon became one of the richest in France as the many products from pine trees brought large returns (see under Agriculture, *qv*).

The forest under threat – For maritime pines the greatest danger, which in a dry climate can never be entirely eliminated, is fire, especially when allied with wind. Today the pine forest covers nearly a million hectares - 2 350 000 acres in the Landes, and to preserve it a special corps of forest firefighters has been created. Numerous observation posts linked by telephone and radio ensure the rapid detection of an outbreak of fire. Air assistance can be called up. Water hydrants are in place, and everything possible has been done to facilitate the firefighters' access in all weathers and with the least delay. To establish wider rides and fire-breaks, and to encourage the local population to remain, the range of agricultural activity has been extended. Commercial developments, access for traffic and especially camping are, however, strictly controlled.

Parc Naturel Régional des Landes de Gascogne

A **Regional Park** differs from a National Park both in concept and in kind as it is a populated area selected for development in three separate but related fields : the improvement of the local economy (encouragement of traditional crafts, expansion of high-quality tourism); the maintenance of the national heritage and local customs (museums, architecture etc); the introduction of the pleasures of nature and the countryside to visitors here.
Regional Parks are administered by organizations whose members are drawn from elected representatives; a charter drawn up with the approval of the local people defines the aims and limits of the project in each region.
The **Landes of Gascony Regional Park** (Parc Naturel Régional des Landes de Gascogne), which was established in 1970, encompasses 290 000ha – over 700 000 acres in the heart of the Gascon forest massif. It extends from the eastern extremity of Arcachon Lagoon, via Val d'Eyre to the valleys of the Grande Leyre and Petite Leyre in the south (fishing, canoeing), and the woodland zones of the Greater Leyre (footpaths and bridle-paths). A 330km – 205 mile circuit enables cyclists to explore the entire park; the roads, peaceful and with very little traffic, offer many stopping places and shelters.
To encourage environmental awareness and the appreciation of wildlife, various museums, nature reserves and study centres have been established in the Park : the Écomusée de la Grande Lande (at Marquèze, Luxey and Moustey), Le Teich bird sanctuary...

The typical Landes house, to be found throughout the Park, is a charming building: it is usually low-built, with no upper storey but an attic with a small dormer window under a tiled roof; the roughcast-covered walls are painted in pastel colours; a wide gable, supported by wooden beams, shelters the façade and the ground-floor *estandad* (veranda). Most stand in a clearing, surrounded by a kitchen garden and a maize patch.

AGENAIS

Agenais is a transitional region lying between the southern part of Périgord, Bas-Quercy (Lower Quercy, to the east) and the Landes. This fertile area is lent a certain unity by the valley of the River Garonne.

In the damp northern sector herds of dairy-cows graze in the pastures covering the clays; further east, pinewoods and plantations of oak and chestnut appear. In the area around Fumel, on the River Lot, a number of small metallurgical works exploit the local sands rich in iron ore.

Pays des Serres – This area stretches as far as the southern part of the Lot *département.* Abandoning the generalized agriculture of Quercy, the farmers here in "greenhouse country" tend to specialize. On the muddier plateaux of Tournon-d'Agenais wheat is the most important crop; the hillsides are used for the cultivation of vines.

Lot Valley – The Lot Valley is one immense orchard punctuated by nurseries and fields of tobacco. Fresh peas, green beans and the melons of Villeneuve-sur-Lot are among the renowned local products.

Valley of the Garonne – The alluvial soils and mild climate here allow more delicate crops, most of them grown on terraces, to flourish; each town and village has its speciality. Agen, for example, is famous for its onions and its prunes : hand-picked, specially-graded fresh plums, grown on grafted trees, are subsequently dried either naturally or in a slow oven to produce the **Pruneaux d'Agen.** The use of grafted plum trees here dates back to the Crusades. In the 16C the monks of Clairac, near Tonneins, were the first to foresee the commercial possibilities of the plum, and 200 years later the market had grown to such an extent that it had to be government-controlled. The plum variety used almost universally in the region today is the *"Robe-Sergent"* (Red Victoria plum). Marmande is famous for its tomatoes and pumpkins; Ste-Marie produces peaches and cherries. Since the 18C even poplar trees have been pressed into service : plantations on land subject to flooding provide wood used in carpentry and the manufacture of paper.

GASCOGNE

The Aquitaine basin is part of a series of French sedimentary beds which resulted from the silting up of an ancient ocean depth; what distinguishes Gascogne (Gascony), the region lying between the Pyrenees and the River Garonne, is the upper covering provided by enormous masses of debris washed down by the rivers after the erosion of the mountains during the Tertiary era.

The most common formation in Gascony is known as the **molasse** – layers of sand frequently cemented into a soft yellow sandstone penetrated by discontinuous marl and limestone beds. This geological structure has resulted in a hilly landscape of mixed topography.

From an agricultural point of view the soils here vary between **terreforts,** which are clayey and heavy to work, and **boulebènes** – lighter and slightly muddy, but less fertile and more suitable for grazing and cattle-breeding.

The hills of Gascony – The rivers, all tributaries of the Garonne, fan out northwards from the foothills of the mountains and cut through the hills of Armagnac in thin swathes. Those emerging from the major Pyrenean valleys – the Neste d'Aure and the Gave de Pau (Aure and Pau torrents) for instance – are already discharging the deposits they carry, and this material, mixed with the detritus from ancient glacial moraines, has produced a soil that is relatively poor. As a result there is a succession of moors between the high **Plateau de Lannemezan** and Pont-Long, north of Pau, via the Ger Plateau on the western side of Tarbes.

In the hills themselves, careful watering has led to the establishment of market gardens specializing in such "exotic" produce as strawberries and melons.

Vines in this region form only a part of the traditional polyculture; the part played by such *Appellation Contrôlée* wines as the Jurançon and Madiran whites and reds, as well as the lower-rated VDQS *(Vins Délimités de Qualité Supérieure)* from Béarn and Tursan, remains limited.

Adour country – The great curving sweep of the River Adour – northwards from its source, then west and finally back towards the south – creates a major demarcation line on the hydrographic chart of the region; the convergence towards Bayonne of all the rivers within this arc is evidence of a continuous sinking of the earth's crust beneath the ocean, which has persisted since the end of the Secondary era.
Within the area encompassed by the Adour is a hilly landscape cut through by the tributaries of the river. The lower slopes of the valleys are terraced as they drop towards the cultivated alluvial strips flanking these streams.

THE PYRENEES

The customary division of this mountain range into three large natural areas succeeding one another from west to east is justified by major differences in structure, climate and vegetation. The distinction is underlined by the race and language of the inhabitants.
(Part of the Central Pyrenees and the whole of the Mediterranean section of the chain are described in the Michelin Green Guide Pyrénées-Roussillon-Albigeois, in French).

Formation of the chain – The remarkable view from the town of Pau of the Pyrenean mountains rising above the hills of the Béarn district presents a seemingly endless series of finely-serrated crests – a mountain barrier revealing at that distance neither individual peaks, apart from Pic du Midi d'Ossau, nor saddles.
The barrier itself, stretching 400km – 248 miles from the Atlantic to the Mediterranean, is relatively narrow (30 to 40km – 19 to 25 miles on the French side of the frontier) yet also massive and continuous: the average height of the Pyrenees is 1 008m – just over 3 300ft.

History of the range – Approximately 250 million years ago a Hercynian (Paleozoic) mountain mass similar to the Massif Central or the Ardennes stood on the site occupied by the Pyrenees today; however, whereas the central and northern heights experienced a relatively tranquil existence, this chain between the Atlantic and the Mediterranean was sited in a particularly unstable zone. Already vigorously folded, and then partially levelled by erosion, the Hercynian block was submerged about 200 million years ago beneath a continental sea and covered by Secondary era sedimentary deposits, before being totally resurrected – and literally shaken from top to bottom – by the Alpine folding, the earliest spasms of which occurred here.
Under the enormous pressure of this mountain-building movement the most recent beds, still comparatively pliant, folded without breaking but the rigid ancient platform cracked, broke up and became dislocated. Hot springs burst through near the fractures; mineral deposits formed and metal-bearing ores appeared.
During the geological eons that passed while this was occurring, the mountain mass, now tortured and misshapen, was ceaselessly worn down by erosion, and the material torn from it washed out by rivers across the plains below.

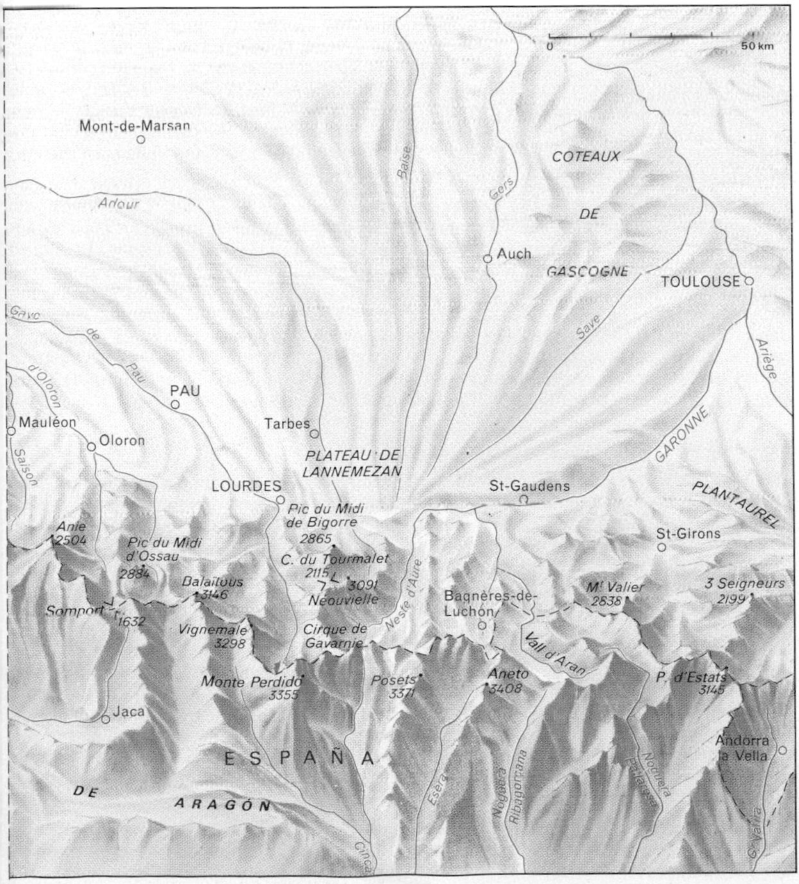

Central Pyrenees

The overall structure of the Pyrenean region is characterized by the juxtaposition of large geological masses arranged longitudinally. Starting from the Upper Garonne, the relief encompasses :

– the rises known as the Petites Pyrénées, of only medium height but remarkable for the alignment of limestone crests pleated in a fashion typical of the Jurassic period;

– the real foothills, formations of the Secondary era (either Cretaceous or Jurassic), with folded beds more violently distorted;

– the **Axial Zone,** the true spine of the Pyrenees along which granitic extrusions, recognizable by sharply defined peaks chiselled by glacial erosion, thrust through the Primary sediments : the Balaïtous, the Néouvielle and Maladetta massifs, the Luchon Pyrenees. The summits however are not made up entirely of granite, since patches of extremely hard schist and limestone exist which are even more resistant to erosion;

– the southern Secondary era sediments, under-thrust to a height of more than 3 000 m – 9 840ft at Monte Perdido, which are to be found largely on the Spanish side of the frontier. Two "masterpieces" of mountain scenery stand out among this limestone relief : in Spain the canyon of the Ordesa Valley (a National Park); in France the lower part of the Gavarnie amphitheatre, with its gigantic platforms of horizontal strata piled one upon the other.

Valleys – The inner part of the chain lacks a channel, parallel to the backbone of the range, which could link up the many transversal valleys. This makes internal communications difficult, a problem exacerbated in the Central Pyrenees by the fact that most passes are impracticable in winter. Each of these valleys was therefore isolated for much of the time, and this led to a survival of socially autonomous lifestyles of the kind still to be found in such *"petit pays"* districts as the Couserans, the Quatre Vallées (Four Valleys) region, and the Pays Toy. The valleys are nevertheless far from being inhospitable : despite being hemmed in, they seem no more than a hilly extension of the plains of Lower Aquitaine – with the additional advantage of a sheltered climate.

Glaciers – A hundred centuries ago the ancient glaciers thrust their abrasive tongues across the mountain landscape, gouging out the terrain as far as the present sites of Lourdes and Montréjeau. Since then these giant ice-floes have shrunk to negligible proportions (less than 10km^2 – 4 sq miles for the Pyrenees, against 400km^2 – 155 sq miles in just the French part of the Alps). There is only one "whole" glacier, complete with tongue and terminal moraine, in the entire range : the Ossoue, on the eastern slopes of the Vignemale.

Many of the most dramatic and appealing features to be found at the heart of the Pyrenees were formed by the old glaciers : hanging valleys, amphitheatres, canyons transformed into pastoral sweeps, jagged crests and scatters of huge boulders, lakes (over 500 in the French Pyrenees), cascades, bluffs, sudden morainic platforms...

The glacial sculpturing of the landscape has also resulted in powerful waterfalls, some of which are harnessed for the production of hydro-electric power.

Summits – The frontier between France and Spain is marked by the peaks of Balaïtous (3 146m – 10 321ft) and Vignemale (3 298m – 10 820ft), though the greatest heights of the Pyrenees are located on the Spanish side of the border : the impressive massifs of the Maladetta (3 404m – 11 168ft) and Posets (3 371m – 11 059ft). The French side nevertheless boasts Pic du Midi d'Ossau (2 884m – 9 462ft), which owes its majestic silhouette to the extrusion of volcanic rocks, and Pic du Midi de Bigorre (2 865m – 9 400ft), notable also for the way it towers over the plain below. The Massif de Néouvielle (3 192m – 10 472ft at Pic Long) includes an extraordinary "water tower", the contents of which are now almost totally reserved for the hydro-electric installations in the valleys of the Pau and Upper Neste torrents.

Picturesque Pyrenees – The Cauterets Valley perfectly illustrates those traditional and well-loved aspects of the Pyrenees which have inspired so many artists : steep-sided, narrow valleys opening up in the higher reaches of their rivers into huge upland pastures, gently sculptured, jewelled with lakes and webbed with torrents both turbulent and limpid. Such attractions, added to the benefits of the hot springs, the individuality of local customs and the exoticism of nearby Spain, appeal to romantic natures. Despite the progressive abandonment of temporary dwellings (mountain refuges, summer sheepfolds etc), of upland tracks and some of the highest pastoral slopes, the Central Pyrenees retain – at least in the Axial Zone – that "friendly" and characteristic image of mountains that have been in some way humanized.

Atlantic Pyrenees

This part of the range is characterized geographically by the disappearance of the Axial Zone, which has led to a confusion of the general relief, there being no longer a continuous spine or backbone to act as a "natural" frontier.

It is among the calcareous beds covering the eastern extremity of the Axial Zone that the most noticeable examples of geomorphological disturbance occur. These are the twisted contortions of the 2 504m – 8 213ft Pic d'Anie and the savage gashes of the Kakouetta and Holcarte gorges. The subterranean levels of these fissured limestones riddled with potholes have provided an immense field of exploration and study for speleologists (cave scientists).

The slopes of these Lower Pyrenees are abundantly wooded and relatively difficult to cross (the Forest of Iraty for example).

Nearer the ocean a more placid topography characterizes the Basque Country, the heights of which are typified by La Rhune, Mont Ursava (at Cambo-les-Bains) and the mountains surrounding St-Jean-Pied-de-Port. The landscape between the Adour estuary and Spain mainly comprises hills sculpted from a heterogeneous mass of marine sediments.

Basque Pyrenees – The charm and cohesion of this region derives mainly from its oceanic climate with plenty of humidity, and the colourful language and civilization of the Basque people, so closely interwoven with those in the neighbouring Spanish pro-

PIX

Chaos de Coumély.

vinces of Guipuzcoa and Navarra. Trans-Pyrenean traffic is largely concentrated on the coastal route but the inland passages remain very popular with tourists and locals who have used them ever since the era of the great pilgrimages to Santiago de Compostela in Spain.

Coast – The dunes and pinewoods of the Landes region stretch beyond the mouth of the River Adour, as far as Pointe de St-Martin near Biarritz.
Further south however the coastline bites into the Pyrenean folds, and the rocks – sedimentary beds violently arched over, foliated into thin laminated layers – form the low, slanting cliffs responsible for the picturesque appearance of the Basque Corniche.

Parc National des Pyrénées

The Pyrenees National Park was created in 1967 with the aim of preserving the beauty of the natural environment; it extends for more than 100km – 62 miles along the French frontier region and varies in width from 1km to 15km – $\frac{1}{2}$ mile to 10 miles, at an altitude between 1 000m and 3 298m – 3 250ft and 10 820ft (at the summit of the Vignemale). Including the Néouvielle Nature Reserve, the park covers an area of 45 700ha – 174 sq miles.
The park itself is bordered by a peripheral zone (206 000ha – 795 sq miles) which has been established with the purpose of revitalising the pastoral economy in the mountain villages and improving tourist facilities.
Camping – apart from one-night bivouacs at more than one hour's walk from the road – is forbidden, as are hunting, lighting fires, picking flowers and the introduction of dogs. Fishing, on the other hand, in the numerous torrents and lakes within the Park, is permitted.
The Park is a refuge for over 4 000 chamois (especially in the Ossau and Cauterets Valleys, where they can be seen more easily) and over 200 colonies of marmots. It is now very rare to catch sight of one of the few remaining brown bears but it is not unusual to see vultures, royal eagles or the huge lammergeyers in flight, in this region still frequented by wood grouse, ptarmigan and Pyrenean musk-rats.
Information centres (Maisons du Parc) – at St-Lary, Luz, Gavarnie, Cauterets, Arrens-Marsous, Gabas and Etsaut – can supply details on the park, its flora and fauna, and how to organize mountain excursions. They also hold exhibitions on such varied themes as glaciers, bears, mountain climbing, Pyrenean watercourses...
Over 350km – 218 miles of signposted footpaths and a score of mountain refuges offer numerous opportunities for ramblers. The Sentier de Grande Randonnée (long-distance footpath, *qv*) numbered GR10 crosses the Park in several places. Monitor-guides are available to oversee mountain trips.

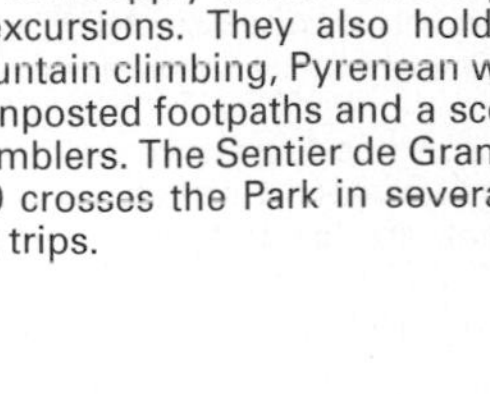

ECONOMY

FISHING AND THE FRUITS OF THE SEA

Since the western part of the region enjoys a favoured situation beside the sea, fishing is naturally one of its principal commercial assets.

Deep-sea fishing – Modern trawlers are ideally suited to fishing on the high seas – a branch of the industry which supplies most of Europe's "fresh fish" and which concentrates its activities at the limit of the continental shelf, where the depth is often 500m – 1 640ft or more. Sole, bream and hake landed by these trawlers play an important part in the economy of La Rochelle, Les Sables d'Olonne, the Ile d'Yeu, St-Gilles and other ports in the northern coastal section.

Tuna fishing – Fishing for the huge tuna fish takes place from June to October, from boats equipped with dragnets and live bait (sardines, anchovies etc). The great white Atlantic tuna, known locally as *germon,* is fished at the beginning of the season between Portugal and the Azores, and the fleets then follow its migration north from the Bay of Biscay as far as the southwest of Ireland. Tuna is the main catch brought back to St Jean de Luz.

Coastal fishing – Though coastal fishing is more limited in its scope than deep-sea fishing, it nevertheless supplies a particular demand – for varieties of fish and seafood which are especially prized when they are absolutely fresh.

Flat fish and round fish –Small trawlers, motor-boats and local fishing smacks bring in sole, whiting, mullet, mackerel, skate etc, according to the season and the locality.

Sardine fishing – For this the fishermen use "turning" nets – seines from 200 to 300m – 656 to 984ft long. The catch is landed daily and sold immediately at quayside auctions. The increasing rarity of sardine banks off the Vendée coast has, however, driven the fleets further towards the coast of Morocco, where ships with deep-freeze compartments have to be used.

Crustaceans – Lobsters, crabs and crayfish are caught – in wicker pots or hoop nets – mainly in the cold waters off the rocky coasts of the Vendée and the Ile d'Yeu. Langoustines (crayfish) are fished further out by the trawlers. Fishermen from Royan and La Cotinière seek out shrimps and prawns on the banks off the Gironde estuary.

Minor fishing – Fishing, whether practised inshore by small boats or onshore by anglers, is common to the entire coast – by line, by cord, by fixed nets, with seine nets from the beach, or even using **carrelets** (suspended nets manoeuvred via pulleys from a landing stage). Carrelets remain popular, particularly in the Gironde estuary, although a certain picturesque quality may weigh more in their favour than any particular effectiveness.

Corte/VLOO

Fishing nets ("carrelets").

Estuary fishing – It is in the spring, when fish swarm upriver to spawn, that the catches of shad and lamprey in the Gironde are at their most plentiful. The eels return at the same time : their tiny **"pibales"** (elvers) are fished from the shore, thousands at a time, with fine-meshed shrimping nets.

Salt marshes – From the 11C to the 18C the marshes, bordering almost the entire Poitou coast, were one of the principal economic assets of that area, especially in the Aunis and Saintonge regions. The salt trade played an important part then in both sea and river traffic. Merchants sailing to northern Europe carried salt as far as the Hanseatic ports, where it was used to preserve fish. Then the receding sea withdrew further still; the marshes silted up and transformed themselves into *gâts* (fever swamps). Today the only salt pans still worked are on Noirmoutier Island and the Isle of Ré, with a few more among the Breton-Vendée marshes. The rest have been turned into pastureland, market gardens, nature reserves or *claires* (basins) for fattening oysters.
The working of salt flats is a delicate operation. The marsh is divided into a grid, squared off with small *bossis* (banks) of earth bearing a large proportion of clay. Sea water, brought by the rising tide, is carried into the grid via narrow canals or *étiers,*

allowed to settle, and then concentrated in a series of reservoirs that become shallower and shallower. The water in the final pans is no more than 5cm – 2in deep. It is here, once the liquid evaporates, that the salt crystallizes.
From May to September the *paludier* (salt-worker) "draws" with the help of a large rake (known as a *las* or *rabale*) the grey salt deposit from the bottom of the pan after his female assistant, the *paludière*, has skimmed the white salt off the surface with a flat shovel. The harvest is then assembled in *mulons* (small heaps) at the side of the pan – often protected against bad weather today by plastic sheeting – to be stocked later in the local *salorges* (special salt stores, usually built of wood).

Oysters

The Marennes-Oléron basin, which extends from the River Charente to the mouth of the Gironde, is among the most important oyster-farming regions in France : the Charente-Maritime *département* alone supplies almost half the national market in these epicurean delicacies. Brittany is the other big oyster-producing area.

History and biology – The two main varieties, the flat oyster *(plates)* and the concave or deep-shelled oyster *(creuses)*, live in their natural state, respectively, on sandbanks or in beds attached to undersea rocks. The **flat oyster** is hermaphrodite and viviparous (the young are produced live and do not have to be hatched). This variety has been known in the region since Gallo-Roman times, and has been gathered or dredged since then; it was a delicacy on the table of Louis XIV, who was a great oyster-lover. In 1920 however the species was almost entirely destroyed by a disease, and flat oysters can only be found now – in very small quantities – in the region of Marennes.

PIX

Oyster beds, Marennes.

The fleshier, richer **deep-shelled oyster**, with a taste that is less delicate and very different, is unisexual and oviparous (the young are hatched from eggs) as well as being less sensitive to changes in the weather. The variety was introduced into the area "accidentally" in 1868 : a ship sheltering from a storm stayed too long in the Gironde on its way from Portugal to England with a cargo of these oysters; the cargo was in danger of going bad and the oysters had to be thrown into the sea. The survivors, having scattered, then imposed themselves on the majority of local farms.
When disease struck again in 1971, these "Portugaises" were in turn supplanted by "Japonaises" *(Crassostrea Gigas)* – oysters bred in the Pacific and imported from Japan or Canada (British Columbia).

Exploitation – **Ostreiculture** (oyster breeding) in France remains very much a "cottage industry" – frequently a family affair – and still a fairly uncertain business : apart from the risk of disease, oyster farms can be destroyed by pollution, silting up, excess salinity, a tempest, an unusually cold spell or degeneration of the oysters – which can also be attacked by crabs, starfish or even winkles.
The **nassain** (young seed oysters or spats), drifting this way and that with the currents, become attached in summer to **collectors** – lime-washed tiles, slates, wooden stakes or stones according to the region; these are then transported to the first "oyster park". After a year or two the oysters are prised off the collectors – a technique known as **détroquage** – and placed in a second "park". They remain a further year or two here, usually in special *pochons* (containers) placed on tables. In the Marennes-Oléron basin the oysters receive a final treatment to mature and refine them, giving them their characteristic pale greenish-blue hue, in fattening pools known as **claires** full of microscopic blue algae. Oysters sold as **Spéciales** have spent longer in the *claires*, and are less densely distributed in them, than the ordinary **Fines de claires**.

Mussels

The mussel is a bivalve with a blue-black shell, and in its wild state lives in colonies on rocks assaulted by the sea. It has been farmed since the 13C and is reared professionally along the coast of the province of Aunis – separated (except in Aiguillon Bay) from the oysters, since the two shellfish are biologically incompatible. The centres of mussel production today are the coast near Brouage, the Isle of Oléron (Boyardville Bay) and the Anse de Fouras to the south of the province; Aiguillon Bay to the north of it.

Mytiliculture – This is the French term for mussel breeding, including their fattening and beautifying for the market. The mussels attach themselves to **bouchots** (stakes) driven into the mud or silt in long lines or arranged in grids, where they fatten and increase in size. The arrangement of the *bouchots* varies from district to district and is subject to strict control. In the Breton Straits the *bouchots à nassain,* for the very young mussels, are well off-shore, and those where the shellfish grow to commercial size much nearer the coast. The *boucholeurs* visit their mussel beds in small, flat-bottomed boats or, if the tide is low, on their *"accons"* – flat wooden crates which they slide across the mud with a hefty kick from their boot.
Gastronomically, mussels serve as the base for the preparation of a regional delicacy known as *mouclade (qv).*

AGRICULTURE

Poitou, the Charentes and the region around Bordeaux all rely heavily on agriculture – crops on the limestone plains, vines on the valley slopes. In the Landes, the forest overshadows everything.

Mixed farming – Mixed agriculture is still the norm in these lands where tenant farming (with a generous percentage of the crop being given to the landlord), although rapidly disappearing, still exists and the average property rarely exceeds 50ha – 125 acres.
Cereals (wheat, maize, oats) in the small farms grow side by side with meadows of clover, alfalfa and other **fodder plants**. There exist also a number of slightly less common crops : in the coastal regions, for example, with their humid atmosphere warmed by the ocean, **early fruit and vegetables** flourish; on the islands (with the exception of the Ile d'Yeu) and in the rich alluvial soil of the marshlands, it is easy to grow new potatoes, artichokes, carrots and peas. The melons known as Charentais also grow in this same area and in recent years these have been so successful that they have spread as far as the Rhône Valley, where they have threatened to supplant the Cantaloupe melon.
Market gardens abound in the lower parts of the Vienne, Thouet and Garonne valleys and those of their tributaries. The Garonne basin, in addition, specializes in tomatoes, various fruits and even tobacco. **Tobacco,** largely a family business, is grown in small fields in the region around Bazas and on the alluvial soil flooring the valleys of the Dordogne, the Lot and the Garonne, where the principal centres are Marmande and Tonneins.

The Landes Forest.

The pines of the Landes – The huge forest covering the Landes *(qv)* consists mainly of maritime pines, although parasol varieties occur here and there. The maritime pine, with its tall bole ringed by tufts of needles, is not a beautiful tree though it does have a certain elegance – and it grows quickly; it has also brought prosperity to what was once a poor and desolate region.
Among other uses it has been since ancient times the base of a traditional activity : **le gemmage** – resin harvesting. Formerly, the *gemmeur* (gum collector) periodically tapped the tree with the aid of a tool known as a *hapchot.* From the wounds made by this the resin bled into small earthernware cups (called *cramponnés* because they were clamped to the trees). Every few weeks the resin was collected, packed into barrels and sent to distilling plants. Today this practice has largely been superseded by the use of sulphuric acid, which activates the process and has the advantage that it does far less damage to the tree. Distillation of the resin is used in the production of turpentine, pitch, transparent wrapping material and other solids.

Even when they are very old, the pines remain useful : after they have been "bled dry" of their resin, they are felled and sent to factories which transform them into parquet flooring, railway sleepers, crates and wood-fibre boards (especially compressed woodchip sheeting). Important installations producing paper, wood pulp and pine cellulose exist in the region (especially at Facturen which alone contributes half of the country's cellulose production).

Ncvali/IMAGE PHOTOTHÈQUE

Resin-collecting.

LIVESTOCK

Cattle – Cattle are reared throughout the region, for their meat or for their milk, in natural meadows or "artificial" ones, sometimes even in intensive production "units". Fattening, particularly of the (white) Charolais breed, takes place in the fields of the Pays de Retz, the Gâtine de Parthenay, the *bocages* of the Vendée, and on the polders of the marshlands. Bressuire and Parthenay, important cattle markets, handle thousands of (tawny) Parthenay beasts and an increasing number of Charolais. Eastwards, towards the Massif Central, the Limousin (chestnut) breed and again Charolais predominate. Lezay, in the south of the Deux-Sèvres *département,* is famous for the trade there in eight-day-old calves and for its cheese industry. Between Poitiers and La Rochelle, and again between the Vendée and the Charentes, lie regions in which French breeds – Black-and-Whites and Normans – supply milk to numerous cooperatives; this area produces cheese, long-life milk and the famous *Beurre des Charentes,* a rich, creamy butter.

Sheep, goats and horses – Sheep, which originally appeared indigenously on the heaths and pastureland of the region, are increasingly important in these otherwise ill-favoured areas. The zones particularly suited to the flocks are the eastern reaches of Poitou, in the Berry district, and also the Gâtine de Parthenay (home of the very tender Charmoise lamb).
Goat rearing has considerably increased in the southern parts of Deux-Sèvres and Vienne, within the framework of a dairy cooperative which produces 50% of all goat-milk products in France. **Chabichou,** the celebrated goat's cheese, is a traditional speciality of the region.
Horse rearing has been in decline since the increase in motorization; breeding racehorses, however, remains a thriving business, especially in the Vendée. The Poitou **baudet** (donkey) and the Mellois mule, on the other hand, have become rare to the point where measures have been taken to preserve them from extinction.

Poultry – From Clisson to Mont-de-Marsan, the farmyards are still full of poultry : Poitou geese, Bressuire and Barbezieux hens, old-fashioned white ducks from Challans. Specialized poultry production is particularly important in the northern part of Deux-Sèvres and in the Vendée.
East and south of the Landes forests is a region of crops (mainly maize) and poultry farming ('yellow', corn-fed chickens; geese, ducks, turkeys) with a flourishing preserved-foods industry which includes in particular a choice variety of *Foie Gras* (prepared duck and goose livers).

WINES AND SPIRITS

The area both to the north and to the south of the Gironde is known throughout the world for its fine wines, fortified wines, cognacs and armagnacs, which have long been exported and play a major role in the local economy.

Wines of Bordeaux

The world-famous Bordeaux vineyards, 105km – 65 miles from north to south and 130km – 81 miles from west to east, cover an area of approximately 105 000ha – 405sq miles.
The region, widely considered the best in the world for fine wines, contains over 8 000 wine-producing "châteaux" (which can mean an estate or simply a property, and not necessarily something resembling a castle) which between them produce wines with 53 different controlled *appellations* under six main "family" headings. Added to these are the Crémant de Bordeaux, a sparkling wine, and the local *digestif* spirit called Fine de Bordeaux. Production breaks down into approximately 75% red wines and 25% white, at an output of some 600 million bottles per year; 40% of the wine is exported to Great Britain, Belgium, Germany and the Netherlands. *For tours through the Bordeaux vineyards and wine cellars see Bordeaux Vineyards (qv) and Practical Information (qv).*

Red wines – According to a local saying, "all the edges are rounded off in the bottle" – and red wines do indeed have a remarkable ability to improve with age. The wines of the region include the elegant wines of the Médoc – the great reds – the delicate, slightly spicy and vigorous Graves to which they have a family resemblance, and the wines of St-Émilion with their strength of character.

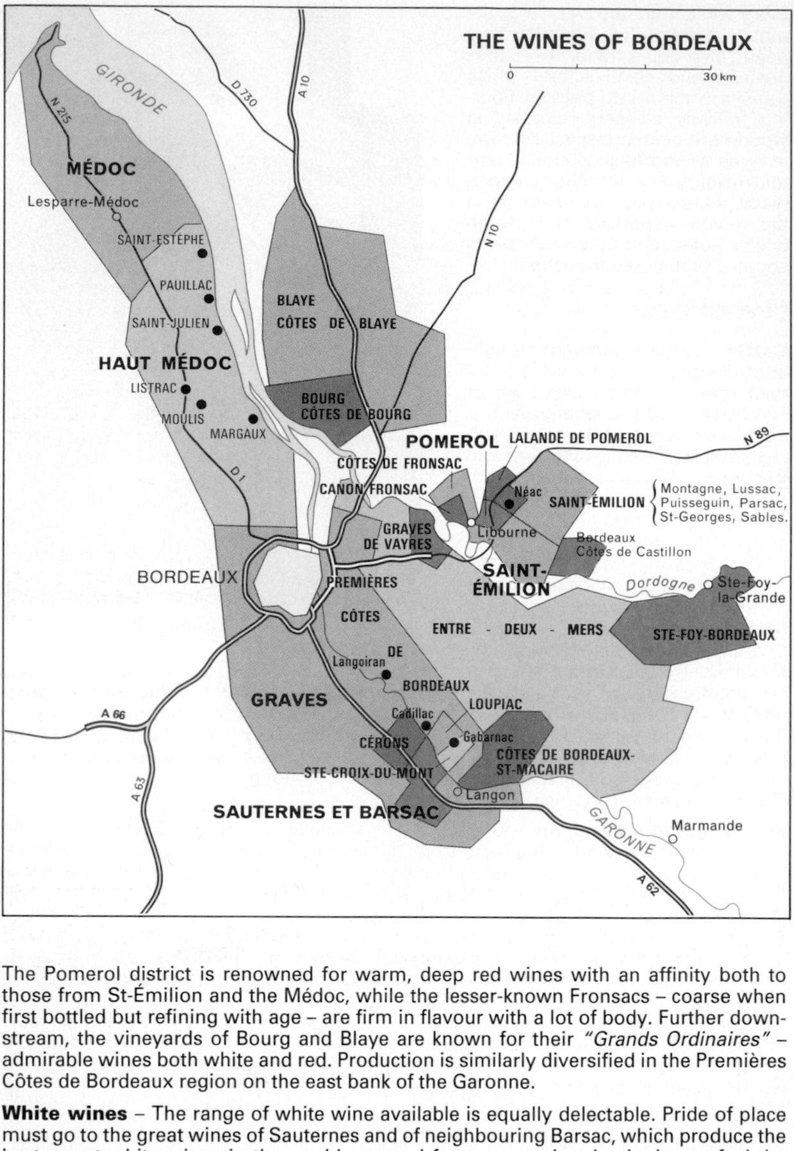

The Pomerol district is renowned for warm, deep red wines with an affinity both to those from St-Émilion and the Médoc, while the lesser-known Fronsacs – coarse when first bottled but refining with age – are firm in flavour with a lot of body. Further downstream, the vineyards of Bourg and Blaye are known for their *"Grands Ordinaires"* – admirable wines both white and red. Production is similarly diversified in the Premières Côtes de Bordeaux region on the east bank of the Garonne.

White wines – The range of white wine available is equally delectable. Pride of place must go to the great wines of Sauternes and of neighbouring Barsac, which produce the best sweet white wines in the world, pressed from grapes just beginning to feel the effects of the famous "noble rot". Less well-known but also of note are the whites of Ste-Croix-du-Mont and Loupiac, on the other side of the Garonne.
At the opposite pole, in the matter of taste, are the dry white Graves – wines of distinction which, for many, typify the whites of Bordeaux : clean-tasting, lightly fruity, vigorous.
The lightly-fragranced products of the Cérons vineyards, ranging from quite dry to slightly luscious, are a link between the best wines of the Graves district and the great Sauternes.
Among the Premières Côtes de Bordeaux *(see above)*, already quoted with the reds, the town of Cadillac produces mellow, velvety white wines that are agreeably fresh. Finally, the huge area known as Entre-Deux-Mers (between two seas : the Atlantic and the Mediterranean), with its wine producers' cooperatives, is a very important supplier of dry white wines and reds which are marketed as *"Grands Ordinaires"*.

Appellations – The term **"Appellation d'Origine Contrôlée" (AOC)** on a wine label is a certification of the wine's supervised origins, carrying with it an implication – though not necessarily a guarantee – of quality.
The Médoc, thanks to the variety of its *terroirs* (soils), is classed into eight zones of *appellation contrôlée* : Médoc and Haut-Médoc, and more specifically St-Estèphe, Pauillac, St-Julien, Moulis, Listrac and Margaux.

Serving Bordeaux wines – The red wines of Bordeaux should not be drunk too young; the whites, on the other hand – especially the dry whites – are at their best relatively soon after bottling. For suggestions of which wines to serve with which foods, see the chapter on Food and Drink *(qv)*.

SEASONAL PROGRESS OF THE VINES : The middle of winter is when vines are pruned. Leaves appear on the vine in April and flowers a month later. By July the grapes are beginning to change colour and are left to ripen quietly for another month. The grapes are usually harvested in mid-September, after which they are taken inside for the wine-making process.

Wines of Béarn

The Béarn region produces three wines of note : the Jurançon, the Madiran and the Rosé du Béarn; see under Béarn *(qv)*.

Muscadet

This well-known dry white wine which forms, with the Gros Plant and Côteaux d'Ancenis, part of the **Vins de Nantes** group, was accorded *Appellation d'Origine Contrôlée (see above)* status in 1936. The vineyards producing the wines of this group stretch away south of the Loire.

Muscadet is made from the Melon grape, which came originally from Burgundy. The vines were imported and planted in the Nantes area after the terrible winter of 1709 because of their resistance to frost.

There are three *appellations,* corresponding to three different regions : the Muscadet de Sèvre-et-Maine, which accounts for the major part of the production, the Muscadet des Côteaux de la Loire (which comes from around Ancenis) and plain Muscadet (from the neighbourhood of St-Philbert-de-Grand-Lieu). All of them yield wines that are light and dry, with an alcoholic content limited to 12%. Served cold, Muscadet is a marvellous accompaniment to fish and seafood.

The **Gros Plant du Pays Nantais** has been classed as a VDQS (*Vin Délimité de Qualité Supérieure* – a superior wine) since 1954. It is made from the Folle-Blanche grapes grown in the Charentes since the 16C. Being a light wine (11%) it complements seafood in general and shellfish in particular.

Cognac

Cognac, famous for centuries throughout the world, is a distillation of white wines produced in the region of the Cognac *appellation* (essentially the Charentes *département*). A good cognac should taste like the very essence of fresh grapes, strong and heady. More than 80% of the production is exported, Britain and the United States alone accounting for 40% of those sales.

History – The distillation of wine to make spirits, practised in the region since the 16C, became generalized in the early 17C. The local vintners at first distilled just the wines that did not travel well but later realised that the process could help turnover, reduce excise duties and facilitate storage (between seven and ten barrels of wine are used to make one barrel of cognac). The taste for the resulting *eau-de-vie* (spirit) spread and it began to be exported, like the wines before it, to the countries in the north of Europe as an adjunct to the salt trade.

Much of the wine trade at that time was in the hands of the English and the Dutch – who, learning that the people of Charentes "burned their wine", dubbed the result *brandewijn* (burnt wine). From this the English coined the word brandy, which has been used in the Anglo-Saxon world ever since. In France the spirit took the name of the town where it was first commercialized, Cognac.

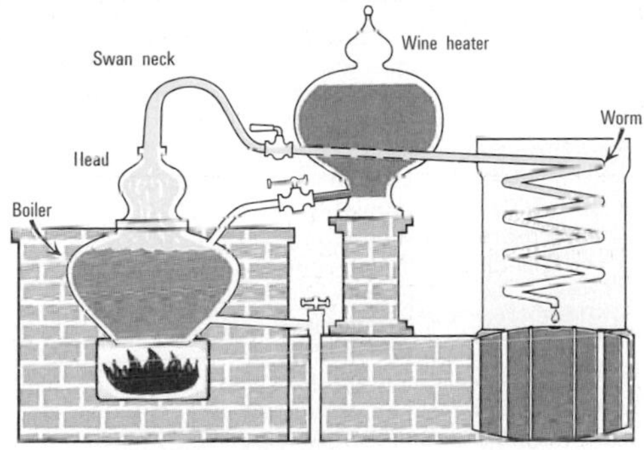

A Charentais Pot Still.

From Cognac the barges and tenders laden with barrels sailed down the River Charente to Tonnay-Charente and La Rochelle, where the cargo was transferred to full-rigged merchantmen bound either for Northern Europe or for the colonies – where the "fire-water" accompanied the baubles and beads used to pacify and bargain with the natives.

Ruined by the devastating outbreak of Phylloxera (American aphids) in the 19C, the Cognac vineyards were replanted by the burghers of Cognac, who had themselves escaped ruin because of the huge stocks they held in store ageing. English merchants and traders played an important part in the promotion of brandy; the names of several famous Cognac brands still have an Anglo-Saxon ring about them.

The vineyards – Almost 90 000ha – 222 400 acres are under the vine, most of them planted with Ugni Blanc (incorrectly termed St-Émilion des Charentes in the region). The vineyards are planted in an area of temperate climate – humid in winter, sunny in summer – and chalky soil similar to that found in the Champagne region, east of Paris. Cognac of maximum finesse, Grande Champagne cognac, is produced from vines at the centre of this region, the area of chalkiest soil; the other five classed *crus* or "growths" – producing more full-bodied and highly flavoured spirit – radiate outwards from it.

Development of cognac – In short, distilling is a means of concentrating the strength and flavour of any alcoholic drink by removing most of the water content. The technique stems from the fact that alcohol in chemical terms is more volatile than water : it boils at a lower temperature. All the alcohol and most of the aromatic elements in a heated wine will therefore be driven off as vapour long before the water boils. If this vapour is collected and condensed, the resulting liquid will contain virtually all the alcohol, certain other volatile elements – known as the congenerics – and very little water.

The system of distilling first came west with the Arabs in the 14C (the Arabic term *al embic* – a still – and *al kohol* are still in use today). For cognac the process is completed in two stages : the alembic or Charentais pot still, made of beaten copper, yields first (after about 8 hours) a liquid containing 25%-35% alcohol, the **brouillis,** which is passed

back into the still after undesirable elements in the congenerics have been drawn off; the second distillate then emerges (after about 12 hours) at a maximum strength of 72%.
The process itself is as follows : vapours compressed in the still head pass into the swan-neck which then passes through the wine heater; this cools the vapours and warms the wine already in there, which will refill the boiler; finally the pipe from the swan-neck leads the vapours to the worm – the coiled copper tubing of the cooling tank, where they condense into liquid.

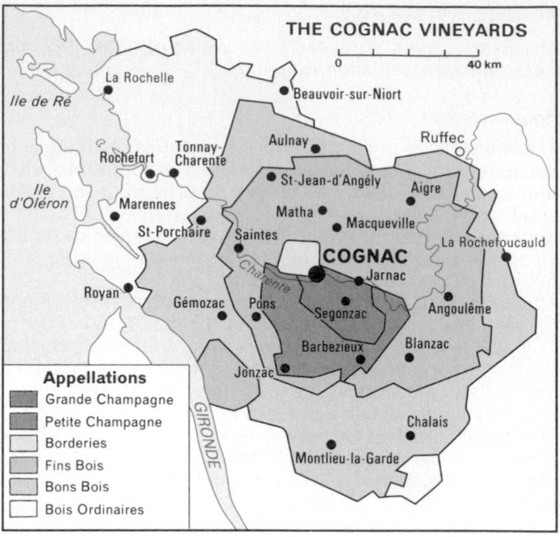

The brandy, fiery but colourless when it leaves the still, is only faintly perfumed; all its character is derived from the maturing process, in barrels left in serried rows in the darkness of the producer's airy *chais* (stores). Here the pale oak of these barrels, brought from the hills of the Limousin, stimulates the oxidization of the spirit, adds tannin and activates the amber coloration. The incredible amount of evaporation from the barrels is equivalent to the loss of 12 million bottles of spirit every year.
The last step before the cognac appears in bottles is taken by the merchants and shippers who put their name on the label : the spirit is diluted with distilled water to the accepted legal strength for the market, cut and blended with brandies of different age, from different crus, and sugar and caramel are added to obtain the required colour, until a consistent quality is arrived at with characteristics recognizable as typical of a particular brand.

Different cognacs – There are several different categories of cognac, classed according to the length of time they have spent maturing in the oak casks.
The three-star label signifies a brandy of normal quality, between five and nine years of age. The acronyms VO (Very Old) and VSOP (Very Special Old Pale) apply to cognacs aged on average between 12 and 20 years. The terms Vieille Réserve, Grande Réserve, Royal, Vieux, XO, Napoleon, Extra etc are used to distinguish cognacs 20 to 40 years old or even more. The words Fine Champagne on the label identify a cognac that is a blend of the Grande and Petite Champagne growths.

Armagnac

Armagnac is very different from cognac both in style and in the technique used to make it. This spirit should be velvety smooth, dry and with a pungent smell; it is considered to have less finesse than cognac.
The region legally permitted to sell its products under the name "Armagnac" extends over a great stretch of land (35 000ha – 135 sq miles), roughly triangular in shape, which is divided into three sub-zones : **Haut-Armagnac** (Upper Armagnac, the hilly region of Auch) in the east; **Ténarèze** (around Condom) in the centre; and **Bas-Armagnac** (Lower Armagnac, the Eauze region) in the west. Armagnac from Ténarèze is fuller and richer while that from Bas-Armagnac is more fruity.
Only white wines made from 10 approved varieties of vine may be distilled to make the spirit, and their common characteristic is a strong, fixed level of acidity. The most popular of these grapes are the Ugni Blanc and the Folle-Blanche (known as Gros Plant in the Nantes area).
It is distilled in a sort of double boiler, at a much lower temperature than cognac, resulting in a stronger flavour and scent which, combined with the effect of the sappy "black" oak casks in which it is stored, adds character (and it matures faster).
Each brand of armagnac has, as for cognac, its expert *Maître de Chai* (Master Storeman) who blends the finished product to give it its particular identity.

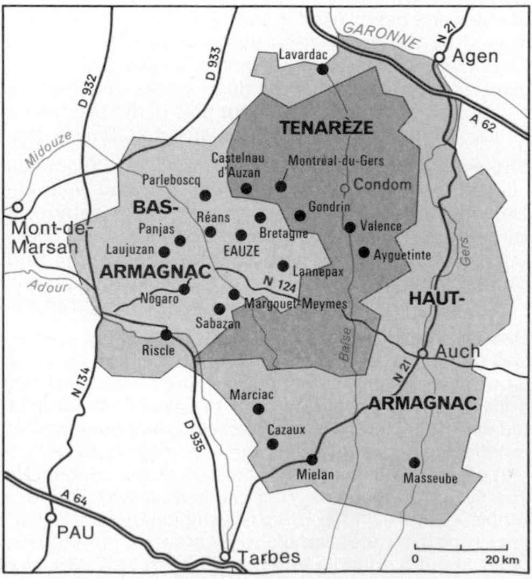

Fortified Wines and Aperitifs

Floc – Floc is the old Gascon word for flower. Floc de Gascogne – a fortified wine between 16° and 18°, about the strength of port or sherry – is drunk chilled as an aperitif, either red or white. Made from selected wines grown in the region of the Armagnac *appellation,* it results from a mixture of the must from these wines with Armagnac at more than 52°. The aperitif is aged in oak barrels.

Pousse-rapière – "Rapier Thrust" is another aperitif, invented in the 16C at Château Monluc, near the town of Condom, by Marshal Blaise de Monluc, army commander and man of letters. The drink consists of Armagnac with the juice of pressed fruits : mixed with Champagne-style dry sparkling wine, it makes an excellent cocktail.

Pineau des Charentes – This is a fortified aperitif wine, classified *Appellation d'Origine Contrôlée* and produced in the same area as cognac; it is made in both red and rosé forms, and it should be drunk very cold.

The aperitif was created by accident in the 16C, when a grower ran a quantity of grape must into a barrel which inadvertently still had some cognac left in the bottom. He was agreeably surprised, some years later, to discover in the barrel a strong wine that was smooth, heady and deliciously fruity.

Pineau is produced from the same growths as the cognac. The musts utilised before the *mutage* (the addition of cognac) should have an alcoholic content of 10%. After the *mutage* the strength of the drink should be at least 16.5%. The blend is then transferred to oak casks and kept for several months in dark stores.

When it has sufficiently matured, it is submitted to an official Commission of Tasters who will decide whether or not it merits the *appellation* Pineau des Charentes.

Pineau sells very well in France and is exported to Belgium, Canada, Germany, Britain, Luxembourg and the United States.

ADDITIONAL ACTIVITIES

Industrial centres – The modernization of the port of Bordeaux extends today all the way downstream from the Aquitaine Suspension Bridge to the mouth of the Gironde : new industries linked to the dock traffic have been installed at Bassens (the foremost outer-port of Bordeaux) and at Blaye, Pauillac and Le Verdon - the oil port and container terminal now known as Bordeaux-le-Verdon.

Ocean-based activities (fishing, sailing) around La Rochelle have increased, though the city is still best known for its traditional industries (shipyards, chemicals, cars, railway rolling stock). Angoulême is well known for its paper production and printing works.

Other industries – In Poitou, Niort is famous for its tanneries, electrical machinery, confectionery and its timber industry. The zone Poitiers-Châtellerault is known for its factories producing car tyres, aeronautical components and various types of machinery, while between Châtellerault and Ligugé there is the Clain "industrial corridor": here, on either side of the Paris-Bordeaux main railway line and route N10, there is a succession of quarries, printing works, chemical refineries and factories processing dairy products and other foodstuffs.

In the Vendée there are uranium mines near Clisson, and factories making furniture, household appliances, agricultural machinery and again tyres at La Roche-sur-Yon, and shoe factories near Les Herbiers. Equally important are the shipyards of La Pallice, the chemical-products companies of Tonnay-Charente and, in Rochefort, manufacturers of plywoods, veneers and more aeronautical components.

The subsoils and substrata of the Landes, long worked for the lignite, rock salt and potassium which can be extracted, have since 1954 also supplied oil in the Parentis district. The gaunt framework of derricks can still be seen from time to time above the forest – or even in the Parentis lagoon itself – when exploratory drilling operations are in progress.

Many of the towns described in this Guide have developed special industrial zones as a result of the present decentralization policies in Europe. These areas are normally, because of their distance from the main commercial and trade centres, used for the establishment of light industries. The pipeline distribution of natural gas near Lacq has also stimulated industrial expansion throughout the Southwest.

HISTORICAL TABLE AND NOTES

Pre-history

In the prehistoric period known as **Paleolithic** (18 000 centuries to 100 centuries BC) human activity existed in the region of what is now Angoulême and around Poitiers (Angles-sur-l'Anglin, Le Grand-Pressigny). Evidence of this presence includes the carvings and leader's staff found in a grotto at Montbron, near La Rochefoucauld; the coastal deposits between Pornic and Pointe de St-Gildas, which reveal signs of a civilization of great hunters; and in the representation of human beings carved on flat stones which were discovered at Lussac-les-Châteaux, southeast of Civaux.
The **Neolithic** period (75 to 25 centuries BC) was marked by the spread of the techniques of polishing and ceramic-making; the development of agriculture (wheat, barley) and stock-raising (sheep, goats), and the decision, by previously nomad populations, to settle in one place; the use of metals (bronze, copper); the construction of megaliths : menhirs, dolmens and tumuli such as those in Bougon and at Ste-Soline (east of Melle).

The Roman conquest

72 BC	Foundation of Lugdunum Convenarum (St-Bertrand-de-Comminges), religious capital of the population south of the River Garonne, by Pompey.
56	Aquitaine conquered by Crassus, Caesar's lieutenant.

Invasions, the rise of the Carolingian Empire and the Hundred Years War

2C-4C AD	Introduction of Christianity in Gaul. St Hilaire elected Bishop of Poitiers.
276	Germanic invasion.
5C	Visigoth kingdom in Aquitaine : continuation of the Latin culture and written Roman law.
End 6C	The Vascons, Basque mountain people from the south, repulsed by the Visigoths, settle in the flat country - "Gascogne" (Gascony).
507	Defeat of Alaric II, King of the Visigoths, by Clovis at Vouillé (north of Poitiers).
732	The Arab advance into Europe halted by Charles Martel at Moussais-la-Bataille.
778	Kingdom of Aquitaine created by Charlemagne.
801	Barcelona taken from the Arabs by Charlemagne and Spanish Marches organized.
820	Start of the Norman incursions. Destruction of Saintes, Angoulême (*c*850) and Bordeaux.
***c*950**	Beginning of pilgrimages to Santiago de Compostela.
1058	Union of the Duchies of Aquitaine and Gascogne. The Southwest under the hegemony of the Comtes (Comtes of Poitiers and Angoulême).
1137	Marriage of Eleanor of Aquitaine to Louis, son of the French king.

Eleanor of Aquitaine (c1122-1204) and the Plantagenet Territories

The marriage in 1137 of Eleanor, the only daughter of **William of Aquitaine,** to Louis, the French *dauphin,* brought with it a dowry which included the duchies of Guyenne, Gascogne, Périgord, Limousin, Poitou, Angoumois and Saintonge, plus suzerainty over the Auvergne and the Comté of Toulouse. Her husband was crowned Louis VII the same year. Fifteen years later, in 1152, the marriage ended in divorce; Eleanor retained all the lands of her dowry.
Eleanor's subsequent marriage to **Henry Plantagenet** in 1154 was a political disaster for the Capetian dynasty : the combined possessions of the bride and groom, extending from the English Channel to the Pyrenees, were as vast as those of the French crown. Henry's crowning as Henry II of England finally upset the fragile international equilibrium : the resulting Anglo-French struggle lasted on and off for 300 years.

Tallandier

Eleanor of Aquitaine.

Later, separating from her second husband, Eleanor left London for Poitiers where she held a brilliant court. From 1173 her various intrigues – she supported her son Richard the Lionheart in the fight against his father, Henry, for example – resulted in her being imprisoned in London by her husband, and she was only released on his death 15 years later in 1189. She took up her plotting again, this time against her youngest son, John (Lackland), and Philippe Auguste, King of France.
Eleanor spent her later life peacefully at her castle on the isle of Oléron and finished her days at Fontevraud Abbey, where she is buried, together with her husband Henry Plantagenet and their son Richard the Lionheart *(for further details of her life, see Eleanor of Aquitaine, qv).*

1224 Poitou attached to the French crown.
1345 Start of the Hundred Years War in Aquitaine.
1356 The French King, Jean le Bon, captured by the English at the Battle of Poitiers and taken prisoner by the Black Prince.
1360 Treaty of Brétigny : the Duchies of Aquitaine, Aunis, Saintonge and Angoulême become possessions of the English crown.
1369 Jean de Berry installed as Governor of Poitou.
1380 Restriction of the English presence in the southwest to Bordeaux and Bayonne, thanks to the formidable Constable Du Guesclin (who had chased the "Grandes Compagnies" – bands of terrorizing mercenaries and brigands – into Spain).
1422 Charles VII proclaimed King in Poitiers.
1450-1500 Dismantling of "English Gascony"; re-attachment of the Comtés of Armagnac and Comminges to the French crown.
1453 Final battle of the Hundred Years War, won by the Bureau brothers at Castillon-la-Bataille. Progressive abandonment of France by the English.

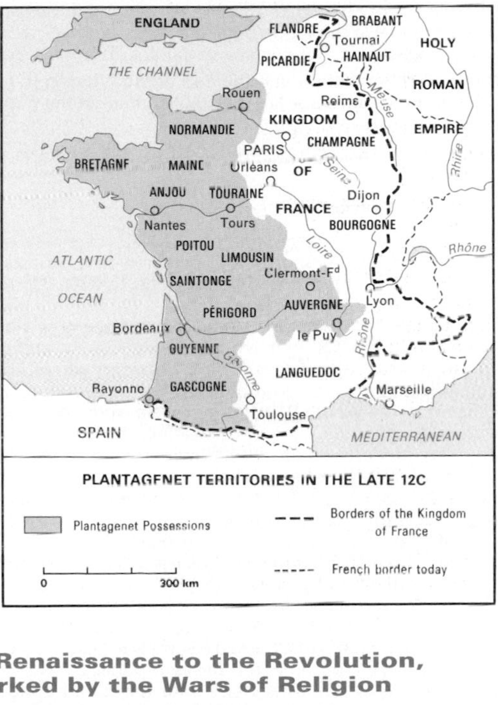

PLANTAGENET TERRITORIES IN THE LATE 12C

From the Renaissance to the Revolution, an era marked by the Wars of Religion

1484 The Albrets – "Kings of Navarre" – become all-powerful in the Gascon Pyrenees.
1494 Birth of François I in Cognac.
1515 Accession of François I. Battle of Marignano : victory for François over the Swiss and the Italians; north of Italy becomes French.
1533-34 The doctrine of the Reformation preached by Calvin in Saintonge, Angoumois and Poitiers (in 1558, from Basle in Switzerland, Calvin tells his fellow Protestants of the Confession of La Rochelle, a sign of the town's early conversion to the principles of Reformation).
1539 The administration of justice re-shaped by the Edict of Villiers-Cotteret, which imposed French as the official language of the judiciary, instead of Latin or the Langue d'Oc.
1555 Jeanne d'Albret crowned Queen of Navarre (reigned until 1572).
1562 Beginning of the Wars of Religion.
1569 Victory for the Duc d'Anjou over the Protestants in the Battles of Jarnac and Moncontour. Poitiers under siege from Protestants.
1570-71 Imposition of the Protestant faith on Béarn by Jeanne d'Albret. Rivalry between her lieutenant, Montgomery, and his Catholic adversary, Blaise de Monluc, in the commission of atrocities.
1579 An attempt made, with "Les Grands Jours de Poitiers", to end religious discord in the region.

1589 Accession of Henri IV, the son of Jeanne d'Albret.

1598 End of the Wars of Religion. Protestants granted freedom of worship, and 100 "safe places" (among them La Rochelle) in which to practise it, through Henri IV's promulgation of the Edict of Nantes.

1608 The future Cardinal Richelieu created Bishop of Luçon.

1627-28 Siege of La Rochelle and eventual submission to Richelieu.

1659-60 Treaty of the Pyrenees. Marriage of Louis XIV and the Infanta Maria Teresa at St-Jean-de-Luz.

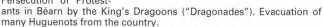

Chantilly, Musée Condé/GIRAUDON

Jeanne d'Albret.

1685 Revocation of the Edict of Nantes by Louis XIV. Persecution of Protestants in Béarn by the King's Dragoons ("Dragonades"). Evacuation of many Huguenots from the country.

18C A decisive impetus to the country's economic development brought during the era of the Intendants (stewards or governors) : the Comte de Blossac in Poitiers, Reverseaux in Saintes, Tourny in Bordeaux.

1789-99 The French Revolution and the end of the "Ancien Régime" (execution of Louis XVI in January 1793); establishment of the Convention.

1793-95 The Vendée War.

1794 Deportation of priests aboard "the hulks of Rochefort".

The Vendée War (1793-95)

By early 1793 a combination of the execution of Louis XVI, years of resentment over the religious issue capped by the rounding up and persecution of priests, the imposition of arbitrary taxes and the Convention's decision to conscript 300 000 men triggered an insurrection and a wave of riots in the west of France.

In Maine, Normandy and Brittany where the rebels were known as the *"Chouans"* and were fairly loosely dispersed, operating in a guerrilla fashion, the authorities did regain control; in the territories south of the River Loire, however, where fewer troops were available and communications were more difficult, the government collapsed. In this area, collectively known as the **Vendée Militaire,** the rebels were able to form the Catholic and Royal Army. Their strongholds were in the Gâtine, the *bocage* and the marshes – difficult country to penetrate, crisscrossed with hedgerows and perfect for ambushes, and in the Retz district, around Grand-Lieu lake.

Led at first by royalists of peasant stock such as **Cathelineau,** a pedlar, and the gamekeeper **Stofflet,** the peasants themselves soon called on their "gentlemen" (local nobles, estate stewards, priests) for help : these included **Gigost d'Elbée,** the Marquis of Bonchamps, Sapinaud, the Chevalier de **Charette, La Rochejaquelein** and **Lescure** among others. They also sought help – with limited success — from the British.

These so-called "brigands", armed at first only with pitchforks and scythes and later with guns taken from the Republicans, worked in "cells" grouped parish by parish, each wearing a cloak bearing the insignia of a Sacred Heart surmounted by a Cross; their flag was white (hence the royalists' nickname, the **Whites;** republicans were known as **Blues**), covered with fleurs-de-lys, and often inscribed with the motto *Long Live Louis XVI.* Their tactics were based on surprise : the good shots, hidden in the hedgerows, would silently surround an enemy patrol and pick off half of them, after which the ambushers would hurl themselves into the attack. If the resistance was too robust, the whole troop would melt away into the depths of the *bocage* – which was bitterly referred to by the Republican general, **Kléber,** as "the labyrinth".

From the spring of 1793 superior Republican troops led by generals Westermann, Kléber and Marceau were deployed in the area. Battles were won by both sides until the winter of 1794 when the Republicans got the upper hand : thousands of Whites were shot or guillotined, while the Blue **"Infernal Columns"** devastated the entire province. Following more battles and treaties the tired rebels eventually submitted to the Revolution through the diplomacy of the astute Republican General Lazare **Hoche.** Stofflet and Charette were finally captured and subsequently shot, the latter with the cry "Long live the King!" on his lips.

From the First to the Second Empire

1804 Consecration of Napoleon I as Emperor of the French, and founding of the town of "Napoleon-Vendée" (today La Roche-sur-Yon).

1806 The **continental blockade,** designed to ruin England by denying the country its economic outlets on mainland Europe, also severely reduced activity in the ports along the Atlantic Coast of France.

1815 Embarkation of the deposed Napoleon for the Isle of Aix.

1822 Plot by the "Four Sergeants of La Rochelle" to overthrow the Restoration government.

1832 Attempts by the Duchesse de Berry to provoke another Vendée uprising, this time against Louis-Philippe.

1845 Birth of the town of Arcachon.

1852-70 The Second Empire – a period of splendour for the Basque coast and country and the spas in the region.

1855 Opening of the Poitiers-La Rochelle railway link.

1860 Opening of the Eaux-Bonnes to Bagnères-de-Bigorre "Thermal Cure" route.

1867 The topography of the Landes revolutionized by the extensive planting of pines.

1868 Appearance of the "Portuguese" oyster in the Gironde.

From the Third Republic to the present day

1870 Installation in Tours and then in Bordeaux of a delegation from the National Defence government, headed by Gambetta.

1876 Phylloxera crisis in the vineyards.

1905 A law separating the Church from the State pushed through by Émile Combes, Mayor of Pons, and Georges Clemenceau, a Deputy in the National Assembly.

1914 President Poincaré, the government and both chambers of the Assembly moved temporarily to Bordeaux before the first German offensive in the First World War.

1929 Death of Clemenceau at St-Vincent-sur-Jard.

1939 End of the Spanish Civil War. Seizure of the Spanish gold reserves (lodged in Mont-de-Marsan) by the Fascist victors; 500 000 refugees flood into the southwest of France.

1940 Refuge again taken in Bordeaux by the authorities of the Third Republic after the German advance southward following the breakthrough at Sedan during the Second World War.

1945 German forces still entrenched in the "Atlantic pockets" (among them Royan) besieged by Free French soldiers and members of the Resistance.

1951 Death of Marshal Pétain on the Isle of Yeu.

1954 Inauguration of the oil wells of Parentis.

1966 Oléron becomes the first French island to be linked to the mainland via a bridge.

1988 Completion of the bridge leading to the Isle of Ré.

1990 Opening of the new high-speed Paris-Bordeaux rail link, with the *Train à Grande Vitesse* (TGV) *Atlantique* making the journey in less than three hours.

ART

ABC OF ARCHITECTURE

To assist readers unfamiliar with the terminology employed in architecture, we describe below the most commonly used terms, which we hope will make their visits to ecclesiastical, military and civil buildings more interesting.

Ecclesiastical architecture

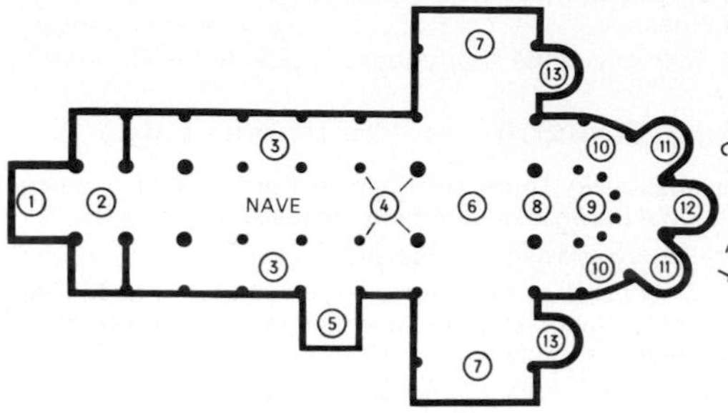

illustration I

Ground plan. – The more usual Catholic form is based on the outline of a cross with the two arms of the cross forming the transept: ① Porch – ② Narthex – ③ Side aisles (sometimes double) – ④ Bay (transverse section of the nave between 2 pillars) – ⑤ Side chapel (often predates the church) – ⑥ Transept crossing – ⑦ Arms of the transept, sometimes with a side doorway – ⑧ Chancel, nearly always facing east towards Jerusalem; the chancel often vast in size was reserved for the monks in abbatial churches – ⑨ High altar – ⑩ Ambulatory: in pilgrimage churches the aisles were extended round the chancel, forming the ambulatory, to allow the faithful to file past the relics – ⑪ Radiating or apsidal chapel – ⑫ Axial chapel. In churches which are not dedicated to the Virgin this chapel, in the main axis of the building is often consecrated to the Virgin (Lady Chapel) – ⑬ Transept chapel.

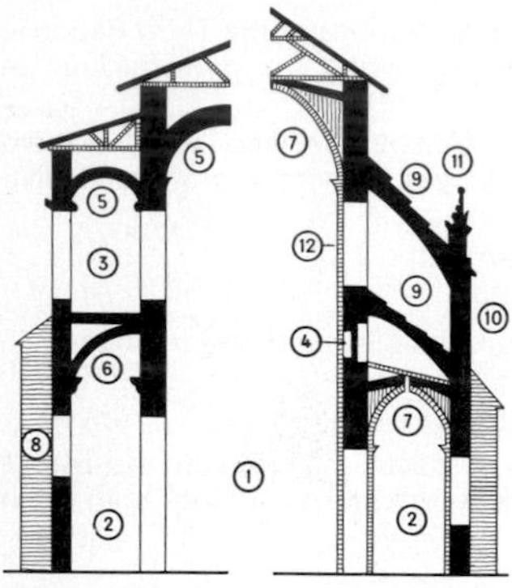

Romanesque Gothic

◄ illustration II

Cross-section: ① Nave – ② Aisle – ③ Tribune or Gallery – ④ Triforium – ⑤ Barrel vault – ⑥ Half-barrel vault – ⑦ Pointed vault – ⑧ Buttress – ⑨ Flying buttress – ⑩ Pier of a flying buttress – ⑪ Pinnacle – ⑫ Clerestory window.

illustration III ►

Gothic cathedral: ① Porch – ② Gallery – ③ Rose window – ④ Belfry (sometimes with a spire) – ⑤ Gargoyle acting as a waterspout for the roof gutter – ⑥ Buttress – ⑦ Pier of a flying buttress (abutment) – ⑧ Flight or span of flying buttress – ⑨ Double-course flying buttress – ⑩ Pinnacle – ⑪ Side chapel – ⑫ Radiating or apsidal chapel – ⑬ Clerestory windows – ⑭ Side doorway – ⑮ Gable – ⑯ Pinnacle – ⑰ Spire over the transept crossing.

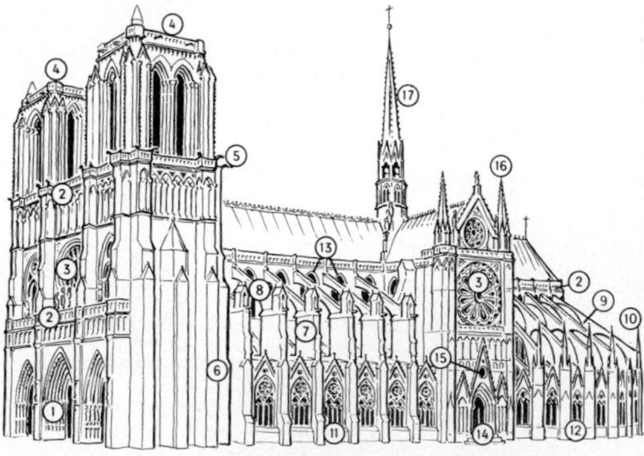

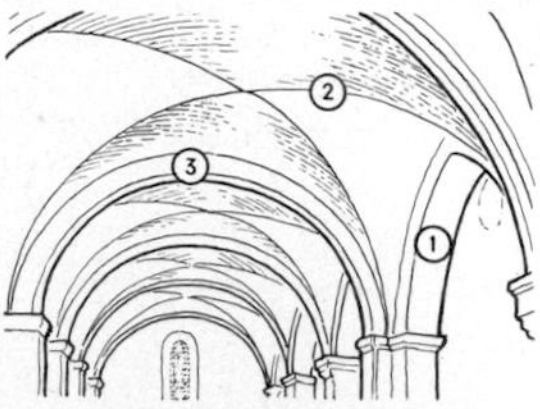

illustration IV

Groined vaulting:
① Main arch – ② Groin
③ Transverse arch

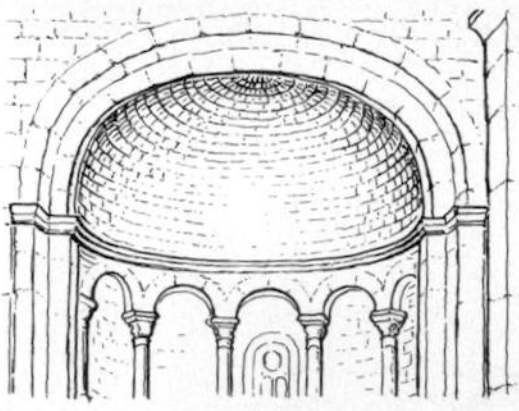

illustration V

Oven vault:
termination of a barrel vaulted nave

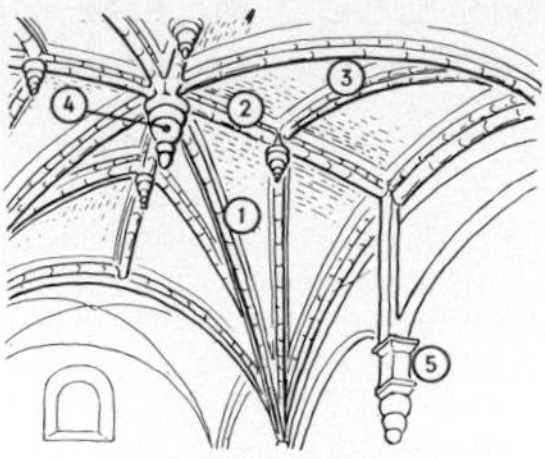

illustration VI

Lierne and tierceron vaulting:
① Diagonal – ② Lierne
③ Tierceron – ④ Pendant
⑤ Corbel

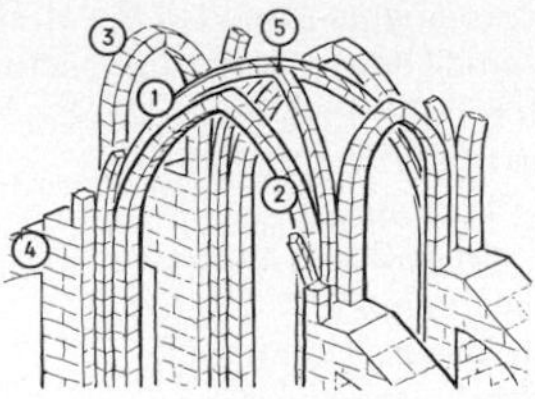

illustration VII

Quadripartite vaulting:
① Diagonal – ② Transverse
③ Stringer – ④ Flying buttress
⑤ Keystone

▼ illustration VIII

Doorway: ① Archivolt. Depending on the architectural style of the building this can be rounded, pointed, basket-handled, ogee or even adorned by a gable – ② Arching, covings (with string courses, mouldings, carvings or adorned with statues). Recessed arches or orders form the archivolt – ③ Tympanum – ④ Lintel – ⑤ Archshafts – ⑥ Embrasures. Arch shafts, splaying sometimes adorned with statues or columns – ⑦ Pier (often adorned by a statue) – ⑧ Hinges and other ironwork.

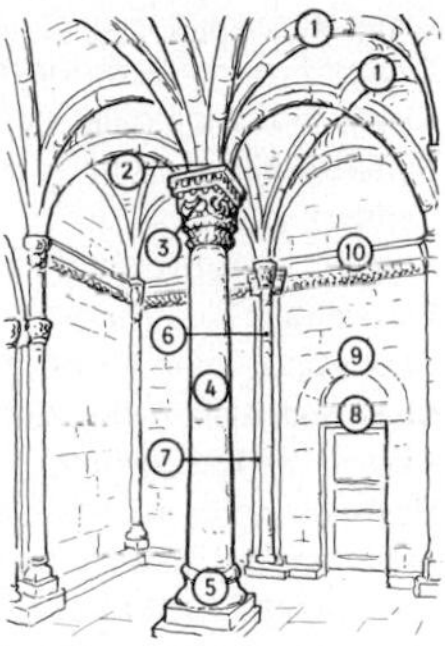

illustration IX ►

Arches and pillars: ① Ribs or ribbed vaulting – ② Abacus – ③ Capital – ④ Shaft – ⑤ Base – ⑥ Engaged column – ⑦ Pier of arch wall – ⑧ Lintel – ⑨ Discharging or relieving arch – ⑩ Frieze.

Military architecture

illustration X

Fortified enclosure: ① Hoarding (projecting timber gallery) – ② Machicolations (corbelled crenellations) – ③ Barbican – ④ Keep or donjon – ⑤ Covered watchpath – ⑥ Curtain wall – ⑦ Outer curtain wall – ⑧ Postern.

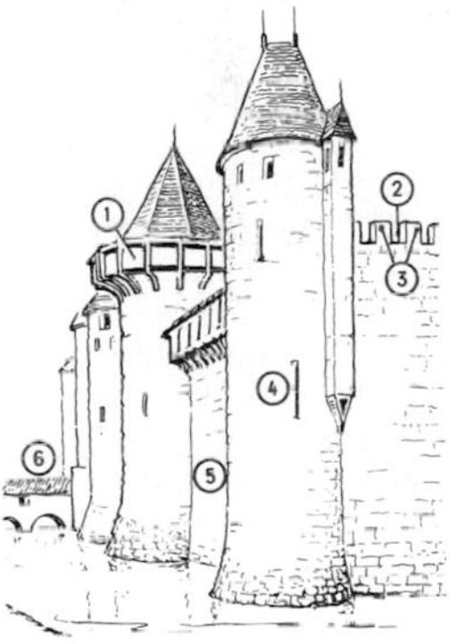

illustration XI

Towers and curtain walls: ① Hoarding – ② Crenellations – ③ Merlon – ④ Loophole or arrow slit – ⑤ Curtain wall – ⑥ Bridge or drawbridge.

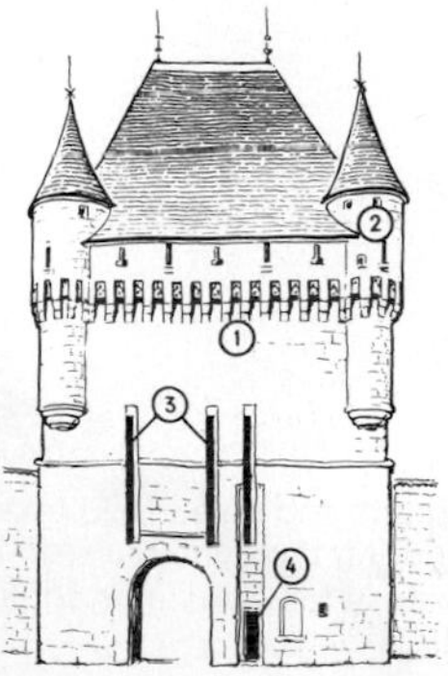

◄ illustration XII

Fortified gatehouse: ① Machicolations – ② Watch turrets or bartizan – ③ Slots for the arms of the drawbridge – ④ Postern.

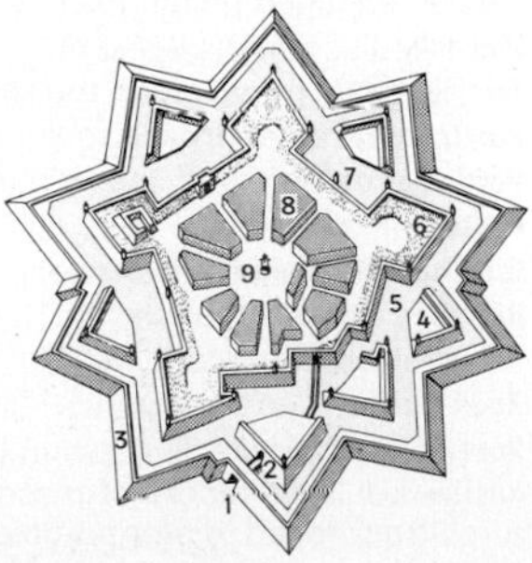

illustration XIII ►

Star fortress: ① Entrance – ② Drawbridge – ③ Glacis – ④ Ravelin or half-moon – ⑤ Moat – ⑥ Bastion – ⑦ Watch turret – ⑧ Town – ⑨ Assembly area.

ART AND ARCHITECTURAL TERMS USED IN THE GUIDE

Acroterion: ornaments placed at the apex and ends of a pediment of a temple.
Aedicule: a small house or room; a niche.
Aisle: illustration I.
Altarpiece or retable: illustration XX.
Ambulatory: illustration I.
Apsidal or radiating chapel: illustration I.
Archivolt: illustration VIII.
Axial or Lady Chapel: illustration I.
Barrel vaulting: illustration II.
Basket arch: depressed arch common to late-medieval and Renaissance architecture.
Bay: illustration I.
Bishop's throne: Gothic chair with a high back.
Buttress: illustrations II and III.
Capital: illustration IX.
Cardo: main street of Roman town running north-south.
Caryatid: female figure used as a column (atlantes are male caryatids).
Chevet: French term for the east end of a church; illustration I.
Cippus (-i): small pillar used to mark a burial place or serve as a sepulchral monument.
Coffered ceiling: vault or ceiling decorated with sunken panels.
Corbel: illustration VI.
Crypt: underground chamber or chapel.
Curtain wall: illustration XI.
Decumanus: main street of Roman town running east-west.
Depressed arch: three-centred arch sometimes called a basket arch.
Diagonal arch: illustrations VI and VII.
Dome: illustrations XIV and XV.
Exedra: niche, usually semi-circular, with a bench around the wall.
Flamboyant: latest phase (15C) of French Gothic architecture; name taken from the undulating (flame-like) lines of the window tracery.
Flame ornament: ornamentation used in classical art representing a vase spewing flames.
Foliated scrolls: sculptural or painted ornamentation depicting foliage, often in a frieze.
Fresco: mural paintings executed on wet plaster.
Gable: triangular part of an end wall carrying a sloping roof; the term is also applied to the steeply pitched ornamental pediments of Gothic architecture; illustration III.
Gallery: illustrations II and III.
Gargoyle: illustration III.
Génoise: decorative frieze under the eaves, composed of a double or triple row of tiles embedded end-on in the wall.
Groined vaulting: illustration IV.
High relief: haut-relief.
Hypocaust: an underground furnace to heat the water for the baths or rooms of a house.
Keep or donjon: illustration X.
Keystone: illustration VII.
Lintel: illustrations VIII and IX.
Lombard arcades: decorative blind arcading composed of small arches and intervening pilaster strips; typical of Romanesque architecture in Lombardy.
Low relief: bas-relief.
Machicolations: illustration X.
Modillion: small console supporting a cornice.
Mullion: a vertical post dividing a window.
Oppidum (-a): Latin word for a fortified agglomeration, usually set on a hill or height.
Organ: illustration XVII.
Oven vaulting: illustration V.
Overhang or jetty: overhanging upper storey.
Ovolo moulding: egg-shaped decoration.
Peribolus (-os): sacred enclosure or court around a temple.
Peristyle: a range of columns surrounding or on the façade of a building.
Pier: illustration III.
Pietà: Italian term designating the Virgin Mary with the dead Christ on her knees.
Pilaster: engaged rectangular column.
Pinnacle: illustrations II and III.
Piscina: basin for washing the sacred vessels.
Porch: covered approach to the entrance to a building.
Portico: a colonnaded space in front of a façade or in an interior courtyard.
Postern: illustrations X and XII.
Quadripartite vaulting: illustration VII.
Recessed arches: see voussoir.
Recessed tomb: funerary niche.
Rood screen: illustration XVI.
Rose or wheel window: illustration III.
Rustication: large blocks of masonry often separated by deep joints and given bold textures (rock-faced, diamond-pointed...); commonly employed during the Renaissance.
Santon: fired and brightly painted clay figurines; traditionally used in the Christmas cribs in Provence.

Segment: part of a ribbed vault; compartment between the ribs.
Semicircular arch: round-headed arch.
Spire: illustration III.
Splay: a slope; applied usually to the sides of a door or a window; illustration VIII.
Stalls: illustration XIX.
Stucco: mixture of powdered marble, plaster and strong glue; used for decoration.
Tracery: intersecting stone ribwork in the upper part of a window.
Transept: illustration I.
Triforium: illustration II.
Triptych: three panels hinged together, chiefly used as an altarpiece.
Twinned or paired: columns, pilasters, windows... grouped in twos.
Voussoir: wedge-shaped masonry in an arch or a vault.
Watchpath or wall walk: illustration X.

Provençal bell cages – Built to resist the mistral which would blow through the wrought iron instead of blowing and knocking down the stones, the Provençal bell cage crowned buildings: religious, civic or military. Either simple (bell-shaped or spherical) or elaborate in shape (bulbous, cylindrical or pyramidial), these wrought-iron cages grace the Provençal sky with their delicate silhouettes.

◀ Illustration XIV

Dome on squinches:
① Octagonal dome – ② Squinch – ③ Arches of transept crossing

Illustration XV ▶

Dome on pendentives:
① Circular dome – ② Pendentive – ③ Arches of transept crossing

Illustration XVI

Rood screen – It replaced the rood beam in larger churches and was used for the preaching and reading the Epistle and Gospel. From the 17C onwards many were removed as they tended to hide the altar.

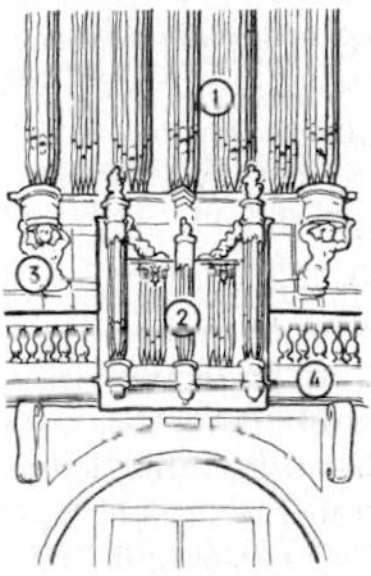

Illustration XVII

Organ:
① Great organ case
② Little organ case
③ Caryatids – ④ Loft

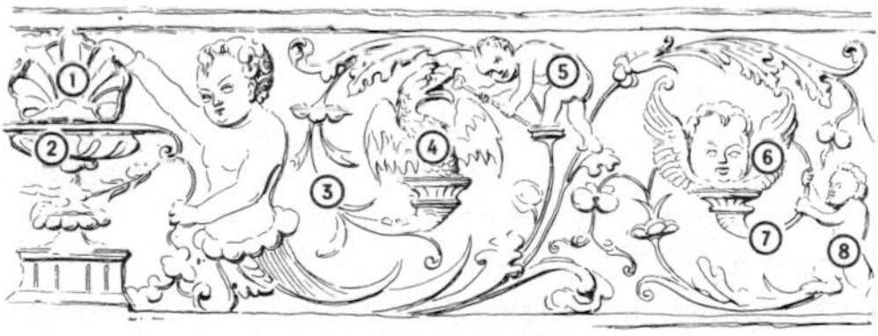

Illustration XVIII

Renaissance-ornament:
① shell – ② vase – ③ foliage
④ dragon – ⑤ nude child
⑥ cherub – ⑦ cornucopia
⑧ satyr

Illustration XIX

Stalls:
① High back
② Elbow rest
③ Cheek-piece
④ Misericord

Illustration XX

Altar with retable or altarpiece
① Retable or altarpiece – ② Predella
③ Crowning piece – ④ Altar table –
⑤ Altar front

Certain baroque retables consisted of several altars; contemporary liturgy tends to eliminate them.

ART AND ARCHITECTURE

Gallo-Roman era

Notre-Dame-la-Grande, Poitiers.

Despite the institutionalized vandalisms of the 19C, many examples still remain of the arts which flourished in the Roman colony of Aquitaine, the capitals of which were Bordeaux, Poitiers and Saintes. The ruins of amphitheatres, theatres, temples and bath-houses, and votive arches scattered throughout these areas offer a broad view of Gallo-Roman civilization.

Romanesque period (11C - 12C)

After the turbulent period of the early Middle Ages, marked by conflicts between the great feudal houses, the year AD 1000 saw a renewal of faith exemplified in the Crusades and the great pilgrimages. In the southwest of France the important religious sanctuaries were all built along the routes leading to Santiago de Compostela in Spain *(see the Way of St James, qv).*

Church Design – In Poitou, Romanesque churches generally comprised a high, barrel-vaulted central nave, buttressed by side aisles which were scarcely less tall. Light entered through the window bays of these aisles.
In Angoumois and Saintonge (the regions around Angoulême and Saintes) the wide, single nave was sometimes barrel-vaulted, sometimes topped by a **line of domes** – showing influence from the Périgord region.

West fronts – The façades were characterized by arcades or tiers of blind arcades. Arcading at the upper level was nevertheless typical more in Angoumois and Saintonge, while churches in Poitou were often distinguished by a tripartite division vertically, with large arcades separated by columnar buttresses (Notre-Dame-la-Grande in Poitiers is an exception).
The west front was usually surmounted by a triangular pediment and flanked by columns or groups of columns sometimes crowned by pierced lanterns with conical roofs. These roofs, and often those of the church belfries, would be covered by overlapping tiles. The façade itself was normally decorated with statues and low-reliefs, intended to deliver a message. Notre-Dame-la-Grande in Poitiers is one of the most successful examples of these "façade-screens" : the story told by the statuary is a page from the Bible and is easily understood.
In Angoumois the west fronts are generally more sober, although that of St-Pierre in Angoulême is famous for its depiction, through 70 different characters, of the Last Judgement.

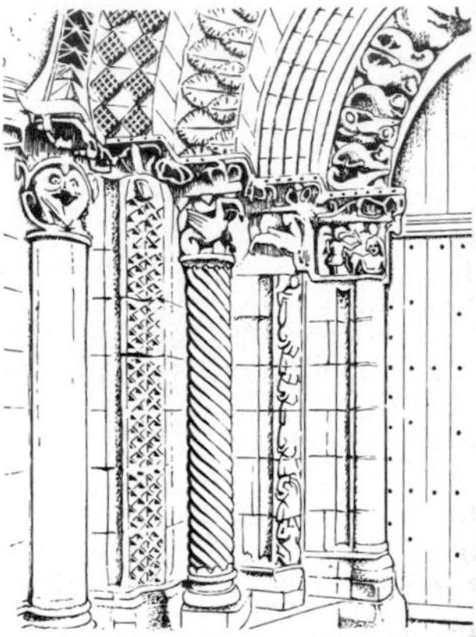

Detail of the doorway, St Nicholas parish church, Maillezais.

Doorways – In Poitou, Saintonge and Angoumois the main doorways are deeply recessed and decorated with lavishly carved covings and capitals. Most of them, on the other hand, lack a tympanum. They are frequently flanked by blind arcades, themselves richly decorated (some believe these arcades to be a development from the Roman triumphal arch).
Many doorways show traces of Spanish-Moroccan influence, largely because of the churches' proximity to the pilgrim routes to Santiago de Compostela; such features include arches which are Moorish, garlanded, clover-leaf or **multilobed** *(illustration see Celles-sur-Belle).*

Belfries – Most Romanesque belltowers in the region have tall buttresses or corner turrets, and are pierced by arcading decorated with open-work at the upper levels.

Belfry-porch (Poitiers)

Central belltower (Saintes)

Melle — Rioux
East ends: Poitevin (left) and Saintongeais (right).

Some of these belfries rise above a porch, like the one at St-Porchaire in Poitiers, but most are placed centrally, marking the transept crossing; Abbaye aux Dames, Saintes, is such an example. The cone-shaped steeple with overlapping tiles which surmounts the church in Saintes is a feature found also in Poitou, and is based on a design originally used by the Romans.

East ends – Churches with an ambulatory at their east end and radiating chapels buttressed by columns are common in Poitou : St-Hilaire, in Melle, is typical. Certain east ends in Saintonge, on the other hand, were built to a simpler design, like the church at Rioux, with a five-faced apse and columnar buttresses; the bays separating the columns have archivolts at the middle level, decorated with a row of blind arcades and miniature columns above. The whole is topped by an elegant frieze running beneath a cornice with carved, double-scroll brackets.

Sculpture – The use of sculpture – on façades, east ends, corbels, arches, consoles and capitals – was facilitated by the nature of the local limestone, which is relatively easy to work; Romanesque edifices are notable for the abundance, variety and finesse of the religious ornamentation. On these surfaces foliage, acanthus leaves in the antique style and pre-Romanesque plaited stonework rival in complexity the bestiary of oriental monsters, biblical illustrations, legends of the saints and scenes of everyday life.
The lavish embellishment of the west front of Notre-Dame-la-Grande in Poitiers stands out in the area; in the Saintonge such sumptuousness in the sculpture is regarded as normal. Whilst the richness of the overall decoration can be almost overwhelming, it is also worth looking closely at the wonderful individual details.

Themes – Some of the themes found in the sculpture are classical and universal, like the Last Judgement, and eminently suitable for illustration on the wide "blank pages" of such façades as Angoulême cathedral; others are more particular to Poitou and Saintonge – Vice and Virtue, for instance, or the Wise and Foolish Virgins. Many covings in the region depict Vices in the form of monsters being overcome by armed women symbolizing the Virtues. The Wise and Foolish Virgins, representing the Elected and the Rejected at the Last Judgement, are shown in the former case as simply dressed and carrying lighted lamps, the latter dressed ostentatiously, with their lamps upside down. On many of the west fronts the legendary **Cavalier,** sheltered beneath an arcade, sits astride a horse which is trampling underfoot a small human figure *(see Melle, qv).*

Frescoes and mural paintings – A fresco (from the Italian word *fresco* = fresh) is a wall or ceiling painting executed on a surface of freshly applied, still-damp plaster, into which the design is incorporated before the plaster dries. The number of colours that can be used is limited, since only pigments made from natural earths and iron oxides suit the technique – allowing the artist yellow to red, and green, violet and cobalt blue.
The most extraordinary murals of the Poitou school are found in St-Savin, where the compositions are remarkable as much for the beauty of the colours, the harmony of the design and the perfection of the technique as for their lively content.

Cemeteries – Charentes is noted for two particular types of monument : the Lanterns of the Dead and the so-called Hosanna Crosses. Each, originally, would have been situated at the heart of the cemetery, though some of the burial grounds have since been displaced.

Lanterns of the Dead – These are stone columns, hollow inside, at the top of which a beacon would have been lit, the flames symbolizing the eternal life of the soul. The structure comprises an underground chamber covering an ossuary, steps leading to an altar at which the priest would recite prayers for the dead, the column itself – usually with a stairway incorporated – the emplacement for the beacon and a conical roof crowned with a cross. The Lantern at Fenioux is a fine surviving example, as is that at St-Pierre-d'Oléron.

"Lantern of the Dead", Fenioux.

Hosanna Crosses – The name of these crosses stems from an old custom under which, on each Palm Sunday, the faithful would commemorate Christ's entry into Jerusalem. At the foot of the cross the priest would chant the Gospel for that day, and then the congregation would form a procession, singing "Hosanna!" as they laid down their branches of palm – their hosannas.
The best-known Hosanna Crosses are those at Moëze, southwest of Rochefort, and at Aulnay.

From Romanesque to Gothic : the Plantagenet Style

In the west of France the Plantagenet style, also known as **Angevin,** marked the transition between Romanesque and Gothic styles; artistically its highest point was at the beginning of the 13C – and by the end of that century it was no more.

Angevin vaulting – In normal Gothic vaulting all the keys are situated at approximately the same height. Plantagenet architecture, however, is characterized by steeply recessed quadripartite vaulting – probably derived from an earlier use of the dome – in which the keystones of the diagonals are higher than the stringer or transverse keys by anything up to 3m – 10ft.
At the end of the 12C these Angevin vaults became lighter as the number of ribs increased and arched more gracefully, springing from slender circular columns. The early 13C saw the style at its finest, the tall, slim pillars supporting an airy tracery of lierne vaulting.

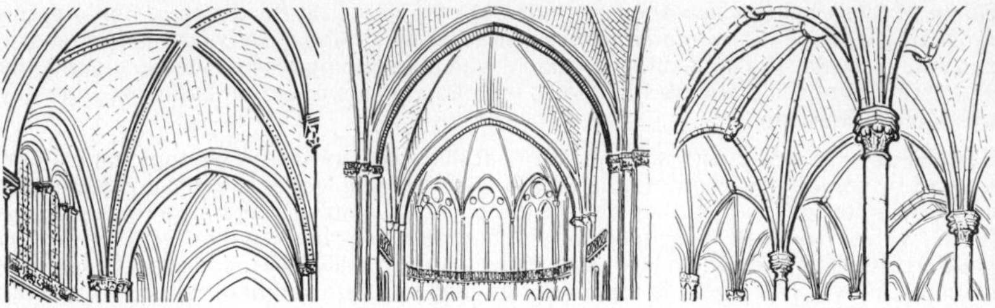

Angevin vaulting

Mid 12C. Late 12C. Early 13C.

Examples of the style can be seen in Vendée, Poitou (Poitiers Cathedral, Airvault, St-Jouin-de-Marnes southeast of Thouars), Saintonge and as far away as the region around the Upper Garonne.

Gothic period (12C – 15C)

Apart from its appearance in the Plantagenet style, which nevertheless retains many elements of the Romanesque, Gothic art raised scarcely an echo in the west and south-west of France; such examples as there are tend to be Southern Gothic, the style of the Mediterranean, characterized by a single, very wide nave and no transept. Certain English influences are evident in the square, Flamboyant towers of a few 14C and 15C churches in Saintonge (St-Eutrope in Saintes, Marennes).

Renaissance period

The Renaissance did not take hold in France instantly following a visit by dignitaries to Rome or Florence, and the traditions of the Gothic style were slow to disappear; the arrival of a score of Neapolitan artists, however, brought from Italy by Charles VIII at the end of 1495, did breathe new life into the French architectural establishment of the time.

Civil architecture – Occurrences of the Renaissance style in the west were the result of members of the court of François I who were natives of Saintonge or Angoumois being influenced by the architecture of the Loire Valley : the "François I Wing" of the Château d'Oiron, for example, displays a characteristic series of basket-handled arches, while the Château de la Rochefoucauld, with its celebrated courtyard surrounded by a three-tiered gallery, is reminiscent of an Italian *palazzo.*

Extensive use of decorative arabesques and grotesqueries – along with a deep nod in the direction of antiquity – distinguishes the châteaux of Dampierre-sur-Boutonne and Oiron : the roofs are tall, with all the slopes on each side at the same angle; the inclusion of splendid staircases accounts for the projecting façades of the central blocks.

Similar features can be found in other châteaux of the region – the old royal Castle in Cognac, for instance (guard-room and gallery) – or in such Renaissance mansions as the Hôtel Fumé in Poitiers and the Hôtel Saint-Simon in Angoulême.

Classical period

The accession of the Bourbon dynasty in 1589, following the era of stagnation which characterized French art and architecture towards the end of the Renaissance, heralded a radical shift in direction : the period of material prosperity which coincided with the reign of Henri IV fired artists eager for change with new ideas, new interpretations of classical, antique themes. Classical art held sway in France from 1589 to 1789.

Classical fortifications

From the 16C onwards fortifications were constructed above all to protect frontier towns, and consisted of curtain walls and bastions surmounted by platforms from which cannon could be fired. Overhanging turrets allowed the defenders to survey the surrounding ditches and keep watch over the terrain beyond.

The acknowledged master of fortifications was **Sebastien le Prestre de Vauban** (1633-1707). Developing the ideas of his predecessors – military engineers employed by the King – he evolved a system based on the use of massive bastions complemented by ravelins or demilunes, the whole being protected by very deep defensive ditches *(illustration p 37).* Vauban's designs are notable for the way he made use of natural obstacles, used only local materials, and added aesthetic value to the functional works he produced, incorporating monumental stone entrance gates, often adorned with sculpture. His talent can be admired at Blaye, where the citadel protecting the entrance to the port of Bordeaux is part of a complex defence system; further south, Bayonne and Navarrenx (south of Orthez) are also examples of the genius of this great military architect.

Louis XVI architecture

Many majestic buildings were built in the Louis XVI style, inspired by the art of antiquity. Those designed by the Parisian architect Victor Louis (1731-1811) are typical of the period : his personal style, noble and sober, is exemplified in the Grand Théâtre in Bordeaux and in numerous châteaux in the surrounding countryside.

Chartreuses – These small châteaux or manor houses dating from the 18C or the early 19C are typical of the Guyenne region and especially around the vineyards of Bordeaux. They were conceived by the local aristocracy desirous of a country retreat that was close to the city yet removed from the noise and bustle of urban life. The *Chartreuses* were low-built, usually without an upper storey, and sometimes included a central block in the form of a pavilion; they opened directly onto a terrace or flower garden. Château Beychevelle, in the wine country, is one of the most charming examples.

MEDIEVAL ARCHITECTURE AND TOWN PLANNING

Military architecture

From the 9C to the 12C the weakness and remoteness of the central power in medieval France contributed to the establishment of powerful Dukedoms and Counties. When the enforced feudalism began to crumble, one of the results was a generalized increase in the scattering of new strongpoints. The southwest and in particular the former Aquitaine, which had been disputed for three centuries by two different crowns, became peppered with fortresses. Outside the towns where, through the consolidation of existing Gallo-Roman protective enclosures, defence could usually be assured, crude new strongholds proliferated in the open countryside : a surrounding ditch, a palisade, a wooden tower – later built of stone – rising on a hillock, these were enough to provide at least basic refuge.

Keeps – Rectangular keeps built of stone made their appearance in the early 11C. Their role initially was purely defensive : the stonework was not particularly thick, there were no loopholes with a field of fire. The ground-floor level, which was dark, served as a store. The keep could only be entered at first-floor level, via either a ladder or a retractable footbridge. This design (illustrated by the keep at Bassoues), which persisted until the 14C, explains why the spiral stone staircases of so many of these structures only started at the higher level.
Before the Hundred Years War there was a 13C-14C Gascon variant of the keep known as a **"salle"** – a fortified dwelling flanked by one or two rectangular towers, set along the diagonal if there were two. Again, only the upper storeys were inhabited and provided with windows.

Castles of brick – Certain castles in the Béarn district bear the trademark of **Sicard de Lordat,** a military engineer employed by Gaston Fébus *(qv),* the 14C overlord of Béarn. For reasons of economy they were built of brick rather than massive stonework. The single square tower astride a polygonal defensive perimeter served both as a keep and as a gateway. The living quarters and the barracks were built against the inside of the curtain wall.

D'après photo Art Pyr/PIX

Fortified church, Luz.

Fortified churches – Fortress-churches occupy a special place in the history of French military architecture, and are numerous in the southwest.
Two types of machicolation were employed in their construction : the classic variety supported by corbels, and another in the form of arches curving between the buttresses (as at Beaumont-de-Lomagne, *see map overleaf*). They appeared for the first time in France in the late 12C, in the Langue d'Oc country.
The churches were traditionally places of asylum, refuges for the hunted, with their robust architecture and their belfries which could be used as watch-towers; moreover the "Truce of God" ordered by the Vatican Council in the 10C and 11C stipulated a "zone of inviolability", extending for 30 paces around each church, in which refugees might not be touched. The Council's orders forbade the waging of war on certain days of the week and during Advent, Lent and Easter week. Violation of the Truce was punished with excommunication.
Examples of these fortified churches still exist in the Upper Pyrenees, in the valleys once subject to cross-frontier raids from Aragon; the best-known are Luz church, enclosed within a crenellated curtain wall, and Sentein church, which has three towers.

"New Towns" of the Middle Ages

Medieval urban development in southwestern France has left only three sites still substantial enough today to be called towns : Montauban (southeast of Agen), founded by the Comte de Toulouse in 1144; the lower part of Carcassonne (1247), built on the west bank of the Aude by St Louis to shelter the homeless after the town was sacked; **Libourne** (east of Bordeaux), named after Sir Roger Leyburn, Seneschal to Edward I of England (1270). *For details of Montauban and Carcassone, see the Michelin Green Guide Pyrénées Roussillon Albigeois (in French).* Aquitaine, however, at first strewn with *sauvetés* and *castelnaux* (refuges and fortified towns, *see below*), was above all characterized by an abundance of *bastides* – those new towns, half "urban", half rural and characterised by a geometric ground plan, which remain today even at their most important no larger than a county town.

Sauvetés and Castelnaux (11C and 12C) – The **Sauveté** (Sauvetat, Sauveterre etc) usually arose as the result of an ecclesiastical initiative. Prelates, abbots or dignitaries of a military Order of Chivalry would found the village or hamlet; the inhabitants would clear, prepare and cultivate their lands; a "host" or overseer, installed perhaps in a small manor house, would supervise the work. These rural townships also provided sanctuary for fugitives.

In a similar fashion, the **Castelnau** (Châteauneuf, Castets etc) originated with the dependencies built by a seigneur around his château. Auvillar (southwest of Agen), Mugron and Pau were once *castelnaux.* In Gascony the name Castelnau is completed by the name of the local fief : Castelnau-Magnoac, Castelnau-Barbarens etc.

Bastides (1220-c1350) – The *bastide* was an entirely new concept, a true purpose-built and efficiently-planned place where people could live. By the middle of the 14C something like 300 *bastides* had been created between Périgord and the Pyrenees. In Gascony and Guyenne these "new towns" were so numerous that it suggests that at one time they were the most important form of collective habitation in the region. Although not all of them were fully developed, and despite their relative lack of importance today – some have disappeared altogether – the *bastides* in their time were a genuine response to demographic, financial and economic needs as well as to military and political imperatives.

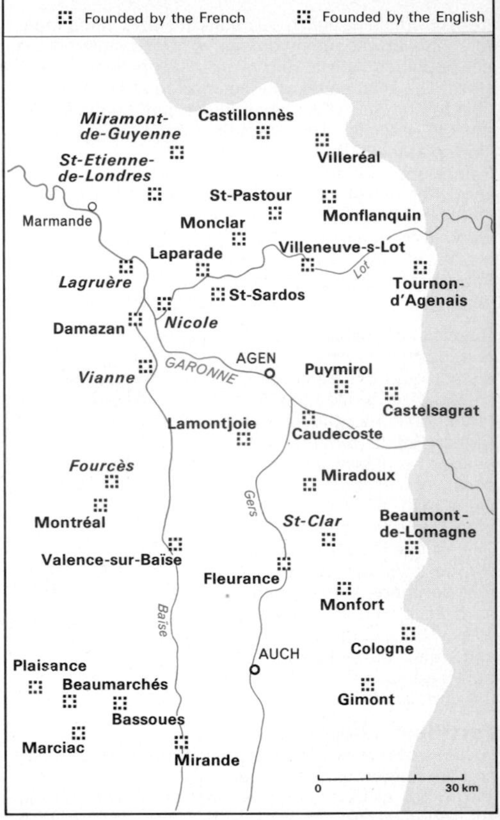

SOME BASTIDES IN GASCOGNE AND GUYENNE

The construction of many *bastides* arose from a contract of *paréage.* Such contracts, frequently drawn up between the King and a local seigneur or between an abbot and a lay seigneur, could also permit two neighbouring seigneurs to detail the rights and powers of each over territories they might hold in common; or they could stipulate that a less powerful seigneur would enjoy the protection of his stronger neighbour in return for a fixed proportion of the former's revenues. The contracts also affected the inhabitants of the *bastide,* establishing their status, outlining the allotment of building plots, specifying the taxes to be paid. To encourage people to move into the *bastide,* new arrivals were granted – among other privileges – the right of asylum and exemption from any military service due to the seigneur. The "immigrants" were free to bequeath property to their inheritors and dispose of their other possessions as they wished. Penalties, on the other hand, could be imposed on those who were slow to build.

Creation of the Bastides – There were three great founders of this system of "rural urbanization" :

– The brother of St Louis, **Alphonse de Poitiers** (1249-71), who became Comte de Toulouse. From the Comminges to the Rouergue district (bordering the River Lot), he multiplied the construction of these new settlements, thereby ensuring a healthy flow of funds to the state coffers and contributing to the "Frenchifying" of the region.

– The Seneschal of Toulouse, **Eustache de Beaumarchais** (1272-94), during the reigns of Philippe le Hardi and Philippe le Bel. The *bastides* he founded in Gascony are particularly well planned, either in traditional chessboard form (Mirande, Marciac) or in a more unusual design, as at Fleurance which is triangular.

– The Duc d'Aquitaine and King of England, **Edward I Plantagenet** (1272-1307) and his Seneschal, Jean de Grailly, who held the stewardship of the Agen region. Their aims were mainly strategic, and their *bastides* were built to counter the French examples on the far side of the "frontier".

Toponymy – Place-names of the *bastides* followed three different principles. They could evoke the settlement's status – Villefranche (Free Town); they could carry the name of the founder – Montréjeau (Mount Royal), Beaumarché, Hastingues (Hastings); or they could suggest a symbolic twinning with some famous foreign city – Valence (after Valencia in Spain), Fleurance (Florence), Cologne, Tournay etc.

Town planning – *Bastides* were fairly rigidly planned, based on the model of a right-angled grid, either square or rectangular (with the exception of Fourcès, a rare circular *bastide*). Variations on this plan were due either to the relief of the chosen site or to considerations of defence. The use of professional surveyors at the planning stage is evident in the rectilinear layout of the streets, always meeting each other at right-angles to form a symmetrical pattern of equal-area lots. Those moving in were allowed so much on which they could build, so much for a garden, and – outside the built-up area but not too far away – an allotment which they could cultivate.
The road system was ahead of its time : the principal streets were usually 8m – 26ft wide, a generous size when none of the buildings had more than two floors.

In the centre of the grid was the main (and only) square, normally closed to traffic and reserved for markets; many of the central, covered market-places still stand today. The square was effectively an open lot islanded among the regular ranks of buildings : the four streets framing it passed from the open air to the *couverts,* and then out again on the far side, retaining their continuity and frequently their street-names. The **couverts,** most of them unfortunately now truncated or lost altogether, were covered passages surrounding the square running beneath either stone-built arcades or projecting upper storeys supported by wooden pillars.

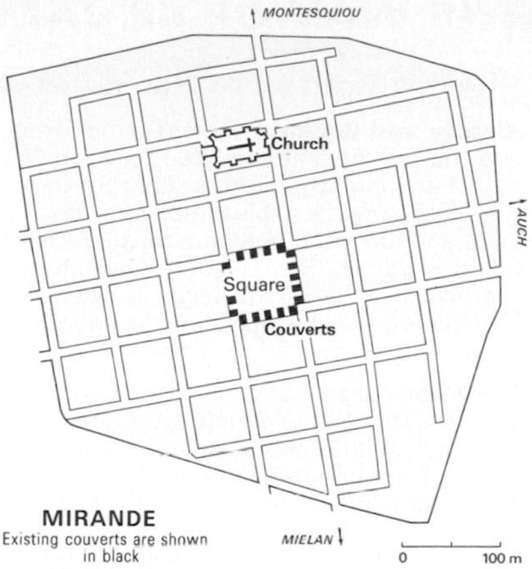

MIRANDE
Existing couverts are shown in black

Bastide Churches – The proliferation of *bastides* from the 13C onwards led to the construction of many new churches. They were built either close to the market square or out on the periphery of the grid, on the specified lot assigned for church and cemetery; here, therefore, the Languedoc single-nave-no-transept style was particularly suitable. Churches in Gascony share a "family likeness", with their belfry-porches (Mirande, Marciac) and their wide, dark naves lit mainly through the clerestory windows of a cramped apse.

Apa/PIX

Circular bastide, Fourcès.

MICHELIN GREEN GUIDES

Architecture
Fine Art
Ancient monuments
History
Geography
Picturesque scenery
Scenic routes
Touring programmes
Places to stay
Plans of towns and buildings

A collection of regional guides for France.

THE WAY OF ST JAMES

Pilgrim Routes to Santiago de Compostela

History and legend – St James the Great, beheaded in Jerusalem in the year AD 91, was the first Apostle martyred for his beliefs; according to legend, his body and head were transported to northwestern Spain in a "stone boat" and buried on the coast of Galicia. On the site of his tomb, miraculously re-discovered in the early 9C, a church was built, and around it grew the town of Compostela. When the Moors were driven from Spain St James (San Tiago in Spanish) became the patron saint of Christians : in the year 844, it is said, at the height of a decisive battle at Clavijo in Rioja, he appeared on a white charger and vanquished the enemy – a manifestation which earned him the nick-name of *Matamore* (Moor-slayer).

The Pilgrimage – Soon after the building of the church to St James, the faithful from far and wide began flocking to the site to venerate the relics. They travelled from hostel to hostel visiting churches, abbeys and holy places along a number of well-defined routes. Throughout the Middle Ages this traffic grew to such an extent that the church of Santiago in Compostela became a shrine equal in importance to Jerusalem itself or Rome.

The first French pilgrimage was led by the bishop of Le Puy in the year 951. Subsequently millions of **Jacquets,** Jacquots or Jacobites (Jacques in French = James) set out from Paris, Tours, Le Puy, Vézelay and Arles, which developed into assembly points for pilgrims from all over Europe.

Pilgrims to Santiago wore a uniform of heavy cape, eight-foot stave with a gourd attached to carry water, stout sandals and a broad-brimmed felt hat, turned up at the front and marked with three or four **scallop shells,** the badge of the saint, which identified the pilgrim's destination. The shells, found in great banks along the Galician coast and still called *Coquilles St-Jacques* (St James's Shells) in France today, were also used as a receptacle to collect alms. A scrip or pouch, a bowl and a small metal box for papers, passes etc, completed the equipment. The network of hostels and hospices where pilgrims could find food and shelter for a night, or receive attention if they were sick, was organized by the Benedictine monks of Cluny, the Premonstratensians and other orders; the Knights Templars and the Hospitallers of St John with their commanderies policed the routes, marked with carved mileposts or cairns : everything was done to ensure the pilgrims' welfare, both spiritually and temporally.

There was even a *Pilgrims' Guide,* the first "tourist" guide ever written, which was produced in Latin in *c*1135, probably by Aymeri Picaud, a monk from Parthenay-le-Vieux. This outlined local customs, gave advice on the climate and weather conditions to be expected, spiced the more mundane information with comments on the morals and mentality of the inhabitants of each region, and listed the most interesting routes and the sights on the way – the pilgrim in those days was in no hurry and frequently made detours which took weeks or months to complete, to visit a sanctuary or shrine (*Le Guide du Pèlerin de St-Jacques-de-Compostelle,* edited by Jeanne Vielliard (Vrin, Paris) is a translation into French of the 12C Latin handbook).

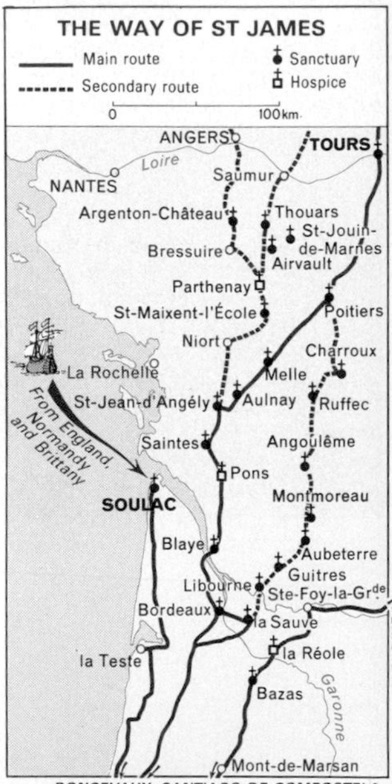

The main routes all converged in the Basse-Navarre district before crossing the Pyrenees. The most important junction was at Ostabat; St-Jean-Pied-de-Port was the last halt before the climb towards the frontier. The pilgrims reached Roncesvalles by a mountain route which was once part of the Roman road linking Bordeaux with Astorga, if possible via the Valcarlos defile – the only road (D 933) still practicable today from one end to the other. The bell of the monastery at Ibañeta pass would toll when it was foggy – or sometimes for much of the night – to signal the right direction to those pilgrims who might have got lost or lagged behind.

With the passage of time, however, the faith that fired people to set out on pilgrimages began to wane; false pilgrims seeking gain by trickery and robbery, and known as "Coquillards", increased; the Wars of Religion, when Christians fought among themselves, reduced the faithful even more. In the late 16C, when Francis Drake attacked Corunna, the relics were removed from the Cathedral to a place of safety, after which the pilgrimage was virtually abandoned. By the 18C anyone wishing to make the journey to Santiago de Compostela was obliged to provide the authorities, when requested, with a letter of introduction from their parish priest and other documents certified to be true by a police official or signed by the pilgrim's local bishop.

For more information on the legend and history of the shrine of the Apostle James the Greater, consult the Michelin Green Guide Spain (see under Santiago de Compostela).

FOOD AND DRINK

Visitors to the Atlantic Coast region of France have a rich variety of choice local products to feast themselves on *(see also Eating Out, qv).*
All along the coast itself good, fresh seafood is available while inland, in Poitou and the Charentes, the "simple, honest and direct, even rustic" cuisine – according to the great chef Curnonsky (1872-1956) – uses healthy raw materials, well prepared. In the Bordeaux region the accent is naturally on wines and wine sauces.

HORS-D'ŒUVRES

For lovers of seafood the obvious starter must be oysters from Arcachon or Marennes, or perhaps mussels from Aiguillon; *pibales* (elvers) from the Gironde, either grilled or *à la ravigote* (with a highly-seasoned white sauce) are a delicious alternative.
Those who prefer *charcuterie* might like to try the famous Bayonne ham or that from Poitou, or, further south, such Basque specialities as **loukinkos** (miniature garlic sausages) and **tripotcha,** a mutton boudin or blood sausage not unlike a small black pudding. Gourmets will also delight in the rich *foies gras* (prepared goose and duck livers) of Gers and the Landes.
A glass of chilled Pineau des Charentes may be taken as an aperitif or savoured with *foie gras,* while a chilled white wine such as a Graves or an Entre-Deux-Mers served at 8° to 10°C is a delightful accompaniment to oysters, fish, crustaceans and other shellfish.

FISH DISHES

This area favoured with an abundance of water – both fresh and salt – offers the choice of sole or turbot from the *Pertuis* (straits), fresh sardines from Royan or Les Sables d'Olonne, and stuffed carp in the Poitou fashion. A dish of **chipirones** – tiny cuttlefish, stuffed or cooked in a casserole – may be tried instead.
Near Bordeaux the choice is usually from fish caught in the Gironde estuary: shad, smelt, salmon, sturgeon, eels or the delicate-fleshed lamprey.

J.-C. Mayer/VLOO

Seafood specialities.

MEAT, POULTRY AND VEGETABLES

The quality of meat in the region, whether it be *chevreau* (young goat), Charmoise mutton or lamb from Pauillac, is invariably excellent. Many dishes around Bordeaux are served with a wine sauce; tender steaks accompanied by this sauce will be described on the menu as *"à la Bordelaise".*
The superb quality of vegetables grown in Charentes help form the base for the delicious *pot-au-feu* (beef stew) known locally as **le farci**; the luscious local broad beans, haricots, peas and Chinese cabbage can equally well be cooked *à la crème* (with cream) or with *beurre de Surgères* (a butter sauce).
Poultry specialities include *poule-au-pot* (chicken stew), Poitou goose with chestnuts, Challans duck and green peas, Barbezieux capon or chicken, and wood-pigeon *salmi* (casserole or ragout). Duck, if it is not conserved in its own fat (the delicious *confit de canard*), may be roasted or served as a *magret* (slices of breast).
Red wines from Médoc or Graves, served cool (cellar temperature) are an ideal complement to poultry, white meat and light dishes, while those from St-Émilion, Pomerol or Fronsac, served at room temperature, are wonderful accompaniments to game, red meat, mushrooms and cheese.

CHEESE

In Poitou, Vendée and Charentes it is quite normal to start off the dessert course with cheeses, for the local varieties are essentially unsalted cottage cheeses made from curdled milk or cream which can be taken with sugar if desired; they include **Caillebote d'Aunis,** a crustless sheep's cheese, and **Jonchée Niortaise**, a goat's cheese served on a rush platter. Equally delicious is the Poitou **Chabichou,** another strongly-flavoured goat's cheese. Some of these varieties may not be restricted to a single source – Caillebote, for instance, can be from goats', cows' or sheep's milk, depending on availability. The sheep's cheeses of the Basque country and Béarn remain characteristic local products.

FRUIT AND DESSERT

A good meal may be finished with a Charentais melon, with walnuts from Poitou or the Angoulême region, with peaches or plums from the valley of the Garonne, or with succulent prunes steeped in armagnac. Desserts include Poitou baked cheesecake *(tourteau fromager),* macaroons from St-Émilion, Charentais gâteau, and *clafoutis* (dark cherries baked in a sweet batter). Sweetmeats include Poitiers nougâtines, chocolate *marguerites* and *duchesses* from Angoulême, and angelica-based sweets from Niort.
The exquisite dessert wines of Sauternes, Barsac, Ste-Croix-du-Mont and Loupiac, served very cold (5°C), are the perfect accompaniment to sweet dishes; a fine cognac makes an excellent digestif.

agneau	lamb
alose	shad
anguilles	eels
à point	medium rare
bette	beet
bien cuit	well-done, well-cooked
boudin	blood sausage
brebis	sheep
canard	duck
carpe	carp
cèpes	boletus mushrooms
chapon	capon
charcuterie	cold meats
chèvre	goat
chevreau	kid
éperlan	smelt
escargots	snails
esturgeon	sturgeon
farci	stuffed
fèves	broad beans
frais, fraîche	cold, chilled or fresh
fromage	cheese
grillé	grilled
haricots	haricot beans
huîtres	oysters
jambon	ham
lamproie	lamprey
macaron	macaroon
marrons	chestnuts
moules	mussels
mouton	mutton
noix	walnuts
oie	goose
palombe	wood-pigeon
pêche	peach
pibales	elvers
poularde	poulard
prune	plum
pruneau	prune
ravigote	a highly-seasoned white sauce
rôti	roast
saignant	rare, lightly-cooked
saumon	salmon
tournedos	fillet steak
volaille	chicken

E. Follet

Poule au pot.

Sights

Porte de la Grosse-Horloge, La Rochelle.

J. Benazet/PIX

AGEN

Pop 30 553

Michelin map 79 fold 15 or 235 fold 17 - Local map p 30.

The town of Agen sprawls across the fertile plain lying between the River Garonne and the hills of the Ermitage. This favoured location has enabled it to become an important centre for early fruit and vegetables, especially peaches, Chasselas (white) grapes and plums. **Pruneaux d'Agen,** the local plums in dried form, may be found as prunes steeped either in brandy or in *eau-de-vie,* and are renowned throughout France.

Agen is a modern, well-planned town, with wide avenues and the impressive green space of Esplanade du Gravier. The busy centre lies around the intersection of Boulevard de la République and Boulevard Carnot, and the pedestrian precincts nearby. Midway between Bordeaux and Toulouse, Agen is the chief urban attraction of the Middle Garonne region.

Local plums.

HISTORICAL NOTES

Artists and scholars – Luminaries of the Renaissance shone especially brightly in Agen. **Matteo Bandello** (1485-1561), the monk, diplomat and courtier banished from Milan by Papal proscription after publication of his scandalous stories in the manner of Boccaccio, found peace and tranquillity as an exile on the banks of the Garonne. Subsequently he became Bishop of Agen.

Julius Caesar Scaligero (1484-1558), who was born in Padua but settled in Agen, brought fame to his adopted home through his sparkling personality, his extensive learning and his influence on many literary figures. His tenth son, Joseph Justus Scaligero (1540-1609), who was born in Agen, was an eminent philologist, a humanist and a Protestant philosopher.

Bernard Palissy (1510-90), born locally, was the author of technical and philosophical treatises, though he is better known as a glassblower and potter. Working with endless determination and at great personal sacrifice – he was said to have burned his own furniture to fuel his furnaces – he was able to rediscover the art of enamelling. He created a type of pottery halfway between Italian faience and glazed earthenware, and had great success with his "rustic" bowls, which were decorated with fruit, plants and animals in coloured relief. One of his clients was Catherine de' Medici, for whom he designed a ceramic grotto.

Early fruit and vegetables – Much of Agen's economy is based in the **"Pays des Serres"** (Greenhouse Country), an undulating region between the valleys of the Lot and the Garonne rivers. The area, part of the natural link between the Atlantic and the Mediterranean, enjoys a remarkably mild climate in which the local market gardening and fruit farming concerns flourish.

OLD TOWN *2 hours*

The itinerary below, starting from Place Docteur-Pierre-Esquirol, leads through some of the most interesting parts of the old district.

Place Docteur-Pierre-Esquirol (**AY 10**) – Bordering this square, named after a former Mayor of Agen, are the town hall – the office of the provincial governor in the 17C – the Ducourneau Theatre, and the Fine Arts Museum.

★★ **Musée des Beaux Arts** (**AXY M**) – The Fine Arts Museum is made up of elegant 16C and 17C mansions – the Hôtels de Vaurs, de Vergès, de Monluc and d'Estrades – which, though internally reorganised to provide space for the exhibits, have largely retained their original façades.

Basement – The cellars of the Hotel de Vaurs, once used as the local gaol (note the chains and shackles still fixed to the walls), today house the museum's **Prehistoric Collections.** These range from the oldest-known dressed stones to the most sophisticated examples of the Neolithic period, and include the minerals of the Maisani Bequest.

Ground Floor – In the large hall dedicated to Medieval Archeology, the main exhibit is the **Tomb of Étienne de Dufort and his wife.** The prone effigies lie on a plinth surrounded by carved figures framed within trefoil arches.
Romanesque and Gothic capitals carved with leaves and fantastic animals adorn the walls. Note also the 16C Brussels tapestry titled *The Month of March,* and the various funerary stones.
Among the mosaics, amphorae and small bronzes of the Gallo-Roman archeology section stands the **Mas Venus,** the finest exhibit in the museum. This 1C BC Greek marble is noted for its elegant contours, perfect proportions and the graceful flow of its draperies. It was discovered near the Mas D'Agen in the 19C.
In a neighbouring room, endowed with a monumental Renaissance chimneypiece, the twin themes are *War* and *The Hunt.* Among the ancient weapons on show is a 16C hunting dagger with a scabbard decorated with a Dance of Death. The 17C tapestry, *The Stag Hunt,* is after a cartoon by Van Orley, and the 15C marble profile of a woman is attributed to Mino da Fiesole.
First Floor – A fine spiral staircase in the Hotel de Vaurs (itself designed on a circular plan) leads to the paintings and decorative arts section. The bronze Minotaur in the centre of the hall is the work of a local artist, François-Xavier **Lalanne.**
Here, beside a reconstruction of the old Agen hospital dispensary with its flasks and crocks of Bordeaux faience, hangs a collection of 16C and 17C French and foreign canvases, notable among them *The Fête* by Teniers the Younger. Also on view are displays of porcelain and **glazed earthenware,** both French and foreign, dating since the time of Bernard Palissy *(see above).* On the same floor is a striking series of

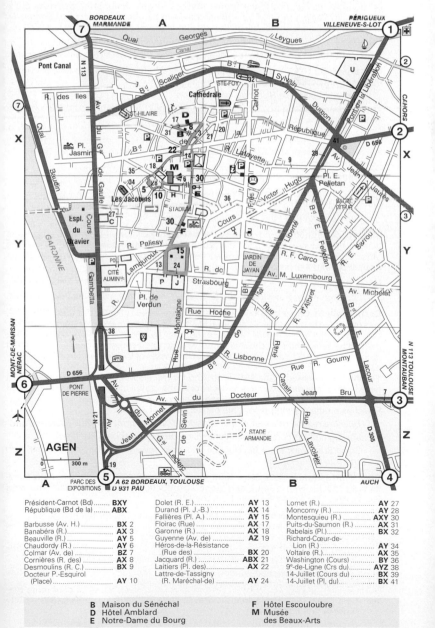

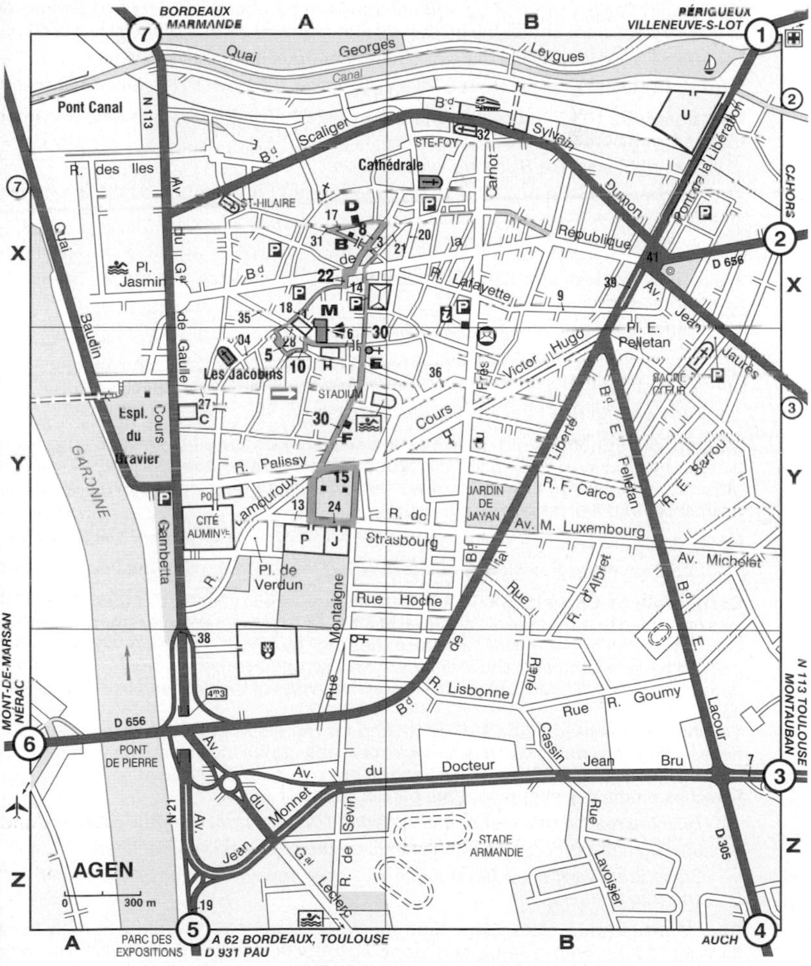

B Maison du Sénéchal
D Hôtel Amblard
E Notre-Dame du Bourg
F Hôtel Escouloubre
M Musée des Beaux-Arts

cameo incrustations (porcelain cameos embedded in glass), on religious, historical and mythological themes, by Boudon de Saint-Amans (1774-1856), a local artist who was also responsible for the unique examples of faience intended to rival the products of the English porcelain factories.

French painting of the 17C and 18C can be found in rooms at the end of a corridor displaying a portrait of Madame du Barry. They contain more fine portraits (in particular François de Troy's *Comte de Toulouse*), and paintings by Watteau *(The Storyteller)*, Nattier Lancret and Hubert Robert. The highlight of this section, however, is a **series by Goya** which includes an expressive *Self Portrait* – showing a keen, lively look emerging from beneath rather heavy features – the *Ascent of a Montgolfier Balloon* and a small, almost surrealist picture, in which horrified human beings are flown over by a donkey, a bull and an elephant in a strange, mysterious light. The room also includes paintings by other Spanish artists and a fine canvas, *The Dying Page,* by Tiepolo. French painting in the 19C is represented by a Corot masterpiece, **The Lake at Avray**; by Courbet and Isabey; by a collection of pre-Impressionists (numerous views by Boudin) and Impressionists (Lebourg, Caillebotte). The *Head of a Romanian Peasant Woman* was the work of the Romanian artist Grigoresco.

Second Floor – The exhibition of 19C paintings continues with fine Impressionist landscapes by Sisley, Guillaumin and Lebasque. The 20C is ushered in by a Picabia, *On the Banks of the Loing,* which is unusual for its Impressionist flavour. In a beautiful room with twinned windows, drawings and paintings by Le Moal and Manessier contrast with stained glass and still-lifes by **Bissière,** who was born in the region.

The Lalanne Room displays prints donated by the artist Lalanne *(see above)* and, beyond, the Docteur-Esquirol Room houses paintings, furniture and Asiatic figurines from the bequest of the former Mayor of Agen. Among the paintings are a blue-toned *Virgin and Child* by Philippe de Champaigne; the *Portrait of Charles IX* and *Portrait of Anne of Austria* by Clouet; and a fine *Head of a Child* by Greuze.

Third Floor – Works by local artists of different periods are exhibited here.

Terrace – From the tower there is a lovely view over the town to the hills of Gascony.

Rue Beauville (**AY 5**) – Local council offices are housed in the fine timber-framed building with corbels at No 1 Rue Beauville.

Turn right into Rue Richard-Cœur-de-Lion.

At the crossroads with Rue Moncorny stands another half-timbered building (tobacconist shop).

Rue Garonne leads into Place des Laitiers.

Place des Laitiers (**AX 22**) – This square, with its arcades and shops, lies at the heart of the town's oldest part.

Cross Boulevard de la République.

Rue des Cornières (**AX 8**) – Half-timbered buildings (Nos 13, 17 and 19) and stone houses built over arcades lend this busy shopping street a picturesque air.

Turn left into Rue Puits-de-Saumon.

Maison du Sénéchal (**AX B**) – The upper storey of this 14C steward's house is pierced by Gothic windows. On the ground floor, various items from the Fine Arts Museum (sarcophagi, 17C busts of women, the bell of the former town hall) are on display beyond a glass door.

Hôtel Amblard (**AX D**) – This is a handsome 18C town house at No 1 Rue Floirac.

Continue along Rue Floirac and turn left at the junction with Rue des Cornières.

Cathédrale St-Caprais (**BX**) ⓥ – This former collegiate church, founded in the 11C, was upgraded to the status of cathedral in 1802. Its most remarkable feature is the 12C east end, which comprises an apse flanked by three radiating chapels each pierced by semicircular arched windows with scrolled corbels in the form of carved human and animal heads. There is an excellent view of the east end from Place Raspail.

The interior, restored in the 19C, is striking for the disproportion between the short nave – which has only two bays and was probably unfinished – and the vast transept crossing, which was originally destined to be covered by a dome.

Frescoes on the walls represent the patron saints of Agen.

Take the road southwest of the cathedral and turn right into Rue Jacquard.

A charming half-timbered building stands on the corner of Rue Banabéra.

Cross Boulevard de la République and head towards the covered market (left) and Rue Montesquieu.

Rue Montesquieu (**AXY 30**) – Note the picturesque 13C-14C church, **Notre-Dame-du-Bourg** (**AY E**), with a brick and stone construction and a belfry-wall. The **Hôtel Escouloubre** at No 12 (**AY F**) dates from the 18C.

Place Armand-Fallières (**AY 15**) – The Préfecture, the 18C former bishop's palace, stands next to the imposing 19C Law Courts in this shady square. The 18C Hôtel Lacépède, on the north side, houses the public library.

Return along Rue Montesquieu and turn left under a vaulted arch into Rue Chaudordy, which leads back to Place Docteur-Pierre-Esquirol.

In passing, the fine twinned windows of the Hôtel Monluc (visible also from inside the Musée des Beaux Arts, *see above*) can be admired.

►► Pont Canal (**AX**); Esplanade du Gravier (**AY**); Église des Jacobins (**AY**) – Huge redbrick Gothic church.

Excursion: Moirax (9km – $5\frac{1}{2}$ miles south) – 12C Romanesque church★.

★ AINHOA

Michelin map 85 fold 2 or 234 fold 33 – 8km – 5 miles southeast of Cambo-les-Bains. Facilities.

Aïnhoa, a typical Basque village, grew up around a walled redoubt founded in the late 12C by monks of the Premonstratensian order (a brotherhood from northern France uniting evangelism and parish duties with the contemplative life). The redoubt was used as a staging post on the pilgrims' route to Santiago de Compostela.

★ **Main Street** – The picturesque main street is lined with traditional houses, their projecting roofs, often asymmetric, covered with old tiles. The sunlit façades are freshly whitewashed each year for the Fête of St John, the shutters and half-timbering painted and the main beams sometimes embellished with inscriptions. Vines and climbing flowers add a further note of gaiety.

Church – This traditional Basque church is notable for its two-tiered galleries, its wooden ceiling and the gilded woodwork in its chancel.
The war memorial at the entrance to the cemetery bears the characteristic disk motif of Basque headstones.

B. Hennequin/VLCO

Basque houses, Aïnhoa.

★ Ile d'AIX

Pop 199

Michelin map 71 fold 13 or 233 fold 14.

The Isle of Aix (the final x is not pronounced) is a small island in the Atlantic, only 133ha – 329 acres in area; it benefits from a mild climate and clear skies which, combined with its historical associations, its attractive town planning and its sophisticated fortifications, make it an alluring destination for visitors.
As the boat approaches the Isle of Aix, sandy beaches and impressive cliffs are revealed along the coast. Inland, pine trees, ilex and tamarisk, encouraged by the mild climate, lend the landscape an almost Mediterranean air.

Access ⌚ – The island can be reached by boat only, from **Pointe de la Fumée** (Smoke Point) and, in season, from La Rochelle and the isles of Oléron and Ré. The direct route from the Point *(25min)* offers interesting views – northwards along the coast up to La Rochelle and towards the Isle of Ré; westwards to the offshore forts of Enet and Boyard *(qv)* and to the Isle of Oléron. Boats arrive at Pointe Ste-Catherine, where the jetty lies under the watchful gaze of the fort commanding the roadstead.
Motor traffic on the island is restricted to service vehicles.

HISTORICAL AND GEOGRAPHICAL NOTES

Memories of Napoleon at the time of his fall are inseparable from this solitary isle still so steeped in the past.
Fishing for shrimps, prawns and other shellfish is one of the islanders' main occupations, and a local craft in mother-of-pearl has also developed (workshop opposite the church). Special beds for the "fattening" of oysters *(qv)* have replaced the old salt-marshes.
The island's resources include, in addition to fishing and the tourist industry, fruit farming, market gardening and the cultivation of vines which produce a light, dry white wine with an accent typical of grapes grown on sandy soil.
From the point of view of maritime traffic, the Isle of Aix occupies a strategic position : it is not only the key to the Charente estuary and the Antioche Straits (Pertuis d'Antioche) but also commands the approaches to La Rochelle, Rochefort and Brouage – a fact which the British were well aware of when they destroyed the ramparts here during the Seven Years' War (1756-63); these were subsequently repaired by a team of engineers which included Choderlos de Laclos, the future author of *Les Liaisons Dangereuses.*

It was the British again who, in April 1809 during the Napoleonic war, sank a squadron of the French fleet from Brest, after the latter had put in to Rade des Basques, the roadstead off the island's northwest coast, on their way to the West Indies. On this notorious "Day of the Fireships" (Jour des Brûlots), the action was won by floating flaming barrels of tar, and thirty small boats crammed with explosives, their fuses already lit, among the French men-of-war.

Call of Destiny – It was on the Isle of Aix that **Napoleon Bonaparte** had his last contact with French soil. In July 1815 the frigate which was supposed to take the exiled Emperor to America anchored off Fort Enet : a potentially threatening British naval force was cruising in the Antioche Straits, blocking the exit to the open sea.
The following day Napoleon landed on the Isle of Aix and visited the fortifications, to wild acclaim from the islanders and the garrison of 1 500 sailors (he had previously inspected the stronghold in 1808, at the height of his power). On returning to ship, he learnt of the options open to his guards : if combat with the British could be avoided, sail past to the ocean; if it could not, discuss terms. Negotiations lasted three days, during which time the Emperor's envoys were assured – falsely – that he would be permitted to seek asylum in England. Finally, escape appearing impossible, Napoleon accepted the advice of his officers and decided to surrender himself to the magnanimity of his adversaries.
On 12 July Napoleon had gone ashore again to stay with the garrison commander, and on 14 July he wrote his now-famous letter *(see below)* to the Prince Regent in London. The next day he donned the green uniform of a colonel in the Imperial Guard – the uniform he had worn at the Battle of Austerlitz – and embarked on a brig which was met by an admiral's barge which in turn took him to the warship *Bellerophon,* where he was taken aboard... after which came that sad last voyage carrying him to exile on that other small island, St Helena, where he was to end his days.

An island prison – The Isle of Aix itself subsequently became a prison, and a variety of "lodgers" were accommodated within the walls of Fort Liédot, on the northern coast : Russian prisoners from the Crimean War, Prussian prisoners from the War of 1870, convicts whose boat had foundered on the rocks on the way to Devil's Island, Russian prisoners, again, during the Great War of 1914-18. During the Second World War the island served as a base for Franco-German negotiations aimed – without success – at the surrender of pockets of resistance holding out at La Rochelle, Royan, and the isles of Oléron and Ré. More recently Ben Bella, one of the leaders of the outlawed National Liberation Front (FLN) of Algeria, was detained here for seven years, along with colleagues, during the Algerian War in the late 1950s and early 1960s.

CENTRE *2 hours*

Wide streets with junctions at right-angles, protected by a double line of fortifications separated by deep dykes, lend the built-up area the atmosphere of a large town, but the small church and the single-storey whitewashed cottages surrounded by hollyhocks could only belong to a village where the sight of a motor vehicle is still a rarity. From here, visitors may take a round tour of the island on foot *(2 hours 30min),* or experience a **horse-drawn carriage ride** ⓥ.

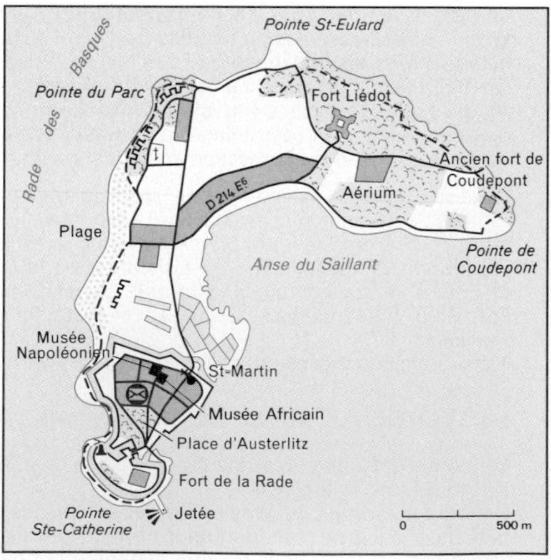

Place d'Austerlitz – At the inner end of Pointe Ste-Catherine a gate with a drawbridge leads to this pleasant open space, once the parade ground, with its shady walks between rows of fine cypress trees. Just beyond the drawbridge, on the right, stands the arcaded harbour office.

Fort de la Rade – This citadel overlooking the harbour was originally designed in 1699 by Vauban *(qv),* the brilliant military architect. Work on the five bastions and ring of fortifications was completed in 1702 but 55 years later the greater part was destroyed by the British *(see above).* The island's strategic importance was again recognized in 1773 by the powerful *Comité de salut public* (State Security Committee), although it was not until 1810 that Napoleon gave the order for rebuilding to start; this was completed in 1837.
The fort today is an isle within the island, completely surrounded by a wide, water-filled moat and a circle of anti-siege defences. There are two lighthouses on the fort. From the jetty below there is a view of the elongated mass of Fort Boyard (3km – 1 3/4 miles away) rising straight from the sea.

Musée Napoléonien ⓥ – The museum (part of the Gourgaud Foundation) is installed in the house where Napoleon took refuge in July 1815; it had been built on his orders in 1808. The house, one of the few buildings on the island with an upper storey, is surmounted by the imperial eagle; two classical columns frame the entrance. Baron Gourgaud, great-grandson of the Emperor's aide-de-camp, bought the building in 1925 and left it to the nation.
The ten rooms contain numerous souvenirs which relate to Bonaparte, his family and his entourage : weapons, works of art, clothes, furniture, documents, and portraits by Isabey, Gros, Appiani and others. In the garden stands an oak grafted to an elm by Napoleon himself in 1808, and a classical-style bust of the Emperor which once served as a ship's figurehead.
Napoleon's room on the first floor is particularly evocative, as nothing in it has been changed since the days when he stood outside on the balcony, watching through his spyglass the manoeuvres of the British fleet off-shore. It was in this room that he composed the famous letter to the Prince Regent in London:
"Faced with the factions dividing my country and with the enmity of the great powers of Europe, I have ended my political career and I come, like Themistocles, to seat myself at the table of the British people. I place myself under the protection of their laws and the indulgence which I crave from your Royal Highness as the most powerful, the most steadfast and the most generous of my enemies."
General Gourgaud was entrusted with the mission of delivering this letter to London, but he was refused permission to land at Plymouth. Napoleon made the General a gift of the document. A facsimile of the Emperor's rough draft of the letter is on view in the museum.

Musée Africain ⓥ – This museum (another part of the Gourgaud Foundation) is housed in a series of former army barracks; it displays ethnographic and zoological items collected by Baron Gourgaud in Africa between 1913 and 1931.
Interesting examples of African fauna are illustrated with the use of dioramas. The white dromedary ridden by Napoleon during the Egyptian campaign was later taken to the Jardin des Plantes in Paris and stuffed after its death. It was transferred to Ile d'Aix in 1933.

Église St-Martin – This was once the church of a priory occupied by Benedictine monks from Cluny. All that remains today is the transept, the apse and the apsidal chapel. The 11C crypt has fine columns with foliate capitals.

★ ANGLES-SUR-L'ANGLIN — Pop 424

Michelin map 68 northeast of fold 15 or 238 fold 25.

The village of Angles, built above the River Anglin, rises in tiers to the foot of a ruined castle. It owes its name to the Angles, a warlike tribe from Germania who in the 5C invaded the island which came to be known as England (Angleterre). It was in the 9C, however, that Charlemagne sent the descendants of those who had remained in Germania south to settle on the banks of a tributary of the River Gartempe. The tributary was named the Angla, and subsequently the Anglin. The inhabitants here are known as Anglais.
"Les Jours d'Angles", a highly-prized form of drawn-thread embroidery, is still made in the village today.
Archeological excavations carried out in neighbouring rock shelters have unearthed important carvings dating from the Magdalenian (Late Paleolithic) era.

A cardinal sin – Like the proverbial victim "hoist on his own petard", **Cardinal Balue,** a native of Angles born in 1421, was condemned by Louis XI to be locked up in a *"fillette"*, a small, uncomfortable type of iron cage originally designed, it is believed, by Balue himself.
Balue came from a modest family but rose rapidly, gaining wealth and power, to become successively Chaplain to the King, Financial Steward, Secretary of State and then Bishop of Evreux. Subsequently he became Bishop of Angers, after which he was created Cardinal. Foolishly, Balue abused the confidence of the King and sold state secrets to the Duke of Burgundy; unmasked, he was sentenced to prison for treason. Eleven years later he was freed at the request of the Pope, emigrated to Rome, and lived another eleven years, showered with honours.

SIGHTS

★ **Site** – From the southeastern end of the bluff on which the castle stands, near a roadside cross and a small Romanesque chapel, there is a splendid **view★** of the whole village. Beyond a breach in the cliff are what remains of the walls and towers of the old castle; to the north, on another promontory, the Romanesque belfry of the upper church rises above the roofs; at the foot of the escarpment the River Anglin, with its reeds and water-lilies, winds peacefully between two rows of poplars. Beyond the turning wheel of an ancient watermill a stone bridge leads to the Sainte-Croix quarter, where the former abbey church has a fine 13C doorway.

★ **Castle ruins** ⓥ – Angles Castle, an important stronghold in the Middle Ages on account of its commanding position and the strength of its defences, was abandoned in the 18C. The Revolution (1789) added to its downfall by allowing local builders to use the place as a stone quarry.

The towns and sights described in this guide are indicated in black lettering on the local maps and town plans.

★★ ANGOULÊME

Pop 42 875

Michelin map 72 folds 13, 14 or 233 folds 29, 30.

From route N 141, northwest of the town, there is a fine view of Angoulême and its impressive **site★** above the River Charente.

A citadel town – Like many towns with a long history Angoulême is divided into two separate parts, an upper and a lower town, corresponding roughly to the old and the new.

The **Upper Town,** ringed by ramparts and known locally as "Le Plateau", is built on a promontory separating the Charente from the tributary Anguienne. The northern district, Old Angoulême, is a maze of narrow streets which have been sensitively restored. The Préfecture district, to the south, strikes a contrast with wide 18C-19C avenues bordered by stately façades. The shopping area to the east has been transformed into a pedestrian precinct.

The **Lower Town,** the business and industrial region, includes most of the outlying areas. It is here that the paper-making which was the traditional activity of Angoulême was based. In the 17C, thanks to the renowned purity of the river's waters, nearly 100 papermills exported reams of watermarked paper to Holland from the warehouses of l'Houmeau. It was to Holland that many artisans working in the trade fled when the Edict of Nantes – allowing Protestants in France freedom of worship – was revoked by Louis XIV in 1685.

Today, only Puymoyen's Moulin du Verger and Fleurac mill at Nersac nearby continue to produce handmade paper, although specialized factories making fine papers (onionskin, tissue etc) and writing paper are still in business at Ruelle, St-Michel and La Couronne.

A festival each January crowns Angoulême as the world capital of the Bande Dessinée (Strip Cartoon), a form of graphic art celebrated in a museum here. To its south, the town also boasts the Lycée de l'Image et du Son, a high-school specializing in the audio-visual arts.

HISTORICAL NOTES

Angoulême, part of the province of Aquitaine under the Romans, was evangelized by St Ausone and by St Cybard, to whom a score of churches in the diocese are dedicated.

The town was the fief of local counts before it was established as a possession of princes of the royal blood; the younger branch of the Valois family, which was to produce the sovereign François I, was awarded the title.

Marguerite of Angoulême – Marguerite de Valois, the sister of François I and nicknamed by him **Marguerite des Marguerites** *(qv),* was also known as Marguerite of Angoulême as she was born in the town in 1492 and spent much of her youth here. She was a woman of great culture and learning – her *Heptameron,* a collection of stories in the manner of Boccaccio, won her a permanent place in French literature – yet equally famous for her fêtes and parties, and was an important influence at court.

She is still evoked in the names of two kinds of local confectionery : *Marguerites* (a type of chocolate) and *Duchesses* (nougatines stuffed with almond paste).

The two Balzacs – The author **Guez de Balzac** (1597-1654), who was born in Angoulême, returned to the town to indulge his moody temperament and vanity : a rigorous stylist, he was dubbed "the man who restored the French language". The other writer, **Honoré de Balzac** (1799-1850), the genius who created *La Comédie Humaine* (The Human Comedy), was adopted by Angoulême and described the town in his famous work *Les Illusions Perdues* (Lost Illusions).

★★ UPPER TOWN *2 hours*

★★ **Promenade des Remparts** – *Start this walk around the old fortifications from Place des Halles and follow the escarpment in an anti-clockwise direction.*

From the round towers and rectangular bastions forming a balcony above the Charente an immense panorama unfolds below.

North Face – Here there are swooping perspectives of the river bridge, the suburb of St-Cybard, the valley of the Charente and the industrial concerns dotted along it. In 1806 General Resnier (1728-1811), who was born in Angoulême, launched himself from the top of the Ladent Tower equipped with a device of his own invention, thereby becoming the first man to effect a non-powered flight. Since he broke a leg landing, however, the General abandoned his plan to exploit the invention – conceived, it is said, with the idea in mind of a future airborne invasion of England by the Imperial army. A commemorative plaque recalls General Resnier and his exploit.

Place Beaulieu – This esplanade is at the end of the promontory, where a school has replaced the old Benedictine abbey. It offers views of the St-Ausone district and the church of the same name, built in the 19C by **Paul Abadie** (1812-84), one of the architects responsible for the Sacré-Cœur Basilica in Paris, and, beyond, of the confluence of the Charente and the Anguienne. Immediately below lies a small park, a popular place for a stroll.

South Front – From here the view is of the Anguienne Valley and its wooded slopes.

★ **Cathédrale St-Pierre** (Y F) – St Peter's Cathedral dates from the 12C. Partially destroyed by the Calvinists in 1562, it was restored in 1634 and, more completely, by Abadie from 1866 onwards.

★★ **Façade** – The impressive façade, decorated in the "Poitiers style", resembles an enormous sculpted picture in which 70 characters, as statues or in low-relief, illustrate the theme of the Last Judgement. The ensemble is presided over by a glorious

Christ in Majesty surrounded by angels, saints in medallions and the symbols of the Evangelists. Both archivolts and friezes above and around the side doors are decorated with intricately-carved foliage, animals and figures. On the lintel of the first blind doorway, on the right, are strange scenes of combat based on episodes from the *Song of Roland (qv).*
The tall tower with six diminishing storeys which rises above the far end of the north transept was partly restored by Abadie.

Interior – Inside, there are some impressive features : the flight of domes resting on pendentives is an extremely bold concept; in the north transept a huge chapel sits beneath the Abadie tower, its supporting columns adorned with remarkable capitals.
Also of note are the Romanesque low-relief in the nave which represents a Virgin and Child, and the 18C organ loft.
In the chancel, the capitals with floral decoration originate from the original 9C cathedral built by Grimoald de Mussiden.

Hôtel de Ville (YZ H) ⊙ – Abadie built this Gothic-Renaissance town hall on the site of the old castle which was the seat of the Counts of Angoulême *(see above).* All that remains of the castle today is the so-called "polygonal tower" – a 13C and 14C keep from which a fine **panorama** can be enjoyed – and the 15C round tower in which Marguerite of Angoulême was born.
South of the town hall, beyond the flower gardens, the vista along the tree-shaded Place de New York ends in a monumental statue of Carnot.

Ancienne chapelle des Cordeliers (Y B) ⊙ – This chapel was once a convent church belonging to the Cordeliers religious order. In 1556 one of the monks, André Thevet, brought the first samples of tobacco – which he called "Angoulême grass" – back from Brazil. He was followed by the lexicographer Jean Nicot, after whom the poisonous alkaloid nicotine is named.
The chapel, attached today to the municipal hospital, has an elegant Gothic belfry with a projecting side supported on two small squinches. In the nave is the tomb of Guez de Balzac *(see above),* who was buried in 1654.

Town Houses (Y) – A number of fine old town houses can be seen around the cathedral and near the law courts. These include 79 Rue de Beaulieu (majestic 1783 façade with Ionic columns and three square turrets); 17 Rue du Soleil (Louis XVI façade overlooking a courtyard); 15 Rue Turenne (Louis XIII entrance opposite the gateway of a 1739 former Carmelite monastery); 15 Rue de la Cloche-Verte, the Hôtel St-Simon (pretty Renaissance courtyard).

Espace St-Martial (YZ 45) – This pleasant modern square designed as a pedestrian precinct is near St Martial's church with its 19C belfry-porch. Benches, a pool and contemporary sculptures add to the attractions of this peaceful corner.

ANGOULÊME

Louvel (Pl. F.) .... Y 31
Marengo (R.) .... YZ 33
Paris (R. de) .... Y
Périgueux (R. de) .... Z
Postes (R. des) .... Y 39
St Martial (Espace et Rue) .... Z 45

Aguesseau (Rampe) .... Y 2
Barthou (R. L.) .... Y 3
Beaulieu (Remp. de) .... Y 4
Bouillaud (Pl.) .... Z 5
Briand (Bd A.) .... Y 6
Champ-de-Mars (Pl.) .... Y 9
Churchill (Bd Winston) .... Z 10
Cloche-Verte (R. de la) .... Y 12
Denis-Papin (R.) .... Y 16
Desaix (Bd) .... Z 20
Gambetta (Av.) .... Y 25

Gaulle (R. Gén. de) .... Y 26
Halles (Pl. des) .... Y 27
La Rochefoucauld (Rue de) .... Y 29
Lattre-de-T. (Av. de) .... Y 30
Midi (Remp. du) .... Y 34
Pasteur (Bd) .... Y 37
St-André (R.) .... Y 42
Soleil (R. du) .... Y 49
Turenne (R.) .... Y 50
3-Fours (R. des) .... Y 53

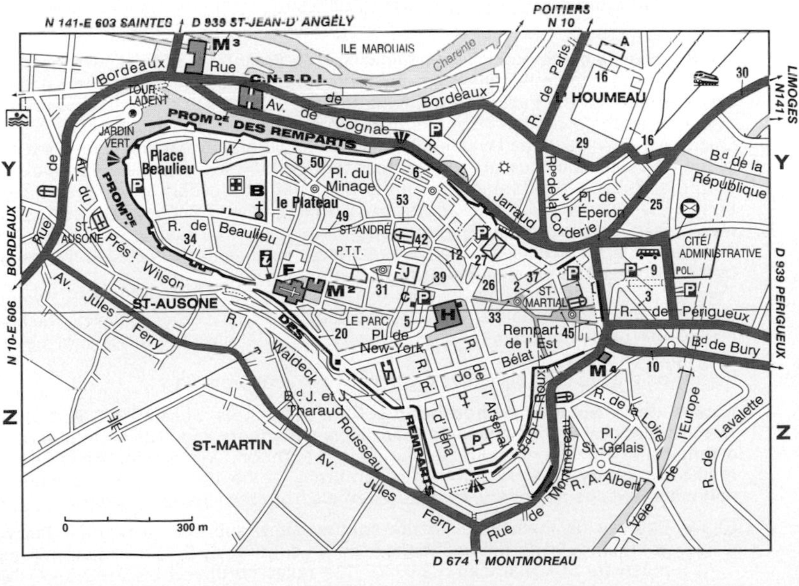

B Ancienne chapelle des Cordeliers
F Cathédrale St-Pierre
H Hôtel de ville
M² Musée municipal des Beaux-Arts
M³ Atelier-musée du papier
M⁴ Musée de la Société archéologique

★ Le CNBDI – STRIP CARTOON CENTRE (Y) ⊙ *allow 1½ hours*

Entrance : Rue de Bordeaux. Alternatively, a stairway rises from Avenue de Cognac.

The initials stand for **Centre National de la Bande Dessinée et de l'Image.** The centre, housed in a group of turn-of-the-century industrial buildings which the architect Roland Castro has remodelled with resolutely modernistic elements, looks as fictional as anything in the works it exhibits.

Inside, the **Médiathèque** *(1st floor)* houses almost all of French strip cartoon production from 1946 onwards. Since 1982 examples of all strip cartoons published in France have been legally registered here for reasons of copyright. Its important stock of material (video cassettes, cartoon albums, magazines etc) may be freely consulted.

Asterix and Obelix.

In the museum a rich collection of plates and original drawings is displayed in rotation. Rooms on the ground floor pay tribute to the Grand Masters of the strip cartoon (through one or more plates or original designs, or through an illuminated screen with a recorded commentary). Videos retrace the significant moments in the history of the strip cartoon.

Among the pioneers there are the Swiss Töpffer (mid-19C), Christophe *(The Fenouillard Family,* 1889), Pinchon (*Bécassine,* 1905), Forton (*The Nickelled Feet,* 1908) and Alain St Ogen (*Zig and Puce,* 1925). Among innumerable subsequent talents represented are the Belgians Hergé (*Tintin,* 1929) and Franquin (*Gaston Lagaffe,* 1957), the Americans Raymond (*Flash Gordon,* 1934) and Schulz (*Peanuts,* 1950), and the French artists Goscinny and Uderzo (*Asterix,* 1959). The host of contemporary creators include : Gotlib, Claire Bretécher, Reiser, Wolinski, Loustal, Bilal, Baudoin, Tardi, Teule...

ADDITIONAL SIGHTS

Musée municipal des Beaux-Arts (Y M^2) ⊙ – The Fine Arts Museum is situated in the 12C former Bishops' Palace, which was remodelled in the 15C and 16C.

The ground floor houses the famous **Casque d'Agris** (Agris Helmet), a masterpiece of the Celtic goldsmith's art dating from the 4C BC, a collection of medieval treasures (capitals, crosses, sculptures), ceramics (mainly regional) and French paintings of the 18C and 19C.

The upper floor contains an eclectic selection of 17C Italian and Flemish paintings, and French works from various periods (orientalists, local artists and members of the Barbizon School). The museum is best known, however, for the quality and richness of its African and Oceanic exhibits (ritual statues from the Congo, masks, Kota reliquaries etc).

Atelier-musée du Papier (Museum-Workshop of the Paper Trade) (Y M^3) ⊙ – The former Bardou-Le-Nil papermill, which specialized in the production of cigarette papers, operated here on the banks of the Charente until 1970. It has since been converted into a museum devoted to the industry which made the region prosperous.

One of the six metal-vaned waterwheels which powered the machinery until the end of the 19C, when electrical energy replaced them, is on view, together with an exhibition detailing the different stages in the industrial production of paper and cardboard. The raw material – rags at first, then wood and waste paper – is transformed into a paste and subsequently into a continuous sheet by means of the machine invented in 1797 by Nicolas Robert. Once dried, this sheet is subjected to numerous other treatments before the final product is obtained.

Two other exhibitions – one devoted to the industry as a whole in the Charente *département,* from the earliest times to the present day, the other following the history of the paper trade worldwide – give a comprehensive overview of papermaking.

Rooms on the 3rd floor also have displays of contemporary art.

Musée de la Société archéologique (Z M^4) ⊙ – This museum devoted to the work of the local archeological society displays, indoors and outside in a garden, examples of prehistoric finds in the neighbourhood, along with Gallo-Roman mosaics, lapidary collections from Roman times to the 18C, and various regional antiquities (weapons, pottery, trinkets, enamels from the Limousin area).

⊙ ►► Château de l'Oisellerie (in the southwestern suburbs by N 10) – Planetarium. Moulin de Fleurac (in the western suburbs by D 699) – Paper mill and museum. St Cybardeaux (21km – 12½ miles northwest by D 939) – Gallo-Roman theatre at Les Bouchauds.

⊙ *Excursion :* Grottes de Quéroy★ (16km – 10 miles east via D 699 and D 412) – Labyrinth of impressive caves.

★★ ARCACHON Pop 13 664

Michelin map 78 folds 2, 12, 71 fold 20 or 234 fold 6 - Local map p 137 - Facilities.

The town of Arcachon, which lies on the southern shore of a huge lagoon open to the Atlantic, was formerly a spa celebrated for the health-giving properties of the local Abatilles springs; today it thrives as a seaside resort and is well-known for its oyster farms. Arcachon may be divided into two quite separate districts offering between them the advantages of beauty and tranquillity together with the more sophisticated diversions of a modern holiday centre.

The **Summer Town** borders the lagoon and attracts tourists with its casino, sailing and windsurfing facilities, power-boat racing and regattas. A large marina crowded with pleasure boats sits beside the busy fishing port with its regular stream of trawlers.

The **Winter Town** ⓥ, further inland and better sheltered from the sea breezes, is a quiet, pine-shaded region of broad avenues bordered by handsome late 19C and early 20C villas. Public gardens and a large park add to the appeal of this gracious retreat.

A forerunner of Brémontier – Arcachon Bay and the region immediately to the south of it were once the fief of the Buch family, seigneurs of the neighbouring town of La Teste. Warlike minor nobles, the Buch knights fought mainly in the service of the English occupiers in the 14C. The best-known, John III, was defeated by Bertrand du Guesclin (*c*1320-80), the French general largely responsible for chasing the invaders from this part of the kingdom.

Louis XVI determined to establish the bay as a military port, but before work could begin it was necessary to stabilise the constantly shifting sand dunes surrounding the anchorage. The task was entrusted to the marine engineer Charlevoix de Villers : his solution, proposed in 1779, was to cover the dunes with plantations. However, the engineer, a victim of court intrigues, was disgraced and the project was only put into practice nine years later by Nicolas Thomas Brémontier (1738-1809) *(qv)*. Under the latter's direction the dunes bordering the Bay of Biscay were finally immobilized by a carpet of vegetation mingling pine trees with bushes of broom.

Birth of Arcachon – In 1841 a new branch line extended the railway from Bordeaux to La Teste, a favourite bathing place by the lagoon for holiday-makers from the wine capital. In 1845 a deep-water landing-stage was constructed 5km – 3 miles north of La Teste; a road across the salt-marshes linked the two. Villas were subsequently built along the road, and so Arcachon was born.

The Bordeaux-La Teste line was not profitable, however, and by 1852 when the Pereire Brothers set up the Compagnie des Chemins de Fer du Midi (Southern Railway Company) and incorporated the line, it was hovering on the brink of bankruptcy. The brothers nevertheless extended the line to Arcachon and successfully promoted it; as a result the town developed substantially.

From 1866 Arcachon, already established as a summer resort, gained a reputation as a desirable winter destination and from then on its success was assured.

Oyster Country – Arcachon oysters were known to Rabelais as early as the 16C but the industrial organization of beds in the lagoon and around L'Ile aux Oiseaux (Bird Island) dates only from 1856.

In 1922 the beds were decimated by disease; the flat-shelled oysters or *Gravettes*, an Arcachon speciality, were almost entirely wiped out. The oyster farmers were forced to replace them with the tougher, more resistant *Portugaises*. Since 1972, however, French beds have been largely restocked with Japanese and Canadian varieties.

The town's annual production of some 10 000 to 12 000 tonnes of oysters makes Arcachon one of the most important centres of ostreiculture in Europe.

ARCACHON

Gambetta (Av.) .... BZ
Lamarque-de-Plaisance (Cours) .... ABZ

Lattre-de-Tassigny (R. Mar.-de) .... AZ 38
Plage (Bd de la) .... ABZ

Balde (Allée Jean) .... AZ 6
Chapelle (Allée de la) .... AZ 16
Héricart-de-Thury (Crs) .... BZ 31

Lamartine (Av. de) .... BZ 35
Legallais (R. François) .... AZ 39
Molière (R.) .... BZ 53
Pompidou (Espl. G.) .... BZ 64
Prés.-Rossevelt (Pl.) .... BZ 65
Thiers (Pl.) .... BZ 71

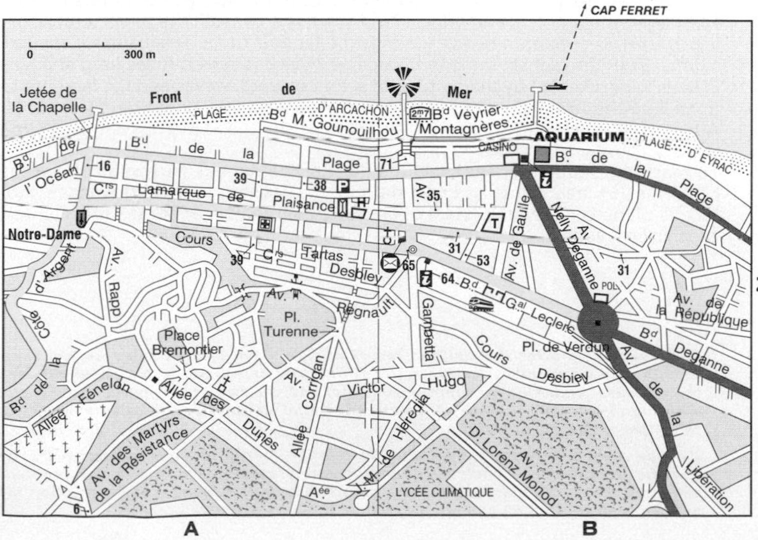

A B

SIGHTS

Sea-front – The pleasant promenade along the tamarisk-shaded Boulevards Gounouilhou and Veyrier-Montagnères, by the Thiers landing-stage, overlooks Arcachon's fine sandy beach. The jetty offers a general **view★** of the resort and the lagoon.

Aquarium et musée (**BZ M**) ⏲ – The aquarium, on the mezzanine floor, displays within its 30 glass tanks marine life typical of the lagoon and the nearer reaches of the ocean beyond.
The museum upstairs boasts a special section devoted to the cultivation of oysters, as well as collections of birds, fish, reptiles and invertebrates native to the region. Another section displays finds from local archeological digs.

Église Notre-Dame (**AZ**) – This 19C church dedicated to the Virgin, the third building in a sanctuary founded by a Franciscan monk in the 16C, is located along the axis of Jetée de la Chapelle (Chapel Jetty), just beyond the Sailors' Cross. Inside, the **Chapelle des Marins** (Sailors' Chapel), adorned with numerous thanksgiving offerings, houses the revered statue of Our Lady of Arcachon.

★ **Boulevard de la Mer** – This charming seaside walk, bordered by pine trees which rise from the sandy ground, skirts Pereire Park and offers fine views of Cap Ferret peninsula.

Dune du Pilat.

EXCURSION

★★ **Dune du Pilat** – *7.5km – 4½ miles south. Leave Arcachon to the southwest and follow D 218.*
The road passes through the adjoining resort of **Moulleau** and then **Pyla-sur-Mer** and **Pilat-Plage**, where hotels and villas stand scattered beneath the pines, before climbing in a series of hairpin bends towards the famous dune. This colossal sandhill, at 114m – 374ft the highest dune in Europe, is 2.7km – over 1½ miles long and 500m – 550yds wide. Created by the combined action of wind, waves and the land itself, the dune is still constantly undergoing change. The west face slopes gently towards the Atlantic rollers while the hollowed landward side to the east drops almost sharply to the woodland pines below.
To reach the summit, either scale the flank of the dune (a fairly difficult ascent) or climb the 154-step stairway. From the top, the **panorama★★** over the ocean and the forests of the Landes – the finest of all views over the Silver Coast – is breathtaking, especially at sunset.

Spas (so-named after the Belgian resort of Spa) have existed since Roman times, though they were most popular in the 19C, partly as a result of the development of the railways, which made them accessible, and the rise of a wealthy middle class who found the combination of treatment, social exclusivity and leisure away from the cities extremely appealing.

Various resorts became known for the relative merits of their waters in treating specific complaints – back pain, low blood pressure, gynaecological problems, exhaustion, nervous complaints etc – though it is widely felt that the rest, good food and fresh air offered also play a large part in the restorative process.

★ Bassin d'ARCACHON

Michelin map 78 folds 1, 2, 11, 12, 71 folds 19, 20 or 234 fold 6.

Arcachon Lagoon (le bassin d'Arcachon), a vast, triangular-shaped inlet, is the only major indentation along the length of the Côte d'Argent or Silver Coast; it is almost cut off from the sea by the narrow promontory of Cap Ferret, which leaves an exit channel barely 3km – 1¾ miles wide.
Several small rivers flow into the bay, the most important being the **Eyre** which irrigates the Landes de Gascogne Regional Park *(qv)*; the northern limits of this protected area stretch as far as the lagoon.
The inlet extends over an area of 25 000ha – almost 100 sq miles, four-fifths of which is exposed at low tide. The 9 500ha – 23 475 acres which remain above water at high tide contain the dykes retaining the "fish reservoirs" of Audenge and Le Teich, and include the low, almost treeless relief of the **Ile aux Oiseaux** (Bird Island), surrounded by oyster farms. The island, 5km – 3 miles in circumference, is dotted with fishermen's dwellings that are visible from Arcachon, and two houses built on stilts which are isolated at high tide (their picturesque quality makes them a frequent subject of local postcards).
The 80km – 50 miles of shoreline enclosing the lagoon, flat to the east and south and bordered by wooded dunes on either side of the entrance channel, include a number of small oyster ports and attractive bathing resorts among the pine trees and mimosa plantations.
The region's prosperity is based on oyster-farming, pine plantations (sawmills, papermills), fishing and tourism (note the many weekend cottages, holiday homes and camp sites). The cultivation of oysters, which takes up 1 800ha – 4 447 acres of the lagoon's surface, is unquestionably the main business.
Although the roads cited in the itinerary below offer few glimpses of the water, they are never far from a stretch of shore or a small jetty affording at least a partial view of the great lagoon.
Fishing smacks can be hired for **boat trips** ⊙ around the lagoon.

FROM CAP FERRET TO ARCACHON

66km – 41 miles : about 5 hours

Cap Ferret – *See Cap Ferret.*

Leave Cap Ferret by Avenue de la Vigne, heading north towards Bordeaux.

The road winds between wooded dunes scattered with stylish villas.
Route D 106 skirts l'Herbe dune and runs between the edge of the forest and the western shore of the lagoon. There are views of the bay from the small fishing port of Piraillan and at the entrance to Claouey.

Arès – A Romanesque church stands on the town's central square; inside, the carved capitals of the columns are illuminated by modern stained-glass windows. The round tower (restored) on the water-front was once part of a windmill.
Arès was originally a port designed for the oyster fisheries, and now also harbours pleasure boats.

From Arès to Biganos the road passes through a recurring landscape of pines to link the towns and villages along the lagoon's eastern shore.

Andernos-les-Bains – This sheltered site at the far end of the lagoon has been inhabited by man since prehistoric times. Today the town here is one of the major local resorts, with beaches which stretch for over 4km – 2½ miles and a casino, and is very popular in summer.
Opposite the beach and beside the small church (St-Éloi), with its 12C apse, lie traces of a 4C Gallo-Roman basilica.
The landing-stage by the casino offers extensive views over the lagoon, the town's oyster port and the marina.

Lanton – The restored Romanesque church (12C apse and nave walls) incorporates an oven-vaulted, raised apse of a restrained and unified design. Framing the central bay, twinned columns support capitals decorated with pine cones and herons *(left)* and stylized leaf motifs *(right)*.

Audenge – The town, a centre of ostreiculture, is known also for its "fish reservoirs" (a system of locks retaining the catch at low tide).

Beyond Biganos take D 3^{E12} to join D 650; opposite the junction is the impressive, smoking bulk of the **Cellulose du Pin** papermill, visible for miles around. The route crosses the inner end of the marshy Eyre delta (bridge over the river) and follows the lagoon's southern shore, which remains pleasantly leafy all the way to the outskirts of Le Teich.

★ **Parc Ornithologique du Teich** – *See Le Teich.*

Gujan-Mestras – This busy town with its six oyster bases is the ostreiculture capital of the Arcachon area. It is extremely picturesque with tile-roofed cabins, canals crowded with fishing smacks, oyster "disgorgers" and waterfront kiosks where oysters can be sampled, ordered and dispatched to family or friends.

Parc de loisirs de la Hume – The park, situated at the crossroads of N 250 and D 652, offers a range of leisure facilities which include : **"medieval" miniature golf**; the **Village médiéval** ⊙, a re-creation of a traditional Landes village where numerous artists and craftworkers (blacksmiths, basket-weavers, sculptors, glassblowers etc), dressed in period costume, ply their trades; **Aquacity** ⊙, a water park, and **La Coccinelle** ⊙, a menagerie, for younger visitors. In the **Marinoscope** ⊙, which is devoted to model ships, there is a remarkable 1:100 scale model **port★** harbouring 156 ships of different tonnage.

La Teste – La Teste was once the capital of the former kingdom of the Buch family and is now part of one of the biggest *communes* (18 000ha – 44 500 acres) in France. Settled by the Boli or Boians before the Roman colonization, it was later developed by the English and subsequently became an important oyster port. Today the *commune* includes the ancient forest of La Teste, Cazaux and its lake *(south)*, and the resorts of Pyla-sur-Mer and Pilat-Plage with its famous dune *(southwest)*.

Fishermen's huts, La Teste.

G. Marineau/TOP

Note, near the tourist information centre in Place Jean-Hameau, the façade of the 18C **Maison Lalanne,** adorned with representations of an anchor, rigging and the heads of the owner's children. The huge belltower of **Église St-Vincent** stands on the site of a chapel which once formed part of the Buch family castle.

★★ **Arcachon** – *See Arcachon.*

ARCHIGNY

Pop 992

Michelin map 68 folds 14, 15 or 232 fold 47.

The name of this village is inextricably linked with the story of the Acadians – early 17C emigrants from the Poitou region who settled in the eastern part of French Canada.

Acadia, corresponding roughly to the present Canadian provinces of Nova Scotia and New Brunswick, was ceded to the British in 1713. After the Treaty of Paris at the end of the Seven Years War (1763), the British government of Canada decided to colonize the area and, in 1773 and 1774, forcibly repatriated the 10 000 French living there to make room for English immigrants.

Returned to Poitou, the dispossessed Acadians settled southeast of Châtellerault on fallow land put at their disposal by the Marquis de Pérusse des Cars.

La Ligne Acadienne – "The Acadian Line" was the name given to a series of similar farm properties built on the heathland between Archigny and La Puye: 58 clay and brushwood houses on rubble foundations, which the ex-colonists hoped eventually to own. Some, impatient because the charter they awaited was delayed, moved later to Nantes and subsequently to French Louisiana. Those that remained received their title deeds only in 1793.

Today, 38 houses from "the Line" are still standing. They are identified by special signs, as are the sites of the 20 which have disappeared. Each year, in the hamlet known as **Huit-Maisons** (Eight Houses), descendants of the Poitou Acadians organize a fête on 15 August to commemorate this period in their history.

ACADIAN FARM ⏲ *30min*

An old Acadian farm at Huit-Maisons *(6km – 3 ½ miles east of Archigny; signposted)* has been transformed into a museum. Here, all under the same roof, visitors can see living quarters with furniture of the period, a cowshed containing agricultural implements, and the barn, where documents relating to the history of the Acadians and their return to Poitou are on display.

Outside the building is a plaque donated by the State of New Brunswick in honour of the people of Poitou, ancestors of the original Acadians.

ARGELÈS-GAZOST

Pop 3 229

Michelin map 85 fold 17 or 234 fold 43 – Local maps pp 83 and 90 – Facilities.
Town plan in the current Michelin Red Guide France.

The largely 19C residential town and hot springs resort nestles in a pleasant mountain-valley setting known for the mildness of its climate. The Argelès basin, meeting point of the most beautiful valleys of the Lavedan region *(qv)*, is studded with many attractive villages and picturesque sanctuaries.

The isolated site, remote among the valleys of the upper Bigorre to the north and the high valleys of Cauterets and Luz to the south, is an example of those internal basins in the Greater Pyrenees which benefit from gentle atmospheric conditions.

The upper town, the oldest and busiest part, stands above the Gave de Pau (Pau Torrent) and the resort proper with its thermal establishments. From this part of Argelès the drama of the **panorama** unfolding on every side is heightened by the jagged teeth of the Viscos, between the Luz and Cauterets gorges, and the nearer peaks of the Néouvielle Massif. There is a particularly fine **view** of the valley of the Azun torrent and the surrounding mountains from the viewing table on the terrace "des Étrangers" (Foreigners' Terrace) off Place de la République.

EXCURSIONS

★★★ **Pic de Pibeste** – *4.5km – 2½ miles north via N 21 and D 102 (left) as far as Ouzous. Park in the car park near the church. Allow at least 4½ hours on foot Rtn. See Pic de Pibeste.*

★ **Route du Hautacam** – *20km – 12 miles east. Leave Argelès via D 100, which crosses the Azun and climbs, after Ayros, the eastern slope of the Argelès basin.*

Artalens – Beyond the village, at an altitude of 800m – 2 625ft, the road crosses a small valley where the stream is flanked by five ancient water-mills; the last mill downstream still has its wheel. Hundreds of these small family concerns could be found all over the Bigorre district in the 19C.

After Artalens the road leaves the summer grazing grounds and takes on a more panoramic character, offering distant **views★** which include, to the southwest, the Vignemale beyond the Cauterets valley, and the Balaïtous which towers above the mountains surrounding the valley of the Arrens. Beyond Hautacam ski station *(right)*, the road reaches a crest from which the foothills of Pic du Midi de Bigorre can be seen and, far below, the pastoral basin closing off the Gazost Valley.

Donjon des Aigles (Eagles' Keep) ⌚ – *6.5km – 4 miles southeast. Take D 100 and then D 13 as far as Beaucens. Park at the far end of the village in the car park at the foot of the castle.* The **Beaucens ruins** provide a fitting setting for the display of raptors (vultures, eagles, falcons, kites, buzzards, owls etc) and other exotic species. The star attraction here is the flight of the birds of prey.

Abbaye d'ARTHOUS

Michelin map 78 east of folds 17, 18 or 234 fold 30 – 2km – 1¼ miles south of Peyrehorade.

The 12C Arthous Abbey, built at the foot of a range of hills angling towards nearby Hastingues, was converted into farm buildings in the 19C and has since been extensively restored. The abbey dependencies had already been attractively rebuilt in the traditional half-timbered Landes style in the 16C and 17C. Premonstratensian monks opened the gates of the abbey to pilgrims on the way to Santiago de Compostela; today part of the complex serves as a hostel for students, particularly those studying archeology.

Abbey church ⌚ – The Romanesque east end has been returned to its original purity. The decoration of the apse and two apsidal chapels includes cornices with a moulded frieze supported by ornamental corbels, geometric decorations reminiscent of the Pipes of Pan, interlacing, and numerous figures, often twinned. Corbels in the south radiating chapel feature the Seven Deadly Sins. The chancel with its oven vaulted apse has a number of capitals decorated with interlacing. The southwestern pillar of the transept crossing is topped by a carved capital representing a centaur with the body of an elephant (late 12C).
Two fine 4C mosaics from a Gallo-Roman villa can be seen in the cloisters : one is made up of geometric patterns, the other shows birds in a vine.

Museum ⌚ This is housed in the lower rooms of the abbey dependencies and has finds from archeological digs in the Landes, the Béarn and the Basque country on display.
The main focus is on the prehistoric site at Duruthy, near Sorde-l'Abbaye *(see below)*, where the quality and richness of the finds echo those of famous sites in the Dordogne. The excavations have uncovered a remarkable assortment of bone and horn implements and tools (harpoons, needles, spear heads), and items decorated with animals or geometric designs which can be dated from the Magdalenian era, 12 000 years ago. One of the finest exhibits is a sandstone sculpture of a kneeling horse.

►► Sorde-l'Abbaye (7km – 4½ miles east via Peyrehorade) – old *bastide (qv)* and traces of the former abbey.

★ AUBETERRE-SUR-DRONNE — Pop 388

Michelin map 75 fold 3 or 233 folds 40, 41.

Aubeterre is an ancient village with steep, narrow streets, huddled in a semicircle at the foot of its castle, high above the green pastureland of the Dronne Valley. It is built on the slopes of a hollow breaking the line of white chalk cliffs which gave the place its name (*Alba Terra* in Latin = White Land).
The village is centred on Place Trarieux, a quiet square overlooked by the bust of Ludovic Trarieux, native of Aubeterre and founder of La Ligue pour la Défense des droits de l'homme et du citoyen (the League for the Defence of the Rights of Man). From here, visitors can climb up to St James' Church or walk down to the monolithic church.

CHURCHES *1 hour*

★ **Monolithic Church** ⌚ – This church is one of a rare type which has been hewn from a single, solid block of rock. There is a similar example near Bordeaux, at St-Émilion *(qv)*.
Work on the church, which is dedicated to St John, probably started in the 12C. It was built to house relics from the Holy Sepulchre in Jerusalem brought back from

Under the Revolution the church was used as a saltpetre works and later – until 1865 – as the local cemetery.
The 12C nave, running parallel to the cliff, gives the impression of being extremely tall, though the vaulting rises to no more than 21m – 69ft. It is flanked by a single aisle, at the end of which a series of galleries communicates with the castle on the cliff edge above. At one end of the nave an apse surrounds a monolithic Romanesque monument, carved from a block left in place when the church was hollowed out, and shaped into a lantern at its upper limit; it displayed the shrine containing the holy relics for the worship of pilgrims.
At the other end of the nave is a primitive 6C chapel, transformed into a necropolis in the 12C after work on the church was completed. Excavations have revealed a series of tombs hollowed from the rock and an ancient font.

Église St-Jacques – St James' was formerly a Benedictine abbey church which later became a collegiate church for a chapter of canons. The Romanesque façade, punctuated by arcades and blind arcades, is decorated with finely sculpted geometric motifs based on Arabic designs. Left of the central doorway a carved frieze presents the labours of the months.
Below the church a battlemented tower protects the 16C chapter-house.

★ AUCH Pop 23 136

Michelin map 82 fold 5 or 235 fold 29 – Local map p 30.

Auch has always been a trade crossroads, busy since Roman times with the heavy traffic plying between Toulouse and the Atlantic, before the route of the Middle Garonne was used. The town was revived in the 18C by Intendant (Steward) Étigny and its appearance enhanced under the Second Empire. The bustling street life and the busy Saturday markets underline its position as administrative capital of Gascony.
The streets at right-angles to the main axis of the town converge on Place de la Libération; the episcopal district stands apart, on the eastern side of the River Gers.

The real d'Artagnan – The statue in the town honouring d'Artagnan represents him as the famous musketeer immortalized by the novelist Alexandre Dumas. The real-life character, Charles de Batz (born *c*1615), borrowed the name d'Artagnan from the Montesquiou family on his mother's side : he was about to join a French Guards regiment and the name was more suitable for court use.
The cadet, already favoured by Cardinal Mazarin (1602-61), Richelieu's successor, divided his time between battle campaigns, diplomatic missions and the bawdy life of the back streets. Having gained the confidence of Louis XIV he was entrusted with the arrest of the powerful Finance Minister Jules Fouquet, who had grown extremely rich at the State's expense – a mandate d'Artagnan is said to have carried out "with great delicacy". He died a hero's death, by then a Captain-Lieutenant in the 1st Company of the King's Musketeers, during the Siege of Maastricht in 1673.
In 1700 an apocryphal "autobiography", *Mémoires de Monsieur d'Artagnan,* was published, which pandered to the public taste for news of "indiscretions" in high places. The book had lain forgotten, gathering dust on the shelves of libraries, when Dumas (1802-70) rediscovered it and used it as background for his world-famous novel in which, with *The Three Musketeers,* d'Artagnan lived again as the classic Gascon hero.

OLD TOWN *2 hours 30min*

★★ **Cathédrale Ste-Marie** ⊙ – Construction of St Mary's Cathedral started in 1489 with the east end, which rests on a crypt to compensate for the lie of the land; work was not completed until two centuries later. The whole marks the beginning of what became known as "French" Gothic : the nave is higher than the side aisles, the triforium positioned between large arcades and clerestory windows. The quadripartite vaulting, dating from the mid 17C, lends the interior a certain stylistic unity.
The axial chapel is flanked on the north side by the Chapel of the Holy Sepulchre which houses an enormous early 16C *Christ Entombed* and on the south side by St Catherine's Chapel with its stone altarpiece dating from the 16C.
The chancel, as vast as the nave, is graced by two extremely fine features : the stained-glass windows and the choir stalls. These are best admired by starting a tour of the ambulatory on the north side.

★★ **Stained-glass windows** – Eighteen works by the Gascon painter **Arnaud de Moles** embellish the windows of the ambulatory chapels. The windows (early 16C) are noted for their rich colours, unusually large panes and big, expressive figures – some of the men's faces are almost caricatures – the decoration incorporating medallions and brace-like ornamentation with Flamboyant Gothic canopies, all of which combine to produce one of the masterpieces of early 16C French art. Vignettes of daily life adorn the lower parts of the windows.
The distribution of subject matter conforms to prevailing theological doctrines at that time linking the Old Testament, the New Testament and even the pagan world – note the representation of the Sibyls.

★★★ **Choir stalls** – This huge artistic project took the wood carvers of Auch 50 years (*c*1500-52) to complete. The 113 stalls – of which 69 are high-backed beneath Flamboyant canopies – are decorated with over 1 500 characters exquisitely carved from the seasoned oak. The general theme again demonstrates the theological parallelism evident in the stained-glass windows : motifs drawn from the Bible, from secular history, from myths and from legends all find their place.

The statues crowning the apse side of the 1609 reredos closing off the chancel originally adorned a rood screen demolished in the 19C; noteworthy among them is a scene representing the four Evangelists at table.
In the penultimate side-chapel on the north side there is a funerary monument to Intendant d'Étigny, which was restored after the Revolution.
The splendid tones of the great organ (1694) may be heard each June during the recitals of classical music which are held as part of the annual Auch Festival.

Mary Magdalene
(detail of a choir stall),
Auch cathedral.

D'après photo Raymond Montané

West front – The solid 16C and 17C west front, with its recessed upper levels producing a slightly tapering effect, presents a carefully-balanced relationship between its pilasters, columns, cornices, balustrades and niches. The doorways are sheltered by a vast porch offering a good view of the interior with its dividing arches constructed to look like antique triumphal arches.
On summer evenings an audio-visual show highlights the best features of the cathedral.

Monumental staircase – The 232 steps of this impressive stairway link Place Salinis, the square next to the cathedral which overlooks the Gers Valley, with the quays below; the statue of d'Artagnan, dating from 1931, is halfway down. Climbing back up the steps offers a fine view of the 14C Tour d'Armagnac (the 40m – 130ft high watchtower of the municipal prison) and the arrangement of abutments and double-course flying buttresses around the cathedral.

Place de la Libération – This is the hub of activity in the upper town. The square is closed on the northwest by the Town Hall and the Allées d'Étigny, which were both completed between 1751 and 1767 by the benevolent administrator whose statue stands at the top of the stairs.

From the Tourist Information Centre housed in the 15C half-timbered **Maison Fédel** (off Place de la République) take Rue Dessoles, which was the town's main street before d'Étigny laid out his great thoroughfares.

Turn right into Rue Salleneuve (stone steps).

The route through the square occupied by the Halle aux Herbes (fruit and vegetable market) leads back to the north side of the cathedral. On the left, the Préfecture occupies the **old Archbishop's Palace** (1742-75) with its classical façade punctuated by tall fluted pilasters.

At the southwest corner of the cathedral take Rue Espagne.

At the end of this street two old houses (Nos 20 and 22) form a picturesque ensemble.

Turn left into Rue de la Convention.

The street, lined with ancient dwellings, leads to the **Pousterles,** a series of narrow stepped alleyways. In medieval times *pousterles* was a word used to designate the posterns set in the walls of the fortified upper town. At the end of the road, a left turn and a few steps lead to Porte d'Arton, which was once the main entrance to the town. Beyond this, Rue d'Églantine skirts the ancient walls of the lycée – formerly a Jesuit college founded in 1545 – before joining Place Salinis.

⊙ ▸▸ Musée des Jacobins : Gallo-Roman archeology; South American colonial art.

EXCURSIONS

★ **Circuit des Bastides et des Castelnaux (Fortified villages and small castles)** – *138km – 86 miles : allow 1 day. Local map under Mirande, qv.*

Leave Auch via N 124 west, towards Mont-de-Marsan. After 5km – 3 miles turn left into D 943, signposted "Route des bastides et des Castelnaux".

The itinerary from Barran to Mirande via Beaumarchès is described in the chapter on Mirande *(qv)*. The return journey from Mirande to Auch is via N 21.

Round trip through the heart of Gascony – *72km – 45 miles: allow half a day. Leave Auch via N 21 north and after 8.5km – 5 miles turn left into D 272. Passing to the right of Roquelaure, take D 148 along the crest route. Continue beyond Mérens along D 518 to Lavardens.*
The road runs through a gentle, undulating landscape, offering a fine **view★** of Lavardens.

Lavardens – This picturesque village with narrow streets is noted for its imposing castle and attractive church belfry; traces of the ramparts and the towers which were part of its encircling walls may also still be seen.
The **castle** ⊙ was razed in the 15C and its rebuilding never completed. The structure standing today is pierced with mullioned and transomed windows, and juts out boldly to the west where the façade is flanked with square towers.

J.-L. Barde/SCOPE

Lavardens.

A stairway hewn out of stone leads up to the main vaulted rooms, some of which have their 17C floors of brick and stone laid in geometric designs. From the top floor there is a panoramic **view** over the neighbouring hills.

Continue along D 103 west.

Jegun – The village on a rocky spur stands within a *bastide (qv)* which still has its ground plan; it was once Church property. Along the main street stand the old market and various ancient houses, one with fine half-timbering. To the east is the 13C collegiate church of Ste-Candide, supported by powerful buttresses.

Continue west.

Vic-Fézensac – This town holds busy markets and fairs. St Peter's Church, with its octagonal belfry crowned by a lantern, contains a Romanesque oven-vaulted apse and traces of 15C frescoes (south apsidal chapel); the marble font left of the entrance is a graceful 18C sculpture of three children supporting a basin.

Leave Vic-Fézensac to the southeast via N 124 towards Auch. At St-Jean-Poutge turn right into D 939 towards l'Isle-de-Noé.

After about 4km – 2½ miles, before turning left into D 374, note the unusual **Gallo-Roman pier** with a niche; its purpose is uncertain.

Biran – In this small *castelnau (qv)* rising on a spur, a single road links the fortified gateway to the remains of the keep. The **church** ⊙ shelters a monumental stone altarpiece carved with scenes on the themes of the Pietà, the Descent from the Cross and the Entombment.

Continue along D 374 and rejoin N 124 to return to Auch.

Other local *bastides* of interest include : Fleurance (24km – 15 miles north); St-Clar (35km – 21 miles northeast via Fleurance); Cologne (39km – 24 miles northeast via Mauzevin); Beaumont-de-Lomagne (50km – 31 miles northeast via Mauzevin).

Château de St-Cricq, Gimont, Castelnau-Barbarens – *57km – 35 miles : allow half a day. Leave Auch via N 124 east and follow signs to "Château de St-Cricq".*

Château de St-Cricq ⊙ – This 16C château is now the town's Reception and Conference Centre. The pentagonal tower shelters a spiral staircase which leads to the main chamber on the 2nd floor and the large rooms on the ground floor which contain imposing fireplaces made from local stone.

Continue along N 124 towards Toulouse.

After 7.5km – 4½ miles there appears, on the left, beyond a meadow, the long south façade of **Château de Marsan** (18C-19C), owned by the Montesquiou family.

Continue along N 124.

Gimont – This *bastide (qv)* founded in 1266 has a typical ground plan which has been narrowly adapted to the relief of a pocked hill. The main road passes directly through the site of the old market. Important *foie gras* preserving businesses and twice-weekly markets throughout the winter ensure the town's gastronomical fame. The church here is an example of southern Gothic architecture, with a single nave and a brick tower in the Toulouse style which is visible from afar. Inside, the treasury (1st chapel on the left) contains a Renaissance triptych which reveals, when open, the Crucifixion flanked by the Virgin and St Lazarus. The outer panels are painted with effigies of Mary Magdalene and St Martha, the former richly dressed and carrying an anointing vase of perfume, the latter taming the Tarasque, a legendary amphibious monster that lived in the Rhône *(see the Michelin Green Guide to Provence).* Note, on either side of the main altar, the two Renaissance towers with lanterns in which the Holy Sacrament (bread and wine) and holy relics were preserved.

Leave Gimont to the southwest via D 12 and continue for 12km – 7½ miles to Boulaur.

Boulaur – Boulaur, a village perched above the valley of the Gimone, has a monastery founded in the 12C by monks from Fontevraud; it is today inhabited by Cistercian monks. The abbey church has a tall east end of stone and brick, and a series of blind arcades which runs under the roof of the south wall.

Join D 626 north of the village and head westwards to Castelnau-Barbarens.

Castelnau-Barbarens – This old village founded in the 12C has houses standing in concentric arcs radiating from the hill on which the church rises. All that remains of the old castle is a tower which now serves as the belfry. The terrace offers a panoramic **view** over the Arrats valley and the neighbouring hills.

Continue to Auch.

After 2km – about 1 mile, on reaching the plateau, D 626 offers a fine **panorama**★ towards the Pyrenees. The route crosses **Pessan,** an old *sauveté* (a rural township founded by a monastery as a sanctuary for fugitives) which developed around an abbey founded in the 9C.

★★ AULNAY

Pop 1 462

Michelin map 72 fold 2 or 233 fold 17.

The church of St Peter of the Tower, standing on the borders of Poitou and the Saintonge, along the age-old pilgrims' route to Santiago de Compostela, rises in solitary state among the sombre cypresses of its ancient cemetery.

★★ ÉGLISE ST-PIERRE-DE-LA-TOUR ⏲ *45min*

The rare unity and harmony of the composition, the abundant and ornate yet controlled decoration, and the warm patina of old stone combine to make this 12C church a masterpiece of regional Romanesque architecture.
The far end of the cemetery, just left of the axis from the centre of the west front, offers the best overall view.

West front – The west front is crowned with small lanterns and includes, at its centre, a porch of broken arches flanked by blind arcades forming funerary niches. The Crucifixion of St Peter is carved on the tympanum of the northern arcade; on the southern tympanum Christ in Majesty is seen with two figures presumably representing St Peter and St Paul.
The receding arches behind the archivolt are carved with graceful sculptures illustrating themes favoured by the Poitou "image makers" : 1st arch *(below),* angels worshipping the Lamb of God; 2nd arch, Virtues exterminating Vices; 3rd arch, the Wise *(left)* and Foolish Virgins; 4th arch, signs of the Zodiac and labours of the months. The central blind bay on the upper level of the front once framed a statue of the Emperor Constantine on a horse *(see Melle, qv).*

Transept – The square belfry-tower, which stands over the transept crossing, served as a landmark for pilgrims and other travellers. The arching over the **north transept doorway** features rows of superbly-carved figures and animals. The carvings represent :
Outer arch : mythological characters and creatures – the musical ass, a goat, a deer, an owl, a Siren etc;
3rd arch : the Old Men of the Apocalypse – 31 here instead of the usual 24 – each holding a phial of perfume and a musical instrument. The intrados (underside) of the arch is carved with kneeling atlantes;
2nd arch : the Disciples of Christ and the Apostles (seated atlantes adorn the intrados);
Inner arch : animals (centaurs, griffins) and foliage of largely oriental inspiration in light relief.
A tall opening above the porch features a central arch adorned with four fine sculptures of the Virtues conquering the Vices.

LAUROS-GIRAUDON

Detail of the north transept doorway, Église St-Pierre, Aulnay.

Apse – On each side of the apse's axial window, strange wreaths of foliage in the oriental style encircle enigmatic figures.

Interior – The nave is roofed with broken-barrel vaulting and buttressed by tall aisles : note the unusually deep openings, narrower on the north side than on the south, and the massive pillars cut by two layers of capitals.
A handsome dome on pendentives crowns the inside of the transept crossing, its ribs radiating from a circular opening through which the bells in the tower above can be rung.
The capitals in the church, especially those in the transept, are exceptionally fine. The carvings on them include elephants with tiny ears *(south transept, by the entrance to the aisle),* Samson, sleeping, bound by Delilah while a Philistine cuts his hair with enormous scissors *(northwest pillar, transept crossing),* imps pulling the beard of a poor man *(north transept, entrance to the aisle)...*

Cemetery – The burial ground, strewn with tombstones in the form of sarcophagi, still has its 15C **"Hosanna Cross"** *(qv)* complete with lectern from which the priest read the lessons on Palm Sunday, and the canopied statues of the saints Peter, Paul, James and John.

AURIGNAC — Pop 983

Michelin map 82 fold 16 or 235 fold 37 – 10km – 6 miles northwest of Boussens.

This old fortified village lies along one of the last ridges of the Lesser Pyrenees west of the Garonne River. Its name, which was ascribed a century ago to one of the Paleolithic civilizations (the Aurignacian), is now familiar to scholars of prehistory the world over.

A stroke of luck – In 1852 a local workman digging near the road leading to Boulogne-sur-Gesse hit upon an old burial place beneath a rock. The find was not thought significant as religious wars had already multiplied the number of such mass graves in Gascony. The skeletons unearthed were re-buried in the communal cemetery.
Eight years later the find came to the attention of **Édouard Lartet** (1801-71), a paleontologist from Gers, who subsequently organized a dig in the area of the workman's discovery. The harvest of bone and flint implements which emerged was extensive enough to enable the scholar to sketch out a rough chronology of the Paleolithic era. It was the start of a great scientific adventure marked, during Lartet's lifetime, by the discovery at Les Eyzies – not far from Sarlat and Lascaux (where the now-famous cave paintings were discovered) in the Dordogne – of skeletons identified as Cro-Magnon, the race defining the Aurignacian period.

SIGHTS

Musée de Préhistoire ⊙ – The museum's central display cases are devoted to Lartet and the excavations around Aurignac. The exhibits include implements and tools (especially the "keeled" scrapers typical of the Aurignacian period), animal bones (bear, hyena, rhinoceros, lion) and other discoveries made near the original grotto by F Lacorre in 1938 and 1939. Additional showcases display tools from the Paleolithic as a whole.
A visit to the prehistoric burial place, on the Boulogne-sur-Gesse road at the exit to the village, completes the tour.

Church – The belfry forms a fortified gateway. Only the porch and its doorway, in the Flamboyant Gothic style, are of particular interest.
The porch, with its four twisted columns, comes from an older church now destroyed. The capitals, trimmed into segments of a hexagon on the exterior, are shaped like dice inside. On the pier of the doorway and the tympanum two statues stand one above the other : a 17C *Virgin and Child,* and *Christ Waiting for Death* (15C).

Keep – The **panorama★** from the old castle keep opens out on either side of the summit of the Cagire, a bulky, wooded mountain typical of the region in the middle distance. On the left are the Pyrenees of the Ariège, and the Maladetta Massif with Pic d'Aneto; to the right the view stretches away to the Luchon and its glacier, the Arbizon and Pic du Midi de Bigorre.

★ BAGNÈRES-DE-BIGORRE — Pop 8 423

Michelin map 85 fold 18 or 234 fold 40 – Local map p 90 – Facilities.

Bagnères-de-Bigorre lies in a lovely pastoral setting north of the Campan Valley, on the west bank of the River Adour. As well as being a picturesque spa, the town is also a lively industrial centre (Pyrenean cloths, electrical and refrigerating equipment, railway rolling stock).
The waters of the recently remodelled cure centre, which are rich in calcium and sulphur salts, are drawn from 13 new bores. These, together with the 38 existing hot springs, are used in the treatment of respiratory, rheumatic and psychosomatic disorders.
Bagnères-de-Bigorre is also a nucleus around which much Pyrenean folklore is centred, and was the home of a well-known 19C literary society specializing in works inspired by the mountains, whose members were known as the "Chanteurs Montagnards" and who travelled to London, Rome, Jerusalem and Moscow.

BAGNÈRES-DE BIGORRE

Coustous (Allées des)	BZ	7
Foch (R. Maréchal)	BY	8
Lafayette (Pl.)	ABY	22
Strasbourg (Pl. de)	BZ	32
Thermes (R. des)	AZ	34
Victor-Hugo (R.)	AZ	35
Alsace-Lorraine (R. d')	BZ	2
Arras (R. du Pont d')	AZ	3
Belgique (Av. de)	AY	4
Costallat (R.)	BY	6
Frossard (R. Émilien)	BZ	12
Gambetta (R.)	AY	13
Joffre (Av. Maréchal)	AY	17
Jubinal (Pl. A.)	BZ	20
Leclerc (Av. Général)	AY	23
Lorry (R. de)	BZ	25
Pasteur (R.)	BY	26
Pyrénées (R. des)	BZ	27
République (R. de la)	AY	28
Thermes (Pl. des)	AZ	33
Vigneaux	BY	37
3-Frères-Duthu (R.)	BZ	39

B Tour des Jacobins
D Ruines du cloître St-Jean
E Maison à colombage
M Musée Salies
M¹ Musée du Vieux-Moulin

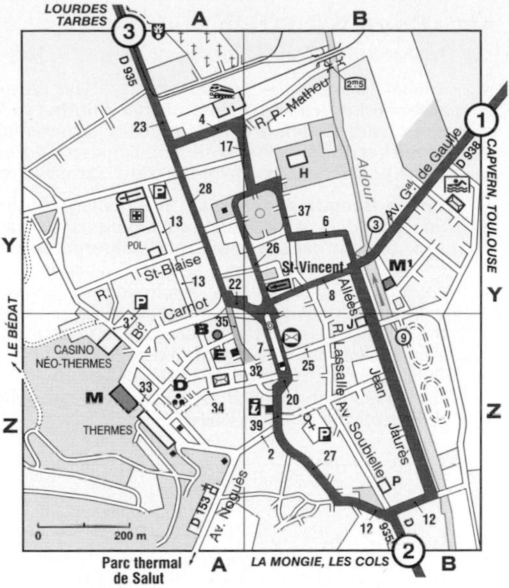

SIGHTS

Old town – Among the attractions of this area – bordered to the east by Les Allées des Coustous, the busiest part of the town – are **St Vincent's Church,** a 16C church with a belfry-wall pierced by three rows of arcades, the **Tour des Jacobins** (**B**), a tower which is all that remains of a 15C monastery destroyed during the Revolution, and the **cloister ruins** (**D**) on the corner of Rue St-Jean and Rue des Thermes. The charming **half-timbered house** (**E**) at the junction of Rue du Vieux-Moulin and Rue Victor-Hugo dates from the 15C.

Musée Salies (AZ M) ⊙ – The Fine Arts department of this museum includes an interesting collection of ceramics, and paintings by Joos van Cleve, Chasseriau, Jongkind, Picabia and others. There are also temporary exhibitions of natural history and photography.

Musée du Vieux Moulin (BY M¹) ⊙ – The old watermill is now used as a museum focusing on crafts and folk traditions of the Bigorre mountain region (traditional tools used in weaving and the wool trade, agricultural implements etc).

★ **Parc thermal de Salut** – *45min Rtn on foot.*
A gateway at the end of Avenue Noguès *(south of the town plan)* marks the entrance to this 1 000ha – 2 470 acre park which offers pleasant walks under fine, shady trees. The central avenue crosses the park and skirts the glade leading to the former Établissement Thermal de Salut – the old spa centre.

EXCURSIONS

★★ **Grotte de Médous** – *2.5km – 1½ miles south via ② on the plan. See Grotte de Médous.*

★ **Le Bédat** – *1½ hours Rtn on foot.* At the junction of three by-roads north of the Casino *(AZ on the town plan),* a path to the left leads to the Fontaine des Fées (Fairy Fountain) and the statue of the Bédat Virgin. Behind the statue, another path follows the crest as far as the viewing table (alt 881m – 2 890ft).
The impressive **view** stretches over the Baronnies and the Lannemezan plateau *(east)* and across the Campan valley to the summits of the Central Pyrenees *(south).*

LA MOUCLADE

This dish from the Charentes region takes its name from mussels known locally as "moucles". There are many variants of the recipe; here is one :

For 4 people. Scrape and wash 4 pints of mussels. Cook them in the "marinière" style – that is, in a saucepan or casserole with a bouquet-garni and a glass of white wine. Once they have opened, remove a half shell from each and arrange them in a flat ovenproof dish.

Gently fry 4 onions, then cover with half the liquid from the mussels; reduce by simmering for half an hour. Add pepper and a pinch of saffron.
Away from the heat, blend 2 egg yolks with 100g - 3½ oz fresh cream. Add this to the onion mixture and then pour over the mussels. Brown for a few minutes in a hot oven and serve immediately.

★★★ Pays BASQUE

Michelin map 85 folds 1 to 5 and 13 to 15 or 234 folds 29, 30, 33, 34, 37, 38, 42.

The landscape of the Basque Country (Pays Basque) presents a dramatic contrast to that of Bordeaux and the moors to the north : suddenly, the mountains are near; the coast, with its cliffs and rugged rocks, differs markedly from the long, level strands of the Landes *(qv);* the hinterland consists of green valleys studded with traditional white houses, and is one of the most attractive regions in France.

Seven Basque provinces – The geology of the Basque region, which marks the final shudders of the Pyrenean folding, is naturally varied. The valleys are tortuous and communications between the different basins difficult; one 17C chronicler described it as "a very bumpy country". This partly explains the former division of the country into small "states" each with its separate identity. The seven Basque provinces nevertheless share a single race and a single tongue, on both the French and the Spanish sides of the Pyrenees; their common motto, in the Basque language, is *Zaspiak-bat* – the Seven that make but One.
This guide describes areas of the three provinces on the northern side of the frontier, those in the French sector of the Basque Country : **Le Labourd, La Basse Navarre** (Lower Navarre) and **La Soule.**

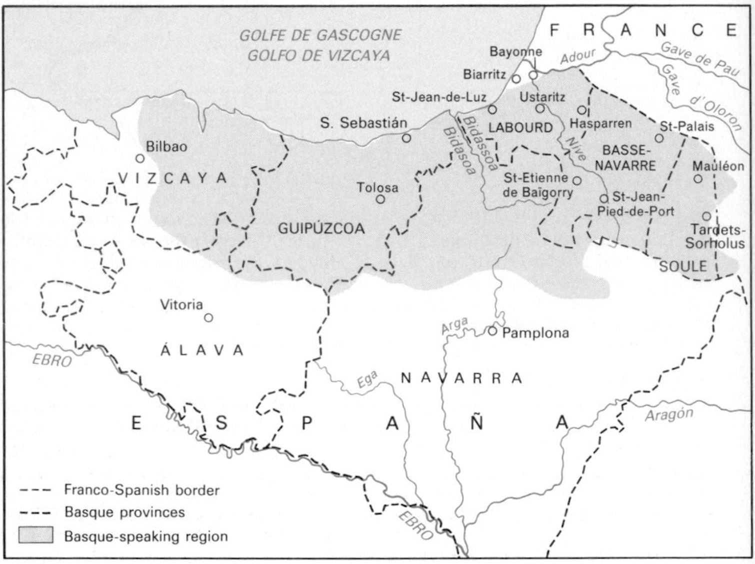

Spanish or French name and its *Basque* equivalent

Bayonne/*Baiona*
Biarritz/*Miarritze*
Bilbao/*Bilbo*
Hasparren/*Hazparne*
Mauléon/*Maule*
Pamplona/*Iruñea*
St-Jean-de-Luz/*Donibane-Lohizun*
St-Etienne-de-Baïgorry/*Baigorri*
St-Jean-Pied-de-Port/*Donibane-Garazi*
St-Palais/*Donapaleu*
San Sebastián/*Donostia*
Tardets-Sorholus/*Atharratze-Sorholüze*
Ustaritz/*Uztaritze*
Vitoria/*Gasteiz*

LIFE IN THE BASQUE COUNTRY

A mysterious race and language – The origin of the Basque people and their common tongue, which curiously bears a resemblance to Finnish, has always been a mystery. All that is known for sure is that they were driven out of the Ebro valley in Spain by the Visigoths and founded the kingdom of Vasconia in the western Pyrenees. The Vascons of the plain then intermarried with the local peoples of Aquitaine and were called Gascons. Those who remained in the mountains fiercely safeguarded their own traditions and their language, **Euskara,** which binds the race together; it has few words but subtle constructions.

Basque houses – The typical house of the Labourd is the most attractive of the traditional Basque dwellings, and has inspired the design of many suburban villas and holiday homes. Its exposed wooden framework, usually painted a reddish-brown, contrasts with the walls of cob (compressed loam, clay or chalk reinforced with straw) coated with whitewashed rough-cast. The front, facing east to avoid the rain brought by the west wind from the Atlantic, is sheltered by a huge overhanging tile roof.
The houses in Basse (Lower) Navarre have a stone framework and semicircular balconies; the darker, slate roofs found in Soule are an indication of the region's proximity to the Béarn region *(qv).* Basque houses all share the characteristic white finish, and many proudly carry over their front doors the date of their construction or their owner's name.
Nowhere else is the family so closely connected with the home. The master of the house, the *Etcheko Jaun,* reigns supreme, and his greatest preoccupation is to preserve the continuity of the family and its estate. The house is bequeathed to the child, boy or girl, designated by the father the "eldest" – not necessarily the oldest in years.

The other children, seeking their fortunes elsewhere, have often headed for the New World, especially Latin America, where the Basques are particularly well-received. During the 19C more than 90 000 French Basques moved to the far side of the Atlantic. Once successful, the "Americanoaks" either return to their native country or invite their relations to join them.
The Basque veneration of the family home, lovingly maintained in perfect order from generation to generation, has preserved the traditional aspect of Basque villages and towns, and has spared them the horrors of modern suburban development. Typical Basque furniture and furnishings may be seen in the Musée Basque, Bayonne.

Basque churches – The church plays a major part in Basque life : the entire village is symbolically grouped around it. Many of the faithful attend services – often in the Basque language – every day.
External architecture, although always simple, is varied. The churches of Soule are built with curious triple belfries and three identical gables – representing the Holy Trinity – surmounted by the Cross of Golgotha *(illustration p 000)*. The internal arrangements common to the three French provinces are equally unusual : a wide nave is surrounded by two or three tiers of galleries, with the pulpit an extension of the lowest gallery; the altar, surmounted by an ornate Baroque reredos, is invariably placed high; sometimes the sacristy is located beneath the rostrum on which the altar stands. During services the nave is reserved for women; the men sit in the galleries.
In the flower-filled cemeteries the most characteristic Basque tombstones, and the oldest (some pre-16C), are disk-shaped : the plinth supports a stone circle usually engraved with the "Basque Cross" (a cross of Hindu origin with bended arms, similar to a distorted swastika).

Disk-shaped Basque tombstones.

D'après photo Ezkila

Pelota – The traditional game of the Basque people has similarities with the games of squash, rackets, real tennis and fives : a ball, the *pelota,* is hurled against the high wall of the *pelota* court, and returned by the opponent full pitch or after it has bounced once within limits marked on the floor of the court. The game *(illustration p 263)*, involving two teams of three players, became fashionable through the exploits of Joseph Apesteguy (1881-1950), who reached international fame as Chiquito de Cambo.
Since the 19C the version most popular with tourists has been the *"Grand Chistera"* which derives its name from the long, curved wicker scoop which extends from the players' protective gloves. In different versions of the game, the ball is struck with the bare or gloved hand, hit with a bat – the *pala* – or caught in the *chistera* and flung from that. A spectacular and athletic version imported from Latin America is the *cesta punta* or *jai alai,* which is played within a covered court. In the game of *pasaka,* played with a glove, the adversaries face one another across a net. The *sare* variation uses an Argentinian racket or *paleta.*
The *pelota* itself, which is slightly larger than a tennis ball, consists of a rubber or boxwood core, wrapped in wool and then encased in leather – calf or kidskin, which does not stretch. The seams must be perfectly smooth.
The *pelotaris* (players) of the two rival teams, wearing white shirts and trousers and rope-soled shoes, are distinguished by the colours of their sashes (blue or red). They bound around the court hurling the ball with powerful sweeps of their arms while the *chacharia* (crier) calls out the points scored in a resonant voice, sometimes adding a satirical couplet commenting on the play. Games are played before excited crowds, and in important matches heavy betting may take place.
The history of the game is retraced in the museum in Bayonne.

Outcasts – In the Basque country, as in the regions of Béarn and Bigorre, certain trades (wood-cutting, carpentry, masonry, weaving...) were in the past reserved for *chrestiaas, agotaks* or *cagots* (pariahs or "untouchables"). From the Middle Ages to the beginning of the 19C these descendants of lepers and plague victims were treated as outcasts, no doubt because of fears of transmitted defects, deformities and possible epidemics. They had to live apart and wear a distinctive badge in the form of a goose foot on their clothes. A special door and stoup were reserved for them in church; if they married outside their caste, the offence was punishable by death.
The gradual acceptance of the *cagots* into the community began when they intermarried with gypsies expelled from Spain in the 16C and continued later when their activities broadened to include the selling of fish and the formation of groups of itinerant musicians.

Folklore – The Basque people, typically silent and serious by nature, express themselves in their dancing, singing and group activities. The young men – most of the traditional dances do not include female partners – travel from village to village for the local fêtes. In the evening, as they return home, their rallying cries echo from mountain to mountain.
The dances, numerous and complex, are generally danced to the sound of a *tchirulä* (three-holed ocarina or flute) and a *ttun-ttun* (small drum) or a stringed tambourine, though they are sometimes replaced by an accordion, a cornet or a clarinet. The

famous Basque Leaps, danced by men only, have many different steps; common to all of them is the striking contrast between the stillness of the torso, the impassivity of the features and the incredible agility of the legs.

The **Fandango,** a dance described as "both chaste and passionate", refers to man's eternal pursuit of his female ideal : the movements of the woman's arms and the upper part of her body harmonize with alternating rhythms representing invitation and flight.

For the celebrated "Wineglass Dance", the fleet-footed men of Soule wear dazzling costumes : the *zamalzain,* who thanks to a wicker frame appears as both a horse and its rider, and the other dancers perform complicated steps around a glass of wine placed on the ground, each finally standing for a fraction of a second on the glass, without breaking it or spilling a drop of its contents.

Basque dance.

Basque songs are primitive, direct and inspired by everyday life, in much the same way as the American Blues, and are set to poetic melodies. French Basques sometimes sing *Guernikako Arbola* (The Tree of Guernica), the sacred song of the Spanish Basques which has become practically their national anthem. In it the Oak of Guernica – the Basque village devastated by Fascist air raids during the Spanish civil war and immortalized by Picasso – symbolizes the *fueros,* or local freedom.

Pastorales in the Basque country, like musical versions of the medieval English Morality Plays, recall the mysteries of the Middle Ages, allegorically opposing the Good to the Bad. Performances can last several hours.

Basque feast-day banquets also often end with improvisations which sometimes turn into song competitions, all on a single theme and set to a single tune.

Pigeon hunting – This is a favourite "sport" in the Basque country. The birds, a species of wild pigeon, migrate from the north to Spain in the early autumn, in flocks of up to several thousand.

In the Landes, wood pigeons are tamed to act as decoys; in the Basque country no live decoys are used. Instead, *pantières* (nets) are hung between the tallest trees across the birds' usual flight path, frequently in a mountain pass. Beaters posted in nearby trees or on drystone cairns chivvy the pigeons when they approach by uttering guttural cries, hustling them in a certain direction; sometimes they brandish white flags and throw dummy hawks made of wood in front of the birds. As a result the birds take fright, dive low and fly into the nets, which then collapse on them.

TOURS OF THE REGION

The following are recommended itineraries and visits within the French Basque provinces :

★ LE LABOURD

From Bayonne to Cambo-les-Bains via La Rhune – *See Le Labourd.*

★ **Route impériale des cimes** – *See Napoleon I's Scenic Highway, Bayonne.*

★ LA BASSE NAVARRE

St-Jean-Pied-de-Port – *See St-Jean-Pied-de-Port.*

Grottes d'Isturits and d'Oxocelhaya – *See Isturits and Oxocelhaya.*

★ LA SOULE

★ **Lower Soule** – Round tour from Mauléon-Licharre. *See La Soule.*

★★ **Upper Soule** – Sights and villages in alphabetical order. *See La Soule.*

Michelin Tyre PLC
Tourism Department
The Edward Hyde Building
38 Clarendon Road
WATFORD - WD1 1SX
Tel : 0923 415 000
Fax : 0923 415 250

Abbaye de BASSAC

Michelin map 72 folds 12, 13 or 233 folds 28, 29 – 7km – 4½ miles southeast of Jarnac.

Bassac Abbey, founded soon after the year 1000 and ravaged during the Hundred Years War and the Wars of Religion, was used by Benedictine monks. A number of important relics were preserved here, among them the Holy Bonds said to have been used to tie up Christ during the ritual Flagellation.
The abbey was abandoned at the time of the Revolution, fell into private hands in 1820 and was returned to religious life in 1947 by the Missionary Brothers of St Theresa of the Infant Jesus.

TOUR *1 hour*

Enter the abbey courtyard : opposite stands the church; to the right, the monastery.

★ **Abbey Church** – In the 15C the interesting façade in the Saintonge Romanesque style was given special defences : a gable pierced by loopholes and flanked by watch-towers. During the Revolution some patriotic hand inscribed on the wall the words of Robespierre : *The people of France recognize the Supreme Being and the immortality of the soul.* The square tower was designed with four levels, each rising progressively more recessed and with more open-work. The top storey is crowned by a spire decorated with tiles arranged in a fish-scale design.
Inside, the single nave with its convex vaulting and its flattened east end testifies to the far-reaching influence of the Angevin Gothic style.
On the southern side there is a 17C painted panel representing the Entombment, and a statue of St Nicholas – probably 13C – the feet of which have been worn down by the touch of hopeful young girls keen to find a husband.
The enormous monks' chancel was remodelled in the early 18C. The 40 delicately-carved stalls, the monumental eagle lectern, the high-altar reredos and two small altarpieces backing the choir screen are all the work of Benedictine fathers helped by local artisans. This sober and elegant decoration perfectly complements the medieval architecture of the sanctuary.

Monastery buildings ⊙ – These were rebuilt in the 17C and 18C. A majestic doorway framed by Ionic columns, followed by a long passageway with diagonal vaulting, leads to the old cloisters.
The cloister galleries were demolished in 1820 (marks where the charges were rammed in are visible) but the monastic buildings still exist, surmounted by attractive dormer windows with pediments. On the ground floor, a tour leads through the kitchens, the calefactory, a balustraded staircase in the south wing, and the old chapter-house, today used as a chapel (fine 17C vaulting; modern – 1954 – stained-glass windows). There is a small garden and a terrace in front of the façade overlooking the Charente river.

★★ BAYONNE

Pop 40 051

Michelin map 78 fold 18 or 234 fold 29 – Local map p 158 – Facilities.

Bayonne lies near the coast on the boundary between the Landes and the Basque country, where the River Nive joins the Adour. This strategic position has made it an important port and as a result the economic capital of the Adour Basin.
The heart of this lively and interesting town combines good shopping facilities with picturesque old streets, ramparts and quays on the south bank of the Adour. The main ramparts extend from the 16C Château Vieux (Old Castle) to the Spanish Gate. **Parc de Mousserolles,** on the eastern side of the town near Château Neuf (New Castle) but outside the ramparts, offers a pleasant place for a stroll, beside its games areas and its small lake. The citadel dominating the suburb of St-Esprit, on the northern bank of the river, was built by Vauban *(qv).*
At the beginning of August, **traditional fêtes★** – *corridas,* fairs and folklore activities – go on day and night. "For six days, boys and girls frolic from the Nive to the Adour."

HISTORICAL NOTES

In the 12C Bayonne was part of the dowry of **Eleanor of Aquitaine** *(qv),* so when Eleanor's second husband, Henry Plantagenet, assumed the crown of England in 1154 Bayonne became English; it remained so for three centuries.
During the Hundred Years War *(qv),* a naval force from Bayonne served with the English fleet. The port was inundated with merchandise and the town flourished.
The integration of Bayonne within the Kingdom of France, however, after the city fell to the French in 1451, brought heavy penalties : a war indemnity – reparations – had to be paid; the English market, which had made the town prosperous, was lost; the French Kings encroached more on local liberties than the distant sovereigns of England – laws and legal documents, they decreed, had now to be written in French and not in Gascon, which produced long-lasting resentment in the people of Bayonne.
In the 16C Charles IX decided to re-open the port, which in the meantime had silted up. The direct channel to the sea was completed in 1578 and trading began again.

Zenith – The prosperity of Bayonne reached its peak in the 18C. The Chamber of Commerce was founded in 1726. Trade with Spain, Holland and the West Indies together with cod-fishing off Newfoundland and local shipbuilding gave the port as much business as it could handle.

Bayonne was declared a free port in 1759, and this trebled its traffic; in the same year it was included in the famous series *Great Ports of France* by the painter Joseph Vernet. Prizes from war on the high seas were fabulous and the affluent citizens commissioned many privateers. The Ministers of Louis XIV – Seignelay, the eldest son of Colbert, and Pontchartrain – fixed, by official decree, the system of dividing the spoils : one-tenth was to go to the Admiral of France, two-thirds to the ship-owners, and what was left to the crews. A sum was also set aside for widows, orphans and ransoms to release prisoners from the Barbary pirates.
The town's Corporation of Ironworkers and Armourers is well-known : it was their members who invented the **bayonet** – named after Bayonne and first used by the French infantry in 1703.

Hard times – The Revolution abolished the free port. The Spanish wars and the Continental Blockade had disastrous effects on the town's sea-borne trade.
It was in Bayonne, in 1808, that Napoleon received the Spanish sovereigns who renounced their right to the crown in favour of Joseph Bonaparte, the Emperor's brother. In 1813 Wellington, at the head of a combined British, Spanish and Portuguese army, marched from Spain into France. Part of the force laid siege to Bayonne while the remainder advanced on Orthez, where the French Marshal Soult was defeated. The British General Hope had meanwhile been captured during a courageous sortie by the Bayonne garrison.
In 1814 Bayonne was besieged again but resisted victoriously. The Allies entered Paris, however, Louis XVIII was proclaimed King of France and Bayonne was obliged at last to yield. This episode was the final chapter in the town's military history.

Port activity – In recent years the port has been extensively redeveloped, and the docks can now handle ships of over 20 000 tons. Work included the building of a new 850m – 930yd quay which has reduced the silting up of the channel, allowed dredging in any weather, and improved access by ensuring a stretch of calm water at the mouth of the Adour.
The mainstay of the port, which now exports more than it imports, is the traffic in raw materials in bulk. Bayonne is the country's chief exporter of sulphur (over a million tons a year, from Lacq – *qv)* and of maize, which is grown in the valleys of the Adour and the Pyrenean torrents and exported to the countries of the European Community. The town holds the largest stock of chemical products on the Atlantic seaboard. The production of cements and fertilizers, and the manufacture of components for the aeronautical industry have also made a big impact on the port area of Boucau-Tarnos, which until recently concentrated on iron and steel-making.

River-boat cruises (**BY**) ⊙ – Cruises along the River Adour are available aboard the cruiser *Bienvenu.*

OLD TOWN *3 hours*

Place de la Liberté (**BY 73**) – This is a busy square at the western end of Pont Mayou, the bridge which crosses the River Nive at the northern end of the Old Town. The town hall, the sub-Préfecture and the theatre, all under the same roof, stand at one end of the square.

Cross the bridge and follow Rue Bastiat as far as Rue Laffitte.

★★ **Musée Bonnat** (**BYZ M**[1]) ⊙ – A chronological tour of the museum's works of art begins on the second floor, where the Primitive and Old Master paintings hang. Among those dating from the 14C and 15C are a *Head of Christ Dead* from the Venetian School and a *Virgin and Child with Pomegranate* attributed to the School of Botticelli. The carefully-lit Rubens Room contains canvases showing *Apollo and Daphne* and *The Triumph of Venus.*
The 17C and 18C artists represented include Poussin (a *Nymph* and a *Satyr*), Ribera *(Woman Tearing Out her Hair)* and Murillo (*San Salvador de Horta and the Inquisitor of Aragon* – one of 11 paintings destined for the cloisters of the Monastery of Seville). From the Spanish and English schools of the late 18C and early 19C are works by Goya *(Portrait of Don Francisco de Borja),* Constable *(Hampstead Heath)* and Hoppner *(Head of a Woman).* Pre-19C French paintings include *The Oath of the Horati* (School of David) and two works by Ingres : *The Virgin and the Host* and *Portrait of Charles X.*
On the first floor hang 19C paintings by Delacroix, Géricault, Degas, Puvis de Chavannes and Bonnat – the artist who assembled this superb collection during his long lifetime (1833-1922) and left it to his native town.
The works of Léon Bonnat himself are exhibited in a gallery surrounding the ground floor terrace (late 19C-early 20C wrought-iron balconies). Among several large portraits, note that of Mme Stern, and a pathetic *Job,* in which the emaciated old man is depicted beseeching the heavens for guidance.
The museum's Drawings Department houses a selection by the Grand Masters, French and foreign, which is displayed in rotation.

Return to Pont Mayou, turn left, and follow the east bank quay to Rue Marengo.

★★ **Musée Basque** (**BZ M**[2]) ⊙ – This museum is housed in Maison Dagourette, a typical Basque building, and is one of the finest regional ethnographic museums in France. A visit is indispensable for anyone interested in the Basque country as a whole, its history, geography and traditions. Every aspect of artistic and cultural life is represented : sacred art (disk-shaped tombstones – *qv*), costumes, the traditional cane or *Makhila,* furniture (a bedroom, a kitchen with brasswork, copperware and faience), information on dances and games, and displays on different professions (innkeeper, shepherd). There is a quantity of documentation on Bayonne itself – its site, its history, its place in literature, painting and song – and on the writers who have lived in the Basque country, including Pierre Loti *(qv)* and Maurice Ravel, the composer. Even Basque shipping finds a place with a display of model boats.

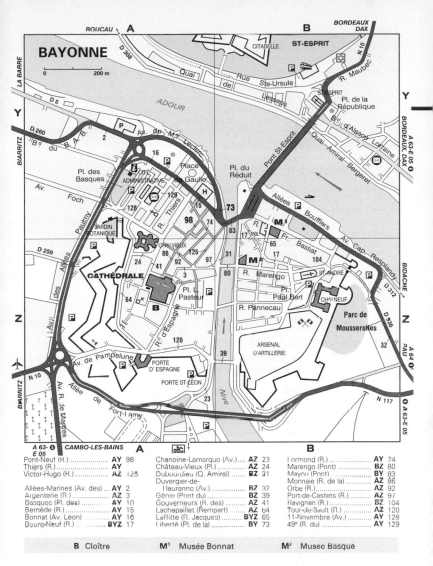

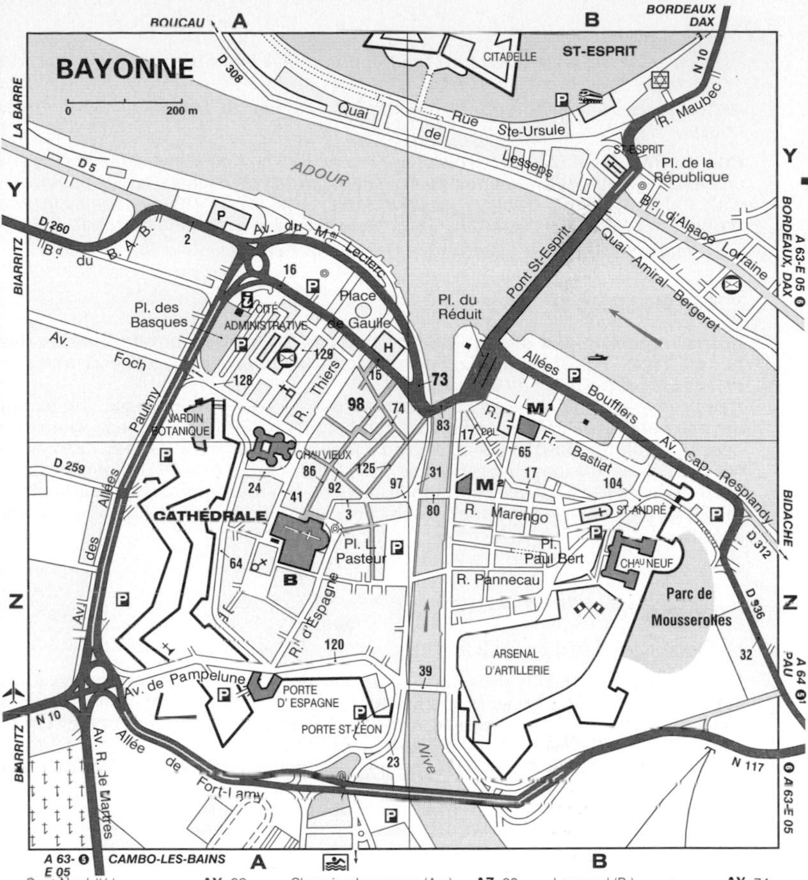

Pont-Neuf (R.)	AY	98	Chanoine-Lamarque (Av.)	AZ	23	Lormond (R.)	AY	74
Thiers (R.)	AY		Château-Vieux (Pl.)	AZ	24	Marengo (Pont)	BZ	80
Victor-Hugo (R.)	AZ	125	Dubourdieu (Q. Amiral)	BZ	31	Mayou (Pont)	BY	83
			Duvergier-de-Hauranne (Av.)	BZ	32	Monnaie (R. de la)	AZ	86
Allées-Marines (Av. des)	AY	2				Orbe (R.)	AZ	92
Argenterie (R.)	AZ	3	Génie (Pont du)	BZ	39	Port-de-Castets (R.)	AZ	97
Basques (Pl. des)	AY	10	Gouverneurs (R. des)	AZ	41	Ravignan (R.)	BZ	104
Bernède (R.)	AY	15	Lachepaillet (Rempart)	AZ	64	Tour-de-Sault (R.)	AZ	120
Bonnat (Av. Léon)	AY	16	Laffitte (R. Jacques)	BYZ	65	11-Novembre (Av.)	AY	128
Bourg-Neuf (R.)	BYZ	17	Liberté (Pl. de la)	BY	73	49e (R. du)	AY	129

B Cloître **M¹** Musée Bonnat **M²** Musee Basque

The pilgrims' routes to Santiago de Compostela are illustrated with a large wall map. One corner is reserved for witchcraft and sorcery – much of the information is based on evidence collected by Pierre de Lancre, who was ordered by Henri IV to act against suspects in the region.

A special section on **Basque Pelota** *(qv)* displays paintings, prints, models of different courts and a collection of *pelotas*, gloves, *chisteras* and rackets.

Cross Pont Marengo and continue into Rue Port-de-Castets and then Rue Argenterie, which leads to a charming square planted with magnolias.

★ **Cathédrale Ste-Marie** (**AZ**) – St Mary's Cathedral was built between the 13C and the 16C in the style of the churches in the north of France. Initially there was only one tower, to the south. The north tower and both steeples were added in the 19C.

A 13C chased knocker, known as the sanctuary ring, is fixed to the north door, which leads into the transept : any fugitive criminal who grabbed the knocker was assured of sanctuary within the church.

Inside, the windows in the nave incorporate fine examples of Renaissance stained glass. In the second chapel on the right (dedicated to St Jerome) a splendid window dating from 1531 depicts *The Canaanite's Prayer*. The two donors are shown kneeling; above is the figure of a salamander, the symbol of François I.

In the 6th chapel a commemorative plaque (1926) recalls "the Miracle of Bayonne" - a celestial apparition in 1451, when English Bayonne was under siege : according to legend, a great white cross surmounted by a crown appeared in the sky... and then the crown turned into a fleur-de-lys, the emblem of France. The townsfolk interpreted this as a sign from God that He wished them to be French, and so discarded the banners and pennants bearing the red cross of St George in favour of some bearing the white cross of France instead. The following day Bayonne surrendered.

The harmony of line and the beauty of the proportions within the cathedral can best be appreciated from the central part of the nave. The chancel and triforium are also noteworthy.

★ **Cloisters** (**AZ B**) ⊙ – *Entrance from Place Louis-Pasteur.* The three galleries which remain form a fine ensemble of 14C Gothic, with attractive twinned bays. A number of ancient funerary stones can be seen.

From the south gallery there is a fine view of the Cathedral and its windows, celebrated for their vast dimensions and unusual design.

Leave via the west door, turn right and then left into Rue de la Monnaie; continue as far as Rue du Port-Neuf.

At the junction with Rue Orbe, on the left, stands an attractive half-timbered house.

Rue du Port-Neuf (AY 98) – This charming pedestrianized street is flanked by low arcades, beneath which famous pastry-shops and confectioners tempt passers-by with mouth-watering displays of chocolates. The art of chocolate-making was brought to Bayonne in the 17C by Jews banished from Spain and Portugal.

Return to Place de la Liberté.

EXCURSION

★ **Route impériale des cimes (Napoleon I's Scenic Highway)** – *From Bayonne to Hasparren, 25km – 15½ miles. Leave Bayonne to the southeast by D 936 (BZ); at the far end of St-Pierre-d'Irube turn right into D 22.*
Napoleon I had this sinuous route carved out as part of a strategic link joining Bayonne and St-Jean-Pied-de-Port via the heights lying between them. The **view★** opens out on the Basque coastline and the summits of the Pyrenees nearest the sea : La Rhune, the jagged crest of Les Trois Couronnes, Le Jaizkibel – which at this distance looks like a steeply contoured island. As the road approaches **Hasparren** *(qv)* the Basque Pyrenees of the upper Nive basin spread out from La Rhune to L'Artzamendi.

★ BAZAS

Pop 4 379

Michelin map 79 fold 2 or 234 fold 15.

Bazas stands encircled by decaying Gothic ramparts on a narrow promontory forming a prow above the valley of the Beuve. The town is the capital of this region of fertile hills and has been the seat, since the 5C, of a bishopric (the title of which, since 1937, has belonged to the archbishop of Bordeaux).
The 4C Latin poet **Ausonius,** who was born in Burdigala (Bordeaux), stayed here several times.
Recent excavations have brought to light foundations of the old *oppidum* (settlement) which date back to the 7C BC.
Industry in the town includes confectionery, ceramics, metal and electrical installations, carpentry and joinery; it is also a regional market for beef and veal.
Throughout the year there are events in Bazas, among them the Procession of the fatted oxen in March, St John's Day fireworks in June, the historical pageant in summer (see Calendar of Events, *qv*) and the feast of St Martin in November.

★ **Cathédrale St-Jean** – The cathedral dates from the 13C-14C and was built on the model of the great Gothic sanctuaries of the North of France. The blood of John the Baptist was venerated here. Following the destructions perpetuated by the Huguenots, bishop Arnaud de Pontac and his successors had the cathedral restored between 1583 and 1636. The west front is attractive and has a unity despite the differences in style between the three levels : the first dates from the 13C, the second from the 16C and the crowning floor the 18C.

Doorways – Their tympana and coving still have fine 13C sculptures which the locals saved from religious vandalism through a payment of 10 000 *écus.* The themes and the style of the scenes portrayed were influenced by those from churches in Ile de France (the region around Paris). The central doorway shows the Last Judgement and the story of John the Baptist, those on the sides the Virgin and St Peter.

Interior – The perspective along the long, narrow nave, uninterrupted by any transept, gives a striking impression of grandeur; its vaulting is reflected in the waters of the font by the main door. The nave was entirely rebuilt after the Wars of Religion, apart from the last four bays : standing at the level of the 6th bay on the right, it is possible to see the difference between the pillar on the left which is 13C and that on the right which is late 16C. The blind triforium with a flattened arch is of a rare design, the only other example in the region being at the cathedral in Auch.
In the chancel, the Louis XV main altar in different-coloured marbles is in a slightly mannered style. In the axial chapel there is a 17C paschal chandelier, and paintings by François Lemoyne (18C) : St Gregory and St Basil *(right),* Chrysostom and Athanasius *(left).* Near the sacristy is a painted wooden figure of St Christopher (16C) and, near the font, a 16C Pietà in stone.

EXCURSIONS

★ **Collégiale d'Uzeste** – *11½km – 7 miles west by D 3 towards Villandraut.* The collegiate church in this village in some ways rivals Bazas cathedral. **Pope Clement V** played a major part in building the church – which was raised to a collegiate church by him in 1312 – and named it in his will as the site for his tomb.
Outside, note the arrangement of the east end and the belfry, the latter completed only in the 16C.
Enter the church by the south door, with its tympanum decorated with a fine Coronation of the Virgin. The interior consists of a nave and side aisles with sexpartite vaulting, and a chancel with an ambulatory and radiating chapels; there is no transept. Behind the altar, which supports a Crucifix thought to date from the 15C, lies the white marble figure of Clement V, which was damaged by the Protestants. In the axial chapel is a 13C figure of the Virgin which was venerated by Pope Clement in his youth and, in the neighbouring chapel, a funerary effigy from the 14C.

★ **Château de Villandraut** ⊙ – *$13\frac{1}{2}$ km – $8\frac{1}{2}$ miles west by D 3.* This is a striking example of castle architecture from the Gothic period. A fairly large space was allowed for residential use, following the norm in medieval castles in Italy or the Middle East. It was built for **Pope Clement V** who often stayed here and is rectangular in shape, measuring 52m by 43m – 170ft by 141ft. The curtain walls linking round towers are protected by a ditch 6m – 19ft deep; two more towers flank the entrance which faces south. The eastern face is more spectacular due to the alignment of its four large towers, the one on the right having been levelled in 1592 on the orders of the *Parlement* of Bordeaux.
A central postern, where the channels for the portcullis and the place for the bludgeons can still be seen, gives access into the interior courtyard, surrounded by a gallery with five arcades and three main sections of the building, ruined but with the pointed arches of the bays still visible : under one of them there is a huge chamber, the old workshop, with a fine broken-barrel vaulted ceiling.
The towers, once crowned by wooden platforms, were built to the same design : guardroom on the ground floor over a cellar, and vaulted living room with monumental chimney and carved keystone on the upper floor (one of the keystones, in the southwest tower, shows the bearded figure of the pope himself sitting between two angels).

★ **Château de Roquetaillade** ⊙ – *11km – 7 miles northwest by D 3 and D 223 (right).* This imposing medieval castle was built in 1306 by Cardinal Gaillard de la Mothe, a nephew of Pope Clement V, and is part of an ensemble made up of two forts from the 12C and 14C within one single set of enclosing walls. Six enormous round towers, crenellated and pierced with arrow slits, surround a rectangular main body; two of them flank the entrance. In the courtyard there stands a powerful square keep and its turret. The twinned and trefoiled bays recall other castles belonging to Pope Clement; there are also huge vaulted rooms and monumental chimneys.
The bartizans aligned along the curtain walls and, inside, the decorative paintings (among them those in the chapel) and the furniture represent an excellent example of the restoration of medieval buildings as conceived by Viollet le Duc during the Second Empire, who was assisted here at Roquetaillade by the architect E Duthoit.
The park contains hundred-year-old trees and a small **farm** ⊙ evoking 19C rural life.

Château de Cazeneuve ⊙ – *10km – 6 miles southwest by D 9.* The château rises on a rocky spur not far from Ciron Gorge. The original 11C encampment was superseded by a castle which became the stronghold of the seigneurs of **Albret** *(qv)* in the 13C. It was protected in the 14C by a polygonal enclosure and passed in 1572 to Henri III of Navarre, the future Henri IV of France; the castle was transformed into a residential château in the 17C and today still belongs to descendants of the Albrets.
The only trace of the former town of Cazeneuve is a triumphal arch; beyond this old entrance is the castle's south front, flanked by two square towers linked by a stone balustrade, and overlooking a dry moat. The gateway with a broken pediment leads through to the main courtyard, which is surrounded by two-storey medieval buildings crowned with balustrades.
Inside, the tour leads through the Consistorial Chamber and the beautifully furnished apartments of the east and south wings; the contents include a particularly striking 17C Italian statue of carved walnut portraying *Le Fou* (The Madman).
A stroll through the grounds reveals bamboo trees, oaks, sequoias and North American redwoods among the parasol pines.

★★ Le BÉARN

Michelin map 85 folds 5 to 7 and 15 to 17 or 234 folds 35, 39, 42, 43 and 47.

Béarn, the largest of the Pyrenean States, is crossed diagonally by the Pau and Oléron Torrents; meadows and ploughed fields rise in terraces on either side of these watercourses, while orchards and vines flourish on the lower slopes of the long ridges above, themselves mainly areas of *"touyas"* (moorland).
In the southern part of the region, the Pyrenees rise to the dramatic heights of Pic du Midi d'Ossau (alt 2 884m – 9 462ft) and Pic d'Anie (alt 2 504m – 8 215ft). The route to the pass, Col d'Aubisque (alt 1 709m – 5 610ft), linking Béarn to the Bigorre region through the mountains, is the most picturesque in the area.

HISTORICAL NOTES

Morlaàs Law – In the year 820 Béarn was raised to the status of a viscounty by Louis le Débonnaire. When the capital, Lescar, was sacked by the Saracens in 841, the small town of Morlaàs took its place.
The Béarnais, like most of the Pyrenean peoples, had always shown a keen taste for freedom : the overlord, whether King of England, of France or of Navarre, was obliged to ride the small state with a very loose rein. In Béarn itself the Vicomte had to give guarantees to his subjects. In the 11C Gaston IV the Crusader promulgated the **"For de Morlaàs"** (Morlaàs Law) – a political and judicial charter which limited the powers of the seigneurs but subjected every inhabitant to a local tax. All the Vicomtes of Béarn had to swear "the Oath of the For" on their accession.
In 1194 the capital changed again : Morlaàs was replaced by Orthez. In 1464 Pau was designated capital of Béarn instead of Orthez, and remained so until the Revolution.

Gaston Fébus – In 1290 the ruling house of Foix acquired the viscounty of Béarn through marriage. The most famous of the Comtes de Foix and Vicomtes de Béarn was Gaston III, known as Gaston the Hunter (1331-91). At the age of 30 Gaston adopted the surname Fébus (or Phoebus) – signifying "the brilliant", "the golden" – on account of his remarkable head of blonde hair. His motto in the Basque tongue was *Toque-y si gauses* (Touch if you dare).

Fébus was a striking character, full of contradictions. A man of letters and a poet, he liked to surround himself with writers, artists and troubadours, but he was also a cunning and ruthless politician, wielding absolute power and scorning the *Fors* he had sworn. He was responsible for the assassination of his brother and he killed his only son during a quarrel. Fébus was a keen lover of the chase and wrote a treatise on the art of venery (hunting). He kept 600 hounds and at the age of 60 could still kill a bear single-handed. It was on his way back from a hunting expedition that he was struck down by a cerebral haemorrhage and died.

Stag hunt (from the Livre de la Chasse de Gaston Fébus).

Marguerite des Marguerites – Thanks to the protection of the Kings of France, and as a result of advantageous marriages, the Albret family – minor nobles from the Landes – found themselves in the 16C in possession of the lands of Foix, Béarn and Lower Navarre. Henri d'Albret (Henri II of Navarre) married **Marguerite of Angoulême,** the sister of François I, in 1527.

Marguerite's beauty, intelligence, charm and kindness were all celebrated by contemporary poets : for them she was "the Marguerite of Marguerites", the "Fourth Grace", "The Tenth Muse". It was said of Marguerite that she had "the body of a woman, the heart of a man and the head of an angel". She used her influence over her brother to protect religious innovators and liberals who were too outspoken, among them Marot and Calvin. Her castle at Pau *(qv),* always alive with banquets and balls, was one of the most active and brilliant cultural centres in Europe. Marguerite's own intellectual achievements included corresponding with Erasmus in Hebrew, Latin and Greek; she spoke good Spanish and Italian; and, inspired by Boccaccio's *Decameron* which she greatly admired, she wrote the *Heptameron,* a collection of 72 slightly risqué love stories, though she held the strictest moral beliefs herself.

Tough Queen Jeanne – Contemporaries were less lyrical on the subject of Marguerite's daughter, **Jeanne d'Albret** *(illustration p 34)* : "The only feminine thing about her is her sex!" was one remark. Jeanne married Antoine de Bourbon, a descendant of St Louis; when the Valois branch of Louis' descendants died out with Henri III, Jeanne's son subsequently inherited the legacy and became Henri IV of France.

The young wife was made of stern stuff : despite being pregnant she accompanied her husband when he fought against Charles V in Picardy; as the pregnancy came to term, she returned to Pau (a 19-day journey over more than 800km – 500 miles of very rough roads) so that the infant might be born in the family castle.

Jeanne succeeded her father to the throne of Navarre in 1555, the Salic Law – excluding females from dynastic succession – not applying in the Pyrenean states.

Her rule was harsh : the romantic indulgences of the previous reign were at an end; there were no more brilliant fêtes, no more pageants and public dancing. In 1560 Jeanne renounced Catholicism for the Protestant faith, with the result that in Pau the churches were transformed into chapels, sculptures were smashed and carvings burned, priests imprisoned or hanged and the Catholic faithful persecuted.

When Charles IX, King of France and a staunch Catholic, sent an army to seize the town in 1569, the Calvinists suffered ruthless reprisals. Jeanne fled to La Rochelle. Five months later, her army re-took Pau and it was the turn of the "Papists" to swing from the gallows (it was not until 1620, when Louis XIII annexed Béarn to the French Crown, that stability returned to the region).

Jeanne d'Albret died in Paris in 1572, two months before the marriage of her son to Marguerite de Valois, a daughter of Catherine de' Medici and Henri II, which Jeanne had arranged to ensure the future of her line and her religion.

Henri the Béarnais – The childhood of the young prince, Jeanne's son, was spent deep in the Béarn countryside, roaming the neighbourhood bareheaded and barefoot, being fed on brown bread, eggs, cheese and garlic and speaking only Gascon. He was accepted into the Protestant Church at the age of 13. Six days after his marriage to Marguerite de Valois in 1572 (Henri had succeeded to the throne of Navarre on the death of his mother, and left his sister Catherine as Regent when he led the Huguenot forces during the wars), France was rocked by the St Bartholomew's Day Massacre : on 24 August and the days following, Protestants all over France were put to death on the orders of Charles IX. In Paris alone 3 000 were murdered on the first day. The massacre, described by Pope Gregory XIII as a "victory", fuelled the fires of hatred separating the two denominations. Henri himself only escaped death by a public recantation of his faith. Later he returned to Protestantism but was again obliged to renounce it through a "solemn abjuration" on his accession to the throne

of France as Henri IV in 1589. To humour the independent spirit of the Béarnais, he announced : "I give France to Béarn, not Béarn to France" – and to underline the distinction he proclaimed himself "King of France and Navarre".
For years prior to this *Lou Noustre Henric* – "Our Henry" as he was affectionately called in Béarn – had solaced his unhappy political marriage through an intimate friendship with Corisande, Comtesse de Guiche. It was from her, during his military campaigns, that he received not only tenderness but also unlimited support : she pawned her jewels and mortgaged her estates to help pay his troops. Friendship outlived love, and until his death at the hands of an assassin in 1610 the King kept up a faithful correspondence with his Comtesse.
(For further details see Pau, qv.)

LIFE IN BÉARN

Pastoral democracies – The mountain people of the valleys of the Aspe, Ossau and Baretous (an area between Béarn and the Basque country), enjoying a collective ownership of their upland pastures, were untouched by the feudal system. Burdens such as serfdom, the salt tax and seigneurial harassment were unknown to these communities protected by local *fors* (laws) granting them, to all intents and purposes, complete political autonomy.
From the 11C, however, troubles over land encroachment – seasonal transference of livestock to the winter quarters of the moorland north of Pau was vital to the economy of the Ossau region – led to innumerable raids, trials and legal battles. The matter was finally settled in 1829 by an act which satisfied the people of the Ossau uplands, fixing for ever the grazing rights over the moorland, sharing them equally, *commune* by *commune*.
The rules governing the use of such territory were a model of pastoral legislation : the pastureland owned collectively by each *commune* was divided into three sections, and a triennial rotation of allocations enabled each shepherd or herdsman to benefit from each of the divisions.

Vineyards of Béarn – The sunny slopes of the chalk ridges are perfectly suited to the cultivation of vines. The best-known vintage is the **Jurançon,** a heady wine with an "amber" or "maize" colour much admired by connoisseurs.
The Jurançon vineyards extend along the west bank of the Pau Torrent, downstream from the town, encompassing 25 different *communes.* The wine ages well and is not impaired by long journeys. The late-ripening grapes are frequently left unharvested until after 1 November, when the condition known as "noble rot" *(qv)* has set in. This produces a sweet wine, drunk on its own or with *pâté de foie gras.*
More recently a great deal of dry white wine has been produced, which is a perfect accompaniment to fish and shellfish.
The wines of the **Vic-Bilh** (Old Villages), which had almost disappeared from the market, are flourishing once again thanks to new plantations of the traditional Cabernet grape. The wine-growing area extends northeast as far as the borders of the Hautes-Pyrénées and the Gers *départements.* The Gers is itself known for the red wines of **Madiran.**
Béarn **Rosé** also has a long pedigree. In the 17C it was exported to Holland and sometimes even as far as Hamburg. Produced mainly near Salies and Bellocq, it is a light and fruity wine which goes very well with the regional recipes of Béarn.

Houses – In the country, permanent dwellings never encroach on arable land. The buildings are generally very large, with steeply sloping roofs. A common feature is the wide, arched coach doorway leading into the barn, which also serves as a stable and log store; from here an internal staircase rises to the living quarters. Homes sometimes contain fine old pieces of furniture with "diamond-point" decoration – the work of Béarnais craftsmen.
Stones rounded and polished by the Pau Torrent are often used for the walls of houses, as well as being basic material for enclosing paddocks and yards.

The Béarnais – The people of Béarn are used to an isolated existence; meeting a Basque, however, they may become effusive and converse in a variant of the old Gascon tongue. Despite their apparent brusqueness, the people of Béarn are both courteous and witty.
Traditional Béarn can be seen most clearly during the 15 August procession at Laruns, in the Ossau valley. The men wear red jackets, waistcoats with wide lapels, knee breeches, gaiters and berets. The women are dressed in wide, pleated skirts, black or brown in colour and partly covered by a small lace apron; they also wear an embroidered shawl and a silk-lined, scarlet hood which falls to the shoulders. A white traditional *bonnette* crowns the women's plaited hair. Only "heiresses" can wear a red skirt and they alone can wear the gold jewellery which remains always in the family.
Young men and women dance the Ossau *Branle* (swing or shake) to the music of the three-hole *fluto* (a flageolet like the Basque *tchirulä*) and tambourines – both played by the same musician.

★GAVE D'ASPE

From Oloron-Ste-Marie to Col du Somport

66km – 41 miles : allow 3 hours. Local map pp 82-83.

"The Valley of the Aspe is an important area because of the regular passage of merchants and men-at-arms between our country and Spain, a passage which has existed since the earliest times," wrote the 17C Béarn historian Pierre de Marca. "Noticeable among the Aspois [the people of the region] is that particular independence which makes hill peoples, secure in their natural fortifications, as high and mighty as the rocks of their mountains." The judgement was still true, in the 19C, of one of the most isolated pockets in the entire Pyrenees.

Today, despite improvements to the roads and the opening in 1928 of a Trans-Pyrenean railway (currently not operating south of Bedous), the glaciated valley of the Gave d'Aspe (Aspe Torrent) – narrowing into wild gorges, opening out sometimes into fertile basins – retains all the harshness of its mountain heritage. The villages here make no concession to being picturesque or charming; bears (these days protected by the National Parks authority) still roam the lonely forests. The population of the long valley now numbers less than 5 000. One of its famous emigrants was Pierre Laclède (1729-78), who was born in Bedous and later founded the city of St Louis, Missouri.

★ **Oloron-Ste-Marie** – *See Oloron-Ste-Marie.*

Leave Oloron to the southeast via Rue d'Aspe.

The road, following the east bank of the Aspe, crosses a rural valley planted with maize and wheat, divided occasionally by windbreaks of poplar trees. Ahead, Pic Mail-Arrouy (alt 1 251m – 4 100ft) appears to be blocking any passage south.

St-Christau – The air in this small spa is fresh and cool. The recently-modernized Cure Centre, where the waters are rich in iron and copper, specializes in treating troubles of the mucous membrane. The Centre stands in a 60ha – 148 acre park.

Escot – This is the first Aspois village, strikingly perched on a terrace at the mouth of the Barescou Valley. In accordance with the local *for,* the Vicomte de Béarn was obliged to exchange hostages with representatives of the valley before setting foot in Escot. Louis IX, on a pilgrimage to Notre-Dame-de-Sarrance, indicated that from here he was leaving his own kingdom by ordering his sword-bearer to lower his blade.

Continue south along N 134.

The road enters Escot Gorge, gateway to the Urgonian limestone massif.

Sarrance – This is a local pilgrimage destination. It is here that Marguerite des Marguerites wrote her *Heptameron.* The church was rebuilt in 1609; it has an octagonal belfry-porch of Baroque inspiration topped by a lantern. The attractive 17C cloisters of the old monastery have side gables with tiled roofs.
At Bedous, a pronounced hogsback rise allows a sudden view of the valley's central basin and its seven villages. Bedous and Accous, historically the county-town, each claim to be the most important. Four volcanic extrusions rise from the floor of the basin. In the background the crests of Arapoup are visible and, to the right in the distance, the first summits of the Lescun amphitheatre (Pic de Burcq).

Turn left to Aydius.

Aydius – This small mountain village has houses attractively staggered across the steep slope.
Across the torrent there is a "weeping rock" – a phenomenon caused by the formation of spongy accretions in a tributary stream.

Return to N 134 and continue south.

The road again enters a narrow gorge.

Turn right to Lescun.

★ **Lescun** – Lescun is a favourite village with mountain lovers owing to the surrounding amphitheatre with its needle-sharp limestone peaks. To admire the full **panorama★★**, park in the car park behind Hôtel du Pic d'Anie and walk to the viewpoint *($\frac{1}{2}$ hour on foot Rtn) :* follow the GR10 footpath as far as the church then take another path, heading east.
Beyond a public wash-house flanked by a cross, the footpath winds around a hillock. From here, turning around, there is a fine view of Pic d'Anie (ahead, in the middle distance) and, to the left, of Le Billare and Dec de Lhurs, which rise in front of the sharp peaks of the Table des Trois Rois *(right)* and Pic d'Ansabère *(left).*

Lescun.

The **Route du Somport★** (N 134) continues to climb the valley, which is now an almost continuous succession of gorges and narrows. The villages, built in pairs on opposite sides of the valley, seem designed to watch over one another (Eygun and Cette, Etsaut and Borce).

Chemin de la Mâture – *From Pont de Sebers (see map overleaf) : 3 hours Rtn on foot along GR10 footpath. This route is not for those who suffer from vertigo. The path, completely exposed to sun and wind, twists above sheer drops with no railings or other protection.* Naval engineers carved out this passage, often blasted from the solid rock, to give access to the trees of Le Pacq Woods. The timber was then transported along this route down to the Apse Valley. When the Apse Torrent was in flood, the wood was assembled into timber rafts and floated down to the naval shipyards in Bayonne.
From the pathway there are views of the upper part of Portalet fort.

Turn back once the meadows of the upper basin are reached.

Fort du Portalet – The strongpoint is perched on a sheer cliff above the river in one of the narrowest, most steep-sided sectors of the valley. It was built in the early 19C and later used for the internment of prominent anti-Nazis during the Occupation (1941-45). From the road, the walled ramps leading to the casemates commanding the access to Urdos can be seen.
At the exit from the gorge, the peaks marking the Spanish frontier appear : a jagged crest notched by the Aspe pass and overlooked by Pico de la Garganta (alt 2 636m – 8 660ft), which is usually flecked with snow.
Beyond Urdos, on the left, the Arnousse viaduct underlines the altitude to which the railway, thanks to a spiral tunnel, has climbed. On the far side of the Forges d'Abel basin the line plunges once more into a tunnel – the Trans-Pyrenean – which is almost 8km – 5 miles long. The road continues to climb through beechwoods before levelling out in the pastureland of the Peyrenère Cirque.

★★ **Col du Somport** – Alt 1 632m – 5 351ft. This pass, the only one in the Central Pyrenees accessible the whole year round, has been famous since the passage of the Roman legions. Until the 12C it was used by pilgrims on the way to Santiago de Compostela. The important staging post at that time was the Hospice de Ste-Christine (now vanished) which was on the southern slopes of the range.
From the high ground behind the restaurant there is an impressive view of the Aragon Pyrenees on the far side of the frontier, heavily indented in the Sierra de Aspe, on the right, more massively stacked along Rio Aragón.
The blues of this distant panorama contrast pleasantly with the green of the forests and the reddish tones of the rocks in the foreground.

★★ GAVE D'OSSAU

From Oloron-Ste-Marie to Gabas

52km – 32 miles : allow 2 hours

This mountain trip can be extended by a visit to the Upper Ossau (qv).

Oloron-Ste-Marie – *See Oloron Ste-Marie.*

Leave Oloron via N 134 east towards Pau then turn right into D 920.

The road follows the former valley of the Lower Ossau, which runs parallel to the present one. The Torrent was long ago diverted by the frontal moraine of the Ossau Glacier, downstream from Arudy, and obliged to carve out an alternative route. Beyond Buzy the road crosses this old moraine barrier (the huge boulders on either side are vestiges of that ancient geological obstruction). Ahead now, covering the lower slopes of the Pyrenean foothills, is Bois du Bager (Bager Wood). The road reaches the entrance to the main Ossau Valley.

Arudy – Industrially, this is the most developed town in the Lower Ossau, thanks to the surrounding marble quarries and the various factories (components for aircraft landing gear, cold lamination) on the outskirts.
The **Maison d'Ossau** ⏲, a 17C house near the east end of the church, contains in its basement displays on the pre-history of the Pyrenees (diagrams, charts and exhibits from excavations illustrate the evolution of tools and implements). The former living-rooms on the ground floor include an exhibition on the flora, fauna and geology of the Ossau Valley.
Displays on the attic floor are devoted to the history of the valley and the life of the local shepherds.

Continue south.

In the distance, once beyond the bridge to Louvie-Juzon, the great mass of Pic du Midi d'Ossau comes into view.

Bielle – This former local capital, split in two by a tributary of the Ossau Torrent, retains a certain sleepy dignity. Several 16C town houses can be seen in the south bank district, between the main road and the church; on the north bank stands a castle built by the Marquis de Laborde (1724-94), a banker accredited to Louis XV and the Duc de Choiseul.

Bilhères – *Drive right through the village.* This is a scattered village containing some houses with 16C and 17C decorative elements – embellished keystones, for example, in the arched doorways.

★ **Plateau de Bénou** – Above Bilhères the view opens out southwards as far as Pic de Ger. The Chapel of Notre-Dame-de-Houndaas, shaded by two lime trees, appears in a **site★** which is kept fresh by running water from several important springs. The road then runs into the pastoral Bénou basin where, in summer, large numbers of sheep graze.

Return to D 934 and continue south.

Beyond Laruns is the wooded Gorge du Hourat, followed by the small spa village of Les Eaux-Chaudes.

Gorges du Bitet – *1 hour on foot Rtn, via a wide forest track : after Miégebat power station, just beyond the bridge over the Bitet, turn right.* A climb through this shady gorge passes a succession of fascinating cascades, rapids and pools. A hydro-electric pressure pipeline marks the end of the walk.

Continue along D 934.

2km – 1 mile before Gabas, at the "Chêne de l'Ours", there is a fine view of Pic du Midi.

Gabas – *See Gabas.*

★★LE HAUT OSSAU

(UPPER OSSAU) – *See Le Haut Ossau.*

★LA FRANGE DES PYRÉNÉES (THE THRESHOLD OF THE PYRENEES)

From Pau to Bielle, via Asson

49km – 30 miles : about 2½ hours – local map opposite.

★★★ **Pau** – *1 day. See Pau.*

Leave Pau to the southwest via the Jurançon district, ④ on the map. The road, N 134, follows the valley of the River Nez. At Gan turn left into D 24.

Notre-Dame de Piétat – Opposite the 17C pilgrims' chapel, at the end of the esplanade, is a roadside cross. Behind this is a viewing table from which a **panorama★** of the valley of the Pau Torrent and its many villages opens out : Pic du Midi de Bigorre is visible in the distance *(southeast),* beyond the line of wooded foothills, along with the Vignemale, Grand Gabizos and Caperan de Sesques *(south).* The local **zoological park** ⓥ contains many exotic species of birds and animals.

Continue to D 37 and turn right along the valley.

Between Pardies-Piétat and Nay the road passes through several pretty Béarn villages of splendid houses with gateways decorated with piers surmounted by stone urns. The church in Nay, which dates from the 16C, has projecting buttresses and star vaults roofing the apse.

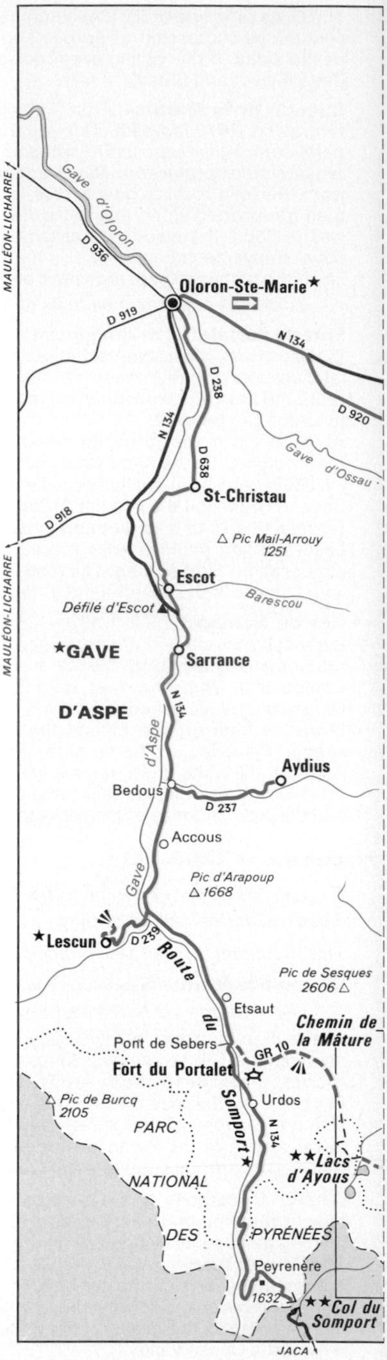

Asson – *3km – 2 miles west of the village (towards Bruges) a road branches off to the Jardin Exotique.* This one-time agricultural show-place, now converted into a **zoological park**ⓥ , is home to a raucous and colourful collection of parrots, parakeets, pink Cuban flamingoes, emus, slender loris, chimpanzees and gibbons, as well as a colony of lemurs from Madagascar.

The glasshouse, which was originally an exhibit at the Paris Exposition Universelle (World's Fair) in 1889, houses 3 500 species of cacti and succulents.

Bruges – A large central square, out of proportion with the size of the village surrounding it, and its link – by name – with a more prestigious town, attest to Bruges' past as one of the southwestern *bastides (qv).*

The road continues through a series of villages with flower-filled gardens. Fields of maize make way for orchards, and these in turn are succeeded by trellised vines. As the road drops down finally to the depression of Lower Ossau, the stone belfry of **Louvie-Juzon church,** with its distinctive outline of an inverted chalice, comes slowly into view. Soon after that the outskirts of Bielle appear.

D 934 (south) leads to Bielle.

Bielle – *Description above.*

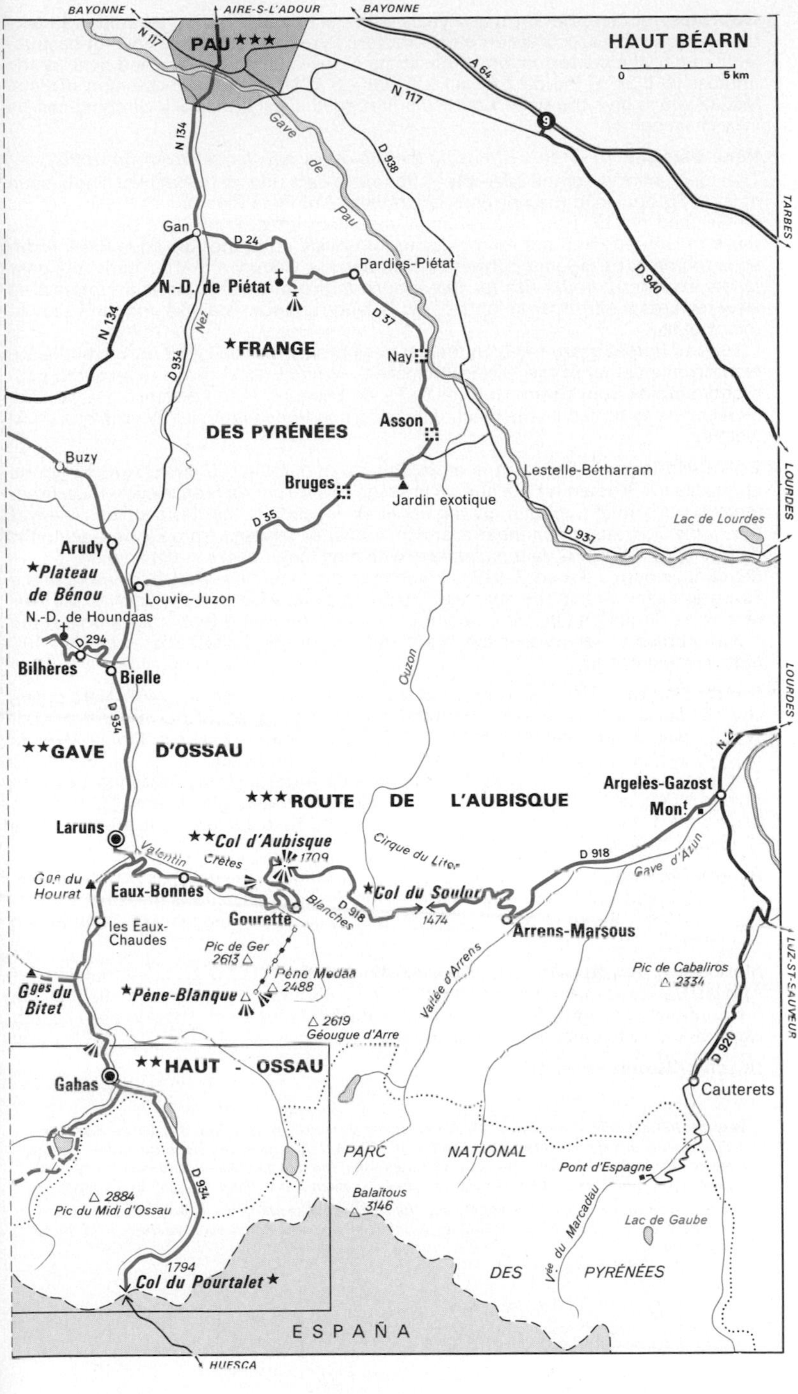

★★★ ROUTE DE L'AUBISQUE

From Laruns to Argelès-Gazost via Col d'Aubisque

48km – 30 miles : allow $2\frac{1}{2}$ hours. Local map above.

As a rule Col d'Aubisque (Aubisque Pass) is blocked by snow from November to June. Between Col d'Aubisque and Col du Soulor there is one-way traffic which changes direction every two hours.

The road, D 918, climbs rapidly above the Laruns basin and continues along one of the most beautiful and spectacular routes in the Pyrenees.

Eaux-Bonnes – This spa, the waters of which are used to treat respiratory problems, sits at the bottom of a wooded valley. The hub of the small town, with its elegant 19C promenades – vestiges of a bygone age – is the esplanade of the Darralde gardens, bordered by mansions in typically Empire style.

The road crosses the River Valentin (note the cascade) and starts the long haul up the flank of the mountain, offering splendid views of the Pic de Ger massif, especially in the early morning and at dusk when the play of colours can be superb.

Gourette – A favourite for many years with the skiers of Béarn, Gourette remains the classic winter sports resort of the western Pyrenees. It lies in a bowl of pastureland among the contorted limestone strata of the mountains, watched over by the impressive bulk of Pic de Ger (alt 2 613m – 8 573ft) and the rocky fang of Pène Médaa which give the **site★** a particularly rugged aspect (the rock climbing can be very challenging).

★ **Pène Blanque** – *1½ hours Rtn using the cable-way which rises from Gourette.*
The upper platform of the **cable-way** ⊙ (the cable-cars ride up the longest single-span hoist in Europe) is in the northern amphitheatre of Pène Blanque, at the foot of Pic de Ger and not far from several small mountain lakes. From here there is a fine **view★** of Gourette and the road twisting tortuously up to the Aubisque Pass. A difficult footpath, zigzagging between Pic de Ger and Géougue d'Arre, leads to a pass *(allow an extra 2 hours Rtn for this excursion)* from which there is an interesting view towards the frontier heights of the Balaïtous. Below is a lake and the valley of the Artouste.
Cows and horses graze freely in the pastures beside the road. Not far beyond Gourette, from a corner of the "Crêtes Blanches" (White Crests) bends, a splendid panorama unfolds from Grand Gabizos to Pic de Sesques. In the distance, Pic du Midi de Bigorre can be seen – the mast of its television transmitter clearly visible in good weather.

★★ **Col d'Aubisque** – The pass is at an altitude of 1 709m – 5 608ft. Among sports enthusiasts it is noted for the annual passage of the Tour de France cycle race. From the mound behind the hotel, by the upper ski-lift station, there is a striking view of the whole Gourette amphitheatre, and an immense **panorama** from Pic de Gers to Pic de Montaigu *(due east, in the distance)* with nine major peaks in between.
Beyond the pass the road (D 918), carved from the mountainside, offers views of the Ferrières valley and, in the distance, the Béarn plain. After that the **Corniche des Pyrénées** skirts Cirque du Litor at a height of almost a thousand feet : this is one of the most impressive sections of the run – and one of the boldest road-works of 19C highway engineers.

★ **Col du Soulor** – The pass is reached at an altitude of 1 474m – 4 740ft. Here grass-covered peaks with spiky tips form the foreground to an enormous mountain landscape. Once more, beyond the Azun Valley, the summits between Pic du Midi de Bigorre and, further to the left, Pic de Montaigu rise into view.
The road then begins its long descent towards Argelès-Gazost, twisting down to Arrens-Marsous. The Balaïtous (3 146m – 10 322ft) and its glacier are visible at the beginning of the descent, on the right. Later the road sweeps into green valleys shaded by oak, ash, beech, birch, chestnut...

Arrens-Marsous – This peaceful small town nestling in the valley is both a holiday destination and a centre for high-altitude rambles to the Balaïtous massif.
Beyond Arrens the road passes through a succession of villages with picturesque churches.

Monument des Géodésiens (Surveyors' Monument) – This tower on the outskirts of Argelès-Gazost is in the form of a geodetic instrument; it was built in 1925 on the hundredth anniversary of the first ascent of the Balaïtous crest. The successful climb was made by a team of military surveyors.

Argelès-Gazost – *See Argelès-Gazost.*

Despite the fact that the species is protected, the European Brown Bear (Ursus Arctos) exists in France only in very small numbers, here in the Western Pyrenees. His favourite haunts – more precisely his places of refuge – are the rocky slopes and the forests of beech and pine, which overlook the Aspe and Ossau valleys at heights between 1 500m and 1 700m – 5 000ft and 6 000ft.

Once a carnivore, subsequently a vegetarian, the bear is now an omnivore, eating, according to season, tubers, berries, insects, acorns and small animals – and sometimes even, to the rage of the hill farmers, sheep.

★★ Grottes de BÉTHARRAM

Michelin map 85 north of fold 17 or 234 fold 39 – Local map p 90.

The Bétharram Grottoes constitute one of the most famous natural phenomena of the Pyrenees, and have been carefully adapted to deal with large numbers of visitors.
They were discovered in 1819 by local shepherds and explored the same year by interested naturalists from Pau. A more systematic examination, begun in 1888 by three speleologists from the same town, eventually lasted ten years and revealed 5 200m – over 3 miles of underground galleries cut through the limestone mountain by the river. In 1898 the caves came to the attention of Léon Ross, a painter from Britanny who had settled in Bigorre *(qv)*. For four years this fascinated enthusiast worked tirelessly to provide access for tourists coming on a regular basis. In 1919 he completed the boring of an exit tunnel.
Today, as well as being of speleological interest, the grottoes offer the opportunity to take a fascinating subterranean trip and to ride in a miniature train.

TOUR ⊙

The underground tour covers 2.8km – a little over $1\frac{1}{2}$ miles leading through five separate galleries, one above the other. The topmost level, comprising huge interconnected chambers hollowed from the rock, is the largest. The most interesting feature of these caves is their porous roofs, which have led to the formation of beautiful stalactites in the *Salle des Lustres,* and a characteristic stalagmite column. The collapsed pot-hole into which the subterranean stream finally plunges is 80m – 262ft deep. It is marked by scattered boulders and a curious "Romanesque cloister" gouged from the limestone. At one point the tour follows the old river bed, a deep and narrow fissure in which different examples of erosion can be seen. The lowest galleries are on the same level as the river is now, and this section is visited by boat. The underground river, once it has emerged from the mountain, hurls itself into the Pau Torrent.
A miniature train takes visitors back to the open air through Léon Ross' tunnel.

★★★ BIARRITZ

Pop 28 742

Michelin map 78 fold 18 or 234 fold 29 – Facilities.

Biarritz, which stands on the borders of the Basque country, is the most fashionable and the most frequented seaside resort in southwest France. The setting is magnificent – Atlantic rollers dashing themselves against rocks and reefs, impressive cliffs, a small port, and superb bathing beaches.
The town's International status is underlined by the fact that there are six golf courses within a short distance, plus two casinos and numerous sporting facilities in the town itself.

Empress Eugénie's town – At the beginning of the 19C Biarritz was a small, poor coastal town without pretensions; the people of Bayonne, when they started to come here to bathe, made the three-mile journey on donkeys or mules. Then Spanish nobility from the far side of the border discovered its charms, and from 1838 onwards the Comtesse de Montijo and her daughter Eugénie made a habit of coming each year. When Eugénie became Empress of France she persuaded her husband, Napoleon III, to accompany her on her annual visit to the Basque coast : the Emperor in his turn was seduced by the place. Their first trip together was in 1854; the following year he had a house built here and named it Villa Eugénie (today it is the Hôtel du Palais). Suddenly Biarritz was famous.
The charm of the town, its reputation for discreet luxury, its celebrity, drew the rich, the famous and the noble from all over Europe : few seaside resorts can boast such an illustrious list of past visitors.

Herque/IMAGE PHOTOTHÈQUE

Grande Plage.

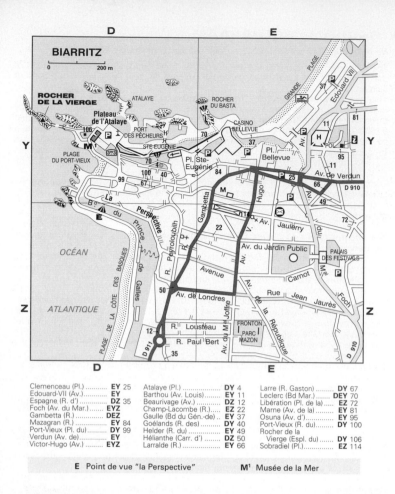

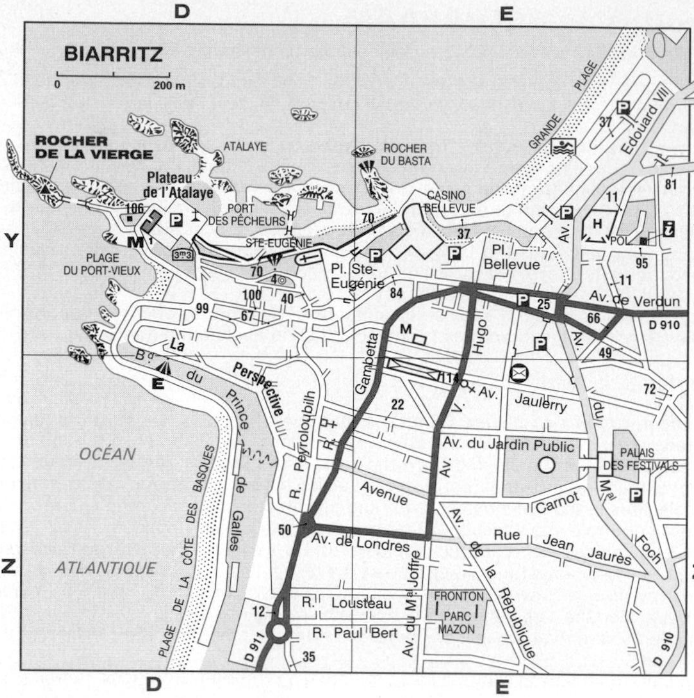

Clemenceau (Pl.) EY 25	Atalaye (Pl.) DY 4	Larre (R. Gaston) DY 67
Edouard-VII (Av.) EY	Barthou (Av. Louis) EY 11	Leclerc (Bd Mar.) DEY 70
Espagne (R. d') DZ 35	Beaurivage (Av.) DZ 12	Libération (Pl. de la) EZ 72
Foch (Av. du Mar.) EYZ	Champ-Lacombe (R.) EZ 22	Marne (Av. de la) EY 81
Gambetta (R.) DEZ	Gaulle (Bd du Gén.-de) EY 37	Osuna (Av. d') EY 95
Mazagran (R.) EY 84	Goélands (R. des) DY 40	Port-Vieux (R. du) DY 100
Port-Vieux (Pl. du) DY 99	Helder (R. du) EY 49	Rocher de la Vierge (Espl. du) DY 106
Verdun (Av. de) EY	Hélianthe (Carr. d') DZ 50	Sobradiel (Pl.) EZ 114
Victor-Hugo (Av.) EYZ	Larralde (R.) EY 66	

E Point de vue "la Perspective" M[1] Musée de la Mer

Resort – The town, colourfully planted with hydrangeas, owes much of its charm to the garden-promenades laid out alongside the cliffs, on the rocks and above the three superb beaches of fine sand which have become one of the most important rendezvous for the international surfing fraternity.

Beaches – The largest and the most fashionable strand is **Grande Plage** (**EY**), overlooked by two casinos (the old casino and the Bellevue); it is extended to the north by Miramar Beach. One hundred years ago, only the most daring of bathers would swim here, which led to its now-forgotten nickname of *Plage des Fous* (Madman's Beach). Most bathers in the resort's "heroic" era at the turn of the century headed for the calmer waters off the small **Plage du Port Vieux** (Old Port Beach) (**DY**); today it remains a family beach and a favourite with local people. The **Plage de la Côte des Basques** (Basque Coast Beach) (**DZ**), the most exposed and consequently the most "sporting", owes its name to an old "ocean pilgrimage" which brought together Basques from the interior each 15 August for a collective bathe. It lies at the foot of a cliff which periodically has to be shored up against landslides. South of the town two more beaches, Plage de Marbella and Plage de Milady, have been opened more recently.

Promenades – The promenades offer a leisurely stroll along gentle slopes shaded by tamarisks, with views of the ocean breaking on the reefs; they can lead to Rocher du Basta (**EY**), with its view over thundering breakers, or to the famous **Rocher de la Vierge★** (Virgin's Rock) (**DY**), crowned by a statue of the Madonna. This is the most famous of the Biarritz rocks, surrounded by shelving reefs and joined to the shore by a wooden footbridge which cannot be used in rough weather because the sea breaks over it. From the rocky projection, lashed by foaming waves, there is a view of the coast all the way from the estuary of the River Adour *(north)* to the Spanish frontier. The bridge to the rock was Napoleon III's idea, and indeed a romantic *Belle Époque* atmosphere characteristic of his period still lingers over much of Biarritz today.

SIGHTS

★ **Musée de la Mer** (**DY M[1]**) ⏲ – This marine museum and scientific research centre stands opposite the Virgin's Rock, adjoining the Plateau de l'Atalaye.
In the basement an impressive aquarium reveals the remarkable richness and variety of the ocean fauna in the Bay of Biscay.
The natural science exhibitions *(ground and first floors)* include sections on marine ethnography, terrestrial phenomena and seafaring life around Biarritz throughout the centuries. From the second floor, visitors can look up into two pools on the terrace above, one stocked with seals, the other with selachians (sharks, rays etc). The terrace itself offers views of the wave-battered Virgin's Rock, the Landes coast and the Basque coast as far as Cap Machichaco in Spain.

The ornithological department includes an aviary with different birds native to the region, and audio-visual displays familiarizing visitors with birdsong and the birds of prey of the Pyrenees.

Plateau de l'Atalaye (**DY**) – This open stretch of ground lies between Basta Rock and a promontory on which the town's remaining *atalaye* stands. This is a watch-tower with a chimney, one of a number used in the past to send smoke signals to fishermen when whales were sighted out at sea (the last Biarritz whale was caught in 1686).
From the plateau there is a view down over the tiny fishing port.

"La Perspective" (**DYZ**) – This fine promenade overlooking the long Basque Coast Beach offers a splendid **view**★★ (**E**) looking south towards the summits of La Rhune, Les Trois Couronnes and the Jaizkibel massif.

Pointe St-Martin ⏲ – There are pleasant gardens laid out on this headland at the far end of Miramar beach (north of Grande Plage, **EY**), but the visit is worthwhile above all for the **panorama**★ visible from the top of the **lighthouse.** The tower is 44m - 144ft high and overlooks the sea from a height of 73m – 240ft. The view (248 steps up) extends all the way from the Spanish coast to the Silver Coast *(qv)* and includes an interesting perspective of Biarritz itself.

★ ANGLET

Pop 33 041 – Facilities.

Anglet forms a link between Biarritz and Bayonne and is, effectively, a vast suburb of each. Its success as a resort and tourist centre followed that of Biarritz during the Second Empire. The site nevertheless belongs geographically more to the Silver Coast north of the Adour estuary – long straight strands bordered by dunes, a flat hinterland planted with pines.
The Olympic skating rink at La Barre, the pool and tennis courts at "El Hogar", the marina and the Atlanthal Complex (a cure centre specializing in sea-water therapy) are lively centres of activity, but Anglet is also known for its excellent facilities for such "open-space" sports as surfing, horse-riding and golf.
Just off Plage de la Chambre d'Amour, the main beach, steps lead to the Chambre d'Amour itself : a cave where two lovers, caught unawares by the rising tide, were trapped and died.
Each summer an International Festival of Humorous Drawings is held in Anglet. The festival was founded in 1979 and features amateur as well as professional artists *(see Calendar of Events, qv).*

★ BIDART

Pop 4 123

Michelin map 78 fold 18 or 234 fold 19 – Facilities.

The small resort of Bidart, halfway between Biarritz and St-Jean-de-Luz, is built on the highest site of the Basque coastline, on the edge of a cliff. Rue de la Grande-Plage and Promenade de la Mer lead steeply down to its beach.

★ **Panorama** – From Chapelle Ste-Madeleine (accessible from Rue de la Madeleine) the clifftop view embraces the Jaizkibel (a promontory closing off the Fontarabia roadstead), the Trois Couronnes and La Rhune *(qv).*

Place Centrale – The charming main square is framed by the church, the *pelota* court *(qv)* and the town hall. Local *pelota* matches and competitions are always watched by enthusiastic crowds.
The church is typically Basque in style with its belfry-porch, its fine wooden ceiling, its superimposed galleries for the men attending services, and its enormous, brightly-coloured 17C altarpiece.

★★★ La BIGORRE

Michelin map 85 folds 8, 9 and 17 to 19 or 234 folds 39, 40, 43, 44, 47, 48.

Bigorre is a former regional and historical unit which, together with the neighbouring Pays des Quatre Vallées (Four Valleys Region – *see below*) forms part of the Central Pyrenees – the most attractive sector of the range with the remnants of ancient glaciers and with the tallest summits : Vignemale (3 289m – 10 817ft), Pic Long (3 192m – 10 469ft) and the **Balaïtous** (3 146m – 10 322ft).
This is a region of wild and craggy landscapes, of enormous natural amphitheatres among the peaks, of foaming, fast-running torrents. All of it lies within the boundaries of the Parc National des Pyrénées *(qv)*.
The few frontier "*ports*" (small passes) which allow communication with Spain are scarcely less high than the summits; some can only be used by local mountain people and their mules. Since 1976 the Bielsa tunnel, at the head of the Aure Valley, has given access in summer to traffic between Gascony and Aragon in Spain.
The busiest parts of the Bigorre region are centred on the area between the mountain zone and the flat-lands – in the basins of Lourdes and Bagnères and on the Tarbes plain. The prosperity here contrasts with the poverty on the Lannemezan and Ger plateaux, immense areas of debris piled up over the millennia by the Pyrenean torrents, which are extended to the north by the fan-like formation of the hills of Gascony.

HISTORICAL NOTES

Comté of Bigorre – In 1097 Comte Bernard II promulgated the *Fors de Bigorre* - local laws confirming the two-way relationship between the people and their seigneur. The *fors* contained the proclamation : "We, who are each worth as much as you, and who together can do more than you, make you our overlord on condition that you respect our rights and privileges; if not, not."
The Salic Law – which in the north prevented women succeeding to the French Crown – did not apply in the Pyrenean states; there were therefore comtesses who ruled the region in their own right, many of them formidable women. One of them, Constance, fought hard against Philippe le Bel who claimed Bigorre in 1292; another, Comtesse Petronilla, married five husbands within 13 years – and had daughters by each one of them; the problems of succession must have been extremely complicated.
In 1292 Philippe le Bel sequestered the comté but the Treaty of Brétigny in 1360 confirmed it as an English possession. In 1406, however, the "intruders" were put to flight after a war of attrition waged by the people of Bigorre (Bigourdans). The region then passed to the House of Foix, and through them eventually to Henri of Navarre *(qv)*. Bigorre was definitively united with the French Crown in 1607.

Lavedan – The mountainous part of the Bigorre region, from south of Lourdes to the Spanish border, was known as "the Seven Valleys of the Lavedan". In the 10C this was administered by Vicomtes, who were direct vassals of the Comtes of Bigorre; in practice, however, the valleys were autonomous. The largest of these, known then as the Barèges Valley, lies in the middle (Luz). Four others – Azun, Estrem de Salles, Bats-Surguère and **St-Savin** (Cauterets) – were on the western flank of the Pau Torrent. The remaining two, less important, were on the east : Davant-Aygue and **Castelloubon** (the Néez Valley). On his accession, the Comte de Bigorre would visit each valley to swear an oath to the Lavedan people, undertaking to respect their customs; in return they would swear loyalty to him. As a precaution, hostages, taken from the most prosperous families in the community, were detained in the château at Lourdes until the safe return of the Comte.

Fighting spirit – The mountain dwellers of Bigorre, who are characteristically small, dark and wiry, are a robust people, and used to boast of being "always kings in our own country".
Men from the Barèges Valley helped to storm the castle in Lourdes and drive the English out of Castelnau-d'Azun in 1407, and the Bigourdan warriors were as difficult with their own countrymen : later in the 15C a King's officer whose zeal had exasperated the inhabitants was thrown over a cliff.
Colbert provoked several revolts by trying to apply the salt tax in the region – where the population in any case obtained their salt from Béarn or in Spain. A local gentleman, Audijos, enrolled 7 000 Bigourdans under his banner and defied the King's commissioners for 12 years. Eventually the application of the tax had to be modified.

Religious Bigorre – When Bernard I placed his Comté under the protection of Notre-Dame du Puy-en-Velay (southeast of Clermont-Ferrand) in 1062 he could not have foreseen that, eight centuries later, the fame of a sanctuary in Bigorre would far outshine that of his patroness : since the time that the Virgin appeared to Bernadette Soubirous, however, Lourdes has drawn literally millions of the faithful from all over the world. In this Bigorre "blessed by God" the important part played by the abbeys of St-Pé-de-Bigorre *(qv)*, St-Savin *(see below)* and St-Orens (south-east of Condom) should not be forgotten either.

Pastoral life – The sheep in the region are mainly nomadic, the Campan breed crossed with Merinos. The finest wool is sent to Tourcoing, the weaving centre in the north of France, and the rest kept for Pyrenean use. All of the sheep yield good meat.
Bigorre is a cattle-raising area too. Two breeds are found in the mountains : the Lourdaise, with a pale, whitish hide, and the Central Pyrenean in the Aure Valley – small beasts of a fine greyish-chestnut colour. The Gascony breed, with a marked, grey hide, is raised in other parts both for traction and for the whiteness of its veal. In the valley of the Adour, the cattle are mainly black and white Friesians bred for their milk.
Pigs, large and of fine quality, are the mainstay of mountain grassland farms.

★★★ LOURDES and Excursions – *See Lourdes.*

GORGE DE LUZ

From Argelès-Gazost to Luz-St-Sauveur

18km – 11 miles : allow 1 hour – Local map overleaf.

This itinerary can be extended, at Pierrefitte-Nestalas, into the Vallées de Cauterets excursions (Pont d'Espagne, Lac de Gaube, Marcadau) – the great "classics" of the Pyrenean tourist routes.

Argelès-Gazost – *See Argelès-Gazost.*

Leaving the lower part of the Argèles basin, D 101 climbs through a chestnut forest.

St-Savin – This village was at one time one of the biggest religious centres in Bigorre. The **terrace** alongside the main square offers good views over the Argelès basin.

The **church** here was once part of a Benedictine Abbey, the abbots of which were seigneurs of "St-Savin Valley". The 11C and 12C building, fortified in the 14C, still has its internal watchpath; a lantern-belfry crowns the 14C tower. The west front has a fine Romanesque doorway with a tympanum carved with a rare representation of Christ, surrounded by Evangelists, in priestly garments. Inside, the small 12C Romanesque font with caryatids was possibly reserved for the untouchables, the *cagots (qv)*. The organ loft (16C) is decorated with masks that have eyes and mouths which used to move when the organ was played, and next to it is a fine Spanish carved wooden figure of Christ (13C and 14C). The **treasury** contains capitals from the old cloisters, Romanesque representations of the Virgin and a 14C silver-plated copper shrine of particular note.

Beyond the village the Piétat Chapel, perched on its rock, comes into view.

Chapelle de Piétat – *Cars can be parked only before the curve in the road skirting the spur.* This sanctuary sits in an extremely poetic **site★**. From a small terrace shaded by lime trees, on the edge of a short but steep escarpment plunging towards the green Argelès basin, there is a fine view of St-Savin church emerging from a thicket of chestnut trees. Among the orchards on the far bank of the torrent are the reddish ruins of Beaucens Castle, once the favourite residence of the Vicomtes of Lavedan. In the distance Pic de Viscos (alt 2 141m – 7 024ft) dominates the junction, at Pierrefitte-Nestalas, of the Cauterets and Barèges valleys.

Pierrefitte-Nestalas – At the northern end of this small town stands the **Musée Marinarium du Haut-Lavedan** ⏲. Here, unexpectedly, is a collection of tropical marine fauna from all over the world, including, in an aquarium, the teeming life of a coral reef.

The road, which has been narrow and winding, now runs out into a fine amphitheatre into which the Pau and Cauterets torrents flow through steep-sided gorges. After Pierrefitte there is the Gorge de Luz, sombre and superb, with dark walls of vertical shale to which a few thickets cling. Cascades tumble here and there.

Before this route was marked out, in the middle of the 18C, the only way to reach Luz was via an extremely precarious mule track known as **Les Échelles de Barèges** (The Barèges Stepladder) – which explains why well-heeled visitors customarily preferred, to the dismay of their toiling porters, a longer detour via Le Tourmalet.

Pont de la Reine – a bridge named in honour of Queen Hortense (1783-1837), the wife of Louis Bonaparte – marks the end of the enclosed sector, and the first Napoleonic milestone in the Barèges Valley. Beyond the bridge is the "Pays Toys" (Luz basin) with its villages nestling amongst the trees. Soon the foothills of the Néouvielle massif appear, left of Pic de Bergons. Then, shaded by ash trees, the route finally reaches Luz – or, remaining on the west bank of the torrent, St-Sauveur.

★ **Luz-St-Sauveur** – *See Luz-St-Sauveur.*

★★ VALLÉES DE CAUTERETS – *See Vallées de Cauterets.*

★★ VALLÉE DE GAVARNIE – *See Vallée de Gavarnie.*

GÈDRE – *See Gèdre.*

★★ ROUTE DU TOURMALET

From Luz-St-Sauveur to Bagnères-de-Bigorre

48km – 30 miles : about 3 hours – Local map overleaf.

This route follows a mountain road which can seem forbidding, on the slopes near Barèges. Col du Tourmalet (Tourmalet Pass) is usually blocked by snow from November to June.

The road follows Bastan Valley, passing the ruins of Château Ste-Marie on the left. The landscape soon becomes bleaker and the hills steeper before Barèges.

Barèges – *See Barèges.*

The road crosses the desolate Escoubous Valley, where the stream winds between stony pastures. After Pont de la Gaubie, a view behind, through the opening of a small valley, takes in Pic de Néouvielle, its craggy pyramid flanked by a glacier. Before long, a line of bold rocky crests appears to the south. To the north, left of the road, Pic du Midi de Bigorre is visible, crowned by its television transmitter and observatory.

★★ **Col du Tourmalet** – Alt 2 115m – 6 937ft. The name Tourmalet in the local dialect means "bad detour". Until the 17C Tourmalet Pass could be crossed only on foot or by sedan chairs with porters; the first vehicles to get through made the journey in 1788 when the road through the Luz Gorge was cut as a result of the Pau Torrent flooding.

From the pass, the mountain **panorama** is remarkable for the ruggedness of the summits it reveals, especially towards Barèges. In the distance, beyond the minor Ardiden range, rises the great mass of the Balaïtous and its glacier.

★★★ **Pic du Midi de Bigorre** – *See Pic du Midi de Bigorre.*

After the detour to see Pic du Midi, the road beyond Tourmalet Pass drops down through grassland which contrasts vividly with the rocky crags and ravines of its western side. Above the road, on the left, a series of hairpin bends looping across the mountainside marks the course of the old track followed by the sedan chairs of the Duc du Maine and his governess Mme de Maintenon *(qv)* when they went from Bagnères de Bigorre to take the waters at Barèges. Below the road, at an altitude of 1 800m – 5 905ft, the pyramids of La Mongie-Tourmalet residential centre mark the entrance to the winter sports resort of La Mongie.

★ **La Mongie** – This high-altitude (1 800m – 5 900ft) winter sports resort enjoys a superb position in a mountain amphitheatre and benefits from continuous snow from December to late April. It is the most specialized centre in the Pyrenees, offering downhill runs, cross-country ski trails and guided ascents which connect with the ski slopes above Barèges *(illustration p 272)*.

There is a cable-car link to **Le Taoulet**★★ (alt 2 341m – 7 681ft), a spur off Pic du Midi de Bigorre which offers splendid **views**★★ of the Néouvielle massif, the Arbizon and the valley of the Campan.

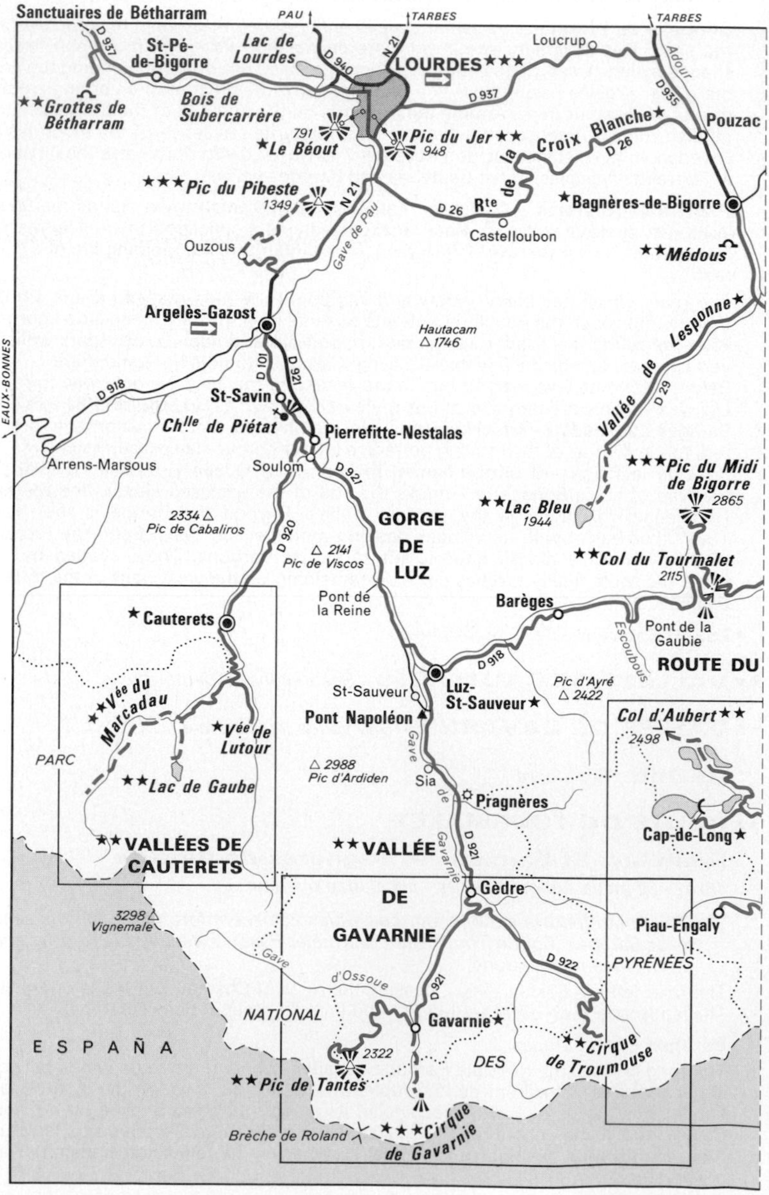

Beyond the resort the road drops more steeply through terraced woodlands, and then leads to a wide sweep through the tributary valley of the Garet. Subsequently it crosses in succession the Tourmalet stream and its tributary, the Arises, which here flows in a series of falls. The Artigues plateau – a pretty hollow of pastureland partly drowned by a reservoir – opens out on the right, below.

★ **Cascade du Garet** – *Park by the Hôtel des Pyrénées in Artigues. Walk through the hamlet and cross a small bridge upstream from the power station.*
A footpath rises into the Garet tributary valley and then passes into a wood of fir trees. Here steps cut in the rock lead down to a viewpoint from which the falls can be admired.

The road then follows the fresh, pretty **Vallée de Campan★**, bordered by meadows of an intense green. Houses and barns with gables stepped in the Flemish style and thatched roofs can be seen dotted here and there in the fields. This scattering of buildings continues as far as Campan.
After Ste-Marie-de-Campan, the road (D 935, north) drops into the Adour Valley. There are glimpses from time to time of the massive summit of Pic du Midi de Bigorre, always identifiable by the tall pylon of its television transmitter.

Campan – The small town includes a 16C covered market, an 18C fountain and a 16C church : left of the porch which leads into the old cemetery (galleries with marble columns) stands a 14C Christ from an old abbey in the region. Inside the church there is fine 18C woodwork.

Beyond Campan, D 29 (left) runs along the Vallée de Lesponne.

★ **Vallée de Lesponne** – This charming valley offers views of Pic du Midi de Bigorre and Pic de Montaigu, which are especially attractive in spring and autumn when they are snow-capped. From Chiroulet near the top of the valley a walk *(4hrs Rtn)* leads to **Lac Bleu★★**, a lake-reservoir in a splendidly isolated spot.

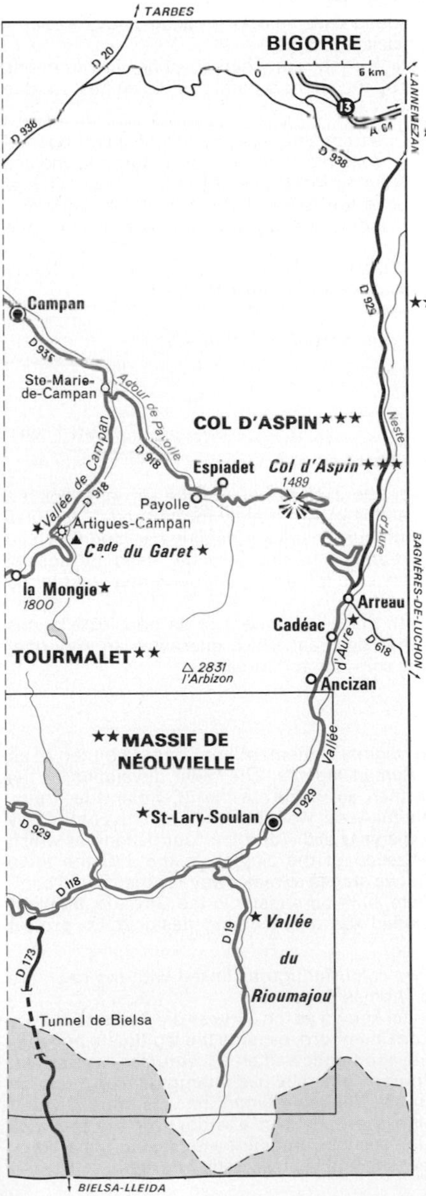

★★ **Grotte de Médous** – *See Grotte de Médous.*

After Médous D 935 continues to Bagnères.

★ **Bagnères-de-Bigorre** – *See Bagnères-de-Bigorre.*

★★★ COL D'ASPIN

From Campan to St-Lary-Soulan

61km – 38 miles : about 3 hours – Local map opposite.

From December to April Col d'Aspin (Aspin Pass) can be closed to traffic for anything from 12 to 48 hours; this is because the clearing of snow is discontinuous and is not a matter of priority.

Campan – *See above.*

Beyond Ste-Marie-de-Campan, the run south through the pretty valley of the Adour de Payolle is similar to the Campan valley, though the "highland atmosphere" is a little more pronounced. In front and to the right, the 2 831m – 9 288ft high Arbizon remains almost constantly in sight. Pic du Midi reappears, behind, when the road passes through the **Payolle** basin (cross-country ski centre).

Espiadet – This is a hamlet at the foot of the famous Campan marble quarry. The green stone, veined with red and white, was used for the columns of the Grand Trianon at Versailles and, in part, for those of Garnier's opera house in Paris.
After Espiadet the road rises continuously all the way to Col d'Aspin. At first, offering occasional glimpses of the Arbizon Massif, the road snakes through beautiful pinewoods; then the trees thin out to reveal surroundings of mountain pastures.

★★★ **Col d'Aspin** – Alt 1 489m – 4 884ft. Despite being at a considerably lower altitude than the three other passes (Tourmalet, Aubisque, Peyresourde) along the Route des Pyrénées, the Aspin Pass offers an incomparable **panorama** with a wider view than any of them. The attractive grouping of the mountain masses and the contrast between snowy peaks and the blue distant forests combine to form an unforgettable picture.
After the pass, the narrow road drops steeply in hairpin bends : in less than 13km – 8 miles it falls from 1 489m to 704m – 4 884ft to 2 309ft. To the right is a bird's-eye view of the well-tilled valley sheltering the village of Aspin; the southern slopes lend themselves well to cultivation. There are views, again, of the Arbizon massif and the Arreau basin.

Arreau – This is a pleasant small town of slate-roofed houses, well-sited at the confluence of the Aure and Louron torrents, at the junction of main routes and between passes; it was once the capital of the Pays des Quatre Vallées *(see below)*.
Beyond Arreau the road follows the **Vallée d'Aure**★. At one time there was a Vicomté of Aure, under the sovereignty of the Kings of Aragon. Then, in the 14C, it was linked with the valleys of Magnoac, Neste and Barousse to form the **Pays des Quatre Vallées** (Four Valleys Region), which fell, in 1398, to the House of Armagnac. In 1527 it was taken over by the Albret family *(qv)*.
The road – D 929 – follows the Aure torrent upstream along the floor of a wide and pleasant valley.

Cadéac – At the far end of the village the road passes beneath the porch of La Chapelle de Notre-Dame-de-Pène-Taillade (the Chapel of Our Lady of the Sheared Rock).

Ancizan – A group of 16C houses recalls the former prosperity of what was once a small town : a long time ago this part of the valley supported a thousand weavers, all producing the local *cadis* (a coarse, thick cloth of undyed wool).
Beyond Ancizan the valley floor is studded with hillocks – called *pouys* locally – which are the remnants of an ancient glacial moraine.
Just before Guchen the road crosses the Aure torrent. There is a fine view from this point of the mountain horizon, pierced by the sharp pyramid of Pic de Lustou (due south).

★ **St-Lary-Soulan** – This town stands on the trans-Pyrenean route which was opened up with the Bielsa Tunnel. It developed during the 1950s as a ski resort, making use of the rises west of the Aure Valley; its sunny location and liveliness make it very attractive. Access to the ski slopes above the town at Pla d'Adet (alt 1 680m – 5 512ft) is either via a cable-car or via a longer, northern route by road taking in the villages of Espiaube and La Cabane.
In summer it is a centre from which mountain walkers set off to explore the Néouvielle massif and the valleys of the upper basin of the Aure torrent.

★★ MASSIF DE NÉOUVIELLE – *See Massif de Néouvielle.*

BLAYE

Pop 4 286

Michelin map 71 folds 7, 8 or 233 folds 37, 38 – Local maps pp 28, 111 – Facilities.

Blaye (pronounced "Bly") is situated on the eastern bank of the Gironde, 36km – 22 miles downstream from Bordeaux, and is known mainly for its citadel, its Côtes de Blaye wines and its harbour. The harbour includes a deep-water landing-stage and an extended dock basin, at right-angles to the Gironde, used by coastal steamers and sailing ships. Fishing boats land lampreys, sturgeon and shad in the spring.
Industrial growth in Blaye is linked with the development of its port installations (despite being 64km – 40 miles from the open sea) which guarantee an important traffic in cereals, fertilizer, heat-resisting soils, tar and molasses.

HISTORICAL NOTES

From the Romans to Vauban – The original settlement here formed on top of an escarpment used as a camp by the Roman legions. The town developed in the Gallo-Roman period and was known then as Blavia. In the 8C Roland le Preux, Comte de Blaye, and his lady, the beautiful Aude, were buried here in the old Abbey of St-Romain, which was founded in the year 350 – and the foundations of which exist today beneath the St-Romain bastion of the citadel. In the 17C the town perched on its rock was demolished in two stages to make way for the citadel completed by Vauban *(qv)* in 1689. Fort Pâté, built on an islet in the Gironde, and Fort Médoc *(qv)* on the west bank concluded the defence ring designed to protect Bordeaux from the English fleet.

The Duchess and the General – Two colourful figures linked with the town are Marie-Caroline de Bourbon-Sicily and Thomas Bugeaud.
Marie-Caroline de Bourbon-Sicily is better known as the 34-year-old **Duchesse de Berry** whose son, under the name of Comte de Chambord, became the legitimate pretender to the French throne. Marie-Caroline, a romantic and an adventuress, was arrested at Nantes – she was hiding in a chimney – after she had attempted to provoke an uprising against King Louis-Philippe in the Vendée region. She was imprisoned in Blaye on 15 November 1832. Although she had been a widow for the previous 12 years, at the time of her incarceration she was pregnant with a child fathered by Comte Lucchesi (to whom, she claimed, she had been secretly married).

M. Guillard/SCOPE

The Citadel.

Général Bugeaud – Marquis de la Piconnerie, Duc d'Isly and a veteran of campaigns in North Africa – was appointed Governor of Blaye by Louis-Philippe so that he could keep an eye on the Duchesse. Bugeaud was a fearless soldier and a good administrator, but he was also vain and ill-tempered, and his lack of tact was legendary. Not only did he keep an eye on his prisoner : he spied on her, even going to the lengths of searching her clothes and linen.

The prisoner's life was brightened by a young officer – the future Marshal St-Arnaud – and her doctor, a friend of Balzac, who between them contrived to cheer up her time in captivity. When, in May 1833, Marie-Caroline gave birth to a girl, the scandal of her apparently illegitimate pregnancy had effectively rendered her no longer dangerous politically. On 8 June that year she was put on a boat in Blaye harbour and sent back to Palermo in Sicily.

★ CITADEL *1 hour 30min*

Access on foot via Porte Dauphine to the south, by car through Porte Royale to the east; both gateways are decorated with shields carrying fleur-de-lys, both protected by demilunes in the curtain wall.

The citadel, still partly inhabited, is a real "town within a town" and lively in season thanks to the craftsmen who still work there.

The landward side, which is 45m – 148ft above the river, is defended by bastions themselves protected by a dyke.

Château des Rudel – This medieval castle, triangular in shape, has a romantic history. It was the birthplace of the 12C troubadour **Geoffroy** (or **Jaufré**) **Rudel**, who fell poetically in love with "a distant princess", Melisande of Tripoli, without ever seeing her. According to legend, he sailed across the sea to join her, fell ill on the voyage, and died on arrival in the arms of his beloved.

Only two towers of the castle still stand but the bridge which led to the entrance and the foundations of the walls are also visible. In the middle of the courtyard the coping around the ancient well can be seen, grooved by the constant rubbing of the chain or rope which lowered the bucket. From the top of the tower, Tour des Rondes, there is a good **view** of the town, the Gironde estuary and the surrounding countryside *(viewing table)*.

Tour de l'Aiguillette – From the side of this tower, which rises at the northwestern end of the citadel, there is a fine **view★** of the estuary, studded with islets as far as the open sea.

Take the pathway on the western side of the Citadel.

Place d'Armes – From the esplanade on the edge of the cliff overlooking the Gironde there is another view of the estuary and the islands. Near Place d'Armes (the old parade ground) there stands a former monastery belonging to the mendicant order of Minims, complete with its chapel and cloisters. The semicircular arcading of the cloisters rests on square pillars.

Pavillon de la Place (Maison de la Duchesse) ⊙ – At the citadel's centre is the house, once used by the Captain of the Guard, where the Duchesse de Berry was held captive. It now contains a museum devoted to the history and culture of the region around Blaye.

Europe on a single sheet : ***Michelin Map 970***.

★★★ BORDEAUX

Pop 210 336

Michelin map 71 fold 9 or 234 fold 3 – Local map p 28 – Facilities.

Bordeaux, set 98km – 61 miles upriver at the first bridging point of the tidal River Garonne, is France's eighth largest city and one of the most important ports in Europe. As a trade centre, the town is renowned not only for the export of the world-famous **wines of Bordeaux** *(qv)* and the spirits distilled in the southwest of France but also for its farming, food-processing and timber connections, and for its place in the high-tech world of aeronautics, electronics and chemicals. Additionally, Bordeaux is part of a powerful communications network which was further enhanced by the completion, in autumn 1990, of the TGV high-speed rail link with Paris. The development of international exhibition sites and the construction of such projects as the World Trade Center and La Cité Mondiale du Vin (the World Wine Headquarters) testify to the economic dynamism which has made the regional capital of Aquitaine an important junction between Northern Europe and the Iberian peninsula.

HISTORICAL NOTES

Dukes of Aquitaine – Bordeaux (the ancient Burdigala before it was colonized and developed under the Romans) was built on a choice site repeatedly attacked by Visigoths, Normans, Saracens and Moors. It was "Good King" Dagobert who, in the 7C, regained the town and the surrounding territory for the Frankish empire and the Merovingian dynasty, creating a Duchy of Aquitaine with Bordeaux as its capital. One of these Dukes of Aquitaine was the legendary **Huon of Bordeaux,** who is said to have killed, without knowing who he was, one of the sons of Charlemagne : exiled by the Emperor, Huon was subsequently involved in a number of adventures before he eventually married the daughter of the Emir of Babylon. A celebrated 13C *chanson de geste* (a series of epic minstrel songs featuring the same hero) was based on an embroidered version of this amorous exploit : according to the myth, the hero's pardon by the Emperor depended on Huon going to Babylon, cutting off the Emir's beard and bringing it back, together with four of the potentate's molars, to Charlemagne. The task was successfully accomplished with the help of Oberon – that same King of the Fairies used by Shakespeare three hundred years later in *A Midsummer Night's Dream.*

Another Duke of Aquitaine was Guillaume Tête d'Étoupe ("William the Scruffy-Haired"), whose daughter married the French king Hugh Capet in the 10C and founded the Capetian dynasty, which lasted until the early 13C.

Eleanor's Dowry – In 1137 Louis, son of the French king, married **Eleanor of Aquitaine,** the only daughter of another Duke William of Aquitaine. The bride's dowry comprised the Duchy of Guyenne, the regions of Périgord, Poitou, Limousin, Angoumois, Saintonge and Gascony – practically the whole of southwestern France – together with the suzerainty of the Auvergne and the Comté of Toulouse. The marriage was solemnized in Bordeaux cathedral; it was not, however, a success. Louis, who became King Louis VII, was a monkish man, an ascetic; his queen, in contrast, was frivolous and enjoyed the good things in life. After 15 years of unhappy marriage, Louis returned from the Crusades and obtained a divorce (1152) through the Council of Beaugency. The settlement gave Eleanor her freedom... and she retained the whole of her dowry. Two years later she married **Henry Plantagenet,** Duke of Normandy, Count of Anjou, ruler of Maine and Touraine.

Politically, this marriage was a disaster for the Capetians : Henry and Eleanor's combined territories covered an area as vast as that ruled by the King of France. When, barely two months after the marriage, Henry succeeded to the throne of England and became Henry II, the resulting imbalance proved too much for the French. The conflict it provoked lasted, intermittently, for three centuries.

The Claret connection – It was the Romans who introduced the cultivation of vines to the Bordeaux region. The red wine, christened "Claret" by the English occupiers, was much appreciated by the Plantagenets : one thousand casks were set aside for the coronation celebrations.

The grape at that time was a sacred fruit – the punishment for thieves was the loss of an ear – and the quality of the wines even then was all-important : six sworn tasters testified to its excellence or otherwise, and no innkeeper dared broach a barrel before it had been submitted for their approval. Merchants who adulterated the wine were severely punished and so were coopers whose casks proved to be defective.

Black Prince's territory (14C) – Bordeaux was known as the capital of **Guyenne** (an old English corruption of the word Aquitaine, which remained in use until the French Revolution). Under English rule the town had the right to choose its own mayor and its councillors or *"jurats"*, and throughout the Hundred Years War trade continued to flourish in the port : wine was still exported to England, and the Bordelais (the people of Bordeaux) cheerfully sold arms to belligerents on both sides. At the same time nobles and *jurats* built themselves substantial stone houses, known as *"taules"* or *"hostaux"*, and the son of the English King Edward III, known as the Black Prince possibly because of his dark armour, established his headquarters and held court here.

The Black Prince was one of the most talented military leaders of his time and one of the most savage plunderers. From his Bordeaux base he sallied forth for one campaign after another, terrifying in turn the people of the Languedoc, Limousin, Auvergne, Berry and Poitou regions. A victim of dropsy, however, the heir to the English throne died before having reigned anywhere but in Bordeaux.

In 1453 Bordeaux and the whole of Guyenne was retaken by the French army; the Hundred Years War was over.

Bordeaux and the "Intendants" – These high-ranking provincial representatives of the French Crown, or "stewards", first appointed by Richelieu during the reign of Louis XIV in the 17C, were made an effective instrument of central government by Jean-Baptiste Colbert (1619-83), the King's Secretary of State, Controller-General of Finances and Superintendent of Buildings. In the 18C the Intendants' broad vision of a spacious, well-planned city to replace the tangle of medieval streets in Bordeaux brought them into conflict with the short-sighted and penny-pinching representatives of the local population, but they succeeded in their aims : the work of Claude Boucher, the Marquis of Tourny, Dupré and St Maur transformed a maze of narrow, twisted and stinking lanes surrounded by swamps into one of the most beautiful towns in France. In Bordeaux's old town, between the St Michael and Chartrons districts, there remain today around 5 000 stone-built houses dating from the 18C. The grandiose urban concepts such as Tourny's avenues, the Bordeaux quays, the Stock Exchange complex and monuments like the Customs House, the City Hall and the Grand Theatre also date from this period. Once the new Bordeaux was established, its position bordering the Atlantic was exploited to the full, and it soon became the premier port in France.

Girondins – During the French Revolution the Bordeaux *députés,* chief among them Pierre Victurnien Vergniaud (1753-93), formed a political grouping known as the Girondins. Essentially bourgeois in attitude, they enjoyed a majority in the Legislative Assembly and during the first few months of the Convention (1793). Because of their federalist tendencies, however, the Girondins were accused of conspiring against the unity and indivisibility of the Republic – of being, in short, anti-revolutionary. Twenty two of them, including Vergniaud himself, were subsequently tried, condemned to death and executed.

Trade boom – The Empire period (early 19C) was a bleak time for the city, as the maritime trade on which it depended was badly affected by the Continental Blockade. The Restoration, however, revived the fortunes of the Bordelais; the great stone bridge and the huge Quinconces Esplanade, projects which the Intendants had no time to complete, date from this era.
Under the Second Empire the city's role as a trade centre continued to develop, largely because of improved communications and the drainage of the Landes marshes to the south.
In 1870 during the siege of Paris, in 1914 before the German offensive and again in 1940 the French government fled south to take refuge in Bordeaux – dramas which earned the town the nickname of "the Tragic Capital". After the Second World War Bordeaux once again found the dynamic spirit of enterprise that its shipbuilders, financiers and merchants had enjoyed in the 18C.

BORDEAUX TODAY

The new-look town – Contemporary projects have concentrated on rejuvenating the old town while simultaneously developing new areas of the city, for example the district around Le Lac, Pessac-Talence university campus, the Grand-Parc and La Benauge developments on the outskirts; the Meriadeck area and the Préfecture gardens in the city itself.

Le Lac – This attractive lake (covering 160ha – 395 acres) to the north of the city offers excellent facilities for sailing and rowing. Tennis courts and a golf course are among the amenities surrounding the lake, along with fine hotels, a conference hall and an exhibition centre which hosts the Bordeaux International Fair, the annual World Wine and Spirit Week and the city's International Flower Show (last held in 1992).
From the district around Le Lac there is direct access to the A 10 motorway to Paris via the suspension bridge, **Pont d'Aquitaine.** This masterpiece of engineering spans the River Garonne 55m – 180ft above the river's highest high-watermark; it is 1 767m – over a mile long.

Meriadeck Area (CY) – This ultra-modern complex includes offices, administrative buildings, apartment blocks, a skating rink, the municipal library and a shopping centre in a series of constructions based on the cube and the circle. In the middle, on Esplanade Charles-de-Gaulle, formal gardens with pools and fountains complement the architectural ensemble. The mirror-walled Préfecture building closes the perspective to the west. Concrete footbridges give access to the roads bordering the complex.

Life in Bordeaux – City life unfolds between wide, tree-lined avenues, and along imposing perspectives down long esplanades bordered by elegant buildings. In the lively city centre, the busiest area is bounded by Place de la Comédie, Cours de l'Intendance – a favourite place with the locals for a stroll – Cours Clemenceau, Les Allées de Tourny and Place des Grands-Hommes, where luxury-goods shops stand alongside the crowded terraces of famous cafés. Nearby, the pedestrianized precincts of the bustling Rue Ste-Catherine and Rue Porte-Dijeaux are bordered by large department stores.
Bordeaux's cultural prestige is reaffirmed by the annual Musical May concerts and the SIGMA Festival, which attract the world's greatest orchestras and most celebrated soloists *(see Calendar of Events, qv).*

The Port – Bordeaux stands strategically upriver of the estuary known as the Gironde, just 98km – 61 miles from the coast, and commands the shortest land link between the Atlantic Ocean and the Mediterranean Sea, via the valley of the Garonne and the Midi Canal (240km – 149 miles long) which incorporates the Naurouze Pass. The city's importance as a port dates back to the blossoming of the wine trade during the English domination, when the exportation of claret began. This was sensibly augmented in the 18C by a heavy traffic in colonial products from the French West Indies.

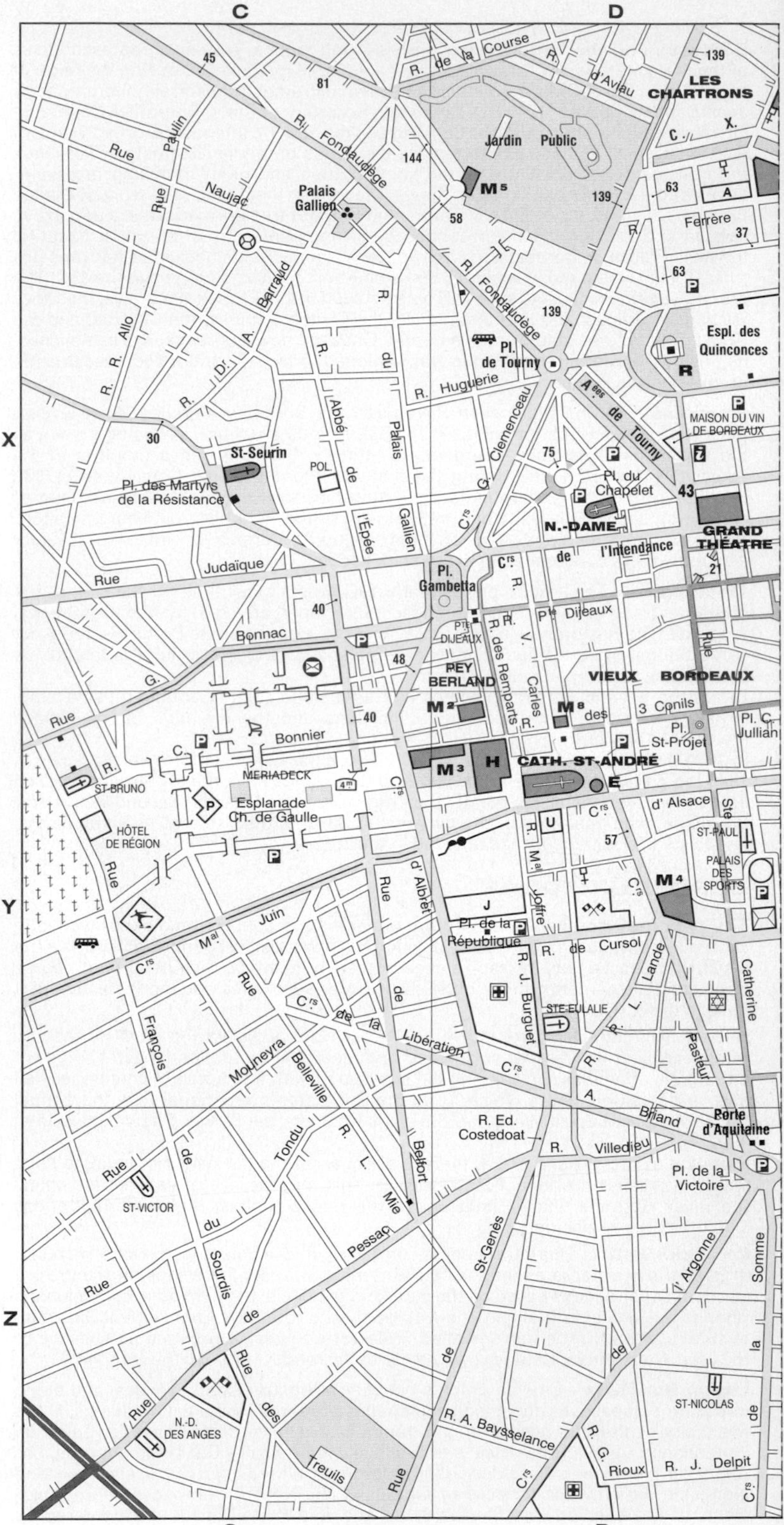

B Tour St-Michel
D Porte de la Grosse-Cloche
E Tour Pey Berland
H Hôtel de Ville
L Ancienne Maison Bordelaise
M1 Musée des Douanes
M3 Musée des Beaux-Arts
M4 Musée d'Aquitaine
M5 Musée d'Histoire naturelle
M7 Musée d'Art contemporain
M8 Centre Jean-Moulin
R Monument aux Girondins

Local maps and town plans in Michelin Guides are oriented with north at the top.

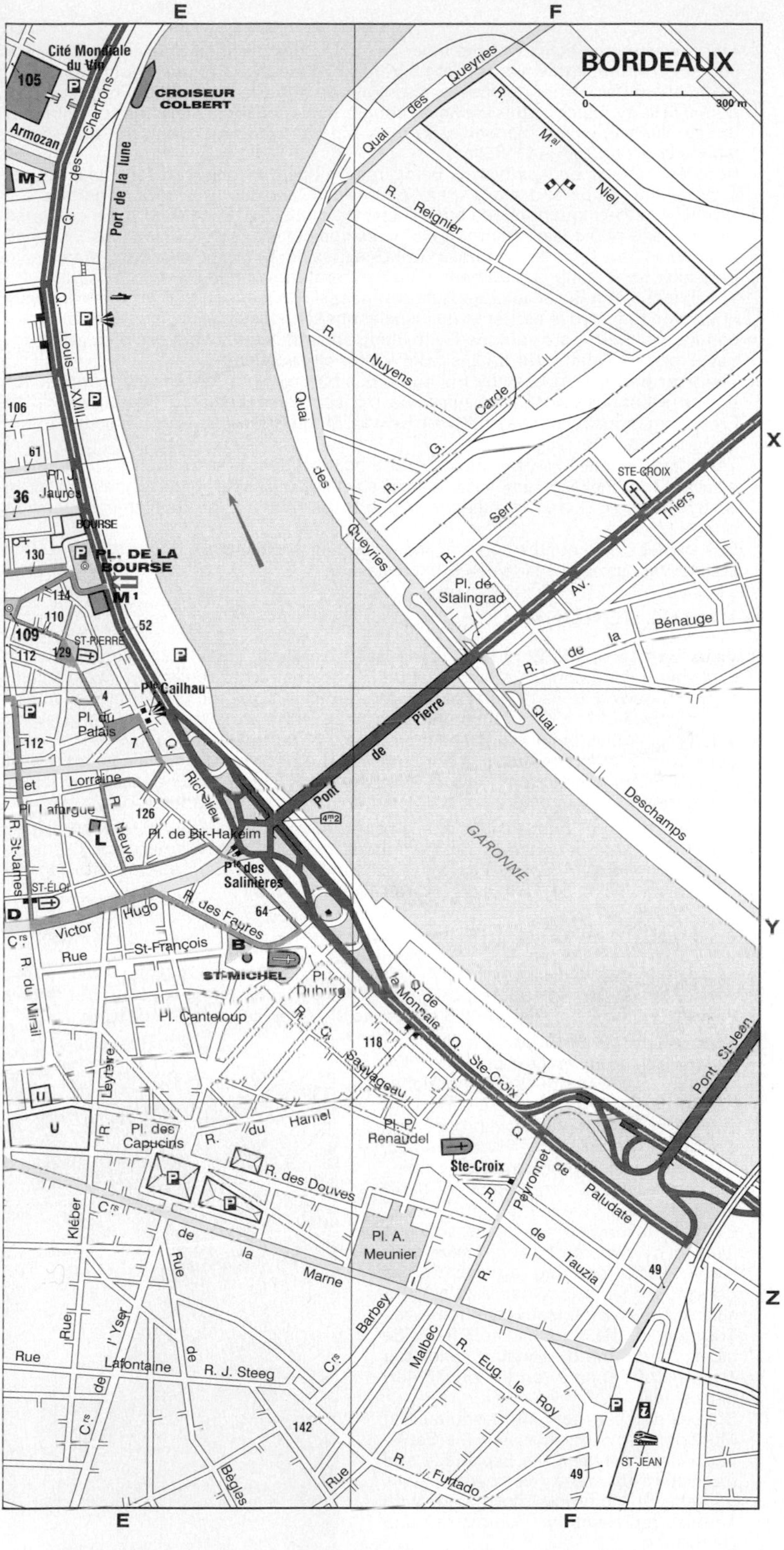

E
F
BORDEAUX
0
300 m
X
Y
Z
Cité Mondiale du Vin
105
CROISEUR COLBERT
Armozan
Q. des Chartrons
Port de la lune
Q. Louis XVIII
106
61
Pl. J. Jaurès
36
BOURSE
PL. DE LA BOURSE
130
114
110
109
112
129
ST-PIERRE
52
Pte Cailhau
4
Pl. du Palais
7
112
Lorraine
et
Pl. Lafargue
126
R. Neuve
L
R. St-James
ST-ÉLOI
D
Crs Victor Hugo
Rue St-François
R. du Mirail
R. des Faures
64
B
ST-MICHEL
Pl. Dubourg
Pl. Canteloup
Leyteire
U
Pl. des Capucins
R. du Hamel
R. des Douves
Crs de la Marne
Kléber
Rue de l'Yser
Rue Lafontaine
R. J. Steeg
Crs de Bègles
142
Rue
Q. Richelieu
Pl. de Bir-Hakeim
Ptes des Salinières
Pont de Pierre
GARONNE
Quai des Queyries
R. Mal Niel
R. Reignier
R. Nuyens
R. G. Carde
R. Serr
STE-CROIX
Av. Thiers
Pl. de Stalingrad
R. de la Bénauge
Quai Deschamps
Q. de la Monnaie
Q. Ste-Croix
R. C. Sauvageau
118
Pl. P. Renaudel
Ste-Croix
Pl. A. Meunier
Q. de Paludate
R. Peyronnet
R. de Tauzia
R. Barbey
R. Malbec
R. Eug. le Roy
R. Furtado
49
ST-JEAN
Pont St-Jean

More recently the activity of the inner-city docks has declined in favour of the new container terminal downstream at Le Verdon where the Gironde meets the ocean. Today the outer harbour at **Bassens** also plays an important role in the regional economic activity. Much of this traffic is brought down the River Garonne to Ambès, at the confluence, where the waterway then widens, accommodating the port installations at Blaye *(qv)* and Pauillac.

Bordeaux's west bank, which is being redeveloped, is reserved for ocean liners, large sailing ships and naval craft. Alongside Quai des Chartrons, opposite the World Wine Headquarters, the **battle-cruiser Colbert** (**EX**) ⊙ is berthed : the disarmed *Colbert,* one of the last important 20C warships put into service (she was launched in 1959), is now open to the public. The Queyries docks on the east bank are used in particular for loading and unloading timber, fertilizers and heavy goods in bulk.

The independent Bordeaux Port Authority keeps a division of dredgers continuously employed to improve access to its installations. The tidal basins, closed to ordinary commercial traffic, are equipped with lifting apparatus and two types of dry dock for naval repairs. Tidal Basin No 2 is reserved for pleasure craft.

The river port is kept busy by the numerous barges from Ambès with supplies for the oil refineries; by those sailing via the southern canals to Toulouse, and to France's national waterway network by way of the Rhône, or to the Mediterranean through Sète.

The liners – about 15 a year, mostly cruise boats or special wine excursion steamers – dock in the **"Port de la Lune"** (Moon Port), so-called because it flanks a crescent formed by the river. A marina has been built at the river's edge near the suspension bridge.

Boat **cruises** ⊙ around the port and along the river are available, departing from Quai Louis-XVIII near Esplanade des Quinconces.

★★ VIEUX BORDEAUX

Vieux Bordeaux (Old Bordeaux) comprises an area of 150ha – 370 acres which is currently undergoing large-scale restoration in an effort to return the city's ancient ochre stonework to its original golden splendour. Among the properties scheduled for this "face-lift", most of them dating from the 18C, are those lining the **quayside** : these prestigious buildings, standing in a row of perfect unity, follow the curve of the River Garonne for over half a mile (there is a fine **view** from the eastern end of Pont de Pierre, the stone bridge). A stroll through Old Bordeaux gives an overview of the trends in architecture and town planning over the centuries.

Two different tours of the old town are suggested below : one of the Quinconces area bounded by the triangle formed by Cours Clemenceau, Cours de l'Intendance and les Allées de Tourny; the other through the maze of narrow streets linking St Peter's and St Michael's districts.

Quinconces District (DEX) *1 hour*

Esplanade des Quinconces (**DEX**) – The sheer size (about 126 000m – 150 700 sq yds) of this large, rectangular esplanade is very impressive. It was laid out during the Restoration (early 19C) on the site of the old Château de la Trompette.

Monument to the Girondins (**DY R**)– This allegor-ical group, erected between 1894 and 1902, serves both as a memorial to the Bordeaux *députés* guillotined at the end of the Revolution and as proof of the city's fidelity towards the Third Republic. It is an astonishing sculptural ensemble : the centrepiece is a column 50m – 164ft high, crowned by a statue representing Liberty throwing off her chains, which is flanked by two remarkable **bronze fountains★**, each featuring aquatic horses drawing a chariot crowded with personalities. The two tableaux symbolize the Triumph of the Republic (on the side facing the Grand Theatre) and the Triumph of Concord (on the public gardens side).

Statues of the writers Montesquiou and Montaigne *(qv)* preside over the Esplanade itself; between the Esplanade and the waterfront stand two rostral (ship's figurehead) columns, decorated with figures representing Commerce and Navigation.

Ducasse/TOP

Detail from a fountain of the Monument to the Girondins, Bordeaux.

Cross Quai Louis-XVIII and, a few yards to the right, climb the 20 steps leading to the terrace in front of the covered car park.

From the terrace there is an overall view of the river and Port de la Lune.

Southwards, to the right, is **Pont de Pierre,** the stone bridge which was completed in 1822; until the opening of Pont St-Jean, upriver, in 1965 it was the only bridge in Bordeaux. The high-slung roadway of the suspension bridge, **Pont d'Aquitaine** *(see above),* which is visible in the distance to the left, followed two years later in 1967.

Place de la Comédie (**DX 43**) – This square, lying on the site of the ancient Forum, was once flanked by a Gallo-Roman temple demolished on the orders of Louis XIV. It was on the temple foundations that the Grand Theatre was built. The square, together with Place de Tourny and Place Gambetta, encloses the heart of one of the city's finest urban developments.

★★ **Grand Théâtre** (**DX**) ⓥ – The recently-restored Grand Theatre is among the most beautiful in France, and is a potent symbol of the richness of both French architecture and French cultural ideas at the time.

The building was commissioned by the Duc de Richelieu (at that time Governor of Guyenne), designed by the architect Victor Louis (1731-1802) and built between 1773 and 1780. From the outside it is distinguished by its Classically-inspired columnar peristyle. The stone façade comprises 12 Corinthian columns surmounted by an entablature, a balustrade supporting 12 statues, and a terrace surrounding an attic floor. The statues, by the sculptor Berruer, represent goddesses and muses.

Two side galleries have arcades surmounted by windows housed in bays separated by monumental pilasters.

Inside the theatre, the coffered ceiling of the foyer is supported by 16 columns. Beneath the dome at the far end, a handsome staircase rises in a single flight then divides into two (an arrangement copied by Garnier when he designed the Paris Opera House).

The panelled auditorium with its 12 gilded columns provides a splendid interior which is acoustically perfect. From the centre of the ceiling, painted by Rogancau after the primitive frescoes of Claude Robin, hangs a chandelier glittering with 14 000 drops of Bohemian crystal.

Outside, follow Cours de l'Intendance as far as No 19, then take Passage Sarget (open to the public since 1878), which leads to Place du Chapelet and Notre-Dame church.

★ **Église Notre-Dame** (**DX**) ⓥ – This church dedicated to the Virgin was formerly a Dominican chapel; it was built between 1684 and 1707 by the engineer Michel Duplessy.

The **façade,** in typical Jesuit style, is organized around a projecting central block comprising two superimposed orders surmounted by a triangular pediment. The wide entablature, decorated with a frieze of acanthus leaves, helps to emphasize the different masses while pilasters, engaged columns and carved ornamentation animate the surface to give an interesting play of light and shade.

The name of the square – Place du Chapelet – derives from the low-relief above the entrance to the church, which depicts the Virgin presenting the rosary *(chapelet)* to St Dominic.

The stonework in the **interior** is especially impressive : barrel-vaulting, pierced by the lunettes of the clerestory windows, for the nave; groined vaulting in the side aisles; an organ loft extended on each side by gracefully curving balconies. The quality and design of the wrought-ironwork – note in particular the gates around the chancel – provide a fitting complement to the architecture.

Allées de Tourny (**DX**) – These avenues offer a splendid perspective from the Grand Theatre down to a late 18C mansion crowned by a terraced gallery. A wide esplanade leads to **Place de Tourny** (**DX**) in which stands a statue of Louis de Tourny, the apostle of urban regeneration, who was Intendant of Bordeaux from 1743 to 1758.

Cours Clemenceau, a wide street lined by shops ranged along coloured pavements, links Place de Tourny with Place Gambetta.

Place Gambetta (**DX**) – This square was formerly known as Place Dauphine. The houses bordering it were all built in the Louis XV style (with arcades at street level and mansard roofs), giving a pleasing architectural unity. An attractive garden in the English style has been laid out at the centre of the square which, during the Revolution, was the site of the scaffold.

Off a corner of the square stands Porte Dijeaux, one of the town gates, which dates from 1748; it leads to the shopping street of the same name.

Cours de l'Intendance and Cours du Chapeau-Rouge (**DEX**) – Cours de l'Intendance is the main street for high-fashion and luxury-goods stores. By No 57 there is a fine view, along Rue Vital-Carles, of the towers of Bordeaux cathedral. No 57 itself, the house where the artist Goya lived and died (1828), is now a Spanish cultural centre.

Where the street meets Place de la Comédie and Rue Ste-Catherine it becomes Cours du Chapeau-Rouge and continues down towards the quayside and the river; it has borne this name since 1464, when the famous Chapeau-Rouge (Red Hat) tavern stood along here.

Round Tour starting from La Bourse *allow 2 hours 30min*

★★ **Place de la Bourse** (**EX**) – Now named after the Stock Exchange (La Bourse), this magnificent square was formerly called Place Royale and was the work of the architect Jacques Jules Gabriel (1667-1742) – *Premier Architecte du Roi* – and his son Ange-Jacques (1698-1782).

The eastern side gives onto the symmetrical façades lining the quays, while to the north rises the Stock Exchange itself; the southern side is graced by the former Hôtel des Fermes (tax inspectorate) which has, on its upper floors, triangular pediments supported by columns – a formula also used on the western pavilion. The majesty of these façades and the variety of their carved decoration combine to form one of the most splendid architectural examples of the Louis XV style.

An equestrian statue of the King by J B Lemoyne, which dominated the square until 1792 when revolutionaries had it removed, was replaced in the 19C by a Fountain of the Three Graces.

Musée des Douanes (**EX M**[1]) ⊙ – The Customs Museum, which recounts the history of the Customs service in France, is housed in a large hall with fine vaulting (restored). To the right, the administration's development is followed chronologically with the help of documents, uniforms, an old Customs Director's office, professional equipment, and prints and paintings including a portrait of St Matthew, the patron saint of Customs officers (he was employed as a tax collector and Customs inspector when he first met Jesus).
On the left, different themes are presented : the Customs Armed; Customs in the cinema, in literature and in strip cartoons; Customs Activities (seizure of drugs, the arrest of counterfeiters); the life of a Customs Brigade (*The Customs Inspectors' Hut; afternoon* by Claude Monet). The tour ends with a display on the Customs officers' latest weapon : the computer.

Continue, via Rue F.-Philippart, to Place du Parlement.

★ **Place du Parlement** (**EX 109**) – This, Parliament Square, was once a royal market. The pleasant quadrangle of Louis XV buildings is arranged around a central court-yard paved with old cobblestones (restored). A Second Empire fountain plays in the centre of the square. Many of the houses are very fine : some have ground-floor arcades, delicate fanlights and mask decorations. They are surmounted by open-work balustrades.

Place de la Bourse.

Take Rue du Parlement-St-Pierre to Place St-Pierre.

Hôtel de Sèze on the square is among many 18C houses in the St Peter's district which have been restored recently. The 14C-15C church, Église St-Pierre, was altered substantially in the 19C.

Follow Rue des Argentiers.

The house at No 14, known as **Maison de l'Angelot,** dates from *c*1750. The carved ornamentation of the façade includes a high-relief of a child, and keystones in the Louis XV rough-cast style known as *rocaille.*

Continue to Place du Palais.

The square owes its name to the old Palais de l'Ombrière, which was built by the Dukes of Guyenne in the 10C, rebuilt in the 13C, used subsequently by the English crowned heads (who were also Dukes of Aquitaine) and which finally, under Louis XI, became the seat of the Bordeaux Parliament in 1462. The Palace was demolished in 1800 to make way for the present Rue du Palais.

Porte Cailhau (**EY**) ⊙ – The name of this triumphal arch derives either from the Cailhau family, who were members of the Bordeaux nobility, or from the *cailloux* (pebbles) washed up around its base by the Garonne and used as ballast by ships. The arch is built on the site of an ancient city gate, east of the old Palais de l'Ombrière, and was completed in 1495, the year of the Battle of Fournoue which was won by Charles VIII, to whom the structure is dedicated; this might explain the juxtaposition of the decorative and defensive elements (conical roofs, windows surmounted by interlaced arches, machicolated parapets).
Inside, on three different levels, an exhibition retraces the history of Old Bordeaux, outlines the important stages of urban expansion and reveals plans for the future (videos). The top floor, under the rafters, offers an unusual **view** across the quays of the Garonne to the stone bridge.

Follow Rue Ausone, cross Cours d'Alsace-et-Lorraine and fork right; turn right into Rue de la Rousselle.

This street is lined with the shops in which the city's wine merchants, grain sellers and cloth wholesalers once plied their trade : the buildings are characterized by tall ground floors surmounted by low-ceilinged mezzanines. No 25 was the city home of the 16C philosopher-essayist Montaigne *(qv).*

Turn left into Rue Neuve and continue to the cul-de-sac (right).

The city's **oldest house** (**EY L**), dating from the 14C, survives here. The stone tracery of the windows is typical of the period.

Continue to the end of Rue Neuve and turn left; on reaching Rue de la Rousselle again, turn right.

Crossing Cours Victor-Hugo there is a view of **Porte des Salinières** (Salt-Sellers' Gate), formerly Porte de Bourgogne (Burgundy Gate).

Take Rue de la Fusterie, opposite, to Place Duburg and St Michael's Basilica.

★ **Basilique St-Michel** (**EY**) ⊙ – The construction of St Michael's Basilica, begun in 1350, lasted for two centuries during which time the original design was much modified. The side chapels were added from 1475 onwards.
The generous dimensions of the restored basilica are impressive : inside, the two-storey elevation is emphasized by high arcades topped with tall clerestory windows, and wide side aisles. The lines of the flattened east end are barely affected by the three small chapels.

J.-L. Barde/SCOPE

In the first chapel off the south aisle stands a statue of St Ursula sheltering a number of people beneath her cloak. On the north side, the fourth chapel – dedicated to St Joseph – contains a richly worked stone and alabaster altarpiece dating from the 16C. The modern stained-glass windows, behind the high altar, are by Max Ingrand. The moulded coving of the north transept doorway frames a tympanum decorated with an allegorical scene representing Original Sin *(left)* and Adam and Eve expelled from the Garden of Eden *(right)*. The organ loft and pulpit date from the 18C; the latter, mahogany with marble panels, is surmounted by a statue of St Michael slaying the dragon.

Tour St-Michel (EY B) ⊙ – The people of Bordeaux are justly proud of this hexagonal Gothic belltower, which stands apart from the basilica : at 114m – 374ft tall it is the highest tower in the whole of the south of France (the tallest tower in the country belongs to Rouen Cathedral : 151m – 495ft). This tower easily dwarfs the cathedral's Pey-Berland tower which also stands separate and is a mere 50m – 164ft. Beneath the slender spire and superbly decorated façades lies a circular crypt.

Take Rue des Faures to Cours Victor-Hugo and turn left.

★ **Porte de la Grosse-Cloche** (EY D) – The 15C arched gateway (Great Bell Gate) with three round turrets and conical roofs is another source of local pride. The accompanying clocks date from 1592 (inside) and 1772 (outside); the bell was cast in 1775. The gateway stands on the site of an older structure, the St Éloi (Eligius) Gate, which was one of the entrances to the 13C walled town. From the belfry of the gateway the announcement of the wine harvest was rung out every year.
It is said that when the King wished to punish the people of Bordeaux, he would have the Great Bell and the two clocks removed.

Follow the narrow Rue St-James, which passes through the gateway, cross Place Lafargue to Rue du Pas-St-Georges and continue to Place C.-Jullian; turn left and continue to Rue Ste-Catherine.

At Place St-Projet there is a baroque fountain which was used, in the 17C and 18C, to distribute water from the higher parts of the town.

Turn right (north) into Rue Ste-Catherine.

Further along the street a number of houses are built over ground-floor arcades, with wide semicircular bays opening at first-floor level. At the junction with Rue de la Porte-Dijeaux note the Galerie Bordelaise *(opposite)*, a covered passageway or shopping arcade built by Gabriel-Joseph Durand in the 19C.

Rue St-Rémi, on the right, leads back to Place de la Bourse.

PEY-BERLAND DISTRICT (CDXY) *allow half a day*

St Andrew's Cathedral, with its famous tower, stands in the middle of Place Pey-Berland, which is flanked by the city's most important museums.

★ **Cathédrale St-André** (DY) ⊙ – St Andrew's Cathedral is the most impressive of all the religious buildings in Bordeaux. The floor-plan extends over 124m × 44m – 406ft × 144ft at the widest part (Notre Dame Cathedral in Paris : 130m × 48m – 427ft × 157ft). The 11C-12C nave was altered in the 13C and again in the 15C; the Radiant Gothic chancel and the transept were rebuilt in the 14C and 15C. During the era of prosperity which the town enjoyed while under English occupation, plans were made to enlarge the original Romanesque church (by then considered too small); however, funds ran

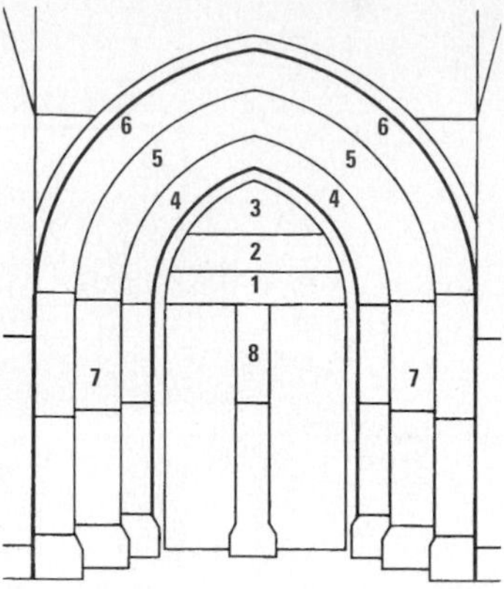

North Doorway.

1. The Last Supper – 2. The Ascension
3. Christ Triumphant – 4. Angels
5. The Twelve Apostles
6. Fathers of the Church and Prophets
7. Statues of Prelates
8. St-Martial

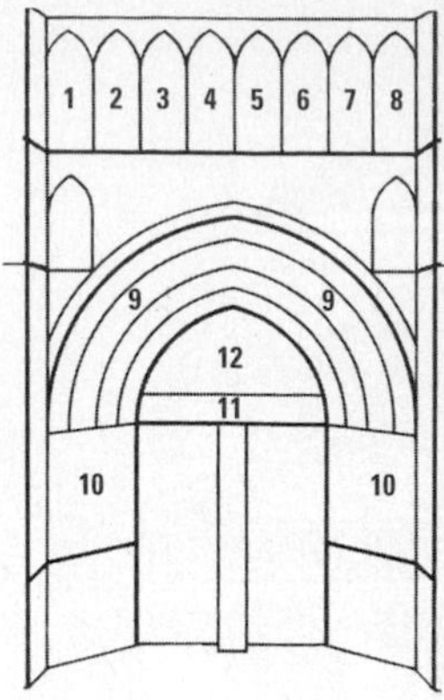

Royal Doorway.

1. to 6. Bishops – 7. A King
8. A Queen – 9. The Celestial Court
10. Ten Apostles
11. The Ressurection
12. The Last Judgement

out before the new nave was completed and the two structures were simply joined together. Later, when the vaults of the nave threatened to collapse, the building was strengthened by buttresses and flying buttresses added at irregular intervals.

Approach the cathedral from the north and circle it to the left (clockwise).

★ **Royal Doorway** – *Illustration below.* This 13C entrance to the right of the North Doorway is renowned for its sculptures, inspired by the outstanding statuary adorning religious buildings in Ile-de-France (the region surrounding Paris, where Gothic architecture originated). Most remarkable are the Twelve Apostles in the entrance bay and, on the tympanum, the fine Gothic *Last Judgement.*

North Doorway – *Illustration below.* The sculptures here are partially hidden by a wooden porch. The north transept is surmounted by sharply pointed spires.

East End – The exterior is distinguished by its fine proportions and by its elevation : the two-tiered flying buttresses soar over the side aisles; between the supports separating the axial chapel from the one on the left, note the statues of St Thomas, patron saint of architects, holding his set-square, and Mary Magdalene, in 15C costume, with her jar of perfume.

★ **Pey-Berland Tower** (**DY E**) ⏲ – The tower, crowned with a belfry and lavishly decorated, was built in the 15C on the orders of Archbishop Pey-Berland. It has always stood separate from the main body of the cathedral, beyond the east end. The steeple, truncated by a hurricane in the 18C, now supports a copper figure of the Virgin.
From here it is worth standing back a little, to the south, for an overall view of the twin spires above the north transept of the cathedral and, in the foreground, the massive, square, terraced towers flanking the south transept.

South Transept Doorway – This entrance to the cathedral is below a pediment pierced by an oculus and three rose windows. The upper part, embellished with trefoil arcades, also boasts an elegant rose window set within a square. The west front, destroyed in the 18C and then rebuilt, remains unadorned.

Interior – The impressive nave features late-Gothic upper parts resting on 12C bases; note the lierne and tierceron vaulting over the first three bays. The pulpit, fashioned from mahogany and coloured marble, is 18C. The different height of the **chancel★**, also Gothic, contrasts with the nave and is accentuated by the slenderness of the tall arches, above which a blind triforium is illuminated by Flamboyant clerestory windows. An ambulatory with side chapels encircles the chancel.

Enter the ambulatory from the southern side.

Against the 4th pillar to the right of the chancel there is a charming early 16C sculpture group depicting St Anne and the Virgin. The axial chapel closes off the 17C choir stalls. Opposite, a fine 17C door of carved wood separates the chancel from the nave. Nearby, set into the wall enclosing the chancel, is a 14C funerary niche in polychrome alabaster dedicated to St Martial, the 3C Bishop of Limoges. Above the altar in the side chapel north of the chancel stands a 14C figure of the Virgin and Child made from English polychrome alabaster.
On the inner face of the west front is the Renaissance **organ loft.** Below it two low-reliefs reveal the development of Renaissance sculpture : the group on the right shows Christ, harried by pagan deities from Hell, descending to Limbo, while that on the left shows the Resurrection, with the Saviour mounted upon an eagle like Jupiter.

Centre Jean-Moulin (**DY M[8]**) ⏲ – This museum, devoted to the Resistance and deportation under the German occupation, presents a panorama of the Second World War; it also has extensive archives relating to the period 1939-1945. Jean Moulin, the most famous of France's Resistance heroes, became President of the clandestine National Resistance Council after a secret visit to General de Gaulle in Britain. Subsequently betrayed, he was caught by the Gestapo, tortured and murdered in 1943.

On the ground floor the Centre displays Resistance pamphlets, secret communications, underground newspapers, illegal radio transmitters and other items – particularly relating to Jean Moulin – which appeared as a result of the Nazi occupation. The first floor concentrates on the spread of Nazi tyranny and the deportations which followed : photographs of concentration camps, prisoners' uniforms, various models, and a series of moving canvases by Jean-Jacques Morvan on the theme of *Night and Fog* (Nuit et Brouillard). The displays on the second floor are devoted to the men of the Free French Forces and their exploits, and include the boat *S'ils-te-Mordent* (If They Bite You) which, crammed with volunteers, linked the Brittany fishing port of Carantec with England. There is also a reconstruction of Jean Moulin's secret office.

Hôtel de Ville (**DY H**) ⊙ – The City Hall is installed in the former bishop's palace, built in the 18C for Archbishop Ferdinand Maximilian de Meriadek, Prince of Rohan. The building marks the introduction of neo-Classicism to France.
The **main courtyard** is separated from the street by an arcaded gateway. The opposite side is bounded by the façade of the palace, its rather solemn lines enlivened by a projecting central section and corner pavilions.
Inside, the most notable features are the state staircase, the salons with their fine 18C panelling, and a banqueting hall decorated with *grisailles* by Lacour.
The rear elevation of the palace overlooks a garden bordered on two sides by galleries transformed into a museum.

★ **Musée des Arts décoratifs** (**DY M²**) ⊙ – The Lalande mansion which houses the Museum of Decorative Arts was designed by Laclotte in 1779; it has tall slate roofs and dormer windows. The dependencies on the left are reserved for temporary exhibitions.
A tour of the right wing begins with the Jeanvrot Collection (items relating to the lives of the last kings of France), presented in a setting furnished in 19C fashion, and continues through rooms of elegant woodwork and fine furniture to reveal a wide range of decorative arts : splendid 18C decanters and flasks, and a display of late 17C and early 18C apothecary's pots and jars in the first-floor Yellow Room; double-curved cabriolet chairs – a Bordeaux speciality – and sparkling 16C and 17C glassware in the Green Room with its *rocaille* panels; an opulently-appointed early 19C bourgeois interior, with a Louis XVI black marble clock and furniture of Cuban mahogany, in the Salon Bordelais. A stone staircase with fine wrought-iron banisters leads to the second floor where superb examples of *faïence* (glazed and decorated earthenware) from France and elsewhere may be viewed. Ornamental ironwork and items typifying the locksmith's craft are displayed on the attic floor.

★★ **Musée des Beaux-Arts** (**DY M³**) ⊙ – The Fine Arts Museum in the north gallery bordering the gardens of City Hall contains a fine collection of 15C to 20C paintings which are exhibited in rotation.
Among works of the Italian Renaissance are *The Virgin Adoring the Christ Child* by Ortolano and, most notably, Titian's *Tarquin and Lucretia* and *Penitent Magdalene*. The wide range of 17C canvases include a Baroque *Virgin and Child* by Pietro da Cortona; Flemish paintings such as Rubens' *Martyrdom of St George* and the joyful *Wedding Dance* by Jan 'Velvet' Brueghel; Dutch works including *The Lute Player* by Ter Brugghen, Van Goyen's impressive *Oak Struck by Lightning,* and David de Heem's 1636 *Still Life.*
An elegant *Portrait of Princess Louise of Orange-Nassau* by Tischbein and *The Embarkment of the Galley-Slaves* by Magnasco are among the 18C exhibits.
The Delacroix *Ruins of Missolonghi* (1826) and Isabey's maritime disaster, *Fire Aboard the Steamer Austria,* are typical of the emotionally-charged paintings of the Romantic Movement.
19C works by landscape painters of the Barbizon School and artists from Bordeaux include Corot's graceful pastoral scene of *Diana Bathing; On the Banks of the Oise* by Daubigny; the Bordeaux-born Diaz de la Peña's *Forest of Fontainebleau; Landscape of the Landes* by Auguin and Auguste Bonheur's *Return from the Fair.*
The beginnings of Impressionism are visible in Henri Martin's *View of St-Cirq-Lapopie,* the snow-covered landscapes of Luigi Noir *(La Porte des Lilas),* Renoir's luminous *Cagnes Landscape,* and *Low Tide at Étaples* by Eugène Boudin.
Among the 20C canvases *Notre-Dame Church, Bordeaux* by the Austrian Ex-pres-sionist Kokoschka is of particular note, as is *The Port, Bordeaux* and *Naples : the Sailing Boat* by Albert Marquet. In *Entrance to the Tidal Basin in Bordeaux,* the local artist André Lhote integrated concepts of Cubism into figurative painting.
The **Galerie des Beaux-Arts** ⊙ in nearby Place du Colonel-Raynal holds temporary exhibitions of works of Fine Art.

★★ **Musée d'Aquitaine** (**DY M⁴**) ⊙ – *20 Cours Pasteur.* This regional museum, housed in the former Literature and Science Faculty and laid out on two levels, traces the life of Aquitaine Man from prehistoric times to the present day.

Level 2 – The collections in the pre-history section contain precious relics of the arts and crafts practised by the hunters of the Stone Age. Among these is the famous "Venus with a Horn" (20 000 BC) from the Great Grotto at Laussel, and the bison from the Cap Blanc grotto (Middle Magdalenian Age). A display of axes unearthed in the Médoc region illustrates the variety of tools fashioned by the metallurgists of the Bronze Age (4 000-2 700 BC). Iron Age spoils include funerary items (urns, jewellery, weapons) discovered in the Gironde burial grounds or Pyrenean tumuli, and the prestigious **Tayac Treasure** – a quantity of gold artefacts comprising coins, small ingots and a remarkable torque (necklace or collar) which dates from the 2C BC.
In the Gallo-Roman section, which includes an important group of inscriptions (note the poignant funeral stone of the child Laetus), aspects of day-to-day religious and economic life in the Aquitaine provincial capital are illustrated through ceramics,

glassware, mosaics and fragments of cornices and low-reliefs grouped around a reconstruction of part of Burdigala's ancient ramparts. Of particular note are a grey Pyrenean marble altar, an imperious **statue of Hercules** in bronze, and the **Garonne Treasure** which comprises 4 000 orichalque (bronze alloy) coins bearing the effigies of emperors from Claudius to Antonin the Pious.
Early Christian times and the Middle Ages are evoked by grey marble and limestone sarcophagi and mosaics, including a 4C representation of *The Holy Sepulchre*. Excavations and public works in the city have uncovered significant pieces, which have been added to the collections on Anglo-Gascon Aquitaine during the medieval period : Romanesque capitals from St Andrew's Cathedral, 14C English alabaster, a Flamboyant Gothic rose window from the Carmelite monastery. Restored to the French, Guyenne became in the 16C the cradle of Humanism under Montaigne *(qv)* : the museum displays armorial bearings from the former Feuillants (Cistercians') monastery, and an imposing cenotaph.

Level 3 – Exhibits relating to Aquitaine in general and the city of Bordeaux in particular cover the period from 1715 to the present day. Bordeaux's golden age saw the development of grand urban projects and the building of splendid mansions which were luxuriously furnished (superb Bordeaux cabinet from Gayon Château; fine glassware and ceramics). Several displays focus on country life and farming in former times. The accent is always placed on the natural resources of Aquitaine, which embraces the rural landscape of Béarn, the Landes (moors) of Gascony, the Gironde and its vineyards, and of course Arcachon and the ostreiculture (oyster farming) inseparable from it. Beyond the rooms dotted with quotations from famous writers, several chambers evoke 19C Bordeaux (the port, the town, colonial trade) and modern Aquitaine.
A section on the cultures of Oceania, Africa and the world of the Eskimoes completes the museum's wide-ranging ethnographic survey.

ADDITIONAL SIGHTS

Les Chartrons District (DEX) – The name stems from a former Carthusian monastery founded here in the late 14C. The district, in the northern sector of the city centre, lies between Cours de Verdun and Quai des Chartrons, and is bounded by Cours Portal to the north. The area's heyday was during the 18C when it became fashionable for members of Bordeaux high society to build their mansions here. Today the heart of the district, which is being restored to its former glory, has become the centre of the city's antiques trade. The nearby Cité Mondiale du Vin provides a permanent exhibition and market-place for wine traders.
The Chartrons area is bordered to the south by **Cours X-Arnozan** – formerly known simply as *le pavé* (the cobbled street) – which reflects the wealth of the great merchant and wine-growing families of the 1770s, who had sumptuous town houses built conveniently close to but removed from the noisy bustle of the port. Such private projects, independent of any overall town planning, nevertheless combined to form an architectural ensemble of remarkable unity. The three-storey Classical façades have arches at ground level; above, squinches support magnificent **balconies★** with ornamental wrought-iron railings.

Musée des Chartrons (**BU** M^{6}) ⏲ – *41 Rue Borie, just north of Cours de Verdun (use Rue Notre-Dame).* The small museum, which traces the history of the maritime wine trade, occupies part of a lavishly-appointed wine-merchant's home, built *c*1720 for an Irish dealer called Francis Burke; it is the only house in the district to have its store-rooms and bottling plant above street level. An elegant staircase with a wrought-iron balustrade leads to the *"plancher"* (floor) – a name customarily used in wine-cellars to designate the sector where bottles are packed. Here the evolution of bottling, labelling and packaging techniques is followed alongside the developments in the wine trade. Many different types of bottles, flasks, jars, stencils and lithographed labels are on view.

F. Delpech

"La Maison" by Jean-Pierre Reynaud, Musée d'Art Contemporain.

★ **Musée d'Art Contemporain** (**DEX M**[7]) ⓥ – *Entrance at 7 Rue Ferrère.* The former **Lainé warehouse**★★, built in 1924 for storing goods imported from the French colonies, has been successfully remodelled into a Museum of Contemporary Arts. It houses the collections of the Centre d'Arts Plastiques Contemporains de Bordeaux (CAPC), which are particularly strong on works from the 1960s and 1970s; these are displayed thematically and in rotation.
Inside, a tall, twin-aisled central section runs the length of the building; it is flanked by side aisles, each separated into three storeys, and the components are rhythmically linked by great, semicircular arches. The huge amount of space available allows even the largest exhibitions to be mounted here, and the biggest individual works can be accommodated within the architecture. The building itself has had the sober character of its original structure (built of grey limestone, pale red brick and wood) further accentuated by the use of severe black metal in its conversion; the whole blends well and could be compared with the transformation of the old 19C railway terminus in Paris into the Musée d'Orsay.
The museum also functions as a cultural centre staging conferences and debates, offering guided tours on the theme of an artist or an aspect of contemporary art, holding children's workshops and showing films.

ⓥ ►► Église St-Seurin (**CX**) – 11C crypt; Site paléochrétien de St-Seurin (**CX**) – Paleo-Christian site; Palais Gallien (**CX**) – 3C amphitheatre; Musée d'Histoire Naturelle (**DX M**[5]); Église Ste-Croix (**FZ**) – Romanesque façade★ in the Saintonge style; Porte d'Aquitaine (**DZ**).

EXCURSION

Banks of the Gironde (EX) – Downstream, where the waters of the Garonne and Dordogne rivers meet, beyond the spit of land which is **Bec d'Ambès,** they flow into a majestic estuary known as the Gironde River, or the "Bordeaux Riviera". The estuary extends as far as Pointe de Grave, covering about 75km – 46 miles; at its widest point, alongside Mortagne, it spans 10km – over 6 miles.
Le Verdon, just south of Pointe de Grave, is a major shipping container port.

★ Vignoble de BORDEAUX

Michelin maps 71 folds 6 to 8 and 15 to 18, 75 folds 11 to 13, 79 folds 1 and 2 or 233 folds 37, 38 and 234 folds 2, 3, 4, 8 and 11 – Local maps pp 28, 108-109 and 111.

If the name Bordeaux signifies for some just the capital of Aquitaine, for wine-lovers all over the world it is synonymous with the best wines that man can create. The **Bordeaux Vineyards** (Vignoble de Bordeaux) from which this nectar is drawn are the subject of a number of **guided tours** ⓥ.

Distribution of the vineyards – The Bordeaux wine-producing area extends over 135 000ha – 520sq miles of the Garonne and the Dordogne valleys throughout the *département* of Gironde. Between Bordeaux and Pointe de Grave, parallel to the west bank of the Gironde estuary, is the Médoc, an undulating plain entirely planted with vines. Further inland, between Agen and Bordeaux, the waters of the Garonne flow powerfully across another plain and then, after the town of Langon, wind between terraced hillsides covered with vines.
The river could have transformed the Agen-Langon sector of its valley into an enormous lake, the rains and snows falling on the Massif Central frequently resulting in ruinous floods; in fact it was content to lay down a tiered series of pebble and gravel beds, the stream-rounded stones charting successive variations of its course throughout the geological eras. Here the towns and villages have withdrawn from the flat, alluvial valley floor and installed themselves either on these terraces or on the hillsides above. Magnificent poplar groves mark the course of the Garonne; the fields on either side are rich with wheat, maize, fodder crops, tobacco, fruit trees and early vegetables. Here and there the valley – sometimes 20km – 12 miles across – shelters a large farm; the farms, known locally as *bordes,* usually have pigeon lofts. Downstream from Langon the valley narrows and the vines appear. They are planted as densely on the steep limestone slopes of the east bank as they are on the gentler relief of the west bank.

CÔTES DE BORDEAUX

From Langon to Bordeaux *54km – 34 miles : allow 3 hours.*

Langon – The town is a local administrative, commercial and gastronomic centre, an important market for the wines of Bordeaux and an excursion centre for trips to the Garonne Valley and Entre-Deux-Mers in the north, the Sauternes region and the Bazadais in the south.
Leaving Langon, cross the Garonne via the new bridge – from which there is a pretty view of the town – and head for St-Macaire.

St-Macaire – This small, medieval town of dark, narrow streets perched on a rock above the river has town walls which date back to the 12C when the town was founded; it has 15C machicolations. **Église St-Sauveur** ⓥ is a huge, imposing church with an unusual trefoil-shaped Romanesque apse. Other features include the 13C murals by the chancel; the Gothic nave and polygonal belfry; the 13C porch crowned by a Flamboyant Gothic rose window. A 13C priory and its cloisters stand nearby.

Verdelais – The church here, **Basilique Notre-Dame** ⓥ, is an important pilgrimage destination; worshippers come to venerate the 14C wooden statue of the Virgin who is invoked in particular against drownings and for healing paralytics.

M. Guillard/SCOPE

Lafite-Rothschild barrel store.

The cemetery of this small town contains the tomb of the painter **Henri de Toulouse-Lautrec** (1864-1901).
The road crosses the vine-covered hillocks of a district producing fortified white wines. In this area the "châteaux" are hidden in clumps of trees; there are views of Ste-Croix (in the foreground), the valley of the Garonne and the distant forest of the Landes.

★ **Ste-Croix-du-Mont** – This village is noted for its group of strange **grottoes**★ hollowed from a thick fossilized oyster bed laid down by the ocean in the Tertiary era; it also offers far-reaching **views** towards the Pyrenees.

After Ste-Croix-du-Mont, take D 10 north to Loupiac.

Loupiac – Loupiac, famous for its white wines, is built on a picturesque site which was already a small town in Roman times. The Latin poet Ausonius lived in the neighbourhood.
The route continues along the foot of the limestone slopes planted with the vines producing the Premières Côtes de Bordeaux *appellation* (white, red and "clairet" wines).

Cadillac – The town, originally a *bastide (qv)* founded in 1280, is situated on the right bank of the Garonne; it is known for its strong, sweet white wines. The remains of the 14C town walls are still visible. The austere **Château** ⊙ (built 1589-1620 for the Duc d'Épernon, wrecked during the Revolution and later rebuilt) stands within its own defensive walls with bastions at the corners. Inside, there are enormous rooms with coffered ceilings and monumental, richly carved and decorated marble fireplaces. The 17C tapestries relating the history of Henri III were woven in the huge vaulted basement.

Rions – This small fortified town is entered via the 14C Porte du Lhyan, which has preserved all its original defensive features : machicolations, guard-rooms on either side, grooves guiding the portcullis, an *assommoir* (a platform from which objects could be dropped on attackers) etc.

Château de Langoiran ⊙ – All that remains of this 13C castle is a ruined defensive perimeter and an imposing circular keep.

At Langoiran turn right and head for the zoo.

Parc Zoologique ⊙ – This zoo in a pleasant, tree-shaded site *(picnic areas and children's games)* has an interesting collection of birds of prey and, particularly, of snakes (more than 50 species). Smaller members of the wildcat family, monkeys, and various types of bird can also be seen.

Bouliac – The main Bordeaux television transmitter has been installed here because the town is sited high up on a hill. From the terrace of the 12C church there are views of the Garonne Valley and the city.

Floirac – From the public gardens of the town, on the corner of D 10 and the street climbing to the church, there is a fine view of the chateau built against a cliff covered in greenery, surrounded by elegant parasol pines and flower-bordered, velvet lawns. On the high ground opposite the church – the Romanesque apse of which can best be appreciated from the cemetery – is the Bordeaux-Floirac **Astronomical Observatory** ⊙. There is an attractive view of Bordeaux, the Garonne and the Graves district from the observatory terrace.

★★★ **Bordeaux** – *2 days. See Bordeaux.*

St-Julien – This is one of the better known names of the Médoc. The *terroir* includes such famous Châteaux as Lagrange, Léoville, Beaucaillou, Talbot – after the English general who lost at Castillon-la-Bataille – and Gruaud-Larose (the proprietor of which, it is said, used to hoist upon the Château tower a different coloured flag to signal the quality – excellent or otherwise – of each year's vintage).

Pauillac – Pauillac is a riverside town, a port with fine quays equipped to receive cruise liners. It is known above all, however, as an important centre of the wine trade, honoured by such famous vineyards as Château Lafite-Rothschild, Château Latour and Château Mouton-Rothschild. There is also a wine cooperative, La Rose Pauillac, the oldest in the Médoc.

★ **Château Mouton-Rothschild** Ⓥ – At the heart of the vineyards above Pauillac rises Château Mouton-Rothschild, one of the most exalted names of the Médoc; its wine was classed *Premier Cru* in 1973. The **chais**★ are open to the public.
The superbly furnished reception hall of the château is embellished with paintings and sculptures on themes of wines and the vine; the banqueting hall beyond is hung with a magnificent 16C tapestry illustrating the *vendanges.* Also on view is an interesting collection of wine labels commissioned from Braque, Dali, Masson, Carzou, Villon and other "modern artists". The tour finishes at the *Grand Chai,* where the hogsheads of the most recent vintage are stored, and the cellars in which the bottles of the precious wine, thousands upon thousands of them, ageing and aged, are racked.
Another series of very old cellars has been transformed into a **museum**★★. It contains an extraordinary selection of paintings, sculpture, tapestries, ceramics, glasswork etc celebrating the subject of wine and its production; it includes precious stones and a dazzling collection of 16C and 17C gold plate. Among the contemporary pieces note the fine work by the American sculptor Lippold.

Château Lafite-Rothschild Ⓥ – This is perhaps the most famous of the *Premier Grands Crus* of the Médoc. Among the treasured bottles of wine stored in the château's impregnable cellars are some dating back to 1811. The name Lafite corresponds to the Gascon term *La Hite* (originally derived from the Latin *Petra Ficta* = carved stone) and was used initially because the Château was built on a small rise. The terrace on which it stands is planted with fine cedar trees and bordered by an elegant Louis XIV balustrade. It has belonged to the Rothschild family since the Second Empire (1868).
Beyond Château Lafite, on the right-hand side of D2, a curious pagoda-like silhouette appears; this is the 19C **Château Cos d'Estournel,** a replica of the palace owned by the Sultan of Zanzibar with whom the proprietor of this estate once had business dealings.

Turn right (D 2) to St-Estèphe.

St-Estèphe – The small town, clustered around its church, rises like an island in a sea of vines. The wines sold under its name, which include Château Montrose, are much prized by lovers of claret. From the small port on the Gironde, east of the town, the view includes the slopes around Blaye which was, in prehistoric times, the furthest limit of the estuary, and a stretch of marshland on the far side of the water.

Follow minor roads west.

Vertheuil – The 11C Romanesque church, modified in the 15C, is a former abbey church which was once, evidently, of some importance : it has two belltowers, three aisles, and a chancel with an ambulatory and radiating chapels. On the north wall are the remains of a handsome Romanesque doorway with covings decorated with figures (peasants pruning vines, the Old Men of the Apocalypse).
The interior, with its 15C ribbed vaulting and its aisles almost as tall as the nave, is reminiscent of the Poitou style *(qv).* In the chancel, where the vaulting is reinforced by radiating ribs, there are stalls carved with scenes from monastic life, and a suspended gallery, both dating from the 15C. The unusual ambulatory is roofed with a series of transverse barrel vaults. In the nave stands the 15C font, carved from a single stone block.
Impressive 18C buildings remain in the grounds of the old abbey, along with traces of the Gothic cloisters. The village is overlooked by the (restored) 12C keep of a ruined castle.

Turn south along D 104.

St-Laurent-Médoc – The church in this small town shows English influences in the square ground-plan of its Gothic belfry-porch, the parapet and the steeple decorated with crockets.

Continue south.

Moulis-en-Médoc – The Romanesque church here was slightly altered during the Gothic period, the south apsidal chapel being replaced by a round turret enclosing a spiral stairway that led to a belfry with a strong-room. At the angles of the transept crossing, the columns supporting the church tower had at one time to be reinforced, thereby reducing the width of the supporting arches. The remarkable apse has carved modillions and blind arcades on the outside, and blind arcades in the interior, their capitals naively carved with historiated cats and birds; the fourth on the left (Tobias carrying the fish whose venom will cure his father's blindness) is especially noteworthy. The *bénitier* (stoup or font) outside the church, incorporated into the façade, was reserved – according to local history – for lepers.
The wines of Moulis have become well known through the Grand-Poujeaux *domaine.*

Castelnau-de-Médoc – Three features of particular interest distinguish the church in Castelnau : a stained-glass Renaissance window portraying the Crucifixion, a wood carving dating from 1736 representing the Pentecost, and a 14C alabaster low-relief of the Holy Trinity, which hangs above the font.

Return to Bordeaux via D 1.

★★ Tumulus de BOUGON

Michelin map 68 fold 12 or 233 fold 7 – Northeast of La Mothe-St-Heray.

This important Megalithic site, parts of which date back to *c*4500 BC, lies hidden in a wood near Bougon, a village known today for its goat's cheese. The complex comprises five tumuli or barrows (ancient burial mounds), either circular or rectangular in shape, which were built by Neolithic tribes living in the neighbourhood; of the tribes' dwellings, however, little or no trace remains.

A Megalithic Necropolis – The outer faces of the barrows are constructed of concentric, drystone walls. Inside, beneath the earth roofs, are **passage graves** comprising a passageway which leads to a funerary chamber, again circular or quadrangular; its walls are formed of large upright stone slabs, and its ceiling of a horizontal stone slab laid over the uprights.
The 300 or so skeletons found in these chambers were grouped together, in limited numbers, confirming that the barrows were designed as collective burial places, though reserved nevertheless for important members of the tribe.
In addition to their function as burial places, they seem also to have served as places of worship, which would make this group one of the oldest surviving sanctuaries in the world.
The site was abandoned *c*2000 BC.

TOUR ⌚ *About 1 hour*

Tumulus A – This circular construction, the first to be discovered in modern times (1840), dates from *c*3300 BC. The funerary chamber, one of the largest known, is 7.8m – 26ft long. It is roofed with a single stone slab weighing 90 tonnes.
A smaller slab, standing vertically, divides the chamber in two. As well as the 220 skeletons here, this tumulus also yielded a rich collection of funerary objects.

Tumulus B – The shape of this barrow is elongated. The interior revealed two funerary vaults at the east end and two passage graves at the west. Shards of pottery discovered here have been dated to the middle of the fifth millennium BC, which makes this the oldest monument on the site.

Tumulus C – This circular mound is 5m – 16ft high and dates from 3500 BC. It shelters a small passage grave and also has a rectangular platform which may have been used for religious ceremonies.

Wall D – A 35m – 115ft long wall runs between Tumulus C and Tumulus E; it appears to have been designed to separate the sanctuary into two separate zones.

Tumulus E – The barrow contains an east-facing passage which leads to two chambers where bones and funerary objects dating from 4000 to 3500 BC were found. These are the oldest-known passage graves in west-central France.

Tumulus F.

Tumulus F – This, the longest enclosure (80m – 262ft), incorporates two more barrows. F2, to the north, dates from 3500 BC and has a passage grave of the type known here as *Angoumoisin* (in the Angoulême style): the passageway leads to a rectangular chamber. To the south, the chamber beyond the east-facing passage of barrow F0 (dating from *c*4000BC) contains vaulting supported by stone corbels. The sepulchres here have been restored.
West of Tumulus F are the **ditches** from which the small stones used to build the retaining walls of the barrows were extracted. The excavation was accomplished with the help of pick-axes fashioned from stag antlers, some of which have been discovered in the spoil.
A museum relating to this important site has recently opened in the hamlet nearby.

Many campsites have shops, bars, restaurants and laundries;
they may also have games rooms, tennis courts, miniature golf courses, playgrounds, swimming pools...

Consult the current edition of the Michelin Camping Caravaning France.

★ Château de La BRÈDE

Michelin map 71 fold 10 or 234 fold 7.

La Brède Castle rises on the border of the Gironde Landes *(qv)*, in the wine country of Graves, its austere lines mirrored in a moat so wide that the castle looks like a fortified island in the middle of a lake. There has been no change to the property since the days when the angular-faced but kindly figure of **Baron Montesquieu** (1689-1755), the writer and philosopher, could be seen pacing around the outer edge of the moat. Château de La Brède (*brède* in the local dialect means marsh or swamp) still belongs to his descendants today.

A country gentleman – Charles de Secondat, future Baron of Labrède and Montesquieu, was born within these castle walls in 1689. As a sign of family humility he was carried to the baptismal font by a beggarman.

Montesquieu's kinsmen were Bordeaux magistrates and he himself – mediocre by his own admission in that profession – eventually became President of the Bordeaux *Parlement.* As with Montaigne *(qv)* he had a passionate love of the countryside, withdrawing frequently to his castle, which he described as "the most peaceful and beautiful rural retreat that I know". Here he looked after his business affairs (he exported a lot of wine to England), supervised with his steward the cultivation of his vines – conversing with his staff in the local *patois* (dialect) – visited his cellars...

Montesquieu, who was by nature easy-going and even-tempered, found relaxation (again like Montaigne) in scholarship and the intellectual life. "Learning, for me," he said, "is the sovereign remedy against world-weariness; I never suffered a disappointment that could not be dispelled by an hour's reading." Two of his best-known works, *Thoughts on the Rise and Fall of the Romans* and *The Spirit of the Law* were written at the castle.

Every year the Seigneur of Labrède spent the winter in Paris, where he was welcomed by the intellectual élite of the Académie Française, to which he himself was elected in 1727. It was in the capital that he died, quite suddenly, of an attack of fever, on 10 February 1755.

TOUR ⌚ *30min*

Castle – A wide avenue laid out by Montesquieu skirts the moat and leads, indirectly, to the austere bulk of the 12C-15C Gothic castle. The original interior court-yard was transformed into a terrace during the Renaissance by levelling one section of the building.

Small bridges which link two ancient fortifications, their doorways surmounted by Latin inscriptions, cross the moat and lead to the vestibule supported by six spiral columns. From the vestibule, which contains the Baron's travelling chests, visitors pass into the salon adorned with family portraits and a fine 16C cabinet.

Montesquieu's own simple **sanctuary** remains exactly as it was when he was alive; a sculpted bust of the writer, his cane and various mementoes are among the items on view. A worn mark visible on one side of the chimneypiece was the result of Montesquieu's shoe repeatedly rubbing against it – he used to sit by the fire here and write with his papers in his lap.

His **library,** which has panelled barrel-vaulting, houses 7 000 books, several of his manuscripts and his writing desk. Each May, as part of the Bordeaux music festival *(see Calendar of Events, qv)*, concerts are held in this room.

Park – Montesquieu took a great interest in his park. He once wrote to Abbot Guasco : "It will give me such pleasure to bring you to my Labrède estate, where you will find a castle – Gothic it must be said, but set in a charming landscape, which I modelled around ideas I found in England... Here, Nature is in its nightgown, just getting out of bed."

BRESSUIRE

Pop 17 827

Michelin map 67 fold 17 or 232 folds 43, 44.
Town plan in the current Michelin Red Guide France.

Bressuire is the chief town of the Vendée *bocage* – a patchwork of farmlands criss-crossed with hedges and woods south of the River Loire. It is an important agricultural market, as attested by the huge dimensions of Place Notre-Dame, the size of the covered food market, and the *foirail* (cattle market) in which big local sales are held every Tuesday. Bressuire also produces preserved meats and school equipment.

The low-built houses here, roofed with convex tiles, cling to a hillside on the banks of the River Dolo – which becomes, downstream, the Ton, before it flows into the Argenton.

Ravages of war – The Vendée wars (1793-96) *(qv)* raged as the result of an anti-revolutionary insurrection involving Royalist-Catholic forces in southwestern districts of the Loire. The rebellion was originally provoked by a levy of 300 000 men demanded by the Convention in Paris on 23 February 1793. Bressuire at that time was under the sovereignty of the Royalist **Marquis de Lescure,** the "Saint of Poitou" and lord of Clisson; the town consequently became the headquarters of the Royalist forces. As a result it was set ablaze and attacked, on 14 March 1794, by the "Infernal Columns" of General Grignon – a former cattle merchant who kept a scrupulous tally of the number of Royalists killed by his men and who prided himself on the fact that 200 were massacred in a single day on the outskirts of Bressuire.

SIGHTS

Église Notre-Dame – The architecture of this church resembles that of sanctuaries in the Val de Loire : the single, very wide nave with Gothic vaulting but with doorways and capitals still in Romanesque style is characteristic of the 13C Plantagenet (Angevin) style *(qv)*. In addition, the huge quadrangular chancel in Flamboyant Gothic style appears also to show an Angevin influence, despite the fact that it dates from the late 15C.
The tower, conceived as a whole in the 16C, achieves a harmonious marriage between Gothic and Renaissance styles – the latter manifesting itself in the upper part. Crowned with a dome and lantern, it recalls the belfries of Tours Cathedral.
The tower rises above the town and surrounding farmlands to a height of 56m – 184ft.

Musée Municipal ⊙ – This small museum devoted to the history and culture of the region is housed in a former granary. It stands near the town hall (built in the early 19C on the site of a Franciscan monastery) in a pretty square. Inside, in a typically regional setting, the displays include collections of local faiences, and mementoes of the Vendée wars.

Château ⊙ – On the western side of the town stands the castle, now partly in ruins, which was once the headquarters of the powerful Barony of Beaumont-Bressuire. It comprises two separate enclosures punctuated by 48 semicircular towers. The outer enclosure, dating from the 13C, is *c*700m – 770yds in circumference. Following it on the left for just over 100yds, the visitor is rewarded with a romantic view of curtain walls and crumbling towers. The inner enclosure dates back to the 11C. A postern leads into the seigneurial courtyard.
The ruined 15C domestic quarters, which were burned down during the Revolution, have since been replaced with a building in the "troubadour" style *(qv)*.
There is a fine view of the castle and its defensive walls from the bridge across the River Dolo *(on the road to Cholet)*.

EXCURSIONS

Château de la Durbelière; Mauléon – *31km – 19 miles northwest on N 149.*

Château de la Durbelière – *Before Mauléon, turn right to St-Aubin.* The old 15C-17C château, now in ruins, formed part of a vast rural development. The seigneurial lodgings, surrounded by a water-filled moat, were flanked by massive square pavilions. In one of these, in 1772, **Henri de la Rochejaquelein** was born.
It was in the courtyard of this château that "Monsieur Henri", at the age of 21, rallied two thousand peasants, calling upon them to follow him to the Vendée Wars under the Royalist flag with the memorable words :

If I advance, follow me;
If I retreat, kill me;
If I die, avenge me!

In October 1793 the handsome La Rochejaquelein was created the very young Generalissimo of the Royalist-Catholic army. After the army moved into Brittany, he was killed by a Republican at Nuaillé, near Cholet, in 1794.

St-Aubin-de-Baubigné – There is a statue here in homage to La Rochejaquelein, who was buried in the church near his cousin, the Marquis de Lescure *(see above)*, head of the Vendée forces. The statue, dating from 1895, was the work of the sculptor Falguière.

La Rochejaquelein.

Mauléon – From May to October 1793 Mauléon – which at that time was called Châtillon-sur-Sèvre – was the capital of the **Vendée Militaire** *(qv)*, the area which was a stronghold of Royalist support during the Revolution. There were even "Royal Bonds" printed to correspond with the Revolution's *assignats* (banknotes).
The town now boasts a **museum** ⊙, installed next door to the town hall in the old Abbey of the Trinity. This is a fine granite building, remodelled during the 19C in Louis XIV style.
The most interesting exhibits are the eight engraved Vaux Rocks : over 200 of these stone blocks, decorated by prehistoric man with crosses, circles, stars and stylized figures, were discovered locally in the 19C. The exact date when the work was done – and by whom and for what purpose – remains a mystery.
The upper floor houses an ethnographic department.
Of Mauléon's **feudal castle** *(western end of the town)* nothing remains but the 12C entrance gateway, flanked by two towers.

★ BROUAGE

Pop 498

Michelin map 71 fold 14 or 233 fold 14.

The ramparts of Brouage, still extremely well-preserved despite being constantly assaulted by the sea winds, soar above the desolate marshland around them. Memories of lost love and lost wars haunt the old walled town now sunk into silence and fated to be no more than a memorial to the friendship between France and Quebec – note the old flags flapping in the ocean breeze.

HISTORICAL NOTES

Grandeur and decadence – In medieval times Brouage played an important commercial role : the town, sheltered by the isle of Oléron at the inner end of "the finest haven in France", was the salt capital of Europe. 8 000ha – 19 768 acres of salt-marshes provided the precious mineral which was to be refined and sent abroad – particularly to Flanders and Germany.

At some time between 1567 and 1570 a son, **Samuel de Champlain,** was born to a Protestant family living in Brouage. The boy became an expert navigator and, on the orders of King Henri IV, sailed away to colonize parts of Canada. In 1608 he left Honfleur in Normandy to found Quebec, opening up the fur trade in beaver and mink. A monument (**B**), erected in 1970, marks the place in Brouage where he was born.

During the siege of La Rochelle *(qv)* in 1628, Brouage became the arsenal of the royal army, and Cardinal Richelieu instructed the Picardy engineer Pierre d'Argencourt to rebuild the fortifications. By the time the work was finished ten years later, Champlain's birthplace, with a garrison of 6 000 men, was the most impregnable stronghold on the Atlantic coast.

At the end of the 17C Brouage entered a period of decline : the founding of Rochefort *(qv)* and the re-establishment of La Rochelle as a base removed most of the military reasons for its existence. Vauban *(qv)* nevertheless undertook to reinforce the ramparts once more, but the haven silted up, the salterns degenerated into "rot-marshes", the breeders of fever, and the garrison was reduced.

During the Revolution Brouage was used as a prison for refractory priests, most of whom soon died of disease.

Love affairs and Affairs of State – In 1659 the 21-year-old Louis XIV was in love with **Marie Mancini,** the raven-haired niece of Richelieu's successor, Cardinal Jules Mazarin. The young couple wanted to get married – but their idyll was destroyed : the Cardinal had decided that, for "Reasons of State", the King must marry the Infanta of Spain to guarantee the peace brought by the Treaty of the Pyrenees, recently signed by the two countries. Marie Mancini was sent to La Rochelle, where she heard with despair of the forthcoming marriage. From September to December that year she withdrew to Brouage, where another of her uncles was Governor, "because solitude is the only solace for my broken dreams". Mazarin subsequently allowed her to return to Paris.

Six months later, after the royal marriage in St-Jean-de-Luz *(qv)*, Louis contrived to absent himself from the official cortège returning to the capital and rode to Brouage, where he occupied the room in which Marie had stayed, pacing the ramparts in turn as he too sighed for the love he had lost.

Racine was inspired by this melancholy episode to write his tragedy *Bérénice*.

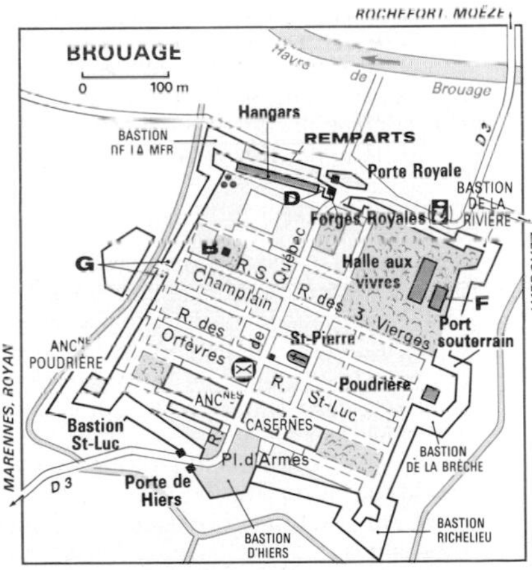

B Emplacement de la maison de Samuel de Champlain
D Escalier Mancini
F Ancienne Tonnellerie
G Courtine de la Mer

★★ RAMPARTS *45min*

Pierre d'Argencourt's ramparts (remparts) at Brouage, constructed between 1630 and 1640, are a perfect example of the art of fortification before the Vauban era. They describe an exact square measuring four times 400m – 440yds, and are protected by seven massive bastions, themselves equipped with gracefully-corbelled bartizan turrets. The walls, 13m – 43ft high, are topped by a brick parapet pierced with apertures for cannon fire. Two gateways, Porte Royale and Porte de Hiers, allow access to the enclave. The western rampart is additionally protected by a demilune detached from the curtain wall.

The northern side of the ramparts was originally the sea-front, overlooking the haven (Havre de Brouage) – today reduced to a single channel. The parade ground (Place d'Armes) was to the south, by the old military quarters (anciennes casernes). Though most of the houses in Brouage, including the Governor's mansion where Marie Mancini and Louis XIV stayed at different times, have disappeared, the military dependencies have better resisted the erosions of time.

Watchpath – It is possible to make almost an entire circuit of the town along the top of the old ramparts, now carpeted with grass. From here the neat rectilinear layout of the plan is apparent, and there is a good view across the marshes to the isles of Aix and Oléron.

Porte Royale – Tunnelling through the northern **Bastion Royal,** this gateway once opened onto the quays. On the right-hand wall of the vaulted passage, leading out, ancient graffiti showing different types of ship can be seen. The outside of the gateway is surmounted by a pediment with the armorial bearings – partly worn away – of France and Navarre. On the left of the gateway there are traces of the ironwork between the stone blocks which helped to strengthen the walls.

Forges Royales – The old blacksmiths' forges back onto Bastion Royal. In the middle of the one occupied today by the tourist information centre, an imposing furnace chimney can still be seen. Left of this forge, **Escalier Mancini** (**D**) is the stone stairway that was used by the King's beloved each time she climbed to the ramparts to dream her solitary dreams. Parallel to the steps is a ramp which was used to hoist up cannons.
To the left are the **Hangars** of Porte Royale, a row of one-time sheds, workshops and stalls, transformed today into shops. The Governor's mansion was just south of this.

►► Église St-Pierre; Halles aux Vivres – restored market; Poudrière de La Brèche – old powder magazine; Bastion St-Luc; Port souterrain – underground harbour; Ancienne tonnellerie – old cooper's workshop.

CAMBO-LES-BAINS

Pop 4 128

Michelin map 78 fold 18 or 234 fold 33. Facilities.
Town plan in the current Michelin Red Guide France.

Haut Cambo, the upper, residential district of this small spa, has groups of hotels and villas on the edge of a plateau overlooking the River Nive, while Bas Cambo, the lower town, is an old Basque village nestling in a wide curve of the river. At one time Cambo was the navigable limit for barges bringing cargoes inland from Bayonne. Further upstream, the thermal cure centre is active once again.
It is the exceptionally mild climate – plus a visit by the well-known poet and writer, Edmond Rostand (1868-1918) – which made Cambo a fashionable cure resort at the turn of the century. Arriving for the first time in the autumn of 1900, Rostand at once fell in love with Cambo and decided to live here permanently. He built a huge villa with beautiful gardens (now open to the public) overlooking the Bayonne road. Rostand was inspired by his walks in the Basque countryside around Cambo to write *Chantecler,* the successor to his *Cyrano de Bergerac.*

★ **Arnaga** ⊙ – This **villa** in the Basque-Labourdin style was built under Rostand's supervision between 1903 and 1906. It stands on a promontory which the writer transformed with formal gardens in the French manner. "It was here," said the Comtesse de Noailles, herself a poet, "that his spirit returned to Nature itself... to the tortoise-shell and jasper-coloured mountains and to the placid waters of the long, quiet Nive."
Inside the "modern-style" house, with its great Basque roof, decorative paintwork and wooden balconies, a collection of Rostand's possessions is on display : furniture, documents, the original costume designs for *Chantecler,* portraits of Rostand and Rosemonde Gérard by Pascau and Caro...

EXCURSIONS

★ **Artzamendi** – *15km – 9 miles south via D 918. Allow 3 hours.*
The road climbs out of the last cultivated bowl of the Lower Nive.

★ **Itxassou** – The cottages in this village are dispersed among cherry orchards. The rustic-looking **church★** standing alone near the River Nive has three tiers of galleries adorned with statues and turned balusters, an 18C giltwood altarpiece and a fine pulpit with decorations picked out in gold. It was here in the 17C that a young *curé,* Jean Duvergier de Hauranne, preached to the villagers; the *curé* later became the Abbot of St-Cyran, made famous by the Jansenist dispute (which opposed Papal theories of Divine Grace).

North of the village, take the road leading to the gliding school (terrain de vol à voile).

Mont Urzumu – From the viewing table, near a statue of the Virgin, there is a remarkable **panorama** of the Basque Pyrenees and the coast from Pointe Ste-Barbe to Bayonne.

Return to Itxassou and continue south.

The minor road, narrowing now, runs along the west bank of the Nive.

Pas de Roland – Park where the road widens, just beyond the parapet with a roadside Cross. Beyond the Cross there is a view down to the Pas de Roland, a pierced rock which forms a kind of gateway. The aperture was opened up, according to legend, by a kick from the horse being ridden by Roland *(qv)* when he was being pursued by the Vascons. A path leads to the site.

Turn right at Laxia; the road becomes very narrow, with steep rises and tight corners.

★ **Artzamendi** – From the approaches to the telecommunications station on this 914m – 3 000ft height near the border with Spain, the **panorama★** extends northwards towards the Lower Nive Valley, the Nivelle basin and its upland pastures, and southwards, beyond the border, to the slopes above the Bidasoa Valley.

Consult the Map of Places to Stay at the beginning of the guide to choose a suitable location.

CAP FERRET

Michelin map 78 fold 12 or map 234 fold 6 – Facilities.

The long thin promontory of Cap Ferret runs north-south at the entrance to Arcachon Lagoon *(qv)*, sheltering the narrow straits leading into the basin. The area has been developed into a seaside resort, with hotels and holiday villas scattered among the pines. It is also a centre of ostreiculture *(qv)*, with the most accessible oyster beds in the lagoon.

Lighthouse ⊙ – This landmark (rebuilt 1947) is 52m – 171ft high, with a revolving lantern which can be seen 50km – 31 miles out at sea. From the platform (258 steps) there is a fine **panorama★** embracing the whole of the peninsula, the lagoon, the straits, the open sea and Pilat Dune *(qv)*.

Plage de l'océan ⊙ – A narrow-gauge railway service operates between Bélisaire landing-stage (eastern side) and this splendid beach on the ocean side of the promontory.

Villa Algérienne – *4km – 2½ miles north.* This site, named after a building in the Moorish style which was demolished in 1965, offers a good view over the lagoon and Bird Island. The oriental influence remains in a chapel, built about 150 years ago, looking out across the sea.

D'après photo J.-D. Sudres/SCOPE

The Chapel of the Algerian Villa, Cap Ferret

★ CAUTERETS

Pop 1 201

Michelin map 85 fold 17 or 234 fold 43 – Local map p 90 – Facilities.
Town plan in the current Michelin Red Guide France.

Cauterets is one of the great Pyrenean thermal and climatic resorts, standing further into the mountain mass than any of the others. The sulphurous waters of the ten springs which bubble out here at temperatures between 36°C and 53°C (97°F and 127°F) are used by the cure centres to treat respiratory disorders; according to a local saying, however, *A Cautarès, tout que garech* (At Cauterets, you can be cured of anything). The town is a bustling summer resort, a popular excursion and mountaineering centre, and an expanding winter sports resort.
As the gateway to the central zone of the Parc National des Pyrénées *(qv)*, Cauterets is within easy reach, for the contemplative tourist, of Marcadau and the Lac de Gaube; the more sporting visitor can enjoy the Vignemale and the foaming torrents of the Cauterets, Cambasque, Gaube and Lutour valleys. The success of the town as a winter resort is due in part to its long season : the sun-drenched ski slopes are open as late as May in Le Lys Cirque, west of Cauterets, at heights of between 1 850m and 2 300m (6 070ft and 7 550ft).

Town – People have been coming to Cauterets for cures since the 10C. The original settlement was higher up the mountain slope but by the 14C it had become cramped and so local monks transferred the church, houses and baths to the present site on the plateau overlooking the torrent. Cauterets blossomed as a tourist centre following the establishment at the end of the 19C of two electrified railway links : between Gare des Œufs and La Raillère (discontinued in 1970) and between Cauterets and Pierrefitte-Nestelas (abandoned in 1949). The tall houses of the thermal district crowd the narrow streets of the torrent's east bank below Les Thermes de César (Caesar's Baths). The west bank has been developed only since 1870. It was the famous Hotel d'Angleterre (1879-1954) which gave this part of the town its fashionably "palatial" aspect, followed by the casino in its tree-shaded esplanade.
Famous visitors to the town have included Gaston Fébus, Marguerite of Navarre, Jeanne d'Albret, the Duchesse de Berry, George Sand and Chateaubriand.

★★ VALLÉES DE CAUTERETS

★★ Val de Jéret – *8km – 5 miles : about 3 hours – local map overleaf.*

Leave Cauterets by D 920, on the west bank behind the casino. After La Raillère cure centre (right), park in the official car park beyond the Pont (bridge) de Benquès.

★★ Cascade de Lutour – A footbridge spans the pool below the four separate falls, the last jumps of the waters of the Lutour Torrent before they join the Cauterets Torrent.
The road continues up the valley, narrow, steep and heavily wooded, strewn with huge boulders and splashed with the torrent's waterfalls.

★★ Cerisey, Pas de l'Ours and Boussès Cascades – These three attractive falls present very different appearances. Above the Boussès cascade the river divides around "Sarah Bernhardt's Island" *(parking in the glade)*.

★★ Pont d'Espagne – *Parking.* The road bridge offers a view of the rocky site known as "the Meeting of the Falls" (confluence of the Gaube and Marcadau Torrents).

Monument Meillon – *15min on foot Rtn. Behind the Pont d'Espagne hotel, leave the road and take a stony footpath on the right. Further on, the path branches off to the right to the monument (Parc National des Pyrénées signpost).* Through the fir trees there is a glimpse of the main falls at Pont d'Espagne and of the Vignemale (south).

★★ **Lac de Gaube** – *1½ hours on foot Rtn by footpath signposted GR10 : departure immediately downstream from Pont d'Espagne. A chairlift from Pont d'Espagne ⏲ can be used for part of this walk.* This has become almost a ritual excursion for Pyrenean enthusiasts for the past 150 years. The lake occupies an austere and beautiful site, with a view of the distant walls of the Vignemale massif where hanging glaciers are visible.

A footpath following the west bank of the river, after the inn, arrives at a view-point from which the Pique Longue of the Vignemale can be seen. At 3 298m – 10 820ft, this is the highest point of the frontier chain between the Atlantic and the Mediterranean.

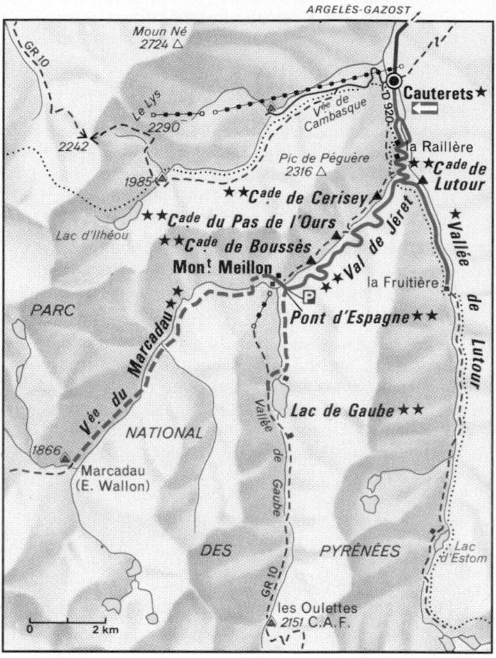

★★ **Vallée du Marcadau** – *7.5km – 4½ miles : 5 hours on foot Rtn. Local map p 90. Take the route to Pont d'Espagne and park in the car park.*

This is an easy valley for walkers and at one time was a favourite route for crossing into Spain. The track rises between an alternation of shelved meadowlands, where the limpid torrent meanders over beds of gravel, and rocky constrictions where the path climbs more steeply through mountain pinewoods. The Wallon refuge, this ramble's destination, stands at a height of 1 866m – 6 122ft. Beyond it is a cirque of pastureland, the upper hollows of which are scattered with small lakes *(exploring these is a matter of whole-day excursions).*

★ **Vallée de Lutour** – *6km – 3½ miles : local map overleaf. Take the Pont d'Espagne road only as far as the series of hairpin bends; beyond them, just before the Bains du Bois establishment, take the sharp left turn into the narrow, very steep forest road to La Fruitière.*

The track offers several glimpses, between the trees, of the upper Lutour falls, and then emerges from the forest into a tranquil pastureland with grazing herds and occasional patches of rock and scree. Here and there however the pines continue up to an altitude of 2 000m – 6 500ft.

Consult the Index to find an individual town or sight.

CELLES-SUR-BELLE

Pop 3 425

Michelin map 72 north of fold 2 or 233 fold 6 – Facilities.

The small town of Celles grew up in the shadow of the tall and sturdy belltower of an old Augustinian abbey built on a terrace above the valley of the River Belle.

The nearby **Base de Lambon** *(3km – 1½ miles north)* is a popular holiday centre offering many leisure activities and sports facilities; these include a sailing club, a lakeside beach, swimming, *pédalos,* children's games and a miniature train providing trips around the lake.

SIGHTS

Église Notre-Dame – This former abbey church is the site of a pilgrimage to the Virgin known as the *Septembresche,* which takes place on the first Sunday of each September. King Louis XI was a regular worshipper here. The church was destroyed by the Huguenots in 1568 but rebuilt a century later, in 15C style, by the architect **François Leduc.**

The Romanesque main **doorway★** of the original abbey church, visible inside the narthex, is most unusual : its multi-lobed arching, decorated with grimacing masks, betrays an oriental influence which can be seen throughout France on the pilgrims' route to Santiago de Compostela.

Inside, the church is striking for the luminosity of the nave and aisles, and for the purity of line seen in the pillars soaring towards the high, curving vaulting.
The 17C statue of Notre-Dame-de-Celles stands at the far end of the chancel.

Church doorway, Celles.

Abbaye ⓥ – *Access to the abbey via the main doorway below the church.*
Three of the presiding abbots here left their mark on history : Geoffrey d'Estissac *(qv)*, Cardinal de La Rochefoucauld, who was Louis XIII's prime minister, and the famous minister Talleyrand.
The monastic buildings and their dependencies were, like the church, the work of Leduc – whose architectural preference for the Tuscan order earned him the nickname François the Tuscan. The attractive main façade (85m – 279ft long) features Ionic columns resting against scrolled buttresses; the right wing of the building was unfortunately never completed. Inside, there is a fine staircase, the old refectory, the kitchen and a cloister gallery, all dating from the 17C. The ruins of the old parish church of St Hilaire (St Hilary), with its 12C crypt, can be seen in the abbey grounds.

EXCURSIONS

Maison du Protestantisme Poitevin – *11km – $6\frac{1}{2}$ miles north.* Michelin map 68 fold 12. *Follow D 103 to Vitré and turn right into D 108.*
This title refers to two Protestant churches, at Beaussais and La Couarde, which together form a religious centre managed by the Poitou Regional Park.

Beaussais – The **temple** ⓥ, a former Catholic church with a Romanesque oven-vaulted chancel, now houses a small Protestant museum. Panels and displays at the entrance relate to the activities of Protestants in the 20C, while those in the nave trace the history of the movement in France, with special emphasis on Poitou. A "Huguenot footpath" links Beaussais with La Couarde *(4km – $2\frac{1}{2}$ miles, details from the museum).*

Take D 10 north to La Couarde.

La Couarde – This section of the **Maison du Protestantisme Poitevin** is housed in a church consecrated in 1904. The showcases and displays concentrate on the period known as "the desert", the period of clandestinity and repression which followed the revocation of the Edict of Nantes *(qv)* in 1685. Among the exhibits are *méreaux*, secret tokens used by Huguenots at that time to identify themselves as members of the faithful. There is a reconstruction of a "Desert Assembly" (a meeting or service held in secret) with a collapsible pulpit which could be quickly dismantled and hidden. Videos *(in French)* are shown.

La CHALOSSE

Michelin map 78 folds 6, 7, 17 or 234 folds 26, 27.

Chalosse, a hilly region nestling within the great curve of the River Adour, has yet to be discovered by the crowds. Fertile patches of "wild" sand – visible in cuts and ditches – stud the region. Despite the modest aspect of the smallholdings and villages, which are in the Landes style, the agriculture is productive and well balanced.
Chalosse has a long history : it is in this region that Paleolithic man fashioned such primal masterpieces as the celebrated Lady of Brassempouy *(qv)*; later, pilgrims passed through on their way to Santiago de Compostela.
The town of Hagetmau *(qv)*, which stands at the centre of Chalosse, is a useful base for excursions. St-Sever, the one-time "city of scholars", is the departure point of a corniche road (D 32) winding above the *Barthes* (local meadows bordering the course of the Adour).

★ TOWNS AND VILLAGES IN CHALOSSE

From St-Sever to Montfort-en-Chalosse

30km – $18\frac{1}{2}$ miles : allow $2\frac{1}{2}$ hours

St-Sever – The town offers good views of the River Adour and the enormous sea of pines which covers the neighbouring Landes *(qv)*. The Romanesque abbey **church** (partly restored in the 17C and 19C) features a chancel with 6 apsidal chapels of decreasing depth, and transept arms which end in galleries resting on a single column which develops, above, into a purely decorative arcade. The marble columns of the chancel and transept were taken from the old palace of the Roman governors of Morlanne : their remarkable **capitals**★ include water-leaf (11C) and lion designs, historiated capitals *(inside the west front)* showing Herod's banquet and the beheading of John the Baptist, and a mixture of figures symbolising the

predominance of the New Testament over the Old. The sacristy leads to the cloisters, only two sides of which remain. Outside, the east end of the church is crowned with a dome and lantern, and surrounded by the Romanesque apsidal chapels which have amusing modillions.
Among the smart 18C town houses of Rue de Général-Lamarque note the old Jacobin monastery (now a cultural centre) with its late 17C brick cloisters, and the **archeological museum** ⏲ which focuses on the *Apocalypse of St-Sever*, an 11C illuminated manuscript.

Take D 32 west out of St-Sever.

Montaut – The main street of this old fortified village runs along the crest crowning the last fold of the Chalosse plateau; its charming houses look out over the plain of the Adour and the forests of the Landes. The church tower, which is also the gateway to the town, was rebuilt after the ravages perpetrated by the bands under Montgomery *(qv)*. The two altarpieces inside the church reveal interesting stylistic differences : that on the right-hand (south) side features a strict rhythm of perpendiculars, in contrast with the sinuous, flowing lines of the Baroque reredos on the left. The former dates from the early 17C, the latter from the 18C.

Continue west.

Between Montaut and Mugron there are frequent views of the rear of the plateau, the promontories dropping down in succession towards the Adour and the *pignada* (a local term for the forest of maritime pines).

Mugron – This small town is the "county town" of the region and is heavily involved in the development of agriculture in the Chalosse (wine co-operative, grain silos). At the time of the Intendants *(qv)*, the small port on the Adour nearby used to export the local wine as far as Holland. From the public gardens around the town hall, once the hillside home of a rich bourgeois family, there are fine **views★** of the valley with its stands of poplars, the stone bridge over the Adour, the neighbouring smallholdings and the old-rose rooftops of the town.

Continue west on D 10.

Laurède – The most interesting feature in this village is the **Maison Capcazalière Peyne★** ⏲ (the dialect word *capcazal* signifies a property inhabited since ancient times) : this 17C house in typical Chalosse style has preserved much of its charm. The interior is adorned with a fine balustraded staircase, good provincial furniture and Louis XIV woodwork, and tall chimneypieces of carved stone.
The village **church** boasts a striking Baroque interior. Of particular note are the monumental high altar surmounted by a baldaquin, the pulpit and lectern, and the woodwork in the sacristy.

Continue west along D 10, passing the 17C Poyanne Château (right); turn left into D 7 to Montfort.

Montfort-en-Chalosse – The nucleus of this small town is a height crisscrossed by narrow lanes and steep, stepped streets. The **Musée de la Chalosse** ⏲ and the nearby Médiathèque are both devoted to country life and the economy of this pleasant rural region.

★ CHARROUX — Pop 1 428

Michelin map 72 fold 4 or 233 fold 19.

Charroux, lying 50km – 31 miles south of Poitiers in a valley on the east bank of the Charente, grew up around a Benedictine abbey dedicated to St Saviour, much of which is now in ruins. A 15C wooden hall stands in the town square.

HISTORICAL NOTES

Holy relics : a source of wealth – The success of St Saviour's Abbey was assured from the start because the original monks were under the patronage of Charlemagne himself. Ecclesiastical Councils were held here from time to time, one of which, in 989, laid the foundations for "the Truce of God". The abbey church was consecrated by Pope Urbain II in 1096.
The abbey, the guardian of priceless relics (flesh and blood of Jesus Christ, parts of the True Cross), became the object of a pilgrimage so important that at one time 25 000 of the faithful would visit it each June. Notables who made the pilgrimage enriched the treasury with gifts of money and magnificent works of art; eventually the abbey possessions stretched as far as England.

Decline – The Wars of Religion in the 16C put an end to the prosperity : the abbey was sacked. In 1762 its function was suppressed altogether and by the beginning of the 19C over half of it had been demolished. The preservation of what remained is due to Mérimée, the Inspector-General of Historic Monuments under the Second Empire. Excavations and restoration work carried out between 1946 and 1953 have exposed the ground plan of the abbey church and revealed the crypt; the cloisters have been restored. Building works in the chapter-house led to the discovery of sarcophagi containing a fine collection of funerary items.

★ ABBAYE ST-SAUVEUR ⏲ *1 hour*

Abbey church – The ground plan here allied the traditional Latin cross outline with the circular design of the Holy Sepulchre church in Jerusalem. The church comprises a narthex, a nave, a transept with side chapels, and an apse with radiating chapels. In the centre of the transept crossing was a circular "sanctuary" surrounded by three concentric aisles, positioned above a crypt. It was surmounted by a tall tower (still standing). The building as a whole, which was 126m – 413ft long, suggested certain early oriental churches.

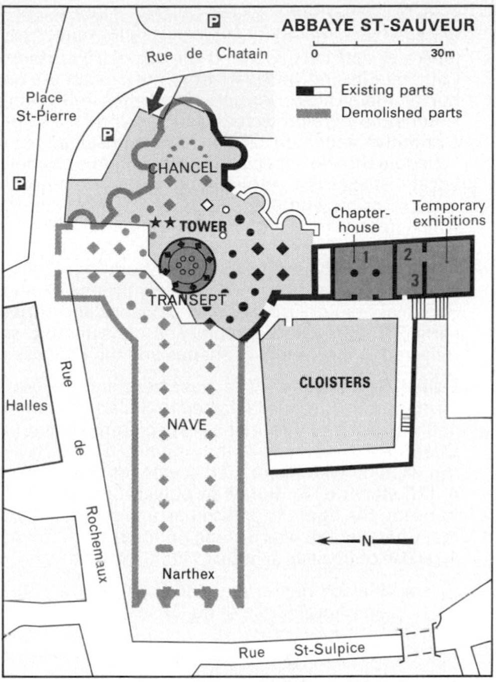

The church was built in the Poitou Romanesque style *(qv)* with the exception of the west front which was Gothic. Several elements from this façade are incorporated in the walls of a house nearby.
The polygonal **tower★★** dates from the 11C and was in the exact centre of the church. It stands like a gigantic canopy above the rotunda sheltering the high altar, which itself surmounts the crypt in which the sacred relics were displayed. The first two storeys of the tower, which are hollowed out, were actually within the church; the upper part was probably crowned by a spire.

Cloisters – The cloisters – today open to the sky and extensively plundered – were reconstructed in the 15C under the direction of Abbé Chaperon, whose heraldic arms, three copes, are reproduced on the capitals of the columns in the chapter-house.

Chapter-house – The large, impressive building houses a number of excellent 13C **sculptures★★** which once adorned the main doorway of the west front. These include *Christ in Judgement* (**1**), originally on the tympanum, and several figures decorating the arching : kings, prophets, past abbots of Charroux, and those delightful statuettes of *The Wise and Foolish Virgins* (**2**) so often seen in the Poitou region. These works are attributed to the sculptor responsible for the doorways of the cathedral in Poitiers.

★ **Treasury** (**3**) – The treasury houses a fine collection of Romanesque pastoral staffs and pieces by Gothic goldsmiths and silversmiths. The staffs, either T-shaped or in the form of a crook, are fashioned from ivory and were discovered in the abbots' tombs excavated beneath the chapter-house. Two magnificently worked silver-gilt reliquaries stand out among the gold and silver plate : one, dating from the 13C, was undoubtedly used as a ciborium or pyxide (a vessel for conveying the Host to communicants who were sick); the other, made in Venice in the 14C, is cylindrical, with sides of near-transparent horn supported by figures of the four Evangelists. The reliquary is closed by a lid bordered with seven miniature gables.

CHÂTELLERAULT

Pop 34 678

Michelin map 68 fold 4 or 232 fold 47.
Town plan in the current Michelin Red Guide France.

The city which has developed on the banks of the River Vienne at the upper limit of its navigable reach owes its name to Ayraud, Vicomte of Poitou, who built a château on the site in the 10C.
The growth of the modest local metal-working trade – concentrated since the 13C on the banks of the River Clain, south of Châtellerault – led to the establishment of a cutlery industry in the city in the 18C. Later (1820) the metallurgy business expanded into an arsenal and arms manufactory safely removed from France's frontiers. The latter, which operated until 1968, played an important role in the economic success of Châtellerault; since then, other companies have established themselves in the nearby industrial zones.

SIGHTS

Pont Henri-IV – The bridge (144m – 472ft long and 21m – 69ft wide) was built between 1575 and 1611 by Charles Androuet du Cerceau, a member of a famous family of architects. Two massive slate-roofed towers, once linked by a central block, protected the entrance to the west end – a wise precaution so soon after the Wars of Religion *(qv)*. In the middle of the bridge, on the upstream side, a cross from which two anchors hang is a reminder of the time when river transport inland thrived and was all-important. Such traffic continued until the mid-19C.

Musée Municipal ⌚ – *Rue Sully.* The museum stands at the far end of a splendid courtyard, in the Hôtel Sully, a mansion built in the 17C by Androuet du Cerceau. Collections of weapons, knives, and 17C to 19C porcelain and earthenwares are on

view, together with carved wooden chair backs, sculptures, paintings and other works of art. One room is devoted to Rudolph Salis (1851-97) who was born in Châtellerault and later founded the famous Parisian cabaret, Le Chat Noir (The Black Cat) : menus and wine lists from the cabaret are on display with posters and a number of metal shadowgraph silhouettes representing an army on the march (the silhouettes were projected in succession on a screen, producing an effect rather like a primitive animated cartoon. Salis himself added a spoken commentary; one of his "shadow theatre" specialities was an entire Napoleonic saga).
Local history from prehistoric times to the present day is traced in another department : prints and engravings of Châtellerault; bills from coaching inns, some of which itemize food and lodging for the traveller's horse.
Documents, photos and explanatory tableaux in a section on the Acadians *(qv)* follow their odyssey to the New World and back, and examine the economic and cultural role played by Acadia (New Brunswick and Nova Scotia) today.
Regional headdresses, bonnets, shawls and christening robes from the 18C to the early 20C can also be seen. The considerable skill of the local linen workers is reflected in the variety of shapes and the richness of the embroidery.

Église St-Jacques – The west front and the two neo-Romanesque towers of this former priory church dedicated to St James date only from the 19C, but the transept and the east end with its buttress-columns are original (12C-13C).
Quadripartite vaulting in the Angevin Gothic style roofs the nave; lierne and tierceron vaulting with historiated keystones covers the south side chapel.
A 17C statue of St James in polychrome wood stands in the northern arm of the transept; the figure is dressed as a pilgrim on the way to Compostela, emphasizing that Châtellerault was a stage on the road to Santiago (St James').
A **carillon** of 52 bells is housed in the north tower.

⊙ ►► Maison Descartes – 16C family home of the philosopher; Musée de la Moto, de l'Automobile et du Cycle – Car, motorbike and cycle museum.

★ CHAUVIGNY — Pop 6 665

Michelin map 68 folds 14, 15 or 233 fold 9 – Facilities.

Chauvigny, a much-battlemented town in the Vienne Valley, developed as a trade and industrial centre specializing in the manufacture of porcelain wares. Traditional exploitation of local freestone – a fine-grained limestone with regular cleavage – has also remained important.

★ UPPER TOWN ⊙ *45min*

The upper town (ville haute), standing on a spur, is itself surmounted by the jagged ruins of forts and castles dominated by the elegant belfry of St Peter's Church.

Château baronnial – This 11C baronial castle, built when the Bishops of Poitiers were also seigneurs of Chauvigny, in turn comprises both an upper part – with an enormous keep – and a lower part surrounded by ramparts revealing traces of the Château Neuf (New Castle) ruins.

Château d'Harcourt – The castle originally belonged to the Vicomtes of Châtellerault, who had it built between the 13C and 15C, on the crest of the promontory. Massive ramparts with a fortified entrance gate still exist.

★ **Église St-Pierre** – The construction of this former collegiate church, founded by the seigneurs of Chauvigny, started in the 11C with the building of the apse and was completed in the following century by the erection of the nave. The style is Romanesque; the building material a fine grey stone. There are two different levels of open-work in the square belfry. The east end, richly decorated with sculptures, is notable for the pleasing proportions of the apse and chapels.
The interior has unfortunately suffered from over-enthusiastic 19C repainting. The capitals of the columns supporting the broken-barrel vaults in the nave are decorated with palm leaf designs. The **capitals in the chancel**★★ are particularly interesting, embracing a fascinating selection of biblical, evangelical and mythical scenes : the Annunciation, the Adoration of the Magi, the Weighing of Souls, the Arrival of the Shepherds, the Temptation and other religious subjects alternate with an extraordinary phantasmagoria of winged monsters, sphinxes, sirens and demons subjecting resigned humans to the worst possible torments. These tableaux, in a highly stylized but extremely expressive manner, are the products of an artistic imagination still haunted by the terrors of the first millennium.

Donjon Gouzon – *Just north of the church.* This keep is all that remains of a castle acquired in the late 13C by the Gouzon family and subsequently (1335) bought by Bishop Fort of Aux. The square keep was originally supported by rectangular buttresses, which were later surmounted by rounded buttresses. Now restored, the keep is to house a national museum of Industrial Archeology.

⊙ ►► Église Notre-Dame – 14C fresco; St-Pierre-les-Églises (2km – 1 mile south) – Pre-Romanesque church with 9C-10C frescoes.

Admission times and charges for the sights described are listed at the end of the guide.
Every sight for which there are times and charges is identified by the symbol ⊙ in the Sights section of the guide.

CIVAUX Pop 682

Michelin map 68 folds 14, 15 or 233 fold 9.

The number of rare archeological treasures found around Civaux confirms the importance of this modest village in relation to the spread of Christianity in the Poitou region.

SIGHTS

★ **Nécropole Mérovingienne** – This ancient burial ground dates from Merovingian times (AD *c*500-750) when the Frankish dynasty founded by Clovis reigned over Gaul and Germany. The boundaries of the site occupied by the cemetery today, bordered by carved stone sarcophagi, are less than 350 years old and contain only a fraction of the original necropolis, which included over 15 000 graves and covered an area of almost 3ha – 7½ acres. The remaining sarcophagi, arranged on several different levels, are now confined to a small rectangle.
The origin of the burial ground remains a mystery. It is thought that the graves might have been those of warriors who fell in a battle between Clovis and Alaric, the King of the Visigoths, or perhaps they were the tombs of penitents who had expressed a wish to be buried at the place of their conversion.
A ruined chapel, dedicated to St Catherine, had been remodelled several times since the Romanesque period.

Musée archéologique ⊙ – This small museum not far from the cemetery contains exhibits from the Merovingian and Gallo-Roman eras (stelae, tombstones, ceramics, funerary items). Of special interest are the reconstructions of various types of grave discovered in the necropolis : with and without coffins, straight into the earth or surrounded by a drystone frame, in sarcophagi or in simple cairns.

Église St-Gervais et St-Protais – The church was built on the site of a Roman temple, in the ruins of which a loggia transformed into a baptistery can still be seen. The apse, which dates from the 4C, has a stone belfry adorned with two tiers of blind arcading. In the barrel-vaulted nave (10C), the cylindrical columns are topped by **historiated capitals** embodying themes which reflect fears of hell and damnation. Sealed into the south wall of the apse is a 4C funerary stone engraved with the Greek letters Alpha and Omega on either side of a *Chrisme* (a monogram formed from the first two letters of the Greek word for Christ).

CLISSON Pop 5 495

Michelin map 67 fold 4 or 232 fold 29.

Clisson stands on a picturesque **site**★ at the convergence of the River Moine and the Sèvre Nantaise. In 1794 the "Infernal Columns" *(qv)* of the Republicans attacked the town and set it ablaze so savagely that by the end of the Revolution virtually every inhabitant had fled. In the early years of the 19C Clisson rose Phoenix-like from its ashes, largely owing to the enthusiasm of the Brothers Cacault, who were natives of nearby Nantes, and the sculptor Frédéric Lemot : they had spent some time in Italy, and under their influence the restored town was progressively "Italianized". Today, houses in Clisson itself and a number of watermills and small factories in the neighbourhood – recognizable by their brick dressed, rounded-arch windows – are evidence of that architectural trend, the first examples of which appeared in Garenne-Lemot park *(see below)*.

OLD TOWN *1½ hours*

Bridges – From the viaduct carrying route N 149 across the Moine there is an attractive view of the castle, the river with its green banks, and the 15C Pont St-Antoine (St Anthony's Bridge). From this second bridge, spanning the Sèvre, there is an equally picturesque vista of the river overlooked by the great bulk of the castle.

Les Halles – The covered market originated in the 15C, though the fine timber framework was fashioned from oak in the 17C and 18C.

Château ⊙ – The ruins rise impressively above the Sèvre Nantaise. The castle, sited on the border of the Duchy of Brittany, was designed to repel attacks from both Anjou and Poitou. The first overlords were the Sires of Clisson, among them the famous Constable, Olivier de Clisson (1336-1407) *(see Michelin Green Guide Brittany)*. In 1420 the castle was confiscated by the Duc de Bretagne.
An earlier castle had been built in the 11C and 12C. This was enclosed within a polygonal structure flanked by towers in the 13C. A keep, also polygonal, was added in the 14C (a section of wall topped by machicolations still exists). The kitchens, the chapel and the seigneur's living quarters also date from the 14C.
The Duc de Bretagne François II modernized the fortifications in the 15C with the addition of a second enclave which included a prison and a huge gateway; this new entrance was protected by a drawbridge, replacing the ancient barbican. Finally, fearing an attack by the Catholic League, the seigneurs strengthened the defences still further in the 16C by building three new bastions.
In the middle of the central courtyard stands a well into which, in 1794, the Republicans flung 18 citizens of Clisson who had sought refuge in the castle.

LA GARENNE-LEMOT ⊙ $1\frac{1}{2}$ *hours – Access via N 149.*

In 1805 Frédéric Lemot acquired the Bois de la Garenne, a wood just southeast of Clisson, and employed the architect Mathurin Crucy to carry out a number of projects in the Italian style.
In the middle of the park stands the **Villa Lemot,** built in neo-classical style and fronted by a semicircular colonnade recalling the famous Bernini columns in front of St Peter's in Rome. The villa is now the home of a contemporary arts organization and the venue of art exhibitions. The terrace behind the villa offers good **views** over the town, the castle, the river and the Temple of Friendship, a columned building in which the remains of Frédéric Lemot lie.
On the right, near the entrance to the park, is the **Maison du Jardinier** (Gardener's House) ⊙. This building with its dovecote tower is a replica of a typical rustic house in Italy, and served as a model for a number of others in the area. It is the headquarters of a study group specializing in local traditions and the Italian influence in architecture. Inside, a model of the park is on display and there is a permanent exhibition devoted to Italian architecture in Clisson.
Scattered throughout the **park** are statues and follies with an antique theme (a Temple of Vesta imitating that in the Tivoli Gardens in Italy, an oratory, a military monument, a tomb...), the Grotto of Héloïse *(see below),* two rocks engraved with poems and, notably, a charming rock-bordered site on the banks of the Sèvre known as The Baths of Diana.

EXCURSIONS

Muscadet country – *Round tour of 40km – 25 miles northwest : about 2 hours.*
Clisson is one of the gateways to the vineyards of the Sèvre-et-Maine region which produces the popular Muscadet wine *(qv)* and the lesser-known Gros Plant white wine. The growers' *domaines* (estates) extend along the slopes of the green and fertile Sèvre Nantaise valley as it twists its way northwards.

Leave Clisson via D 59, northwest.

Monnières – The church in this village dates from the 12C and 15C but the interesting stained-glass windows are modern, with wine and the vine providing the main decorative motifs.

La Haie-Fouassière – The village probably derives its name from *La Fouace* – a kind of pancake – which is a local speciality. Near a water-tower is the **Maison des Vins de Nantes** ⊙, the seat of a local growers' association which provides information on local wines and offers wine-tasting. Nearby there is a picturesque view of the hillsides, studded with villages, above the Sèvre Valley.

Le Pallet – A former chapel in this small town now accommodates the **Musée du Vignoble de Nantes** ⊙. The museum is divided into four sections : arts and folk traditions of the Nantes wine country, methods of wine exploitation, production and transportation; the history of Le Pallet and its neighbourhood from Gallo-Roman times to the present; the life of Barrin de la Galissonnière, a local man who became Governor of Canada in the reign of Louis XIV and was famous for his talents as a botanist; the personality and work of **Pierre Abélard** (1079-1142), one of the founders of scholastic moral theology, whose dialectic genius profoundly marked the thinking of his time – and who became equally celebrated on account of his love for **Héloïse,** who bore him a child, but whose enraged family wreaked a terrible revenge on him; it was ten years before the tragic lovers met again, by which time Abélard had committed himself entirely to studying *(see Michelin Green Guide Champagne-Ardennes, in French, and also "Héloïse and Abélard" by George Moore, published in 1921).*

Mouzillon – South of the church in this village is a **Gallo-Roman bridge** across the River Sanguèse.

Vallet – This town is considered to be "the Muscadet capital".

Take D 756 west towards La Chapelle-Heulin and turn right after 2km – 1 mile.

Château de la Noë de Bel-Air ⊙ – This elegant château, rising above the vineyards, was destroyed during the Revolution and rebuilt in 1836; it now comprises an enormous loggia faced with Tuscan columns on the front overlooking the grounds. The brick dressing of the orangery and outbuildings is reminiscent of the houses in Clisson.

COGNAC

Pop 19 534

Michelin map 72 fold 12 or 233 fold 28 – Local map p 30.

Cognac, the birthplace of François I and cradle of the fine brandy *(qv)* which bears its name, is a peaceful town; near to its famous cellars and stores the buildings stand darkened by the microscopic fungi which thrive on the fumes of alcohol.
Place François I, a busy square with an ornamental fountain, links old Cognac, crowded on the slope above the River Charente, with the huge spread of the modern town. Not far from here, at No 10 Place Jean-Monnet, is the **"Cognathèque"** (**Z B**). Among the town's industrial companies is the St-Gobain verrerie **(glassworks)** ⊙.

Royal childhood – The literary and artistic House of Valois-Angoulême held court in the town from the late 14C until the accession of **François I** in 1515; it was here that François, the son of Charles of Angoulême and Louise of Savoy, was born "about ten hours after midday on the 12th day of September" in 1494. Part of his youth was spent in the Valois château here near the Charente, where he lived a carefree life with his sister Marguerite of Angoulême *(qv)* and Charles' two illegitimate daughters, Madeleine and Souveraine, who were brought up alongside the legitimate children, as was the custom at the time.

BARREL STORES

The cellars and barrel stores *(chais)* spread out along the riverside quays, near the port and in the suburbs, shelter the casks in which the slow alchemy between the alcohol and oak occurs, bestowing on the brandy of Cognac its distinction and subtlety. Many of these stores, linked to famous names, may be visited.

Otard – *See Town Centre, "Ancien Château" below.*

Hennessy (**Y D**) ⊙ – After 12 years' service with Louis XV's Irish Brigade, Captain Richard Hennessy, wearying of army life in 1760, discovered the Charente region and settled in Cognac.
Seduced and conquered by the allure of the delicious elixir distilled here, he sent several casks to his relatives in Ireland and, in 1765, founded a company of shippers which was an immediate success. The Captain's descendants still head the company today.
The **Musée de la Tonnellerie** (Cooperage Museum) is devoted to the handmade construction of brandy casks (different stages of manufacture; tools and implements). The trunks of oak trees from the Limousin in central France – wood in which the proportion of tannin is of paramount importance – are personally selected by the *Maître de Chai* (Cellar-master) and then sawn into calibrated sections *(douelles)* not unlike small planks. These are left to season for 5 or 6 years in the open air. The *douelles* are then assembled into barrels, and held in place with iron hoops. The tour of the museum ends with a visit to the barrel stores on the other side of the river.

Camus (**Y F**) ⊙ – *29 Rue Marguerite-de-Navarre.* The tour offered by this company of shippers, founded in 1863, concentrates on the history of cognac, its distillation, its ageing and its blending. Visitors are subsequently conducted through the *tonnellerie* and the *chais* before watching the bottling process.

Remy Martin ⊙ – *4km – $2\frac{1}{2}$ miles southwest via ④ on the map, then left towards Merpins.* This firm, the origins of which go back to 1724, creates its cognac exclusively from the élite Grande Champagne and Petite Champagne vintages. A **miniature train** takes visitors on a tour of the plant. In the *tonnellerie* – the largest in Europe – coopers can be seen at work on the casks, and then the train travels through a section of vineyard and various cellars used for stocking and ageing the spirit. Two different commentaries *(in French)* illustrated with slides punctuate the journey.

Martell (**Z E**) ⊙ – This house, the oldest of all the Cognac distilleries, owes its name to Jean Martell, who settled in the town in 1715. Here it is possible to visit the cellars and also to watch procedures in the bottling and packing departments. An audio-visual presentation traces the history of the brandy.

Prince Hubert de Polignac ⊙ – *4km – $2\frac{1}{2}$ miles southeast by* ①. This co-operative (established 1949) unites a number of local growers. A tour can be made of the different installations in the Pavillon du Laubaret.

TOWN CENTRE *1 hour*

Quartier Ancien (**Y**) – The Old Town was once surrounded by ramparts. Two main thoroughfares cut through the ancient network of lanes, alleys and courtyards : the steep, twisting slope of Grande-Rue and the straight, shop-lined length of Rue A.-Briand.
The lower part of the Old Town seems almost abandoned, and the mooring rings of the river port, at one time crowded with lighters loading salt or brandy, are used these days only for the occasional skiff or pleasure boat.

Ancien Château ⊙ – This 15C and 16C château recalls the memory of the Valois family and François I, who was born here. It became the property of the Comte d'Artois (the future Charles X) under Louis XVI and was sequestrated by the Republicans during the Revolution. Since 1795 it has been used as a barrel store by the firm **Otard,** which was originally founded by an old Scottish family.
The façade overlooking the Charente has a fine balcony, known as "the King's Balcony", the supports of which are sculpted with salamanders, François' emblem.
Inside the old château it is possible to visit the Helmet Hall, where Richard the Lionheart married his son Philip to Amélie of Cognac; the chamber contains a magnificent chimneypiece surmounted by a helmet, the work of Jean le Bon. In one corner are traces of the Lusignan family's original 13C feudal castle. The huge rooms, with their ribbed vaulting – including the Guards' Room – are extremely elegant. The tour ends with a visit to the barrel stores.

Porte St-Jacques and Grande-Rue (**15**) – The restored 15C gateway, flanked by two round towers with machicolations, once commanded a bridge which has disappeared; it still however leads to Grande-Rue, originally the main street in Cognac. On the left, at the foot of the hill, is a Renaissance fountain. The street is typically medieval, with a winding course and 15C houses with projecting, half-timbered upper floors.

Rue de l'Isle-d'Or (**16**) – This street is lined with town houses dating from the 17C with fine façades (restored).

Rue Saulnier (**25**) – In contrast to Grande-Rue, Rue Saulnier is bordered by aristocratic Renaissance buildings; its name recalls one of the traditional activities of Cognac – the salt trade. The street, which was very wide for the period, has retained its irregular cobblestone surface and its handsome 16C and 17C houses. At the far end is a Renaissance house with a shop.

Musée Municipal (**Y M**) ⊙ – The museum is housed in the Dupuy d'Angeac mansion, which stands in the Town Hall grounds – an undulating garden area with lawns and rockeries.

Ground Floor – The displays here cover the history and civilization of the Cognac area from the earliest times to the present through maps, plans, prints and photographs; headdresses, bonnets and traditional costumes; glasswork and bottle-making; fine glazed earthenwares; fossils – mainly shellfish – found in the Secondary limestone formations in the region. In a section devoted to archeology there are stone, bronze, bone and ceramic items from prehistoric times, and pottery, statuettes and bracelets from the Gallo-Roman period.
There is also a reconstruction of the interior of a rural house, evoking the life of a local wine grower *c*1875.

Basement : Musée du Cognac – The exhibits on this floor concentrate on brandy-making, giving a historical perspective, illustrated by documents. A succession of six rooms illustrates, with the help of tools and machines, the culture of vineyards and the making of wine; distillation of spirits; the trade in brandy and the Pineau des Charentes apéritif; the workforce; cooperage; saddlery. Another room is devoted to traditional agriculture in the Cognac area.

First Floor – This section houses paintings, sculpture, furniture and *objets d'art*, both French and foreign, from the 15C to the 19C.
On the landing, interesting works in molten glass by Émile Gallé (1846-1904), one of the principal pioneers of Art Nouveau, are on view.

COGNAC

Angoulême (R. d') .... Y 3
Armes (Place d') .... Y 4
Briand (R. A.) .... Y
Victor-Hugo (Av.) .... Z
14-Juillet (R. du) .... Z 26
Allées (R. des) .... Z 2
Bayard (R.) .... Z 5
Bazouin (R. Abel) .... Y 6
Boucher (R. Cl.) .... Y 8
Chalais (R. de) .... Z 9
Cordeliers (R. des) .... Y 10
Crouin (R. des) .... Y 12
François-Ier (R.) .... Y 14
Grande-Rue .... Y 15
Isle-d'Or (R. de l') .... Y 16
Lattre-de-T. (R. de) .... Y 18
Lusignan (R. de) .... Y 20
Magdeleine (R.) .... Y 21
Martell (Pl. Ed.) .... Z 22
Monnet (Pl.) .... Z 23
Saulnier (R.) .... Y 25

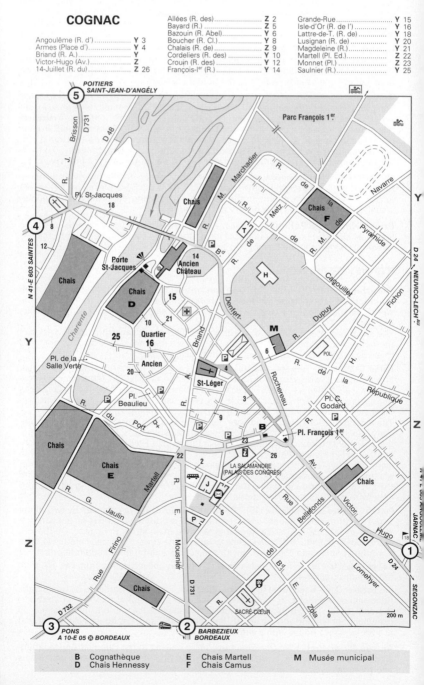

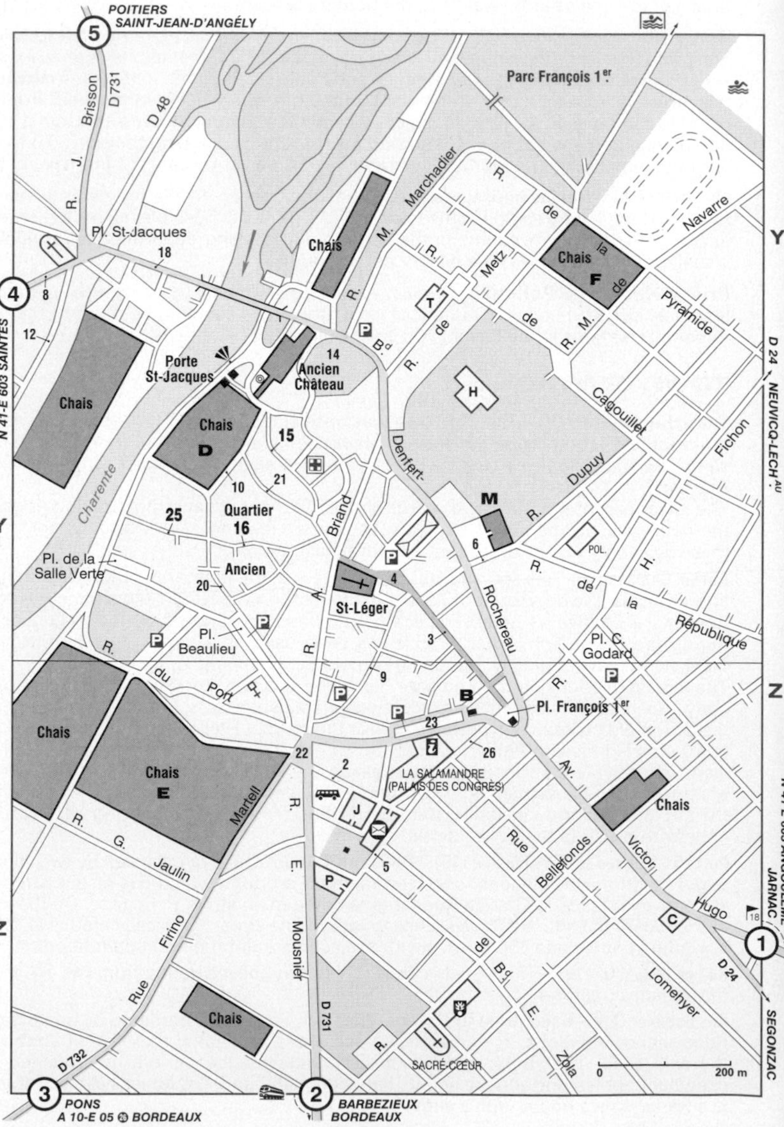

B Cognathèque
D Chais Hennessy
E Chais Martell
F Chais Camus
M Musée municipal

The period paintings originate from countries which were clients of the Cognac brandy trade. Particularly noteworthy are two works from the 16C Antwerp school : *Lot and his Daughters* by Jan Massys, and *Adam and Eve* by Frans Floris. One room on this floor has a display of contemporary paintings.

Église St-Léger (Y) – This 12C church has been extensively remodelled. The most interesting part is the Romanesque west front, pierced in the 15C with a large Flamboyant Gothic rose window. The archivolt of the doorway below is adorned with carvings representing the signs of the Zodiac and the labours of the months. The vast nave inside dates from the 12C. In the south transept hangs a fine 17C painting, *The Assumption of the Virgin*.

Parc François-Ier (Y) – This park, bordered to the west by the River Charente, was part of the former castle grounds, prolonged by a thicket of tall trees. So dense was the growth in this wood, much of it made up of oak trees, that Louise of Savoy used to call it her "dedalus" (maze).

EXCURSIONS

Richemont - Château-Chesnel - Migron – *24km – 15 miles north. Leave Cognac via ⑤ on the map.*

Richemont – The church and the castle ruins here rise half-hidden among the trees crowning a spur. The **church** is built on the site of an ancient stronghold – the loopholes and arrow slits of which are still visible – and contains a delightful pre-Romanesque crypt (10C). A small archeological museum in the sacristy contains a model of the original fortress.

Continue to Cherves, and to Château-Chesnel beyond.

Château-Chesnel – This curious residence was built between 1610 and 1625 by Charles Roch-Chesnel. Architecturally the château seems to hesitate between the Renaissance style and 17C classicism, whilst nevertheless retaining a strong flavour of medieval military architecture – for example, in the deep dry moats around it. The central block and the towers at each corner are crowned with a battlemented parapet. The complex as a whole forms a huge square, surrounded by large agricultural buildings.

Return to D 731 and continue north; at Burie turn right (D 131) to Migron.

Migron – The small **Éco-musée du Cognac** ⓥ *(2km – 1¼ miles north; signposted)*, located among vineyards, is dedicated to the process of making brandy.
There is a reconstruction of a home distillery, complete with ancient pot still, alembic, and the domestic distiller's – or "moonshiner's" – bed, which had to stay nearby during the entire operation. Also on view are wine presses, one of them for use with feet, a cooper's workshop, wine-growers' tools and examples of the huge copper alembics still used in the trade.

Gensac-la-Pallue – *9km – 5 miles southeast via ① N 141, then turn right.* Before arriving at Gensac, route D 49 skirts the *pallue* (marshland) from which the small town derives its name. The interesting 12C **church** has a Romanesque west front decorated with reliefs of the Virgin (left) and St Martin (right), the patron saint of the church, both of them being carried heavenwards by angels. The Romanesque nave, roofed with four domes supported by pendentives, leads to a Gothic chancel.

Neuvicq-le-Château – *19km – 9 miles northeast via D 24 to Ste-Sévère.*

Macqueville – This peaceful village in the heart of the Fins Bois vineyards northeast of Cognac has modern distilleries which deal exclusively with the production of cognac. The white houses, roofed with tiles, have Empire-style porches and closed courtyards. In the shady square, **Église St-Étienne** (St Stephen's church) is a charming example of the Romanesque art which flourished in the ancient province of Saintonge during the 12C. The north transept is replaced by a belltower with radiating chapels; the east end is flattened; the archivolt of the north doorway is carved. Equally characteristic are the semicircular blind arcades of the walls and the amusing modillions on the cornices. Inside, recessed pillars with elegant capitals support the Gothic vaulting of the wide nave; the ribbed transept crossing is magnificent.
A gabled façade with one pepperpot turret is all that remains of the 11C Boucherau castle.

Neuvicq-le-Château – This is another village of picturesque low houses with tiled roofs. The château, which overlooks a small valley and gave the village its name, incorporates a 15C main block with a charming staircase-tower, and a 17C pavilion crowned by a tall, steep, typically-French roof. It today houses the post office.

★ Les COLLINES VENDÉENNES

Michelin map 67 fold 16 or 232 fold 42.

This line of hills – the Hills of the Vendée (Collines Vendéennes) – sparsely populated and somewhat austere, forms the backbone of the Vendée *département*. Rising between the Sèvre Nantaise river and the belt of mixed woodland, hedges and pastureland known as **le bocage,** the chain embraces a series of summits stretching from the town of Les Herbiers to St-Pierre-du-Chemin, southeast of Pouzauges, with a southern extension (the Gâtine heights) as far as Parthenay.
These granite crests carpeted with bleak moorland, washed with the pale gold of furze and broom once winter is over, are in fact foothills of the Hercynean chain in Brittany. They have a northwest-southeast orientation.
The highest part of the chain, irrigated by rainfall from the cloud masses rolling in from the Atlantic, rises in the northwest to overlook the *bocage* stretching 50 miles away to the sea. It is here that the most important "mountains" can be found : Mont des Alouettes (alt 231m – 758ft), Puy du Fou, **Mont Mercure** (at 285m – 935ft the highest summit in the range), Bois de la Folie (alt 278m – 912ft) and Puy Crapaud (alt 270m – 886ft).
In the past these heights offered both strategic and tactical advantages to the military. The Romans built a road linking the crests, and a temple crowned Mont Mercure.

Windmill country – For centuries the Vendée hills were dotted with countless windmills which worked, sometimes throughout the night, grinding wheat and rye from the fertile plains nearby everytime the sea winds blew. During the Revolution, however, the Royalist supporters here used their mills as a kind of rural semaphore system, altering the position of sails and vanes to telegraph information concerning the movements of the enemy; as a result many were burned down by Republican troops. Mechanization in the 19C put those which had been restored out of business.
Many mills are again being restored to working order.
A typical example is stone-built, cylindrical in shape, and topped by a movable, conical roof covered with shingles (this type is known as a tower mill because of its fixed, tower-like base). The four sails are fixed to the revolving roof and there is frequently a **"guivre"** (a long beam reaching to the ground) attached, which can be used to help turn the sails to face the prevailing wind. The sails' wooden armatures are covered either with canvas (hemp in earlier times) or wooden slats articulated according to the Berton System, invented in 1848.

B. Chemin

The windmill and chapel, Mont des Alouettes.

FROM POUZAUGES TO LES HERBIERS

41km – 22 miles : allow about 2½ hours.

Pouzauges and its surroundings – *See Pouzauges.*

★★ **Puy Crapaud** – *See Pouzauges.*

Leaving Pouzauges in the direction of Les Herbiers the route passes the two mid 19C, shingle-roofed tower mills of Terrier-Marteau (right).

Bois de la Folie – *See Pouzauges.*

A sweeping curve, followed by an attractive loop in the opposite direction, leads D 752 down into a small valley which develops into the depression separating Pouzauges from St-Michel-Mont-Mercure.

★ **St-Michel-Mont-Mercure** – The granite houses of this town, the highest in the Vendée hills, are gathered around a church dedicated to St Michael (who was often associated with high places), built on a site previously venerated by worshippers of Mercury, the protector of travellers.
The church, dating only from 1898, reaches a height of 47m – 154ft. It is surmounted by a huge copper statue of the saint, itself 9m – 30ft tall. Church and statue can be seen in the distance from viewpoints for miles around. From the top (194 steps) of the **tower** ⓥ an immense **panorama**★★ stretching as far as the ocean can be admired. At this height, the complex pattern of the *bocage* appears almost like a continuous forest. The crest-line of the hills is clearly visible, bordered to the south by the trees of Bois de la Folie, near Pouzauges, and to the north by Mont des Alouettes, not far from Les Herbiers.

Moulin des Justices ⓥ – This mill owes its name to the fact that it is perched on top of a bluff from which, in former times, justice was administered. It stands 3km – 1¾ miles along the road to Les Herbiers, on the left of which, again, there are fine **views** of the *bocage*.

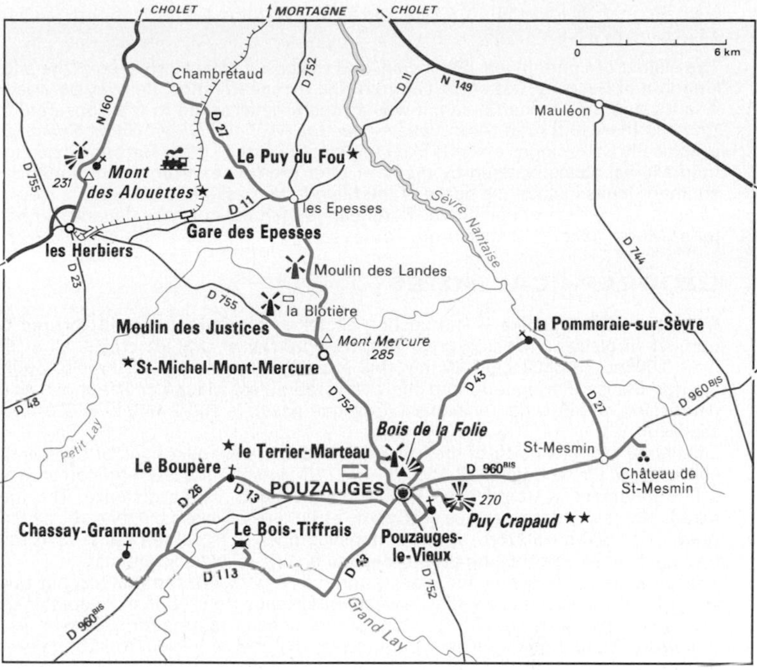

The mill, built at the end of the 19C, rises 275m – 902ft above sea level. Movement of the shingled roof is effected by a winch inside the building. The width of the sails can be varied via the articulation of wooded slats designed on the Berton System. Production at this mill is concentrated today on the refinement of organic flour.
From the garden of the neighbouring inn there is a view looking north to Les Épesses, the Moulin des Landes and the Château de la Blotière.

Return to St-Michel and take the road leading to Les Épesses.

Beyond St-Michel, hairpin bends lead D 752 into and out of a valley, after which the road passes near a bluff crowned by a windmill with no sails (the Moulin des Landes). Soon afterwards the two churches of Les Épesses, built side by side, come into view.

★ **Le Puy du Fou** – *See Le Puy du Fou.*

★ **Mont des Alouettes** – This wild stretch of moorland marks the northwestern limit of the Vendée hills. The name derives from the bronze skylarks *(alouettes)* which decorated the helmets of Gallic warriors when they were enlisted in the Roman legions based in the area. In 1793 the seven mills on these moors were among those most frequently used to send signals by the "Whites" (Royalists); subsequently all were set alight by the Republicans. Three of them have now been restored.
The mills are all typical of the region, with their rough-hewn oak *guivres* or tails and shingled candle-snuffer roofs. One of them is dedicated to the Vendée writer Jean Yole; another **mill** ⊙, nearby, still grinds corn, thanks to its canvas-covered sails. The small granite chapel in the style known as "Troubadour Gothic" *(qv)* was started in 1823 in honour of the Royal and Catholic Army. It was neither enclosed nor furnished with windows until 1968.
From this height, the enormous **view★★** stretches away towards Nantes, the Atlantic Ocean and, towards Pouzauges, the rest of the chain dominated by the church of St-Michel-Mont-Mercure. It is from here, too, that the impressive, almost mysterious effect of the *bocage,* with its intricate mixture of copse and spinney and hedgerow, is most strongly felt.
Driving down from the moors offers a good, almost aerial view of the town, far below, of Les Herbiers.

Les Herbiers – The town stands on a mound overlooking the Grande Maine river with its grassy banks; local industries make furniture, shoes, clothes and pleasure boats. The **church** is fronted by a powerful belfry-porch with Flamboyant doorway flanked by the figures of St Peter and St Paul.

Gare des Épesses – This is a typical early 20C village station. The station building now houses the **Musée de l'Histoire des Chemins de Fer en Vendée** ⊙ which, through posters, documents and objects, retraces the recent past and revolutionary developments of the railways.
The **Puy du Fou train à vapeur (steam train)** ⊙ operates along the old Mortane to Les Herbiers track (22km – 13 miles), stopping at Gare des Épesses, and is an enjoyable way of discovering the *bocage.*
An old carriage from the original Orient Express train provides refreshments.

Use the Index to find more information about a subject mentioned in the guide – towns, places of interest, isolated sights, historical events or natural features.

★★ Le COMMINGES

Michelin map 82 folds 15, 16, 17, 85 fold 20 and 86 folds 1, 2, 3, 11; or map 234 folds 44, 48 and 235 folds 41, 45.

The district of Comminges, historically and ecclesiastically a province of the ancient kingdom of Gascony, lies at the centre of the Pyrenean range, halfway between the Atlantic and the Mediterranean. It was at one time attached to the Couserans area *(qv)* and the Vall d'Aran (Aran Valley – *see the Michelin Green Guide Spain*). Geographically Comminges extends from the heights of the Upper Garonne basin to the mild alluvial plains watered by the river after it emerges from the mountains; the southern limits include the peaks of the Maladetta massif (Pic d'Aneto, at 3 404m – 11 164ft, is the highest point in the Pyrenean range), the northern flatlands stretch as far as Muret, 19km – 12 miles from Toulouse.

GEOGRAPHICAL NOTES

Granites and marbles – The Luchon sector of the Pyrenees, still scoured by a number of glaciers, forms a great east-west barrier of granitic crests, all of them over 3 000m – 9 850ft high. Within this massif lie the valleys of the Oô (Spijoles, Gourgs Blancs, Perdiguère) and the Lys (Crabioules, Maupas). The most marked depression, the Port de Vénasque (Vénasque pass), is still 2 448m – 8 030ft above sea level.

Limestone foothills north of the Marignac basin, on the east bank of the Garonne, culminate in Pic de Cagire (alt 1 912m – 6 272ft), which rises from the forest to form a fine landmark in front of the snow-covered crests in the distance. The forest, mainly beechwoods, continues eastwards as far as the Massif d'Arbas (Pic de Paloumère : alt 1 608m – 5 276ft), which is honeycombed with subterranean cavities and frequently used as a training ground for speleologists (cave scientists).

The lower part of Gascony, for years ignored by sightseers and tourists, has revealed during the past century evidence of an important colonization in Paleolithic times (Aurignac; the Save and Seygouade Gorges, near Montmaurin), as well as the remains of Gallo-Roman villas (Montmaurin, *qv*). It was here in the 5C, before the first barbarian invasions, that the era of grand properties in Aquitaine, furnished with marble from the quarries of St-Béat, drew to a close.

Pyrenean Garonne – In the Aran Valley, on the Spanish side of the frontier, the word *Garona* is used to name several different mountain torrents. The most important, the Río Garona de Ruda, rises near Monte Saboredo (alt 2 764m – 9 068ft), south of Puerto de la Bonaigua (Bonaigua Pass). Several tributaries flow into the torrent, notably the Río Garona de Jueu, itself appearing in the middle of a forest as a spring gushing from rock fissures in a fan of cataracts 30m – 100ft high. According to the speleologist Norbert Casteret, who made a study of the north face of the Maladetta in 1931, the waters are in fact a resurgence of melted ice from glaciers higher up the massif.

The Garonne arrives in France at Pont du Roi. At this point it is no more than a typical high mountain stream, with a steeply sloping bed and a variable flow, shrunken in winter and swollen in May and June. In the Comminges region it is broadened by the Pique, the Ourse and the Aure torrents. At Montréjeau, flowing into a regular channel lying along the foot of the range from La Barthe-de-Neste to Boussens, it curves suddenly eastwards to cross the St-Gaudens plain. The Boussens cluse (transverse valley) marks the Garonne's definitive exit from the Pyrenees.

HISTORICAL NOTES

A creation of the Romans – In the year 76 BC the Roman Triumvir Pompey, on his way to a campaign in Spain, annexed the upper valley of the Garonne and incorporated it in the Roman province of Transalpine Gaul. On his return four years later he founded the town of Lugdunum Convenarum (today St-Bertrand-de-Comminges, *qv*) and settled there a population of *Convenae* – "people of all origins" – largely drawn from the ranks of brigands, mountain dwellers and shepherds. The town prospered and grew rapidly.

In the more remote valleys of the Pyrenees local devotion to pagan deities was intense, yet these cults managed to survive for many years alongside both Celtic and Imperial divinities, dying out only gradually under the influence of Christianity. Most of the mountain churches in the Luchon area – especially in the Oueil and Larboust valleys – have stonework built into their walls which once formed part of the fabric of pagan temples. Recent excavations in the Haute-Garonne *département* have revealed the remains of villas built by the Gallo-Roman aristocrats who ruled the region in the 2C and 4C AD. The *villa urbana,* where the master lived, was luxuriously appointed with baths and heated by hot air flowing up from beneath the mosaic floors and between the walls, and surrounded by gardens, gateways, and basins filled with water-lilies. There would have been many works of art in the house. The *villa rustica* housed the land workers. Crops were stored in the *fructaria* and the whole complex was enclosed by a high wall. Land not worked by the master was divided among smallholders, each of whom was obliged to yield a proportion of his crop to the landowner.

Comté of Comminges – Comminges, which at first formed part of the Duchy of Aquitaine, was joined in the 10C with Couserans *(qv)* to create a county under the suzerainty of the Comtes of Toulouse. The treaty of Corbeil, concluded between St Louis of France and Iago (James) I of Spain in 1258, reserved the claim of Aragon, Spain, to the Aran Valley – a cession confirmed *de facto* in 1659 by the Treaty of the Pyrenees *(qv)*. Comminges reverted to France in 1454.

Failing agreement on the delineation of a new *département* to be called the Central Pyrenees, the district was incorporated into the Haute-Garonne in 1790.

★ROUTE DE PEYRESOURDE

From Arreau to Luchon

41km – 26 miles : about 3 hours – Local map below.

Arreau – *See Arreau.*

Leave Arreau via D 618 southwest.

The road ascends the valley of the Louron torrent, at first hemmed in by two wooded slopes and then running out, south of Avajan, into an upland basin scattered with villages, most of them in a damp environment and partly abandoned. This depression, closed off to the south, is overlooked on the left (east) by Pic de Hourgade (2 964m – 9 724ft), a mountain complex broken up into sharp spines separating snow-filled valleys.

Génos – *15min on foot Rtn. At the top of the hill, just before the entrance sign, take the ramp leading to the church.* A path skirting the cemetery on the left leads to the castle ruins. There is a **view** from here, across a lake where there are facilities for various watersports, of the mountain mass closing off the end of the valley.

Turn back. At the foot of the dip in which the ruins stand, cross the torrent and, by way of Armenteule and Estarvielle, rejoin the D 618 heading east.

Beyond the turn-off to Mont there is a fine panorama westward over the Louron Valley. The road – which runs on a ledge carved from the mountainside – continues to the pass, Col de Peyresourde, which is reached at an altitude of 1 569m – 5 148ft via a combe, one slope of which is shaded by the magnificent Balestas pine forest.

Peyragudes – Alt *c*1 600m – 5 250ft. This is a ski centre served by mechanical hoists on either side of the crest. From the hilltop a little above the "altiport" there is a marvellous **view★** over the Néouvielle massif with its lace-work of snow and over the attractive countryside.
It is worth leaving D 618 for the corniche road leading to Gouaux-de-Larboust, if only for the **views★★** over the Oô Valley and the slate roofs of Oô village : the fresh valley with its burgeoning ash and walnut trees contrasts with the mountain landscape typical of the Luchon massif – mainly sombre rock masses (Spijoles, Les Gourgs Blancs, Pic du Portillon d'Oô) dotted with the glitter of small glaciers.

Cazeaux-de-Larboust – The **church** in this hamlet is decorated with paintings – 15C murals, most of them heavily re-touched. Facing the entrance there is a curious *Last Judgement* showing the Virgin succouring Christ, to lighten his suffering and calm his anger. The sword of justice falls from the hands of the Divine Judge.
Leaving Cazeaux there is a charming view of the church and houses of Castillon.

Chapelle St-Pé (St-Pierre-de-la-Moraine) – This is a pleasant place to stop. The walls of this chapel and particularly the buttresses incorporate many fragments of pagan funerary monuments. Here, as in all the upper parts of the Comminges district, there are many traces of ancient religions, notably Celtic and Roman.

St-Aventin – *See St-Aventin.*

The shaded road continues its descent towards the Bagnères-de-Luchon basin.

★★ **Bagnères-de-Luchon** – *See Luchon.*

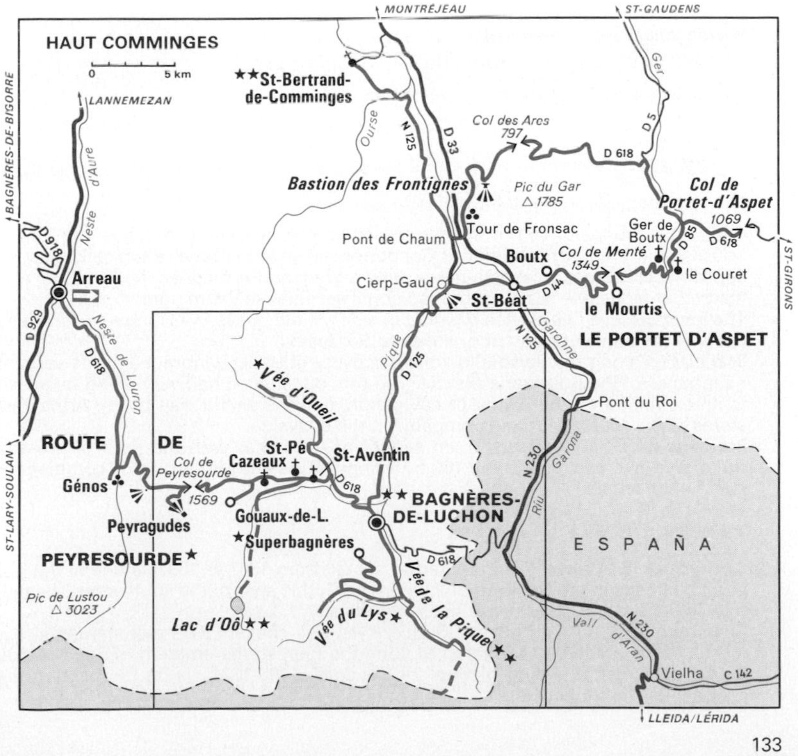

★★ EXCURSIONS AROUND BAGNÈRES-DE-LUCHON

For local map and descriptions see Luchon.

LE PORTET D'ASPET

From Luchon to St-Bertrand-de-Comminges

94km – 58 miles : about 3 hours – Local map overleaf.

Leave Luchon via D 125 north.

After Luchon, the first stage of this excursion follows the valley of the Pique. There are particularly fine views, just before Cierp-Gaud, of the mountain mass forming the frontier (southeast); of the limestone Gar massif, surmounted by a large Cross (northeast). The Garonne (north) flows into the wide Marignac basin.
At Cierp-Gaud turn right into D 44 to cross this depression, which is overlooked by the escarpments of Pic du Gar. The road passes the famous marble quarries and approaches St-Béat Gorge.

St-Béat – This old strongpoint, the "key to France" as it was known (note the town arms), commanded the opening of the Aran Valley into Gascony; it was the home of **Marshal Gallieni** (1849-1916), military governor of Paris and later War Minister.
The grey houses splashed by the torrent stand in an arc at the bottom of the gorge. On the right bank, the keep – now used as a clock tower – is all that remains of the 14C-15C citadel. The local white and grey marble was used for many of the pools and statues in the gardens of Versailles, and features here in the door and window surrounds of the houses.
The road east climbs quickly above the slate roofs of the village of Lez.

Boutx – There is an attractive view of the huddled, tightly-packed roofs of this village.

Beyond, the road rises in a series of hairpins through a forest of conifers and arrives at **Col de Menté** (alt 1 349m – 4 426ft).

Le Mourtis – The chalets and apartment blocks here, inhabited mainly during the skiing season, are scattered beneath a forest of ancient, lichen-festooned fir trees – part of an enormous belt of woodland straddling the valleys of the Garonne and the Ger.
Descending the eastern slope of Menté Pass, the road passes through the narrow valley of the Upper Ger, strewn with isolated barns and villages perching on the slopes, their churches displaying unusual triple-spired belfry-walls **(Ger de Boutx, Le Couret)**.
Ignoring the turn-off to Henne-Morte, on the left, the route climbs again, more steeply.

Col de Portet d'Aspet – Alt 1 069m – 3 507ft. From the slopes in front of the chalet-hotel by the pass a mountain panorama opens out, with the dark, gently sloping pyramid of Mont Valier (alt 2 838m – 9 311ft) in the background.
The Couserans district *(qv)* extends from the eastern side of the pass.

Turn back and continue the itinerary along D 618, going through Henne-Morte.

The route again follows the valley of the Ger, this time via a spectacular wooded gorge. From Col des Ares (alt 797m – 2 615ft) the road continues to descend through the pretty Frontignes countryside.

Bastion des Frontignes – From the hairpin bend just before the village of Antichan there is a fine **view** of the Luchon massif and its glaciers. *Viewing table.*
Skirting the flanks of Pic du Gar, the route now offers more and more extensive views, northwards over the Garonne Valley, southwards to Bagnères-de-Luchon and the mountain cirque surrounding it. The ruins of the **Tour de Fronsac,** which appear on the left, are all that remains of an ancient fortress of the Comtes of Comminges.

At Pont de Chaum (Chaum bridge) turn right into N 125.

★★ **St-Bertrand-de-Comminges** – *See St-Bertrand-de-Comminges.*

CONDOM

Pop 7 717

Michelin map 79 fold 14 or 234 fold 24 – Facilities.

Condom is the major centre in an area rich in attractive rural churches and manor houses, and the old mansions of Condom itself give the town a typically Gascon appearance; its economic activities – selling grain and Armagnac, flour-milling and the timber industry – are also the traditional activities of the region.
The River Baïse, a fine stretch of water beside the old quays, was long ago canalised to allow the transportation of brandies to Bordeaux.
Boat trips ⓥ along the Baïse allow the discovery of Barlet windmill and the verdant river banks of the Bouquerie district. The trip, punctuated half-way along by a visit to an exhibition on the histoy of navigation, finishes with a visit to the Armagnac stores of the Jean du Vignau company on the quayside.
Pousse-rapière ("Rapier Thrust"), an aperitif of Armagnac with the juice of pressed fruits, was invented here in the 16C by Marshal Blaise de Monluc, army commander and man of letters.

TOWN CENTRE *1½ hours*

★ **Cathédrale St-Pierre** – This cathedral, rebuilt from 1507 to 1531, is one of the last great buildings in the Gers region built in the Gothic style of the southwest. The belfry with its quadrangular tower rises majestically.
The south door, in Flamboyant Gothic style, still shelters 24 small statues in the niches of the archivolt : the lamb of John the Baptist, the emblem of Jean Marre; Marre, the great "building bishop" of Condom (1496-1521), is on the base of the central pier's empty niche.

The nave is illuminated by windows which include, in the chancel, Flamboyant tracery following the style of the local school (1858); those south of the nave have stained glass (1969) from a major workshop in Limoges. The ribs of the vaulting are articulated around historiated keystones : at the 5th bay the arms of the "building bishop" are visible; at the 7th, St Peter.
The neo-Gothic enclosure around the chancel has large statues of angels and saints made from terracotta moulded in 1844.

Go round the chancel to the left.

Above the door to the sacristy a fine marble plaque commemorates the consecration of the cathedral in 1531. The Lady Chapel, at the east end, is a Gothic sanctuary which was once part of the old cathedral.

★ **Cloisters** – The cloisters were largely rebuilt in the 19C. St Catherine's Chapel – now a public passageway – off the eastern gallery of the cloisters has attractive keystones on the polychrome vaulting.

Musée de l'Armagnac ⊙ – This museum contains rare tools and machinery used in the old days by local vinegrowers (18-tonne press, grape-crushing roller), a complete set of cooper's tools and of bottle samples produced by Gascon gentlemen-glassmakers, various alembics... The old Armagnac export routes along the River Adour and the Garonne are shown on a map.

►► Hôtels de Polignac, de Cugnac and de Riberot (fine 18C mansions).

EXCURSIONS

★ **La Romieu** – The entrance to the late 12C-early 13C collegiate **church**★ here is through the cloisters with their interesting – though damaged – decorative motifs and through a doorway beneath a machicolated arch; the **eastern tower** ⊙, an octagonal structure, stands apart. 14C murals may still be seen in the sacristy : 16 angels adorn the vaulting. A spiral staircase (153 steps) leads up to the platform, from which there are good views of the rooftops of the village, the belfry-tower and the cloisters.

Larressingle, Montréal – *Circuit of 40km – 25 miles west of Condom : allow half a day. Leave Condom via D 15 towards Montréal.*

Larressingle – This 13C fortified village is enveloped within walls in the middle of which there remain a keep, a church and some restored old houses. A bridge straddling the moat and a fortified gate allow access to the centre. The ruined keep consists of three storeys linked by a spiral stair. The Romanesque church, also defensive in structure, has been reduced to two encased chancels. A path outside the ramparts leads around the fortifications.

Montréal – This *bastide (qv)*, one of the earliest built in Gascony (1256), stands in a picturesque site above the valley of the Auloue. Though severely damaged during the Wars of Religion, it has retained a fortified Gothic church and a central square bordered by houses with arcades, one of which houses the **Musée archéologique** ⊙ *(access through the Tourist Information Centre)*. Inside there are several items (pottery, iron objects, Merovingian buckles) found at Séviac *(see below)*, among them the "Mosaic with Trees" which incorporates motifs of fruit trees and fleur-de-lys.

2.5km – 1¼ miles south are the ruins of **St-Pierre-de-Genens church**, where the Romanesque doorway is surmounted by a 7C-8C white marble chrism.

Gallo-Roman Villa, Séviac ⊙ – The archeological digs in this site since the last century have revealed the foundations of an important and well-appointed Gallo-Roman villa of the 4C, intermingled with the vestiges of paleo-Christian and Merovingian buildings, all of which indicate permanent occupation here from the 2C to the 7C. The main residence, on a slightly-elevated chalky plateau, is arranged around a square courtyard surrounded by galleries with mosaic-covered floors. To the southwest lie the vast hot baths with chambers above hypocausts (hollow, hot-air-filled spaces forming part of an under-floor heating system) and swimming pools richly-decorated with coloured mosaics and marble.

D 29, at the northern exit of Montréal, follows the course of the River Auzoue.

★ **Fourcès** – A small bridge crossing the Auzoue, bordered by a 15C and 16C castle, leads to this picturesque *bastide* founded by the English in the 13C. The unusual village with its circular ground plan *(illustration p 45)* still has half-timbered houses, above stone or wood arcades, grouped around a large shaded central square with a stone cross at its centre. Traces of the old town walls remain and the old clocktower. Fourcès is a riot of colour during the Spring flower festival season.

Return to Condom via D 114.

★ Phare de CORDOUAN

Michelin map 71 fold 15 or 233 fold 25.

Access ⊙ – The lighthouse can be reached either from Royan or from Pointe de Grave *(qv)* where there is a museum devoted to this extraordinary structure.

History – The light, as fascinating for its architecture as for its isolated setting, watches over the approaches to the Gironde estuary, which are frequently rough and at the mercy of dangerous currents. The rocky boss on which it stands once formed part of Pointe de Grave (Grave Point) but was separated from the mainland and reduced to an islet during the 16C and 17C. Today the ancient land link is revealed only at times of exceptionally low tides.

In the 14C the Black Prince *(qv)* ordered an octagonal tower to be built on the promontory, on the top of which a hermit was to keep a beacon alight at all times. A chapel and a few small cottages were added around the base of the tower. At the end of the 16C, however, the main structure was in danger of collapsing and so the local governor called in the architect-engineer **Louis de Foix,** who had just completed the diversion of the River Adour *(qv)* which was a gigantic undertaking for that period. De Foix arrived with a workforce of more than 200 and constructed on the rocky base a belvedere surmounted by domes and lanterns protected by platforms with balustrades.

In 1788 the engineer Teulere remodelled the upper part of the structure in the Louis XVI style, resulting in a vivid contrast between the earlier richness and flamboyance of the lower levels and the later architectural restraint.

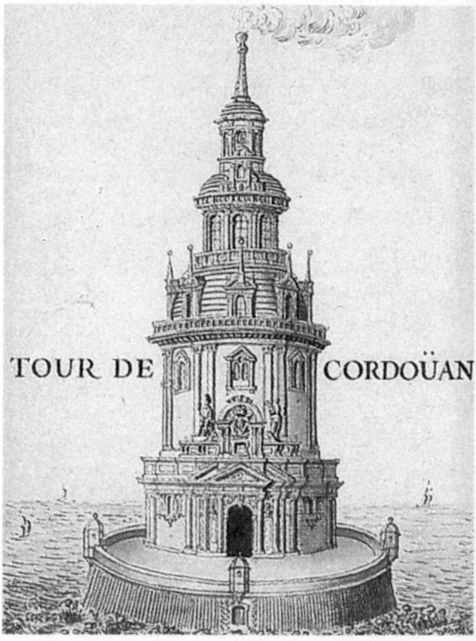

Cordouan lighthouse in the early 17C.

Tour ⊙ – The combination of Renaissance storeys below and a Classical upper portion, separated by a balustrade, lends the lighthouse an air at the same time bold and majestic.

Below the 66m – 216ft tower, a postern leads into the circular bastion which protects the complex from the fury of the seas. Within this are the lighthouse-keepers' quarters. On the ground floor of the tower itself a monumental doorway gives access to the vestibule from which 301 steps lead to the modern lantern (which houses an intermittently-flashing light). On the first floor, which is surrounded by an outside gallery, is the King's Apartment. There is a **chapel** on the second floor, again circled by a gallery, and this is crowned by an elegant dome. The bust above the entrance door is of Louis de Foix.

★ CÔTE D'ARGENT

Michelin maps 71 folds 15 to 20, 78 folds 1 to 6 and 11 to 18, 233 folds 25 and 36, or 234 folds 2, 6, 10, 14, 17, 18, 21, 22 and 25.

The Côte d'Argent or **Silver Coast** is the name given to the part of the Aquitaine shoreline which extends virtually in a straight line from the Gironde estuary in the north to the mouth of the Bidasoa River on the Spanish border; the coastline of the Landes *(qv)*, from the Gironde to the River Adour, forms the major part of it and provides some of the best beaches in Europe.

The north-south itinerary suggested below, from Pointe de Grave to Capbreton, takes in the principal lakes and coastal lagoons as well as the main seaside and lakeside resorts of the Landes. From Bayonne to Hendaye, the Côte d'Argent is better known under the name of the Côte Basque (Basque Coast).

LES LANDES GIRONDINES

From Pointe de Grave to Arcachon

175km – 108 miles : allow 4 hours. Local map opposite.

This route runs between the coast and the moors (landes) of the Gironde area.

Pointe de Grave – *Park the car by the memorial.* Pointe de Grave (Grave Point) is the tip of the headland at the northernmost limit of the Landes which curves across to narrow the mouth of the Gironde. It lies directly across the water from the resort of Royan.

The monument which now stands here replaces a 75m – 246ft pyramid erected to commemorate the landing of American troops in 1917, which was demolished by the Germans in 1942. The Point was one of the Atlantic Coast strongpoints where German forces stationed in western France held out after the Allied landings in 1944; it was not overcome until April 1945, only weeks before the armistice.

The old blockhouse on top of the end dune offers a vast marine **panorama★** over Cordouan lighthouse 9km – 5 miles out to sea, the peninsula and lighthouse of La Coubre, the Gironde and the port installations at Le Verdon, the coves around Royan and the splendid expanse of the Atlantic.

Another lighthouse, on the Point itself, contains the **Musée du phare de Cordouan** ⊙. This museum highlights the exceptional architecture of the off-shore Cordouan beacon *(qv)* and gives some idea of the daily life of the keepers. Children's drawings on the theme of lighthouses, and an aquarium with exotic marine species complete the exhibition, and the gallery offers a fine view of the estuary.

A small **scenic railway** ⊙ operates from Pointe de Grave to Soulac *(see below)* and there are also **boat trips** ⊙ available, particularly to the Cordouan light.

Le Verdon-sur-Mer – Le Verdon is an important container terminal standing in a privileged position at the mouth of the estuary, protected from the ocean by Pointe de Grave. It benefits from a deep-water port unrestricted by locks or tides, and offers direct access up the Gironde; its location, combined with the excellent facilities available – including fast cargo handling and good warehousing and equipment – makes it particularly suitable for the huge container ships and oil tankers which dock here before sailing for Central America, South America, West Africa or the Indian Ocean.

Soulac-sur-Mer – The seaside resort bordered by pine-covered dunes is partly protected from the surge of the ocean by a high sandbank on which once stood the ancient city of Noviomagus, which was engulfed by the waters in the 6C. Until the 16C Soulac had an important roadstead opening on the Gironde estuary, where pilgrims to Santiago de Compostela *(qv)* would alight, and which was clogged up in the 17C by marshes.

A scenic railway returns from here to Pointe de Grave.

The **Basilique Notre-Dame-de-la-Fin-des-Terres** was a Benedictine abbey church which, at the end of the 18C, was almost entirely swallowed up by the sands; it was uncovered and restored in the 19C. The church includes elements of 12C Romanesque architecture and has a 14C belfry which replaced one which stood over the transept crossing. The Poitou style of building is apparent in the nave without any openings, dimly lit by windows in the side aisles which are almost as tall as the nave itself. Some of the historiated capitals remain : three show the tomb and shrine of St Veronica *(left pier before the chancel)* who evangelised the Médoc region and died in Soulac; one portrays St Peter in prison *(at the entrance to the chancel, left)*; another has Daniel in the lions' den *(inside the chancel)*. The polychrome wood statue of The Virgin at the Land's End is the object of pilgrimages.

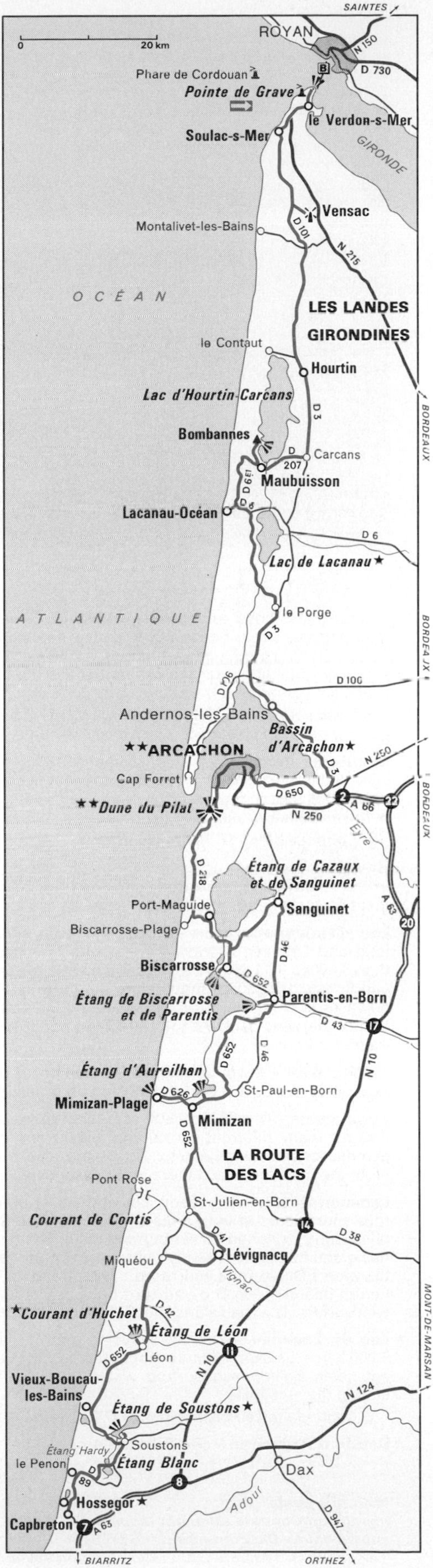

Lacanau lake.

The town also boast an **Archeological Museum** ⌚ displaying flint axes, chisels, decorated pottery, arrow heads etc from the neolithic and bronze ages, and from the Gallo-Roman period military ensigns, money, ceramics, glassware...
A modern building near the casino houses the **Fondation Soulac-Médoc** ⌚ : on view inside are paintings and sculptures by contemporary local artists.

Head south along D 101 for about 10km – 6 miles and take D 101^{E6} (left), following the orange signposts to Vensac windmill.

Moulin de Vensac ⌚ – This traditional 18C windmill consisting of a stone tower with a conical roof was moved to its present position in 1858. Visitors can follow the different stages in flour-making from the grinding of corn to the final sifting; some of the machinery, fashioned from oak, is as old as the mill itself.

Continue along D 101 to Hourtin.

Hourtin – The village, the starting-point for the network of lakes, lagoons and canals in the southwest suitable for canoeing, has now also become, with the development of Hourtin-Port at the lake's edge, a base for pleasure boats.

Lac d'Hourtin-Carcans – This huge, wild and isolated lake, 19km – 12 miles long and between 3 and 4km – about $2\frac{1}{2}$ miles wide, covers an area of more than 6 000ha – 14 800 acres. It is like an inland sea set within a landscape of moors and forests, fringed by marshes to the north and parts of the east (most of which however is sandy terrain); dunes, sometimes reaching a height of 60m – 197ft, border the west bank. At the northern end, at Le Contaut, there is a French Navy training centre.

Maubuisson – A wooden building here houses the **Musée des Arts et Traditions populaires des Landes** ⌚, a museum focusing on local life in and around the forest.

Bombannes – This 200ha – 500-acre **"open air centre"** among the pines provides facilities for many different sports and leisure activities : boating, tennis, swimming, gymnastics, archery, games... There are also a cultural centre and picnic areas. From the northern beach there is a pleasant view of an extensive reach of the lake.

Lacanau-Océan – The resort lies at the foot of sand dunes, facing the sea which rolls shorewards in long lines of breakers. The dunes are carpeted with maritime pines, long exploited for timber and resin. The geometrically-arranged plantations, rising and falling over sandy valleys known as *"lèdes"*, offer a pleasant contrast to the wide spaces of the enormous silver strand.
Return inland along D 6 and turn right before Le Moutchic, a resort popular with windsurfers. The road skirts the west bank of Lacanau Lake.

★ **Lac de Lacanau** – This attractive stretch of water covers an area of 2 000ha – 5 000 acres. Its 8km – 5 mile length teems with freshwater fish, including eels, pike and perch. Sailing, windsurfing, water-skiing and the hiring of boats or *pédalos* are among the amenities.

Continue to Le Porge and take D 3 towards Arcachon and its lagoon.

★ **Bassin d'Arcachon** – *See Bassin d'Arcachon.*

With this guide,
use the appropriate Michelin Maps (scale 1 : 200 000)
shown below the contents table on page 3.
The common symbols will make planning easier.

LA ROUTE DES LACS

From Arcachon to Capbreton

200km – 124 miles : allow 1 day. Local map p 137.

This itinerary passes the numerous lakes and lagoons along the coast south of Arcachon.

★★ **Arcachon** – *2 hours. See Arcachon.*

Leave Arcachon via D 218 to the southwest.

★★ **Dune du Pilat** – *See Arcachon.*

2km – $1\frac{1}{4}$ miles before Biscarrosse-Plage turn left (D 305) inland towards Port-Maguide.

The road dives down towards Cazaux and Sanguinet Lake, following the shoreline as far as Navarrosse after passing the small pleasure beach of **Port-Maguide.**

Étang de Cazaux et de Sanguinet – This fine stretch of water, with Sanguinet at its eastern limit, is linked with the neighbouring Biscarrosse and Parentis Lake by a canal. From Navarrosse to Biscarrosse the road runs through a pine forest.

Biscarrosse – Near the lake, four pavilions joined by three galleries house the **Musée historique de l'Hydraviation** (Seaplane and Flying Boat Museum) ⌚. The evolution of these machines, which reached its high point between the wars when concrete runways did not yet exist and the landing gear was increasingly unable to support the weight of the larger aircraft, is faithfully traced here. Numerous documents, models and original parts (engines, airscrews etc) tell the story of water-borne aircraft, the pioneers who designed them, the inauguration of an aero-postal service, the Biscarrosse seaplane base, the first long-distance flights, and the evolution of larger and larger civil and military types. An 18-minute film *(in French)* on the birth and death of the giant flying boats can be watched.
Opposite the museum actual seaplanes and flying boats can be viewed in a huge glazed hangar. It is also possible to visit a laboratory where remnants of aircraft shot down during the war are protected by electrolysis against corrosion.

Étang de Biscarrosse et de Parentis – The lake is a magnificent waterway spreading over an area of 3 600ha – 8 890 acres.

From Biscarrosse head northeast along D 652.

Sanguinet – The interesting **Archeological Museum** ⌚ in the village displays finds from local digs and excavations in and around the lake.

Take D 46 south to Parentis-en-Born.

Parentis-en-Born – The name of this small town is well-known in France today because of its links with petroleum. **The Musée de Pétrole** ⌚ established by Esso REP shows some of the technicalities and problems associated with the prospecting and production of the twentieth century's "black gold".

Follow D 652 southwest to Ste-Eulalie and continue (left) to St-Paul-en-Born; turn right into D 626.

Étang d'Aureilhan – There are attractive views of this lake from Aureilhan.

Mimizan – Most of the original town was buried beneath the rising dunes in the 18C. On the road to Mimizan-Plage lie the ruins of a Benedictine abbey where the remorseless advance of the sandhills was finally stopped : this feat was the work of a local man named Teixoëres, who was the first to use couch-grass and rushes as a means of consolidating – and so halting – the shifting dunes. The belfry of the old abbey church, built in the 13C, is still standing.

Mimizan-Plage – At the very end of D 626 turn right into Rue de la Poste and then left into Rue Assolant-et-Lotti. At the end of this street, on the left, a short flight of steps leads to a monument commemorating the landing here of the aviators Lefèvre, Assolant and Lotti on 16 June 1929 after their epic North Atlantic flight. The top of the dune offers splendid views.

Rejoin D 652 south via D 67.

Courant de Contis – Several streams emerging in the Landes are led to the ocean via this sinuous waterway, which passes through areas of vegetation as dense as they are varied. The "Current" clears a passage down to the marshes, and finally between the dunes, winding its way sometimes beneath a canopy of fresh leaves, sometimes between high natural hedges of bracken, reeds and alder bushes, with wild vines tangled between. Cypress trees, poplars, cork-oaks and pines mark the contrasting landscape above the high banks, although nearer the sea, downstream from Pont Rose, the pines predominate.

At St-Julien-en-Born take D 41 southeast to Lévignacq.

Lévignacq – This charming village, typical of the Landes, boasts an ancient church and low, timber-framed houses with tiled roofs. The church, fortified in the 14C, is unusual : the porch and doorway are in the Louis XIII style and the belfry is fashioned like a keep; the **wooden vaulting★** in the interior was decorated in the 18C with paintings representing the Nativity, the Holy Trinity and the Ascension; in the chancel is an altarpiece surrounded by twisted columns, while in front of the altar itself there is a giltwood representation of Jesus in the Garden of Olives.

Return via D 105 to D 652, turning left at Miquéou. Just before Léon, take D 142 (right) to the lake.

Étang de Léon – The cool, clear water in a peaceful countryside setting attracts tourists and watersports enthusiasts.

★ **Courant d'Huchet** – This capricious coastal river, full of eels, runs through lush, exotic-looking vegetation and offers a pleasant setting for **boat trips** ⊙, especially on summer mornings. Its winding course meanders beside rushes and water lilies, black cypresses, vines, wild hibiscus...

Continue along D 652 south.

Vieux-Boucau-les-Bains – Almost abandoned in 1578 when the course of the River Adour was changed, the town of Port d'Albret was renamed Vieux-Boucau (Old Estuary in the local dialect) and subsequently reborn as a tourist resort centred on a lagoon covering 60ha – 148 acres. The saltwater, sandwiched between the coastal sands and the pines, is topped up each day via a dam and a system of lock gates following the rhythm of the tides.
Le Mail is an attractive promenade, especially at night when the illuminations bring the place a charm of its own.

Continue along D 652.

★ **Étang de Soustons** – The shape of this fine stretch of water, and the fact that it is fringed by reeds and surrounded by dense pinewoods, means that it is never possible to see the whole lake at once. All parts of it however are easily accessible through the woods : to reach it from Soustons, follow Allée des Soupirs *(left of the church)* and then Avenue du Lac as far as the landing stage, where the banks are attractively planted with flowers. From here there is an excellent view of the narrowest part of the 730ha – 1 800-acre lake, and across to the other bank. For a view of the widest part, leave the jetty and walk through the pines along the southern shore *(30min Rtn on foot).*

Rejoin D 652 towards Tosse; after 4km – $2\frac{1}{2}$ miles turn right into the road to Gaillou-de-Pountaout (signposted Étang Blanc), which passes between Étang Hardy and Étang Blanc.

Étang Blanc – This delightful "white pool" is bordered by fishermen's huts and circled by a narrow road offering pretty vistas of the site and the surrounding countryside. From the final corner it is possible to look down on the neighbouring Étang Noir (Black Pool).

Turn right into D 89.

The road leads to **Le Penon,** a seaside resort offering accommodation ranging from apartments along the waterfront to villas among the forest pines.

Continue southwards.

★ **Hossegor** – *See Hossegor.*

Capbreton – The town, separated from Hossegor by Boudigau Canal, was an important port up until the diversion of the River Adour *(qv).* Decline followed but today, thanks to its attractive residential buildings, its marina and its fine-sand beach, the town is an important seaside resort. The landing-stage offers good views over the coast, the Pyrenees and the mouth of the canal.
Capbreton is also known for its **"Gouf"** or swallow-hole – a phenomenon of underwater topography which is invisible from the surface, but the existence of which fishermen, centuries before its discovery, had sensed during storms. It is the main geomorphological trait of the continental shelf in the Bay of Biscay. The swallow-hole is an east-west chasm running for over 60km – 37 miles from the exit of the harbour; it is 3-10km – 2-6 miles wide and reaches 3 000m – nearly 10 000ft in depth. The reasons for its existence have led to various hypotheses – for instance, that it is the result of a complex process of underwater fluvial erosion; a fracture linked to the rising up of the Pyrenean mountains; a canyon gouged by the River Adour during the great glaciations of the Quaternary Age when sea levels lowered – though none has yet been conclusively proved.
Above the municipal casino, the **Écomusée de la Pêche et de la Mer** ⊙ is a museum which focuses on marine geology and the history of the fishing industry around Capbreton and the Landes coast (aquariums, models, photos, films). Note the skeleton of an arctic whale beached near Le Penon in 1988. From the terrace there are **panoramic views** over the area.

LA CÔTE BASQUE

From Anglet to Hendaye *41km – 25 miles : about 2 hours.*

The southern stretch of the Côte d'Argent is known as the Côte Basque (Basque Coast); descriptions of its attractive towns and villages – **Anglet★**, **Biarritz★★★**, **Bidart★**, **Guéthary**, **St-Jean-de-Luz★★** and **Hendaye★** – may be found under their separate chapter headings.

★ COULON

Pop 1 870

Michelin map 71 north of fold 2 or 233 fold 5 – Facilities – Local map p 173.

This small town is the capital of the **Marais Poitevin** *(qv)*, that huge area of fertile Poitou marshlands south of the Loire and inland from Les Sables-d'Olonne.
The Poitou marshlands are divided into the *Marais Desséché* (Dry Marsh) and the *Marais Mouillé* (Wet Marsh). Coulon, which lies on the edge of the latter, more easterly section, is the main embarkation point for **boat trips** ⊙ through this attractive "Green Venice". Land exploration of the marsh country can also be made from the town in a **miniature train** (le Pibalou) ⊙ or by **minibus** (le Grenouillon) ⊙.
From the bridge across the Sèvre Niortaise there is a pleasant view of the canalized river flowing peacefully between quays lined with boatmen's houses.

SIGHTS

Église – This church, Romanesque originally but remodelled later in the Gothic style (west and south doors), is one of very few in France to have a preacher's pulpit outside in the open air – in the form here of a small canopied tower.

Aquarium ⓥ – The aquarium is installed in a house overlooking the church square and displays over 2 000 varieties of river fish, including a *Silure* – a kind of catfish and the largest freshwater fish in the world – weighing more than 20kg – 44lbs, and exotica from the tropics.
Slides and a diorama provide visitors with an excellent perspective on the Marais Poitevin as a whole – the flora, the fauna, the agriculture, the marshlands throughout the seasons etc.

Maison des Marais mouillés ⓥ – *Place de la Coutume.* The name of the square in which this museum stands recalls the fact that, in days gone by, boatmen used to stop here to pay their *Droit de Coutume* (customary dues), a tax levied on goods in transit. The small museum explains the formation of the Wet Marsh, and focuses on the traditional occupations here, particularly eel fishing, and the local inhabitants since prehistoric times (artefacts from the Bronze Age have been found at Coulon, including a cart wheel, now in the Musée du Donjon at Niort).
A small aquarium is home to some fish; a video on the Marais may also be watched.

Le COUSERANS

Michelin map 86 folds 2, 3, 13 or 235 folds 41, 42, 46.

This region just north of the "axial zone" or backbone of the Pyrenees was closely linked with the neighbouring district of Le Comminges *(qv)* in medieval times, even though it was independent enough to have its own bishop at St-Lizier. "Couserans of the 18 valleys" corresponds geographically with the basin of the Upper Salat torrent, with St-Girons at the centre as the equivalent of county town. The relatively soft sedimentary rocks of the area, particularly the schists, have been gashed by tributaries of the Salat torrent to form heavily indented mountain massifs separated by wide valleys. Luminous skies above a fresh green landscape with abundant vegetation characterize this upland country, but life in the mountains is precarious and in the absence of any industrial exploitation the region is becoming progressively depopulated.
The frontier chain, marked by the pyramid silhouette of Mont Valier (alt 2 838m – 9 314ft) which is visible from as far away as Toulouse, remains a favourite haunt for the sturdier and more determined hill-walkers and mountaineers (most of the recommended walks require at least ten hours).
The prehistoric painted grottoes of the Volp Valley discovered by Comte Henri Begouën (1863-1955) are closed to the public.

BIROS AND BETHMALE VALLEYS

1 From Audressein to Seix

46km – 29 miles : about 2 hours – Local map overleaf.

Audressein – This is a pleasant small village at the convergence of the Bouigane and Lez rivers. The pilgrims' **church** (mainly 14C) dedicated to Notre-Dame-de-Tramezaygues is crowned by an open-work belltower. The central porch is decorated with 15C murals, many of them votive offerings by way of thanks from those who had narrowly escaped a violent death or a prison sentence. Much of the painting has worn away but there are recognizable images of John the Baptist, St James and four angel-musicians.
The route follows the Lez Valley upstream.

Castillon-en-Couserans – The small village on the east bank of the Lez is built along a river terrace at the foot of a wooded hill.

Les Bordes – At the entrance to the village, by a roadside Cross, there is a pretty view of the oldest bridge in the Couserans area and of the Romanesque church at Ourjout.

Vallée de Biros – The Biros valley is watered by the Lez river. Continuing up the valley, the road passes a number of tributary valleys on the south side, at the far end of which are glimpses of the frontier chain and its peaks. Among these are Mont Valier, seen at the head of the Riberot valley, and Mail de Bulard (valley of the Orle).

Sentein – Sentein is a tiny thermal spa and a good mountain excursion centre. The church with its fine three-storey belfry crowned by a spire is flanked by two square towers, all that remains of a fortified enclosure which had a circumference measuring 200m – 220yds.

Turn back down the valley and return to Les Bordes. Turn right.

★ **Vallée de Bethmale** – This valley is wide and picturesque, its humpbacked slopes scattered with barns and, on terraces beside the road, small villages where the steep streets burrow between a huddle of interconnected houses. *(Avoid the detours signposted to Arrien and Aret.)*
The *commune* of Bethmale (which in 1990 had only 96 inhabitants) used to be known for the imposing bearing of its population and their distinctive dress : the traditional men's jackets, for example, were made of raw wool with multicoloured facings – a fact which continues to intrigue ethnologists and experts in folklore, for similar garments exist as part of ceremonial peasant costume in the Balkans.

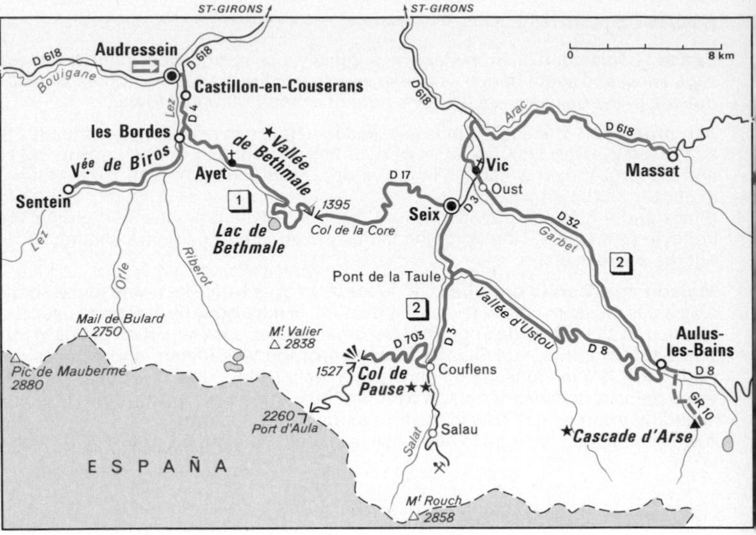

Ayet – In the church, which is built on a raised site, there are examples of 18C "primitive" woodwork – note especially the Rococo open-work carving (in poor condition) in the baptistery chapel.

About 5km – 3 miles further on, park by the roadside near a sharp bend to the left and walk into Bethmale Forest.

Lac de Bethmale – *15min on foot Rtn.* The lake sits in an attractive setting surrounded by beech trees.

Gaining height in an amphitheatre of pastureland, the road reaches Col de la Core (alt 1 395m – 4 577ft) from which there is a view back over the Bethmale Valley. East of the pass is the Esbints valley, where the landscape is wooded and wilder. To the southwest, the secondary chain of the Mont Valier massif is visible. The road descends, once again passing orchards and barns as it leads towards the confluence of the Salat and Garbet torrents near Oust, the geographic centre of the Upper Salat region.

Seix – The village is overlooked by a 16C château.

★ UPPER SALAT AND GARBET VALLEYS

2 From Seix to Massat

84km – 52 miles : allow 1 day – Local map above.

From Seix the road south following the Upper Salat upstream continues as far as Salau, not far from the Spanish border, where there are important tungsten mines. For 10km – 6 miles beyond Seix, this itinerary follows the course of the torrent in a narrow, steep-sided valley then branches off at the entrance to Couflens towards Col de Pause and Port d'Aula. *This is a narrow mountain road, climbing very steep slopes. The surface is poor and rutted over the final 3km – $1\frac{3}{4}$ miles (generally obstructed by snow from October to May).*

The track climbs above the impressive, forested Angouls Valley. Off to the south, through the gap carved by the Salat, the summits of the valley's terminal amphitheatre can be seen above Salau; the highest is Mont Rouch (alt 2 858m – 9 377ft). The route continues beyond the strikingly situated village of Faup, perched on a rocky ledge, to the pass.

★★ **Col de Pause** – Alt 1 527m – 5 010ft. A climb above the pass on the right-hand slope beneath Pic de Fonta offers a different **view** of Mont Valier on the far side of the Estours Valley breach : from here the chasms gashing the summit's east face and the ridges of its northern foothills are clearly visible.

Beyond Pause Pass the impressive route follows a road in very poor condition which cannot be recommended : motorists should be aware of the risk of possible damage to vehicles. Return to Pont de la Taule and turn right into D 8.

The road follows the **Vallée d'Ustou,** climbs for a few miles, and then drops down again in a series of sharp bends to Aulus-les-Bains. There are fine views during the descent.

Aulus-les-Bains – This ancient hydro-mineral spa was known to the Romans but became popular again only in the early 19C. It still retains a cure centre, in the gardens of which waters used for treating urinary disorders, gout and obesity can be drunk. Aulus is a convenient starting point for excursions into the three tributary valleys of the Garbet (the Fouillet, the Arse and the Upper Garbet), all of which have waterfalls and small lakes.

Continue southeast up the Garbet Valley. After 1km – $\frac{1}{2}$ mile park the car and take footpath GR10, on the right.

★ **Cascade d'Arse** – *10km – 6 miles Rtn on foot.* Crossing the river and winding south, GR10 leads to the foot of these superb falls which plunge 110m – 360ft in three separate stages.

Return to Aulus and take D 32 northwards down the Garbet Valley.

The **Vallée du Garbet★** is one of those most scored by former glaciers in the Upper Couserans – and in one of the best locations. It is sunny and scattered with pretty hamlets often boasting thatched cottages with stepped gables, and was once known locally as *"Terro Santo"* (sainted land) on account of the large number of chapels and wayside shrines to be seen.

At the far end of the valley, beyond Oust, the road leads to the village of Vic.

Vic – The **church** here is typical of those in the Ariège *département,* with its belfry-wall and its Romanesque triple apse. In the small square by the entrance a wrought-iron Cross, testimony to the skill of the Ariège ironsmiths, commemorates the fallen in the two world wars.
Inside the church, the 16C coffered and painted ceiling of the nave and aisles is echoed in the murals covering the vaulting above the chancel.
The Salat, now joined by the Garbet torrent, runs through a narrowing valley, the banks becoming higher and steeper. After the Kercabanac tunnel, the itinerary leaves D 32 to turn sharply right into D 618 following the sinuous Arac torrent. Soon after Castet, these winding gorges describe a particularly pronounced curve; here, especially on the *"soulane"* (sunny side of the valley), the varied green of the trees contrasts vividly with the red of the rocks and the russet tints of the dried bracken. Finally the channel widens out into the Massat basin.

Massat – This small local capital boasts a church with a gabled west front flanked by an elegant 15C octagonal tower. At the top level (the tower reaches 58m – 190ft), the muzzles of decorative cannons project through diamond-shaped apertures. Above the entrance there is a fine wrought-iron grille.

DAMPIERRE-SUR-BOUTONNE

Pop 335

Michelin map 72 folds 1, 2 or 233 folds 16, 17 – 8.5km – 5 miles northeast of Aulnay.

This village, pleasantly situated in the green valley of the River Boutonne, is known for its Renaissance château, built in an ideal setting on an islet in the river. Since 1981 Dampierre has also become famous as a breeding centre for the celebrated *"Baudets"* (donkeys) of Poitou.

SIGHTS

Giraud/RAPHO

Poitou donkeys.

Château ⊙ – Of the four blocks originally framing the castle's inner courtyard, only the one housing the living quarters remains; it is flanked by two massive towers designed to defend the building from outside attack. From the courtyard itself the aspect of the château is less severe. The most impressive feature is a two-tiered gallery of basket-handle arches, the two levels being separated by a frieze of carved foliage. The upper gallery features a coffered ceiling, the 93 sections of which are carved with crests (a swan pierced by an arrow, the emblem of Claude of France, wife of François I), insignia (Catherine de' Medici and Henri II), and allegorical scenes and symbols (a labyrinth, a cherub astride a chimera...). These are often bordered by scrolls bearing mottoes, most of them in Latin. An interpretation and explanation of these decorations was offered in 1931 by the author Fulcanelli in his alchemist study, *Les Demeures Philosophales.*
Among the furnishings on view in the apartments are fine Flemish tapestries and a superb Italian ebony cabinet (16C). In the guardroom, the chimneypiece bears the inscription : *"Estre, se cognestre et non parestre"* (To be is to know oneself rather than be known).
There are two exhibitions in the castle reception : *Art and Alchemy* (which analyses details of the coffered ceiling) and *Dali's Horses* (paintings inspired by the ceiling).

Maison de l'Âne de Poitou ⊙ – *At La Tillauderie, 5km – 3 miles northeast on D 127 towards Chizé.*
The **Baudet du Poitou,** an unusually large donkey, reddish-brown in colour with a long, woolly coat, has been bred in this region for centuries. Crossing a mare with the male ass of this breed produces a hybrid, sterile mule known as a *Mule Poitevine* which is particularly suited to carrying heavy loads over difficult terrain. Most were bred at the "animal workshop" at St-Martin-les-Melle, near the town of Melle, and were in great demand until the beginning of this century, when motorized methods of transport took preference.
Since the 1950s the Poitou donkey has been threatened with extinction; the establishment of a national research centre, near Dampierre, may however save the race, which has been greatly weakened by inbreeding.
Display panels and video in the small museum illustrate the history of the Baudet and the efforts being made to preserve the breed. Nearby, she-asses from Portugal and local Baudets can be seen grazing peacefully together. The robust, mule-producing stallion belonging to the centre may also be seen in the stables.

★ DAX

Pop 19 309

Michelin map 78 folds 6, 7 or 234 fold 26 – Local map p 137 – Facilities.

Dax is a popular spa town, much favoured by those with rheumatic or lymphatic complaints. The effectiveness of its celebrated mud baths – composed of silt from the Adour river and medicinal waters from the town's hot springs – is due to the algae with a strong radioactive content which proliferate in the mixture.
Standing on the boundary between the Chalosse district and the forests of the Landes, Dax is also an important commercial and agricultural centre specializing in farm produce and resins from the pine forests. Riverside walks, colourful public gardens, interesting churches, even bullfights, combine to make the town an enjoyable stopping place for tourists.
A lake village, with houses on stilts, once stood on the site where Dax is built today, but little by little alluvia from the Adour silted up the lake and the village was able to spread out over dry land.

HISTORICAL NOTES

From Augustus to Louis XIV – Once the Romans had settled in the Dax region, the hot springs became famous : Emperor Augustus brought his daughter Julia here for a rheumatic cure; the town received favours from Rome and prospered.
An English possession after Eleanor of Aquitaine *(qv)* married Henry Plantagenet (Henry II of England) in 1152, Dax became French again only in 1451 when the Comte de Foix took possession of it in the name of Charles VII.
After the celebration of the marriage between Louis XIV and Maria Teresa at St-Jean-de-Luz *(qv)*, the king and his bride stopped at Dax on their way home to Paris. The townsfolk set up a triumphal arch at the entrance to the town as a sign of welcome : the painting on it of a dolphin emerging from the water, and the Latin inscription, was a message punning on the words dolphin and *dauphin,* hoping that the couple's stay in Dax would be a fruitful one.

A great Saint – In 1581 **Vincent de Paul** was born, in a hamlet not far from Dax *(see Excursions below).* From a poor peasant family, he worked as a shepherd from an early age; in 1595 the intelligent child was sent to one of the Franciscan schools in Dax; five years later he was ordained a priest at Château-l'Évêque. He was appointed *curé* at Châtillon-les-Dombes, where he founded the first Brotherhood of Charity. In 1625 he created an organization, known as the Lazarists, to teach and help the poor, and eight years later, with Louise de Marillac, founded the Sisters of Charity who succoured the sick.
Throughout his apostolic ministry "Monsieur Vincent" fought to combat the terrible poverty of the times. When Louis XIII appointed him Chaplain-General to the galleys, he lavished consolation and spiritual help on the convict-slaves. Horrified by the filth of existing hospitals, he founded the Bicêtre, the Salpétrière, the Pitié and Enfants-Trouvés (Foundling) hospitals in Paris, as well as a hospital for convicts in Marseille.
It was Vincent de Paul who attended Louis XIII on his deathbed. At the request of the Regent, Anne of Austria, he sat with the "Council of Conscience" and helped with the reform of the Catholic Church. During the *Fronde* (the French civil war which raged between 1648 and 1653) he tried to restore peace, organized food supplies for towns threatened with famine, and set up soup kitchens and public employment centres.
This forerunner of modern social services died in 1660, at the age of 79. He was canonized in 1737.

SIGHTS

Fontaine Chaude (Hot Fountain) – This spring at the centre of town is the main attraction in Dax. The water, which has been tapped since Roman times, gushes at a temperature of 64°C – 147°F into a huge basin surrounded by arcades.

Banks of the Adour – The riverside walks are particularly pleasant. Upstream from the bridge, the Th.-Denis Park contains the ruins of an arena (les arènes) and fragments of the 4C ramparts, now developed as a promenade shaded by plane trees. Downstream are the Potinière Gardens and the Baignots' Avenue and Park.

Cathédrale – The cathedral was built in the Classical style in the 17C to replace a collapsed Gothic church, of which a fine doorway remains, now part of the inner façade of the north transept. The embrasures of the double doorway are decorated with twelve columns supporting large statues of the Apostles; an effigy of Christ adorns the pier. Both the tympanum and archivolt are richly embellished.

Musée de Borda ⊙ – The museum, housed in a 17C mansion, takes its name from **Jean-Charles Borda** who was born in Dax in 1733. The naval engineer, mathematician, geometrican and accomplished seaman was responsible for major developments in nautical observation and calculations.
The rooms display prehistoric, archeological and numismatic (coin) collections. One room is devoted to regional folklore, another to the Landes races.

Crypte Archéologique ⊙ – Recent archeological digs opposite the museum have uncovered the podium of a 2C Gallo-Roman temple.

St-Paul-lès-Dax – *North of the town centre : take the Bayonne road, then follow the signposts.* Of particular interest on the church are the 11C low-reliefs decorating the exterior of the east end. From left to right, the naive, early Romanesque works represent : the Holy Women at the Tomb; the Trinity *(on a buttress);* a trio of fantastic beasts; the Last Supper; the Kiss of Judas; the Crucifixion; Samson riding a lion *(on a buttress);* St Veronica; a dragon; an allegory of Heaven.
Inside the church, the chancel with its stone stalls is impressively austere.

EXCURSIONS

Berceau de St Vincent de Paul et Notre-Dame de Buglose (St Vincent de Paul's birthplace and Buglose Church) – *9km – 5 miles northeast. Leave Dax by N 124 (east) and turn left into D 27.* Buildings belonging to the charitable and educational institutions founded by the saint are grouped around a modern church in neo-Byzantine style. The complex was built in 1864 to honour "Monsieur Vincent".
On the approximate site of the saint's birthplace, on the left of the square, is an old house built with surviving relics of the original cottage, which can be visited. Inside are numerous mementoes relating to "Monsieur Vincent"; outside, the ancient oak tree was already standing when Vincent de Paul was a child here.

Continue along D 27.

Notre-Dame de Buglose – The church is a centre of pilgrimage. Above the altar of the modern basilica, built in the Romanesque style, is the venerated Virgin : a statue in multicoloured stone discovered in 1620. The church tower houses a carillon of 60 bells.
A lane leads to a spring and to the small chapel (now enveloped within a larger, modern chapel) which was built where the statue was found.

Préchacq-les-Bains – *16km – 10 miles northeast. Leave Dax by N 124 (east) and at Pontonx-sur-l'Adour turn right into D 10, and right again.* The village stands among oak woods on the south bank of the Adour and specialises, like Dax, in the treatment of rheumatism and respiratory complaints. The small spa, which was visited by the writer Montaigne *(qv)*, boasts hot springs (63°C – 145°F) impregnated with calcium sulphate, and a cold sulphur spring at 18°C – 64°F. In the gardens beyond the thermal treatment centre, pools of the vegeto-mineral mud used can be seen.

Lesgor – *22km – 14 miles northeast. Leave Dax by N 124 (east); beyond Pontonx turn left into D 425.* The small village has a picturesque fortified church in the local Landes style.

ESPELETTE Pop 1 661

Map 85 fold 3 or 234 fold 33.

This village dates from medieval times and remains a sprawling collection of houses lining narrow, winding streets, which is unusual in the Labourd district.
Worth noting in the **church** are the grilles at the Communion table. 17C and 18C disk-shaped Basque crosses can be seen in the adjacent cemetery.
Espelette specializes in growing red peppers (capsicums) but there is also a brisk local trade in **Pottocks** the ponies which live in herds in a semi-wild state on the uninhabited slopes of the frontier mountains.

Pottok pony.

D'après photo M. Fraudreau/TOP

These animals, resembling in some ways Britain's own New Forest ponies, were once exported to England, because of their diminutive stature, to haul trucks in the underground galleries of coal mines. Today the breed has been "improved" for riding purposes and to provide horsemeat.

★ FENIOUX Pop 133

Map 71 fold 4 or 233 fold 16 – 8km – 5 miles southwest of St-Jean-d'Angély.

The village, a scatter of small houses on a hillside overlooking a valley, is known for its church and its *Lanterne des Morts* (Lantern of the Dead).

Church – This charming country church with a single nave dates back, in part, to the Carolingian epoch (9C). Typical of the period are the small number of openings, the small-size stonework and the thin slabs of masonry, pierced to form an interlacing design, known as *fenestrelles.*
The west front is in Saintonge Romanesque style *(qv)*. Grouped columns frame an immense doorway, deeply recessed, with ten supports for the archivolt carved with (from top to bottom) the labours of the months, the signs of the Zodiac, the Wise and Foolish Virgins, Angels adoring the Lamb, and the Vices overcome by Virtue. On the north side of the façade a small doorway is charmingly decorated with floral and foliate designs. The open-work belltower holds a special place in the history of Romanesque art because of its bold yet light design, and has been much copied by late 19C architects. Over-zealous restoration has unfortunately exaggerated the austerity of its attenuated lines, which now appear almost spindly.

★ **Lanterne des Morts** – *Illustration p 41.* This tall, elegant and robust monument stands in the middle of a former cemetery; a vaulted sepulchre adjoins it. It is composed of eleven columns grouped together to support a small lantern, itself encircled by 13 smaller columns. It is topped by a pyramid-shaped roof of overlapping tiles and surmounted by a Cross. Inside, a spiral staircase *(37 steps)* ascends to the top.

★ Abbaye de FLARAN

Michelin map 82 north of fold 4 or 234 fold 24 – 8km – 5 miles south of Condom.

Flaran Abbey was founded in 1151 as part of the expansion of the Cistercian Order throughout Gascony. Thanks to the benevolence of local seigneurs it prospered rapidly, before falling under the domination first of the English and then of the French. It was spared neither by the Wars of Religion *(qv)* nor, later, by the exigencies of the Revolution.
The abbey, situated on the outskirts of Valence-sur-Baïse, has now been transformed into a **cultural centre** hosting concerts, exhibitions and seminars throughout the year. Each summer an audio-visual presentation, *Flaran, Pierres Vivantes* (The Living Stones of Flaran) recalls the eventful past of this fine monastic complex *(see Calendar of Events, qv).*

TOUR ⏲ *1 hour*

Abbey lodgings – The building was constructed in the 18C for the use of the Prior and his guests, and has the charm of a small Gascon château. It stands adjacent to the part of the abbey which replaced the lay brothers' wing on the west side of the cloisters in the early 14C. The reception area and the salon (**1**) are decorated with fine plaster mouldings. From the main courtyard, bordered on the west side by the stables (**2**) and outhouses, visitors can admire the west front of the abbey church at close quarters. The upper part of the façade is pierced by a rose window encircled by a chequered pattern; unusually, the semicircular arched entrance below has no tympanum above the door.

Abbey church – The church (built between 1180 and 1210) comprises a nave flanked by single aisles, a transept which is wider than the nave is long, and a chancel, parallel to which are four transept chapels. The broken-barrel vaulting which covers the nave and aisles terminates in an oven vault above the chancel. Powerful transverse arches are supported by engaged twinned columns emerging from rectangular pillars. The ornamentation of the double capitals is very simple, following Cistercian tradition : either smooth foliage or scrolls and interlacing, all highly stylized. The semicircular east end and rows of blind arcades festooning the four chapels (best seen from the garden) are characteristic of early Romanesque art in the south. A foretaste of the Gothic style, however, can be seen in the rib vaulting above the transept crossing.
The **sacristy** (**3**) opens off the north transept. It is a very light, square room, notable again for the rib vaulting springing from a central column. A stone staircase outside the entrance leads to the monks' dorter.

Cloisters – Entrance from the church is via a doorway surmounted by a fine *chi-rho* (the XP monogram from the Greek spelling of the word Christ), a favourite motif of Gascon artists during the Romanesque period. Of the four original cloister galleries, only that on the west side (early 14C) remains today. The framework of the structure resembles that favoured by contemporary architects in the Toulouse area : the pointed arches of the arcades rest on twinned columns, the capitals of which are decorated either with foliage or with human or animal faces.

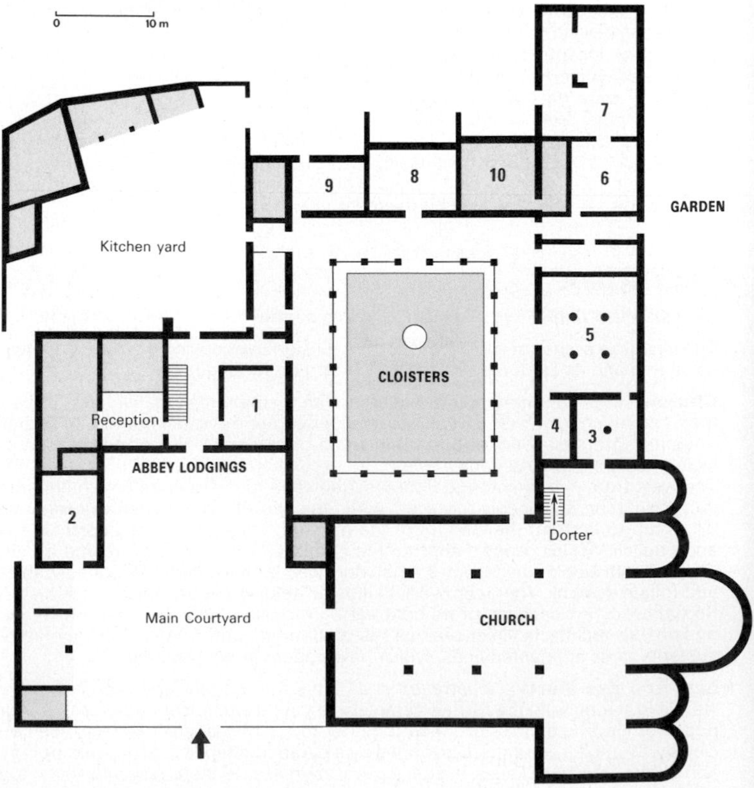

Monastic buildings – These extend from the northern arm of the transept. The **armarium** or library (**4**), next to the sacristy, is entered via the **chapter-house** (**5**) in which the quadripartite vaulting is supported by beautiful columns of different-coloured Pyrenean marble; three openings with arching resting on colonnettes give onto the cloisters.
Beyond a passageway that leads to the garden, the former **monks' common room** (**6**) and the **store-room** (**7**) house an exhibition on the section of the pilgrims' route to Compostela that lies within Gascony. The exhibits include maps, sculptures, funerary crosses of fallen pilgrims, a 17C statue of St James in polychrome wood...
On the floor above, reached by a staircase from the north transept, the old **monks' dorter** (dormitory) was transformed into separate cells in the 17C. These communicate with the Prior's apartments and the upper gallery of the cloisters, from which there is a fine view of the abbey as a whole.
In the centre of the northern wing stands the **refectory** (**8**), flanked by **kitchens** (**9**) and the **calefactory** (**10**), originally the only heated room in the complex, where the monks would have kept warm while reading and writing. The refectory was remodelled in the 18C; it is decorated with fine stucco-work, particularly above the chimneypiece where the motif is a phoenix rising from its ashes.

Garden – This is in two parts : a formal garden in the French style and, near an old mill, a herb garden stocked with medicinal and aromatic plants. There is a good view of the eastern wing of the monks' building and the east end of the abbey church.

Ferme de la Magdeleine – The farm buildings – barns, stables, farmer's quarters etc – adjoin each side of an old square tower, southwest of the abbey proper; they are all that remain of the 14C fortifications. Between the farm and the monastery a 5C Roman mosaic, recently uncovered from a villa nearby, can be seen.

⊙ ►► Armagnac Country : Mouchan (northwest) – Romanesque church; Cassaigne Château (northwest) – Tour of the barrel stores; Château du Busca-Maniban (southwest); Valence-sur-Baïse (southeast) – 13C *bastide* with 14C church; Monluc Château (southeast) – Medieval fortress and the cradle of *pousse-rapière,* an armagnac-based liqueur.

FONTENAY-LE-COMTE

Pop 11 456

Michelin map 71 fold 1 or 233 fold 4 – Local maps pp 173 and 176 – Facilities.
Town plan in the current Michelin Red Guide France.

Fontenay lies sheltered in a fold of land on the banks of the River Vendée, bordering the plain, the *bocage (qv)* and the Poitou marshlands. Its limestone houses, sometimes coated with rough-cast, sprawl between two main axes perpendicular to the river. Place Viète is effectively the town centre and lies on the site of a bastion which formed part of the ancient fortified enclosure. East of it, particularly in the areas around Notre-Dame Church and St-Jean Church (beyond Rue des Loges), is the Old Town. The modern part of Fontenay extends southwest of the line drawn by Rue Clemenceau and Rue de la République.
Fontenay remains essentially a market town, despite the establishment of a large industrial zone southeast of the town.

HISTORICAL AND LITERARY NOTES

In the Middle Ages and during the Renaissance Fontenay, the capital of Lower Poitou, was a stronghold accustomed to violent attacks. A local heroine, Jeanne de Clisson, defended it in 1372 against Bertrand du Guesclin, one of the generals responsible for chasing the English from France. At the end of the 16C the town was the scene of struggles between *Parpaillots* (Protestants) and Papists. Two centuries later, Republicans twice fought the Royalists of the Vendée beneath its walls.

A fountain of fine spirits – In the 16C Fontenay (the name is derived from the Quatre-Tias fountain – *see below*) was a centre of Renaissance exuberance.
In 1520 the young **Rabelais** knocked at the gates of the Cordeliers (Franciscans') headquarters, which stood on the site of the present town hall. He had left the Cordeliers of Angers and hoped to study Greek literature under Friar Pierre Amy, a precursor of the Reformation. Amy put him in touch (by letter) with the Hellenist scholar Guillaume Budé (1467-1540), a humanist whose later *Correspondance* with Rabelais and others became an important document in the literary history of the period.
At Fontenay Rabelais and his friends would meet at the home of **André Tiraqueau** (1480-1558), learned legal writer, proud father of 30 children and author of a treatise on matrimonial laws for which Rabelais composed an epigraph in Greek verse. In 1523, however, Rabelais was constrained to seek refuge with the Benedictines of Maillezais *(qv)* after his Father Superior discovered books favourable to the Reformation among Rabelais' belongings.
In the second half of the century other Fontenay humanists found fame, among them Barnabé Brisson, President of the Parliament of Paris, who was hanged in 1591 during the disputes concerning the Catholic League *(qv)*, and François Viète (1540-1603), the brilliant mathematician who invented algebra. The poet and strict magistrate **Nicolas Rapin** (*c*1540-1608) was another major local figure : during the "Grands Jours" of Poitiers *(qv)* he took part in a poetry competition, the theme of which was to be a flea frolicking on the snow-white bosom of Mademoiselle de Roches, a noted Poitou bluestocking. Rapin won the prize with his piece *La Puce* (The Flea), which was followed by *L'Anti-Puce.* Later, in Paris, he was one of the chief instigators of *La Satire Menippée* (a political pamphlet directed against the Catholic League and published in 1594) before retiring to his country residence, the Château de Terre-Neuve *(see below)*.

SIGHTS

Musée Vendéen ⓥ – *East side of Place Viète.* The ground and first floors of this regional museum contain collections of archeology (Gallo-Roman glassware from local tombs), ornithology (stuffed birds, photographs of their natural habitat) and ethnography (southern Vendée furniture).
The second floor is devoted to the history of the town and to artists with Vendée connections, among them the painters Paul Baudry *(Diana Surprised),* August Lepère *(The Squall* – the arrival of a storm over the sea – and *Views of the St-Jean-de-Monts Dunes)* and Charles Milcendeau *(View of the Wet Marsh, The Embroideresses, The Spinning-Wheel).* Also on view are Lepère sketches which served as a basis for engravings.
A small modern art department includes work by Émile Lahner (*The Kitchen, The Egyptian Woman* and highly coloured abstracts dating from 1959 and 1960). A huge sculpture by the brothers Jan and Joël **Martel** represents *An Olonne Woman Wearing a Shawl.*

Église Notre-Dame – *East of the Musée Vendéen.* The church is marked by a slender and elegant 15C **belltower★** which was remodelled in 1700 by the architect François Leduc. The 82m – 270ft tower, crowned by a spire decorated with crockets, is similar to that of Luçon cathedral *(qv).* The main doorway is Flamboyant Gothic, with a large stone filigree opening replacing the tympanum. Wise Virgins with upright lamps and Foolish Virgins with their lamps upside down are carved in the coving. A delicate 19C Madonna adorns the pier niche.
A Louis XVI pulpit is among the features worth noting inside the church; others include the Brisson chapel and the apsidal chapels, dating from the time of François I, and now partly concealed by the outsize 18C altarpiece.
The small 9C crypt, discovered by chance in the 19C, is a rare and important example of early architecture in the Lower Poitou region. Roman mortar was used for the groin vaulting; the capitals of the supporting pillars are in Byzantine style.

Take the small street at the southeastern end of the church.

Rue du Pont-aux-Chèvres – A number of interesting old houses can be seen in this street. The former Benedictine priory at No 3 has a staircase tower. At No 6, the Villeneuve-Esclapon mansion is adorned with a monumental Louis XIII entrance surmounted by a Laocoon (an antique sculpture group representing Laocoon, the priest of Apollo, strangled with his two sons by serpents; the original is in the Vatican). The figures are flanked by statues of Hercules and Diana. No 9 boasts a fine balustraded staircase; the property belonged in the 16C and 17C to the Bishops of Maillezais. No 14 is a splendid example of a Renaissance private house, though recently deprived of its left wing. It belonged once to André Rivaudeau, mayor of Fontenay in the late 16C and author of the tragedy *Aman,* which inspired Racine to compose *Esther.*

The northeastern end of the street leads into a small square.

Place Belliard – The statue in the quiet square represents General Belliard (1769-1832) who saved the life of Napoleon Bonaparte at Arcole by shielding him with his own body. The General was born at No 11.
Five interesting houses (three of them with arcades) flanking one side of the square were built by the architect Jean Morisson in the reign of Henri IV. Morisson himself lived at No 16 : the pediment is crowned by a statue of the architect holding a pair of compasses, the emblem of his profession. His personal motto, *Peu et Paix* (literally, Few and Peace, roughly equivalent to "Less is More") is carved above the first-floor bay.

Leave the square at its northern end and turn right into Rue Guillemet; take the second turning on the left into Rue de la Fontaine.

Fontaine des Quatre-Tias – In the local patois, the word *tias* means pipes. The fountain, built in 1542 by the architect Lienard de Réau, bears the Latin inscription *Fontanacum Felicium Ingeniorum Fons et Scaturigo* (The Fountain and Source of Fine Spirits) – a motto bestowed on the town by François I. The King's coat of arms, complete with emblematic salamander, is engraved on the pediment. The fountain is also inscribed with the names of famous magistrates who have sat on the bench in Fontenay, including that of Nicolas Rapin *(see above).*

Return to Rue Guillemet and cross the bridge, Pont aux Sardines.

Rue des Loges – In the 18C this street, flanked by quaintly named lanes and alleys – Rue du Lamproie (Lamprey Lane), Rue de la Grue (Crane Street), Rue de la Pie (Magpie Alley) – was the town's main street. Today Rue des Loges is a pedestrian shopping precinct, still bordered by a number of houses with fine old façades. Among these are the house at No 26 with wrought-iron balconies and carved human faces; No 85, with an impressive late 16C doorway of carved stone; and No 94, a medieval building with projecting upper floors. On the corner of Rue St-Nicolas stands a carefully restored early 16C half-timbered house.

Return to Place Viète.

Château de Terre-Neuve ⓥ – *Take Rue Rabelais west out of Place Viète and turn first left into Rue Brisson to the château.*
Morisson, who built the houses in Place Belliard *(see above),* was also the architect of this country retreat commissioned by his friend Nicolas Rapin at the end of the 16C. It was here that Rapin wrote his well-known work, *Plaisirs du Gentilhomme Champestre* (The Pleasures of a Country Gentleman). The archeologist and engraver Octave de Rochebrune restored the château *c*1850, adding to the decoration and collecting together a number of works of art which lent the property as a whole

a fine Renaissance air tempered by Classical influences. The building comprises two main blocks at right-angles to one another, with turreted bartizans at each corner. The façade is adorned with Italian Renaissance muses in terracotta and a porch which was originally part of another château.
The **interior★** features a number of remarkable elements : Louis XIV woodwork from Chambord Château on the Loire, a door from François I's study, fine Louis XV and Louis XVI furniture, 17C and 18C paintings and a handsome chimneypiece, designed by Philibert Delorme, with carvings evoking the symbolic system devised by the Renaissance alchemists. Weapons, costumes, mortars, keys and a collection of carved ivory pieces are on display. The Renaissance decoration of the dining hall includes a monumental doorway with a splendid frame, an imposing chimneypiece supported by two griffins, and a coffered ceiling of carved stone.

★★ Le FUTUROSCOPE

Michelin map 68 folds 13, 14 and 232 fold 46 (southeast) - at Jaunay-Clan.

This vast 70ha – 173 acre development at the northern gates of Poitiers was created to introduce the public to the realities of modern technology and to give it an insight into the coming developments in a world dominated by screen images.
The complex, the **European Park of the Moving Image** or more simply **Le Futuroscope,** presents a modernistic architectural universe of steel and glass which was conceived by the French architect Denis Laming; it is dominated by a symbolic sphere above the Communication Pavilion. Numerous attractions, both educational and purely entertaining, are on offer.
Aside from the park and its amusements, Le Futuroscope comprises a teaching complex with an innovative pre-university high-school, an Open University college, a number of other higher-education institutes and the ENSMA (*École Nationale Supérieure de Mécanique et d'Aérotechnique* – a college of aerospace instruction). The site also contains an industrial sector including a teleport (a state-of-the-art telecommunications centre), a conference centre and a number of hotels and restaurants.

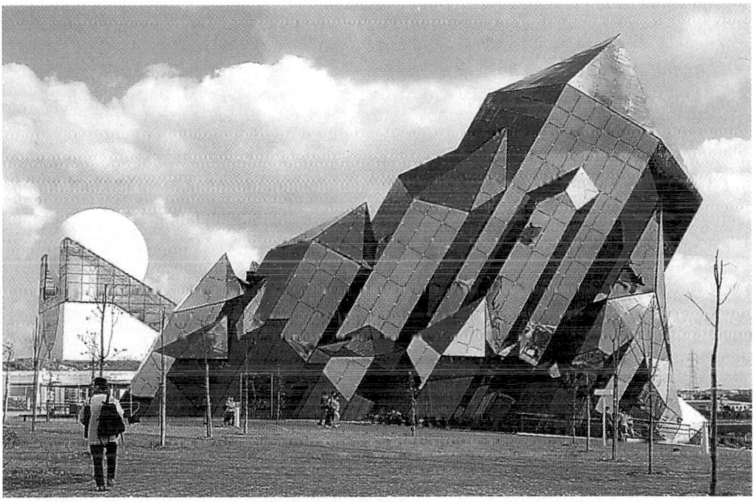

M. Baret/RAFHO

The Kinémax.

Tour ⌚ *Allow 1 day.*

The **Monde des enfants** (Children's World) invites young visitors to simultaneously play and learn in its magical setting. Nearby, the **Lac enchanté** (Enchanted Lake) and its **théâtre alphanumérique** present performances and productions incorporating the technology of the future.
Advances in the field of communications are on display in a number of different buildings and halls : they include 3-D films; the "Showcan" showing films shot at 60 frames per second; **Cinéma Dynamique,** which is a thrilling action simulator; the huge **Kinémax,** a futuristic building in the form of gigantic rock crystals, in which films are shown on a screen measuring 600m^2 – 718 sq yds; **Omnimax,** the hemispherical cinema; Tapis magique (Magic Carpet), a cinema with two screens, one of which is on the floor; the 360°, a full "circular cinema". In the Cinéautomate the audience can become involved with the film by intervening to alter the scenario.
A lift travelling in a spiral carries visitors to the top of the **Gyrotower** (45m – 146ft), from where there is a global view over the whole of this striking architectural project.

★★ Vallée de GAVARNIE

Michelin map 85 fold 18 or 234 folds 47, 48. Local map p 90.

The Vallée de Gavarnie and the Cirque de Gavarnie (a great geological amphitheatre) from which its head-waters flow are known all over the world. The landscape is so forbidding that it provoked the visiting Baroness Dudevant (the author George Sand) to write, not without exaggeration : "From Luz to Gavarnie is primeval chaos; it is hell itself." Victor Hugo described the track through the neighbouring Chaos de Coumély as "a black and hideous path"...
Great hollows – the Pragnères, Gèdre and Gavarnie basins – were gouged out by glaciers during the Quaternary Age; the waters then sliced through the rock between the basins to create narrows, the most typical of which is St-Sauveur Gorge. Temporary dwellings perch on the resulting ledges; torrents rush down in cascades from the tributary valleys.

★★ GAVARNIE VALLEY

From Luz-St-Saveur to the Cirque de Gavarnie

20km – $12\frac{1}{2}$ miles : about $3\frac{1}{2}$ hours. Local map below.

★ **Luz-St-Sauveur** – *See Luz-St-Sauveur.*

Leave the town via D 921 south. Avoid, in the holiday season, the line of excursion coaches which forms at around 1500hrs near Pont Napoléon.

Pont Napoléon – The single arch of this bridge, built on the orders of Napoleon III in 1860, spans the gorge channelled by the Pau Torrent; a marble memorial column surmounted by an eagle stands at its eastern end. The bridge offers an impressive view over the sunken stream and the scrub-covered gorge.
The road, carved from the bed-rock, twists through another gorge; passing through the hamlet of Sia *(bridge)* it approaches the service cableway which rises alongside the pipelines supplying the power station.

Centrale de Pragnères (Pragnères Power Station) ⊙ – This is the most powerful hydro-electric plant in the Pyrenees. The turbines are fuelled by waters collected from the Néouvielle massif and from the west bank tributaries of the Pau Torrent – the former with a water-head of 1 250m – 4 101ft, the latter with a fall of 900m – 2 953ft. The Néouvielle water supply is stored in Cap de Long reservoir, more than half of which is filled with the help of two pumping stations.
Visitors to the power station are shown the machine room with its turbines, and a model, illustrated with illuminated circuits, of the complex and its supply lines.

Just before Gèdre, the jagged peak of Pimené (alt 2 801m – 9 190ft) appears, beyond and to the right of the Montagne de Coumély (streaked with another hydro-electric pipeline). Piméné is the final peak before the Cirque de Gavarnie.

Gèdre – *See Gèdre.*

★★ **Cirque de Troumouse** – *15km – 9 miles southeast of Gèdre. See Gèdre.*

Return to Gèdre and continue along D 921.

The scenery again takes on a wild aspect. Above, to the right, is the glacier-created hanging valley of the Aspé Torrent (Gave d'Aspé). The stream dashes itself down into the main valley via the spectacular Cascade d'Arroudet. The road crosses the rock-strewn Chaos de Coumély (*chaos* is a French geological term referring to an accumulated scattering of irregular rocks and boulders) at the foot of the **Montagne de Coumély** and begins the final ascent towards Gavarnie.
Beyond and to the left of the Fausse Brèche and Pic des Sarradets (in the foreground) the upper reaches of the amphitheatre come into view, with its snow-covered ledges, and the summits of Le Casque, La Tour and Pic du Marboré.
The hamlet of Bareilles appears next *(right)* and then, on the Turon de Holle, at the mouth of the Ossoue Valley, the monumental statue of Notre-Dame-des-Neiges.

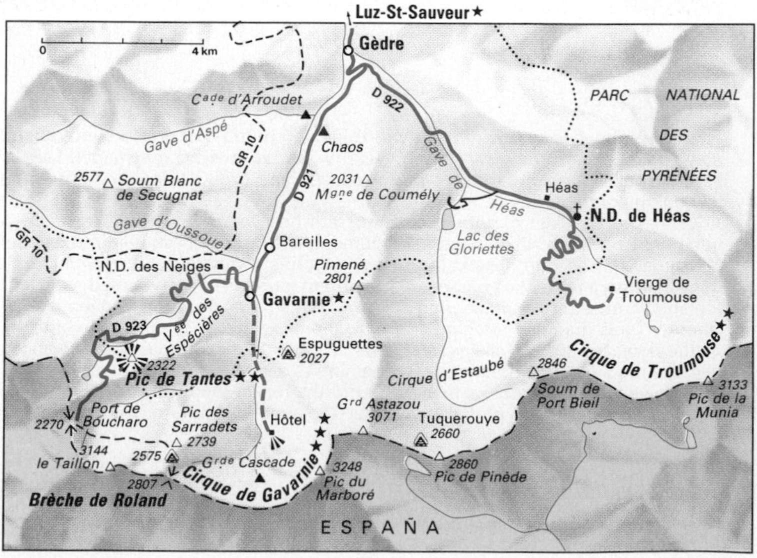

★ GAVARNIE

In the summer season the small village experiences a phenomenal influx of visitors : strictly the end of the road as far as wheeled traffic is concerned, Gavarnie has since 1864 provided a large and varied assortment of mounts for the trek to the Cirque. Once the day-trippers have gone, however, and the mules, donkeys and ponies have been returned to their pastures, Gavarnie resumes its identity as a climbers' centre, a base for mountaineers.
The installation of ski-lifts in the neighbouring Vallée des Espécières (alt 1 500-2 000m – 4 920-6 562ft) is helping to turn Gavarnie into something of a winter sports resort.

Church – The 14C church was once part of a priory founded by the Hospitallers of St John of Jerusalem, and stands on the old pilgrims' route to Port de Boucharo (Boucharo Pass, alt 2 270m – 7 448ft). The three 17C giltwood statues at the entrance represent the Virgin, St Joseph and John the Baptist. To the left of the high altar at the entrance to the Chapelle du Bon Port stands a polychrome statue of St James of Compostela. Inside the chapel, two statuettes of Compostela pilgrims flank the 14C statue of Notre-Dame-du-Bon-Port. The Virgin holds a pilgrim's water flask.

★★★ CIRQUE DE GAVARNIE

2½ hours Rtn on foot (mounts – horses or donkeys – can be hired ⓥ).

This colossal, amphitheatre-like formation *(illustration p 15)* has been hollowed out from a rock mass comprising three superimposed layers of horizontal strata rising in giant steps from the floor of the blind valley. Snow-covered ledges separate the tiered formations one from the other, gleaming white against the ochre cliff faces.
The Cirque is 3.5km – over 2 miles wide at its base and 14km – 9 miles around the crest line (from Astazou in the east to Pic des Sarradets in the west). The floor level is, on average, 1 676m – 5 503ft above sea level; the surrounding summits rise to more than 3 000m – 10 000ft. It has been estimated that, were the entire hollow to be used as an arena, over 15 million spectators could be accommodated; the drama festival held here each summer *(see Calendar of Events, qv)* attracts more modestly-sized audiences.
The amphitheatre was formed by glacial action upon a previous degradation of Secondary Age sediments, when waters released from the Monte Perdido massif pushed back the head of the valley and undermined the surrounding cliffs. Subsequently the Gavarnie glacier – of which only fragments remain on the upper ledges – pierced out the amphitheatre and carried away the debris of the earlier erosion.
The mounted excursions today end at the Hôtel du Cirque but it is possible to continue, on foot *(1 hour Rtn)*, as far as the Grande Cascade. This, the most impressive of the innumerable waterfalls silvering the walls of the circus, is fed by a melt-water overflow from the frozen lake, 2 592m – 8 500ft up on Monte Perdido on the Spanish side of the frontier. The cascade drops a clear 422m – 1 385ft into the void.
From the hotel there is a spectacular view of the Cirque and its surroundings, one of the most magnificent mountain landscapes in all Europe. Gazing with wonder at the majesty of the sheer rock walls and tiered snow platforms, Victor Hugo exclaimed : "It is both a mountain and a rampart; it is the most mysterious of structures by the most mysterious of architects; it is Nature's Coliseum – it is Gavarnie!"

★★ PIC DE TANTES

11km – 7 miles, by the Port de Boucharo road.

Leaving Gavarnie in the direction of Luz (north), turn left just before the bridge. The road skirts the statue of Notre-Dame-des-Neiges at the mouth of the Ossoue Valley, then transfers to the Espécières valley (winter sports facilities) before climbing to the pass known as Col de Tantes. Leave the car at the saddle and continue on foot to the rounded summit of Pic de Tantes (alt 2 322m – 7 618ft), to the northeast.
From the summit there is a breathtaking **panorama★★** of the peaks surrounding the Cirque de Gavarnie (the floor of the circus is not visible from here). Among the most remarkable is Pic du Marboré, gashed by the course of the Cascade glacier. Further west the rocky spine of Les Sarradets, in the foreground, slightly masks the Brèche de Roland *(see below)* before the frontier

F. Gohier/EXPLORER

La Brèche de Roland.

crest reappears at Le Taillon and the peaks of Les Gabiétous. More distant still, far off to the northwest, rises Le Vignemale, which shoulders the Ossoue glacier. In the northeast the Néouvielle massif stands in front of Pic du Midi de Bigorre (recognizable by its television transmitter).

The road continues, clinging to the cliff edge above the wild Pouey Aspé valley. It ends at Port de Boucharo, at a height of 2 270m – 7 448ft. This is the departure point for the mountain path leading to the 2 800m – 9 800ft high **Brèche de Roland** (Roland's Breach). According to legend, the vast fracture in the rock face was made by Roland (a gallant 8C knight who was a nephew of Charlemagne) when he tried to break his trusty sword Durandal to prevent it falling into the hands of the Saracens. The *Chanson de Roland* **(Song of Roland)** was the first of the epic French *Chansons de geste (qv).*

The path leading to the breach is a difficult one, passing by Les Sarradets refuge. The climb should be attempted only in exceptionally fine weather, and then only by those experienced in mountain walking, with suitable footwear. Allow at least half a day.

GÈDRE

Pop 317

Michelin map 85 fold 18 or 234 fold 48 – 9km – 5 miles south of St-Sauveur. Local map p 90.

This village lies in a basin of green meadows cut by long lines of poplar trees, at the confluence of the Héas and Gavarnie torrents. Gèdre makes a charming halt on the route to the Cirque de Gavarnie *(qv)* and is also a starting point for excursions to the Troumouse and Estaubé cirques. From the Hôtel de la Brèche de Roland there is a view of the legendary Brèche de Roland *(qv)* in the mountain wall and, further to the right, the snow-filled hollow of the "False Breach", from which a single pillar of rock known as *Le Doigt* (the finger) points upwards.

EXCURSION

★★ **Cirque de Troumouse** ⊙ – *15km – 9 miles plus 15min on foot Rtn. The (toll) road approaching the amphitheatre is usually obstructed by snow from December to April.* The road climbs through the pastures of the Héas Valley, the grassy slopes of which are punctuated by a *chaos*, a scattering of boulders which have tumbled from the Montagne de Coumély and, higher up, a second *chaos* in which the largest rock serves as a pedestal for a statue of the Virgin.

Héas – The **chapel** ⊙ beyond this village, its dome rising amid the last clump of trees in the valley, is the site of regular pilgrimages (15 August, 8 September, Fête of the Rosary, 1st Sunday in October). The original building was swept away by an avalanche in 1915 and rebuilt ten years later. The north aisle of that original chapel still remains, along with statues, paintings, the 1643 bell, a font and an 18C processional Cross. The venerated statue of Notre-Dame-de-Héas, recovered intact from the debris of the avalanche, now stands in the chancel.

From the road winding up the southern slope of the valley there are interesting views of the "trough" hollowed by the ancient Héas glacier. The escarpment on the northern side above Héas chapel is notched by a mountain torrent falling from a pool at the bottom of a swallow-hole.

To the south a semicircle of mountain crests appears – a rock formation notable for the extraordinary wave-like structure of its pale, tightly folded strata.

★★ **Cirque de Troumouse** – The best view of this amphitheatre is from a rocky spur, in the centre of which stands a statue of the Virgin, the Vierge de Troumouse *(15min on foot Rtn).* The amphitheatre is enormous – large enough, it is claimed, to accommodate three million "spectators". Its floor of meadowlands, slightly convex on the whole, is enclosed by an almost unbroken rampart of mountains 10km – 6 miles around. The highest point is Pic de la Munia (alt 3 133m – 10 279ft), identifiable by the remains of its hanging glacier.

Below this, on the left, are twinned rock pinnacles known locally as "the Two Sisters".

★ Écomusée de la GRANDE LANDE

Michelin maps 78 folds 1 to 5 and 79 folds 1 to 11 or map 234 folds 6, 7, 10, 11, 14, 15, 18 and 19.

The Grande Lande Open-air Museum comprises three separate sites near the villages of Marquèze, Luxey and Moustey, in the heart of the Parc naturel régional des Landes de Gascogne (Landes of Gascony Regional Park, *qv*). Between them they evoke the daily life and traditional activities of the region in the 18C and 19C.

Marquèze ⊙ – Map 78 fold 4 or 234 fold 18. *Access only by train from Sabres. The train runs for almost 5km – 3 miles through the forest and then leaves visitors in the Marquèze clearing.* This sector of the museum covers almost 70ha – 173 acres in the protected region of the Eyre valleys and comprises a delightful collection of traditional buildings – some original, others reconstructions on their former site – from the 30 or so structures which stood here when the clearing was occupied by three families.

The **airial,** for centuries an oasis in the bleak moorland and subsequently a glade in the pinewoods which replaced the moorland, is a sort of huge esplanade, mainly planted with oak trees, where the houses and farm buildings were grouped. It is

Nova i/IMAGE PHOTOTHÈQUE

Chicken coop and Le Mineur.

here that the master's house **(Marquèze),** dating from 1824, stands. It combines stout beams, cob walls and a three-pitched roof, and, like the other buildings, has no foundations, relying on sound timber construction for its stability.
Nearby, the more modest house with less massive beams was where the servants **("brassiers")** were lodged. Beyond is the tenant farmer's house with its barns, pig sties, beehives and chicken runs.
A path beneath the trees leads to the miller's house (1834) and the **Mill** itself, with its two separate millstones for grinding the smaller and the larger varieties of grain.
The woodland walk ends at the **charbonnières** (charcoal burners), where old trees were burnt very slowly to produce charcoal, before returning to the *airial* where an information centre presents a selection of documents, maps, models and an illustrated commentary *(in French)* on the museum and the agricultural and pastoral life of the region. A nearby sheep-fold contains a flock of grazing sheep : they were once used to clear the moorland for agricultural use and enrich it with their droppings.
On the other side of the railway, between an aviary and an ancient well, there is a second "big house", known as "Le Mineur", which was transferred from another *airial,* and an exhibition explaining the old agri-pastoral system. In the **model orchard** over 1 600 species of fruit trees native to the Grande Lande are tended; they include varieties of apple, plum, cherry, medlar, quince...

Luxey – Map 79 fold 11 or 234 fold 15. The **Jacques and Louis Vidal Resinous Products Workshop** ⏲ illustrates the traditional local industry based on resin products which dates from the beginning of the Industrial Revolution; the workshop operated commercially from 1859 to 1954. Visitors may follow every stage from the arrival of the tapped pine-tree sap to the final storage of refined turpentine.

Moustey – Map 78 fold 3 or 234 fold 14 – *North of Pissos.* Here the former Notre-Dame Church, recently restored, houses a **Musée du Patrimoine Religieux et des Croyances Populaires** ⏲ in which an exhibition devoted to the region's religious heritage and popular beliefs reveals a lesser-known aspect of rural life.

Le GRAND-PRESSIGNY

Pop 1 120

Michelin map 68 fold 5 or 232 fold 48 – Facilities.

This small hilltop town is picturesquely situated below the walls of a medieval castle, facing the confluence of the Claise and Aigronne rivers.
To scholars of pre-history the area is renowned for the numerous craftsmen who worked in flint. In the Late Neolithic period flint tools produced here in quantity were "exported", by way of trade or barter, to many different regions; examples have been discovered as far away as Switzerland.

★ **Musée départemental de Préhistoire** ⏲ – The **museum,** founded in 1910 by Dr Édouard Chaumié, is housed within the splendid precincts of the **castle,** which still shows signs of its fortress origins : a walled 13C defensive enclosure studded with round towers, a fortified gateway, the two remaining sides of a square 12C keep. The 16C seigneurial residence, standing among well-kept gardens, is adorned on the side nearest the keep with an elegantly arcaded Renaissance façade.
The museum illustrates the major stages in the development of pre-history through discoveries made at the more important sites in the Touraine region.
The exhibits are separated into different *espaces* (areas) or sections. Section I defines the broad divisions of pre-history as a whole. Section 2 is devoted specifically to the Archaic Paleolithic and Lower Paleolithic periods : a film *(in French)* analyses the series of sediments extracted from a sand-pit at Abilly. The Middle Paleolithic is evoked through discoveries from two sites near Tours (Section 3) : a model here illustrates the life of hunters, based on discoveries at Moustier in the Dordogne, in the second half of the last interglacial period.

The Upper Paleolithic (Section 4) and particularly the life of hunters in Burgundy at that time are detailed next, and then the Neolithic and Late Neolithic (exportation of flint implements) in Section 5.
Finally, in Section 6, the Bronze Age is recalled with examples from the bronzes of Azay-le-Rideau, material from sites in the Creuse Valley etc. Consultation of a computer software program *(in French)* completes the tour.
An annex houses a special section on paleontology which displays fossils found in the Touraine area, notably in marine deposits north and south of the Loire.

★ GUÉTHARY

Pop 1 105

Michelin map 85 fold 2 or 234 fold 29 – Facilities.

This pretty seaside resort has grown up around a picturesque Basque fishing village between Biarritz and St-Jean-de-Luz. The holiday villas, most of them built in a more sophisticated version of the local Labourd style, stand in well-tended gardens. There are fine views of the Basque countryside, the mountains and – from the promenade above the beach – the coast as far as Biarritz.
The main square, with its *pelota* court and its town hall in the local style is worth a visit.

Church – This church, built above the N 10 coast road on the height of Elizaldia, is one of the most impressively situated in the region. Noteworthy inside are a 15C processional Cross, a 17C Christ crucified, and a *Pietà* from the same period.
The tombstone of Monsignor Mugabure (1850-1910), a local priest who became the first Archbishop of Tokyo, is in the church. The poet P-J Toulet (1867-1920), who was born in Pau, is buried in the cemetery outside.

HAGETMAU

Pop 4 449

Michelin map 78 east of fold 7 or 234 fold 27.

Imposing public buildings (colleges, a covered market) in 1950s style testify to the post-war prosperity of Hagetmau, a trade centre for the grain grown and the pigs raised in the Chalosse district *(qv)*, and a major chair-manufacturing base.

Crypte de St-Girons – This crypt, which was a halt on the pilgrims' road to Compostela *(qv)*, is all that remains of an abbey built to house the relics of St-Girons, the 4C evangelist who preached the Gospel in the Chalosse region. The ceiling of the crypt rests on four central marble columns and eight engaged columns around the walls. The tomb of the saint lay between the marble columns. Scenes carved on the 12C capitals represent his battle against the forces of evil and the dangers surrounding his missionary activities.
Other capitals in the crypt show the deliverance of St Peter – an angel cuts the captive's bonds with the tip of his lance – and the parable of the rich man : in front, the feast; on the left, the rich man, dying of thirst amid the flames of Hell, begs for mercy from the soul of Lazarus, who is being carried by angels to Abraham's bosom. In a third scene figures are seen overcoming monsters, snatching away the fruit that the beasts hold in their jaws.

EXCURSIONS

Brassempouy – *12km – 7½ miles west. Leave Hagetmau to the southwest via the road to Orthez; after 2.5km – 1½ miles turn right into D 2. Just before St-Cricq turn left into D 21.* This small Chalosse village, the main street of which appears to be straddled by the stone tower of the Romanesque-Gothic church, is among the world's most important prehistoric sites. On a limestone hillside west of the village is **La Grotte du Pape** (the Pope's Cave) ⊙, where the first works of art ever created by man were discovered at the end of the 19C. They include the earliest known representation of a human face, carved *c*23 000 years BC – the celebrated 3.6cm – 1½ inch ivory carving known as the **Dame de Brassempouy** or Dame à la Capuche (Lady with the Cowl) *(see Michelin Green Guide Flanders, Picardy and the Paris region : St-Germain-en-Laye Museum)*. Though many important discoveries had been made here during the past hundred years, huge archeological tracts still remained largely intact when excavations were resumed in 1982.

Musée de la Préhistoire ⊙ – The museum displays some of the prehistoric discoveries made in the Chalosse district (a millstone, polished axe-heads) along with items found at Brassempouy since excavations were resumed (tools, bones and the remains of animals which had been eaten). Period documents recall the original 19C excavations. An exhibition of prehistoric female statuary includes reproductions of the world's most famous statuettes and copies of nine figurines discovered at Brassempouy itself.

Samadet – *10km – 6 miles east.* The hey-day of this small town was from 1732 to 1811 when its *faïences* (glazed earthenwares) were known throughout the world. The factories here were able to produce both deep and strong tones using the Grand Feu technique (high-temperature firing) and more delicate colours using the more gentle Petit Feu. The **Musée des Traditions rurales et Faïences au 18ᵉ s** ⊙, in the old abbot's house, contains rare and beautiful collections of celebrated Samadet wares; there are items decorated with roses, carnations, butterflies, and dishes in green monochrome with grotesques or chinoiseries. An 18C bourgeois interior, 18C costumes, various workshops and reconstructions of the Royal *faïencerie* are also of interest.

★ HENDAYE

Pop 11 578

Michelin map 85 fold 1 or 234 fold 33 – Facilities.
Town plan in the current Michelin Red Guide France.

Hendaye is a border town lying on the east bank of the Bidasoa river, which forms the Franco-Spanish frontier at that point. The town comprises three separate districts : Hendaye-Gare, Hendaye-Ville and Hendaye-Plage, corresponding to the area around the railway station, the town proper, and the sea-front. At high tide the sharply curving estuary is transformed into a semicircular lake, known as the Baie de Chingoudy, with Hendaye on one side and the Spanish town of Fuenterrabia on the other.

The resort of **Hendaye-Plage** benefits from uninterrupted views over the open sea and a climate which encourages luxuriant vegetation : magnolias, palm trees, tamarisk, oleanders, eucalyptus and mimosa line the avenues and shade the gardens everywhere. The casino, built in a Moorish style, looks almost out of place among such tropical growth.

From the beach, the coastal view to the northeast is blocked by the rock outcrops known as Les Deux Jumeaux (the Twins, *illustration below*), just off Pointe de Ste-Anne. In the other direction Cabo Higuer (fig-tree cape) marks the mouth of the Bidasoa.

Mopy/RAPHO

Basque coastline with Les Deux Jumeaux and La Rhune.

L'île des Faisans (Pheasant Island) – This river isle downstream from the Spanish frontier post at the Behobia bridge is today no more than a wooded strip increasingly threatened by the current; no trace remains of the important historical role it once played. As early as 1463 Louis XI met Henry IV, the King of Castile, on its banks; in 1526 François I, held prisoner in Spain after the battle of Pavia, was exchanged here for his two sons. Since the island was deemed suitable for occasions in which royal and diplomatic etiquette were involved, it was used again in 1615 as "neutral" ground on which two royal brides-to-be could officially be introduced to their new countries : they were Elizabeth, the sister of Louis XIII chosen as the wife of the Infante of Spain (the future Philip IV), and Anne of Austria, the Infante's sister, chosen for Louis XIII himself.

The **Treaty of the Pyrenees** *(qv)* was signed on Pheasant Island in 1659. A commemorative stone recalls the event.

Nuptial preliminaries – In the spring of 1660 the island was the scene of feverish preparations. The painter Velasquez (who died soon afterwards of a chill caught during the work) decorated the pavilion in which the marriage contract, provided for in the Treaty of the Pyrenees, was to be signed by Louis XIV and Maria Theresa, the daughter of Philip IV of Spain. As each delegation wished to remain on its own soil – protocol in fact forbade the King of Spain to leave his own territory – the building on the mid-stream islet was divided inside by an imaginary frontier line. Volleys of musketry, fired simultaneously on both banks of the river, celebrated the conclusion of these formalities, which had lasted from 4 to 7 June *(for details of the wedding see St-Jean-de-Luz, qv)*.

►► Hendaye-Ville : Église St-Vincent – 13C Grand Crucifix★.

EXCURSION

Biriatou – *5km – 3 miles southeast. Leave Hendaye via Rue de Béhobie, N 111.* Beyond Béhobie the road follows the course of the Bidasoa before twisting up towards this tiny village, where it ends beside a parking area. The small square with its *pelota* court *(qv)*, its adjoining inn and the church at the top of a flight of steps makes a charming ensemble. The view here embraces the wooded mountains, the frontier river below and the first few miles of Spain on the far side.

★ HOSSEGOR

Pop 2 829 (with Soorts)

Michelin map 78 fold 17 or 234 fold 25 – Local map p 137 – Facilities.

Hossegor is a pleasant seaside and climatic resort bordered by Boudigau Canal, which separates the town from neighbouring Capbreton *(qv)*. It is thanks to the efforts of successive generations of local architects, writers and painters that, since the beginning of the century, this choice natural site wooded with pines, cork-oak and arbutus has been carefully developed into a holiday centre complete with parks, gardens, hotels, casino and a golf course.
Various climatic conditions influenced by the coast, the lake and the forest, combined with an ideal humidity level, have endowed the town with a microclimate that is particularly reviving.
Some way off-shore is the famous Gouf de Capbreton *(qv)*, an undersea canyon 3 000m – 9 800ft deep and over 60km – 37 miles long. The huge groundswell produced by this submarine phenomenon has made Hossegor a playground for surfing enthusiasts and each summer, in the second fortnight of August, the professional surfers' World Championship – the *Rip Curl Pro Landes* – is held here.

★ **Le Lac** – This long salt-water lake, ringed by the pine forest with its villas in the local style, occupies a space in which the since redirected River Adour *(qv)* once flowed. As it is linked by Boudigau Canal (constructed in the last century) directly with the ocean, the lake is affected by the tides.

G. Cranham/RAPHO

Surfing.

★★ Grottes d'ISTURITS et d'OXOCELHAYA

Michelin map 85 fold 3 or 234 fold 34.

These two **grottoes** ⓥ are located between St-Palais and Hasparren; they can be reached from the village of St-Martin-d'Aberoue *(turn left down Rampe des Grottes)*. The caves, one above the other, correspond to two different levels, each long-abandoned, of the subterranean course of the River Aberoue. A single visit encompasses both.

Grotte d'Isturits – It is through this upper cave that visitors penetrate the limestone stronghold of the mountain. It is mainly of scientific interest : traces of occupation by Paleolithic Man from the Mousterian period to the Magdalenian have been discovered, showing an exceptional continuity. Excavations have revealed semi-rounded staffs incised with curvilinear ornamentation, and a number of carvings, examples of which are on display in the local museum.

Grotte d'Oxocelhaya – The second stage of the tour, in the lower cave, reveals a fascinating series of chambers richly decorated with natural rock concretions : stalactites, stalagmites, columns, discs, translucent "draperies" and a glittering petrified cascade.

OYSTER-EATING THROUGH THE AGES

The Greeks ate oysters either roasted in mint and honey, or more simply fried in oil; the Celts also ate them, and the Romans swallowed them raw with a little seasoning. During the Renaissance they were sautéd in oil and mashed with peas, bread and wine, a recipe which may have been developed to disguise any lack of freshness in the oysters.

JARNAC
Pop 4 766

Michelin map 72 fold 12 or 233 fold 28.

Jarnac stands on the north bank of the River Charente, in a pleasant wooded site on the edge of the "Grande Champagne" district, not far from Cognac *(qv)*; the local economy is based on the distillation and shipping of brandies.
The town was the birthplace of the French President, François Mitterrand.

HISTORICAL NOTES

Jarnac Thrust – In 1547 Gui Chabot, Baron de Jarnac, having been insulted by La Chataigneraie (a close friend of Henri II and one of the finest swordsmen in Europe), challenged him to a duel. The encounter, organized as a "single combat" affair subject to the Will of God, took place on 10 July at St-Germain-en-Laye near Paris, in the presence of the King, the Queen, Diane de Poitiers and the entire Court. Jarnac, on the point of losing, vanquished his opponent with a thrust that was within the rules but entirely unexpected, severing La Chataigneraie's hamstring. The term **Coup de Jarnac** (Jarnac Thrust) has been used to describe this type of attack ever since – but with an added sense of treacherousness which may seem unfair, in the circumstances, to the memory of the battling Chabot.

Battle of Jarnac – As a result of Calvin having stayed several times in the region during 1534 and 1535, Aunis, Saintonge and the Angoulême district rapidly became hotbeds of Protestantism. On 13 March 1659, during the Wars of Religion, a battle subsequently known as the Battle of Jarnac was fought near the village of Triac (just east of the town). The Catholic forces led by the Duc d'Anjou (the future Henri III) routed the Huguenots of the Prince de Condé. Condé, wounded during a cavalry charge and fallen from his horse, was finished off on the orders of the Duc d'Anjou by Montesquiou, the Captain of the Guard.

SIGHTS

Maison Courvoisier – *Place du Château.* A small **museum** ⓥ (entrance near the bridge) traces the history of spirit distillation and the different stages in the production and refinement of Cognac. The silhouette of Napoleon I on the bottles of the Courvoisier brand recalls that Emmanuel Courvoisier, the founder of the company, supplied the Emperor himself, and that in 1869 the firm was appointed purveyor to the Court of Napoleon III by Royal decree. A visit to one of the brandy *chais* (storehouses) includes a slide show projected onto a sphere.

Church – This former abbey church dating from the 11C has a square tower adorned with blind arcades. The upper level is pierced by two openings with small columns. In the 13C crypt the remains of mural paintings can be seen.

★ Le LABOURD

Michelin map 85 folds 1, 2, 3 or 234 folds 29, 33.

Labourd is one of the seven old provinces of the Basque country *(qv)*, three of which are in France and four in Spain. The region extends along the Atlantic coast between the mouths of the Adour and the Bidasoa rivers; inland the boundary corresponds roughly with the course of the River Joyeuse.
The 30km – 19 miles of Labourd coastline offer a picturesque alternation of rugged cliffs and sandy coves; away from the ocean rollers the landscape is one of gentle hills and wide moors known as *touyas*. Mountains stand out against the clear skies but they are not high : La Rhune, the culminating peak in the range, rises to no more than 900m – 2 953ft above sea level.

1 FROM BAYONNE TO CAMBO-LES-BAINS VIA LA RHUNE

70km – 44 miles : allow 1 day. Local map overleaf.

★★ **Bayonne** – *See Bayonne.*

Leave Bayonne to the southwest and take D 932 towards Cambo-les-Bains; pass beneath the motorway and then turn right towards Arcangues (D 3).

The road climbs through a stretch of hilly country.

Arcangues – This picturesque village is particularly attractive around the church, the inn and the *pelota* court *(qv)*. A commemorative bust of the singer Luis Mariano (1914-70) stands at the entrance to an open-air theatre, near the village car park. Inside the church, with its carved galleries, there is a large Empire-style chandelier and a low-relief representing the beheading of John the Baptist, patron saint of the parish. The cemetery offers a panoramic **view**★ of the Basque Pyrenees.

Continue along D 3, heading south.

The winding road snakes through Ustaritz Forest. Beyond, the descent towards St-Pée offers distant glimpses of La Rhune, the Irun depression, the promontory of Jaizkibel and the sea. To the east, the minor Artzamendi range closes off the upper Nivelle basin.

St-Pée-sur-Nivelle – The ruins of a 14C-15C castle stand at the eastern exit of this village.

Turn right (west) into D 918.

★ **Ascain** – The pretty village square, with its church, *pelota* court, traditional houses and welcoming hotels, has a great deal of character. The Basque church with its three-tiered galleries is preceded by a massive belfry-porch; on the right of the

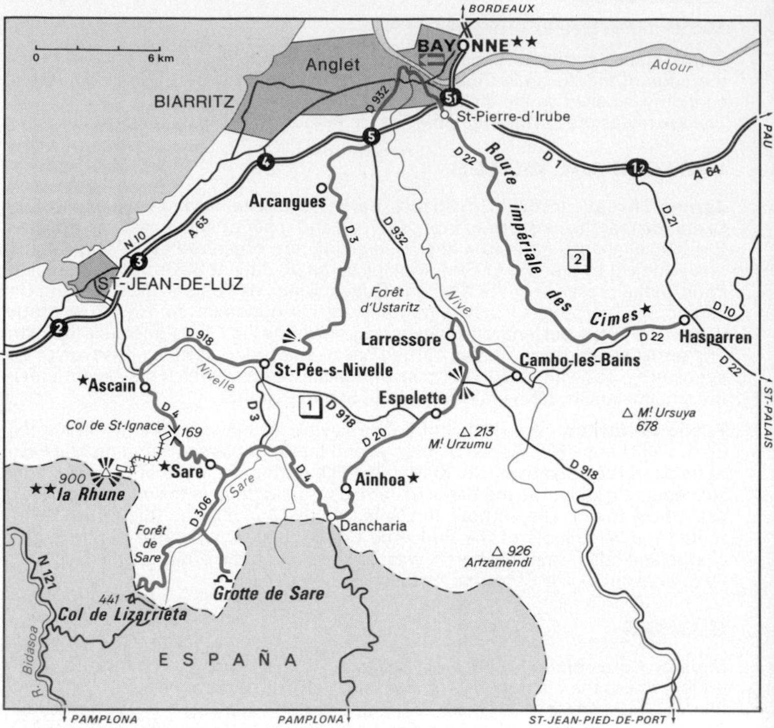

cemetery behind it is an interesting disk-shaped stele dating from 1657. In one of the Ascain restaurants there is a *trinquet* – a rectangular indoor court marked out for a variant of *pelota,* reminiscent of the English game of fives.

Continuing south through a moorland landscape, the road (D 4) rises beside an attractive valley to reach Col de St Ignace (St Ignatius Pass), at an altitude of 169m – 555ft.

★★ **La Rhune** ⓥ – *From Col de St Ignace : 1 hour Rtn by rack and pinion railway.* La Rhune (in Basque *Larrun :* "good pastureland") is regarded as the symbol of the French Basque country. From the summit (alt 900m – 2 952ft; television transmitter) of the frontier-mountain there is a superb **panorama★★★** over the ocean (Bay of Biscay), the Forest of the Landes, the Basque Pyrenees and, southwards, the Bidasoa valley.

The road down through the *touyas* has cut through and exposed the red sandstone of the mountain, which is used as the local building stone. There are views of the Artzamendi and the upper Nivelle to the east.

★ **Sare** – This charming village was described, under the name of Etchejar, by the author Pierre Loti *(qv)* in his novel *Ramuntcho* (1897). The high wall of the *pelota* court, the shaded streets, and the fine galleried church with its raised chancel and Baroque altarpieces are all typical of the Basque country.

Sare is also known as "wild pigeons' hell" due to the local method of snaring the migratory birds as they fly south in the autumn.

The upper Sare valley, a pastoral landscape of sheep and dairy cattle between scattered hamlets with some fine dovecotes is particularly appealing.

Take D 306 south.

Grotte de Sare ⓥ – The grotto or *"Lezea"* (a Basque word meaning cave) is part of a vast series of galleries gouged from the limestone at the beginning of the Quaternary era by waters hurtling down from Pic d'Atchouria. Corrosion, abrasion and dissolution of some of the rock's mineral constituents have produced over the millennia every kind of karstic cavity. The discovery here of flint tools and the remnants of bones shows that many of these caves were at one time occupied by humans, particularly during the Upper Perigordian period (20 000 BC).

The enormous entrance, which opens to the northeast, leads into a subterranean labyrinth illuminated by blue lights. The natural marvels to be seen on the 900m – $\frac{1}{2}$ mile or so tour are explained in an audio-visual presentation *(in French).*

Return to D 306 and turn left.

The road continues beside attractive undergrowth flourishing on the banks of a stream, then rises into the oak-filled Forêt de Sare.

Col de Lizarrieta – Alt 441m – 1 447ft. The pass, with its hides and snare centres all along the crests, is a hive of activity during the pigeon-shooting season.

Return to Sare and take D 4 east.

★ **Aïnhoa** – *See Aïnhoa.*

Head northeast along D 20.

Espelette – *See Espelette.*

Before the road plunges down into the valley of the Nive, the view opens out again onto the Basque Pyrenees, La Rhune and the Artzamendi *(behind)*, and the heights of Cambo-les-Bains and the gentle green slopes of Mont Ursuya *(ahead)*.

Turn left (D 20) to Larressore.

Larressore – From 1733 to 1906 a seminary founded in this village by Abbot Daguerre trained many Basque priests. Beside the *pelota* court is the **Atelier Ainciart-Bergara** ⊙, a workshop established before the Revolution by a craftsman of that name and still staffed today by members of the same family. The workshop produces, using ancient family techniques, the traditional Basque staff or *makhila*, made from the wood of the medlar tree which is seasoned and decorated with a pattern of dried sap which has oozed from specially made cuts.

Cambo-les-Bains – *See Cambo-les-Bains.*

★ 2 ROUTE IMPÉRIALE DES CIMES (NAPOLEON I's SCENIC HIGHWAY) –

See Route Impériale des Cimes.

★ LANDES DE GASCOGNE

Michelin map 78 folds 3 to 5 or 234 folds 14, 15, 18, 19.

The ancient province of the Landes (moors), divided since the Roman occupation by invasions, feudal disputes and the Wars of Religion, took a long time to establish its identity. The area was once a marine depression, subsequently filled with fine sands – quite distinct from those on the coast – during the Quaternary era; the vast tract is poorly drained and below the surface is a hard impermeable layer, further reducing its fertility.
Development of the region since the Second Empire *(qv)* has concentrated on the extension of the forest at the expense of the barren *Lannes* (the Landes of olden times). The great mantle of pinewoods and deciduous forests that carpet the land so thickly between the Gironde Landes and the River Adour do give way eventually to a variety of other landscapes throughout the old Gascon province. Part of this territory has now been given special protection as the Parc naturel régional des Landes de Gascogne (Landes of Gascony Regional Park, *qv*).
In the middle of this area are the **Grandes Landes,** extending from the Gironde to the outskirts of Dax, an enormous woodland zone from which the carefully-managed pine forests supply various wood-based industries (sawn timber, veneers, paper pulp, wood charcoal, wood alcohol). This is particularly the case around Sore, Pissos, Sabres and Morcenx, less so in the smaller villages which nestle in forest clearings or within the picturesque valleys of the Eyre.
Hard by the eastern limits of the Grandes Landes are the **Petites Landes,** which offer a contrasting landscape of gentle undulations patterned with attractive hamlets among the patchwork of meadows and cultivated fields.
Further south the **Marsan** region, irrigated by the River Midouze and its tributaries, is characterized by steep-sided valleys and their complement of terraced meadows, with cornfields and vines between the smallholdings and their cattle.
Bas-Armagnac, the western, "lower" part of the Armagnac region, is a hilly country of mixed farming with fine vines among the other crops, especially in the neighbourhood of Villeneuve-de-Marsan and Labastide-de-l'Armagnac. On the northern fringe of this area lies the **Gabardan,** a landscape of moors and forest which includes, from Estigarde to Losse and Lubbon, a zone of lagoons and drained marshes. Eastwards, hemmed in by the Petites Landes and the Grandes Landes, is **Albret,** an area which was favoured in the 13C by the local seigneurs who extended its boundaries to the sea. Here the forest, punctuated by occasional fields or meadows, covers a high proportion of the territory.
The regions of Born, Marensin and Marenne comprise what is now known as the Côte d'Argent (Silver Coast, *qv*). **Born,** from Biscarrosse to a point south of Mimizan, is an area of huge lagoons, swollen by streams from the interior, and an attractive coastline. Behind the lakes the forest is lush, with a thick undergrowth of broom, bracken and furze. Orchards and cornfields flourish around the larger villages.
Marensin, which extends to the north of Soustons, has much the same general aspect as Born, with its beaches, lakes and streams, but its landscape has the added variety of extensive plantations of cork-oak, and the presence of cattle and cereal crops on the richer soil inland where the larger farms are.
Maremne, boasting attractive lakes in a woodland setting and the charming resorts of Hossegor and Capbreton, has the mildest climate of the three regions. A rich vegetation of oleanders and mimosa proliferates among the ever-present cork-oaks. The fertile land is also particularly suited to growing maize.
On the banks of the Adour, the spas of Dax, Préchacq and Tercis mark the southern limits of the Landes forest and the beginning of the **Chalosse** district *(qv)*. On each side of the fast N 10 throughroute, delightful side roads tempt the visitor to explore this fascinating countryside, so poetically evoked by François Mauriac in the novel *Thérèse Desqueyroux* and so inspiring to the painters of the Barbizon School.

TOWNS AND VILLAGES

Belhade – Michelin map 78 fold 3 or 234 folds 14, 15. The name of this hamlet means "beautiful fairy" in the Gascon tongue. The church, built in the Landes style with a belfry-wall, has a porch with handsome carved capitals.

Belin-Béliet – Michelin map 78 fold 3 or 234 fold 10. Eleanor of Aquitaine *(qv)* was born in this village in 1123. A low-relief in her memory stands on the site of the castle built by the Dukes of Aquitaine.

★ **Côte d'Argent** – *The Lake Route : Arcachon to Capbreton – See Côte d'Argent.*

★ **Dax** – *See Dax.*

★ **Écomusée de la Grande Lande** – The fascinating open-air museum is based at three sites : **Marquèze, Luxey** and **Moustey.** *See Écomusée de la Grande Lande.*

Mont-de-Marsan – *See Mont-de-Marsan.*

Pissos – Michelin map 78 fold 4 or 234 fold 14. Route de Sore, which runs through an old Landes estate, leads to **La Maison des Artisans** ⊙ where contemporary arts, local gastronomic specialities and crafts are exhibited : furniture made from local pine-wood, wrought-iron ware, copper pieces etc. Opposite the centre an old shepherd's fold has been transformed into a **glassblowers' workshop** ⊙.

Préchacq-les-Bains – This village on the left bank of the River Adour lies in the midst of an oakwood; its hot baths (Bains) are used to treat rheumatism and respiratory problems. The waters, rich in calcium sulphate, bubble out at temperatures of 18°C – 64°F (the cold spring) and 63°C – 145°F. There are mud baths in the gardens beyond the cure centre.

Roquefort – This was once a fortified town; it still has its old ramparts and 12C and 14C towers. The **church** was founded by Benedictines in the 11C and later became an Antonin Commandery – where those of the devoutly faithful who suffered from a violent fever known as "St Anthony's fire" were tended. The largely Gothic building has defensive loopholes visible on the apse and on the square tower which served as a keep. The south door, in Flamboyant Gothic style, is decorated with the arms of the town – three rocks, three stars. Beside the church is the old priory.

Sabres – Michelin map 78 folds 4, 5 or 234 fold 18. The village contains a Renaissance church with a tall open-work belfry, ribbed vaulting inside and an interesting porch and doorway.

Solférino – Michelin map 78 folds 4, 5 or 234 fold 18. The ancient estate in which this hamlet sits was granted to Napoleon III in 1857. The land, once barren and marshy but now drained and replanted or reafforested, is a good example of the regeneration in this region. The **museum** ⊙ in the old village hall exhibits souvenirs of the Second Empire and the royal family, and has displays relating to the Landes in the 19C.

Abbaye de LIGUGÉ

Michelin map 68 fold 13 or 233 fold 8 – 8km – 5 miles south of Poitiers.

Ligugé claims the title of the Oldest Monastery in the West. After more than three centuries of interruption, monastic life here on the west bank of the River Clain was resumed in 1853 by Benedictine monks from Solesmes.

Under the sign of St Martin – In the year AD 361 a soldier born in what is now Hungary established a monkish cell here in the ruins of a Gallo-Roman villa in the Clain Valley; this was the man who later became St Martin, the patron saint of France.

Martin was a young officer in the Roman army when he encountered one day at the gates of Amiens a beggar who was numbed with the cold; he at once took off his cloak, sliced it in two with his sword and gave half to the shivering pauper. Subsequently, having seen in a dream Christ Himself wrapped in the shared cape, he had himself baptized.

Martin became a disciple of Hilaire (Hilary), the Bishop of Poitiers, and spent almost ten years here at Ligugé. His burning faith and profound sense of charity were soon spoken of throughout the region, and in the year 370 the inhabitants of Tours entreated him to become their bishop. Not far from Tours, he founded the monastery of Marmoutier.

St Martin died at Candes, on the banks of the Loire, in 397. The monks of Ligugé and those of Marmoutier disagreed over who was to have charge of the body, but the men of Tours had their way by placing the corpse in a boat and rowing silently away after nightfall while their rivals slept. It was then that the miracle occurred : although it was November, as the vessel neared the town leaves appeared on the trees, flowers blossomed, birds sang – it was St Martin's Summer.

TOUR ⊙ *45min*

Excavations – The digs here, which were started in 1953 in front of and beneath the nave of the present St Martin's Church, have revealed an exceptional series of pre-Romanesque structures which incorporate the remains of a Gallo-Roman villa, an early basilica (discovered in 1956) dating from before the year AD 370, a 4C *Martyrium* (votive chapel), a 6C church and a 7C basilica.

Items which may be viewed include :

– On the left, the wall of one room of the Gallo-Roman villa, with a floor made of some kind of concrete. On the right is an arcade of the *Martyrium,* which succeeded this room.

– The south transept of the 7C basilica, which forms the foundation of the present belfry; a vault dating from AD 1000; a 4C Ionic capital (re-used); a model and plans of the original buildings.

– Beneath the present nave, the crypt of the 7C basilica. Behind this is the apse of the primitive basilica built by Martin in the 4C.

– The southern apsidal chapel of this same 7C basilica. The ornamental tiling, enamelled segments in geometric patterns, is the oldest of its kind in France.

Église St-Martin – Today this is the parish church of Ligugé. It was rebuilt in the early 16C by Geoffroy d'Estissac *(qv)*, at that time Prior of Ligugé.
The **west front** and its belfry, both in the Flamboyant Gothic style, are extremely elegant. On one leaf of the carved Renaissance doors St Martin is depicted dividing his cloak.

Monastery – A number of ancient features are included within the monastery as a whole. A round tower in the outer wall is known as the Rabelais Tower because the celebrated story-teller spent a lot of time here between 1524 and 1527, when he was working as secretary to Geoffroy d'Estissac.
A community of 40 Benedictine monks inhabits the monastery today. The site so impressed the writer **J-K Huysmans** (1848-1907) that he stayed here as an oblate – a lay person attached to a religious community in order to benefit from its spiritual support – in 1901. The painters Rouault and Forain and the poet Louis Le Cardonnel were received at the same time. The poet Paul Claudel, brother of the sculptress Camille Claudel, was also a postulant here.
In the **Galerie d'émaux** ⊙ there is an exhibition of the enamel-work from the studio here which has made this monastery famous throughout the world.
The visit ends with a tour of the small **museum** in which the monastic history and geography of the area is illustrated.

★★★ LOURDES

Pop 16 300

Michelin map 85 folds 17, 18 or 234 fold 39 – Local map p 90 – Facilities.

The town of Lourdes, pleasantly situated on the banks of the Pau torrent, is famous the world over as a religious and curative centre. It is in the summer months, during the season of pilgrimages, that the great ceremonies, the processions, the throng of believers and the invalids buoyed up by faith and hope lend the town its particularly moving spiritual atmosphere. It is said that no other pilgrimage – whether to Rome, Jerusalem, Santiago de Compostela or even Mecca – draws such crowds.

J.-D. Sudres/SCOPE

Basilica.

THE PILGRIMAGE

Bernadette Soubirous (1844-79) – The Soubirous family was poor and the parents, millers, brought up their four children with difficulty. Bernadette, the eldest, was born in Lourdes but spent her first few months with a wet-nurse at Bartrès, not far from Lourdes. In early 1858, when she was 14, she was living with her parents in their single room and attending a school for poor children run by the Sisters of Charity. At weekends, preparing for her First Communion, she went to parish Catechism classes. On Thursday 11 February, a school holiday, Bernadette was gathering wood on the river bank near a local landmark known as Massabielle Rock, accompanied by one of her sisters and a neighbour. It was then, in a grotto hollowed out from the rock, that she saw for the first time the vision of the "Immaculate Conception"; the beautiful "Madonna" was to appear to her 18 times in total.

Massabielle Grotto – Although Massabielle Rock was not easily accessible at the time, a crowd of believers and unbelievers alike began to form around its cave, and increased daily as news of Bernadette's vision spread. During the ninth "apparition" Bernadette began to scrabble with her fingers in the earth floor of the cave and suddenly a spring, never before suspected, gushed forth and continued to flow in front of the startled spectators.
In 1862 the Church decided that a sanctuary should be built around the grotto. The first procession was organized in 1864 during which a statue dedicated to Our Lady of Lourdes, and lodged within the cave where the apparitions occurred, was officially blessed.

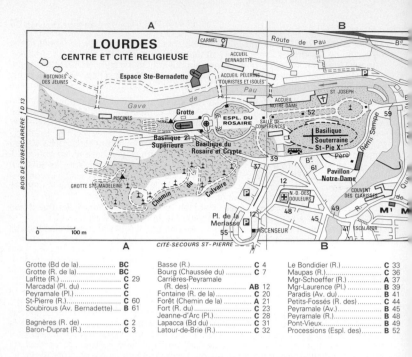

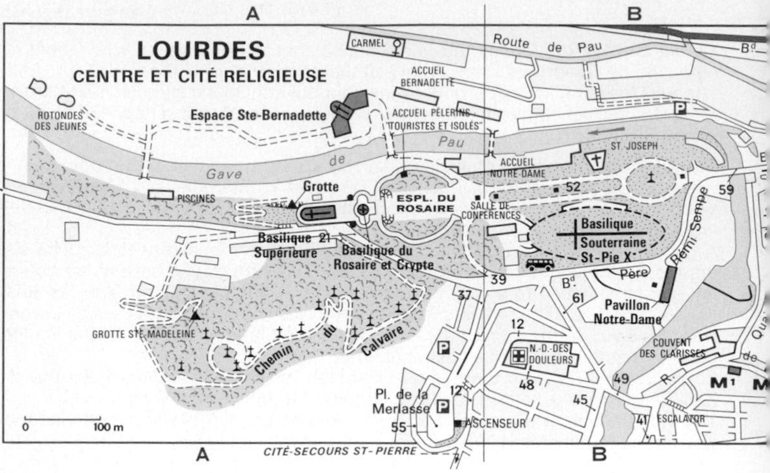

Grotte (Bd de la) .... BC
Grotte (R. de la) .... BC
Lafitte (R.) .... C 29
Marcadal (Pl. du) C
Peyramale (Pl.) C
St-Pierre (R.) .... C 60
Soubirous (Av. Bernadette) .... B 61

Bagnères (R. de) .... C 2
Baron-Duprat (R.) .... C 3
Basse (R.) .... C 4
Bourg (Chaussée du) .... C 7
Carrières-Peyramale (R. des) .... AB 12
Fontaine (R. de la) .... C 20
Forêt (Chemin de la) .... A 21
Fort (R. du) .... C 23
Jeanne-d'Arc (Pl.) .... C 28
Lapacca (Bd du) .... C 31
Latour-de-Brie (R.) .... C 32
Le Bondidier (R.) .... C 33
Maupas (R.) .... C 36
Mgr-Schoeffer (R.) .... A 37
Mgr-Laurence (Pl.) .... B 39
Paradis (Av. du) .... B 41
Petits-Fossés (R. des) .... C 44
Peyramale (Av.) .... B 45
Peyramale (R.) .... B 48
Pont-Vieux .... B 49
Processions (Espl. des) .... B 52

In 1866 Bernadette entered as a novice the Convent of St Gildard, in Nevers, the home of the Sisters of Charity who educated her; she took the veil the following year under the name of Sister Marie-Bernard. She died on 16 April 1879.
Bernadette was beatified in 1925 and canonized in 1933.

World's Largest Pilgrimage – The earliest visits, at first at parish and then at diocesan level, were expanded in 1873 into a national event organized by the Fathers of the Assumption in Paris. A year later, the second "National" included arrangements for 14 invalids to be treated at Lourdes. From then on, attention to the sick and the lame became a priority in the "miracle town" (in 1963 the first special pilgrimage was organized for poliomyelitis victims; in 1990 over 70 000 of the $5\frac{1}{2}$ million registered visitors were sufferers from a serious complaint).
Since the celebration of Bernadette's centenary in 1958 and the Vatican II Council, the planning of organized pilgrimages has taken a new turn. All the great traditional events, such as the Holy Sacrament Procession and the Torchlight Procession, have been retained but there have been new initiatives concerning meetings, the reception of pilgrims etc. The grotto has been relieved of certain "accessories" and the Basilique du Rosaire, renowned for its organ and its acoustics, is now thrown open for secular concerts and musical events.

VICINITY OF THE GROTTO *Appropriate dress essential.*

Two avenues which lead to Esplanade du Rosaire in front of the semicircular religious centre are used for important church rites and processions. A large statue of the crowned Virgin stands at its head.

Sanctuaries and places to pray – The neo-Byzantine **Basilique du Rosaire** (**A**), consecrated and blessed in 1889, occupies the lower level of the centre, between the two curved arms of the semicircle approach. The basilica (2 000m^2 – 2 392 sq yd) can accommodate a congregation of 2 000. Mosaics in the flanking chapels represent the Mysteries of the Rosary.
Between this building and the Upper Basilica lies the **crypt,** reserved in the daytime for silent prayer. Bernadette was present when the crypt was consecrated on 19 May 1866.
The neo-Gothic **Basilique Supérieure** (**A**), slender and white, was dedicated to the Immaculate Conception and consecrated in 1871. The interior comprises a single nave divided into five bays of equal size. There are 21 altars, and numerous votive offerings decorate the walls. The vaulting in the side chapels carries inscriptions quoting the words Bernadette heard from the Virgin.
Below this Upper Basilica, beside the river, is **La Grotte** (**A**), the cave where the visions appeared; a Virgin in Carrara marble marks the spot. Nearby are taps from which spring water can be drawn and, a little further downstream, the pools where ailing pilgrims bathe.
Two bridges span the river to give access to the north bank meadow where **l'Espace Ste-Bernadette** (**A**) has been built. The church in this complex, which is again in the form of a semicircle, was consecrated in 1988. It is large enough to accommodate 7 000 worshippers. The Assembly of French Bishops meets here each year in plenary session.
Larger still is the colossal **Basilique Souterraine de St-Pie X** (**B**), the underground basilica consecrated on 25 March 1958 to solemnise the official centenary of the apparitions. The huge oval hall built beneath the esplanade, on the side of the southern avenue, can hold up to 20 000 pilgrims – more than the entire population of Lourdes. It is one of the largest churches in the world, measuring 201m × 81m – 660ft × 266ft at its widest point and covering an area of 12 000m^2 – 14 350 sq yds. Engineers point out that it is thanks to the use of pre-stressed concrete that such low vaulting was able to be installed without intermediate supporting columns.

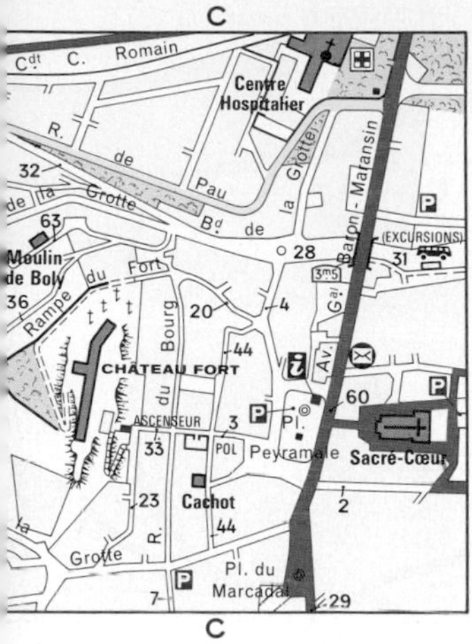

M[1] Musée Grévin de Lourdes
M[3] Musée du Gemmail

The **Chemin du Calvaire** (Road to Calvary) (**A**) starts beside the grotto and winds up through the trees past fourteen "Stations" of bronze statuary. It ends at the Cross of Calvary. Nearby are the grottoes of St Madeleine and Our Lady of Sorrows (Notre-Dame-des-Douleurs), in the natural cavern on the flank of Mont des Espélugues.

Pavillon Notre-Dame (**B**) ⊙ – On the ground floor of this building is a **museum** dedicated to "Bernadette and the Message of Our Lady". Mementoes of the young saint, together with pictorial material on the site of the 18 apparitions and on the history of the pilgrimages, can be seen.
The basement houses the **Musée d'Art Sacré du Gemmail** ⊙ (Gemmail is a technique which involves the juxtaposition and superposition of coloured glass fragments illuminated from the interior by artificial light, to produce a form of stained glass window without the lead armatures). The museum compares this contemporary expression of sacred art with more traditional examples in the same material hroughout the ages.
A gallery annex opens on alternate (odd) years to display the work of the winner of the biennial festival and competition devoted to religious art in this medium. The laureate is authorized to use the title "Painter of Light".

COMMEMORATIVE SITES

Cachot (**C**) ⊙ – *15 Rue des Petits-Fossés.* This single room in a disused prison – referred to by the family as "the cell" – was where the Soubirous family lived in a state of penury at the time of the apparitions.

Centre Hospitalier (**C**) ⊙ – *Beneath the colonnade, follow the signposts marked "Visite Chapelle".* Formerly the hospice run by the Sisters of Charity, this hospital complex is where Bernadette attended classes before being admitted as a boarder from 1860 to 1866. Photographs and personal souvenirs of the saint are on view in the parlour; in the small adjoining chapel where she took her first Communion are her communicant's cape, her Catechism and Holy Bible, and her prayer stool.

Moulin de Boly (**C**) ⊙ – *Rue Bernadette-Soubirous.* This old mill, which was Bernadette's mother's dowry, was where Bernadette was born on 7 January 1844. It now contains an exhibition on the Soubirous family.

Église du Sacré-Cœur (**C**) – The building of this parish church started in 1867 on the orders of Monseigneur Peyramale, *curé* of Lourdes at the time of the apparitions. According to records it was at the font here – transferred from another sanctuary which was demolished in 1908 – that Marie-Bernard (Bernadette) Soubirous was baptised two days after her birth.

Bartrès (**Y**) – *3km – 1¾ miles north.* It was to the wet-nurse Marie Aravant-Lagües in this village that Bernadette was confided as a baby. She returned here occasionally either for health reasons or to help out with some minor chore. Mementoes of Bernadette's visits can be seen in **Maison Lagües** ⊙. Period examples of country furniture are on display in the old kitchen.
Returning to Lourdes, park near the wayside shrine to St Bernadette and climb to the **bergerie** (sheep-fold) where, until 1858, the young girl kept sheep.

SIGHTS

★ **Château Fort** (**C**) ⊙ – *Access via a lift, via the Saracens' Staircase (131 steps) or up the castle ramp from Rue du Bourg. The third route passes the small Basque cemetery on the side of the slope, with its disk-shaped headstones.*
The castle is perched on the last boss constricting the ancient glaciated valley of the Lavedan. The glacier's terminal tongue, 400m – 1 312ft thick, petered out where Lourdes is today. The fortress, guarding the gateway to the Central Pyrenees, imposed feudal law on the turbulent hill-men of the Lavedan region *(qv)* and was subsequently, in the 17C and 18C, used as a state prison.
From Pointe du Cavalier (Rider's Bluff), at the castle's southern extremity, a vast panorama unfolds of the valley of the Pau torrent and the whole Pyrenean chain.
Inside the fortress a **Pyrenean Folk Museum**★ displays items from the regions lying between Bayonne to the west and Perpignan to the east. Among the exhibits on local customs and folk arts are costumes, musical instruments, fine ceramics, a Béarnaise kitchen and a collection of *surjougs* (wooden attachments with small bells fitted to the yoke of oxen). There are also sections on paleontology and pre-history.
The castle chapel, on the eastern side, contains woodwork, an altar and 18C polychrome statues from the original (demolished) parish church in Lourdes. On the esplanade several 1 : 10 scale models illustrate Pyrenean architectural styles from both sides of the Franco-Spanish frontier. The castle itself, with its square keep towering above the rock, is a fine example of medieval military architecture.

★★ **Pic du Jer** – A **funicular** ⊙ on the southern side of the town climbs this peak. A gentle 10-minute walk from the upper station leads to the 948m – 3 110ft summit, which offers a fine **panorama** of the Central Pyrenees.

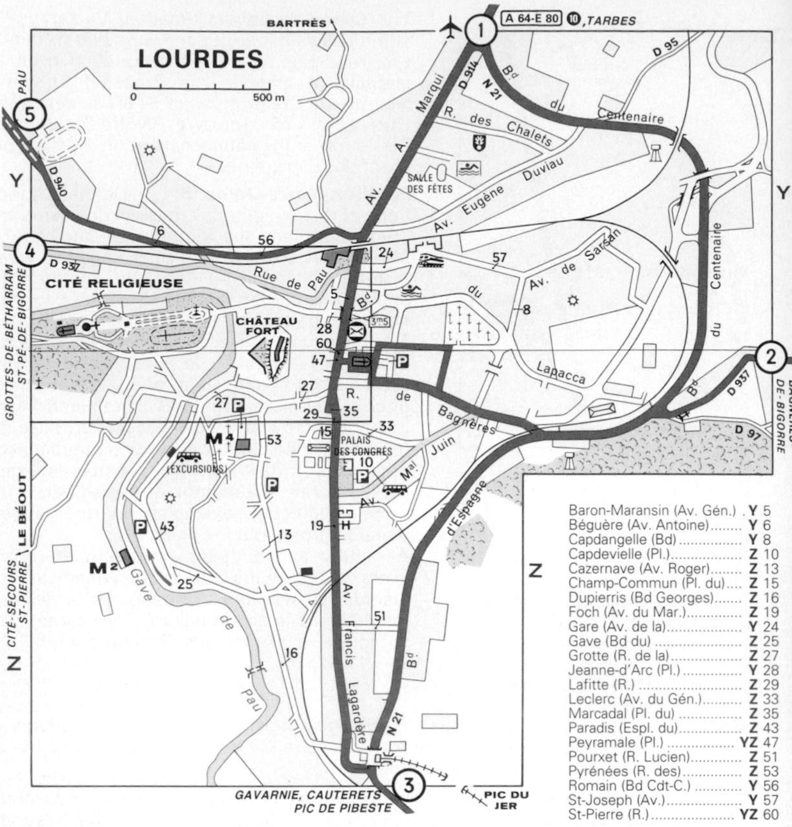

Baron-Maransin (Av. Gén.)	Y	5
Béguère (Av. Antoine)	Y	6
Capdangelle (Bd)	Y	8
Capdevielle (Pl.)	Z	10
Cazernave (Av. Roger)	Z	13
Champ-Commun (Pl. du)	Z	15
Dupierris (Bd Georges)	Z	16
Foch (Av. du Mar.)	Z	19
Gare (Av. de la)	Y	24
Gave (Bd du)	Z	25
Grotte (R. de la)	Z	27
Jeanne-d'Arc (Pl.)	Y	28
Lafitte (R.)	Z	29
Leclerc (Av. du Gén.)	Z	33
Marcadal (Pl. du)	Z	35
Paradis (Espl. du)	Z	43
Peyramale (Pl.)	YZ	47
Pourxet (R. Lucien)	Z	51
Pyrénées (R. des)	Z	53
Romain (Bd Cdt-C.)	Y	56
St-Joseph (Av.)	Y	57
St-Pierre (R.)	YZ	60

M² Musée du Petit Lourdes M⁴ Musée de Lourdes

The walk can be extended (30min Rtn) by leaving the tarred path to the observatory at the first right-hand bend on the way down. A narrow track branches off to climb to the mountain's southern peak.

From here, the impressive view includes the junction of the Argelès and Castelloubon valleys.

★ **Le Béout** – *Take the cable-car on the southern side of town then ¾ hour Rtn on foot, or take the footpath from Cité-Secours-St-Pierre, the rescue centre, which is reached via a road south of the religious complex* (**A**). The mountain (alt 791m – 2 595ft) offers a splendid **view** of Lourdes, Pic du Jer, Pic de Montaigu, the Argelès Valley and the valleys of Bat-Surguère and Castelloubon. Great, oddly-shaped boulders are scattered along the crest, testifying to the power of the Quaternary age glaciers under which the mountain was completely submerged. At the far end the view takes in Pic du Midi de Bigorre, the lake west of Lourdes, the Marboré "cylinder", Monte Perdido and, among the more distant summits, Pic Long in the Néouvielle massif, the highest point (alt 3 192m – 10 473ft) of the French Pyrenees.

⌚ ►► Musée Grévin de Lourdes (**B M¹**) : waxworks museum; Musée du Petit Lourdes (19C Lourdes in Miniature Museum) (**Z M²**); Musée du Gemmail (**B M³**); Musée de Lourdes (**Z M⁴**).

EXCURSIONS

Lourdes, lying between the Béarn and Bigorre regions, can be used as the departure point for many tourist itineraries. Consult the Principal Sights map *(qv)* and the local map in the chapter on Bigorre *(qv)*.

★★★ **Pic de Pibeste** – *13km – 8 miles south. Leave Lourdes by ③ and take N 21 south for about 10km – 6 miles then turn right to Ouzous (D 102). Leave the car in the village car park near the church. Allow at least 4½ hours walk Rtn. See Pic de Pibeste.*

★★ **Grottes de Bétharram** – *16km – 10 miles west. Local map p 90. Leave Lourdes by ④, D 937 west. Allow 2 hours.*

St-Pé-de-Bigorre – The small town, popular as a base for outdoor activities, grew up around an abbey dedicated to St Peter (from which the Gascon name "Pé" derives). The Romanesque abbey, built on the pilgrims' route to Santiago de Compostela by Cluniac monks, was at one time the finest and the largest religious monument in the Pyrenees; the Wars of Religion, however, and the earthquake of 1661 inflicted terrible, irreparable damage on it.

The west end of the abbey church included a transept with a tower above the crossing; all that remains today is a small wing below the tower with Romanesque decoration, which is used as the present baptistery *(left of the entrance)*. A much-revered statue of Notre-Dame-des-Miracles dates from the 14C.

★★ **Grottes de Bétharram** - *See Grottes de Bétharram.*

★★ LUCHON Pop 3 094

Michelin map 85 fold 20 or 235 fold 45 – Local maps pp 133 and 166 – Facilities. Town plan in the current Michelin Red Guide France.

Bagnères-de-Luchon, or Luchon as it is more commonly known, is a thermal and climatic spa lying in a beautiful setting halfway along the scenic Route des Pyrénées. The busiest and most fashionable cure resort in the region, it is also a tourist and winter sports centre with a wide choice of ski runs, climbs and excursions. In the winter the town serves as a base for skiers attracted by the snowfields of Superbagnères – the station's high-altitude annex – or the more distant runs of Peyragudes, Peyresourde and Le Mourtis.

Baths of Ilixo – In Gallo-Roman times the One valley (the land of the Onesii) was already famous for its healing waters. Ilixo, the centre's guardian god, presided over baths so magnificent that they were "the best after those of Naples" according to an inscription in Latin on the wall of the bath-house. Excavations have revealed traces of enormous pools lined with marble, allied to systems circulating warm air and steam. A Roman road linked the baths with Lugdunum Convenarum (St-Bertrand-de-Comminges, *qv*).

The Great Intendant – In 1759 **Baron d'Étigny,** who lived at Auch, visited Luchon for the first time. The baron, who was Intendant (Royal Steward) of Gascony, Béarn and Navarre, was so impressed with the cure town that he determined to restore it to its former glory. By 1762 a carriage road linked Luchon with Montréjeau to the north; the splendid avenue – which today bears the nobleman's name – was given an official opening, and planted with rows of lime trees which had to be guarded by soldiers as the inhabitants were hostile to such innovations.
D'Étigny then replaced the primitive common pool with nine double troughs made of wood, each with a removable cover furnished with holes for the bathers' heads. This was a substantial improvement though those taking the waters still had to undress in the open air, screened only by a board fence. D'Étigny was also the first person to think of appointing a regular doctor to a thermal spa.
The next step was to advertise the town. D'Étigny persuaded the governor of the province, Maréchal Duc de Richelieu, to take a cure. The duke was delighted; the Roman remains enchanted him. He extolled the merits of the spa at Versailles and returned for a second cure : from then on the town's success was assured. Even the premature death of Baron d'Étigny in 1767 did not halt Luchon's development.

Cures – More than 80 springs which rise in the mountain of Superbagnères are tapped in the spa : they emerge at temperatures between 18°C and 66°C (66.5°F to 159°F) and are among the most sulphurous and most radioactive in the world. Especially effective in the treatment of respiratory disorders, the Luchon cures have for a long time been favoured by singers, actors, lawyers and priests suffering from strained vocal cords. More recently the **Radio-Vaporarium** has been successful in treating rheumatic complaints and in physical re-education : it comprises a series of wide cauldrons hollowed out in galleries beneath the rock, where the emanations form a natural Turkish Bath at temperatures ranging from 38°C to 48°C (100°F to 118°F). The Radio-Vaporarium forms part of the most luxurious **thermal cure centre** ⓥ in Luchon.
The spa springs are rich in **barégine,** a colony of algae and bacteria found only in sulphurous water. Cultivated and blended with neutral clay, this organic material is part of the "thermal mud" used for local applications.

The Town – Life in Luchon centres on the **Allées d'Étigny,** the principal avenue leading to the baths. The mansion at No 18, built in the 18C and used for the reception of the Duc de Richelieu, now houses the tourist information centre and the local museum.

Musée du Pays de Luchon ⓥ – The ground floor of this regional museum displays the "Plan Lézat", a three-dimensional relief map of the mountains around Luchon on a scale of 1 :10 000, which dates from 1854. The upper floors are devoted to mementoes of famous visitors, to distinguished Pyrenean climbers and to winter sports on the neighbouring massifs of La Maladetta, Le Lys, L'Oô and the Aran. Iron age artefacts, statues and votive altars from the Gallo-Roman period show Man's long-standing interest in the region. Photographs and reproductions in another room relate to the more recent history of the town, the local casino and the thermal cures. The arts, crafts and folk traditions of the surrounding valleys are represented by a rich and varied collection : weavers' looms, shepherds' crooks, farming tools, religious items...

EXCURSIONS

★★ 1 Vallée de la Pique

11km – 7 miles south. Leave Luchon via D 125 – local map overleaf.

The road follows the Pique Valley upstream, rising first through meadows and then through splendid forests. After crossing the river, turn left into the road (D 125) leading to the Maison Forestière de Jouéu. This lodge, which stands in a plantation of conifers, belongs to the University of Toulouse and is a specialist botanical laboratory used for studying the flora of the fields and forests.

Park the car : owing to a series of landslides, the last 2km – 1 mile has to be travelled on foot.

At an altitude of 1 385m – 4 544ft the Hospice de France is reached. This group of low buildings in the centre of a beautiful upland pasture typical of the Pyrenees is an excellent base for ramblers : the surrounding forest, the abundance of waterfalls, the majesty of the landscape all beckon invitingly.
Walkers in good physical condition who would appreciate a close view of the highest point in the Pyrenees should leave the Hospice very early and take the mule track leading to **Port de Vénasque** (alt 2 448m – 8 032ft). From the first slopes on the Spanish side of the pass *(4½ hours on foot Rtn),* or better still from **Pic de Sauvegarde,** which rises to 2 738m – 8 983ft *(6 hours on foot Rtn),* there is a superb view of the entire Maladetta massif.

★★ 2 Lac d'Oô

14km – $8\frac{1}{2}$ miles southwest : allow $2\frac{1}{2}$ hours. Leave Luchon via D 618, the road to the Col de Peyresourde (described in the opposite direction in the chapter on Le Comminges). Local map below.

St-Aventin – This hamlet boasts a majestic Romanesque **church** ⊙ with some fine fragments of sculpture : 12C Virgin and Child *(pier right of the main door),* a low-relief showing the body of St Aventin being unwrapped from its shroud by a furiously stamping bull *(on a buttress, right),* and Gallo-Roman funerary monuments *(where the nave meets the apse).* Inside, note the pre-Romanesque font carved with symbolic animals (lambs, fish, doves) and the 12C mural paintings.
At Castillon, fork left into the Oô Valley road (D 76) which skirts the base of the huge moraine on which the villages of Cazeaux and Garin are perched. At the far end of the valley (south), the Seil de la Baque glacier is visible. The road runs alongside the Neste d'Oô and crosses a stretch of fine meadowland. Finally it arrives at a shallow depression that was once a lake – an austere setting, surrounded by rocky escarpments on which only scrub and straggly firs grow. At Granges d'Astau (alt 1 139m – 3 737ft) the road ends. The torrent hurtling down on the right of these heights forms a spectacular waterfall known as "La Chevelure de Madeleine" (Mary Magdalene's tresses) – popular imagination seeing in the silver threads of the cascade the long hair of the repentant sinner.

★★ **Lac d'Oô** – Alt 1 504m – 4 934ft. *Footpath signposted GR10 : 2 hours on foot Rtn.* The lake lies in a magnificent setting; in the background, the torrent issuing from Lac d'Espingo falls 275m – 902ft in a superb cascade. The waters of the lake (covering 38ha – 94 acres; maximum depth 67m – 220ft) fuel the Oô hydro-electric power station *(consequent lowering of the lake's water level may render the scene less attractive).*

★ 3 Vallée du Lys

32km – 20 miles south : allow $2\frac{1}{2}$ hours. Local map below.

The full name of this valley is "Bat de Lys" or Vale of Avalanches. D 46, a good road, continues from where the route to the Hospice de France branches off, 5.5km – $3\frac{1}{2}$ miles from Luchon.

After 1.5km – 1 mile, where the road widens, park the car.

Gouffre Richard – There is a good view of this powerful waterfall – where the river plunges into a rocky cauldron formed by a pot-hole in the strata – from the base of an electricity pylon (left).
Continue west, turning off the road to Superbagnères into D 46A (left). The road veers southwards, revealing a **panorama★** of the highest peaks surrounding the amphitheatre at the head of the valley.

Park the car in the (free) car park of the restaurant "Les Délices du Lys".

Centrale du Portillon (Portillon Power Station) – The hydro-electric station is powered by water falling from a maximum height of 1 419m – 4 656ft, a drop which was thought sensational when the station was opened in 1941.

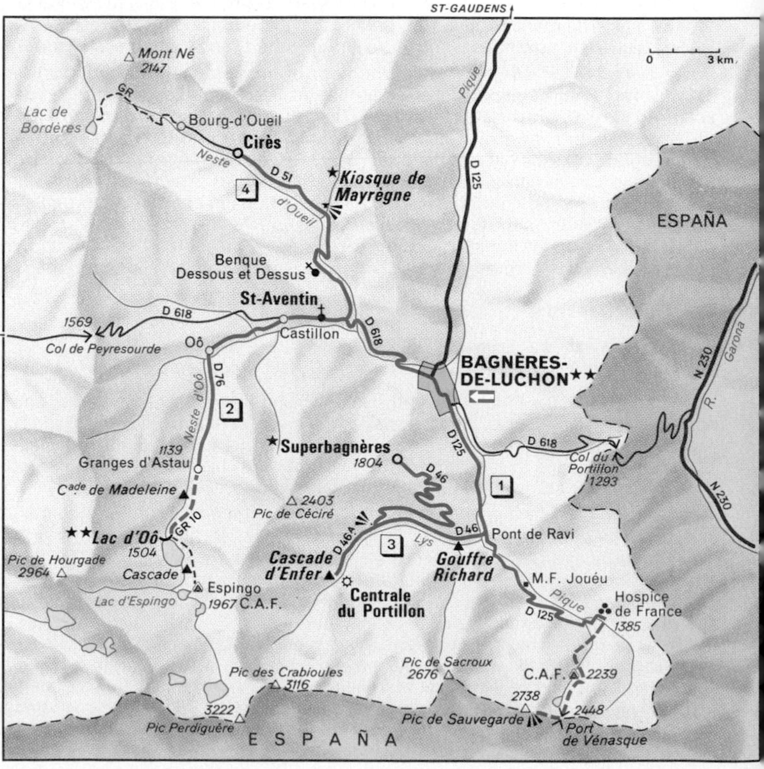

Cascade d'Enfer – "Hell's Waterfall" is the last leap of the Enfer stream.

Return to D 46 and turn left to Superbagnères. The road runs through beech-woods.

★ **Superbagnères** – Alt 1 804m – 5 919ft. Superbagnères is popular in summer as a high-altitude resort but it is better known as a ski station (it stands well above the tree-line). Championships are held on its great snow-fields in winter. From the viewing table in front of the hotel a great **panorama**★ of the frontier crest and the glaciers of the Maladetta massif can be admired.

★ 4 Vallée d'Oueil

15km – 9 miles northwest : 30min. Local map opposite. Leave Luchon by D 618.

After some sharp bends, beyond a chapel commemorating the martyrdom of St Aventin, turn right into D 51. About 2km – 1 mile along, a track *(left)* leads to **Benque-Dessous-et-Dessus.** The church in the upper village contains 15C mural paintings.

The lower **Oueil Valley**★ is noted for its pastoral charm and clustered villages. Fields of wheat, buckwheat, maize and potatoes rise in terraces on the sunny slopes; magnificent meadows, framed by firs, carpet the shaded side of the valley.

★ **Kiosque de Mayrègne** – *Free access to the viewing table on the café terrace.* There is a fine **panorama** over the heights of the frontier chain and the sombre Vénasque massif glittering here and there with glaciers from the Portillon upper cirque to Oô. In the distance, between Pic de Sacroux and Pic de Sauvegarde, the Maladetta range is once more visible, culminating in the 3 404m – 11 168ft Pic d'Aneto, the highest point in the Pyrenees.

Cirès – The houses of this tiny, picturesque hamlet are packed into a mini amphitheatre below a church isolated on its promontory; like all the houses in the valley, beneath their pointed roofs they have high lofts, enclosed by lattice-work, to store the abundant hay.

During the Roman era Cicero ate oysters in the belief that their high phosphorus content would nourish his mind; in the 16C Louis XII made his advisers eat them daily, for the same reason. Marshal Junot, in the early 19C, allegedly downed 300 oysters each morning...

LUÇON

Pop 9 099

Michelin map 71 fold 11 or 233 fold 3 – Local map p 172.

This charming episcopal town on the borders of the Poitou marshlands and the plain was once a seaport; more recently it has become an important trading and agricultural centre.

Richelieu – On 21 December 1608 in the cathedral here a pale-faced young man accepted the homage of a handful of canons : Armand du Plessis de Richelieu, aged only 23, was taking over "the worst bishopric in France, the filthiest and the most disagreeable" – as he himself described it to a friend soon after his arrival.

He was hardly exaggerating as the town had been ruined by the Wars of Religion and by illness and fever brought on by the damp of the surrounding marshes. Such fevers forced the young bishop to retire from time to time to his 16C country château because at the Bishop's Palace, which had been deserted for 30 years, not a single fireplace was in working order.

Richelieu refused to be discouraged, however, and persevered with his mission, restructuring his See and its clergy, restoring the cathedral and palace, founding a seminary. He was also responsible for the building of a town bearing his name southwest of Tours, near the Loire.

Tallendier

Richelieu by Philippe de Champaigne.

At the same time the man who was later to play an important role as state adviser to Louis XIII was enhancing his prospects by intensive study of history and theology; by cultivating friendships with diplomats and such influential figures as Father Joseph (who subsequently became Richelieu's mentor on matters of foreign policy), Cardinal de Bérulle (a major force during the Catholic renaissance in the 17C) and the Abbot of St-Cyran (whom he was himself to have imprisoned, many years later, at Vincennes).

SIGHTS

Cathédrale Notre-Dame – This former abbey church became a cathedral in 1317. As well as Richelieu, the See counts at least one other celebrated bishop on its roll : Nicolas Colbert, the brother of the Minister, who reigned over the bishopric from 1661 to 1671.
The church, built of fine honey-coloured limestone, is largely in the Gothic style, although the northern arm of the transept dates back to Romanesque times. The west front was entirely remodelled in the late 17C under the supervision of the architect François Leduc. The overall balance and strictly classical layout of this façade (superimposed antique orders, scrolled decoration etc) contrast vividly with the slender, tapered Gothic spire which was rebuilt in 1828 and rises to a height of 85m – 279ft. The façade as a whole serves today as a belfry-porch.
The well-proportioned nave and chancel date from the Gothic period; the latter is adorned with ornamental woodwork and a rich canopy. Richelieu himself is said to have preached from a pulpit, delicately painted with fruit and flowers, in the north aisle. In the south transept is a 16C *Descent from the Cross* (recently restored) from the Florentine School. The 19C organ in the gallery is by Cavaillé-Coll (1811-99).

Episcopal Palace – South of the cathedral is the 16C façade of the old bishops' residence. Entrance – via the **cloisters** – is through a doorway surmounted by a Gothic arch framing the armorial bearings of Louis, Cardinal de Bourbon, who was Bishop of Luçon from 1524 to 1527. Galleries juxtaposing both Gothic and Renaissance elements were added in the 16C. The western side, formerly the chapter-house library, is pierced by Renaissance windows.

►► Jardin Dumaine★.

LUSIGNAN

Pop 2 749

Michelin map 68 fold 13 or 233 fold 7 – Facilities.

This small Poitou town lies along the crest of a promontory overlooking on one side the valley of the River Vonne, on the other a depression in which a business district has been built flanking the main road to Poitiers.

Mélusine the fairy – A long time ago, according to legend, Raimondin, the young Comte du Poitou, accidentally killed his uncle with a hunting spear while the two men were grappling with an enraged wild boar. Wandering distraught in Coulombiers Forest, not far from Lusignan, Raimondin saw a spring suddenly well up at the foot of a bluff on top of which appeared the filmy white silhouettes of three enchanting female figures. One of them was the fairy Mélusine, whom the young noble determined to make his bride.
Despite her mortal marriage Mélusine retained her magic powers : the slightest wave of her wand still conjured up dream palaces. In this way she created not only Lusignan Castle, on the spot where she met Raimondin, but also the fortresses of Pouzauges, Tiffauges *(qv)*, Mervent, Vouvant *(qv)*, Parthenay *(qv)* and Châteaumur.
Alas, the fairy bride unfortunately hid a shameful secret : having in the past murdered her own father, she was condemned to be transformed, every Saturday, into a serpent-woman. Nobody should see her in this form.
One fine Saturday, however, consumed by jealousy at Mélusine's repeated absences, Raimondin burst through the door of her room. Stupefied, he discovered his wife changed into a Siren, combing her long golden tresses as she bathed. Mélusine at once dived out of the window, assumed the form of a giant snake, and slithered sinuously three times around the town and the castle before hurtling down onto the gate-house tower of the château... and vanishing into thin air.

SIGHTS

Castle ruins – The fortress was built at the extremity of the promontory, overlooking the steep-sided valley in which the Vonne describes its lazy curves. It belonged originally to the Lusignan family, who claimed to be descendants of Mélusine; members of the same family at one time ruled over Jerusalem and Cyprus.
All that remains of the castle today is a group of buildings occupied by a museum, along with subterranean chambers and the foundations of several towers which were once part of the surrounding fortifications. In the 18C the castle grounds were transformed into the Promenade de Blossac, named after the steward responsible. An avenue of lime trees surrounded by flower gardens now leads to a terrace from which there is an attractive view of the Vonne Valley, spanned by a 432m – 475yd viaduct : the elegantly traced course of the river and the vivid colour contrast with the bright green meadows on either side and the sombre tones of the woods carpeting the slopes above.

Church – This fine example of Poitou Romanesque architecture with particularly impressive proportions was built by the Lusignan family in the 11C. The recumbent statue in the south aisle is Gothic. The high altar stands above a crypt with triple barrel vaulting. Outside, a porch added to the southern elevation in the 15C faces an interesting house with half-timbered, projecting upper storeys which dates from the same period.

★ LUZ-ST-SAUVEUR — Pop 1 173

Michelin map 85 fold 18 or 234 folds 43, 44. Local map p 90. Facilities.

The villages of Luz and St-Sauveur face one another across the Pau torrent in a picturesque mountain setting.

Napoleonic Souvenirs – The inhabitants of this valley, once fierce and unsociable by nature (the ruins of the castle wrested from the English have proved the point since 1404), were nevertheless unable to disguise their gratitude to Napoleon III and Empress Eugénie for the benefits showered on the town and its surroundings by the royal couple. A trip around the Luz basin from Pont de la Reine north of the town to Pont Napoléon in the south, via the Solferino Chapel, is virtually a "Napoleon III tour". The chapel is used for an annual ceremony commemorating the foundation of the Red Cross.

★ LUZ

Luz, the capital of a small mountain canton which for centuries was cut off in winter from the lowlands by the hazards of the route through the avalanche-prone Échelles de Barèges *(qv)*, is today a surprisingly busy and well-equipped tourist centre. Fashionable as a summer resort in the 18C and 19C, the small town boasts a number of distinguished houses dating from that period, white beneath their slate roofs and adorned with carved lintels, cornices and wrought-iron balconies.

★ **Fortified Church** ⓥ – *Illustration p 43.* The church, incorrectly called a Templars' church, was built in the 12C and fortified in the 14C by the Hospitallers of St John of Jerusalem. The defensive features included a watch-path running round beneath the roof, a crenellated wall enclosing an old cemetery, and two square towers. The fine Romanesque doorway is decorated with the figures of Christ the King surrounded by the Evangelists.
Inside, note the 18C woodwork, the small **museum** of religious art in the 17C Chapelle Notre-Dame-de-la-Pitié, and a second **museum** (local curiosities) beneath the "Arsenal" tower.

ST-SAUVEUR

The town's single street, perched above the torrent, is named first after the Duchesse de Berry, leading socialite of the 1828 season, and then after Empress Eugénie, whose visits – particularly that of 1859 – sealed the resort's success.

EXCURSION

Barèges – *7km – 4 miles east.* This pleasant ski resort (at 1 250m – 4 100ft also the highest spa resort) was the cradle of the Pyrenean ski school.

★ MAILLEZAIS — Pop 930

Michelin map 71 fold 1 or 233 folds 4, 5 – Local map p 173.

A little way outside this Poitou village, on the edge of the flat immensity of the marshlands which make up the Marais Poitevin, stand the imposing ruins of Maillezais Abbey.
The abbey was founded by Guillaume Fier-à-Bras, Comte de Poitou, at the end of the 10C. At that time the limestone boss on which it is built was pounded by the ocean – part of the enormous Gulf of Poitou *(qv)*, since silted up and sealed in to become the famous marshes. The abbey, dedicated to St Peter, was at first confided to monks of the Benedictine order, who honoured here the arms of St Rigomer. In the 13C it was sacked by Geoffroi la Grand-Dent, a member of the Lusignan family who claimed to be the son of Mélusine *(qv)* and who was subsequently used by Rabelais as a model for the boisterous and brave giant **Pantagruel** in his novel of the same name.
In 1317 the French Pope John XXII elevated Maillezais to the status of a bishopric but allowed the monks to remain in the abbey. During the Wars of Religion most of the buildings were destroyed and the Bishop of Luçon, Richelieu, ordered the episcopal seat to be transferred to La Rochelle.
A **boat trip** ⓥ through the Wet Marsh district of the Marais Poitevin *(qv)* makes an agreeable complement to the tour of the abbey here.

Two humanists – Between 1518 and 1542 the Bishop of Maillezais was **Geoffroy d'Estissac** *(qv)*, a Périgord man who seemed to collect livings as a hobby : he was Abbot of Celles-sur-Belle, of St-Liguaire near Niort, of Cadouin in Périgord, Prior of Ligugé and Hermanault, near Fontenay-le-Comte, and Dean of St-Hilaire de Poitiers. Geoffroy was a great builder, constantly altering and improving the establishments for which he was responsible; it was he who started the construction of the castle at Coulonges-sur-l'Autize, decorative elements of which were subsequently transferred to the Château de Terre-Neuve at Fontenay-le-Comte *(qv)*.
The erudite and liberal Bishop welcomed Rabelais to Maillezais when the young monk was expelled from Fontenay in 1523, and for three years employed him as secretary. Rabelais followed him to several other ecclesiastical residences in the Poitou region. Later, from Rome, he sent d'Estissac the first seeds of the green vegetable which became known as *Salade Romaine* (Cos Lettuce).
The writer **Agrippa d'Aubigné** (1552-1630) was born in the Saintonge region and later became a close friend of Henri IV; he was the grandfather of Mme de Maintenon *(qv)*. An ardent Protestant, he was condemned to death four different times for his religious views. A scholar as much as a poet, he wrote among many other works a

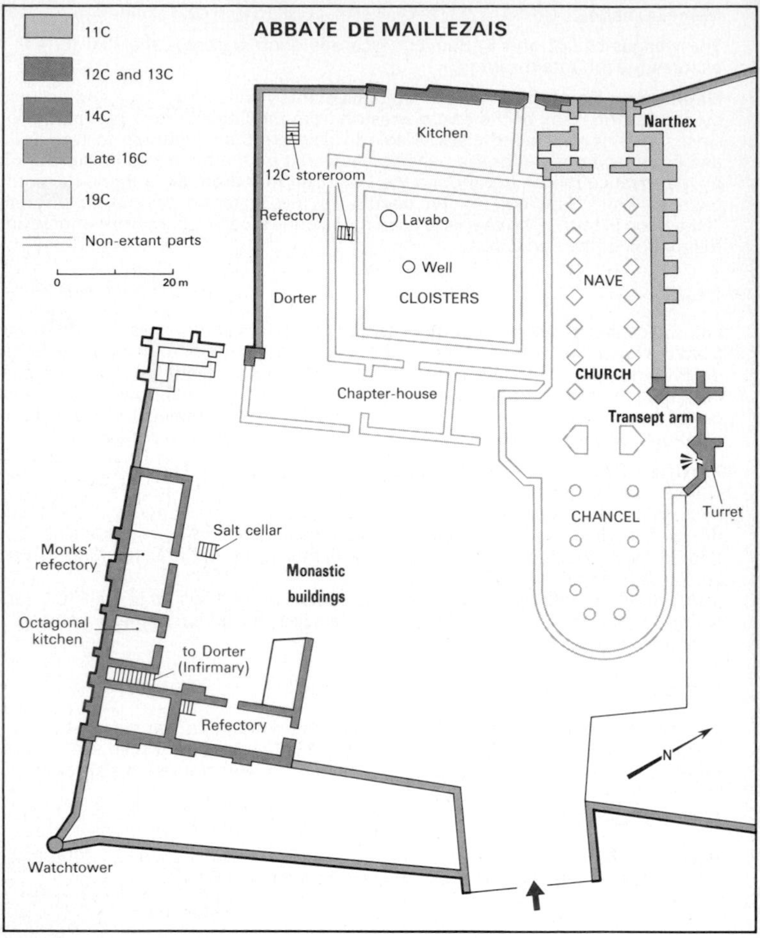

Huguenot *chanson de geste (qv)* entitled *Les Tragiques* (Tragedies), many of whose 9 264 lines have become famous in French literature : a well-known example is *Une rose d'automne est plus qu'une autre exquise* (More than any other is the Autumn rose exquisite).

From 1584 to 1619 d'Aubigné spent much of his time either in his fort at Doignon, near Maillé south of Maillezais, or within the abbey itself, where he was host to Protestant troops fortifying the outer walls.

★ ABBAYE DE MAILLEZAIS ⌚ *45 min*

Much of the fortified wall built around the monastery on d'Aubigné's orders is still standing. The work transformed the abbey into a true fortress : on the left of the entrance a bastion shaped like the prow of a ship faces the Wet Marsh. It was surmounted by a bartizan watch-tower, and since the "prow" pointed due south this was also able to serve as a giant sundial.

Abbey church – Building of the church began in the early 11C, though only the narthex and the wall of the north aisle remain from this period. The narthex was flanked by two square towers, following a pattern established in Normandy where abbey churches were distinguished by tower strongpoints on either side of the west front. The façade of the church here was later incorporated into the fortified wall built by d'Aubigné.

The three tall, crowned openings piercing the existing aisle wall reveal that the nave was altered in the 13C. The aisles were originally topped by galleries – again as in Norman abbeys.

The transept, of which only part of the northern arm remains, was a 14C Gothic addition. It is possible to climb to the top of one of the truncated turrets flanking its gable, from which there is a good general view of the ruins, the village and the marshes. The outlines of the huge chancel, which was rebuilt in the 16C by Geoffroy d'Estissac, can still be made out.

Monastery – Most of the monastic buildings date from the 14C. The foundations of the old cloisters have been uncovered, along with sections of the paving, a 12C storeroom, a *lavabo* where the monks washed their hands before entering the refectory, a well and a number of abbots' or bishops' tombstones.

One wing of the monastery still stands and includes the ancient salt cellar (basement); the octagonal kitchen, now housing an exhibition of items discovered during the excavations – scrolled modillions, capitals etc – and the refectories (ground floor); the guests' dorter (dormitory) and infirmary with its large central fireplace (first floor).

★★ Le MARAIS POITEVIN

Michelin map 71 folds 1, 2, 11, 12 or 233 folds 2 to 5.

Since 1975 the Marais Poitevin (Poitou Marshlands) has formed part of an enormous Parc Naturel Régional (Regional Park, *qv*) which also includes the Val de Sèvre and the Vendée *(qv)*. It is a region of immense, luminous skies, of meadows bordered by poplars and willow trees, of innumerable watercourses along which glide the black boats of the marshlanders. This lush landscape is a popular holiday destination.

Gulf of Poitou and its islands – Aiguillon Bay, an Atlantic inlet itself in the process of silting up, is all that remains of the vast gulf which stretched in ancient times from the limestone plain in the north to the hills of the Aunis *(qv)*. The gulf, which penetrated inland as far as Niort, was scattered with rocky limestone islets (now occupied by such towns as Maillezais, Marans and St-Michel-en-l'Herm). Its shores, which can still be identified via the "dead" cliffs which remain, are now marked out by Moricq, Luçon, Velluire, Fontaines and Benet to the north, and by Mauzé-sur-le-Mignon, Nuaillé-d'Aunis and Esnandes to the south.

The marshland epic – Little by little the rivers Lay, Vendée, Autise and Sèvre Niortaise discharged their alluvium into the gulf, while at the same time sea currents were piling up a clay-like silt known locally as **"Bri"**, and as a consequence the marine inlet was transformed into a huge salt-marsh.
From the 11C onwards monks in the region intervened : they laid out canals and fisheries, built locks and watermills, established agriculture and grazing land. In the 13C the incumbents of the abbeys of Nieul, St-Michel-en-l'Herm, Maillezais, Absie and St-Maixent dredged out the Canal des Cinq-Abbés (Five Abbots' Canal) which drained the northern part of the swamp; for his part Philippe le Hardi, King of France, whose family was from Poitiers, traced out the course of the Achenal-le-Roi (King's Canal).
The work, interrupted by wars, was resumed under Henri IV : an engineer from Bergen-op-Zoom in Holland established a series of waterways known as the Canal de la Ceinture des Hollandais (the Dutch Belt). After that came the Levée des Limousins, the 1771 Dyke and the Village of the Year 7, all testifying to the progressive "colonization" of the marshlands. Around Aiguillon Bay itself Dutch-style polders *(qv)* protected by dykes were reclaimed from the sea between the 16C and the 19C. As the bay slowly silted up, mussel beds *(bouchots, see below)* began to be created, mainly around Esnandes and Charron.

The Marais today – The marshes, stretching away on either side of the Sèvre Niortaise river, cover an area of 80 000ha – 198 000 acres or 310 sq miles.
The general configuration of the Marais includes a network of embankments or dykes, known locally as **"bots"**, along the top of which run roads and tracks and below which are the principal channels (**"contrebots"**). When the rivers draining into the marshes are in spate, excess water surges into subsidiary **"achenaux"** (channels), which divert the flow again into **"rigoles"** and finally **"conches"**, marked by lines of small trees. Between these waterways the land, which is extremely fertile, is used both for crops and for grazing.

Errath/EXPLORER

Cattle transportation in the Marais Poitevin.

The region is divided into "Dry Marsh", nearer the sea, where the Atlantic winds blow, and "Wet Marsh", further inland, bounded on the north by the limestone plain of the Vendée and southwards by the hills of Aunis. The **Wet Marsh,** sometimes called **Venise Verte** (Green Venice), is the more picturesque, particularly east of the Autise, on either side of the Sèvre; it covers some 15 000ha – 37 000 acres or 58 sq miles of the Marais as a whole.
Much of the marshland remains to be explored. A profusion of alders, lofty ash trees, willows and poplars of the species known as "Poitou Whites" lines the banks, and overhangs the labyrinth of narrow channels parcelling the rich fields in which herds of Friesians, Normans and locally-bred cattle graze. The plots under cultivation produce an abundant harvest of artichokes, onions, garlic, melons, courgettes, broad beans and the delicious haricots, usually white, known as **"mojettes"**. Some 90 000 trees growing in this sylvan paradise were destroyed during a terrible storm in 1983.
The **Dry Marsh** presents a very different aspect. A territory of wide open spaces crossed by canals and dykes, it produces wheat, barley and various types of bean despite the fact that the black earth of the *bri* needs constant fertilizing. The pastureland has been given over to the rearing of salt-pasture sheep and cattle. The holdings here are much larger than those in the Wet Marsh.

Marshlanders – The Marshlanders, solemn and thoughtful by nature, live in low, whitewashed houses grouped in villages either on limestone islets or on the dykes, where there is no risk of flooding. Each householder owns some kind of cabin in an isolated spot. Most houses are flanked by a *cale* – a miniature creek in which boats

can be moored. Boats are the normal means of transport, manoeuvred either with a **"pigouille"** (a hooked pole or gaff) or a short oar called a **"pelle"**. There are two types of boat : the slim, lightweight **"yoles"** are used for going to church, to market or to school whereas the larger, more heavily-built **"plates"** take the place of vans or trucks, delivering farm produce or ferrying horses and cows. They are also used for towing rafts or poplar logs being floated inland to the veneering works at Niort and St-Hilaire-la-Palud.
The marshlanders deliver their milk to local co-operatives, which produce a celebrated brand of butter, returning the whey for the fattening of pigs. Fishing brings in mullet, perch, carp, roach, crayfish and eels. Hunting for waterfowl and other game birds (duck, plover, snipe) is restricted to the winter months.

★★ BOAT TRIPS ⊙

A trip by car can show up the contrast between the Wet Marsh, so overgrown with trees that it seems like one vast forest, and the huge, bare flatlands of the Dry Marsh, but the only way to really experience the Wet Marsh, to appreciate its poetry, its silences and its uniqueness, is to go by boat. The vessels, mirrored in the still water, glide in summer beneath a dense vault of foliage filtering the bright light through shades of grey-green to jade. Apart from Coulon, the main tourist centre in the Marais, many other places offer **boat trips** *(see map opposite)*, with or without guides. **Cruises** up the Sèvre Niortaise are also available. Minibus trips or a ride in a miniature train *(see Coulon, qv)* along the earth roads of the marshlands also help visitors to discover the delights of the area.

TOWNS AND SIGHTS *listed alphabetically*

Digue and Pointe de l'Aiguillon – The famous dyke, conceived and built by Dutch engineers, is a slender 6km – $3\frac{1}{2}$ mile tongue of land protected by a breakwater. To the east is the islet of La Dive, with its cliff gashed by old breakers; beyond that are beaches bordered by sand dunes.
Pointe de l'Aiguillon, the southeast extremity of the dyke where there is a wildfowl hunting reserve (Réserve de Chasse maritime), projects into the grey waters of the silting-up bay. The wide **view★** extends from the narrow estuary of the River Lay and Pointe d'Arcay (northwest) to the Île de Ré (southwest) and the port of La Pallice (south). The famous mussel beds are visible only at low tide.

L'Aiguillon-sur-Mer – The low-built houses overlooking the estuary of the Lay, which is separated from the Atlantic by a barrier of dunes (now a national hunting reserve), face a denuded countryside, bleak beneath an immense sky.
The local economy is based on nursery gardening, coastal fishing and the cultivation of oysters and mussels.

Angles – One of the gables on the old abbey church here is adorned with the representation of a large bear which, according to legend, was changed into stone by a hermit named Martin. Inside the church, the chancel and transept are Romanesque while the nave is in the Plantagenet style *(qv)*.

Benet – The church is marked by a square 15C belltower and has a Romanesque west front, which has suffered from the addition of a Gothic porch. The representation of a horseman habitually found in Poitou churches can be seen in one of the side arcades, along with a figure holding a pair of scales. The central bay has historiated arching.

Chaillé-les-Marais – There is an interesting view of this one-time isle in the Gulf of Poitou from route N 137. Built on what is now just a limestone bluff, the town commands the plain which was once under water. It is the centre of the Dry Marsh sector known as Petit Poitou, the first in the province to be drained and dried.
The **Maison du Petit Poitou** ⊙ *(on the road to Luçon)* offers comprehensive information on the drying out of the marshes, their flora and fauna, and the activities of the inhabitants. Video films *(in French)* are shown. Outside, animals whose traditional habitat is the Marais – local donkeys, goats, cows – can be seen.

★ **Coulon** – *See Coulon.*

Damvix – This small marshland village in a pleasant location on the Sèvre Niortaise contains a number of low cottages linked by footbridges which span the narrow canals.

Esnandes – The inhabitants of the low, whitewashed houses here farm mussels and oysters. The first **bouchots** *(qv)* were installed in the 13C, when the captain of a ship wrecked in the bay, an Irishman named Walton, settled here : to survive he caught birds by fixing a net between two posts planted in the silt, and soon he noticed that the posts became covered in small mussels which grew more rapidly than those on the natural banks.

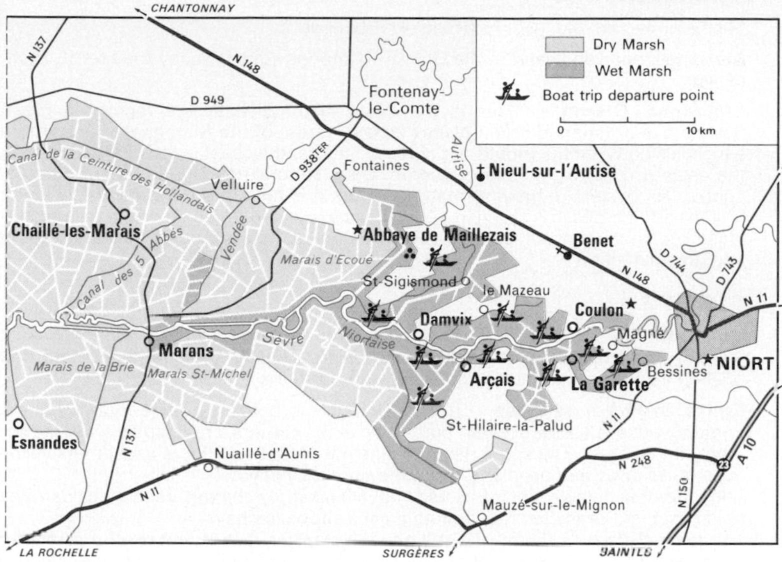

The **Maison de la Mytiliculture** ⓥ traces the history of Aiguillon Bay and the developments in mussel farming since the 15C.

La Faute-sur-Mer – Although it boasts a casino, La Faute remains basically a small family seaside resort, with a long beach of fine sand.
The **Parc de Californie**★ ⓥ *(on D 46, the road to La Tranche-sur-Mer)* is a bird sanctuary : 4ha – 10 acres of greenery and flowers from which more than 300 different species, some of them birds of prey, can be watched flying freely or nesting according to season.

La Garette – The houses of this old boatmen's hamlet on the Vieille Sèvre are characteristic in that each has two entrances : one from the waterway, the other from the road. The bridge across the river offers a view of the Sèvre and its quays.

★ **Maillezais** – *See Maillezais.*

Marans – This is the market town of the Dry Marsh, and noted for its grain storage (silos). Once it was known for the production of pottery; today there are several light industries and pharmaceutical laboratories. The small port, linked to the ocean by a canal, harbours a boatyard. Lock gates maintain the level of the tidal basin, where a number of coasters and pleasure craft are moored.

Moricq – The massive, square, fortified tower (15C), which is today isolated in the middle of a meadow, once defended the small port on the Lay.

Nieul-sur-l'Autise – This village grew around an old abbey founded in 1068; in the 13C monks began to drain the neighbouring marshes. The abbey was secularised in 1715 and soon abandoned. The Romanesque abbey church in Poitou style *(qv)* was restored in the 19C and features a richly carved west front. The square **cloisters**★ ⓥ are original and have Romanesque galleries offering good views.
The **Maison de la Meunerie** ⓥ is a restored old watermill now housing a museum : the mill workings and domestic rooms of the miller and his family are on view.

★ **Niort** – *See Niort.*

St-Denis-du-Payré – The **Réserve Naturelle M-Brosselin** ⓥ *(2km – 1¼ miles east)* encompasses 207ha – 512 acres of marshland frequented by large numbers of birds, either nesting or making a customary halt during their migration. A diorama with slides which can be viewed at the **reception centre** illustrates the various species which can be identified through telescopes from the nearby **observatory.**

St-Michel-en-l'Herm – There is an old **Benedictine Abbey** ⓥ here dedicated to archangel St Michael who appeared to people in high-up places – hence the high position of statues of this saint. The abbey, founded in the 7C by Ansoald, bishop of Poitiers, prospered until the 9C when it was devastated by the Normans. Wars with the English during the 14C and 15C, the Wars of Religion in the 16C and the Revolution brought only more destruction. It was rebuilt each time, though only partly the last time, in the late 17C, when François Leduc was involved. Of particular note are the Gothic chapter-house and calefactory, with a refectory and the monks' building by Leduc.

La Tranche-sur-Mer – This is a seaside resort with an immense beach of fine sand stretching for 13km – 8 miles. Behind, pinewoods extend over an area of 600ha – 1 483 acres. Maupas Lake offers facilities for learning various water sports, including windsurfing, water-skiing, dinghy sailing etc.
Since 1953 nurserymen have, with great success, introduced the cultivation of tulips; **Les Floralies Tranchaises** (local flower shows) ⓥ are organized in a shady 7ha – 17 acre park.
In the summer season there is a choice of **boat cruises** ⓥ starting from La Tranche.

MARENNES

Pop 4 634

Michelin map 71 fold 14 or 233 fold 14 – Facilities.

Marennes, once an island in the Gulf of Saintonge *(qv)*, is today the French oyster capital.

"Marennes-Oléron" – This is the name distinguishing the renowned green-fleshed oyster fattened in the *claires* (special beds) of the Marennes-Oléron basin, which lies between the mouth of the River Seudre, the coast north of Marennes and the eastern coast of the Isle of Oléron. Ostreiculture *(qv)* makes use of so-called "parks" for oysters to grow to maturity in but it is only in the *claires* of this region that the adult mollusc is fattened, refined and subjected to the effects of microscopic algae known here as *Navicules Bleues* which give the seafood its delicate perfume and greenish tint.

SIGHTS

Vidéorama de l'huître ⏲ – *In the tourist information centre.* The video *(in French)* focuses on ostreiculture in the Marennes-Oléron basin, showing interesting material on its history and the activities of oyster farmers.

Église St-Pierre-de-Sales – This 15C church is built in a style known here as English, with a tall square tower, buttressed at the corners, crowned by a spire decorated with crockets. The spire, rising to a height of 85m – 279ft, is a landmark visible from miles away and used as a navigation point by sailors.
The interior is noteworthy for its wide nave flanked by chapels beneath balustraded galleries. Eight-branched rib vaulting arches above the bays.
The **tower platform** ⏲ (55m – 180ft high; 291 steps) offers an impressive **panorama**★ over the oyster farms, the islands, the Avert peninsula and a stretch of the marshes.

Château de la Gataudière ⏲ – *1.5km – 1 mile north.* The château was built *c*1749, in the Louis XIV style, by **François Fresneau** (1703-70), an engineer officer who studied the production of rubber from the hevea tree in French Guiana and returned to France to lay the base for its industrial use. The château stands on the site of a medieval house in the heart of an old marsh village known as Les Gataudières. On the garden front, a terrace with a wrought-iron balustrade runs the length of the façade. A classical pediment embellished with a *Triumph of Flora* (the goddess of flowers) surmounts a central block decorated with trophies symbolizing the resources of the region (oyster farming, salt-marsh agriculture, wine-making etc).
Inside, the main reception floor is notable for the Grand Salon with its stone walls set with fluted Corinthian pilasters representing the arts, the sciences and the four seasons. Fine Louis XV furniture can be seen in the dining hall and the Blue Salon. A building in the courtyard houses an exhibition of horse-drawn vehicles.
A street in Marennes is named after Fresneau, and an inscription on the façade of the Sous-Préfecture pays tribute to his work.

EXCURSION

★ **Brouage** – *6.5km – 4 miles northeast. See Brouage.*

★★ Grotte de MÉDOUS

Michelin map 85 northeast of fold 18 or 234 fold 44 – Local map p 90.

In 1948 three speleologists from Bagnères-de-Bigorre, exploring a gallery which did not penetrate very far into the rock, discovered a blow-hole which suggested the existence of a substantial cavern close by. The site, not far from Bagnères, was near a resurgent spring watering the pools in the grounds of Médous Château. The cavers gouged a larger hole in the rock wall, squeezed through an opening not much bigger than a cat flap... and found themselves in a series of galleries full of marvellous rock formations.

Tour ⏲ – The 1km – $\frac{2}{3}$ mile route twists through an enchanted land of stalactites, stalagmites and broad petrified flows of calcite (carbonate of lime) which have hardened over the ages into fantastic forms evoking waterfalls, hanging draperies, a magnificent church organ etc; the chambers have subsequently been given suitably fanciful names. After the Gallery of Marvels, the Hindu Temple, the Cervin Halls and the Great Organ Chamber, the visit includes a boat trip along a short subterranean stretch of the River Adour : the caverns have been hollowed out over the millennia by waters siphoned off from the main river through a tunnel near Campan, only emerging into the open air again in the grounds of Médous Château.

MELLE

Pop 4 003

Michelin map 72 northeast of fold 2 or 233 folds 17, 18.

Melle occupies a corner site where the narrow, heavily wooded Béronne gorge meets a smaller valley. The best view of this site is from D 950, driving northeast from St-Jean-d'Angély.
The town owes its existence to silver-bearing veins of lead mined in the hills of St-Hilaire, on the west bank of the Béronne, and used in medieval times for the production of coins in a local mint. Melle was won over at the time of the Reformation and enjoyed a certain prosperity after the foundation of its college in 1623.
Melle was, until motorised transport became widely available, a celebrated centre for the rearing of Poitou *Baudets (qv)*, the local type of donkey.
Melle is unusual in having three Romanesque churches. Two of them, originally attached to Benedictine monasteries, accommodated pilgrims on the road to Compostela *(qv)*.

SIGHTS

Librairie Montazeau

Le cavalier de Melle.

★ **Église St-Hilaire** – St Hilary's Church, built in the Poitou Romanesque style at its purest, was part of the Abbey of St-Jean-d'Angély. The sober east end and the west front with its coned pinnacles are particularly attractive.

Above the north doorway stands a carving of a **horseman** ("le cavalier de Melle") which is famous in the history of religious art for the controversy the figure has provoked : the crowned rider whose mount tramples underfoot a small seated figure wearing a long robe has been identified at various times as Charlemagne, as Jesus Christ suppressing the Ancient Law, or even as the Emperor Constantine triumphing over paganism.

The east end *(see illustration p 40)* includes three apsidal chapels with buttress-columns and carved modillions radiating from an ambulatory joined to the transept. Two more chapels lead off the transept itself; above the crossing rises a tower which acts as a belfry.

Interior – The scale of the nave, aisles and ambulatory indicates that the church was designed as a place of pilgrimage. The barrel-vaulting is supported by pillars, quadrilobed in section, with interesting carved capitals : the third on the right, entering from the west front, depicts a wild boar hunt. A doorway leading into the south aisle is – most unusually – decorated on its inner side : on the archivolt, Jesus and the Saints accompanying Him overcome fantasy animals representing the forces of evil. At the far end of this aisle a sound system diffuses a continuous programme of sacred or ritual music from all over the world.

Église St-Pierre – This church dedicated to St Peter once belonged to a priory attached to St-Maixent Abbey. It was built, like St Hilary's, in the Poitou Romanesque style, and stands on a hill overlooking the Béronne. The east end and the side entrance are remarkable for their carved ornamentation : a cornice above the south doorway is supported by historiated modillions (symbols of the Evangelists) between which are carved signs of the Zodiac, and Christ in Glory occupies a niche above this cornice. The east end is noteworthy for the decoration of the bays, the charming modillions of the axial chapel, and – crowning one of the buttress-columns – a capital featuring two peacocks, the symbols of immortality.

Interior – Inside, the aisles are topped with barrel-vaulting, again like St Hilary's. The capital of the third pillar on the north side represents Christ entombed.

Église St-Savinien – This former church, dating from the 12C and deconsecrated in 1801, was for many years used as a prison. Today it serves as an exhibition hall and is also the home of Melle's annual **Music Festival** *(see Calendar of Events, qv)*. The building has an entrance with a lintel roofed like a lych-gate, a rare feature in Poitou. On the lintel itself Christ, haloed, stands between two lions.

Mines d'Argent des Rois Francs (Kings' Silver Mine) ⊙ – The porous limestone on which Melle stands harbours a quantity of geodes – pockets or cavities containing crystallized minerals, in this case lead ore with a small proportion (3%) of silver. The mine from which the ore was extracted, which had been worked since the 5C, became, under Charlemagne, the supplier of silver to a local mint designed to strike the royal coinage. In the 10C the mint was moved elsewhere and the disused mine was forgotten until the 19C.

Since then the build-up of rubble has been cleared from the ancient galleries to render them accessible to visitors. During the underground tour, primitive ventilation chimneys can be seen, along with a number of concretions, a small lake and traces of the oxidization caused by the firing which broke up the rock. Sound effects within the galleries evoke an atmosphere of mining.

Outside, the **Carolingian Garden** contains species of plants which were eaten or used in other ways at the time the mine was in use.

Chemin de la Découverte – Arboretum – This pedestrian only trail, which follows stretches of disused railway line, encircles nearly the whole of the old town within its 5km – 3 mile circuit. Vegetation native to the region alternates with zones in which 650 different species of foreign and exotic trees and shrubs have been planted, all of them labelled for identification purposes. Of particular interest is the **Bosquet d'Écorces** (Bark Grove) north of St Hilary's Church.

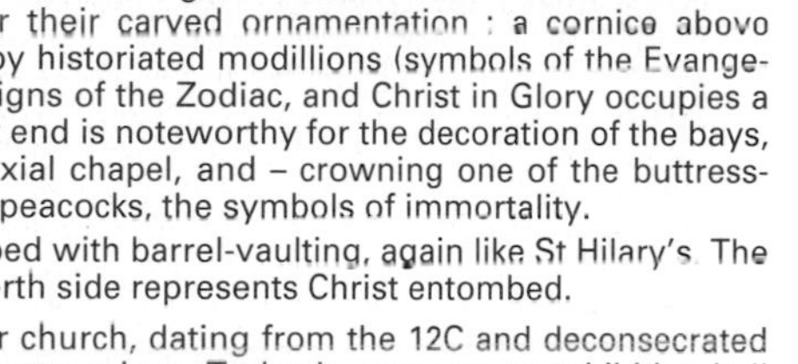

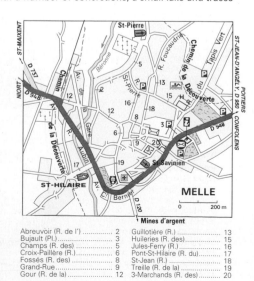

Abreuvoir (R. de l')	2	Guillotière (R.)	13
Bujault (Pl.)	3	Huileries (R. des)	15
Champs (R. des)	5	Jules-Ferry (R.)	16
Croix-Paillère (R.)	6	Pont-St-Hilaire (R. du)	17
Fossés (R. des)	8	St-Jean (R.)	18
Grand-Rue	9	Treille (R. de la)	19
Gour (R. de la)	12	3-Marchands (R. des)	20

EXCURSIONS

Chef-Boutonne – *16km – 10 miles southeast via D 948 and D 737.* The name of this town, meaning "Head of the Boutonne", derives from the fact that the river of that name has its source nearby. The church, in the Javarzay district, dates from the 12C and 16C; it was once part of a Benedictine priory. Nearby are the ruins of the former **château** (built *c*1515) of the Rochechouart family. Of the original fortified enclosure, once marked out with twelve towers, there remains one round tower with machicolations and an elegant fortified entrance flanked by turrets and pierced by Renaissance windows. The Gothic chapel is entered through a Renaissance doorway.

Pers – *20km – 12½ miles east.* In a cemetery adjacent to the Romanesque church in this tiny village stands a tall structure dating from the 13C : the **Lanterne des Morts** (Lantern of the Dead). The monument, elegant in its simplicity and its sobriety, comprises a central shaft of stone flanked by four small columns with capitals, the whole supporting a lantern surmounted by a cross. Beneath the pyramid roof, four arched openings reveal the space in which an oil lamp would burn during burial ceremonies. East of this monument is a group of five sarcophagi, probably 11C and 12C, some of them adorned with carved rosettes.

★ Forêt de MERVENT-VOUVANT

Michelin map 67 fold 16, 71 fold 1 or 233 folds 4, 5.

This National Forest lies at the junction of the Vendée plain and the mixed woodland, farmland and pasture known as **le bocage.** It covers 5 000ha – 20 sq miles of a granitic plateau carpeted with clays and sand, and gashed by deep, steep-sided valleys. Since 1956 three of these – the valleys of the Vendée, its tributary the Mère, and the Verreries stream – have been flooded to form a 130ha – 320 acre reservoir enclosed within four separate dams.

Excavations have revealed the remains of glass furnaces dating from Gallo-Roman times, proving the existence in the region of a civilization that was well established even then.

In the 12C the forest belonged to the house of Lusignan *(qv)* which owned both the Château de Mervent and the Château de Vouvant. The forest was annexed to the royal domain in 1674 and then assigned to the Comte d'Artois in 1778 on a grace-and-favour basis (it would return to the Crown on the death of the family's last surviving male heir). As a result of the Revolution, however, it became the property of the State.

The deep and dark, close-packed thickets of conifers and oak once harboured packs of wolves; today wild boar and deer still roam the forest.

Numerous well-marked footpaths and bridlepaths cross the area.

FROM FONTENAY-LE-COMTE TO VOUVANT

35km – 22 miles : allow 5 hours – Local map below.

Fontenay-le-Comte – *See Fontenay-le-Comte.*

5.5km – 3½ miles north of Fontenay turn right.

★ **Barrage de Mervent** – *Access via a one-way traffic system.* The approach to Mervent Dam is marked by a stone sculpture representing a Siren, the work of the **Martel Brothers** (20C). The 130m – 426ft long dam plugs the valley of the Vendée, retaining a volume of 8 500 000m³ – 11 330 000 cu yds and supplying water to the southern half of the Vendée *département* and several neighbouring towns.

From the dam there is an attractive and picturesque view of the reservoir, curving among the wooded slopes upstream.

Below the barrage is a water purification plant and power station.

Parc Zoologique du Gros Roc ⓥ – This zoo, set on the hills overlooking the Vendée and planted with many different species of tree, is home to a huge variety of animals from all five continents. The park extends over 5ha – 12 acres.

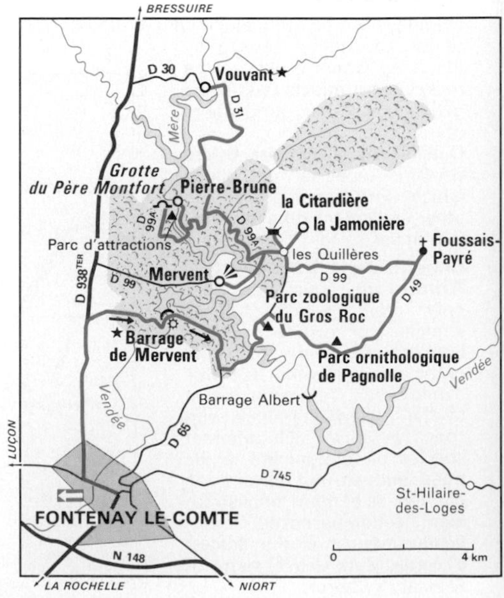

Parc Ornithologique-Animalier de Pagnolle ⊙ – More than 1 000 animals can be seen in this wide, flower-filled area – among them 260 bird varieties, ranging from the tiniest species to the ostrich.

Foussais-Payré – A number of fine Renaissance houses and a 17C covered market distinguish this small town renowned for its annual folklore festivals. The entrance and west front of the **church** feature a remarkable collection of religious scenes carved in the 11C by Giraud Audebert, a monk from the Abbey of St-Jean-d'Angély.

La Jamonière – The **Musée des Amis de la Forêt** ⊙ contains leaflets, books, exhibitions, videos etc on the forest, its flora and fauna, and the traditional local activities.

Château de la Citardière – The château, partly hidden behind a belt of ancient trees, has a fine 17C façade reflected in a wide moat. A restaurant now occupies the interior.

Mervent – The small town is perched on a rocky spur, deep in the heart of the forest. In the Middle Ages the castle *(on the site of the present town hall)* was the seat of the Lusignan family; nothing remains of it today. From the town hall gardens *(near the church square)* there is a fine **view★** down over the reservoir with its beach (swimming, *pédalos* etc) on the eastern shore behind Mervent dam.

Grotte du Père Montfort – Louis-Marie Grignion de Montfort, a humble and devout Catholic preacher from Brittany who was later canonised, took refuge in the forest in *c*1717 because he wished to meditate during a mission to convert Protestants; the cavern in which he found shelter subsequently became a place of pilgrimage. The footpath leading to it starts behind a wayside shrine on route D99^{A}, where cars may be parked.
The grotto opens onto the slope of a valley above the River Mère. From there the path descends to La Maison du Curé, the house to which a later cleric retired. The choice then is either to return directly to the shrine or to walk on *(15min)* to Pierre-Brune, turning right onto a track following the west bank of the Mère.

Pierre-Brune – This picturesque site faces a steep, rocky slope near a small dam; a hotel, restaurants and a **leisure park** (parc d'attractions) ⊙ with a miniature train known as the *Tortillard* have been added to the site.

★ **Vouvant** – *See Vouvant.*

★★★ Pic du MIDI DE BIGORRE

Michelin map 85 fold 14 or 234 fold 44 – Local map p 90.

This mountain peak, a familiar landmark to the Gascons, is distinguished by a silhouette which stands clearly apart from the main Pyrenean chain. Ease of access, a series of outstanding views and a scientific installation of world renown had long established its importance before modern tourism set the seal on its fame.

Access – *From Col du Tourmalet (qv) : 5.5km – $3\frac{1}{2}$ miles, representing 40min Rtn by car or 5 hours Rtn on foot. The toll road is traffic-controlled; parking and overtaking is forbidden. The route, following ledges along the west flank of Pic du Tourmalet and Pic Costallat, can be alarming : the gradient is 7.30% – 1 in 14 as far as Sencours, 8% – 1 in 12 on the hairpins, and 12% – 1 in 8 on the final section.*

The **toll road from Col du Tourmalet to Les Laquets** ⊙ (open from July to 10 October) is one of the highest in Europe; Les Laquets is at an altitude of 2 650m – 8 694ft. As the route climbs, views appear of Pic d'Arbizon, the Néouvielle and Vignemale massifs, and the Gavarnie summits.
From Les Laquets *(inn)* the top of the peak can be reached either by **cable-car** ⊙ or on foot *(1 hour Rtn)* via a pathway looping across the scree.

Summit – Pic du Midi has been cut into at a height of 2 865m – 9 400ft to allow the installation of a television transmitter which serves the whole of southwest France. Of all the views in the Pyrenees, the **panorama★★★** opening out from this point is the most impressive. As the 19C climber and explorer **Henry Russell** (1834-1909) said, there are mornings here "which must make the saints long to be on Earth!". Southwards, the Néouvielle massif stands out like an extraordinary real-life illustration of glacial relief.

There is a viewing table at the entrance to the Observatory.

The Pic du Midi **Observatory and Institute of World Physics** ⊙ lies on a terrace quarried from the bed-rock just below the summit; it is one of the most important high-altitude scientific research centres in the world. The centre was founded in the 19C at the instigation of the French General Nansouty and the engineer Vaussenat, and was transferred to the state in 1882; it was attached to the University of Toulouse in 1903.
Both the observatory and the 85m – 280ft television transmitter serve to identify Pic du Midi de Bigorre from a great distance.

MIRANDE

Pop 4 150

Michelin map 82 north of fold 14 or 234 fold 32 – Local map p 44 – Facilities.

Mirande is one of the most lively and characteristic of France's southwestern *bastides (qv)* – those purpose-built defended small towns. Since its foundation in 1281 by Eustache de Beaumarchais and Bernard VII, Comte d'Alsace, the village has retained the chessboard symmetry of its ground-plan *(illustration p 45)*, with separate 50m – 164ft square blocks of dwellings and the centre of the grid marked by a *place à couverts* (a market place surrounded by arcades where business and trade could be carried out, shielded from sun or rain). The Asbarac family, who were responsible for the medieval Rohan watchtower nearby, gave their name to the central square here. Several fine half-timbered houses have been preserved in Rue de l'Évêché.

SIGHTS

★ **Musée des Beaux-Arts** ⏲ – Most of the carefully-displayed works in this small Fine Arts Museum were donations or legacies from local enthusiasts.

A portrait of Joseph Delort, founder of the museum, hangs in the entrance hall alongside the two handsome 19C Sèvres vases and the keys of the town presented to Napoleon Bonaparte when he visited Mirande in July 1808. The show-cases contain antique ceramics and lustrous 17C-19C glazed earthenwares and porcelain from such renowned centres as Moustiers, Samadet, Dax and Nevers.

Paintings from the 15C to the 19C are exhibited in the Great Hall. Among a collection of small Flemish works painted on copper, note the exceptional 17C *Adoration of the Magi.* The Italian paintings from the same period include a somewhat truculent *Italian Masquerade* by Michelangelo Cerquazzi, while French painting from the 16C is distinguished by Claude Vignon's magisterial *Prophet Zacharia* in which the treatment of the subject, ardent and fiery against a contrast of light and shade, shows the influence of Caravaggio. Three 19C French seascapes, one of them painted on a flat stone, were inspired by Dutch masters of the 17C.

In the middle of the hall, beneath a pyramid roof, one work stands out from a group of interesting portraits : an extremely fine 18C *Study of a Head* from the school of Jacques-Louis David. There is also a display of beautiful gilded porcelain. Beyond, on a single panel, three different schools can be compared : 16C Italian, 17C Dutch and 17C Flemish.

In a smaller room, a slide show presents paintings from the reserve collection, most of them with a local connection.

Church – The picturesque turreted belfry of this early 15C sanctuary served more than once as a shelter for the *bastide's* defenders. The tower is pierced by open-work Gothic bays, the fenestration becoming richer level by level. An outer porch attached to the belfry spans the street. Ribbed vaulting roofs the porch and the ensemble is shored up by two huge arches.

The Gothic nave in the interior was heightened in the 19C.

EXCURSION

★ **Circuit des Bastides et des Castelnaux (Fortified villages and small castles)** – *100km – 62 miles : allow 1 day. Leave Mirande via N 21 northeast towards Auch. After 3km – 1¾ miles turn left into D 939.*

The itinerary suggested below describes a triangle formed by D 943 to the north, D 3 and the Bouès Valley to the west and N 21 to the east. It includes a selection of *bastides* and *castelnaux,* the well-planned villages and towns built by *seigneurs* around their châteaux or strongholds, which are typical of this region.

The route crosses **L'Isle-de-Noé,** a village at the convergence of the Grand Baïse and Petite Baïse rivers, where an 18C château can be seen.

Barran – The main curiosity in this *bastide,* built on the site of an earlier ecclesiastic settlement, is the extremely unusual spiral-shaped spire above the **church.** The village still has a fortified gateway on the east side, and the characteristic covered market in the central square.

Return to L'Isle-de-Noé and continue west.

Montesquiou – This *castelnau* rises on a spur high above the Osse Valley. The village gave its name to the younger branch of the de Fézensac family, from which sprang the seigneurs of d'Artagnan and de Monluc. A gateway at the end of the main street is all that remains of the 13C outer wall; near it stands a picturesque row of half-timbered houses.

Continue west.

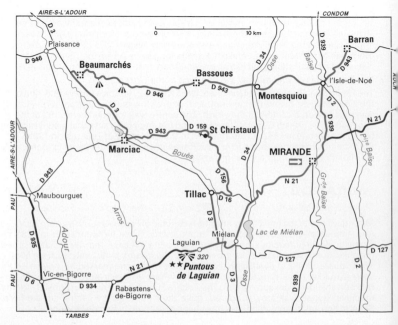

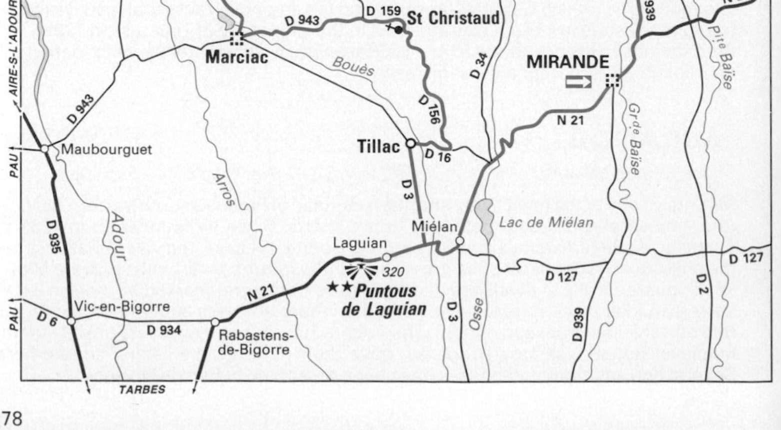

Bassoues – The 14C **keep** ⊙, which can be seen from afar, is a magnificent example of military architecture. Its highly-fortified southeasterly front (restored) contrasts with the well-appointed interior : latrines on each floor, a spiral staircase leading up to vaulted rooms on the first and second floors, a decorated chimney, a sink under an arch, and niches serving for storage space (second floor). Exhibitions in the rooms trace the birth and evolution of Gascon villages. The top-floor platform, where round watchtowers rise between the terrace and the top of the buttresses, offers a good **view★** to the northeast.
The village **church** was remodelled in the 16C and the 19C; it has a single nave extended by a quadripartite-vaulted chancel and contains a fine 15C stone pulpit.

D 946 now descends, via a 12km – 7½ mile **crest route★**, to the "Rivière Basse" depression drained by the Arros. On the way, the view extends through the Adour gap as far as the Pyrenees.

Beaumarchés – This royal *bastide* was founded in 1288 as the result of a *contrat de paréage (qv)* between the Seneschal (Steward) of Beaumarchais and the Comte de Pardiac. The deal – whereby the lesser noble agreed to hand over a part of his revenue, in return for protection, to the greater noble – is illustrated in the **church** on one of the capitals adorned with an escutcheon bearing the arms of France. This Gothic church with its single nave is striking for its massive appearance and its 15C porch, which was planned to become a belfry but was never completed. An interesting frieze of carved male and female heads runs around the upper gallery.

Turn left into D 3, which runs alongside the artificial lake at Marciac.

Marciac – The foundation of this *bastide* dates from the late 13C; until the 19C a large covered market stood in the middle of the arcaded central square. A tall stone steeple crowns the belltower of the 14C Notre-Dame Church. In the summer the town hosts a series of jazz concerts *(see Calendar of Events, qv).*

Head east towards Auch, following the picturesque D 943 which runs above the valley of the River Bouès. At the top of the climb turn into D 159, a crest road with fine views of the Pyrenees.

Northwards (left), there are glimpses of the impressive keep rising above Bassoues.

Turn right into D 156 to St-Christaud.

Here the road crosses the Via Tolosane, which was once the route followed by pilgrims from Provence on their way to Santiago de Compostela.

St-Christaud – The village **church,** built of brick in the Transitional style, stands on a dominant site facing the distant Pyrenees. An unusual feature of the building is the square windows, between buttresses, which have been "turned" through 45° to form a diamond shape.

9km – 5 miles further on, turn right into D 16.

Tillac – This small *castelnau* laid out on the plain has picturesque half-timbered houses with angle-posts along its main street which links a fortified tower with the 14C **church.**

Take D 3 south, following the Bouès Valley, then turn right into N 21 towards Tarbes. After the hill beyond Laguian, fork left to the viewing table (alt 320m – 1 050ft).

★★ **Puntous de Laguian** – This offers one of the most famous views in the Pyrenees : on a clear day the **panorama** extends over a mountain barrier 150km – 93 miles wide. Pic du Midi de Bigorre can be identified by the pylon of its tall television transmitter.

Return to N 21 and turn right, heading east : the road passes through the bastide of Miélan before following the valley of the Osse. A few miles after the Miélan lake-reservoir, which regulates the flow of the shallow river, the road reaches Mirande.

Château de MONTAIGNE

Michelin map 75 fold 13 or 234 fold 4 – 9km – 5 miles northeast of Castillon-la-Bataille.

It was to Montaigne Château that **Michel de Montaigne** (1533-92), the son of a rich merchant, Counsellor to the Parliament of Bordeaux and Mayor of the city and, above all, one of the giants of French philosophy, retired to compose his world-famous *Essays* – erudite works, sceptical yet tolerant, evoking a philosophy of life reflecting the Gascon outlook which combines both wisdom and individuality.
Montaigne, who was born and died in the château, wrote in the tower library where he worked : "The year of Christ 1571, at the age of 38 years... Michel de Montaigne, long wearied by the exigencies of the Court and public life, has withdrawn, while he feels himself still whole, into the bosom of the Muses, there to pass his remaining days in peace and total security."

Michel de Montaigne.

It was said of Montaigne that he "entered" literature as others enter the Church; that his retreat from the world was less out of disgust with public life than because of an insatiable intellectual curiosity, a belief that the human soul must be capable of grander exploits than were available in everyday life. The general conclusion of his works, embodied in his celebrated rhetorical question *Que sais-je?* (What do I know?) is the recognition of the fallibility of human reason and the limitations of human knowledge.
Despite his announced withdrawal from the world, Montaigne did in fact leave the château on a number of occasions – to carry out his municipal functions in Bordeaux, to take the air in Paris, even to visit Italy – but he spent the last ten years of his life on his own land, terminally depressed by the Wars of Religion, and soured by his shrewish wife.

Château – The main living quarters were rebuilt after a fire in 1885, though the original **Library Tower** ⏲ was saved. From his room immediately above the castle chapel the philosopher could hear the celebration of Mass below, thanks to a special opening in the wall. The famous library itself – on the beams of which 54 Latin and Greek precepts are inscribed – is on the top floor.
Walking around the château, visitors can still admire today the peaceful countryside that Montaigne so often contemplated : a landscape of wooded hills, of vineyards which produce an excellent white wine, of the medieval silhouette, on the horizon, of Gurson keep.

MONT-DE-MARSAN

Pop 28 328

Michelin map 82 fold 1 or 234 fold 23 – Local map p 30.

The town lies at the confluence of the Douze and Midou rivers, which join to form the River Midouze, and is the capital of the Marsan region in the southeast of the Landes *(qv)*. It enjoys a climate that is hot in summer, rainy but mild in winter. Palm trees, magnolias and oleanders flourish in the open air, spiced from time to time with the tang of pines carried on the breeze from the forest nearby.
From medieval times to the *"Ancien Régime"* (19C), Mont-de-Marsan was a busy commercial centre but today it is above all an important administrative centre, with a curious collection of public buildings (préfecture, town hall, theatre, prisons) in the style known as *Empire-Restauration.* Although there is still a healthy trade in agriculture (maize, vines, fruits), the local market is dominated by poultry products and *foies gras.* Industrially the town supports a sawmill and an aerial research centre run by the military.
To the north of the town there is a huge racecourse, with local stabling for 300 horses. The twelve meetings a year here include flat racing, steeplechases and trotting events.
The bullfights and contests pitting men against combative cows (in neither of which is the animal killed) which are popular in this region are held in the town arena.

SIGHTS

★ **Musée Municipal** ⏲ – This museum in the heart of the old town is housed in two beautifully restored 14C buildings, linked by a gallery in which temporary exhibitions are held.
Prehistoric discoveries and collections of natural history can be seen in the **Musée Dubalen.** The monumental sculptures in the garden are by Charles Despiau (1874-1946), a native of Mont-de-Marsan who was among the artists promoting the revival of interest in sculpture at the beginning of the 20C.
The **Musée Despiau-Wlérik** is devoted to modern figurative sculpture. Over 700 works by 100 different artists are on display, most of them dating from the 1930s. The museum focuses in particular on works originally exhibited during the 1937 International Exhibition.
The sculptors include Orloff, Bourdelle, Bouchard, Zadkine, Manolo and Gargallo. The upper floors of this old keep with its Gothic windows are reserved for local artists. The stairway linking them is adorned with fine examples of glazed earthenwares from Samadet.
Works by Charles Despiau occupy one whole floor : they include a series of nudes *(Apollo, Eve, The Greek),* several female busts, among them *Paulette,* a marble which was admired by Rodin, and a strikingly naturalistic *Liseuse* (Woman reading). On another floor *The Child in Clogs* is an early work by Robert Wlérik (1882-1944), the Mont-de-Marsan sculptor responsible for the equestrian statue of Marshal Foch in Place du Trocadéro, Paris.
The terrace, reached via a spiral staircase, offers a good view of the town as a whole.

Viewpoint – From the bridge just downstream from where the two rivers meet there is a pleasant view, upstream, of the old houses beside the river banks; downstream, abandoned quays recall the days when Mont-de-Marsan was a river port.

Parc Jean-Rameau – Extending for some distance north of the town, beside the Douze, this shady riverside park with its flower gardens, its fine magnolias and plane trees is a favourite place for a stroll. At one time it was the garden of the Préfecture, and a footbridge *(private)* still links the two.

⏲ ►► Aire-sur-l'Adour – 35km – 21 miles southeast : Église St-Pierre-du-Mas (sarcophagus of Ste-Quitterie in the crypt); Labastide d'Armagnac – 29km – 18 miles northeast : Picturesque 13C *bastide;* Barbotan-les-Thermes – 43km – 26 miles via Labastide d'Armagnac : Hot springs resort nestling in a wooded valley.

MONTMAURIN

Pop 205

Michelin map 82 fold 15 or 235 fold 37 – 10km – 6 miles south of Boulogne-sur-Gesse.

Montmaurin sits in the region of the Gascony hills which is drained by the Upper Save river, offering fine views of the Pyrenees; for tourists, however, the major attraction is archeological : the remains of a Gallo-Roman villa lie just outside the village (1km – $\frac{3}{4}$ mile southeast).

Villa gallo-romaine ⊙ – The descendants of a certain Nepotius (from whose name the region of Nébouzan is derived) inherited near Montmaurin a territory extending over c7 000ha – 17 300 acres. The original *"villa rustica"* built on this land in the 1C AD concentrated the agricultural and rural dependencies around "the big house", in the same way that important farmers on the plains do today. In the 4C, however, this residence was replaced by a marble mansion, which looked inwards and was separated from the agricultural buildings dispersed around the property. For the diversion of the host and amusement of his guests, this *"villa urbana"* was adorned with gardens, colonnades, statues of nymphs... Thermal baths and a system of hot air circulating beneath the tiled floors assured the inhabitants of comfort however inclement the weather. The regular consumption of quantities of oysters was further proof of the epicurean quality of this "country life" existence.
The mansion as a whole comprised 200 rooms arranged around a row of three separate courtyards graced with peristyles and pergolas. The chambers facing northwest on the left of the central courtyard, which could be heated and were near the kitchens and the gardens, were doubtless dining halls. The complex was completed to the northeast by a series of summer apartments set on tiered terraces. The heated bath-house stood near the outbuildings.

Follow the Save Valley downstream for 1km – $\frac{1}{2}$ mile, then cross the river and continue east and then north along D 98.

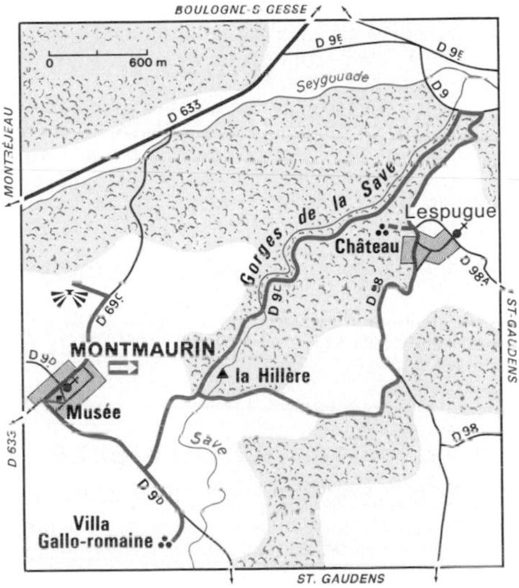

Château de Lespugue – The ruins crown a rocky spur above Save Gorge. They can be reached on foot by descending through an oak grove and then climbing through the woods on the opposite slope of the valley.

Return to the car and continue down to the river. Just before the bridge, turn left into D 9.

Gorges de la Save – The Save torrent, carving a deep channel here through the limestone folds of the Lesser Pyrenees, has hollowed out a number of grottoes or shelters beneath the rock. Several of these, excavated between 1912 and 1922 by the Comte and Comtesse de Saint-Périer, yielded finds dating back from the Magdalenian (late Paleolithic) and Azilian (transitional Paleolithic-Neolithic) periods. Notable among the finds is the statuette known as the *Venus de Lespugue* (the original is now in the Musée de l'Homme, Paris).

La Hillère – On the left, leaving the gorge, the route passes a **chapel** ⊙ in a cemetery in which a huge **polychrome mosaic** dating from the time of Constantine (4C AD) can be seen. Beside the road, archeological digs have exposed a 4C "water sanctuary" comprising temples, baths, a fountain, even a market, associated with a cult involving the worship of water.

Return to Montmaurin.

Museum ⊙ – *Ground floor of the town hall (Mairie).* This local museum is divided into two sections : one is devoted to the prehistoric finds in the region and the archeologists involved in their discovery; the other to the Gallo-Roman civilization in the area. In the latter a model of the villa can be seen, together with discoveries made on the site, including the contemporary bust of an adolescent.

Viewing Table – *800m – 880yds north of the village.* From the viewing table here there is a very wide – but distant – **panorama★** extending from the Pyrenees in the Ariège *département* to Pic du Midi de Bigorre and Pic de Ger. Through the gap carved by the Garonne it is possible to see the Maladetta massif and the glaciated sections of the Luchon heights on the frontier.

This guide, which is revised regularly, is based on tourist information provided at the time of going to press. Changes are however inevitable owing to improved facilities and fluctuations in the cost of living.

MOUILLERON-EN-PAREDS

Pop 1 184

Michelin map 67 folds 15, 16 or 232 fold 42.

Two of the most outstanding men in the recent history of France, **Georges Clemenceau** *(qv)* and **Jean-Marie de Lattre de Tassigny,** were born in this small village typical of the Vendée *bocage (qv)*. It was also the birthplace of the celebrated 19C astronomer **Charles-Louis Largeteau** (1791-1857).

Jean-Marie de Lattre de Tassigny (1889-1952) – The life of Jean de Lattre is interwoven with the history of the first half of the 20C. Scion of an aristocratic Vendée family, he was admitted to the élite St-Cyr military academy; he became a dragoon and then an infantry officer during the First World War. In 1920 he was posted to Morocco, where he distinguished himself in the Rif War. A brilliant tactician, he was promoted to Colonel, and then General in 1939. After the fall of France in the Second World War, he was arrested by the Germans in 1942 but escaped a year later and made his way to London to join the Free French, and from there went to Algiers. In 1944 he led the French 1st Army during the invasion of Provence, subsequently liberating Alsace, crossing the Rhine and advancing as far as the Danube. He was among the Allied leaders who signed the German Act of Capitulation on 8 May 1945. In 1950 he was appointed High Commissioner of Indo-China. De Lattre died in Paris in January 1952; four days later he was posthumously elevated to the rank of Marshal of France.

NATIONAL MUSEUMS ⊙ *2 hours.*

The town hall, which stands not far from the **church** with its 12C belfry (the 13-bell carillon rings daily at noon), houses the **Musée des Deux Victoires.** As much a memorial as a museum, this establishment reviews in parallel the destiny and the career of two extraordinary men, Clemenceau and de Lattre, caught in the maelstrom of two world wars. Among the documents, souvenirs, trophies and other items on display are a walking stick presented to "Tiger" Clemenceau by his *poilus* (soldiers), the handle of which is carved in the shape of a tiger's head, and the head of the eagle which once surmounted the pediment of the Reichstag, presented to de Lattre in 1945 by the Soviet Marshal Zukov.
In the village, commemorative plaques identify the birthplaces of Clemenceau and de Lattre, who was called *Le Roi Jean* (King John) by his troops. The birthplace of the latter is now the **Musée Jean-de-Lattre-de-Tassigny.** The de Lattre family's lifestyle, characteristic of that enjoyed by a generation of Vendée notables, has been carefully recreated. The house retains its original furniture and there are a number of display cases evoking both the home life and the career of the Marshal.
Opposite the house is the cemetery where the body of de Lattre lies beside his son, who was killed in Indo-China.
An old windmill situated on **Colline des Moulins** *(2km – 1¼ miles east)* now serves as a memorial chapel to de Lattre. From this quiet hillside there is a fine view of the *bocage (qv)*.

★★ Massif de NÉOUVIELLE

Michelin map 85 fold 18 or 234 folds 44, 48.

This granitic mountain mass attracts a great number of sightseers and ramblers because of its hundred or so lakes and the clear air around it. The massif offers many examples of glacial relief, culminating in the 3 192m – 10 465ft high Pic Long. Since 1850 tributaries of the Neste d'Aure (Aure Torrent) originating in the Néouvielle have helped regulate the flow of rivers from the hills of Gascony *(qv)*; these waters, held within a natural "water tower" are used today in the production of hydro-electric energy.

E. Follet

Massif de Néouvielle.

FROM ST-LARY-SOULAN TO COL D'AUBERT

70km – 43 miles : about 5 hours.

It is recommended to make this excursion in the early summer, as soon as the road (normally closed from October to early summer) and the path to Col d'Aubert are free of snow, as this is when the waterfalls and the lakes are at their highest level and, as a consequence, most impressive.

★ **St-Lary-Soulan** – This small winter sports resort developed since 1950 along the western slopes of the Aure Valley : there is skiing above the resort, at Pla d'Adet (alt 1 680m – 5 511ft) and the two are linked by a cable car. During the summer the town is a useful base for mountain tours in the Néouvielle region – especially since it lies on the trans-Pyrenean highway completed in 1976 by the opening of the Bielsa tunnel.
After St-Lary the valley narrows to a gorge. Up on the left is the watch-tower village of Tramezaïgues : in days gone by, its castle defended the whole valley against incursions by the Aragonese.

From Tramezaïgues take D 19, a road that is only partly surfaced. Beyond Fredançon, the last 4km – $2\frac{1}{2}$ miles of the road are so narrow that passing is impossible.

★ **Vallée du Rioumajou** – This is a densely wooded valley with numerous waterfalls. Not far from the Spanish frontier the former Rioumajou hospice (alt 1 560m – 5 117ft), now a mountain refuge, stands in a fine amphitheatre with steep grassy or tree-covered slopes.

Return to Tramezaïgues and turn left into D 929.

As the road follows the line of the Neste d'Aure Valley, the silhouette of Pic de Campbieil comes gradually into view. The mountain, one of the highest points in the massif at 3 173m – 10 407ft, is recognizable by its twin-peaked crest underlined by a *névé* (an area of snow not yet compressed into ice at the head of a glacier).

Beyond Fabian turn left into D 118.

The road, climbing alongside the waters of the Neste de la Géla, passes through the scattered hamlets of **Aragnouet.** Below, on the right, the belfry-wall of the 12C **Chapelle des Templiers** ⏲ appears : two ancient statues are housed in this restored Templars' sanctuary.

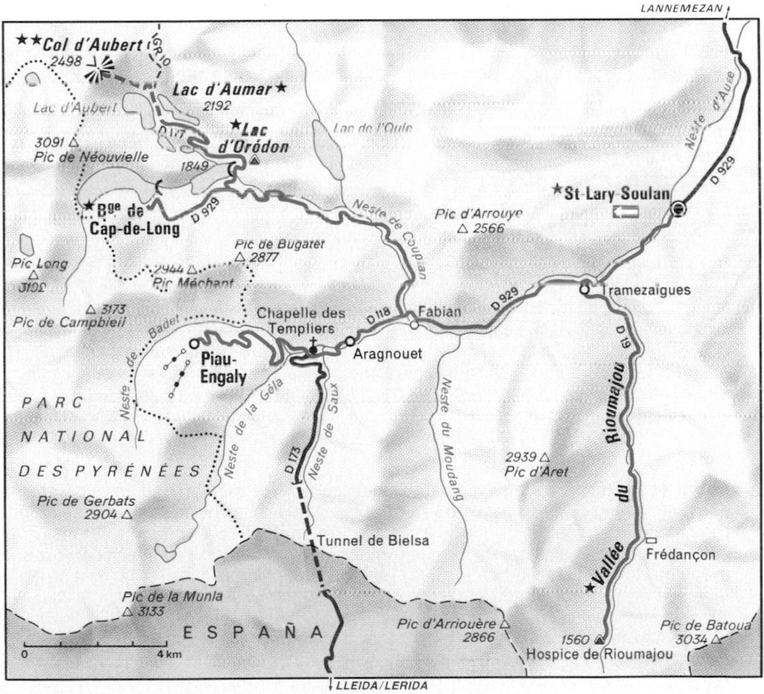

Leave the route leading to the Bielsa tunnel on the left and continue to Piau-Engaly.

Piau-Engaly – The **site**★ of this small ski station, facing the grim escarpments of Pic de Bugatet and Pic Méchant, is impressively austere.

Return to Fabian and turn left into D 929 heading north.

The old road carved out by the French electricity authority to allow access to the Cap-de-Long site *(see below)* is now the start of the scenic "Route des Lacs" (Route of the Mountain Lakes) which leads, for the moment, only as far as Lac d'Aubert.
Climbing up through the valley of the Neste de Couplan, D 929 scales an ancient glacial channel via a series of hairpin bends known as "The Edelweiss".
From the Orédon fork onwards, the narrow road can be quite striking.

★ **Barrage de Cap-de-Long** – The dam (maximum height 100m – 328ft) has created a volume of 67 million m^3 – 89 million cu yds of water and is a major element of the Pragnères hydro-elecric power station. The artificial lake with its inaccessible shores is frequently frozen over until the month of May, and resembles a fjord at the foot of the Néouvielle's rocky walls. It lies at an altitude of 2 161m – 7 090ft.
The Route des Lacs seems almost to plunge towards Orédon lake, crosses an old earthwork dam, and then climbs again towards Aumar and Aubert lakes.

★ **Lac d'Orédon** – Alt 1 849m – 6 066ft. This dammed lake occupies a basin, the scree-covered slopes of which are covered by a forest of firs. The site, which includes a chalet-hotel, is useful as a base for those exploring the mountain. Upstream, the view is blocked by the wall of Cap-de-Long dam.
The road continues to climb and emerges from the forest into an enormous bowl scattered with mountain pines, some of them a century old, overlooked by the sharp ridges of Pic de Néouvielle.

Park the car in the car park at the end of the road, near Lac d'Aubert, and continue the excursion on foot : walk back a short distance and take the public footpath signposted GR10.

★ **Lac d'Aumar** – Alt 2 192m – 7 192ft. This is a peaceful upland lake, surrounded by grassland and an occasional pine, draining into Lac d'Aubert.
At the far end of the lake the summit of Pic de Néouvielle (alt 3 091m – 10 142ft), bordered by a small glacier, comes into view. Leaving GR10 on the right and following a non-signposted track, which in fact follows the course of the future Route des Lacs extension, this route finally crosses a slope of scree *(the route here is marked by cairns or small piles of stones)* to lead to Col d'Aubert.
At the end of the climb rejoin the public footpath, which is clearly visible against the flank of the mountain.

★★ **Col d'Aubert** – Alt 2 498m – 8 196ft. This pass links the depression cradling the Aubert and Aumar lakes with the desolate Escoubous combe on the slopes towards Barèges. There is a remarkable **view★★** of the tiered lakes, and the smaller stretch of water below them known as Les Laquettes, at the foot of Pic de Néouvielle. Far off to the southeast the glaciated ensemble of the Maladetta massif can be seen.

★ NIORT

Pop 57 012

Michelin map 71 fold 2 or 233 folds 5, 6.

Niort rises beside the green waters of the Sèvre Niortaise, distilling a charming air of placid bourgeois prosperity, especially in season when the many flowers around the town come into bloom.
The town is the departure point for excursions in the Poitou marshlands (Marais Poitevin, *qv*).

HISTORICAL NOTES

City site – Niort developed in Roman times around a ford allowing access across the River Sèvre (*Novum Ritum* means new ford in Latin). The town today is built on the slopes of two facing hillsides : on one stands the castle keep and the Church of Our Lady; on the other the former town hall and the St-André district. The heart of the town, Rue Victor-Hugo, crosses the site of the old medieval market in the lowest part of the valley. At the eastern extremity Place de la Brèche, a huge square bordered with trees, is where the main roads leading to the town centre converge. Here ancient houses roofed with round tiles line the narrow, twisting streets climbing the slope, many of which have retained their original names : Rue de l'Huilerie (oil mill street), Rue du Tourniquet (turnpike lane), Rue du Rabot (wood plane street) etc. Rue du Pont and Rue St-Jean were once shopping streets crammed with market stalls.

Local activities – Today, while still a centre of glove-making and *chamoiserie* (tanning and oiling skins to make them supple), Niort is home to more modern industries including veneering and the manufacture of chipboard (one of the most important in France), electro-mechanical machinery, electronics, chemical products, machine tools, central heating equipment and clothing. All the industries are featured at the important annual trade fair, held in the spring.
Since a number of *Mutuelles* (national Friendly Societies) established their headquarters in the town, Niort has also become one of France's insurance capitals.
Local gastronomic specialities include eels and *petit-gris* (snails) from the nearby marshes, delicious cheesecake made from goat's milk, and products made from **angelica** *(Angelica Archangelica),* that aromatic plant whose stalks are crystallized (for confectionery), cooked (in jam making) or distilled (for angelica liqueur).

Madame de Maintenon – **Françoise d'Aubigné,** the grand-daughter of the poet Agrippa d'Aubigné *(qv),* was born in Niort in 1635, in a house in Rue du Pont which stood in the shadow of the castle where her father was locked up for non-payment of debts. Soon "the Aubigné girl" – Bignette to her friends – was sent away to stay with an aunt at Mursay château, on the Sèvre just north of Niort, where she helped to look after the turkeys. Her time at Mursay was the happiest of her unfortunate childhood : the young Françoise subsequently spent some time sharing the fairly miserable life of her mother and her brothers in the French West Indies and then at La Rochelle before being sent to live with various families around Saintes. Her proud and fiery personality, however, was such that she was eventually sent in disgrace to an Ursuline convent. She was still only 14 years old.

She escaped from the convent only to be confined to another, in Paris, before she met and married the poet Scarron, 25 years her senior. After his death the young widow became part of the Court, as governess to the children born to Louis XIV by his mistress Madame de Montespan *(qv)*, and soon caught the King's eye herself : he subsequently created her Marquise de Maintenon. Françoise and the king were secretly married in 1684, the year Madame de Montespan fell from favour.
When the "Sun King" died in 1715, Madame de Maintenon retired to the establishment she had founded in St-Cyr in 1685 : an institution for the education of impoverished daughters of the nobility. She died in 1719.

SIGHTS

★ **Donjon** (AY) – This keep was the most important element in a fortress begun by Henry II Plantagenet in the 12C and completed by his son Richard the Lionheart. It was surrounded by a defensive perimeter 700m – 770yds in circumference, a quadrilateral defined today by the Rues Brisson, Thiers, de l'Abreuvoir and de la Sèvre. The ensemble formed a small "town within the town", which included, apart from the castle itself, houses, gardens and a parade ground flanked by the collegiate church of St-Gaudens, destroyed during the Wars of Religion. Under the Bourbons the keep was used as a state prison.
Today its unusual silhouette still towers over the Sèvre. The plan and elevation are original : two tall, massive bastions, square in shape and linked by a 15C building which replaced the primitive curtain walls, are bordered by turrets which also act as buttresses.
Inside the keep is a **Museum** ⓥ. At the Entrance level, the **Hall of Glove-making and Chamoiserie★** focuses on Niort's traditional trades. The lower rooms, vaulted in the 18C, house the town's **Archeology Collection.** This includes stone tools, an early Bronze Age gold necklace, ceramics discovered during excavations at Bougon *(qv)*, a 9C BC chariot wheel, Merovingian sarcophagi, coins from the Carolingian era found at Melle, a late Gauloise stele, and a 14C knife-handle of carved ivory representing a shepherd playing the bagpipes.
The ethnology department on the upper floor has a reconstructed Poitou interior (*c*1830) complete with costumes, furniture, domestic utensils etc.
From the platform at the top of the keep there is a view of the town and the river.

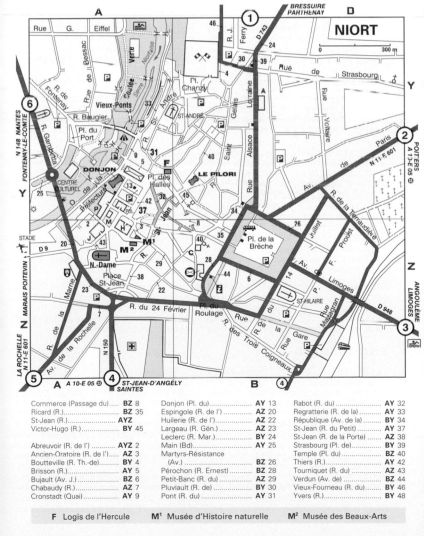

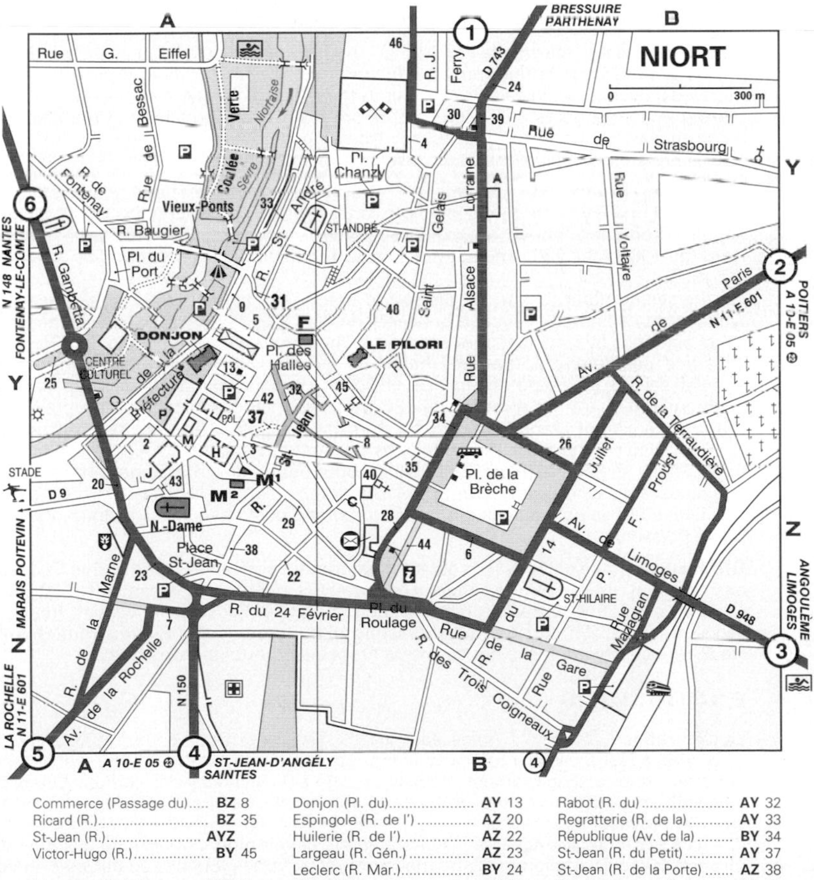

Street	Ref
Commerce (Passage du)	BZ 8
Ricard (R.)	BZ 35
St-Jean (R.)	AYZ
Victor-Hugo (R.)	BY 45
Abreuvoir (R. de l')	AYZ 2
Ancien-Oratoire (R. de l')	AZ 3
Boutteville (R. Th.-de)	BY 4
Brisson (R.)	AY 5
Bujault (Av. J.)	BZ 6
Chabaudy (R.)	AZ 7
Cronstadt (Quai)	AY 9
Donjon (Pl. du)	AY 13
Espingole (R. de l')	AZ 20
Huilerie (R. de l')	AZ 22
Largeau (R. Gén.)	AZ 23
Leclerc (R. Mar.)	BY 24
Main (Bd)	AY 25
Martyrs-Résistance (Av.)	BZ 26
Pérochon (R. Ernest)	BZ 28
Petit-Banc (R. du)	AZ 29
Pluviault (R. de)	BY 30
Pont (R. du)	AY 31
Rabot (R. du)	AY 32
Regratterie (R. de la)	AY 33
République (Av. de la)	BY 34
St-Jean (R. du Petit)	AY 37
St-Jean (R. de la Porte)	AZ 38
Strasbourg (Pl. de)	BY 39
Temple (Pl. du)	BZ 40
Thiers (R.)	AY 42
Tourniquet (R. du)	AZ 43
Verdun (Av. de)	BZ 44
Vieux-Fourneau (R. du)	BY 46
Yvers (R.)	BY 48

F Logis de l'Hercule **M**[1] Musée d'Histoire naturelle **M**[2] Musée des Beaux-Arts

Logis de l'Hercule (AY F) ⓥ – It was in this hostelry, which at one time traded under the sign of Hercules, that the first case of the Plague epidemic that was to decimate the population of Niort for seven months was reported on 6 May 1603.
On the ground floor, vaulted 16C rooms have been furnished in the style of the early Middle Ages, and contain items unearthed in digs (coins, ceramics) and a series of tableaux, with commentaries, which chronicle the town's past.
A miniature **museum** in one room is dedicated to angelica – with the reminder that the plant, brought to Niort by nuns in the 17C, was long believed by pharmacists to be the sole effective remedy against the Plague.

★ **Le Pilori** (BY) – This odd structure is the old town hall, built on the site of a medieval pillory. The building, on a ground plan that is practically triangular, was modified in the 16C by the architect Mathurin Bertomé, who bordered it with semi-circular towers, crowned it with machicolated parapets and pierced it with mullioned windows. The upper part of the belfry dates from the 17C and the pinnacle from the 19C. Le Pilori is now used for displaying temporary exhibitions.

Coulée Verte (AY) ⓥ – This promenade comprises the renovated Cronstadt, La Regratterie and La Préfecture quays and is a pleasant place for a quiet riverside stroll. From the **old bridges** (Vieux Ponts) linking the two halves of the town there is a splendid view of the castle keep.

Église Notre-Dame (AZ) – The elegance of this church's 15C belfry is due in part to a lightening of the square tower by the addition of serrated pinnacles to the buttresses; four of the niches hollowed from these still contain statues. The difference in size between the tower and the spire is further emphasized by the placing of dormers and more pinnacles at the base of the latter. Finally the steeple itself, rising to a height of 76m – 250ft, is reinforced by superimposed relief-arches forming a chevron design.
The north façade, on Rue Bion, has a fine doorway in Flamboyant Gothic style.
Inside the church – the layout was reversed in the 18C – the first chapel off the north aisle contains some curious tombs dating from 1684 : Charles de Baudéan-Parabère, Governor of Niort, his wife and his son, also Governor in his day, are all represented climbing out of their graves on Resurrection Day. In the third chapel hangs *St Bernard Trampling the Decree of Pope Anaclet,* an 18C painting by Lattainville. The early 16C font was used for the baptism of Françoise d'Aubigné. A *Way of The Cross* and the carved wood pulpit in the Gothic style date from 1877.

Musée d'Histoire Naturelle (AZ M[1]) ⓥ – An impressive collection of stuffed birds on the ground floor of this museum includes local species, diurnal birds of prey (buzzards, falcons) and sea-birds including those which frequent estuaries (puffins, herring gulls, penguins etc). Elements of pre-history are explained in the paleontology department and through fossils from the Deux-Sèvres region. On the first floor there are displays of minerals, insects, reptiles, osteology (animal skeletons).

Musée des Beaux-Arts (AZ M[2]) ⓥ – The first floor of the Fine Arts Museum is concerned mainly with the decorative arts. Gothic ivory carvings, gold plate, enamels from the Limousin are exhibited, together with French and German pewter from the 16C to the 18C, oriental pottery, and medallions from the Middle Ages to the 18C.
On the second floor, beyond a display of woodwork painted with Biblical scenes which once decorated a château, a gallery divided into several separate salons presents paintings by excellent minor masters. The first two are devoted to the 17C and 18C, and particularly noteworthy here are a remarkable *St Augustine* from the Spanish school, a number of small Dutch scenes by Mieris, and a large Coypel composition. The charming selection of 18C portraits includes Nattier's *Young Girl as Diana,* a canvas of Marie Leszczynska, and the *Marquis d'Artaguiette Drinking* by Grimou. Also of note are a 17C still-life by the Antwerp painter Coosemans; a tantalizing *Thalia,* the comic muse, by Louis de Boullogne (early 18C); anecdotal scenes and landscapes by Corot, Chintreuil *(Moonlight)...*
The final (19C) salon includes a number of female busts by a local sculptor, Pierre-Marie Poisson.

Old Houses – The oldest and most interesting houses in Niort stand in Rue St-Jean and adjacent streets. Among them are the 15C Governor's residence (No 30 Rue St-Jean) and, at No 3 Rue du Petit-St-Jean, the Hôtel Estissac, an elegant Renaissance mansion. Old houses with projecting upper storeys line Rue du Pont and at No 5, by a courtyard, is the house where Françoise d'Aubigné was born.

EXCURSIONS

Les Ruralies – *11km – 7 miles east via* ③. This enormous complex, conceived mainly as a rest area for motorway users, groups together not only the usual restaurants, shops selling regional specialities, and petrol and service stations but also an hotel, an exhibition centre, the local agricultural Chamber of Commerce and a couple of museums.
The **Musée de la Machine Agricole** ⓥ illustrates the development of farming techniques through the tools, implements and machinery involved : ploughs and harrows, olive oil presses, stills, harvesters, tractors etc. In the section devoted to apiculture it is possible to view through a transparent panel a hive in full production. Video films are shown.
Beside the museum, in the **Maison des Ruralies** ⓥ, a permanent exhibition entitled **L'Aventure Humaine en Poitou-Charente** evokes, with the use of photos, documents, period material, models and reconstructions, life in the region from prehistoric times to the present day. Temporary exhibitions on a variety of different themes are also held.

Forêt de Chizé – *23km – 14 miles south via ④.*

Beauvoir-sur-Niort – The **Rimbault windmill** ⓥ, overlooking the Niort plain from the edge of Chizé Forest, is a tower mill which was built in 1682 and abandoned in 1928; it has now been largely restored. The mobile roof portion, rotating on a greased wooden rail, is back in place; the *guivre* (an exterior beam allowing the sails to be turned into the wind) is in working order; part of the internal mechanism has been replaced; the sails are once more equipped with superimposed wooden slats arranged according to the Berton system.

Villiers-en-Bois – In the middle of the **Forêt de Chizé** (Chizé Forest), all that remains of the vast Argenson Forest which covered almost the whole of this region in the Middle Ages, is the **European Zoorama** ⓥ, where more than 600 animals are collected together in an ideal setting of 25ha – 62 acres largely dominated by oak, hornbeam and beechwoods. This is no ordinary zoo but a specialized project aimed at facilitating the observation and study of fauna peculiar to Europe.
Its inhabitants include mammals such as wolves, lynx, bears, foxes, otters and beavers; birds such as diurnal and nocturnal predators, webfooted species and waders; reptiles and amphibians, which live in conditions as near as possible to their habitats of origin. The larger mammals – wild boar, deer, Poitou donkeys *(qv)*, wild mountain sheep, the rare European bison – wander in huge wooded enclosures.
Of particular interest is the presence of aurochs (a variety of wild ox extinct since the 17C which once roamed much of Europe), recently biologically "recreated" by selective breeding of certain primitive types of domestic cattle.

★ **Château du Coudray-Salbart** ⓥ – *10km – 6 miles north by D 743. The path up to the ruins starts near the bridge over the river.*
The castle, which rises on an escarpment overlooking the Sèvre Niortaise, is an unusual and fascinating example of 13C military architecture. Its construction (1202-25) is linked to the final phase of the battle between the Capetians (Philippe Auguste, Louis VIII) and the Plantagenets (King John, Henry III) for possession of the Guyenne region.

Île de NOIRMOUTIER

Michelin map 67 fold 1 or 232 folds 25, 26, 37, 38 - Facilities.

The long thin isle of Noirmoutier frames the western margin of a gulf south of the Loire estuary, separated from the mainland only by a narrow channel which recedes at low tide. Before reaching the island the attractive marshland countryside of the Breton-Vendée must be crossed.

The low-lying island, blessed with a mild climate, luminous skies and numerous beauty spots, is a delightful and popular holiday retreat. Auguste Renoir, having stayed here with paintbrush and palette, wrote to a friend : "It is an admirable place, lovely as the South, with a sea beautiful in a different way to the Mediterranean."

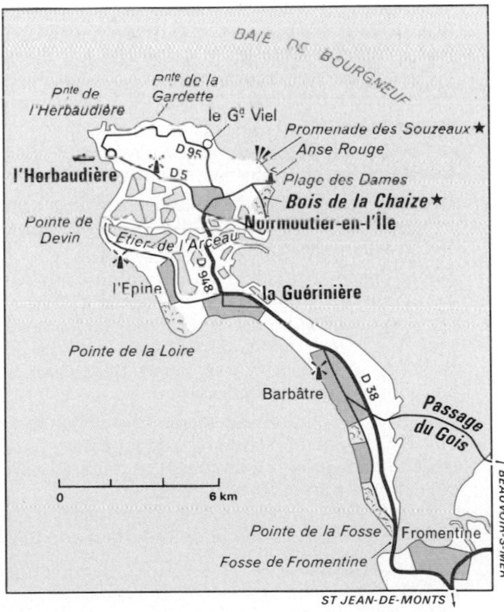

Access ⓥ – The island can be reached either via the picturesque **Passage du Gois** *(see below)* or from Fromentine via a **toll bridge.**

GEOGRAPHICAL AND HISTORICAL NOTES

Since Roman times successive subsidence has been reducing the area of Noirmoutier so that although the island is still 20km – 12 ½ miles long, it is now scarcely 1km – ½ mile wide at La Guérinière – where, in 1882, heavy seas almost cut the place in two.
Noirmoutier comprises three sectors. To the south the Barbâtre dunes stretch towards the Vendée coast, from which they are separated by the **Fosse de Fromentine,** a gap only 800m – 880yds across but scoured by violent currents. The centre of the isle is similar to the Dutch landscape, with **polders** (stretches of land reclaimed from the sea) and salt-marshes below sea-level, protected by dykes. The area is criss-crossed by canals, the most important of which, the Étier de l'Arceau, crosses the island from one side to the other.
To the north, a series of creeks indent a rocky coast carpeted with oak, pine and mimosa – from which the flowers are exported each year by the tonne. Here again there are dunes, planted this time with maritime pines, on which several windmills stand.

Resources – The island's resources are mainly agricultural. The soil, enriched with sea-wrack, favours the production of early potatoes and forced fruit and vegetables which are highly prized. Dry-stone walls, embankments, tamarisk hedges or rows of cypress trees protect the crops from the sea winds.
The riches of the ocean itself, however, are not neglected : oysters are farmed in the Baie de Bourgneuf; fishermen from the port at l'Herbaudière are famed for their catches of sea bass as well as crab, lobster and other crustaceans. The harbour at Noirmoutier-en-l'Île serves mainly as a haven for wintering craft.
The **salt-marshes** *(qv)* glittering beneath the sun yield several hundred tonnes of salt per year. This production is largely due to the unusually high proportion of sunshine, to the generous tidal range and, paradoxically, to bad weather. Of the 700ha – 1 730 acres of salt-marsh on the island, only 100ha – 247 acres are exploited, by 40 *"paludiers"* – proprietors grouped into syndicates or co-operatives which manage the upkeep of the channels and oversee the extraction and sale of the salt.
The islanders live in low-built houses with red-tiled roofs and whitewashed walls. Since 1959 an undersea pipeline has supplied them with fresh water from the mainland.

Passage du Gois – This 4.5km – 2½ mile submersible causeway was the only way wheeled traffic could reach the island from the late 19C until 1971, when the toll bridge was opened.
The Gois passage formed on shoals (its name is derived from a local term, *"goiser"*, which means to wade). The route is marked out by refuge-buoys, allowing people caught out by the rapidly rising tide to hoist themselves to safety and wait... for the tide to fall again.
From the causeway it is possible to see fishermen, oyster farmers and *boucholeurs* *(qv)* busy about their work in the shallows.

Sea cruises ⏲ – These are available from l'Herbaudière to Île du Pilier and towards Île d'Yeu.

NOIRMOUTIER-EN-L'ILE Pop 4 846. Facilities.

Noirmoutier is the island capital, an all-white town, with its pale buildings extending parallel to a canal-port from which the sea withdraws at low tide. The 1km – ½ mile long Grande-Rue (main street) ends at a former parade ground opening onto the port.

Place d'Armes – The royalist **General d'Elbée** *(qv)* was executed by a Republican firing squad on this parade ground in 1794. A little way back from the esplanade, the castle and the church stand side by side on a slight rise. Two fine 18C buildings are nearby : on the right, facing the castle, the Lebreton des Grapillières mansion (now a hotel); on the left the Jacobsen house, named after a Dutch family who worked on the draining of the island during the 18C.

Château ⏲ – The 15C defensive perimeter, bare and austere, forms a rectangle interrupted only by two corner towers with bartizan turrets. Picturesque views of the town, the salt-marshes and the sea can be seen from the covered way running around the castle's circumference. Inside the enclosure are the old Governor's residence and a square 11C keep which houses a **museum.**

Ground floor – Local minerals and ornithology. The comprehensive collection of stuffed birds includes teal, marsh owls and snipe. A geological map explains the ground formation of the island and the bay.

First floor – This section contains a diverse assortment of items connected with the ocean : ships' figureheads, model boats, a boarding party's axe and sabre, an early 19C cross made from seashells...

Second floor – Local history : archeology and the Wars of the Vendée *(qv)*. In a corner turret, the armchair in which **General d'Elbée** was shot is on display : incapable of moving because he had not recovered from wounds suffered in the battle of Cholet *(see Michelin Green Guide Châteaux of the Loire)*, the General was transported in this chair to Place d'Armes, where the executioners waited. A 19C painting by Julien Le Blant illustrates the drama.

Third floor – This houses a splendid collection of English **Staffordshire pottery★** (18C and 19C), some of it known as **Jersey pottery** because it was there that the pieces were stored. The variety of shapes, the decorative motifs and the colours used lend this collection a particular brilliance.
From La Vigie turret there is a **panorama** of Noirmoutier and the coast : the view extends as far as La Baule on the mainland to the north and Île d'Yeu to the south.

Église St-Philbert – This former Benedictine abbey church combines the Romanesque (chancel) and Gothic (nave) styles. Beneath the chancel, flanked by sumptuous Baroque altars, a fine 11C crypt occupies the site of the original Merovingian chapel. The crypt houses the cenotaph of St Philbert – an empty tomb installed in the 11C, the original sarcophagus having been transferred at the time of the Norman invasions.

Aquarium-Seeland ⏲ – Local and tropical sea creatures are on show here in a setting featuring underwater caverns and the hulks of sunken ships. A huge pool is reserved for sea-lions. In front of each display a short explanation *(in French)* enables visitors to familiarize themselves with the different species.

Musée de la construction navale ⏲ – This museum, housed in a former *salorge* (salt loft) once used as a yard by local artisan boat-builders, illustrates the traditional techniques of boat-building.
Plans, blueprints, templates, sails and rigging, and demonstrations of wood-sawing and the construction of hulls faithfully reproduce the atmosphere of the old marine workshop.

ADDITIONAL SIGHTS

★ **Bois de la Chaize** – *Access via D 948; follow the signs towards Plage des Dames.* This wood overlooking the sea could be a corner of the French Riviera : clumps of umbrella pines, ilex trees and mimosa thickets, scenting the air during the February flowering season, combine to give the place its deservedly exotic reputation.

The **Plage des Dames** owes its name to the fact that Gallic Druidesses practised their rites here in ancient times. The sheltered beach, an elegant curve of fine sand, is the starting point of the **Promenade des Souzeaux★** – a charming walk *(45min Rtn)* past the rocky, wooded creeks of the island's northeastern coast.

Bois de la Chaize, Noirmoutier.

Leave the beach via the footpath under the ilex trees on the left of the small landing-stage, then follow the first track climbing upwards, again on the left.

After the lighthouse, pines are again interspersed with the ilex. The rocky cliffs here overlook a sea studded with reefs and there are views of the Côte de Jade (Jade Coast), west of Pornic on the mainland. The clifftop path passes above the pretty Anse Rouge (Red Cove), dominated by Plantier Tower, before leading to Souzeaux beach.

L'Herbaudière – A busy traffic of brightly-coloured boats animates this small fishing port where the catch (lobsters, crayfish, various white fish) is sold daily at quayside auctions. The multi-coloured pennants which serve to mark the position of lobster-pots out at sea give a festive air to the vessels which sink them. A forest of masts rises above the pleasure craft moored in a neighbouring basin.

From the jetty separating this marina from the fishing port there is a view of l'Île du Pilier, a small island crowned by a lighthouse, which was once linked to Noirmoutier by a causeway.

La Guérinière – Here, at the narrowest part of the island, a survey of local activities and folk art in the late 19C and early 20C is presented at the **Musée des Arts et Traditions Populaires** ⓥ. Agriculture, fishing, crafts and life around the salt-marshes are among the subjects treated. The museum also houses reconstructed local interiors, collections of costumes and headdresses, and such local folk art as seascapes painted on fragments of sail-canvas by *cap-horniers* ("Cape-Horners") – sailors who had worked aboard the full-rigged clippers navigating the dangerous seas around Cape Horn in the cargo "races" of the 19C.

★ Abbaye de NOUAILLÉ-MAUPERTUIS

Michelin map 68 fold 14 or 233 folds 8, 9 – 11km – 7 miles southeast of Poitiers.

The remains of this ancient Benedictine abbey are half hidden from the road in a small wooded valley.

Battle of Poitiers (1356) – It was not far from the abbey, on the north bank of the River Miosson, west of the minor road to Les Bordes, that one of the bloodiest battles of the Hundred Years War *(qv)* took place. Known to historians as the Battle of Poitiers, this was the encounter in which the French King **Jean II le Bon** (1319-64) was defeated and taken prisoner by the **Black Prince** *(qv)*, son of Edward III of England. The King, surrounded by a few companions, had advanced onto a knoll known as "Alexander's Field" when he was attacked by the Anglo-Gascon army. Jean, wearing the royal armour garnished with gold fleurs-de-lys, resisted long and bravely, helped by his youngest son Philippe, still only a child, who called out to him warning him of oncoming blows. Eventually, however, totally exhausted and wounded in the face, the King was obliged to give in. To regain his freedom he had to abandon to the English the western half of his kingdom, pay an enormous ransom and allow two of his other sons to be taken as hostages to London. When one of them escaped, Jean himself went to the English capital to replace him, and died there soon afterwards.

TOUR *30min.*

Route D 12 from Poitiers offers an attractive view down over the abbey, the old defensive perimeter of which (walls and towers) has been cleared and renovated. Aside from these walls and towers – some of which have been partly levelled – the abbey was protected by moats fed from offshoots of the Miosson.
A small, charming drawbridge leads to the vaulted north gate and through to the abbey courtyard beyond. The 15C abbot's residence attached to the entrance is served by an attractive staircase turret.

Abbey church – *Best views of the building as a whole are from the left side.* On the right the 12C belfry-porch is lightened by a large bay pierced in the 15C. The lateral wall in the centre has a curious elevation : two levels of arching, superimposed, are themselves surmounted by arches and bays; both sets of features are Romanesque but the lower date from the 11C and the upper from the late 12C. The upper parts of the transept and chancel were altered in the 17C : it was then that the semicircular apse was replaced by a flat east end. The impressive dome on squinches, reinforced by ribs, rises above the first bay of the nave, which is framed by very narrow aisles and has 12C barrel vaulting. Note, near the north entrance, the Romanesque column of blue-grey marble which was re-used during the modification of the church.
A fine ensemble of 17C woodwork (rood screen, choir stalls, lectern eagle) adorns the middle of the church. At the far end of the chancel, behind the 17C high altar, stands an enormous mass of carved and painted stone : the 9C **tomb★** known as the Shrine of St Junien. Staircases on each side of the chancel (restored in the 17C) lead down to the crypt in which the relics of the saint are venerated. In the south transept, another staircase gives access to a necropolis.

Monastic buildings – There remains, south of the church, one wing crowned with a strange Romanesque chimney (said by some to have been a former *Lanterne des Morts – qv*) and, beyond, a 17C building facing the Miosson.

★ OIRON

Pop 1 009

Michelin map 68 fold 2 or 232 fold 45.

The small village of Oiron is the home of two splendid but little-known architectural monuments : the château of the Gouffier family and a delightful Renaissance collegiate church.

The Gouffier Family – Artus Gouffier, chamberlain to François I, accompanied his sovereign to Italy and was so overwhelmed by Italian art that on his return, in the early 16C, he began building a church in the Renaissance style. At the same time he organized the construction of a tower and one wing of the château. Both church and château were completed under the direction of his eldest child, Claude, who also began collecting the works of art which were to adorn the latter. Master of the King's Horse and extremely wealthy, Claude Gouffier held the title of Comte de Caravas : in legend he became the Marquis de Carabas (the fictitious title given to his impoverished owner by "Puss in Boots", the hero of Charles Perrault's fairy tale of 1697). In 1700 Mme de Montespan *(qv)* acquired the château; she stayed here often until her death in 1707.

SIGHTS

★ **Château** ⏲ – The Château d'Oiron is both enchanting and intriguing. Constantly modified, yet in a style always oddly lagging behind its period, it encapsulates two whole centuries of the history of architecture in France.
Beyond two small pavilions stands the main body of the château, comprising a central block roofed in the French style flanked by two square pavilions crowned by balustrades, and two wings – one 16C with an upper floor, the other 17C with a terrace – framing the central courtyard.

Tour – Thanks to a project designed to link contemporary art with the traditional French heritage, the château is being progressively enriched by a collection of works specifically earmarked for it.

The wing with the upper floor was the one started by Artus Gouffier in 1515 and completed by his son Claude. The charming Gothic-inspired gallery with its basket-handled arcades is crowned by marble medallions carved with the profiles of Roman emperors. Panels on the gallery wall show paintings of the finest horses owned by Henri II – commissioned by the Master of the King's Horse himself.
A fine staircase, decorated with a central newel with spiral moulding which acts as a banister, leads to a majestic **gallery★★** on the upper storey. On the walls are 14 paintings, slightly faded but still remarkable for their design and composition, on themes from *The Iliad* and *The Aeneid.* It was Louis Gouffier who commissioned the Louis XIII ceiling, which comprises 1 670 coffered panels painted with different subjects – an encyclopedic collection of birds, mammals, weapons, plants, scientific items... From this gallery the tour leads to the Trophy Pavilion and the former chapel (**1**), adorned with glazed earthenware tiles from the local village.
The central portion of the château, started by Louis Gouffier and finished by La Feuillade, retains the existing 16C constructions, notably a superb Renaissance staircase with straight flights and a hollow core, inspired by the one at Azay-le-Rideau on the Loire. The reception hall known as the King's Salon boasts a splendid ceiling with beams painted with mythological and grotesque characters. The King's Pavilion includes two chambers decorated with an exuberance typical of the Louis XIII style. The King's Room is covered by an extraordinary ceiling groaning with heavy gilded motifs framing painted, coffered panels. The Study of the Muses (**2**) is named after the nine muses who decorate its panelling.

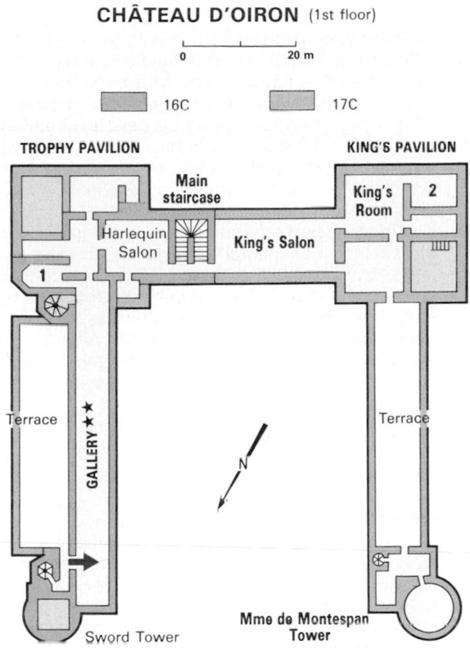

★ **Collegiate Church** – The Renaissance façade includes twinned doors and a large arch surmounted by a pediment bearing the arms of the Gouffier family.
In the transept lie the family tombs, executed by sculptors from Tuscany named Juste, who had settled in Tours. The two largest date from 1537; the smaller pair, from the studio of Jean II Juste, from 1559. In the northern arm of the transept is the tomb of Philippine de Montmorency, second wife of Guillaume Gouffier, who died in 1516. Her recumbent effigy is represented clothed in the garments of a widow. Nearby is the mausoleum of her son, the Amiral de Bonnivet, killed in 1525 while fighting with François I during the French defeat after the siege of Pavia.
The tomb of Artus Gouffier, founder of the church and brother of the admiral, is in the south transept, beside that of his son Claude; the figure of Artus is clothed in armour. A 16C painting after Raphael represents John the Baptist.
The seigneurial chapels, on either side of the chancel, are magnificently decorated in the Renaissance style. The south chapel contains a 16C portrait of St Jerome; the painting of *The Holy Family* in the north chapel dates from the 18C. The keystones in each chapel are very elaborately worked. Also noteworthy are the picturesque 16C statues of the Apostles on the high-altar reredos, the portrait of Claude Gouffier on the north wall of the chancel, and a fine *Resurrection,* painted in the Flemish mannerist style of the 16C, on the south wall.

★ Île d'OLÉRON

Michelin map 71 folds 13, 14 or 233 folds 13, 14 – Facilities.

The Isle of Oléron, which lies just off the coast between Royan and La Rochelle, is a popular holiday resort with families in search of sun, sea, fresh air and the spicy tang of pinewoods.

Pont-Viaduc – Since 1966 Oléron has been linked to the mainland by an elegantly curving road bridge, the longest in France at 3 026m – just over $1\frac{3}{4}$ miles. The viaduct is built of pre-stressed concrete in simple, modern lines and rests on 45 rectangular piles; the central spans, 79m – 259ft wide, rise 23m – 75ft above the highest of high tides. A 7m – 23ft carriageway, two cycle lanes and two walkways for pedestrians are incorporated in the viaduct's total width of 10.6m – 35ft.
From the mainland, the best view of the bridge is from the old ferry landing-stage at Le Chapus *(qv).*

Boat trips ⏲ – Connections with Île d'Aix *(qv)* in season, also round-trip cruises.

GEOGRAPHICAL AND HISTORICAL NOTES

Oléron, a prolongation seawards of the old province of Saintonge *(qv)*, is, apart from Corsica, the biggest of all the French islands (30km – 18 ½ miles long and 6km – 3¾ miles wide). The *Pertuis* (Straits) of Antioche and those of Maumusson, ravaged by dangerous currents, separate it from the Charente coast.
The limestone foundation of the low-lying isle is streaked with areas of sand forming long strings of dunes, wooded in the north (Saumonards Dune) and west (on the Côte Sauvage). The white houses of Oléron are surrounded by mimosas, oleanders, tamarisk, fig trees and the grey-green spines of agave. Here and there old windmills rise above the landscape.

Natural Resources – To the east, the coastline and the lowlands between Boyardville and St-Trojan are exclusively reserved for oyster farming – the island's principal economic asset, along with early fruit and vegetables and the cultivation of vines. The vineyards, mainly grouped around St-Pierre and St-Georges, produce white or rosé wines with an agreeable, slightly iodized flavour characteristic of the region. The salt-marshes, once numerous near Ors, St-Pierre and La Brée, have largely been transformed into oyster *claires (qv)*.
A more recent development on the island is the establishment of several fish farms raising eels, trout and clams.
The most important fishing port on Oléron is La Cotinière on the west coast but an unusual form of coastal fishing also survives around the Chassiron headland at the isle's northernmost extremity. Here, visitors may see the local catch caught in specialized **fish locks** – walled enclosures fitted with grilled apertures at the seaward end, through which the water filters as the tide goes out. At low tide the fishermen wade out in the shallow water which remains and capture their prey with the aid of *fouënes* (a kind of harpoon) or *espiottes* (a type of sabre).
On the Côte Sauvage (Wild Coast), locals go spear fishing – especially in June and September – for bar and meagre *(1)*.
There is a treatment centre specialising in salt-water and sea-air cures at St-Trojan *(see below)*.

"The Rules of Oléron" – In 1199 the 76-year old **Eleanor of Aquitaine** *(qv)*, now a penitent following her turbulent life – in her youth she had provoked scandal through her "wild" behaviour – returned to her island possession and stayed in the château here before retiring to Fontevraud Abbey where she died in 1204.
Now, however, much quietened down, she set about restoring law and order to the island she ruled. The dangerous Côte Sauvage, for instance, had long been at the mercy of wreckers who looted and pillaged ships driven ashore and robbed any survivors from their crews – a practice euphemistically known as *"le droit d'aubaine"* (the right of the windfall). Eleanor decreed that henceforth such brigands must be punished : "They must be put in the sea and plunged under water repeatedly until they are half dead, and then taken out and stoned to death as one would dispose of wolves or mad dogs."
Subsequently the dowager drew up a set of rules "concerning the seas, the vessels sailing upon them, their masters, crew companions and also merchants". This maritime code, known as *Les Rôles d'Oléron,* served as a base for all subsequent charters regulating conduct on the high seas.
After the reign of Eleanor (a statue of her stands in the museum in St-Pierre, *see below*) Oléron was coveted both by the French and the English. In 1372 the English abandoned the isle, taking away with them all the official documents.

The Oléron Pocket – The island was occupied by the Germans in 1940 and liberated on 30 April and 1 May 1945, though not without difficulty : overcoming the stubborn resistance of the 15 000-strong occupiers' garrison and forcing a German capitulation required a large-scale combined operation, which was code-named Jupiter and involved Allied land, sea and air forces.

ST-PIERRE-D'OLÉRON Pop 5 365.

St-Pierre is situated in the centre of the island, on the edge of the marshes, and is both the commercial and the administrative capital of the island. In the summer months the town, with its attractive pedestrian precincts, becomes extremely busy.

Church – A pale-coloured octagonal belfry dating from the 18C serves as a landmark for sailors at sea. On each side of the chancel, a chapel is preceded by cloverleaf arching supported by black marble pillars.
From the platform at the top of the tower (32m – 105ft high), the whole of the island is visible in the foreground of a **panorama★** embracing the Isle of Aix, the Isle of Ré and the estuary of the River Charente.

Lanterne des Morts – This "Lantern of the Dead" *(qv)*, rising to a height of 30m – 98ft, stands in Place Camille-Memain on the site of a former cemetery. The monument was built at the time of the English occupation in the 13C and its slender, sober lines are typical of the early Gothic style. It is crowned by an 18C pyramid roof.
Inside, a staircase still leads to the beacon at the top where the priest used to light the flame symbolizing the immortality of the soul. An altar stands against one of the walls.

Maison des Aïeules – It was in this "ancestors' house", home of his maternal grandparents at No 13 in the street now bearing his name, that the writer **Pierre Loti** *(qv)* spent many of his school holidays. In 1923 Loti was buried – like his Huguenot ancestors – in the family garden, here "beneath the ivy and the oleanders"; his

(1) The map Isle of Oléron *(scale 1/45 000 from Éditions R Quémy, 78510 Triel-sur-Seine) gives details of coastal fishing and places where fishing is practicable on foot.*

Inland waterway, Île d'Oléron.

child's bucket and spade were placed near his body, following his wishes. In front of the town hall a bust of Loti, who was born in Rochefort *(qv)*, commemorates the writer's link with St-Pierre.

Musée Oléronais Aliénor-d'Aquitaine ⊙ – *23 Rue Pierre-Loti.* The museum, built in the local style and named after Eleanor of Aquitaine, focuses on the arts and traditions of the island. The reconstruction of a period kitchen (furniture, utensils, domestic ware, figures in costume) evokes home life in days gone by. There is a section on agricultural and maritime activities, another on vine-growing and wine-making. A collection of sea shells illustrates species of molluscs and crustaceans found around the coast. Documents relating to Pierre Loti are also on display.

ST-TROJAN-LES-BAINS Pop 1 486 – Facilities.

St-Trojan is a pretty seaside resort with Mediterranean-like vegetation. Warm water from the Gulf Stream laps its four sandy bathing beaches; the attractive villas scattered among the trees on the edge of a magnificent pine forest are fragrant with the scent of mimosa from January to March.
A thalassotherapy centre (salt-water and sea-air cures) treats rheumatism and other complaints.

Forêt de St-Trojan – This huge stretch of woodland, thickly carpeted with parasol pines relieved here and there by an undergrowth of ilex or clumps of broom, covers an area of 2 000ha – almost 5 000 acres. Much of it covers dunes, the crests of which sometimes rise up to 36m – 118ft. Forest rides allow cyclists and walkers to explore the forest, which is exploited for its timber.

Grande Plage – *3km – 1¾ miles west of St-Trojan via D 126 E1.* This splendid beach of dune-backed fine sand, exposed to the west wind and the Atlantic rollers of the Côte Sauvage, stretches as far as the eye can see in every direction.

Pointe de Manson – *2.5km – 1½ miles southeast of St-Trojan.* The road to the Point ends by an *estacade* (dyke). From the top of this there are **views** of the viaduct, the headlands of Ors and Le Chapus, the Seudre estuary and La Tremblade peninsula – which frame what is in effect a small inland sea.

Plage de Gatseau – *4km – 2½ miles south of St-Trojan.* The road leads to a delightful beach of fine sand, very popular with bathers. On the way there are fine **views** of the Arvert headland, Ronce-les-Bains and the landmark tower of the church at Marennes *(qv)* on the mainland.

Pointe de Gatseau – This isolated promontory at the southern extremity of Grande Plage, separating it from the more sheltered beach at Gatseau, is one of the most evocative spots on the Côte Sauvage (Wild Coast). Access is by a small **tourist train** ⊙ which runs between St-Trojan and the Côte Sauvage.

TOUR OF THE ISLAND

From St-Trojan-les-Bains *85km – 53 miles : allow 1 day – Local map p 194.*

St-Trojan-les-Bains – *See above.*

Le Grand-Village-Plage – The **Maison Paysanne Oléronaise** ⊙ is an open-air museum showing a local peasant farm as it would have been in the past. The farmhouse – one room, one window – is equipped and furnished to recreate the atmosphere of peasant life in the past. Traditional activities linked with the sea and vine-growing are recalled by the implements and tools on display in the outhouses (wine store, stables, barns). The small **Maison de la Coiffe et du Costume Oléronais★** has attractive displays of the traditional costumes and headdresses worn on the island in the last century.

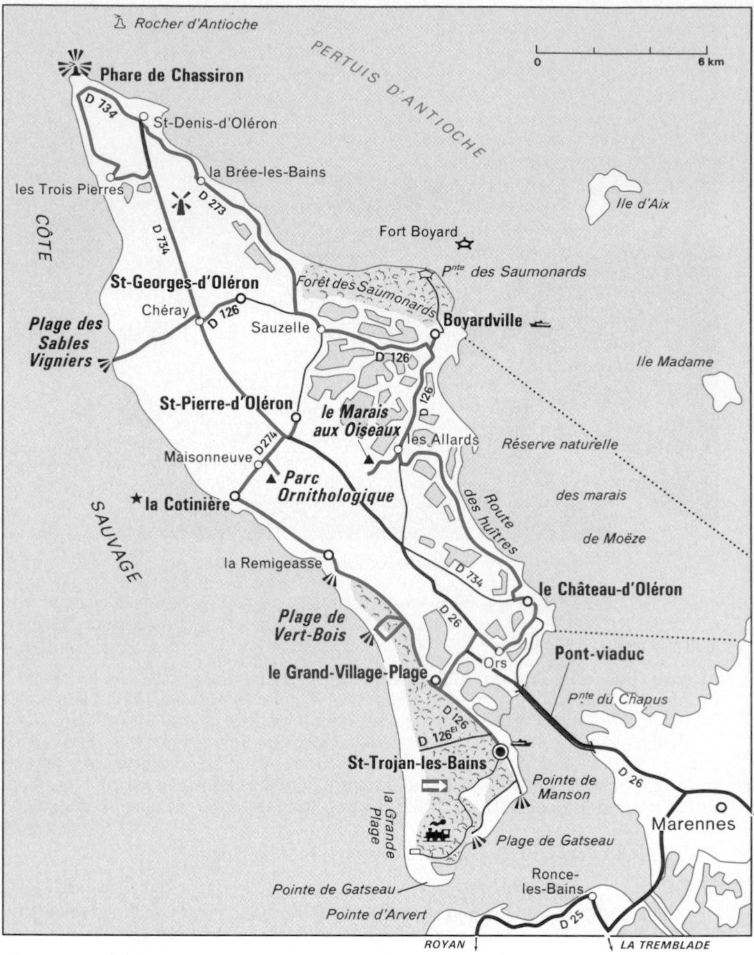

Le Château-d'Oléron – The remains of a 17C fortress, a citadel originally built on Richelieu's orders, stand here. In 1666 the construction of the port at Rochefort led Louis XIV to order the establishment of a *ceinture de feu* (girdle of fire) to protect the Charente estuary leading to this new port. Fouras and the Isle of Aix were therefore heavily fortified and the Oléron citadel re-designed and reinforced. Numerous deportees, both lay and religious, were imprisoned here during the Revolution.

The town is arranged geometrically around a huge central square containing a pretty Renaissance fountain with four cabled columns. The port penetrates the built-up area : a picturesque local sight is the arrival and departure of boats bound for the oyster farms.

The small coast road heading north towards Les Allards is known locally as the **Route des Huîtres** (the oyster road). This narrow roadway permits the servicing of the many canals, sheds and "ports" strung out opposite the east-coast oyster farms – and gives visitors a fascinating insight, especially at low tide, into the island's ostreicultural activity.

Le Marais aux Oiseaux (Bird Marsh) ⓥ – *At Les Grissotières.* This area of former salt-marshes surrounded by oak trees is now a **bird sanctuary** and provides a winter retreat for some species of migratory birds and a nesting site for others. Herons, egrets, pelicans and wild geese are among the numerous species which can enjoy here the swamp conditions of their natural habitat.

Boyardville – The name of the resort derives from a hutted camp established here for the army of workmen building **Fort Boyard,** a curious stone structure rising, offshore, from the shallow sea in the middle of the Straits of Antioche, between the Isle of Oléron and the Isle of Aix. The fort, another project designed to protect the mouth of the Charente, was started in 1804 and completed in 1859 under Napoleon III; progress in the science of artillery, however, which was developing much more rapidly than work on the fort, made it militarily out of date before it was even finished. In 1871 it was used as a prison : a large number of *Communards* (members of a Parisian workers' rebellion who were savagely crushed after the Franco-German war of 1870-71) were incarcerated there before their trial and deportation to New Caledonia.

Boyardville, once a training centre for the crews of torpedo boats, is today enlivened with a small marina. The 8km – 5 mile beach is in fact the seaward side of the Dune des Saumonards, an undulating 450ha – 1 100 acre sand mass covered with plantations of pine trees – an ideal site for ramblers. A forest track leads to the old Saumonards fort (military territory).

Continue west along D 126; beyond Sauzelle turn right towards St-Denis-d'Oléron (signposted Foulerot-Le Douhet-La Brée), passing a number of small seaside resorts. Beyond La Brée, follow the coast road.

Phare de Chassiron ⓥ – This black and white lighthouse built in 1836 is 50m – 164ft high. The 224-step climb to the top is worthwhile for the huge **panorama**★ it reveals : apart from the Isle of Oléron itself, the view takes in the Isle of Aix, the Isle of Ré, the port of La Rochelle, La Pallice and, offshore, the Rocher d'Antioche with its warning beacon, which looks like a town swallowed up by the sea. Below the lighthouse, at low tide, the fish locks around the cape are visible.

Turn south and follow the coast road to St-Georges-d'Oléron.

The road, running above low cliffs which mark the beginning of the **Côte Sauvage**, is flanked inland by a plain scattered with market gardens.

St-Georges-d'Oléron – The façade of the 11C-12C Romanesque church in this small town is attractively decorated with geometric motifs. The crowned arch of the central doorway was rebuilt in the 13C and the Gothic vaulting over the nave dates from the same period. The church as a whole was restored in 1618 and again in 1968. There is a fine covered market in the town square.

Plage des Sables Vigniers – The beach, between two rock spurs at the foot of wooded dunes, offers views of the Côte Sauvage and over a sea that is frequently stormy.

St-Pierre-d'Oléron – *See above.*

Parc Ornithologique de Maisonneuve ⓥ – Over 200 species of birds can be seen in this sanctuary, including, among the brightly coloured exotics, the crowned yellowcrest crane, the toucan, the macaw and the blackheaded lory of New Guinea.

★ **La Cotinière** – This is a busy, picturesque port halfway down the Côte Sauvage. Thirty small trawlers are based in the harbour, fishing mainly (in summer) for shrimps, prawns, lobster, crab and sole. Once landed the catch is sold immediately at **"La Criée"** ⓥ – the local term for a fish auction in the covered market. A Sailors' Chapel (1967) stands on the dune overlooking the port.
The route crosses the Côte Sauvage dunes, passes **La Remigeasse** and then penetrates an area of woodland (pines and holm oaks) offering tantalising glimpses of the ocean.

Plage de Vert-Bois – The road follows a one-way system to loop through another patch of tree-covered duneland fringed with reeds before arriving at this beach; from here is an impressive **view**★ of the ocean, with long lines of breakers rolling shorewards every time the wind rises.

★ OLORON-STE-MARIE

Pop 11 067

Michelin map 85 folds 5, 6 or 234 fold 39 – Local maps pp 82 and 254.
Town plan in the current Michelin Red Guide France.

This is a town of two parts, which were administratively united in 1858. It lies at the confluence of the Aspe and Ossau torrents, which become, once joined, the River Oloron.
Oloron was originally an Iberian and subsequently Roman outpost founded on the hill where the Ste-Croix district now stands. Its name is derived from Iluro, a Pyrenean deity. In the 7C and the 9C, Basque, Norman and barbarian invasions totally destroyed the town, and the surviving inhabitants moved to the far bank of the Aspe and built up the village of Ste-Marie on the flat land where Romans had also settled. In the 11C Centulle IV, Vicomte of Béarn, rebuilt the devastated hill-town and made it a military and trading centre. In the Middle Ages Ste-Marie remained a rural and episcopal centre, only becoming industrialized much later. The bishopric was abolished in 1790.
In the past Oloron was an important stage on the pilgrim's route to Santiago de Compostela, one of the last before the climb to Col de Somport *(qv)*, the pass on the Spanish frontier. In memory of this tradition, contemporary sculptures by artists including Guy de Rougemont, Carlos Cruz-Dies and Michael Warren have been placed at strategic points of historic interest around the town. This unusual urban initiative is part of an overall project to mark out the ancient pilgrims' road, to be continued along the Aspe Valley and from there into Galicia via Hecho (Spain).

SIGHTS

Église Ste-Marie – This former cathedral dates from the 12C and 13C, except for the chancel with its five radiating chapels which was rebuilt in the 14C after a fire.

★★ **Main Doorway** – The belfry-porch shelters a magnificent Romanesque doorway, one of the rare examples of its period which, miraculously, has suffered no serious damage in spite of local invasions and religious wars. This good condition is partly due to the exceptional hardness of the Pyrenean marble used in its construction : over the centuries the stone has become as smooth as polished ivory.
The doorway was built on the orders of Gaston IV "the Crusader", Vicomte of Béarn (1090-1131), on his victorious return from the First Crusade, to glorify the taking of Jerusalem which was made possible by war machines of his own invention. These devices – mobile assault towers on wheels and boulder-throwing catapults – brilliantly deployed by their designer, were also instrumental in the successful storming of Zaragoza during the re-conquest of Spain.

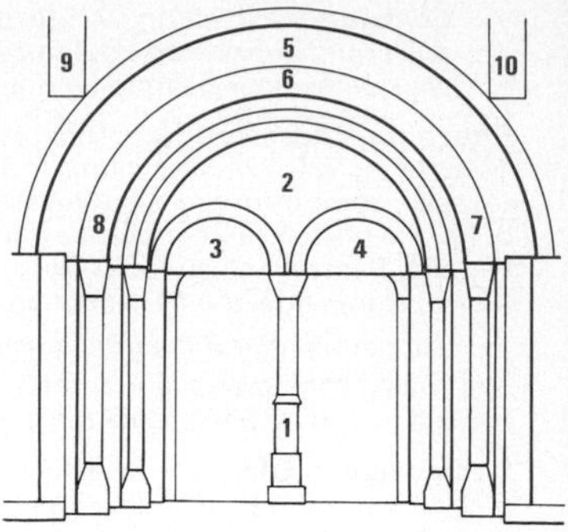

Among the doorway's most impressive features are :

1) Two atlantes in chains (thought by 19C archeologists to be Saracens – an allusion to the Moors Gaston found installed in France on his return from the Holy Land, and whom he subsequently drove out);

2) A Descent from the Cross;

3 and **4**) Lions, symbolizing the Church, persecuted (on the right) and triumphant (on the left) – elements remade in the 12C;

5) Coving representing Heaven : the 24 old men of the Apocalypse, carrying long-necked jars of perfume, are playing violas or *rebecs* – three-stringed violins used by minstrels – as they worship the divine Lamb, which carries the Cross. Evil is represented by a dragon's head. This is a literal translation into sculpture of the Vision of St John in The Apocalypse;

6) Coving representing Earth. The craftsmen used local models to recreate the entire peasant life of the place and the period : boar hunting, salmon fishing and smoking (from 1 000 to 1 500 salmon were caught then *each day* at Oloron), cheese-making, work on the vines and the preparation of hams;

7) An equestrian statue of the Emperor Constantine trampling on paganism (a theme equally popular with the stonecarvers working on contemporary church façades in the Poitou district). The statue was thought in the 19C to represent Gaston the Crusader himself;

8) A monster devouring a man;

9 and **10**) Sentries guarding the Tomb : isolated now but until the 19C posted on either side of a high-relief representing the Ascension of Christ (again, these figures were once believed to be guards posted by Constantine at the doors of Christian basilicas to protect them).

Interior – A lepers' stoup is inset into the first pillar supporting the organ loft (north side). At the entrance to the chancel a gilded oak sanctuary lamp and a 16C lectern are carved from the trunk of a single tree.
Other features of note include the pulpit, dating from 1523, the fine organ loft (1650), a 17C crib with carved wood figures (north aisle) and a large sketch, attributed to Murillo, for an *Assumption of the Virgin* (above the first tall arch on the north side of the nave, near the organ loft). The canvas was brought back from Zaragoza by a local man who was a soldier enlisted in the army of the French Empire.

Quartier Ste-Croix – The Holy Cross district, the old town surrounding the château of the Vicomtes (destroyed in 1644), is built on a projecting spur between the two torrents.

Église Ste-Croix – A massive tower gives this Romanesque church a severe, slightly military aspect (the remains of a covered watch-path can be seen to the east of the building). Inside, there is an unusual Spanish-Moorish dome, added in the 13C, above the 11C transept crossing. Inspired by the mosque at Cordoba, the architects of this dome mounted it above star vaulting supported by columns with historiated capitals.
Near the church are two fine Renaissance houses; lower down in Rue Dalmais is the stately La Grède tower (14C) with its twinned bays. Beside it is a 17C building which houses the **Maison du Patrimoine** ⓥ : departments of archeology, ethnography and mineralogy relating to the town and the Upper Béarn region occupy three floors of this museum, together with paintings and souvenirs of the wartime internment camp at Gurs.

Promenade Bellevue – *West of the church, by the terrace overlooking the Aspe torrent and the Ste-Marie district. Follow, on the right, the route along the top of the old ramparts.* From here there is a striking **view** up the valley of the Aspe to the mountain chain beyond it, which extends westward as far as the Basque country.

ORTHEZ

Pop 10 159

Michelin map 78 fold 8 or 234 fold 30.
Town plan in the current Michelin Red Guide France.

Orthez was the capital of Béarn after Morlaàs and before Pau; today it is a busy and picturesque town, its most interesting architectural feature an ancient fortified bridge. Gaston VII Moncade, Vicomte of Béarn, was behind the town's development in the 13C. After the union of Foix and Béarn *(qv)* Gaston Fébus held court here. The writer and court poet Jean Froissart (*c*1337-*c*1400) described in his *Chroniques* the brilliance of the château receptions after he had been a guest there in 1388 and 1389.
Francis Jammes (1868-1938) was another poet of note associated with Orthez. He lived in the town from 1897 to 1907; the wooden-balconied house that was his home can be seen on the way out of town, on the route to Pau.

SIGHTS

Old Town – In the days of Gaston VII and Gaston Fébus the ground-plan of Orthez did not lie parallel to the river, as it does now : the main axis of the town then was at right-angles, clustered on each side of a line drawn from the fortified bridge to Château Moncade. Reminders of this period remain in the dignified old houses, some with decorated porches, which line Rue Bourg-Vieux, Rue de l'Horloge and Rue Moncade.

★ **Pont Vieux** – The 13C bridge, guarded by a tower pierced with an arched gateway, guarded the entrance to the town; originally a second fortified gate completed the defences on the southern side. The tower was still in use as a defence feature in 1814, at the time of the struggle against Wellington. From the bridge there is an attractive view of the Pau Torrent, tumbling past the huge blocks of limestone half-blocking the river bed.

Tour Moncade – This tower is all that remains of the grandiose fortress built by Gaston VII in the late 13C and early 14C.

Maison Jeanne-d'Albret – *On the corner of Rue Roarie and Rue Bourg-Vieux.* The elegant 16C mansion once belonged to Jeanne d'Albret *(qv)*, the mother of Henry IV. The building has an octagonal tower which adds to the charm of the main entrance, leading to a paved inner courtyard. The steeply-sloping tiled roof is typical of the region. The carefully restored façades reveal the warm tones of the stonework.

Monument du Général Foy – *3.5km – 2 miles north, on the road to Dax.* The monument is a memorial recalling the Battle of Orthez (1814) in which Marshal Soult's 30 000 men were defeated by Wellington's army of 45 000. General Maximilien Foy, the "Citizen Hero" (1775-1825) distinguished himself during this episode, before the town was abandoned. The monument sits in a pleasant location surrounded by fine Béarnaise farms crowned by tall sloping roofs, with views of the distant Pyrenees.

★★ Le Haut OSSAU

Michelin map 85 folds 16, 17 or 234 folds 43, 47.

Upstream from the village of Eaux-Chaudes, the Ossau Valley separates into three different branches – the valley of the Bious Torrent, the Soussouéou Valley and the Valley of the Brousset Torrent – which together are known as Le Haut Ossau (the Upper Ossau region).

Pic du Midi d'Ossau – Alt 2 884m – 9 462ft. This mountain peak, recognizable from as far away as Pau, is in the form of a fang – a silhouette which contrasts with the normal Pyrenean crestline, and which is striking less for its boldness than for its delicacy. The peak is formed from an andesite core, the remains of an old volcanic "chimney" from around which the surrounding strata have been eroded away. A tour of the peak starting from Bious-Artigues (signposted as an alternative to GR10) is a walk which should be attempted only by fit and experienced climbers. It can be broken by an overnight stop at the Pombie **CAF Refuge.**
Hundreds of chamois live on the slopes of the Pic's eastern foothills.

★ 1 FROM GABAS TO BIOUS-ARTIGUES

4.5km – 2 ¾ miles, then 45min on foot.

Gabas – This is a mountain village lying in the hollow where the torrents rushing down from Pic du Midi d'Ossau meet. Sheep's cheese prepared (pressed) in a special way is a local delicacy. The 12C village chapel, with vaulting supported by semi-cylindrical pillars and thick, crossed joints, has been redecorated in a modern style.
After Gabas turn right into D 231; the road climbs very steeply, leading to the dam which has effectively drowned the Bious amphitheatre.

★ **Lac de Bious-Artigues** – Looking south from the west bank of the lake, not far from the dam, there are superb **views★** of Pic du Midi d'Ossau : at sunset the andesite rock-faces fade through every shade of red to deep violet. To the south-west is the impressive bulk of Pic d'Ayous.

★★ **Lacs d'Ayous** – *Climb (on foot) : 2½ hours; descent : 1½ hours; difference in altitude : 560m – 1 837ft. Follow the Parc National signs and the red-and-white markers of footpath GR10.* From the refuge west of these three mountain lakes there are grandiose **views★★★** of Pic du Midi reflected in the waters.

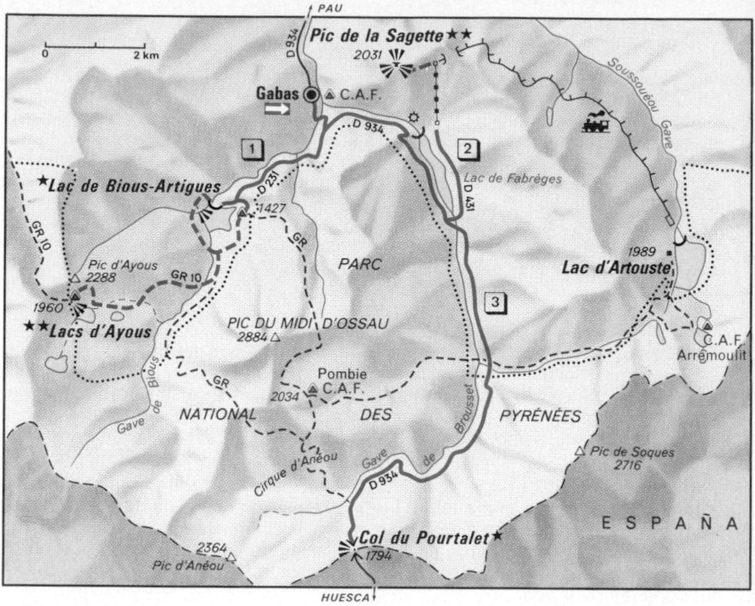

★ 2 EXCURSION TO LAC D'ARTOUSTE *Allow 4 hours.*

This excursion combines a ride in a cable-car to La Sagette, leaving from the eastern side of the Fabrèges reservoir (Lac de Fabrèges), and a trip on the Lac d'Artouste mountain railway. In winter the cable-car services the runs of the Artouste ski station.

Cable-car to La Sagette ⓥ – From the upper station (alt 1 950m – 6 398ft) a marvellous **view**★★ of the glaciated valley of the Brousset far below – partly drowned now by the reservoir – forms part of the same mountain panorama dominated by the silhouette of Pic du Midi d'Ossau. A look at the **Pic de la Sagette**★★ viewing table is worth the climb *(1 hour on foot Rtn).*

From La Sagette to Lac d'Artouste ⓥ – The little train winds and twists its way among the mountain slopes at a height of 1 950m – 6 398ft. The 9km – 5 mile **journey**★★ offers striking views of the Soussouéou Valley, 500m – 1 640ft below. From the terminus (stop limited to 1½ hours) a footpath leads to Lac d'Artouste *(30min Rtn).* A dam has now raised the surface level of the lake, which laps the granite slopes of an amphitheatre surrounded by peaks which rise to 3 000m – 9 850ft.

3 FROM GABAS TO COL DU POURTALET *15km – 9 miles.*

The road skirts the Fabrèges and Artouste hydro-electric power stations then climbs to the level of the Fabrèges reservoir. Ahead, on the Spanish frontier, are the slopes of Pic de Soques – a mountain with a particularly contorted geological structure. Still climbing, the road runs through a narrow channel and leads finally to the Anéou cirque.

★ **Col du Pourtalet** – Alt 1 794m – 5 886ft. This border pass is normally blocked by snow from November to June. Looking back towards the north there is a fine **view**★ of the immense pastoral Anéou cirque – dotted in summer with countless sheep – and, further north still, of Pic du Midi d'Ossau.

★ PARTHENAY

Pop 10 809

Michelin map 67 fold 18 or 232 fold 44.

Parthenay is picturesquely sited on a rocky spur circled by the River Thouet. The town is the capital of the Gâtine region *(qv)*, an agricultural area renowned for its sheep farming, dairy products, apple orchards and above all cattle-breeding. The **cattle market** ⓥ, held every Wednesday in the Bellevue district *(behind the railway station)*, is the second largest in France for animals destined for the butchery trade. The town is also home to a number of aeronautical, mechanical and electronics industries, and its importance is reflected in the number of trade fairs held each year in the Parthenay *Palais des Congrès* (conference and exhibition centre).

HISTORICAL NOTES

Ubiquitous Mélusine – The legendary **Mélusine** *(qv)*, the fairy who turned into a serpent, is said to have presided over the birth of Parthenay – as she is supposed to have done in the case of many fortified towns in the Poitou region. Parthenay is, nevertheless, different : the seigneurs here remained directly descended from Mélusine until the Middle Ages, being members of the Larchevêque family, the younger branch of the Lusignans, themselves supposedly issue of the fairy.

PARTHENAY

Aguillon (R. Louis) .... Z
Jaurès (R. Jean) .... Z 17
Bancs (Pl. des) .... Z 3
Bombarde (R.) .... Z 4
Bourg-Belais (R. du) .... Z 5
Château (R. du) .... Y 6
Citadelle (R. de la) .... Y 8
Cordeliers (R. des) .... Y 9
Donjon (Pl. du) .... Z 10
Faubourg-St-Jacques
(R. du) .... Y 12
Férolle (R.) .... Y 14
Gaulle (Av. Gén. de) .... Z 15
Godineau (R. de) .... Y 16
Marchioux (R. du Fg) .... Z 21
Meilleraie (Bd de la) .... YZ 22
Picard (Pl. Georges) .... Z 27
Place (R. de la) .... Z 29
Poste (R. de la) .... Z 30
Sépulcre (R. du) .... Z 33
Sires-de-Parthenay
(Bd des) .... Z 34
Vau-Vert (Pl. du) .... Y 35
8-Mai-1945 (Bd du) .... Z 36

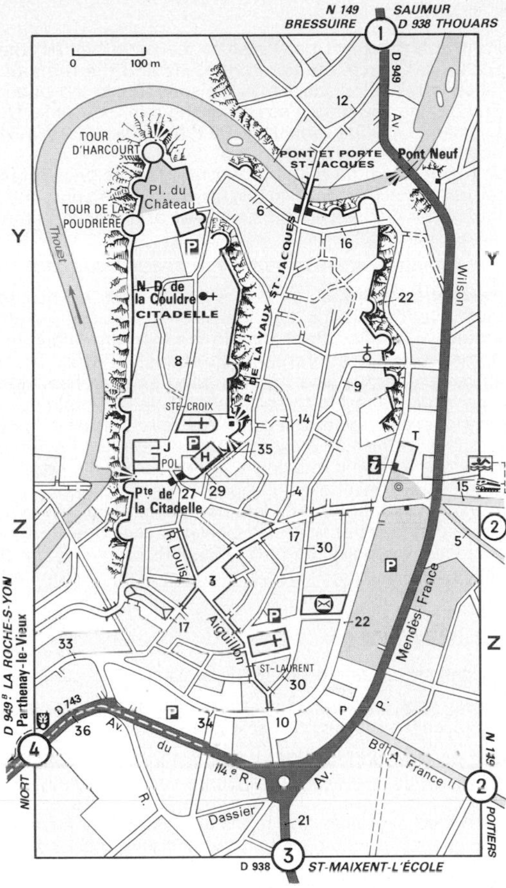

Pilgrims' Way – In medieval times Parthenay was one of the important stops on the pilgrims' route to Santiago de Compostela *(qv)*. Arriving from Thouars, the exhausted travellers would go first to the church hospital (a chapel still exists on the road to Thouars). Having left there those who had fallen ill on the journey, the pilgrims would cross the bridge, go through the fortified gateway and enter the town. Once they had found accommodation in the inns and taverns of Rue de la Vaux-St-Jacques they would then pay ritual visits to the local sanctuaries (there were 16) : churches such as Notre-Dame-de-la-Couldre and Ste-Croix. Once these devotions were completed, the pilgrims were free to disperse among the taverns in the town or to admire the charms of the graceful women of Parthenay, so renowned for their looks that they were celebrated in a popular folk song of the day.

MEDIEVAL TOWN ⏲ *3 hours.*

★ **Site** – From Pont-Neuf (Y) there is a fine **view★** of the oldest part of Parthenay, in particular of the picturesque architectural group formed by Pont-St-Jacques and the ancient fortified gateway beside it.

The citadel perched high up at the extremity of the promontory protects the castle keep, the seigneurial residence and the collegiate Church of Ste-Croix behind its massive ramparts. Down below, the fortifications are strengthened by the natural barriers of the river and the Vaux-St-Jacques valley. In the Middle Ages Parthenay had the reputation of being impregnable.

The St-Jacques district in the hollow of the valley and, higher up, the St-Laurent district were once protected by another fortified enclosure, with Porte St-Jacques *(see below)* as its main feature.

★ **Pont and Porte St-Jacques** (Y) – The narrow 13C bridge across the River Thouet was, and is, the entrance to the town from the north. A drawbridge unites it with the St-Jacques gateway, dating from the same period, which retains its tall, twin towers and its machicolated watch-path.

★ **Rue de la Vaux-St-Jacques** (Y) – This was once Parthenay's main shopping street and links the two town gateways, Porte St-Jacques and Porte de la Citadelle. The street's medieval aspect still recalls the days of the pilgrims. Some of the ancient half-timbered houses with projecting upper storeys have wide bays at street level, marking the location of former shops and stalls.

The road continues up through Place du Vau-Vert (Green Vale Square), skirting the walled citadel – the levelled towers of which are still distinguishable.

Citadelle (Y) – The citadel is the former seat of the House of Larchevêque, and was reinforced with ramparts in the 12C; **Porte de la Citadelle** (or Porte de l'Horloge) – a powerful Gothic fortification framed by pointed towers – leads into the fortress. In the 15C the gateway served also as a belfry; a huge bell dating from 1454 still hangs here.

From a terrace just northeast of the town hall (**H**) there are **views** of the apse of Ste-Croix Church, the tiered gardens and the roofs of the lower town; in the distance, a railway viaduct may be seen. From the public gardens beside the Police Station, the 16C bridge spanning the river is visible. North of the town hall are the two churches : Ste-Croix (12C) and **Notre-Dame-de-la-Couldre** with its fine Romanesque doorway in the Poitou style *(qv)*.
At the northern tip of the promontory is the wide, grass-covered esplanade where the castle once stood (two towers, Tour d'Harcourt and Tour de la Poudrière, are all that remain). There are striking **views** of the bend in the river and over the Vaux-St-Jacques district.

A footpath at the foot of the ramparts leads back to Porte de la Citadelle.

Parthenay-le-Vieux – *1.5km – 1 mile west.* An octagonal belfry which rises on a bluff overlooking the east bank of the Thouet, and which is visible for miles around, identifies Parthenay-le-Vieux priory church. **Église St-Pierre**★ ⓥ has a Romanesque west front, in Poitou style *(qv)*, notable for its symmetry; the entrance doorway and the two blind arcades flanking it are surmounted by three bays suggesting the three aisles inside the building. The figure on the entrance coving is, according to legend, the fairy Mélusine herself. The decorations on the tympana of the side arcades represent Samson overcoming a lion, and a crowned horseman carrying a falcon. Aligned below the cornice are the heads of cats with pointed ears, symbolizing imps.
The harmonious interior combines a central nave with barrel-vaulting, slightly pointed, and side aisles with half-barrel vaults. Over the transept crossing a dome on squinches supports the belfry. Capitals crowning the columns on each side of the chancel are decorated with carvings of lions and goats.

PASSAY

Michelin map 67 fold 3 or 232 fold 28.

Passay, a typical inland fishing hamlet, is the only place from which it is possible to approach the mysterious Lac de Grand-Lieu.

Lac de Grand-Lieu – This was once a true lake but during the past hundred years an insidious invasion of vegetation has gradually converted it into a marsh or swamp, immense and forbidding. The shores of this lake, their exact position concealed by rushes and reeds and clumps of furze, have now developed into an exceptional ornithological site which was officially declared a Nature Reserve in 1980.
The swamp, which is linked to the Loire estuary by the Achenau (*cheneau* is a local word for canal), covers an area of 4 000ha – 9 884 acres in summer and 8 000ha – 19 768 acres in winter. The rocky bottom, at depths of between 1m and 2m – 3ft 4in and 6ft 8in according to season, is in places covered by a thick bed of silt. It is said that beneath this shroud lies buried the ancient town of Herbauge, cursed because of its dissolute morals. According to legend, the muffled tolling of its church bell can be heard coming from the middle of the swamp at midnight on Christmas Eve.
The lake lies directly below one of the regular Atlantic migration routes and is the temporary home of more than 200 species of birds including ducks, geese, teal, snipe, corncrakes and rails, and grebes. It is also an important nesting site for grey herons and the rare spoonbill.

O. Garguil

Common heron.

Two museums (La Maison du Pêcheur, *see below,* and La Maison du Lac at St-Philbert-le-Grand-Lieu) are uniquely allowed to organize the rare **boat trips** around the lake, sorties aimed at discovering the beauty of the wildlife.

Maison du Pêcheur ⓥ – This small museum housed in an observation tower overlooking the marsh and its surroundings reveals the secrets of an eco-system that is unusually rich. The flora and fauna of the area are clearly and simply presented and explained, as are the activities associated with them – especially local fishing techniques. Indigenous species (perch, pike, carp, eels) can be viewed in the museum's aquariums.

Except when otherwise stated,
all recommended town tours are intended as walks.

★★★ # PAU

Michelin map 85 folds 6, 7 or 234 fold 35 – Local maps pp 30 and 83. Facilities.

Pau, the most elegant and most pleasantly situated of all the towns on the fringe of the Pyrenees, was highly prized as a tranquil winter resort by the British in the 19C. Today, as well as offering a consistently "soft and healing" climate, the city has, since the discovery of natural gas at Lacq nearby *(see below)*, developed into a true regional capital.

A new university was established in 1970 and what was a sleepy agricultural market town and administrative centre is now fast expanding industrially across Pont-Long moorland to the north. The town is also an important military garrison, specializing in training paratroopers.

For tourists, Pau's attraction lies in its historical links with Henry of Navarre (Henri IV of France), in its location offering excellent views over the mountains, and in its good leisure and sports facilities including golf, horse-racing, fox-hunting and other pastimes introduced by the British in the 19C. The annual Grand Prix motor race also draws large crowds : the Formula 3000 **Pau Circuit** shares with the Formula 1 course in Monaco the distinction of being one of the few remaining "round the houses" tracks, where the race is run through the streets of the town – a tough test for drivers when each lap measures less than 3km – 2 miles.

International athletics and other top-level sporting events are organized at the **Palais des Sports** in the northern part of Pau; the stadium has a capacity of 7 500 spectators. Nearby, the 5 000-seat **Zenith Centre** is the site of major cultural activities.

HISTORICAL NOTES

The fourth capital of Béarn – Pau was originally a simple strongpoint commanding a ford – a fortified look-out post behind a stockade of *pals* or *paux* (stakes in the Gascon tongue of Oc) which was later replaced by a bridge over the torrent. Gradually a village grew up around the post.

In the 14C Gaston Fébus *(qv)* built a wall around the settlement and laid the foundations of the castle which remains in Pau today. His successors continued his work and, in 1450, the town followed Lescar, Morlaàs and Orthez as the provincial capital of Béarn. It was, however, modest as capitals go : each time the States (provincial assembly) met, there were always some deputies who had to sleep under the stars owing to the shortage of lodgings.

In 1527 Henri d'Albret, King of Navarre, sovereign lord of Béarn and Comte of Foix and Bigorre, married Marguerite of Angoulême, the sister of the French King François I. The celebrated "Marguerite of Marguerites" *(qv)* transformed the castle in accordance with Renaissance taste, surrounded it with luxuriant gardens and used them as background for pageants and plays which she composed herself, and turned the castle into the foremost intellectual centre of the time.

Henri IV.

Birth of Henri IV – Henri and Marguerite's daughter **Jeanne d'Albret** married a descendant of St Louis, and her son, Henry of Navarre, later became Henri IV of France as a consequence *(see Béarn, qv)*.

Jeanne returned from campaigning in Picardy to Pau for the birth of her son : she arrived on 3 December 1553 and was confined ten days later. As Jeanne's father had advised, she sang songs in the Béarnaise tongue during labour so that the child "might neither cross nor tearful be". According to custom, directly Henri was born Grandfather d'Albret rubbed his lips with a clove of garlic and then moistened them with the local Jurançon wine, before laying the baby in the turtle-shell that was to be his cradle.

Beyond the Wars of Religion – Both the fiercely-Calvinist Jeanne and her son Henri were heavily involved in the Wars of Religion, which set Catholics and Protestants in France against each other for 36 bloody years (1562-98), and Pau changed hands several times during this turbulent period. It was not until Louis XIII annexed Béarn to the French Crown in 1620 that stability returned.

Louis XIII formally reinstated Catholicism as the "official" religion in Pau (Jeanne and Henri had persecuted Catholics mercilessly), and numerous monasteries and convents were established to strengthen the Catholic position. Louis was however

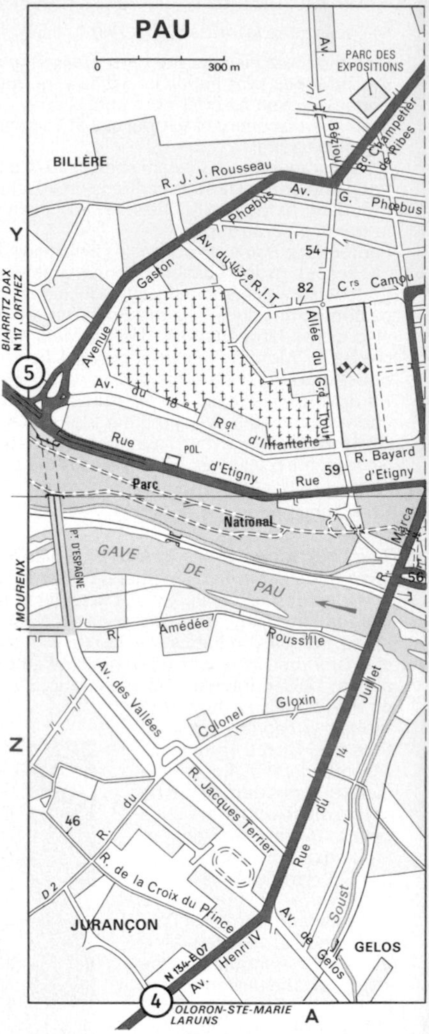

obliged to pander to the separatist spirit of the Béarn province by the grant of special concessions, privileges and local liberties : the Parliament of Navarre was created and sat at Pau. A university was founded.
From this time on it was the *Basoche* who held the ascendancy here (the word embraces the whole machinery of the law : judges, lawyers, notaries, clerks, bailiffs etc), which earned Pau the nickname of "the Quill-pushers' capital". Until the revolution, however, Pau remained a small town.

An English Discovery – As early as the "July Monarchy" of 1830 there were English residents in Pau, and they gradually grew in numbers to form a colony. Some of these expatriates were retired officers who had fought with Louis XVIII on his victorious return from Britain in 1814. It was however a Scot, Doctor Alexander Taylor (1802-79), who brought the town fame and fortune : in 1842 he published his theory – which was rapidly translated into most European languages – that Pau could serve as a winter resort providing cures for various ills, and many visitors came to test his claim; many did indeed find a stay here beneficial.
The local enthusiasm for sports dates from the same period : the colony introduced the steeplechase in 1841 (the racetrack at Pont-Long is, along with the Grand National course at Aintree in England, one of the most important in Europe). Fox-hunting followed a year later and, in 1856, the first golf links on the continent were inaugurated. The year 1889, when Queen Victoria instead chose Biarritz for a one-month visit, saw the start of Pau's decline as an international winter resort.

SIGHTS

★★★ **Boulevard des Pyrénées** (BCZ) – On the initiative of Napoleon I the southern leg of Place Royale, just behind the castle and the statue of Henri IV, was extended as far as **Parc Beaumont** and the municipal casino. The resulting promenade, which forms a splendid terrace overlooking the valley and the torrent, was named Boulevard des Pyrénées – and indeed the **view**★★★ from it of the mountains is spectacular. The panorama extends, beyond the vine-covered slopes of the Gelos and Jurançon foothills, from Pic du Midi de Bigorre to Pic d'Anie, with Pic du Midi d'Ossau standing out especially clearly. In fine weather, particularly in the early morning and evening, the sight can be breathtaking.
The park surrounding the casino has trees of many species and a small lake.

★★ **Château** (BZ) – The castle, built by Gaston Fébus in the 14C on a spur overlooking the river, has lost its military aspect despite the square, brick keep – in typical Sicard de Lordat style *(qv)* – which still towers over it. Transformed into a Renaissance palace by Marguerite of Angoulême, the building gained a state staircase and new façades overlooking an inner courtyard. The castle's present 19C aspect dates from the time of Louis-Philippe and Napoleon III, when the exterior was faced with neo-Gothic cladding. The main gateway, the Louis-Philippe tower, the chapel in the projecting part of the keep and the extensive interior renovations are all from the same period. Today Pau Château is the only royal palace modified by one or the other of these two sovereigns which remains unaltered.

Interior ⓥ – Temporary exhibitions relating to Henri IV and his entourage are displayed on the first floor.
The highlight of the **Royal Apartments** (huge rooms sumptuously redecorated in the 19C) is the superb collection of Gobelins and Flemish **tapestries**★★★ removed from the royal storehouse during the reign of Louis-Philippe.
The tour starts in the elegant 16C kitchen, in which a scale-model of the whole castle can be seen. The "hundred-place dining hall" – with a table large enough to accommodate that number of revellers – is illuminated by neo-Gothic chandeliers which

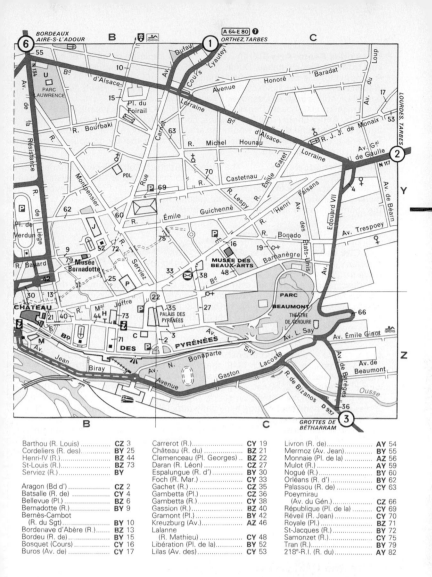

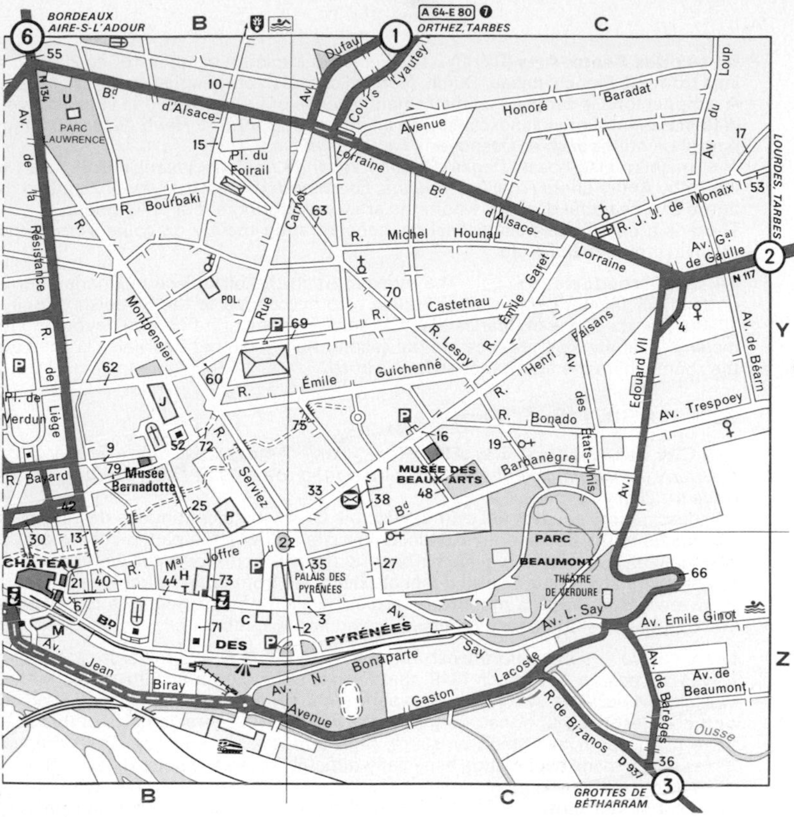

Barthou (R. Louis) .... **CZ** 3	Carrerot (R.) .... **CY** 19	Livron (R. de) .... **AY** 54
Cordeliers (R. des) .... **BY** 25	Château (R. du) .... **BZ** 21	Mermoz (Av. Jean) .... **BY** 55
Henri-IV (R.) .... **BZ** 44	Clemenceau (Pl. Georges) .. **BZ** 22	Monnaie (Pl. de la) .... **AZ** 56
St-Louis (R.) .... **BZ** 73	Daran (R. Léon) .... **CZ** 27	Mulot (R.) .... **AY** 59
Serviez (R.) .... **BY**	Espalungue (R. d') .... **BY** 30	Nogué (R.) .... **BY** 60
	Foch (R. Mar.) .... **CY** 33	Orléans (R. d') .... **BY** 62
Aragon (Bd d') .... **CZ** 2	Gachet (R.) .... **CZ** 35	Palassou (R. de) .... **CY** 63
Batsalle (R. de) .... **CY** 4	Gambetta (Pl.) .... **CZ** 36	Poeymirau (Av. du Gén.) .... **CZ** 66
Bellevue (Pl.) .... **BZ** 6	Gambetta (R.) .... **CY** 38	République (Pl. de la) .... **CY** 69
Bernadotte (R.) .... **BY** 9	Gassion (R.) .... **BZ** 40	Réveil (R. Jean) .... **CY** 70
Bernès-Cambot (R. du Sgt) .... **BY** 10	Gramont (Pl.) .... **BY** 42	Royale (Pl.) .... **BZ** 71
Bordenave d'Abère (R.) .... **BZ** 13	Kreuzburg (Av.) .... **AZ** 46	St-Jacques (R.) .... **BY** 72
Bordeu (R. de) .... **BY** 15	Lalanne (R. Mathieu) .... **CY** 48	Samonzet (R.) .... **CY** 75
Bosquet (Cours) .... **CY** 16	Libération (Pl. de la) .... **BY** 52	Tran (R.) .... **BY** 79
Buros (Av. de) .... **CY** 17	Lilas (Av. des) .... **CY** 53	218e-R.I. (R. du) .... **AY** 82

hang from exposed joists. Splendid 18C Gobelins tapestries representing *The Hunts of Maximilian,* and part of the series of 17C tapestries showing the labours of the months – known, after its creator, as the "Lucas Months Tapestries" – hang on the walls. The Renaissance-style furniture was made by Jeanselme in the 19C. The large and lavish first-floor reception hall, with its coffered, Italianate ceiling, contains the remainder of the Lucas tapestries.

In the royal bedroom stands an unusual, monumental bed fashioned in the Louis XIII style; the chairs are 17C Anglo-Dutch. The turtle-shell which served as a cradle for Henri IV can be seen in the room in which the future king was born. St John's Hall derives its name from the rare 16C tapestry depicting the life of John the Baptist; the room also contains a *Trictrac* set (a dice game not dissimilar to backgammon) made from walnut inlaid with ivory and mother-of-pearl and incorporating Henri IV's royal monogram.

A series of mid-17C tapestries depicting *The Story of Psyche,* from the studio of Raphael de la Planche, ends the tour of the apartments.

Musée béarnais ⊙ – *Third floor, south wing.* The museum offers an insight into the traditions, customs and folk-arts of the former province of Béarn.

Important examples of locally-crafted furniture are on view : a 17C-18C oak table incorporating an open-work bread store; a 1768 walnut cupboard fashioned in the Morlaàs style (different motifs carved on the upper and lower parts of the doors); a walnut chest in Lanceolate Gothic style.

Local activities, craftwork and leisure pursuits are also represented : fabrication of the wide Béarnaise beret, production of the rope soles for espadrilles, farm cheeses, a game of ninepins with 14lb walnut bowls and 7lb beechwood skittles, special costumes for funerals and fêtes, examples of the *herrade* (a water-container made from the hollowed-out trunk of a tree)...

Displays of Pyrenean fauna feature bears, vultures, black grouse and butterflies; local architectural styles and building techniques are illustrated in a typical Béarnaise house; a section on local luminaries includes General Bernadotte, Marshal Bosquet, General Bourbaki, Louis Barthou, Francis Jammes and Simin Palay, a writer in the language of the province.

Footbridges link the terraced castle gardens with the shady woods of the **Parc National.**

★ **Musée des Beaux-Arts** (CY) ⊙ – The Fine Arts Museum exhibits 15C to 20C paintings from the French, Italian, Dutch, Flemish, Spanish and English schools.
A regional tone is supplied by the romantic works of Eugène Devéria (1805-65) who died in Pau (mountain landscapes and an interesting *Birth of Henri IV*), and contemporary paintings such as Desnoyer's *Factories at Lacq*.
The museum also boasts Degas' *Cotton Exchange in New Orleans* (1873). The two works by André Lhote *(The Two Friends, Fourteenth of July in Avignon)* contain the figure of a beautiful dark girl whom the artist met during a fête in Avignon.
There is a fine numismatic collection, concentrating mainly on coins from France and Navarre minted in Pau.

Musée Bernadotte (BY) ⊙ – The museum is in the birthplace of Charles Bernadotte (1763-1844), the Marshal of France who succeeded to the Swedish throne in 1818 under the name of Charles XIV. The salons on the first floor are devoted to the display of family magnificence; on the second floor is an old Béarnaise kitchen and the room where the future monarch was born.

EXCURSIONS

"La Cité des Abeilles" **(City of Bees)** ⊙ – *11km – 7 miles west. Leave Pau by D 2 to Mourenx. At Laroin, take the D 502 hairpin road towards St-Faust-de-Bas and continue for 2km –* $1\frac{1}{4}$ *miles.*
This fascinating, educational centre, which is undergoing continuous development, is devoted to the Bee and its existence. Visitors follow a footpath climbing a slope planted with sweet-smelling, nectar-bearing flowers to discover the world of apiculture, ancient and modern : traditional old beehives from different regions of France; a covered apiary from a monastery; a glass-walled observation hive in which the workers can be studied tending their allotted honeycombs.

Lacq – *25km – 15 miles northwest. Leave Pau by (5) on N 117 towards Orthez.*
It was at Lacq, in December 1949, that France's first commercially viable oil-field was discovered. Two years later an experimental drilling operation here pierced one of the largest pockets of natural gas in the world. The characteristics of this seam were great depth, very high pressure, high temperature and combined chemical gases which made exploitation especially difficult. Today the natural gas is pumped from 30 different wells in the area.
The **Pavillon d'information du Groupe Elf-Aquitaine** (Elf-Aquitaine information centre) ⊙, beside the Elf petrol station on the main road, houses a permanent exhibition dedicated to the site, the drilling and processing methods used and the products obtained here.

The Pau Golf Club, founded in 1856 by four Scotsmen, was the first to be built on the continent; it was also the first golf club in the world to admit women members.

★★★ Pic de PIBESTE

Michelin map 85 fold 17 or 234 fold 39 – Local map p 90.

The Pibeste Peak, despite its relatively modest height (alt 1 349m – 4 426ft), offers one of the finest viewing points in the whole of the central Pyrenees.

Access – $4\frac{1}{2}$ *hours Rtn on foot (2 hours 20min uphill), leaving from Ouzous (on D 102 west of N 21 between Lourdes and Argelès). There is a small car park near the church at Ouzous. It is essential to have stout shoes or boots, warm clothing and a supply of food.*
The footpath, identified with yellow markers, rises gently as far as the level of the panorama over Ouzous, near an arboretum in which different species of pine are being developed; the following section, climbing in hairpin bends, is tougher – and steeper. Beyond Col des Portes (alt 1 229m – 4 032ft) the path separates into two branches which join up again further on to arrive at Pibeste after crossing a beechwood. At the upper station of the old cable-way, staircases climb to the television transmitter.
From the summit there is a magnificent **panorama** southwards towards Pic du Midi de Bigorre, Pic de Montaigu, several peaks rising to more than 3 000m – 9 850ft (Monte Perdido, Vignemale, the Balaïtous), the valleys of the Pau and Cauterets torrents, the frontier chain, and the heights overlooking the road to Col d'Aubisque. To the north the view extends towards Lourdes, Pau and the Tarbes plain.

★★ POITIERS

Pop 78 894

Michelin map 68 folds 13, 14 or 233 fold 8.
Map of conurbation in the current Michelin Red Guide France.

The most impressive view of Poitiers is from the Plâteau des Dunes in the St-Saturnin suburb east of the town, below the cliff on the east bank of the River Clain. The town, perched on a promontory isolated between the Clain and the Boivre, offers lovers of art and architecture a rare choice of fine buildings to admire, while the medieval districts in the heart of the city have much of general interest to sightseers : a busy student life centring on the nearby university additionally lends the district a particular animation, especially around the square in front of the town hall.

HISTORICAL NOTES

Dawn of Christianity – The earliest Christians in the region gathered together in the centre of the Roman city here in the 3C and 4C : St John's Baptistery was one of their sanctuaries. Their first important bishop, the gentle **St Hilaire** (St Hilary, died AD 368), was an outspoken champion of orthodoxy; he also taught St Martin *(qv)*, who was his favourite disciple. Arriving uninvited at the Council of Séleucée, Hilaire found that the monks refused to make room for him – "when suddenly, miraculously, the earth itself rose up and assumed the form of a splendid chair, higher than the others, and all those present were lost in wonderment," according to the chronicler of *La Légende Dorée (The Golden Legend)*.
Another renowned name in the history of the Church in Poitou was **St Radegund,** the wife of Clotaire I, who fled to Poitiers in 559 and founded Holy Cross Monastery – where her confidant, St Fortunat, would recite poems he had written in Latin.

A momentous date – Of the three conflicts known as "the **Battles of Poitiers**" *(qv)*, that in which Charles Martel vanquished the army of the invading Arabs in AD 732 and saved Christianity is by far the most famous – and the most important.
The Arabs – Moors, Saracens – having conquered Spain *(see Michelin Green Guide Spain)* flooded into Gaul from the south. Checked for the first time by Eudes, Duke of Aquitaine, they decimated his forces near Bordeaux and continued towards the centre of the country, sacking and pillaging everything on their way. Eudes asked for help from the Merovingian leader Charles Martel; the Arabs, who had just burnt down St Hilary's Church in Poitiers, found themselves confronted by the Frankish troops a few miles north of the town.
Martel's cavalry cut the Moslem army to ribbons, and little by little the invaders began to retreat from Aquitaine. The year 732 remains as an important symbol of Western Christianity's first true victory over the Moslems.

Jean de Berry's Court – The city of Poitiers, having twice fallen under English domination – in the 12C by Henry Plantagenet and Eleanor of Aquitaine, in the 14C after the second Battle of Poitiers in 1356 – was finally restored to the French crown after General Bertrand du Guesclin (*c*1320-80) had chased the English from the region. The royal representative was the brother of Charles V : Jean, Comte de Poitou and holder of the Berry and Auvergne dukedoms.
De Berry's rule, which extended from 1369 to 1416, brought fame and prosperity to Poitiers. Jean de Berry was ostentatious and sophisticated, a generous patron of the arts, and never travelled anywhere without his menagerie and a retinue of talented artists : men like the architect Gui de Dammartin, a sculptor named André Beauneveu and, later on, painters of miniatures such as the Limbourg brothers.

Poitiers during the Renaissance – The intellectual reputation of the renowned 4 000-student university drew many thinkers and writers to Poitiers.
Following his patron and protector Geoffroy d'Estissac *(qv)*, **Rabelais** stayed here several times between 1524 and 1527; Calvin was also a visitor. This city of monks and priests (there were 67 churches then) – "A big town and confident, teeming with scholars" as it was described at the time – became for a while France's third most important cultural centre after Paris and Lyon. Certain members of the humanist philosophical and poetic group known as *Les Pléiades* came to rub shoulders with the learned at the university. They included the mathematician Jacques Pelletier of Le Mans (a friend of Ronsard, the leading light of the group), the poet Jean-Antoine de Baïf (1532-89), and Joachim du Bellay (1522-60), another poet who modelled his style on the Hellenistic lyricism of antiquity. De Baïf's work, *Les Amours de Francine (The Loves of Francine)* provides the reader with an insight into the life of literary coteries in Poitiers at that time.

"Les Grands Jours de Poitiers" – This title was the name given to a congress of notables which was held in 1579 with the aim of putting an end to religious differences. The meeting gathered together virtually "everybody who was anybody" in the Poitou region, including Nicolas Rapin *(qv)* and Étienne Pasquier (1529-1615), a famous lawyer. The high society of Poitiers opened its doors wide to such distinguished guests.

Four hundred years of sleep – Despite the decisions taken during that 16C congress, Poitiers was not spared by the Wars of Religion. Destruction, misery, famine were visited upon the town, which in addition twice suffered the rigours of a siege. From then on life in Poitiers went into decline : throughout the whole of the 17C and 18C everything stood still, stagnated or regressed; even the university, despite the fame of some of its students – Descartes for instance – shared the same fate. Despite the strenuous efforts of the Intendant **Comte de Blossac,** this "slumber" persisted until after the Second World War.
Since then the influence of a younger generation has injected a new dynamism into the town and has enabled it to reclaim its position as capital of the Poitou-Charentes region.

★ CITY CENTRE MONUMENTS *3 hours.*

★★ **Église Notre-Dame-la-Grande** (DY) – The name of this former collegiate church stems from the Church of Ste-Marie-Majeure in Rome. The building, with its perfect lines and the aesthetic balance of its architectural features, stands as a supreme example of Romanesque art in France. The west front, which has blackened over the centuries, is one of the most famous in the country.
The dimensions of the church are : length 57m, width 13m, height 16.6m (respectively 187ft × 43ft × 54ft).

★★★ **West front** – The elegant west front dates from the 12C and typifies the Poitou Romanesque style – even if the architects were influenced by the art of the Saintonge area *(qv)*. It is densely carved and the lively figures are further accentuated, according to the time of day, by the play of light and shade.
In the centre, at ground level, is an arched doorway with four receding lines of coving, flanked by arcades framing twinned arcatures within. Above these three arched elements are low-reliefs of *(read from left to right and from the lower level to upper)* Adam and Eve (**1**); Nebuchadnezzar on his throne (**2**); the four prophets Moses, Jeremiah, Isaiah and Daniel (**3**); the Annunciation (**4**); the Tree of Jesse (**5**); the Visitation (**6**); the Nativity (**7**); the bathing of the Infant Christ (**8**); the Meditation of St Joseph (**9**). The central doorway is surmounted by a large, very tall arched window bay, itself flanked by a double row of blind arcades housing the Apostles (**10**) and (at the extremities of the upper row) two figures said to be St Hilary (**11**) and St Martin (**12**). The coving of the arcades is decorated with fine carvings representing plants and fantastic creatures.

Christ in Majesty (**13**) gazes down from an oval-shaped frame in the great gable above. The figure is surrounded by the symbols of the Evangelists and crowned by a stylized sun and moon, metaphors for eternity in the Romanesque period.
At each side of the west front a cluster of columns supports a pierced lantern with straight or arched cornices and a roof in the shape of a pine-cone, covered with scales.

North Wall – The chapels flanking this side of the church were added in the 15C (against the chancel) and the 16C (along the aisle). Note the unusual silhouette of the square-sectioned 12C belfry with a pierced turret, again topped by a pine-cone roof.

Interior – The interior of the church, which is in the Poitou style but without a transept, was unfortunately whitewashed in 1851. On each side of the barrel-vaulted nave are very high rib-vaulted aisles. The second pillar on the left, on entering the church, bears a carved and painted group (15C-16C) representing the descendants of St Anne, who was known sometimes as "the Saintly Relative".
A 17C copper goblin can be seen in the chancel. Behind the high altar stands a 16C statue of Notre-Dame-des-Clefs (Our Lady of the Keys), installed to replace the original which was destroyed in 1562 : the statue recalls a miracle said to have occurred in 1202, when the keys of the town were spirited away from the traitor who was going to hand them over to the besieging English. The oven vault above the chancel – painted in the 12C with a fresco depicting the Virgin in Majesty and Christ in Glory – is supported by six heavy, round columns arranged in a semicircle.
The original apsidal chapel, on the south side of the ambulatory, was replaced in 1475 by another, now dedicated to St Anne. This was founded by Yvon du Fou, the Seneschal (Steward) of the city, whose armorial bearings can be seen above the fine Flamboyant funerary niche where his tomb was lodged. In its place now is an Italian version of *The Entombment,* in polychrome stone, which dates from the 16C. The work was once in Trinity Abbey in Poitiers.

Palais de Justice (DY J) ⊙ – The Restoration façade of the law courts masks the Great Hall and the original keep of the ancient ducal palace, rare examples of urban civic architecture dating from the Middle Ages. The early 12C keep, known as **Tour Maubergeon,** was transformed into a residence for Jean de Berry in the 14C.
The **Great Hall**★ (47m – 154ft long and 17m – 55ft wide) was reserved for important trials, solemn audiences and sessions of the Provincial Estates. In 1418, four years before he was proclaimed king, the fleeing Charles VII set up his court and parliament here. In March 1429 Joan of Arc was subjected to a gruelling interrogation by an ecclesiastical commission, to emerge after three weeks with an enhanced sense of her sacred mission – and official recognition that the mission was religiously inspired.

Although construction of the vast hall had started under the Plantagenets, it was de Berry who commissioned the architect Dammartin to build the great gable wall with its three monumental chimneys, its balcony and Flamboyant windows. Up above, four fine statues represent *(left to right)* Jean de Berry, his nephew Charles VI, Isabeau of Bavaria, and Jean's wife Jeanne de Boulogne.
Outside, the three chimney conduits are partially – and very artfully – concealed by the fleurons decorating the upper part of the gables. The best view of this rear elevation of the law courts, with Tour Maubergeon and its statues on the right and the gable wall on the left, is from Rue des Cordeliers. Remains of the original Gallo-Roman defensive wall can be seen in the adjacent square.

Hôtel de l'Échevinage (DY D) – This 15C building with its contemporary chapel was once the town hall. It originally housed first the university's *Grandes Écoles* (seats of higher learning) and then the local magistrature (échevinage).

Église St-Porchaire (DY E) – All that remains of the original 11C church built on this site is the belfry-porch with its four-sided pyramid roof.
Three tiers of arcades and bays stand above the great Roman arch, decorated with Romanesque capitals, which serves as an entrance to the two-aisle church restored in the 16C. The right-hand capital shows Daniel delivered to the den of lions but happily saved by an emissary from God; those on the left portray birds drinking from a chalice and two lions separated by the stem of a plant.
Up in the belfry hangs the great bell of the university, which was cast in 1451. At one time it was used to announce the start of student classes.

★ **Baptistère St-Jean** (DZ) ⌚ – St John's Baptistery, dating from the middle of the 4C, is the oldest example of Christian architecture in France. It is now "buried" to a depth of 4m – 13ft owing to a progressive series of landslips over the centuries and work on embankments carried out in the 18C. The ditches surrounding the site were dug in the middle of the 19C.
Originally the baptistery comprised two rectangular chambers : the baptismal hall and a narthex, preceded by an entrance corridor framed by two changing-rooms.

POITIERS

				DY			DY	
Carnot (R.)	CZ		Abbé-Frémont (Bd)	DY	2	Macé (R. Jean)	CY	50
Cordeliers (R. des)	DY	9	Bouchet (R. Jean)	DZ	7	Marne (R. de la)	DY	55
Gambetta (R.)	DY	19	Coligny (Bd)	DY	18	Mouton (R. du)	DY	63
Grand-Rue	DY	31	Descartes (R.)	DY	23	Oudin (R. H.)	DY	67
Marché (R. du)	DYZ		Gaulle (Pl. Ch.-de)	DY	32	Riffault (R.)	CY	74
		54	Intend.-le-Nain (R.)	DY	40	Solférino (Bd)	CZ	89
			Jean-de-Berry (Pl.)	DY	47	Tison (Bd de)	CY	92
			Jeanne-d'Arc (Bd)		48	Verdun (Bd de)		94

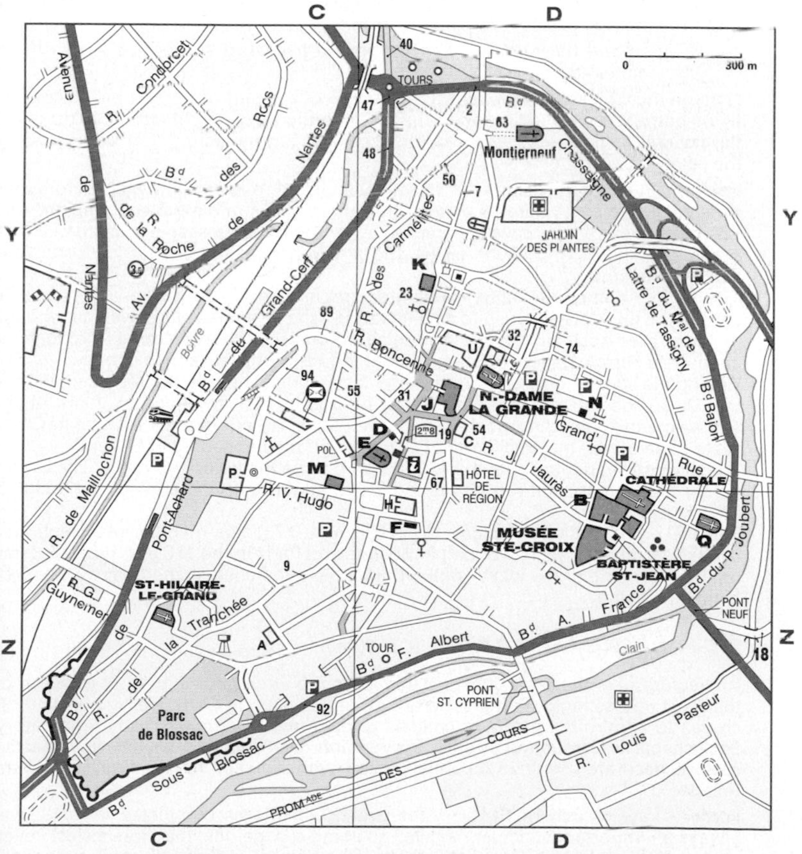

B	Devenir-Espace Pierre Mendès-France	F	Hôtel Jean-Beaucé	M	Musée de Chièvres
D	Hôtel de l'Échevinage	J	Palais de Justice	N	Hôtel de Rochefort
E	Église St-Porchaire	K	Hôtel Fumé	Q	Église Ste-Radegonde

The rectangular baptismal hall still exists, together with a 6C-7C quadrangular apse and two apsidal chapels, originally square but changed to a semicircular shape in the middle of the 19C. The former narthex, however, which was restored in the 10C, is now polygonal. Panels of Romanesque brickwork brace the window embrasures, which are partly blocked up and pierced with oculi. Beneath the gables are strange pilasters with capitals carved in low-relief.

Interior – Inside, the baptistery is notable for the intricately carved capitals of its marble columns, covered with beading, strapwork and foliage in the antique manner; for the colonnettes supporting the arcades; for the three tall arcades, pierced in the wall set back from the entrance doorway, which link the narthex and the baptismal chamber. The apse and its two chapels are surmounted by oven vaults.
In the centre of the baptismal chamber is the octagonal pool which was used for baptism by total immersion : the novice convert, whose clothes would have been removed in one of the changing rooms, was first lowered into the water to receive the ritual unctions from the bishop, then dressed in a white tunic and solemnly received in the cathedral. In the 7C use of the pool was superseded by baptism by affusion (holy water poured over the head) following the installation of a cistern supplying the font; until the 12C this was the only place in Poitiers where baptisms could be consecrated.
Romanesque **frescoes** – partly over-painted in the 13C and 14C – adorn the baptistery walls : an *Ascension* above the apse; *Christ in Majesty* decorating its oven vault; four horsemen, including the Emperor Constantine, on one of the walls in the rectangular chamber; peacocks, the symbol of immortality, on the left-hand wall.
The building now houses an interesting lapidary museum. The exhibits include a fine collection of Merovingian sarcophagi discovered in Poitiers and the surrounding area, inscribed pillars, an ancient *dimière* (a measure used when collecting tithes) carved in stone, and the moulds which were used to produce the decorations adorning the outer walls of the baptistery itself.

★ **Cathédrale St-Pierre** (**DYZ**) – St Peter's Cathedral was begun at the end of the 12C and almost completed by the end of the 14C – the date of its consecration; it is most striking for its huge dimensions.

Exterior – The wide west front, with its rose window and three 13C doorways, is flanked by two asymmetric towers. That on the left (northern) side, supported by a series of engaged colonnettes, retains an octagonal storey topped by a balustrade.
The tympana of the doorways are carved with fascinating sculptures, among them the Crowning of the Virgin (left); the dead hurrying from their graves and the heavenly elect separated from the damned delivered to Leviathan (centre); the teaching of St Thomas, patron of stone-carvers – the miraculous building of a "mystical palace" for the King of India (right).

Walk around the northern flank of the cathedral as far as Rue Arthur-de-la-Mauvinière.

Note on the way around the massive strength of the buttresses and the absence of flying buttresses. At the far end of the building the dizzy height (49m – 161ft) of the flat **east end** can be appreciated – especially as this is emphasized by a falling away of the land.

Interior – On entering, visitors are struck by the sheer power of the architecture : the wide shell of the cathedral is divided into three aisles of almost equal height, and the impression of a perspective soaring away towards the east is accentuated by a progressive narrowing of the aisles and a lowering of the central vault from the chancel onwards.
Twenty-four domed rib vaults – a Plantagenet influence – crown the eight spans of each of the three aisles. Despite its flat exterior, the east end is hollowed out enough to form three apsidal chapels. A cornice embellished with historiated modillions supports a narrow gallery running around the walls above a series of blind arcades.
Among the stained-glass windows at the far east end is a late 12C representation of the Crucifixion showing a radiant Christ flanked by the Virgin and St John. Above and below this are : the Apostles, with their faces raised towards a Christ in Glory, set in a mandorla; the crucifixion of St Peter and the beheading of St Paul.
The **choir stalls★**, dating from the 13C, are said to be the oldest in France. The carved corner-pieces represent the Virgin and Child, angels carrying crowns, the architect at work etc.
The 18C organ, built by François-Henri Clicquot (1732-90), member of a celebrated dynasty of organ-makers working in Rheims and Paris in the 17C and 18C, is located on the inner side of the west front, within a beautiful shell-shaped loft with basket-handled arching.

★★ ST-HILAIRE-LE-GRAND (**CZ**) *30min.*

Archeological enthusiasts consider this ancient church dedicated to St Hilary to be the most interesting in Poitiers. Before going inside, it is worth walking around the church to admire the group of chapels grafted onto the transept and ambulatory. Each chapel is surrounded by columns with intricately worked capitals, and boasts a cornice decorated with modillions carved with horses' heads, small monsters, foliage...

Interior – The church of St-Hilary-the-Great, which was completed in 1049, was always an important sanctuary as well as being a large one; the three aisles, covered with timber ceilings, frequently sheltered members of the earliest pilgrimages to Santiago de Compostela. Unfortunately in the 12C the church was ravaged by fire and the gutted timbers were replaced by stone vaults; however, as the distance it was possible to span in stone was naturally less than it was with wooden beams, the architects charged with the restoration were obliged to narrow the aisles. They

solved the problem by dividing each of the original side aisles longitudinally in two, adding central columns to support the ribbed vaulting above; at the same time two rows of columns were added to the nave, linked ingeniously to the original walls and bearing a whole series of small domes. The final arrangement – the church as it is today – has a central nave bordered by three aisles on either side – the only seven-aisle church in Europe.
Two of the northern aisles incorporate the 11C belfry, the base of which forms an impressive room with massive columns and remarkable archaic capitals. The vaulting is reinforced with huge string courses.
It is from the transept that the vision and originality of the architecture can best be appreciated. Both transept and **chancel** are raised some way above the level of the aisles. The floor at the front of the chancel is covered with a fine mosaic. The pillars framing it have interesting capitals, notably, on the north side, that representing the burial of St Hilary himself (**1**). The ancient frescoes (**2**) on the four pillars preceding the transept represent bishops of Poitiers. In the chapels, more frescoes illustrate episodes in the lives of St Quentin and St Martin.
The chancel is separated from the ambulatory by a semicircle of eight columns, linked at the base by fine 12C wrought-iron grilles. In the ambulatory, on the main axis of the church, is an unusual statuary group of the Holy Trinity (**3**) : God the Father presenting his Son on the Cross, above which stands the dove of the Holy Spirit.
In the **crypt** is a casket (19C) containing the relics of St Hilary.

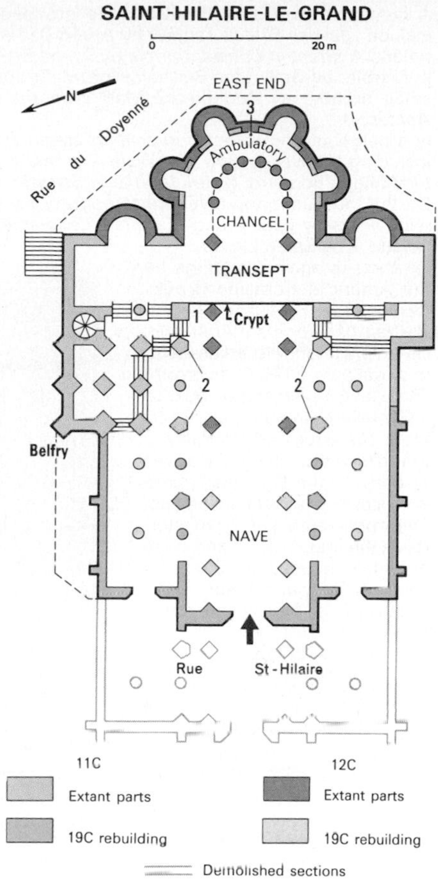

ADDITIONAL SIGHTS

★★ **Musée Ste-Croix** (DZ) ⊙ – The museum is housed in a modern building standing on the site of the former Holy Cross Abbey (Abbaye Ste-Croix).

Folk arts, traditions and customs – *A staircase leads down to this department.* Exhibits evoke rural life in the Poitou region of bygone days, traditional customs and beliefs, and examples of ancient trades.

Archeology – *Basement : access down a staircase at the far end of the first hall.* The collections here concentrate on the Poitou of pre-history to medieval times. The chronology of the Paleolithic era is set out, with displays of flint implements, tools and other items discovered during digs (fragments of a bronze roasting spit from the 7C BC, an ingot of pure copper, objects buried *c*700 BC). A number of Gallo-Roman finds are presented against a backdrop of the remains of antique walls : inscriptions, fragments of columns, low-reliefs and statues, among them the head of a man and a famous Minerva in white marble (1C AD) unearthed in Poitiers. Fine funerary stones from Civaux, including *Man as a Child,* are also on show.
Take the staircase at the end of the gallery. Here a medieval low-relief, *The Stonecutter,* found near St-Hilaire-le-Grand, can be seen. At the top of the stairs is a Renaissance medallion embossed with the features of Christ.

Painting galleries – The exhibits are displayed in a number of rooms on several different levels linked by stairways or steps. The fine collection consists of paintings from the 18C to the present day, and a few sculptures.
The first gallery contains works from several local artists working in the **late 18C**, many depicting mythological episodes, and a series by Géricault entitled *Masculine Anatomy.* In the centre of the gallery is a 17C funerary statue of Claude de l'Aubespine by Nicolas Guillain, a recumbent plaster effigy by James Pradier (*c*1845), a Jean Escoula marble symbolizing *Sleep* (1885) and, beyond, a reconstruction of the studio of the sculptor Jean-René Carrière (1888-1982).
The next gallery *(down several steps)* is devoted to the 19C : Alfred de Curzon, a local painter *(The Convent Garden),* Octave Penguilly-l'Haridan *(The Parade of Pierrot),* Charles Brun *(Portrait of Germaine Pichot),* and Léopold Burthe *(Ophelia).* In the middle of the gallery is an Auguste Ottin marble and a Carrier-Belleuse terracotta.

A number of works by **Orientalists** are grouped together on an upper level. They include : *Jewish Fête in Tangier* by Alfred Dehodencq, *Fantasia* by Eugène Fromentin and *A Street in Constantinople* by André Brouillet. Nearby is a bust of Louis XIII in marble, by Guillaume Berthelot; beside it are three 19C Barye bronzes, and two small bronzes by Rodin *(The Man With the Broken Nose* and *The Despairing Adolescent).*

In a neighbouring gallery *(up several steps)* are three works by Camille Claudel – including the well-known *The Waltz* – an early Mondrian landscape, and paintings by Vuillard, Bonnard, Sisley *(A Village Street)* and others.

On the museum's top level are temporary exhibitions of contemporary art, along with works by Lépine and Marquet *(Les Sables-d'Olonne).* The bust of the writer Colette is by Sarah Lipska.

Downstairs again, paintings by the American Romaine Brooks include *The Poet in Exile* and *Portrait of Gabriele d'Annunzio.* On a small landing adjacent to this gallery, a Maillot bronze *(Prairie Nymphs)* stands next to a Gustave Moreau tapestry cartoon, *The Siren and the Poet.*

In a basement corridor a series of works by the 17C Dutch painter Nicolas Maes is displayed. The works represent the mysteries in the life of Christ and were originally housed in Ste-Croix Abbey (other paintings from the Dutch school have been transferred to the Musée de Chièvres, *see below*).

The Siren and the Poet by Gustave Moreau.

★ **Église Ste-Radegonde** (DZ Q) – This former collegiate church was founded around AD 552 by Radegund with the idea that it would eventually become the last resting-place of her nuns from Holy Cross Abbey. The church is characterized by a Romanesque apse and a belfry-porch which stand at opposite ends of a nave in the style known as Angevin Gothic. The belfry-porch, majestic and massive in its proportions, square in plan and then octagonal, was enhanced in the 15C with a Flamboyant portal in the niches of which today stand modern statues of the patron saints of Poitiers. At the base of the tower there remains a chamber, lined with stone benches, where ecclesiastical justice used to be dispensed.

A small garden east of the church offers an agreeable view of the **east end** and the pleasing lines of the church as a whole.

⏲ ►► Hôtel Fumé (**DY K**) – 16C university building; Église de Montierneuf (**DY**) – 11C church altered in the Gothic and Classical periods; Musée de Chièvres (**CY M**) – Fine 16C-18C furniture, also tapestries, ceramics, and enamels from Limoges; Hôtel Jean-Beaucé (**DZ F**) – Handsome Renaissance building; Hôtel de Rochefort (**DY N**) – Courtyard façade of note; Parc de Blossac (**CZ**) – Plunging view over the Clain Valley; Devenir-Espace Pierre Mendès-France (**DZ B**) – Modern science and technology exhibition centre and planetarium; Faubourg St-Saturnin (east of the city centre).

EXCURSIONS

★★ **Le Futuroscope** – *At Jaunay-Clan : 5 miles north via (1) – See Le Futuroscope.*

★ **Abbaye de Nouaillé-Maupertuis** – *11km – $6\frac{1}{2}$ miles southeast via D 12^C – See Nouaillé-Maupertuis.*

In the Middle Ages dovecotes ("pigeonniers") were built to attract pigeons and doves for two reasons: not only did the birds provide meat but their droppings were also highly-prized as a fertiliser – though it was so rich in nitrates that it could be used only in the rainy season when it would be naturally diluted.

The length of time given in this guide

- ***for touring allows time to enjoy the views and the scenery***
- ***for sightseeing is the average time required for a visit.***

POUZAUGES
Pop 5 473

Michelin map 67 fold 16 or 232 fold 42 – Local map p 131 – Facilities.

Pouzauges stands at the heart of the hills of the Vendée *(qv)*, on the slope of a hill crowned by the Bois de la Folie and overlooking the expanse of the *bocage (qv)*.

SIGHTS

Château – This medieval fortress comprises walls incorporating ten ruined towers, and a square keep, flanked by turrets, which protected the entrance. A cross recalls the 32 Vendée Royalists who were shot here during the Revolution.

Église St-Jacques – St James' Church was built of granite in the Vendée style with a square tower over the crossing; it has a short nave and a 12C transept which is in a transitional Romanesque-Gothic style. The large, Flamboyant Gothic chancel with 3 bays is 15C.

Pouzauges-le-Vieux – *1.5km – 1 mile southwest.* The granite **church** dates from the Romanesque period, apart from the chancel which was remodelled in the 14C, and stands in an attractive landscape dotted with cypresses. The pure lines of its architecture – its strong, simple doorway, extended transept and short, square tower over the crossing – became a model for many other churches in the region. Beneath the broken-barrel vaulting of the interior are a floor paved with funerary stones and walls painted with 13C **murals** : these portray the Meeting of St Anne and St Joachim at the Golden Gate, the Presentation of the Virgin in the Temple, and a Conversation between the Virgin and an angel.

★★ **Puy Crapaud** – *2.5km – 1½ miles southeast.* This is one of the highest points of the chain (alt 270m – 885ft) and is crowned by the ruins of a windmill (now a restaurant). At the top of the mill (ask at the bar) a viewing table identifies the features of the vast **panorama** which stretches over the Vendée as far as the ocean.

Bois de la Folie – *1km – ½ mile by D 752 northwest and a small road to the right.* On the right, before reaching the wood, appear the two windmills of **Terrier-Marteau**★ ⓥ : the two white, shingle-roofed mills were built in the 19C and have since been restored. The *guivre* or tail allows the revolving roofs, to which the arms and sails of the mill are attached, to be positioned into the wind. One of the mills still grinds grain, the other contains a video *(in French)* on the Vendée, various stuffed animals and assorted agricultural tools. There is a fine **view**★ westwards over the surrounding landscape.
The wood itself is made up of oak, pine and beech trees and covers an outcrop of granitic rock. During Roman times it was probably considered to be a *"lucus"* (sacred wood) having previously been a meeting place for druids who collected mistletoe and held sacrificial rites. The thick cluster of trees has been nicknamed the Pouzauges Bouquet or the Vendée Lighthouse and offers a fine **view**★ over the *bocage.*

EXCURSIONS

Round trip to the east – *31km – 18 miles. Follow D 960BIS east to St-Mesmin.*
A short distance beyond St-Mesmin, on the right, stand the picturesquely-sited medieval ruins of the **Château de St-Mesmin.** The machicolations of the keep still remain.

La Pommeraie-sur-Sèvre – Inside the Gothic church, with its elegant Plantagenet vaulting, 15C frescoes show the Seven Deadly Sins. A Roman bridge crosses the Sèvre.

Round trip to the west – *33km – 20 miles. Take D 960BIS west.*

La Boupère – The village has an unusual **church** which dates from the 13C but was fortified in the 15C. The west front is flanked by buttresses pierced by loopholes and crowned by two watchtowers which are linked by a machicolated watch-path. The sides are protected by bartizans.

Prieuré de Chassay-Grammont ⓥ – This monastery, founded around 1196 by Richard the Lionheart, is currently undergoing restoration and is a good example of the architecture of the Grammont Order, members of which were hermits who lived as a community in a secluded spot. They espoused poverty and their monasteries or cells are correspondingly austere.
Here all the monastic buildings, including the church, are grouped in a quadrangle around what was the cloisters. Light in the simple church entered only through the three windows of the apse.
On the ground floor, the chapter-house has Romanesque Angevin vaulting and the large refectory has fine 13C Gothic Angevin vaulting. The monks' dorter is upstairs.

Le Bois-Tiffrais – This château houses the **Musée de la France Protestante de l'Ouest** ⓥ, which traces the history of Protestantism in western France and especially in the Poitou region through documents, display panels and various objects : Bibles, pulpits which could be dismantled in a hurry, clandestine badges identifying followers...

Mussels should be firmly closed before cooking and open up naturally during the process; any that remain closed should be discarded. Oysters may be checked for freshness by lightly touching their edges or moistening them with lemon juice : they should contract. Fresh oysters are hard to open; any not freshly opened should be rejected.

★ Le PUY DU FOU

Michelin map 67 fold 15 or 232 fold 42 – 2.5km – $1\frac{1}{2}$ miles northwest of Les Épesses.

On summer evenings the château sparkles under the lights of its famous *Son et Lumière* show in which a cast of hundreds stages an open-air historical pageant; by day the museum here evokes the entire past of the Vendée region, while various attractions lure visitors into the 12ha – 30 acres of grounds.
The name Puy du Fou is derived from the Latin : Puy (from *podium*) means an eminence, a knoll; Fou (from *fagus*) designates a beech tree. Thus "A hill where a beech tree grows" or, less lyrically, "Beechmount".

Château ⊙ – It is likely that the original castle, built in the 15C and 16C, was never completed; it was in any case partly destroyed by fire during the Wars of the Vendée *(qv)*. There remains nevertheless a fine late Renaissance pavilion at the far end of the courtyard, preceded by a peristyle with engaged Ionic columns. This now serves as the entrance to the museum. The left wing of the château is built over a long gallery.

★★★ **Cinéscénie** ⊙ – The terrace below the rear façade of the château, together with the ornamental lake below it, makes an agreeable background for the spectacular *"Cinéscénie"* in which "Jacques Maupillier, peasant of the Vendée" directs a company of 700 actors and 50 horsemen in a dazzling show. The history of the Vendée is re-lived with the help of an impressive array of special effects, fountains, fireworks, laser and other lighting displays... *(See Calendar of Events, qv)*

★ **Écomusée de la Vendée** ⊙ – In the entrance to the museum there is a fine staircase with straight flights of steps, and a coffered ceiling.
As a preliminary tour of the museum, the chapel and the old guardroom offer interesting views of the château; a film *(in French)* describes life in the Vendée today.
The first section of the museum proper is concerned with the region's past, from its geological formation to the end of the *Ancien Régime :* each main period is evoked thematically, with complementary displays of contemporary objects and reconstructions (a Megalithic tomb, a Gallo-Roman kitchen, a Romanesque façade).
The second (post-Revolution) section begins with an examination of the Wars of the Vendée, an audio-visual montage tracing the military operations from 1793 to 1796. Following this, the emergence of a local "folk memory" based on local fables, memoirs and accounts written in the 18C and early 19C – a corpus of material structured and given official approval under the Restoration – is explained; it found expression in an abundant iconography (portraits of Vendée heroes), a recognizable literary current and indeed royal rewards.
By the end of the 19C, however, a Republican vision opposed to this view had appeared. Revolutionary heroes such as Bara and Hoche were revered, while "official" art imposed a "Breton" image on the combatants in the west.
Finally the museum includes a review of the industrial heritage of the Vendée. One of the most interesting exhibits is an early 20C steam engine designed by Piguet which drives a carding machine.

★ **Le Grand Parcours** ⊙ – The entire Puy du Fou estate extends over 30ha – 74 acres. Numerous paths surrounding the château, skirting lakes or crossing dense woods of chestnut trees offer pleasant walks with a choice of interesting diversions *(a miniature train serves all the attractions mentioned below)*.
Within the setting of a reconstructed **18C village,** complete with windmill and working church bells, the work of artisans in period costume can be admired; from time to time musicians playing traditional instruments will perform a serenade; jugglers vie for the applause of bystanders with feats of skill and virtuosity. In the neighbouring fields, animals from the village farm graze – among them the famous *baudets (qv)*.
The ruins of a 13C **castle** provide the background for a display of falconry – free-flying trained birds. An aviary nearby contains birds of prey.
Additionally, it is also possible to listen to a brass quintet playing baroque music, to control the play of fountains from a distance, to slip inside a tent to watch a 3-D film *(in French)* on the Vendée, or to thrill to the spectacle of a knightly joust.

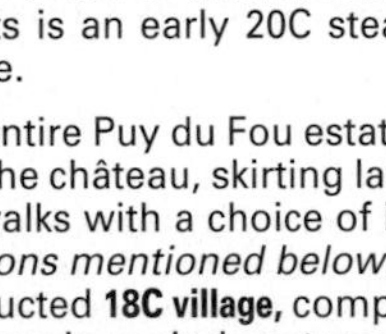

To plan a special itinerary :

- ***consult the Map of Touring Programmes which indicates the recommended routes, the tourist regions, the principal towns and main sights.***
- ***read the descriptions in the Sights section which include Excursions from the main tourist centres.***

Michelin Maps nos 67, 68, 71, 72, 75, 78, 79, 82, 85, 232, 233, 234 and 235 indicate scenic routes, interesting sights, viewpoints, rivers, forests...

★ Île de RÉ

Michelin map 71 fold 12 or 233 folds 2, 13 – Facilities.

The Isle of Ré points a long finger seawards just off the port of La Rochelle, cutting in two the gulf between the Isle of Oléron and the Vendée coast. The island is bordered to the north by the Breton Straits (Pertuis Breton) and to the south by the Straits of Antioche.
This unspoilt island, its surface broken only by vineyards and an occasional pinewood, has, unsurprisingly, become a favourite retreat for summer holiday-makers in search of sunshine, sea air and wide open spaces. Although a bridge now links it to the mainland it retains most of its insular character and its famous salt-marshes. Numerous signposted cycle-tracks allow visitors to crisscross the island in peace and quiet.

The viaduct ⊙ – This gracefully-curving toll bridge, opened in 1988, is one of the engineering marvels of Europe, carrying the road 2 960m – nearly 2 miles across the narrows separating the Île de Ré from the suburbs of La Rochelle. The viaduct reaches a maximum height of 32m – 105ft above the level of the highest tides.

Chesnat/SIPA PRESS

The viaduct to the Île de Ré.

HISTORICAL AND GEOGRAPHICAL NOTES

Anglo-French rivalry – From the Hundred Years War to the fall of Napoleon, the Île de Ré was closely involved in the conflict between the English and the French, during which the "red-coats" (the English) made many attempts to storm its shores : it would have been an invaluable base so close to mainland France. Nor was the isle spared during the Wars of Religion, which brought misery and deprivation to the inhabitants.
In 1625 the brave Marquis de **Toiras** (1585-1636), a deeply spiritual and fiercely warlike man, was governor of the island, which he had wrested from the Protestants and then reinforced by building the St-Martin citadel and the fort of La Prée. At that time, the whole island was under arms. An English fleet commanded by the Duke of Buckingham anchored off Les Sablanceaux and columns of infantry poured ashore to lay siege to the town of St-Martin, defended by 1 400 French, and the fort of La Prée. In no time there was an acute shortage of provisions. There were rations for less than a single day left when the miracle occurred : a squadron of 30 ships from the French fleet appeared in the Breton Straits and, with a favourable wind, managed to penetrate the harbour at St-Martin.
The siege, nevertheless, continued. On 6 November 1625, 6 000 Englishmen, encouraged by a mass singing of psalms, hurled themselves at the town walls. After a bloody hand-to-hand battle they were however repulsed.
It was then that Louis XIII, arriving at La Rochelle, despatched a contingent of reinforcements to the island, under the leadership of Marshal de Schomberg. The English, caught between two fires, were attacked at Pont de Feneau, near Loix, and massacred, leaving 2 000 dead on the field together with 6 cannons and 46 flags. Toiras was created Marshal of France in 1630.

The land and its inhabitants – L'Île de Ré, sometimes known as "L'Île Blanche" (The White Isle), extends in a northwesterly direction for almost 30km – 18½ miles. It largely comprises a series of Jurassic limestone outliers forming islets – principally Loix, Ars and Ré proper – which have become linked together.
In the north the deeply indented bay of Fier d'Ars, and the marshes surrounding it, constitute the **Réserve Naturelle de Lilleau des Niges** ⊙, the home of thousands of different species of birds including grey curlews, widgeon, teal, silver plovers and geese.
In the south a line of sand dunes has formed on a rocky plateau which stretches far away beneath the sea; the jagged cliffs eaten away by the encroaching tides have given rise to the name of this area : La Côte Sauvage (The Wild Coast).
The southeastern part of the Île de Ré, the widest and most fertile, is broken up into tiny smallholdings producing early fruit and vegetables, asparagus and above all vines (the wine, red, white and rosé, is full-favoured, with a hint of algae in the aftertaste). The fortified apéritif-wine made here on the island is as good as the better-known Pineau des Charentes *(qv)*.
To the north and west the vines share the land with pinewoods, as far as La Couarde. Beyond that, Ars-en-Ré is salt-marsh country – although the marshes are fast disappearing *(see salt-marshes, qv)*.
The people of Ré – the Rétais – are landlubbers rather than seafaring folk. Of the riches of the ocean they deal only in *"sart"* (seaweed and other wrack), harvested with huge rakes, shellfish and the prawns which teem on the rocky *platin* exposed at low tide. In addition, oyster farming has been introduced to the Fosse de Loix and Fier d'Ars inlets.

In the past the women of the island wore a long, narrow headdress to protect them against the fierceness of the sun; its name, the **quichenotte,** is said to derive from "kiss not", as its function was also, allegedly, to discourage the advances of amorous invading Englishmen. Today this tradition, like many others, has all but vanished – the island donkeys, for instance, which have disappeared entirely, were bedecked with straw hats and picturesque "trousers" in stripes or squares to keep away flies and mosquitos in the salt-marshes. Such things can now be seen only on postcards in the village shops.

The villages are scattered all over the island, their single-storey houses, dazzlingly white, brightened with hollyhocks and delphiniums and scarlet salvia, or a wisteria on a trellis.

Boat trips ⓥ – There are cruises in season, and direct links to the Isle of Aix.

★ ST-MARTIN-DE-RÉ Pop 2 512.

The island capital, formerly an active port and a military stronghold, has turned gracefully into a charming tourist centre. The narrow streets, quiet, spotlessly clean, still bumpy with cobblestones, have largely managed to retain the atmosphere of the *Grand Siècle* (the 17C in France).

★ **Fortifications** – These date back to the early 17C but were entirely re-fashioned by Vauban *(qv)* after the siege of 1625 *(see above)*. Vauban came to inspect the Île de Ré in 1674 with the aim of strengthening the defences of the naval installations created by Colbert at Rochefort in 1666; the fortifications he designed for St-Martin were completed in 1692.

The walled enclosure was pierced by two monumental gateways, Porte Toiras and Porte des Campani, preceded by ravelins (half-moon defences) and with guard-rooms on the inner face.

The citadel, built in 1681, was used as a prison under the *Ancien Régime* (19C) and later became a religious penitentiary.

The citadel is not open to the public but a walk around the bastions on the seaward side reveals pleasing **views** of the Breton Straits and the mainland; note also the interesting watch-turrets and the cannon embrasures. The strongpoint's main entrance takes the form of a majestic classical gateway with a pediment bearing carved military emblems. The citadel has its own small port, between two bastions in front of this gateway.

Beyond the citadel and the tennis courts below it lies a beach of fine sand.

Parc de la Barbette – This park, sheltered by the fortifications, is a pleasant place for a shady stroll, looking down on the sea and the distant southern coast of the Vendée. Holm oaks, acacias, parasol pines and locust trees lend the park an almost Mediterranean air.

The Port – Trade with Canada and the West Indies brought the port of St-Martin great prosperity during the 17C. Pleasure craft and a few fishing boats have now, however, replaced the tall ships sailing from the north in search of salt or wine, and the schooners from the Caribbean laden with spices. Port and harbour between them girdle the old sailors' district, now busy with shops, forming a picturesque islet which is popular with visitors. The quays are paved with the ballast of long-gone merchant ships.

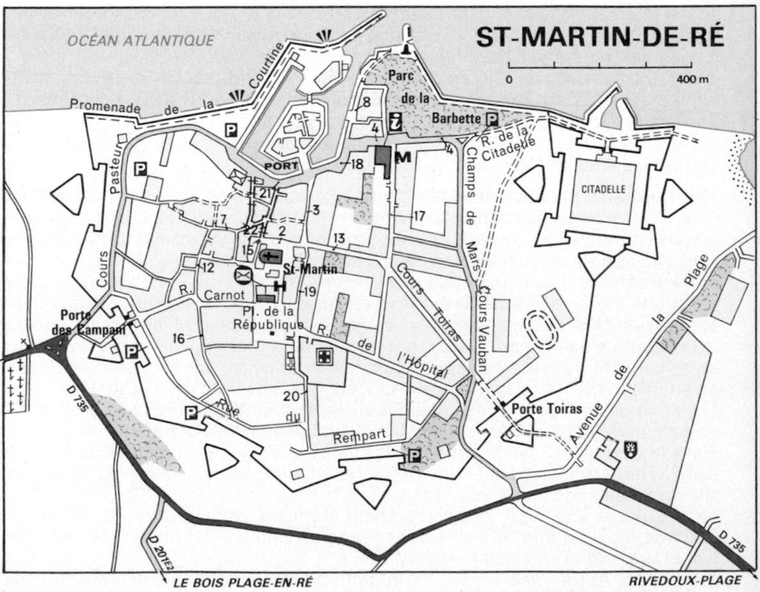

Bailli-des-Écottais (Cours) 2
Baron-de-Chantal (R.) 3
Bouthillier (Av. Victor) 4
Cîteaux (R. de) 7
Clemenceau (Quai Georges) 8
Cohonneau (R. Suzanne) 12
Dechézeaux (R.) 13
France (Pl. A.) 15
France (R. Gaspard) 16
Gabarets (R. des) 17
Job-Foran (Quai) 18
Lapasset (R. du Général) 19
Père-Ignace (R.) 20
Poithevinière (Quai de la) 21
Sully (R. de) 22

Hôtel de Clerjotte (M) – Tall slate roofs crown this fine building constructed in a style midway between Flamboyant Gothic and Renaissance. It was originally the headquarters of an organization owing allegiance to the local ruler, the *Officiers des Seigneurs de Ré,* and was at one time used as the town arsenal.
Today the building houses a museum and the tourist information centre. In the courtyard, bordered with Renaissance galleries, stands a staircase-tower at the foot of which is an elegant Flamboyant doorway.

Musée Ernest-Cognacq ⊙ – The maritime history of St-Martin and the island as a whole is presented through models, ships' figureheads, ancient weapons and tableaux (combat scenes, portraits of mariners, Napoleon's return from the Isle of Elba aboard the brig *Inconstant*...). On the ground floor these seafaring displays are supplemented with a collection of pottery from Delft, La Rochelle and **"Jersey"** *(qv)*, and the reconstruction of a Louis XIII bedroom with furniture of the period.

Église St-Martin – The church dates from the 15C and was nicknamed "the big fort" because of the fortifications (still visible from the transept) which protected it. Ruined by the Anglo-Dutch naval bombardment of 1696, it was restored in the early 18C. A chapel dedicated to sailors contains 18C and 19C votive offerings.

Ancien Hôtel des Cadets de la Marine (H) – This building houses both the town hall and the post office. It was built in the 18C to be used as barracks for a company of naval cadets. At the beginning of the 20C Ernest Cognacq, a merchant who founded the famous La Samaritaine department stores in Paris, made a gift of it to his native town.

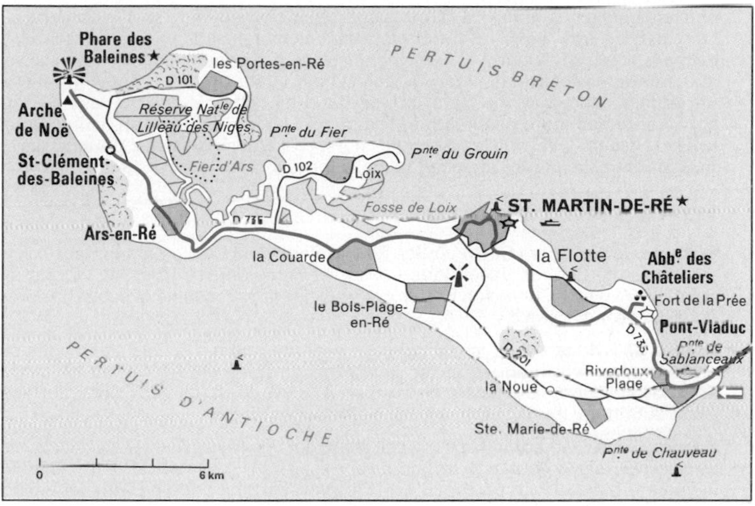

TOUR OF THE ISLAND

From the viaduct to St-Martin-de-Ré

13km – 8 miles : about 30min.

The road, D 735, follows the coast as far as Fort de La Prée, built as part of the ring of defences around La Rochelle, and then forks left into the interior.

Ancienne Abbaye des Châteliers – The ruins of this Cistercian abbey founded in the 12C and destroyed in 1623 stand, with the wind whistling through them, on the bleak moorland carpeting Les Barres promontory. The remains of the abbey church include the west front and walls tracing the outline of a nave and a flattened east end in the style of Citeaux Abbey. The chancel was lit via an elegant window. On the left of the church a series of pillars crowned with the beginnings of ribs indicate that cloisters once stood here. Excavations have unearthed capitals, coins, even skeletons.

From St-Martin-de-Ré to Phare des Baleines

17km – 11 miles : 1 hour.

Ars-en-Ré – This small port with a network of lanes and alleys so narrow that the corners of houses had to be shaved off to allow carriages to turn into them was once frequented by Dutch and Scandinavian vessels loading cargoes of salt.
In the main square, once a cemetery but now covered over and planted with elms, stands **Église St-Étienne** (St Stephen's Church) ⊙, its belfry spire sharp as a needle, painted black and white as a landmark to sailors. A fine Romanesque entrance, partly below the new ground level, leads to a nave of the same period reinforced with thick ribs. The Gothic chancel, longer than the nave, is flanked by wide side aisles. The domed vaulting here is in the Angevin style.
Just south of the church is the Seneschal's (Steward's) House, dating from the Renaissance period and embellished with two corner turrets.

St-Clément-des-Baleines – The **Maison des Marais** ⊙ *(16 Rue de l'École)* is an information centre specialising in the island's flora and fauna. Guided walks are organized to explore the dunes, the coastline and the marshes.

L'Arche de Noé ⓥ – This "Noah's Ark" **amusement park** not far from St-Clément offers visitors a trip through a magical world which presents the history of navigation at sea through models and dioramas, a collection of crustaceans and corals ("Oceanorama"), displays of stuffed birds native to Île de Ré, a maze and exotic animals. The **Naturama★** houses a remarkable collection of stuffed animals from all over the world, grouped according to their habitat; decoratively-presented exotic butterflies and insects; a number of aquariums, and a turtle weighing 537kg – 1 175lbs which was washed up on one of the island's beaches in 1978.

★ **Phare des Baleines** ⓥ – This lighthouse, rising 55m – 180ft above the headland, was built in 1854 to replace a 17C beacon-tower which had a light that did not carry very far. The tower may be reached by a pathway.
A spiral staircase of 257 steps leads to the gallery of the lighthouse. From here there is a splendid **panorama★** over the Breton Straits, the Vendée coast and Pointe de l'Aiguillon to the north and east, over the Isle of Ré to the southeast and the Isle of Oléron to the south. At low tide it is possible to see the **fish-locks** *(qv)* around the cape. East of the lighthouse lies Conche des Baleines, a wide bay backed by dunes which describes a graceful curve indenting the coast.
The use of the word *baleine* (whale) in names in this area derives from the fact that, in Roman times, hundreds of whales were washed up on these shores.

Pays de RETZ

Michelin map 67 folds 1 to 3 and 13 or 232 folds 26 to 28 and 39 to 40.

This area, which is almost a large island stretching south from the estuary of the Loire to the north "bank" of the Breton-Vendée marshlands *(qv)*, is, historically, the extreme south of Brittany. It is a region of only modest heights and large, often marshy depressions, and exudes a melancholic character that is not without charm; the Atlantic side with the Côte de Jade and its cliffs of schist is less austere in appearance and more picturesque. The local economy is based on fishing, tourism (seaside resorts), raising dairy-cattle, nursery gardening in the polders *(qv)* and winemaking : the grapes are used to make the local Muscadet de la région Nantaise.

TOWNS AND SIGHTS

Côte de Jade – From St-Brévin-les Pins to Pornic, embracing a number of seaside resorts, is the Côte de Jade (Jade Coast); its name derives from the vibrant green colour of its waters. Between Pornic and St-Gildas the coastline of schist has created appealing sandy creeks.

★ **Pointe St-Gildas** – *Park in the car park near the marina.* Waves crash against the reefs of schist which emerge from under this grass-covered point, on which traces of the Atlantic Wall are visible. From the tip of the point the view extends from the coast of Brittany (north) to the Isle of Noirmoutier (south).

★ **Pornic** – This is an attractive summer resort set on a narrow creek. It offers sheltered beaches, a golf course, a salt-cure centre *(thalassotherapie)* and attractive villas in gardens planted with parasol pines. From the harbour bobbing with fishing boats, near the old town, there are good views of the houses climbing the hillsides. The Old Castle, nestling in the greenery overlooking the beach, was built of granite in the 13C and 14C; it was remodelled in the 19C. It was originally surrounded by water and access was via a drawbridge, which was later replaced by a bridge. Promenade de la Terrasse, laid out on the old ramparts, provides views all around. Dolmen des Mousseaux is a neolithic tomb and monument (*c*3500 BC).

Bourgneuf en Retz – The **Musée du Pays de Retz** ⓥ *(6 Rue des Moines)* is housed in the 17C buildings of an old monastery. It includes sections on archeology, collections of local headdresses and costumes, reconstructions of traditional workshops etc.

Château du Bois-Chevalier ⓥ – *4km – 2½ miles northeast of Legé.* The central body of this Louis XIV château is crowned by a dome and flanked by six wings with high French roofs; the ensemble is reflected in the waters alongside.

Passay and Lac de Grand-Lieu – *See Passay.*

★ Château de la ROCHE COURBON

Map 71 west of fold 4 or 233 fold 15 – 2km – 1¼ miles north of St-Porchaire.

This château, which stands isolated at the heart of the oakwoods that the author **Pierre Loti** *(qv)* loved so much, overlooks a graceful series of balustraded terraces and formal gardens in the French manner.

"Sleeping Beauty's Castle" – This was the title of an article written by Loti in 1908, which appeared in *Le Figaro* newspaper, to stimulate interest in his campaign to save the woods around the old château, itself long abandoned. Loti recalled the memories of his youth, when his holidays were spent with a friend – later to be his brother-in-law – who became the tax-collector in nearby St-Porchaire. Often as an adolescent, he wrote years later, he would stray "into the density of these oaken groves" sliced by a ravine buried beneath the foliage and pitted with small grottoes where "the greenish half-light filtered through leafy branches"...
The campaign – harnessed to another run by fellow writer André Hallays – was a success : not only was the forest saved from the woodman's axe; from 1920 onwards the château was restored and its gardens brought back to life.

TOUR ⏲ *2 hours.*

The estate is entered via Porte des Lions (Lions' Gate), a monumental 17C structure with three arches, adorned with caryatids on the inside. Having crossed a moat, which was bordered with balustrades in the 17C, visitors pass below the "keep", an ancient machicolated tower which today houses a museum displaying prehistoric finds unearthed in nearby excavations.

Château – The château, like the keep, dates from the 15C but was substantially altered by Jean-Louis de Courbon in the 17C when windows, dormers and skylights were refashioned and arcades added at the foot of the garden façade to support a balcony. This façade is remarkable for the balance of its elements and its balustraded stairway.
Inside, the tour of the château starts with a library-cum-study furnished in Louis XIII style which serves as a gallery for the paintings, most of them from the old chapel : they include Biblical episodes, allegories, landscapes and a series of painted panels illustrating *The Labours of Hercules* which date from the time of Louis XIV.
The 18C Grand Salon, with panelling and furniture from the same period, contains a bust of Hubert Robert after Pajou, and a painting by the Dutch artist Hackaert which shows the château as it was in the 17C.
Visitors then pass through a Louis XVI vestibule hung with rare, early 19C, illustrated panoramic wallpaper, and landscapes painted by Casanova, the brother of the notorious libertine. The tour finishes with two 17C rooms with Louis XIII ceilings : in the first of these is an enormous stone fireplace bearing the Latin inscription : *Fide, Fidelitate, Fortitudine* (By Faith, Fidelity and Courage); the second room is a kitchen-banqueting hall with furniture in the Saintonge style *(qv)* and a curious, very old roasting jack.

★ **Gardens** – Beyond the château formal parterres and basins, separated by clipped yew hedges and graced with statues, form a magnificent and colourful perspective focusing on a double stairway flanking an ornamental waterway.
Skirting these waters and the nymph at their far end, visitors reach a terrace offering a stunning **view**★★ of the château, reflected in the smooth surface of the pool below it. The wide tree-lined walk leads to a column surmounted by a sphere; from here, by turning suddenly around, it is possible to experience that same sense of magic and surprise that so stimulated Pierre Loti.

Salle des Fêtes – Within this "festival hall" there is a superb late 16C stone stairway with balustrades.

Grottoes – *30min Rtn on foot.* The woodland walk ends in an avenue of holm oaks which leads to the narrow valley carved out by the Bruant, a tributary of the River Charente. It is this stream which feeds the pools and waterways in the castle gardens.
The caves in the steep wall of the ravine which intrigued the young Loti were inhabited by Prehistoric man.

★ ROCHEFORT

Pop 25 561

Michelin map 71 fold 13 or 233 folds 14, 15

Noble and austere Rochefort, the "town of Pierre Loti" *(qv)*, has always been associated with the sea and it still breathes out the salt tang of its nautical past. Students of France's School of Naval Aeronautics today throng its public gardens and patrol the wide, straight streets quadrangling the city centre.

HISTORICAL NOTES

In the days of sailing ships – In the middle of the 17C Jean-Baptiste Colbert (1619-83), Louis XIV's minister in charge of the Navy, was looking for a base from which the Atlantic coast could be defended against the incursions of the English. Brouage was silting up and the roadstead of La Rochelle was not sufficiently sheltered. Rochefort, 15km – 9 miles upriver from the mouth of the Charente, seemed the ideal choice. It was protected off-shore, moreover, not only by the isles of Ré, Aix and Oléron, but also by the Fouras and Le Chapus promontories – all of them easy to fortify.
It was decided therefore, starting from scratch, to turn Rochefort into a military port with an arsenal as powerful as the one in Toulon, and from 1666 onwards work started on the docks and fortifications. The man in charge was the minister's nephew, Colbert du Terron, aided by two military engineers, Chevalier de Clerville and François Blondel, who drew up plans for the arsenal and traced out the ramparts. By 1671 Rochefort could boast a population of 20 000, and 13 men-of-war, a galley and several brigantines had been launched.
The town, originally constructed of wood, was rebuilt in stone in 1688 on the orders of the naval governor Michel Bégon – the man who gave his name to the begonia family : these exotic plants discovered in the West Indies by a priest, Father Plumier, were brought back to France at the governor's request *(see below)*.
All that remains of the old ramparts today is a section of wall near the marina and a watchtower bartizan behind the post office.

The Hulks of Rochefort – In the autumn of 1792 the Republican "cleansing" of the clergy began. Hundreds and hundreds of priests who had refused to swear that they accepted the "civil" status of the Church under the new Constitution were sent to Rochefort, where they were destined to embark on ships taking them to the Guyana penal colony in South America. Anchored in the Charente were two

decrepit ships (known as "pontons" or hulks) awaiting them : an antique former hospital ship, the *Bonhomme-Richard,* and an old ship-of-the-line, the *Borée.* In the event the prisoners were transferred to two even more dilapidated slave-traders, the *Washington* and the *Deux-Associés.* The "villains" were crammed between decks in batches of 400, lying on filthy straw, with nothing but sea-water to wash in. A communal tub of broth with a few broad beans floating in it was all they had for food, the *sans-culottes* (revolutionaries) having already sold part of the rations destined for the prisoners.
One day, after a short voyage, the hulks weighed anchor. Instead of deportation to Guyana, the priests found they were kept aboard ship off the Isle of Aix *(qv).* On deck shots were fired and cries of "Long live the Republic! Long live Robespierre!" rang out over the water. By now the deportees, lacking everything, had only one aim : to survive. In January 1794, however, typhus made its grim appearance. Twelve or thirteen priests died every day; at each death there was a noisy celebration by the crew. The corpses, at first thrown into the sea, were later transported to Aix or to Île Madame – a tiny off-shore islet linked to the mainland at low tide : fatigue parties drawn from the surviving priests were forced to carry out this gruesome task; many of them died doing it.
Transferred at last to Île Madame, all of those still living were freed in 1795.

Arsenal – Colbert's arsenal was, by 1690, "the biggest, the most complete and the most magnificent in the kingdom" : 47 warships had been armed and provisioned there with ammunition, among them several three-deckers such as the famous *Louis-le-Grand.*
Between 1690 and 1800 three hundred new vessels slid into the waters of the Charente from Rochefort's naval yards.
The arsenal stretched along the banks of the Charente in two sectors that still exist, interspersed with launching slipways and the entrances to dry docks. Apart from the guns and ammunition supply section there were 11 shipbuilding yards and four refitting basins, including **La Vieille Forme** (**G**), the oldest masonry dry dock (1669) in the world. The complex also housed a foundry specializing in copper-plated nails, a boilermaking shop, forges, sawmills, rope-makers and a cooperage works producing barrels for gunpowder etc, and enormous warehouses for quartermasters' stores. The mast pits could contain up to 50 000m^3 – 65 400 cu yds of wood rendered rot-proof by the briny water. A studio of "marine sculptors" carved figureheads and embellished poops and prows. Between 5 000 and 10 000 workmen were employed in the arsenal, which was entered from 1830 onwards via the famous Porte du Soleil. Each morning and evening the flagship based on Rochefort fired a cannon shot to signal the opening and closing of the gates.
It was from Rochefort, in March 1780, that General La Fayette set sail for the second time to reinforce the "Insurgent" troops in America. In the first half of the 19C the Rochefort yards built the *Sphinx,* the first of the French navy's steam-powered warships, and the *Mogador,* the most powerful paddle-wheel frigate ever built in France.
In 1816 the frigate *La Méduse* sailed from Rochefort for Senegal in West Africa, only to be wrecked off the coast of what is now Mauritania. The loss of the ship inspired Géricault to paint his celebrated dramatic work *The Raft of the Medusa.*
The gates of the Rochefort arsenal closed for the last time in 1926.

SIGHTS

★ **Maison de Pierre Loti** (**B**) ⌚ – The author Pierre Loti (1850-1923), whose real name was Julien Viaud, was born in Rochefort at No 141 of the street that now bears his *nom-de-plume;* he was the son of a town hall official. Loti, a much-travelled naval officer, accomplished sportsman and something of a dandy with a distinguished bearing, was nevertheless a novelist of great sensitivity and an exceptional story-teller. Inspired by his voyages to exotic destinations, he wrote *Pêcheur d'Islande (Iceland Fisherman), Aziyadé, Ramuntcho* and *Madame Chrysanthème,* books which were instrumental in his acceptance as a member of the élite Académie Française at the unusually young age of 41.
Loti's house is in fact two intercommunicating buildings – his birthplace and the house next door, which he acquired as soon as he was able – concealing a remarkable interior behind a relatively plain façade. The rooms are sumptuously furnished and decorated, and full of souvenirs from his many voyages.

Labat/EXPLORER

Pierre Loti's House, Rochefort.

There are two salons on the ground floor. Loti's piano stands in the first, which is hung with family paintings, some by his sister; the second houses Louis XVI furniture and a number of mementoes and *objets d'art*. The **"Renaissance" Dining Room** – furnished in the Spanish style and hung with five 17C Flemish tapestries – includes a huge chimneypiece and a dais for musicians. On the mezzanine floor, the former studio used by the author's painter sister, transformed into a "15C salon", was the site of a famous "Louis XI dinner" in April 1888.
The spartan furnishings of the first-floor master bedroom are in striking contrast to the three apartments around it : the **Mosque,** with décor largely from a mosque in Damascus (collection of prayer mats, candelabra, weapons, a painted cedarwood ceiling); the **Turkish Salon** with its sofas, cushions, exotic wall hangings and a stucco ceiling inspired by the Alhambra in Granada; the **Arab Room,** glittering with enamelwork and adorned with a *moucharabieh* (a carved wood screen placed in front of a window).
Much of the "orientalist" material in the house was brought into the country for Loti by smugglers.

★ **Musée d'Art et d'Histoire** (M[1]) ⏲ – The museum is housed in the former Hôtel Hèbre-de-Saint-Clément.
A large picture gallery and an adjoining exhibition room contain a sketch by Rubens *(Lycaon Changed into a Wolf by Jupiter),* a number of 17C flower paintings, portraits from the 16C Italian School, and others by Roques (Ingres' teacher) and a series of landscapes, portraits and sentimental scenes from the Empire and Romantic epochs. These include Gauffier's *Return of the Prodigal Son* and work by Belloc, Rouget (portrait of Lola Montès) and Michallon. More recent paintings hang nearby.
Fine collections of ethnographic interest from Africa and Oceania, including superb Polynesian masks, may be found in the Lesson Gallery.
In the following room hang seascapes and a copy of Géricault's dramatic work inspired by the *Medusa* tragedy *(see above).* The Local History department has an extraordinary plan of Rochefort, in relief, from 1835, and Vernet's painting, *The Port of Rochefort.* The Camille Mériot Room is reserved for collections of shells.

ROCHEFORT

Audry-de-Puyravault (R.) 2
Gambetta (Av.) 17
Gaulle (Av. Ch. de) 18
La Fayette (Av.) 21
République (R. de la) ....

Benes (Rue) 5
Carnot (R. Sadi) 7
Clemot (Rue) 8
Colbert (Pl.) 9
Combes (R. E.) 12
Dr Pujos (Rue du) 13
Duvivier (Rue C.) 14
Fosse-aux-Mâts (Av. de la) 15
Grimaux (Av.) 19
Lesson (Rue) 23
Pelletan (Av. C.) 25
Port (R. du) 27
Roux (R. A.) 31
Vivres (Quai aux) 37
Zola (R. E.) 38
11-Novembre-1918 (Av. du) 42
14-Juillet (R. du) 43

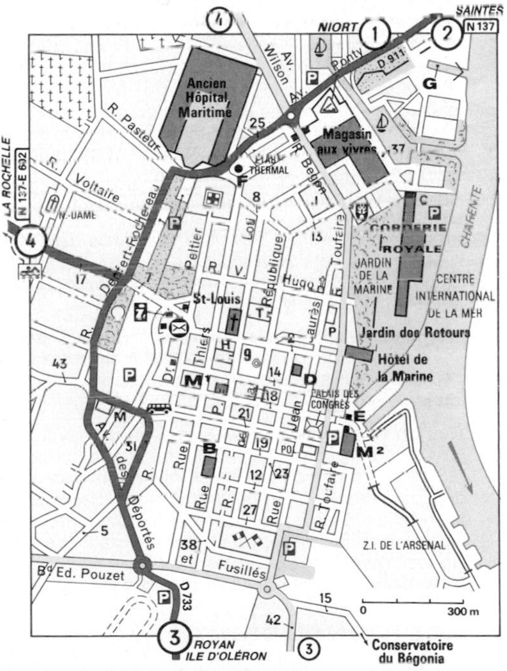

B Maison de Pierre Loti
D Les Métiers de Mercure
E Porte du Soleil
F Ancien château d'eau
G Vieille forme
M[1] Musée d'Art et d'Histoire
M[2] Hôtel de Cheusses

Place Colbert (9) – This fine square, huge and rectangular in shape and bordered by elegant façades, is the true city centre.
On the western side, the town hall is installed in the Hôtel d'Amblimont (named after a former Governor of Martinique, victor in a sea battle with the Dutch fleet in 1674). The 18C monumental fountain on the other side of the square represents the Ocean and the River Charente mingling their waters.
Many of the scenes in the 1967 Jacques Demy musical film, *Les Demoiselles de Rochefort,* were shot in this square.

Église St-Louis – The church was built on the site of a chapel belonging to an old Capuchin monastery (1672). The enormous entrance (Corinthian columns surmounted by a triangular pediment), the three aisles with their vast pillars, the vaults above, are all imbued with the majesty of the classical style.
Four more Corinthian columns support the canopy above the high altar.

Porte du Soleil (E) – This entrance to the arsenal, dating from 1830, is built in the form of a triumphal arch. Vigorously-carved seafaring emblems adorn the inner face of the entrance.

Hôtel de Cheusses (M²) – A magnificent gateway leads to the courtyard of this 17C mansion which was once the local Admiralty headquarters. Today the building is a naval museum.

Musée de la Marine ⊙ – Model ships, ships' figureheads, navigational equipment, paintings, charts, weapons and flags evoke the history of the French Navy from the 17C to the 20C. Maps, documents and explanatory models illustrate the story of Rochefort's old naval dockyard. Particularly impressive are the very large ship models (and those of windmills) in the outer hall.
Of particular note is the enormous capstan from the privateer commanded by René Duguay-Trouin (1673-1736), whose great exploit was the capture of Rio de Janeiro in 1711 with "a feeble fleet".

Hôtel de la Marine – Once the headquarters of the local "maritime Préfecture", this old mansion is now occupied by the officer commanding Rochefort's aero-naval base. Napoleon Bonaparte once stayed here, and the oldest part of the building dates back to the time of Louis XIV. In front of it is a monumental 18C gateway. A tall, square-sectioned tower at one side was formerly used for the exchange of visual signals with ships.

Jardin de la Marine – The tree-lined riverside walks and terraced lime trees of this quiet, sheltered garden date back to the 18C. A handsome staircase terminating in a doorway with three arches leads down to the former royal rope factory.

★ **Corderie Royale** – This rope factory below the garden and overlooking the Charente was founded by Colbert in 1666 and completed four years later; it stands on a kind of "raft", a grid of heavy oak beams, because of the nature of the soil. The factory supplied all the rigging for the entire French fleet from the time the factory was opened until the Revolution; once steam took over from sail, however, its activity declined and it was closed at the same time as the arsenal.
The Corderie Royale was severely damaged during World War II but has been the subject of an extensive restoration programme which has replaced the original lengthy façade (374m – 1 227ft long). This is surmounted by a blue slate mansard roof with pedimented dormers. The rear façade is reinforced by elegant scrolled buttresses. The building as a whole is a classic – and rare – example of 17C industrial architecture.
The Corderie's northern wing houses the present Chamber of Commerce and Industry, its central section the municipal library and "médiathèque", and the southern wing is the office of a coastline and lakeside conservation agency, together with the LPO (a society for the protection of birds) and the **Centre International de la Mer** ⊙, which has a permanent exhibition on ropes and rigging : once the hemp had arrived from the Auvergne it was spun, assembled in strands and then twisted into its final form before being tarred – the length of the building both limiting and conditioning that of the rigging. Among the exhibits is an imposing 19C *machine à corder* (twisting machine) which runs on rails. Temporary exhibitions on maritime themes are also held here.
Around the Corderie now are the **Jardin des Retours,** planted with rare or exotic species; the riverside **Jardin des Amériques,** which includes the **Aire des Gréements** (the Rigging Zone), evoking the vessels of the past; and the **Labyrinth des Batailles Navales,** a maze of clipped yew hedges.

Magasin aux Vivres – This late 17C naval storehouse, next to the provisioning dock and facing the marina, was the site of a bakery able to produce 20 000kg – 44 100lbs of bread each day. The cellars could store 18 000hl – 396 000 gallons of liquid.

Ancien Hôpital Maritime – The former naval hospital standing in the middle of a park was built in the late 18C. The chapel, crowned with a pinnacle, lies behind a façade with a carved pediment. Nearby is a small centre for **thermal cures,** La Source de l'Empereur (The Emperor's Spring). The waters have been used since 1866 but from 1953 onwards they have been drawn from an artesian well drilled to a depth of 846m – 2 776ft. The centre treats rheumatism and dermatitis.
Opposite stands the old **water tower** (**F**), a fine quadrangular structure in stone, dating from 1900, which at one time supplied the whole town.

ADDITIONAL SIGHTS

★ **Les Métiers de Mercure** (**D**) ⊙ – Here a series of workshops and stores dating from 1900 to 1940 have been re-created in meticulous detail within an old warehouse dating from the turn of the century. The picturesque evocation of life in days gone by includes a Rochefort bar with its Belle Époque façade, a pharmacy, a hatter's, a grocery store, a forge etc.

Conservatoire du Bégonia ⊙ – *Take Avenue du 11-Novembre-1918 to the south, turn left into Avenue de la Charente and right into Rue Charles-Plumier.*
Plumier was the botanist priest who first brought begonias back from the West Indies in the 17C. The plant was not, however, commercially available in France until the end of the 18C. Here, in a huge hothouse, over 850 species, natural and hybrid, are grown, cared for and brought to perfection.

Ancien Pont Transbordeur de Martrou – *2.5km – 1½ miles south via Avenue du 11-Novembre-1918.*
This iron transporter bridge, a splendid example of industrial art dating from 1900, is 176m – 577ft long and stands more than 50m – 164ft above the surface of the Charente. The bridge was the last of its type to remain in use in France, but is now closed to traffic. Since 1991 the river has been crossed by a new toll-bridge, the Viaduc de la Charente.

La ROCHEFOUCAULD Pop 3 448

Michelin map 72 fold 14 or 233 fold 30.

La Rochefoucauld is a small town on the banks of the River Tardoire which is lent a picturesque quality by the beauty of its old half-timbered houses.
Near the old fairground (Champ de Foire) is a 17C bridge, slightly humpbacked, with two half-moon ravelins, face to face, built so that pedestrians could get out of the way of carts and carriages. From here there are pleasant views of the river and the old château rising grandly above it.
The prosperity of La Rochefoucauld depends on several small industries, among them the production of *"charentaises"* – a comfortable form of slipper. It was in the time of Louis XIV that this began as a cottage industry, part of the footwear being made then from felt off-cuts from the manufacture of sailors' reefer jackets. The slippers were so successful that they were worn even by members of the Court.

SIGHTS

★ **Château** ⊙ – The Château de La Rochefoucauld, built as the seat of a duchy in 1622, was the home of an illustrious line whose chief has traditionally always had the Christian name of François; the best-known is probably François VI de La Rochefoucauld (1613-80), the pessimistic author of the famous *Maxims*. The château, still the property of the same family, is constructed of soft white stone. The remains of a square Romanesque keep are still visible, but the place as a whole, with its elegant Renaissance façade and fine courtyard, recalls the châteaux of the Loire more than any military stronghold.
The river front is framed by a medieval tower and the castle chapel. Noteworthy here are the pedimented dormers with their candelabra and their tabernacle motifs stamped with a shell.

Ancien couvent des Carmes – *Rue des Halles.* A restored chapter-house and huge cloisters with groined vaulting and trefoil arching supported by delicate small columns comprise the main points of interest in this former Carmelite monastery. Part of the building has been turned into a laboratory of paleontology.

Église Notre-Dame-de-l'Assomption-et-St-Cybard – The church is built in a style rarely found in the Angoulême region : 13C Gothic. Above the portal is a rose window; the belfry is crowned by an octagonal spire.

Ancienne pharmacie de l'hôpital ⊙ – *Place du Champ-de-Foire.* The old pharmacy of the hospital, which dates back to the 17C, houses an interesting collection of chemist's pots, flasks, mortars (16C and 17C) and a complete surgeon's instrument case from the Empire period; its original owner was attached to the army of Napoleon. Also on display are a fine 17C Christ fashioned from ivory; a collection of pewter (porringers, goblets); a 1740 Communion water iron.

EXCURSION

Forêt de la Braconne – *Tour of 18km – 10 miles : allow 1 hour. Leave La Rochefoucauld via D6 northwest and at Pont-d'Agris turn left into D11.*
The Braconne massif is a limestone plateau extensively carved by underground waters which have produced dolines or sink-holes caused by subsidence of the surface. It extends over an area of approximately 4 000ha – 9 884 acres. The best-known – and the most spectacular – of the sink-holes is known as **"La Grande Fosse"** (the big pit), a huge funnel-shaped depression 55m – 180ft deep and 250m – 820ft in diameter. Although it is smaller, **"La Fosse Limousine"** *(southeast of the Grande Combe roundabout)*, hidden by tall beech trees, is also attractive. As for **"La Fosse Mobile"** *(not open to the public)*, legend has it that a wicked son who had murdered his father tried in vain to dump the body in this sink-hole – but the nearer he approached the edge of the depression, the more it moved away from him. In fact the depths of this abyss, which lies in an isolated spot in the silence of the woods, are used as a training centre for local cavers. The subterranean system connects with an underground water supply which leads eventually to the source of the River Touvre.

At the Grande Combe roundabout, take the forest road leading south and return to La Rochefoucauld by N 141.

★★★ La ROCHELLE Pop 71 094

Michelin map 71 fold 12 or 233 fold 14 – Facilities.
Town plan in the current Michelin Red Guide France.

La Rochelle is the capital of the Aunis – a region, once a Roman colony, which changed hands several times between the English and the French in the Middle Ages. It is a town popular with painters, seduced by its atmosphere, the hustle and bustle of its daily life.
The old fortified port, the hidden streets lined with arcades, the ancient wooden houses and stately mansions, whether under the brilliance of summer skies or the most romantic of drizzles, all combine to make La Rochelle the most attractive town on the coast between Nantes and Bordeaux.

HISTORICAL NOTES

A Protestant stronghold – La Rochelle was sometimes known as "the French Geneva" as it was, like its Swiss counterpart, a haven for numerous disciples of **Calvin** before 1540; in the early days of the Reformation his teachings were even preached in the city churches. Between 1562 and 1598 the Wars of Religion brought a bloodbath to the region. In 1565 priests were hurled into the sea from the top of the tall Lantern Tower; in 1568 a former Augustinian monastery was turned into a Protestant church. Three years later a National Synod was held here under the presidency of Calvin's follower, the writer and theologian Théodore de Bèze. The staunchly Calvinist queen Jeanne d'Albret *(qv)*, her son Henri de Navarre (the future Henri IV) and the Prince de Condé took part in the debates. The Confession of Faith of the Reformed Churches, promulgated in Paris in 1559, was ratified in the Aunis capital and became the Confession of Faith of La Rochelle.
In 1573 the royal army, led by the Duc d'Anjou, laid siege to the city. Anjou, the future Henri III, had engaged the services of the Italian military engineer who had been employed by the Protestants to design and build the ramparts of La Rochelle – and who therefore knew the weak points of the defences. But La Rochelle held out. The inhabitants made use of a machine, derisively known as *"L'Encensoir"* (the censer), which drenched the assailants with boiling water and melted pitch. After six months of continued attacks the city still had not fallen, and the royalists had lost 20 000 men, when the siege was lifted.

Hôtel de Ville, La Rochelle/EXPLORER

The Siege of La Rochelle by Henri Motte (in the Town Hall).

The siege of La Rochelle (1627-28) – Some 55 years later a second royalist army stood at the gates of La Rochelle – though this time the town was allied with the English, who had invaded the Île de Ré *(qv)*.
Two equally determined figures were pitted against each other on this occasion : outside was **Cardinal Richelieu,** determined to impose a unity on France, whatever the cost; inside was **Jean Guiton** (1585-1654), a small, abrupt man, uncultivated yet fanatic in temperament, who had been an admiral in the navy and was now Mayor of La Rochelle. At the beginning of the siege, Guiton spoke to the people of La Rochelle, saying "I will be Mayor since you wish it. But you see this dagger? I swear that I will bury it in the bosom of the first man to talk of surrender... and I demand that I should be stabbed with it myself should I suggest a capitulation..."
Unfortunately for Guiton the blockade was organized by a masterly hand, both on land and at sea, from where help for the besieged from the English was expected : Richelieu himself took charge of the siege.
What was in effect a gigantic dyke was erected across the bay to block the entrance to the harbour. This barrier, designed by the marine architect Clément Métezeau, comprised huge, long beams of wood driven into the sea floor, between which stone blocks and rubble were jammed among the breaking waves and the swirl of currents. In the middle an opening was left to allow the tide through. Both infantry and artillery were posted on top of the dyke with the result that the English fleet was unable to sail through and relieve the beleaguered garrison.
At first the people of La Rochelle were not overly concerned at the building of the dyke : storms, they were convinced, would sweep it away. In fact it held, though it took the besiegers 15 months to starve the town into submission. Richelieu made

his victorious entry on 30 October 1628, followed two days later by Louis XIII. Inside the perimeter all was desolation, the houses were full of corpses : of the 28 000 inhabitants living there before the siege, famine and sickness had spared only 5 000, among them the courageous Guiton, who was later to serve the King.

From Rabelais to Fromentin – La Rochelle has always been a popular town with writers. **Rabelais** *(qv)*, one of the first, broke his journey here and described the light from the Lantern Tower in *Pantagruel.* **Choderlos de Laclos,** the author of *Les Liaisons Dangereuses,* was garrisoned here *c*1786 as an engineer officer overseeing the construction of the arsenal. He lived in a house linked, via a concealed stairway and an underground passage, with the mansion owned by Admiral Duperré *(see below).* It can only be guessed at whether de Laclos' marriage to Solange, the Admiral's sister, was in any way connected to this ease of access...

The writer associated more than anyone with La Rochelle is **Eugène Fromentin** (1820-76), who was a painter and an art critic as well as a novelist. He was influenced by the artists Corot and Delacroix, and his painter's eye is obvious everywhere in his one slight but beautiful romance, *Dominique.* In this novel he describes with the precision of a naturalist the life in 19C La Rochelle; the landscapes, the skies and the light of the Aunis are suggested with an incomparable lightness of touch.

Fromentin was a native Rochelais but many other eminent men from other parts of France were also associated with the town. They include Voltaire and Laclos, Corot, the Impressionist painters Signac and Marquet, Joseph Vernet who painted the port, and distinguished naturalists and scientists like Lafaille, d'Orbigny and Bonpland. Jean-Paul Sartre was at school in La Rochelle; Georges Simenon lived here for a while : his novel *Le Voyager de la Toussaint* (The All Saints Day Traveller) is set in the town. An annual convention, held since 1732, brought together some of these eminent figures.

The physicist René-Antoine Ferchault de **Réaumur** (1683-1757), who developed an alcohol thermometer and a scale of temperature to go with it, is one of the scientists who attended the conventions. A man whose curiosity was all-embracing, Réaumur was much concerned also with natural history, researching such diverse subjects as chicken-farming, pearl-bearing mussels and the life of insects. As a metallurgist, he was known for his work on smelting and on steel, suggesting that the microscope be applied to the study of metals. The opaque white glass resembling glazed earthenware, which was developed by him, is still known today as "Réaumur Porcelain".

PORTS AND INDUSTRIES

A trading city – La Rochelle today is particularly well equipped with ports and docks and harbours. The original port – Le Vieux Port – at the inner end of a narrow inlet traded with the North in the Middle Ages (wines and salt exported; cloth and wool imported) and later prospered even more through business with Canada and above all the West Indies. Because of its lack of depth this old port – or "grounding port" – is now reserved mainly for non-industrial or coastal fishing boats. Deep-sea fishing craft and heavy freight are handled at **La Pallice** *(5.5km – 3½ miles west)*, the commercial outlet for the whole of the Aunis region which was established at the end of the 19C : it has a fine roadstead sheltered by the Île de Ré and can accommodate the largest of freighters. The commercial traffic (6 million tons annually) includes imports of hydrocarbons, tropical woods, paper pulp, phosphates and fertilizer, and exports of oil-seeds, cereals and frozen meat. Construction of La Rochelle's new and ultra-modern **fishing port,** which will include an automated and computerized market for fish auctions, was begun in 1993, at **Pointe de Chef de Baie** at La Pallice.

The third of La Rochelle's newer ports is **Les Minimes** *(see below)* on the southern side of the bay, which is entirely reserved for pleasure craft.

Around fifty locally-based trawlers fish the coast from the Bay of Biscay to Portugal, and as far afield as the southern waters of England and Ireland, making La Rochelle an important distribution centre for fresh fish. The deep-sea fleet, using the modern "containerization" technique whereby the catch is frozen and packed on board, is one of the most advanced in Europe.

Regattas and top-class ocean races draw the élite of the world's yachtsmen to La Rochelle. At Whitsun the International Sailing Week provides a splendid spectacle, on land as well as at sea.

A large number of **boat trips** ⊙ upriver or out to sea are available.

Though marine activities seem to predominate here, there are many other successful industries : shipyards, chemical works, and factories producing cars, rolling stock and other material for the railways are among the most important.

★★ VIEUX PORT (Z) *2 hours.*

The old port is divided into five separate sectors : the outer port (Avant Port) or approach road; the shallow inner port with its fishing smacks and pleasure boats (Vieux Port); a small tidal basin (Bassin à flot) where yachts are moored; the larger, outer tidal basin for trawlers (Bassin des chalutiers) where the quayside fish auctions are held every morning; and a variable-level balancing dock (Bassin de retenue) fed by a canal channelling the waters of the Sèvre.

La Ville-en-Bois, west of the larger tidal basin, is an area of low wooden houses mainly used as workshops for ships' repairs or chandlers and spare-part shops.

Quai Duperré – The cafés lining this quay offer a fine view of the waterfront activity. Beyond the masts and the rigging, the embarkations and disembarkations and the manoeuvring of small boats, the perspective is closed by the two towers guarding the harbour mouth – Tour St-Nicolas on the left, Tour de la Chaîne on the right. On the extreme right, the conical roof of the Lantern Tower is visible.

The picturesque Rue du Port and Petite-Rue du Port, inhabited mainly by fishermen and sailors, lead to the quay. On the western side, facing the big clock, stands a statue of **Admiral Duperré**, who was born in La Rochelle in 1775 and commanded the French fleet at the time of the taking of Algiers in 1830.

★ **Tour St-Nicolas** ⓥ – The tower, 42m – 138ft high and leaning slightly, is a fortress in itself. It was built in the 14C on a pentagonal plan, the five corners being reinforced with three engaged circular turrets, one rectangular turret and a square tower, higher still, which acted as a keep. The tower, with its loopholes and bartizans, was for a long time used as a prison. It was named after the patron saint of navigators.
An outside stairway which acts as a buttress leads to the main room, octagonal beneath elegant ribbed vaulting. From here, other staircases within the thickness of the walls mount to a second chamber, off which there are several rooms including a chapel, and then to the lower parapet. Models, dioramas and watercolour maps (from the Musée Maritime, *see below*) trace the evolution of the port area from the 12C to the present day. From the upper parapet, surrounded by high machicolated walls with arrow slits, there are views of the harbour exit, the bay and the Île d'Aix *(qv)*.

Tour de la Chaîne ⓥ – This tower is reached via a quay, bordered with old lime trees, known as Cour des Dames. Behind it are the fine houses once lived in by shipowners. In the past, ships which drew too much water for the old port were able to dock alongside this quay. The tower owes its name to a huge and heavy chain which used to be stretched across the harbour mouth between this tower and Tour St-Nicolas at night, closing the port to ships. According to Rabelais the chain – still visible at the foot of the tower – was used to keep the giant Pantagruel in his cradle.
Tour de la Chaîne, built in the 14C, was for a long time used as a powder magazine. Originally there was a turret attached to it but this was demolished in the 17C to widen the narrow channel. Inside, a superb vaulted chamber houses a **relief map** of La Rochelle as it looked before the siege *(recorded commentary, in French, on the history of the town).*
The tower is linked with Tour de la Lanterne by **Rue Sur-les-Murs,** which follows the top of the old medieval rampart – the only section not demolished by Richelieu, who hoped to use it as a defence against the English (at that time the foot of the wall was at the water's edge).

★ **Tour de la Lanterne** ⓥ – The Lantern Tower is not as old as the other two (it dates from the 15C), and was built with strictly functional concerns in mind, eschewing aesthetic considerations in favour of military imperatives. The great mass of the building, its walls 6m – 20ft thick at the base, contrasts starkly with the elegant octagonal spire and the fine lantern – originally used as a beacon – which surmount it. At ground level is the old guard-room in which the history of La Rochelle is now recounted through illustrated panels.
Within the spire are four rooms one above the other, the walls of which bear **graffiti★** scrawled by soldiers as well as prisoners, mostly dating from the 17C and 18C. The most interesting are protected by glass.
At the second level of the spire a projecting balcony affords a remarkable **panorama★★** embracing the roofs of the old town, the port, the ocean and the off-shore islands. At low tide it is possible to make out the foundations of Richelieu's dyke, level with Fort-Louis, beyond the promenade.

Gabut District – A picturesque residential and shopping development has been built on the site (east of Tour St-Nicolas) of an old bastion which was once part of the town's ring of fortifications (demolished in 1858). The façades with their wood cladding recall the fish-lofts and sheds of old-time sailors, while vivid colours and wide windows lend the place a Nordic air.

★★ OLD TOWN *2 ½ hours.*

The oldest district of La Rochelle, which was built to a regular plan and protected, until 1913, by Vauban's fine ramparts, still exudes an atmosphere part mercantile and part military. The busy, lively **shopping centre** is based around the town hall (**Z H**), its principal axes Grande-Rue des Merciers and Rue du Palais. Narrow streets still paved with ancient stone slabs, secret passages, some of them vaulted, arcades and darkened "porches" where passers-by can stroll sheltered from bad weather – all these give the area plenty of character.
Many of the houses are designed on a plan particular to La Rochelle. Almost all of them have two entrances, one on the main street, the other on a lane parallel to it. At ground-floor level, these buildings have one huge room – often converted into a shop – an interior courtyard with a staircase leading to a balconied gallery, and a rear courtyard surrounded by outhouses. On the upper floor, above the shop, is a room looking out on the street, a kitchen overlooking the courtyard, and a "dark room" with no direct light from outside. **Half-timbering** on the oldest houses is overhung with slates to protect the wood from the rain.
The **"beaux quartiers"** – the fashionable areas – are west of Rue du Palais. The most stately are Rue Réaumur and Rue de l'Escale. Here, behind high walls pierced with imposing gateways and sometimes (Rue Réaumur) topped with balustrades, the old families live in their solemn 18C mansions midway between courtyard and garden.

Follow the itinerary marked in green on the town plan.

★ **Porte de la Grosse-Horloge** (**Z F**) – *Illustration p 49.* This gateway with its outsize clock was the entrance to the town, coming from the port. The original Gothic tower was modified in the 18C by the addition of a belfry surmounted by a dome and lantern. The turrets on either side are decorated with nautical emblems.
On the far side of the gateway is Place des Petits-Bancs, a small square with a statue of Fromentin in the middle. On the corner of Rue du Temple stands a charming house (1654) with a Renaissance façade.

★ **Grande-Rue des Merciers** (**Y 70**) – This shopping street is one of the most characteristic arteries of La Rochelle, bordered by numerous galleries and houses built in the 16C and 17C. The medieval buildings, half-timbered under the familiar slate covering, alternate with Renaissance homes built of stone and distinguished by fantastic gargoyles.
The wood-and-slate house on the corner of Rue du Beurre, and those at Nos 33, 31, 29 and, at the far end, No 17, are all 17C buildings with pedimented windows. No 8 is late 16C, with very narrow windows and heavy pediments; No 5 is early 17C with strange carved figures. No 3 dates from 1628. Mayor Jean Guiton lived in the last two.

Take Rue de la Grille on the right, then turn left into Rue de l'Hôtel-de-Ville.

★ **Hôtel de Ville** (**Z H**) ⓥ – The town hall, a late 15C-early 16C composite building, is notable for its rich decoration. The rectangular central courtyard is protected by a walled Gothic enclosure surmounted by a machicolated watch-path reinforced by a belfry-tower.
The **main façade**★, built in the reign of Henri IV in the Italian style, overlooks the courtyard. Behind its fluted columns the ground-floor gallery of the façade hides a fine coffered ceiling. The decoration includes trophies, medallions and monograms entwining the initials of Henri IV and Mary de' Medici.
Finer still is the upper level, reached via a balustraded stairway. Here there are pillars and niches in the Tuscan manner, the niches housing effigies representing the four cardinal virtues : (left to right) Prudence, Justice, Fortitude and Temperance. At the top of the façade, outside, elegant dormers appear above the cornice.
The **interior** contains Jean Guiton's study, complete with his armchair in Cordoba leather and the desk he struck forcefully with his dagger to emphasize his famous pronouncement before the siege; the walls are hung with Aubusson tapestries.
Henri Motte's 19C painting of the siege can be found in another room, along with a Jacques Callot engraving and a 1628 canvas by Van der Kabel depicting the same tragic event in the town's history.
The rear façade looks out over Rue des Gentilshommes and also dates from the time of Henri IV; it includes a door studded with bosses which is known as the "Porte des Gentilshommes" because it was through here that the city aldermen filed on the day that the mandate granting them each "the style and title of Gentleman" expired. Above the doorway is a carving of the ship which appears as part of the city's coat of arms.

Return to Porte de la Grosse-Horloge via Rue du Temple.

PORT DES MINIMES *2 hours.*

Three thousand two hundred craft of all types can be accommodated at Minimes marina, on the southern side of the bay sheltering La Rochelle, which makes it the largest pleasure port in Europe on the Atlantic side. Three deep-water tidal basins – Bout-Blanc, Marillac and Lazaret – have been developed. Around the port is a zone of artisans : ship-fitters, sail-makers, painters and experts in repair work provide every service needed by the owners of yachts and cruisers. A sailing school of repute is based here, and there is also a residential area with apartment blocks and holiday homes.

A regular waterbus service operates between Les Minimes and Vieux Port.

★ **Aquarium** ⓥ – This important, ultra-modern aquarium founded by René Coutant presents a vast panorama of underwater fauna and flora from around the world. The first three rooms are devoted either to a particular ocean or to a specific marine area (the Atlantic, the Mediterranean, tropical seas etc), their species displayed in superbly arranged tanks. A tunnel with transparent walls allows visitors to wander freely through a tropical marine environment, while an immense basin containing 2 500hl – 55 000 gallons of water accommodates turtles and sharks. There is a small tropical garden (including an aquarium with piranhas).

Musée Océanographique ⓥ – *Lazaret basin.* The museum, with its modern architecture, opens into a huge space reserved for displays of marine mammals : seals, sea lions, whales, dolphins, walruses... There are also skeletons, stuffed specimens and documentation on the biology of the various species. Another department offers a panoramic view of the marine environment and the activities associated with it : scientific and oceanographic exploration, flora and fauna of the sea and the coast, eco-systems, the culture of mussels and oysters, fishing etc.

MUSEUMS

★★ **Musée d'Histoire Naturelle** (**Y**) ⓥ – The museum stands by the entrance to a park, the Jardin des Plantes, and is housed in two separate buildings facing one another :

Musée Lafaille – This fine 18C building, once the home of the Governor, still contains much of its Louis XV woodwork. On the ground floor is the **Cabinet Lafaille,** a study-room in which Clément de Lafaille, a War Controller and natural history enthusiast, assembled a collection of curiosities which he bequeathed to the La Rochelle Royal Academy in 1770; the collection, furniture included, was transferred here in 1832. Against a backdrop of magnificent panelling and woodwork inlaid with coral and carved with scientific objects are glass-fronted cabinets, display-cases and a *coquillier* – an 18C cupboard with numerous small drawers, designed to house a collection of shells – said to be the last one remaining in France. The rare crustaceans, molluscs and other shellfish are worth a close examination.
Stags' heads, antlers and other trophies adorn the wide stone stairway leading to the first floor. The landing is occupied by the stuffed figure of the first giraffe ever brought to France, a gift to Charles X from Mahomet Ali, the pasha of Egypt.

The **Zoological Hall,** created in 1832, is an interesting example of the museological thinking of curators of the period, anxious to offer a complete cross-section of the animal kingdom, which was only then beginning to be classified in a rational manner. The **Ethnology Rooms** contain some exceptional exhibits : a statue of the god Terriapatura brought back from the Gambier archipelago in Polynesia, a bicephalic statuette, "Moaï-Kava-Kava", from Easter Island, a large Kwele mask from the Congo, and terracottas from Chad.

Musée Régional Fleuriau – This second building focuses on the natural history of the La Rochelle area : geology, paleontology, pre-history and zoology. There is an interesting reconstruction of part of a forest with such local fauna as wild boar, otters, roe deer and stags.

★ **Musée du Nouveau Monde** (Y M^{2}) ⊙ – The Hôtel Fleuriau, acquired by a shipowner of that name in 1772, houses within panelled Louis XV and Louis XVI salons a number of collections tracing the relationship between La Rochelle and the Americas since the Renaissance. Shipowners and merchants grew rich trading with Canada, Louisiana and especially the West Indies, where they possessed huge plantations producing spices, sugar, coffee, cocoa and vanilla. They prospered enormously too in the "black gold" trade, known more politely as "triangular commerce" : sale of cloth and purchase of slaves on the African coast; sale of these slaves and purchase of colonial products in America; sale of the latter in Europe.
Among the displays, ancient maps, coloured engravings, allegories of America, wallpapers (*The Incas* by Dufour and Leroy) and everyday objects used by the Indians are of particular interest. Note also the section on slavery, the fall of Quebec, West Indian engraving and relevant literary themes (*Atala* – the novel by Chateaubriand about the impossible love between an Indian and a Christian girl).

★ **Musée des Beaux-Arts** (Y M^{3}) ⊙ – The Fine-Arts Museum occupies the second floor of the old bishop's palace, which was built during the reign of Louis XVI; following local custom the courtyard is separated from the gardens by a high balustraded wall. A wrought-iron staircase with ovoli leads to the alcoved gallery in which the paintings hang. The rest of the palace houses a library, an "artothèque" (a lending department for engravings and photographs of paintings) and a study section. The most interesting work among the older paintings is an *Adoration of the Magi,* the last known painting by Eustache Le Sueur (17C French School). Portraits by local artists dating from the 18C include works by Brossard de Beaulieu and Duvivier. The 19C is represented by Bouguereau, Corot, Maurice Denis and Eugène Fromentin – including several evocative studies of Algeria.
A separate department is devoted to 20C work (glass by Maurice Marinot), some of which is displayed in rotation.

★ **Musée d'Orbigny-Bernon** (Y M^{4}) ⊙ – This museum specialises in local history and ceramics. Mementoes of the siege of La Rochelle include liturgical items used by Cardinal Richelieu when he celebrated the first Mass after the fall of the town. A number of documents relate to the economic prosperity and intellectual life in the Aunis capital during the 18C.
On the first floor an exceptional collection of ceramics centres on the *faïence* (glazed earthenware) of La Rochelle but there are fine pieces also from Marseille, Nevers, Strasbourg and Moustiers. An interesting series of pharmacy flasks and bowls is displayed in a number of 18C medicine cabinets.
The second floor is devoted to the Far East (musical instruments, finely carved ivories, a table inlaid with mother-of-pearl) while the basement houses an archeology section (celebrated 12C tomb).

Musée Maritime : Frégate France I (Z E) ⊙ – Visitors are free to wander wherever they like, from the engine-room to the bridge by way of the galleys, over the five decks of this impressive museum-ship which was formerly a meteorological frigate. Meteorology, fishing and life aboard ship are the subjects of interesting displays. Moored beside the frigate are the *St-Gilles,* an ocean-going tug, and the *Joshua* – the ketch in which Bernard Moitessier competed in the "Golden Globe" (the first single-handed, round-the-world yacht race in 1967 and 1968).
On the quayside is an old wooden lifeboat.

⊙ ►► Musée Grévin (**Z M^{6}**) – Waxworks museum; Musée des Automates (**Z M^{8}**) – Old and modern automata; Musée des Modèles Réduits (**Z M^{5}**) – Model trains, boats and planes; Musée Rochelais de la Dernière Guerre (**Y M^{7}**) – Life in La Rochelle under the German Occupation (1941-45); Musée du Flacon à Parfum (**Z M^{9}**) – Collection of scent bottles, housed above a perfume shop; Parc Charruyer (**YZ**); Temple Protestant (**Z R**) – Religious museum in an 18C temple.

La ROCHE-SUR-YON — Pop 45 219

Michelin map 67 folds 13, 14 or 232 fold 40.

This unusual town, built on a plateau overlooking the River Yon and the *bocage (qv),* was born out of an imperial wish to install – if necessary by force of arms – a strategic military stronghold designed to prevent further uprisings in the Vendée. In 1804 Napoleon transferred the provincial capital from Fontenay to La Roche-sur-Yon, a modest small town which was subsequently renamed "Napoléon". Plans for a military transformation were drawn up by the engineer Duvivier but the lack of stone in the region constrained him to build in cob; as a consequence, when Napoleon passed through in 1808 to have a look at the new fortifications, Duvivier was sacked, being reproached for having created "a mud-walled town".

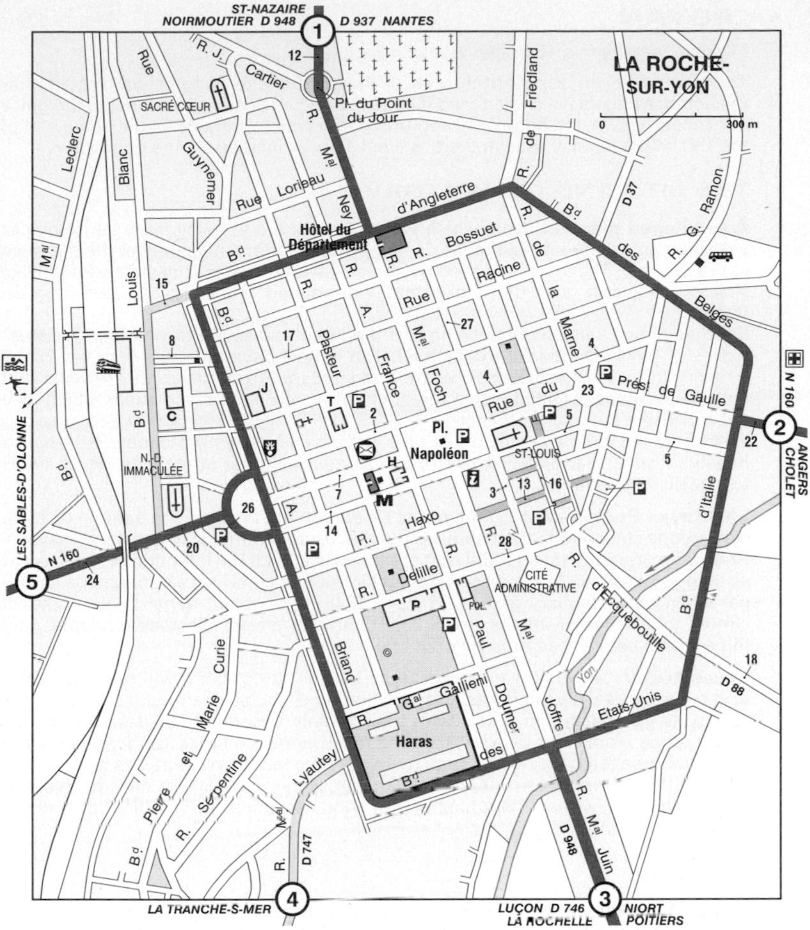

Baudry (R. Paul) 3	Gambetta (Av.) 8	Poincaré (R. Raymond) 20
Carnot (R. Sadi) 5	Gutenberg (R.) 12	Pompidou (R. G.) 22
Clemenceau (R. G.) 7	La Fayette (R.) 14	Résistance (Pl. de la) 23
Halles (R. des) 13	Manuel (R.) 15	Salengro (R. R.) 24
	Marché (R. du) 16	Vendée (Pl. de la) 26
Allende (R. S.) 2	Molière (R.) 17	Victor-Hugo (R.) 27
Berthelot (R. M.) 4	Moulin-Rouge (R. du) 18	93e-R.I. (R. du) 28

It was in fact during the Restoration that La Roche found its definitive shape : a geometric, straight-line plan with a grid of streets crossing each other at right-angles, the wide main arteries converging on a huge esplanade which served as a parade ground or barrack square. This town took the form of an irregular pentagon from which six main routes permitted a rapid rectilinear deployment of troops. This innovation in urban planning reflected precisely the politico-architectural thinking in France in the middle of the 19C.
The name of the town was nevertheless changed several more times : it became Bourbon-Vendée under the Restoration and the July Monarchy, Napoléon-Vendée at the time of the Second Empire and returned to La Roche-sur-Yon in 1870.

SIGHTS

Place Napoléon – The great esplanade, designed to accommodate 20 000 soldiers, is surrounded by neo-Classical buildings : the town hall, the law courts (now a concert hall), the *lycée* (high-school) and the church of St Louis – an imposing monument fronted by heavy Doric columns. In the centre of the square stands an equestrian statue (1854) of Napoleon I.

Museum (M) ⏲ – As well as archeological collections from the prehistoric, Gallo-Roman and medieval periods, the museum offers a panorama of 19C Parisian academic painting and a series of canvases by local artists of the same period – Milcendeau, for instance, who recorded the life around the marshes, and Baudry, who was responsible for the décor of the Paris Opera House.
Work by contemporary artists (Beuys, Boltanski etc) is presented in rotation with a photographic back-up, and there are additional temporary exhibitions by living painters.

Hôtel du Département – This comprises an old Napoleonic hospital in which exhibitions are held and, just behind it, a modern building (1990) by Roland Castro and Jean-Luc Pellerin. The latter, with its immense glass façade scarcely hiding a large pink tower, cuts vividly across the austerity and rigour of the 19C town-planning.

Haras (Stud) ⏲ – This is one of the most important stud-farms in France. A number of thoroughbred stallions and French trotting horses are stabled here.

★★ ROYAN

Pop 18 837

Michelin map 71 fold 15 or 233 fold 25 – Facilities.

The town of Royan, capital of the **Côte de Beauté** (Coast of Beauty), was rebuilt after the bombardments which flattened it in 1945 and has once more found, in the guise of a modern town, the popularity and prosperity which characterized it at the end of the 19C. In the holiday season there is a substantial increase in the population.

THE SITE AND ITS HISTORY

A privileged place – Royan, which was once reputed to enjoy more sunshine per year than anywhere else in France, is ideally located on a headland at the entrance to the Gironde. The town is flanked by choice holiday resorts : the stately Pontaillac, **Meschers-sur-Gironde** and the more family-orientated St-Palais and **St-Georges-de-Didonne.**

Beaches of fine sand curve enticingly at the inner end of the town's four **"conches"** (coves or bays indenting the coastline). The largest cove harbours a strand 2km – 1¼ miles long; the smaller ones, warm and sheltered from the wind, are separated by cliffs or dunes carpeted with a forest of holm oaks and parasol pines which give out a pleasant summer fragrance.

Apart from the natural beauty of the area and a particularly mild climate, Royan also benefits from a seaweed-cure centre and numerous other attractions, which helps to explain its popularity.

The Royan Pocket – At the time of the Liberation of France, in the autumn of 1944, Nazi troops stationed in the southwest withdrew to a number of coastal enclaves – St-Nazaire, Verdon, Royan – and dug themselves in with the intention of holding out as long as possible. Royan was besieged by the French forces of General de Larminat when, on 5 January and 14-15 April 1945, two violent aerial bombardments almost totally destroyed the town. The Germans nevertheless surrendered only three weeks before the armistice on 8 May.

Royan today – Anyone who knew Royan before World War II will remember, not without a certain nostalgia, its ornate villas and chalets half-hidden among the palms, its great Victorian hotels with their heavily decorated façades, the casinos like Baroque temples or palaces from the Renaissance. All that has gone : only the Pontaillac area today can evoke such memories; Royan town centre has been rebuilt following the norms of late 20C town planning. Huge perspectives have been opened up, bordered by apartment blocks with wide balconies and red-tiled roofs in the Charentais manner.

SIGHTS

★ **Église Notre-Dame** (B) – The church was built between 1955 and 1958 to plans by the architects Guillaume Gillet and Hébrard. It is a structure of reinforced concrete coated with resin to protect it from wind erosion. The load-bearing elements, in the form of a V opening outwards, are separated by glass walls.

From Place Notre-Dame, at a slightly lower level, the ascending perspective of the east end, forming a kind of prow, is accentuated by the belfry which soars to a height of 65m – 213ft.

On the left, detached from the nave, is a pyramidal baptistery.

ROYAN

Briand (Av. A.)	B	5
Europe (Cours de l')	C	
Gambetta (R.)	B	
Loti (R. Pierre)	B	
République (Bd de la)	B	40
Alsace-Lorraine (R.)	B	3
Conche-du-Chay (Av. de la)	A	6
Desplats (R. du Colonel)	B	7
Dr.-Audoin (Bd du)	B	8
Dr.-Gantier (Pl. du)	C	9
Façade de Foncillon	B	12
Falaise (Bd de la)	AB	13
Foch (Pl. Mar.)	C	15
Foncillon (R. de)	B	16
Font-de-Cherves (R.)	B	17
Gaulle (Pl. Ch. de)	B	19
Grandière (Bd de la)	C	21
Leclerc (Av. Mar.)	C	26
Libération (Av. de la)	C	28
Notre-Dame (R.)	B	32
Parc (Av. du)	C	35
Pierre-de-Mons (R.)	B	37
Rochefort (Av. de)	B	42
Schuman (Pl. R.)	B	45
Semis (Av. des)	C	46
Thibeaudeau (Rd-Pt du Cdt)	B	48
5-Janvier-1945 (Bd du)	B	52

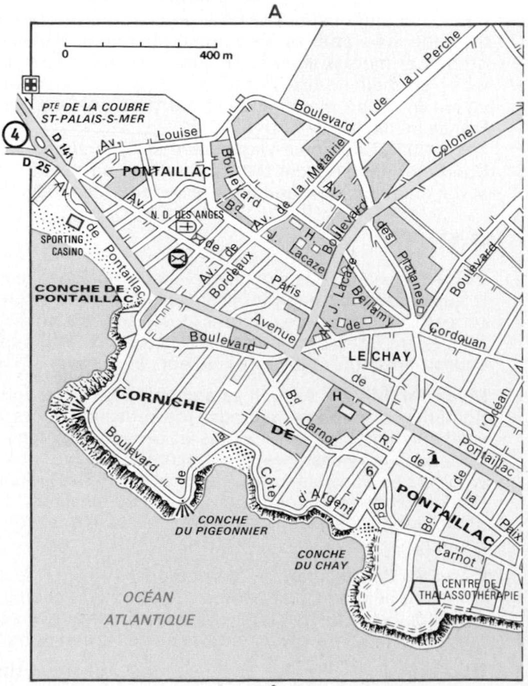

Inside the church, visitors are at once struck by the weightless quality of the single nave, flying away, spacious and light. The height of this nave, bordered by galleries and a triforium, varies from 26m – 85ft in the centre to 36m – 118ft. The great organ, the work of the Poitou master Robert Boisseau, has a case of hammered pewter and is renowned for the quality of its tone.
Two contrasting statues face one another beneath the northern gallery : a 14C carved wood St Joseph with a recumbent Christ, and a modern, copper figure of Joan of Arc.

★ **Front de Mer** (**BC**) – Royan's majestic seafront curves around the northern end of the **Grande Conche** – an imposing crescent of buildings, commercial as well as residential, its line emphasized by a columned peristyle in the shelter of which people can shop or admire the view of the Gironde estuary. Off to the right the distinctive silhouette of Cordouan lighthouse *(qv)* can be recognized.
In the centre of the arc the roof-line is interrupted by a promenade gateway through which, at the far end of Boulevard A.-Briand, the market (Marché Central) – with its dome – can be seen.
At the western end of the seafront is the port. This comprises a dock for trawlers and the sardine boats which fish for the famous *"royan"*, a marina for yachts and cruisers, and a tidal basin with the jetty from which the ferry to Pointe de Grave leaves. In the summer season **boat trips** ⓥ are organized.

★ **Corniche de Pontaillac** (**A**) – *This walk should be taken at high tide for the best views. Follow Boulevard Carnot and Boulevard de la Côte-d'Argent.*
Having skirted the tennis courts and the old Fort du Chay, the route runs above a number of small coves (Conche du Chay, Conche du Pigeonnier) from which there are fine views of the Gironde and the Côte de Beauté, from Pointe de Suzac (southeast) to Pointe de la Coubre (northwest). The walk ends at the **Conche de Pontaillac**★, a sheltered inlet surrounded with smart villas scattered among the sub-tropical foliage. This small beach fringed with a perfect curve of fine sand is the most popular in Royan.

►► Église Réformée (**B D**); Marché Central (**B**) – Market with original fine-concrete dome; Palais des Congrès (**B**) – Glass-walled building.

EXCURSIONS

★ **Pointe de La Coubre and Forêt de La Coubre** – *31km – 19 miles northwest : allow 3 hours.*

Vaux-sur-Mer – On one side of the valley stands a charming Romanesque church rising from an old cemetery planted with elms and cypress trees. Inside, note the capitals at the transept crossing, especially the figure of the bear-leader on the southern side.

Nauzan – A cove with a beach of fine sand, sheltered from the wind by cliffs on either side.

St-Palais-sur-Mer – This small, popular resort with its stylish elegance is surrounded by smart villas scattered among the pines and ilex trees. The **Parc du Marais du Rhâ** *(behind the covered market),* laid out around a lake, is well equipped for leisure activities (miniature golf, cycle-track, tennis, boating, fishing etc). From the cove there is a view of the Cordouan light.

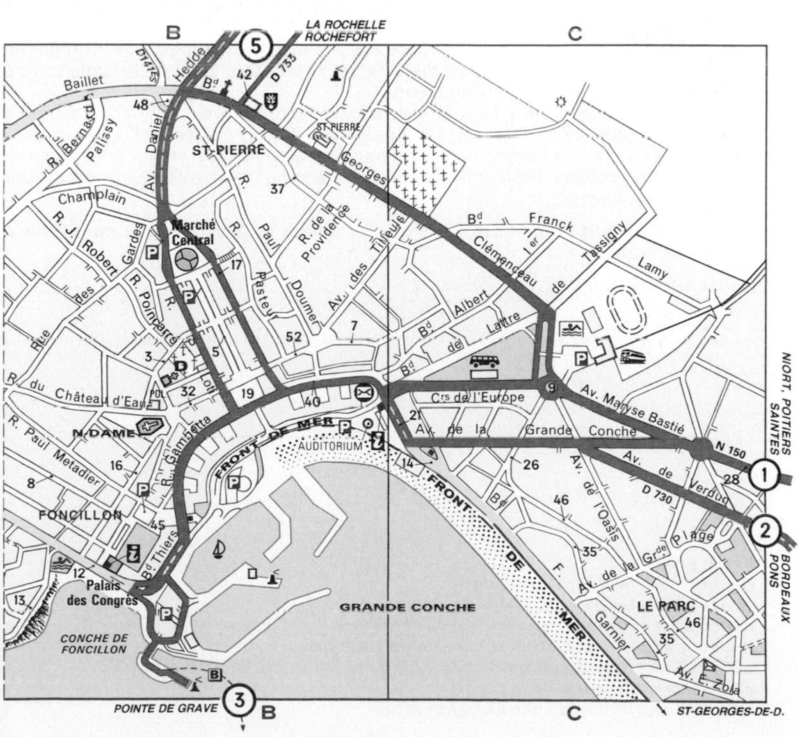

At the far end of the beach (on the right, looking at the cove), take Rue de l'Océan and then **Sentier de la Corniche★** *(signposted, 45min Rtn on foot)*. The path, also known as the *Sentier des Perrières* (path of the slate quarries), twists through the woods and then crosses a gash in the cliff into which, at high tide, the ocean rollers hurl themselves with a thunderous noise. The path ends at a promontory where the jagged rocks have been smashed into bizarre shapes : Monk's Rock, the Devil's Bridge, the Quarrymen.

★★ **La Grande Côte** – *Park in the car park, on the left, where D 25 turns away from the coast and plunges into the woods. Walk to the rock platform. Telescope.*
From this viewpoint, when the weather is bad – or even unsettled – sightseers can enjoy the grandiose spectacle of huge waves breaking violently on the rocks, sending bursts of spindrift jetting high in the air. From left to right, the **view** embraces the Gironde, Pointe de Grave, the Cordouan light, and the promontory and light-house of La Coubre.
A few yards away, on the right, there is a view sideways down onto the beaches and dunes of La Grande Côte, where long lines of breakers roll shorewards and bathing is very dangerous. Rod and reel fishing with cast weights is practised along the almost-deserted strand, especially for bass.

★★ **Zoo de la Palmyre** ⊙ – Pink flamingoes at the foot of a waterfall tumbling down a huge rock greet visitors to this charming zoo. The park, undulating and pleasantly shaded, extends over an area of 10ha – 25 acres which have been carefully adapted to simulate as far as possible the animals' natural habitat.
Panels explain *(in French)* the character and lifestyle of individual species. The creatures on view include lions, panthers, hyenas, bears, rhinoceros and hippopotami, as well as reptiles, penguins and other birds; among the smaller creatures are performing parrots which cavort on bicycles and scooters. The zoo is also involved in breeding species threatened with extinction.
The route emerges from the forest to pass the resort of **La Palmyre** then skirts **La Bonne Anse** – a lagoon refuge for small boats during bad weather, where coastal currents have turned the extremity of Pointe de La Courbe back on itself to form a spit shaped like a shepherd's crook.

★ **Phare de La Coubre** – La Coubre Lighthouse has had to be rebuilt several times because the dune on which it stands is "mobile". The present version dates from 1905 and rises to a height of 60m – 199ft. Its slender, soaring, two-tone tower overlooks the Point from a position near the semaphore station. This is one of the most powerful lighthouses in France, with a beam that carries 53km – 33 miles, signalling the approaches to the Gironde. The walls inside are coloured an opaline blue. From the top – 300 steps and then a metal ladder – there is an extensive **panorama★** over La Coubre Forest and the Isle of Oléron (north and east); the extremity of the point and its coastal spit, La Bonne Anse, and Cordouan lighthouse standing alone on the horizon (south). In the distance Pointe de Grave and the Côte de Beauté as far as the cliffs of Meschers-sur-Gironde are visible.

★ **Forêt de la Coubre** ⊙ – Most of this 8 000ha – 19 768 acre forest is composed of maritime pines and ilex trees; there are still a few deer to be seen. Extensive reafforestation has all but eradicated the traces of the devastating fire which ravaged the area in 1976.
The forest serves to stabilize the dunes along the Arvert coast, better known as the **Côte Sauvage** (Wild Coast), which was studded during World War II with bunkers built by prisoners of war under the German Todt Organization. Cycle-tracks penetrate the woodlands and lead to the beaches.
Half a mile north of La Coubre lighthouse *(car park)* a sandy track twists through the dunes to the strand, from which there is an impressive view of Atlantic rollers crashing against a gently shelving shore.
8km – 5 miles further north, beyond the metallic Gardour tower, there is a wooded knoll on the right of route D 25. Crowning this rise, at the end of a forest road known as Chemin des Fontaines, is a panoramic tower made of wood : this is the **Tour des Quatre Fontaines.** From it there are wide-ranging views over the forest massif and the ocean beyond.

★ **La Côte d'Argent** – *See Côte d'Argent. For details of ferry services see Michelin Red Guide France.*

★ **Phare de Cordouan** – *See Cordouan.*

★★ Les SABLES-D'OLONNE Pop 15 830

Michelin map 67 folds 11 and 12 or 233 fold 1 – Facilities.
Town plan in the current Michelin Red Guide France.

Les Sables-d'Olonne is an important seaside resort on the **Côte de la Lumière** (Coast of Light), built on the sands of what was once an off-shore bar. The town stretches between a small port and an immense beach of fine sand running for more than 3km – 1¾ miles at the foot of the celebrated "Remblai" (an embankment promenade).
The summer season is the only time visitors will see the local girls in their traditional, ancestral costume – in carnival processions and folklore festivals. The costume – "light and short", with pleated petticoats, black stockings, *sabots* with heels, and tall headdresses with quivering "wings" – derives, like the dark features of the local people themselves, from the fact that centuries ago the area was settled by Moors expelled from Spain. The Vertonne depression, where the immigrants settled, is still known as "Saracens' Corridor".

Tempest by the harbour, Les Sables-d'Olonne.

HISTORICAL AND GEOGRAPHICAL NOTES

Origins – In the Middle Ages the site here was no more than an outer port for Olonne, a small town on the Vertonne estuary now a little way inland. Then, little by little, the inlet silted up, finally turning into a swamp and then a salt-marsh *(qv)*; Les Sables-d'Olonne (the sands of Olonne) was created.
Under the patronage of Louis XI, who visited the area with the chronicler Commynes, the Seneschal (Steward) of Poitou, the port was dredged out and shipyards were built. Some of the vessels launched here took part in the great voyages of discovery. In the 17C a local sailor, **Nau the Olonnais**, distinguished himself in the West Indies during the bloody guerrilla warfare fought against the Spaniards by the buccaneers of Turtle Island and the half-privateer, half-pirate "Brothers of the Coast"; he died tragically, devoured by hostile natives.

Economic life – The port comprises a dock for fishing boats, a tidal basin (Bassin à flot) for cargo ships, and a marina known as **Port Olana** with 1 100 berths for yachts and cruisers which lies further upriver, just south of the long, straight by-pass road linking Les Sables with the ancient fishermen's district of La Chaume west of the town. The marina has been established in what was once known as the "bassin des chasses" (*chasse* = flush) – so-called because its waters, abruptly released, would flush away the silt forming on the bed of the estuary.
Port Olona is the starting point for the four-yearly round-the-world race known as the "Vendée Globe" – a tough challenge for single-handed sailing boats with no ports of call allowed and no help on the way *(the next race is scheduled for late 1996)*.
Fishermen from this part of the coast used to fish mainly cod; at one time Les Sables would fit out as many as 100 cod-fishing boats a year. Today the trawlers with their modern gear are engaged in both coastal and deep-sea fishing, generally in the southern part of the Bay of Biscay, although vessels sometimes travel as far north as St George's Channel, between Great Britain and Ireland. Because of the tonnage landed the town ranks 12th among France's fishing ports.
The **salt-marshes** ⓥ north of the town are no longer exploited : plans have been approved to transform them into a zone of aquaculture. Market gardens in La Chaume, on the other hand, well-fertilized with marine compost, continue to produce high-quality early strawberries, artichokes etc.
In the summer season organized **boat trips** ⓥ leave from the port.

During the summer months the sea is warmer and less healthy; it is also then that oysters spawn, and as a consequence their meat loses much of its texture and distinctive flavour. This is why it is said that oysters should be eaten only when there is an "r" in the month.

SIGHTS

★ **Le Remblai** (BZ) – This embankment was built in the 18C to protect the town from the incursions of the sea. Today the fine promenade along its top is bordered by shops, hotels, cafés and luxury apartment blocks with splendid views of the beach and the bay. In the summer, before lunch or during the evening, it is the favourite meeting place of bathers, who have only to cross the road to slake their thirst or do their shopping after they have left the beach. At the western extremity of Le Remblai is the municipal swimming pool and one of the casinos (Casino de la Plage, which includes a 700-seat theatre and a conference hall which can accommodate 1 000). Behind the modern blocks, the narrow streets of the old town beckon.

La Corniche – This southerly prolongation of Le Remblai leads to the new residential district of La Rudelière. After 3km – $1\frac{1}{4}$ miles the clifftop route arrives at **Le Puits d'Enfer** (Hell's Well) – a narrow and impressive cleft in the rock, at the foot of which the sea foams and thrashes.

La Rudelière District – The development is near the **Lac de Tanchet,** with its lakeside sailing school. In the same area are the town's second casino, Casino des Sports, a sea-water cure centre (Centre de Thalassothérapie), sports grounds and a zoo.

Parc Zoologique de Tranchet ⊙ – In this pleasantly laid out "green belt" environment, visitors can observe a variety of wildlife including camels, llamas, kangaroos, monkeys and rare birds.

Église Notre-Dame-de-Bon-Port (AZ B) – The church was built in 1646 by Richelieu. In the nave, which is an excellent example of late Gothic architecture, the Gothic vaults are perfectly complemented by the pilasters of the Corinthian order supporting them.

Musée de l'Abbaye Ste-Croix (BZ M[1]) ⊙ – The old Holy Cross Abbey, founded in the 17C by Benedictine monks, is now a cultural centre. On the ground floor of the museum are two galleries devoted to **modern and contemporary art.** The exhibits include surrealist paintings and sculpture by Victor Brauner and works by Marquet *(Summer,* and *The Beaches at Les Sables-d'Olonne).*
On the first floor are a lithograph by Francis Bacon, works by Gaston Chaissac (one of the leaders of the Art Brut (Raw Art) movement, 1910-64), by Dubuffet, who was influenced by Chaissac, and by Robert Combas of Figuration Libre.
The second floor houses a **Department of Pre-History** and an interesting **ethnologic collection.** This includes a marshland domestic hut interior, traditional costumes from Les Sables and the surrounding marshlands, seascapes by the local painter Paul-Emil Pajot, and a number of model boats. The 17C attics contain more works by Victor Brauner and Chaissac.

Musée des Guerres de Vendée (AZ M[2]) ⊙ – This is a waxworks museum in which the more striking episodes from the vicious local wars are represented. Many contemporary documents are on display.

La Chaume – The redeveloped, former fishermen's district west of the town proper has small houses with tiled roofs which contrast starkly with the planned modernism of the resort.

LES SABLES-D'OLONNE

Bisson (R.) .... AZ 8
Guynemer (R.) .... BZ
Halles (R. des) .... AZ 29
H.-de-Ville (R. de l') .... AZ
Nationale (R.) .... BZ
Travot (R.) .... BZ 60

Bauduère (R. de la) .... BZ 6
Caisse-d'Épargne (R.) .... AZ 10
Collineau (Pl. du Gén.) .... BZ 14
Commerce (Pl. du) .... AZ 15
Dingler (Quai) .... AZ 18
Église (Pl. de l') .... AZ 24
Gabaret (Av. A.) .... BZ 26
Leclerc (R. Gén.) .... ABZ 33
Liberté (Pl. de la) .... BZ 35
Louis-XI (Pl.) .... BZ 36
Navarin (Pl.) .... AZ 40
Palais-de-Justice (Pl.) .... AZ 46
Roosevelt (Bd F.) .... AZ 53

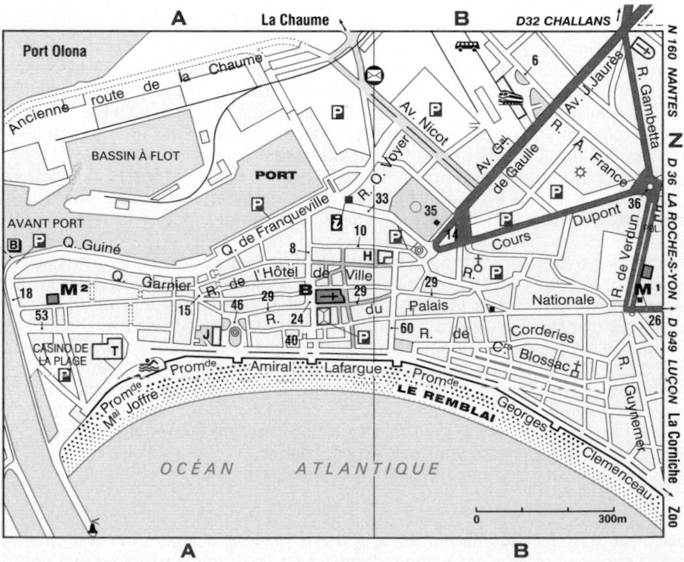

B N.-D.-de-Bon-Port M[1] Musée de l'abbaye Ste-Croix
M[2] Musée des Guerres de Vendée

Tour d'Arundel ⓥ – This tower, once the keep of a fort built in the 12C for Lord Arundel, is used today as a lighthouse. There is a fine view of the bay from the top.

Fort St-Nicolas – The 11C priory chapel, transformed into a fort in 1779, stands on a pleasant site commanding the entrance to the port and offering a splendid view of the bay. It now holds temporary exhibitions.
A garden has been laid out around the building, with a mosaic memorial (1971) to sailors lost at sea. From here it is possible to walk down to the Grande Jetée headland and the beacon at the end of its long breakwater *(illustration above).*

EXCURSIONS

Château de Pierre-Levée ⓥ – *5km – 3 miles northeast via N 160.* This charming 18C folly in the Louis XVI style was built by Luc Pezot, a tax collector for Les Sables district.

Olonne Forest and the Marshlands – *Round tour of 21km – 13 miles. Leave Les Sables via La Chaume and follow D 87^A northwards, crossing the abandoned salt-marsh zone.*

Forêt d'Olonne – This stretch of woodland islanded between the ocean and the Vertonne marshes shimmering beneath the sun extends for 15km – 9¼ miles north of Les Sables. Oak thickets beneath clusters of tall pines carpet over 1 000ha – 2 470 acres of dunes crisscrossed by footpaths, from which herds of deer may occasionally be seen.

Cross D 80 to Champclou and continue to L'Île-d'Olonne.

The road crosses the Olonne marsh, the eastern part of which has been transformed into a bird sanctuary. The marsh was originally formed because of the gradual silting up, in prehistoric times, of what was the Bay of Olonne.

At L'Île-d'Olonne, take the road for Olonne-sur-Mer. After 1km – just over half a mile – turn right towards the observatory (signposted).

Observatoire d'Oiseaux de l'Île-d'Olonne ⓥ – Well-placed on a rise overlooking the marsh, the observatory allows visitors, with the help of telescopes, to study the birds in the **Chanteloup Hunting Reserve.** Every summer the 38ha – 94 acre reserve accommodates, among many other species, an important colony of avocets.

Olonne-sur-Mer – This one-time coastal port now stands a little way inland, owing to the silting up of the Bay.

★★ ST-BERTRAND-DE-COMMINGES

Pop 217

Michelin map 85 fold 20 or 235 fold 41 – Local map p 133 – Facilities.

St-Bertrand is one of the most picturesque villages in the foothills of the Pyrenees, perched on an isolated hilltop at the entrance to the upper valley of the River Garonne. It is encircled by ancient ramparts and dominated by an imposing cathedral; the belfry-porch of this sanctuary, crowned by a defensive wooden gallery, is a landmark visible for miles around.
Apart from its remarkable **site★★**, St-Bertrand is noted for the artistic and architectural treasure it contains, and for the charm of its steep, narrow streets crowded with medieval houses and artisans' workshops. In summer, in conjunction with nearby Valcabrère *(see below),* the village holds a Music Festival.
Today St-Bertrand-de-Comminges, formerly a stopping-place on the pilgrims' route to Santiago de Compostela, remains one of the most impressive sights on any journey through the Pyrenees.

Memories of Herod – The town that preceded St-Bertrand enjoyed a distinguished Roman past as **Lugdunum Convenarum,** capital of the tribe of Convenae in the 1C BC; it is thought to have had as many as 60 000 inhabitants. The Jewish historian Flavius Josephus asserts that it was the place to which Herod, the Tetrarch of Galilee, and his wife Herodias, responsible for the murder of John the Baptist, were exiled by the Emperor Caligula four years after the death of Christ.
Originally no more than a hill settlement, Lugdunum Convenarum subsequently spilled over onto the plain below and eventually spread as far as Valcabrère and the banks of the Garonne. Ongoing **excavations** have unearthed two Roman bath-houses, the remains of a theatre, a temple probably consecrated to Rome and to Augustus, a 5C Christian basilica and a marketplace on one side of a large square flanked by porticoes.

Two Bertrands – The Roman colonial capital was eventually sacked by the Barbarians. Subsequently rebuilt on the hill only and enclosed within a wall, it was however totally destroyed for a second time by the Burgundians in the 6C. For nearly 500 years after that the town stood empty and fell into decay.
Around 1120 the Bishop of Comminges, Bertrand de L'Isle-Jourdain, appreciating the site of the old acropolis, had the ruins cleared and built a cathedral. To serve it he appointed a chapter of canons. The effects of the future St Bertrand's actions were felt almost immediately : the faithful flocked to the town which grew up around the church, and pilgrims broke their journey here. The town adopted the name of the man who had brought it back to life.
By the end of the 13C the cathedral founded by St Bertrand was no longer large enough for its congregation. A namesake, Bertrand de Got, who was himself destined to become Clement V, the first Avignon Pope, continued the Bishop's work; the enlargement of the church was completed by his successors in 1352.

The Cathedral, St-Bertrand-de-Comminges.

★ CATHÉDRALE STE-MARIE-DE-COMMINGES ⏲ *allow 2 hours.*

Park in the car park, then go through Majou Gate, following the old Roman road to the citadel.

The Romanesque part of the cathedral comprises the west front crowned with a belfry, the porch and the three western bays; the rest is Gothic. The tympanum (west door) is carved with an effigy of Bishop St Bernard and an *Adoration of the Magi.*

★★ **Cloisters** – Other cloisters in the region are larger and richer; none, however, are more impressive. The pervading sense of spiritual peace and retreat from the world distilled by the architectural setting is enhanced by the temporal poetry of the splendid mountain landscape visible through the arcades (one of the galleries is open to the outside world, a rare arrangement).

Three of the galleries are Romanesque while the fourth, adjoining the church, was altered in the 15C and 16C; it houses several sarcophagi. The capitals in the cloisters are exceptional for their carvings showing Biblical scenes, foliage and scrolls. In the first gallery, on the right entering the cloisters, a celebrated pillar portrays the Evangelists Matthew, Mark, Luke and John (**1**).

★ **Treasury** – *Above the cloisters' northern gallery.* The treasury includes two 16C Tournai tapestries *(in the raised chapel).* The former chapter-house contains episcopal ornaments, a mitre, two liturgical copes (The Virgin and The Passion), and the shaft of St Bernard's crook, fashioned from a narwhal tusk. The copes, exquisitely worked in broderie anglaise, were the gift of Bertrand de Got on the occasion of the translation of Bishop St Bertrand's relics (1309).

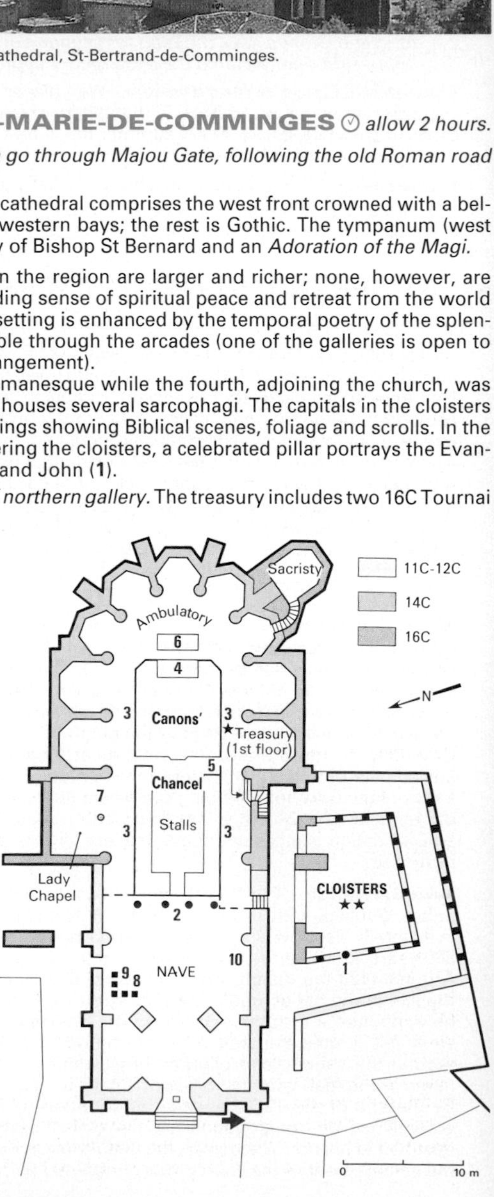

Canons' Chancel – The chancel boasts the superb **woodwork**★★ commissioned from sculptors in Toulouse by Bishop Jean de Mauléon and inaugurated by him in 1535. The carvings include the rood screen (**2**), the choir screen (**3**), the high altar reredos (**4**) – unfortunately disfigured by over-painting – a bishop's throne (5) surmounted by a three-tiered pyramidal dome, and 66 **stalls,** 38 of them with tall backs and canopies. Piety, wit, satire – even lechery – are given free reign in the little world created by the craftsmen, the general theme of which is the Redemption.

St Bertrand's Tomb (6) – The tomb is a 15C stone-built tabernacle in the form of a shrine, which supports an altar.

Lady Chapel – The chapel, a 16C addition on the northern side of the church, contains the marble tomb of Hugues de Chatillon (7), who completed the building in the 14C. The lierne and tierceron vaulting signify the end of the Gothic period.

Nave – Space for the congregation on the outer side of the rood screen is somewhat limited but this is compensated for in the richness of the furnishings : a 16C organ on which, in season, recitals are given (8); a pulpit (9) with classical carvings (16C); the former parish altar (10), which dates from 1621. The imposing altar-front is made of Cordoba leather.
After visiting the cathedral, visitors may go down past the 15C and 16C houses to Cabriole Gate : the old barbican offers a good view of the surrounding countryside and over to Valcabrère *(see below)*.

Follow the old ramparts south, returning to the car park via Lyrisson Gate, an alley on the left and the gardens of the old museum.

EXCURSIONS

★ **Valcabrère** – *2km – 1 ¼ miles northeast by D 26.* The 11C-12C **Basilique St-Just**★ ⏲ stands isolated in the middle of fields, surrounded by its cypress-filled cemetery.

St-Gaudens – *17km – 10 miles northeast by D 26, D 33 and D 8.* The **Musée de St-Gaudens et du Comminges** ⏲ focuses on local history, folklore and customs, porcelain, religious art, and has an important mineral collection.

★★ ST-ÉMILION

Pop 2 799

Michelin map 75 fold 12 or 234 fold 3 – Local map p 28 – Facilities.

St-Émilion is a delightful town built on the slopes of a limestone plateau overlooking the Dordogne Valley, and surrounded by its famous vineyards. Ancient ramparts, monuments, a maze of narrow streets and stone stairways linking picturesque small squares combine to form an overall picture that never fails to impress visitors. In fine weather the sun accentuates the golden tones of the pantiled roofs and old stone walls, while the ever-changing contrasts of light and shade add extra interest to any stroll through the medieval quarters.
The town is known not only for its fine wines but also for the local macaroons.

★ **Site** – St-Émilion faces due south, nestling within a horse-shoe between two hillsides. At the junction of the two slopes, a tall belltower rises above a rocky spur honeycombed with caves, catacombs, a hermitage, a chapel and an extraordinary underground church. At the foot of this promontory, below the church, lies Place du Marché, the main square at the heart of this busy small town. The square acts as a link between the districts sprawled over the two hills, one the site of the royal castle, the other the site of a deanery, reflecting the age-old rivalry between the Church and the State.
The top of the King's Tower *(see below)* offers a fine overall view of the town.

Peace Lovers – Centuries after the Latin poet Ausonius settled in the locality – he had property on the hillside, and his name today remains allied to one of the prestigious wine "houses" – it was a hermit named **Émilion** who found here the peace and tranquillity necessary for meditation. Émilion, originally from Brittany, was a baker by trade before embracing the monastic life at Saujon, near Royan *(qv)*. Withdrawing subsequently to the limestone slopes of the Dordogne Valley, he discovered a grotto watered by a natural spring in the rocky centre of what is now the town bearing his name, and lived there until his death towards the end of the 8C.
Ten centuries later it was a fugitive who sought sanctuary in St-Émilion : **Élie Guadet,** a native of the town and a prominent member of the Girondin Party at the beginning of the Convention *(qv)*. Suspected of "Moderantism" – what today would be termed deviation from the party line – Gaudet became a victim of the Revolutionary leader Robespierre's hatred for the Girondins, and was obliged to flee Paris disguised as an upholsterer. He took refuge first in Normandy and later rejoined a couple of Girondin colleagues in St-Émilion. It was here, one day in 1794, that he was discovered, arrested, and taken to Bordeaux, where he died on the scaffold.

Jurats and the Jurade – In the Middle Ages the famous red wines of St-Émilion *(see also Bordeaux vineyards, qv)* were qualified as "Honorific" because it was the custom to offer them to royalty and persons of note. From then on it was decided that, in order to maintain the excellence and reputation of wines permitted to bear that name, they should be subject each year to evaluation by a committee of professionals. The body appointed by the town council to carry out this task was called the *Jurade* and its members the *Jurats.* The Jurade was re-formed in 1948 and still operates today.
In the Spring of each year, a procession of Jurats wearing scarlet, ermine-trimmed robes and silken hoods attends a solemn Mass and then proceeds to determine whether the previous Autumn's wine is fit to receive their seal of excellence. Once this decision in general has been made, each grower is invited to submit his particular product to the jury for appraisal.
In the Autumn these same Jurats assemble at the top of the King's Tower to proclaim the official start of the grape harvest. Such solemn rites are accompanied by ceremonial banquets – suitably washed down with local wines – held in the Dominican Room of the local wine-growers' association.

SIGHTS

★ **Monolithic Church** – The church, the largest monolithic sanctuary in France to be carved from a single solid block of rock, is a great rarity. It was fashioned between the 8C and the 12C by enlarging natural grottoes and caverns which already existed in the porous strata. The façade above the main square corresponds to the chancel, pierced by three 16C windows which allow light into the three aisles within. The main entrance is on the left of these windows, through a tall 14C Gothic porch decorated on the tympanum with a *Last Judgement* and a *Resurrection of the Dead.* The vaulted passageway beyond is lined with headstones.
The interior of the church is impressive as much for the size of those three aisles carved from the rock as for the perfect symmetry of its vaulting and squared pillars – only two of which support the belltower *(concrete supporting posts have been added temporarily, during restoration work).*
The majestic **belfry** ⓥ, dating from the 12C, 14C and 15C, boasts a tower pierced by imposing Romanesque bays; above, the 15C spire soars to a height of 67m – 220ft. From inside *(198 steps)* there is a fine view of the town, its monuments and the neighbouring vineyards.

Chapelle de la Trinité ⓥ – Holy Trinity Chapel, a miniature sanctuary built by Benedictine monks in the 13C, includes a harmonious – and, in the southwest, rare – example of a timber-framed Gothic apse. Inside, elegant High Gothic ribbed vaulting converges on a keystone embossed with the symbolic Lamb.
Below the chapel, in the same rock mass as the church, is the grotto known as **L'Ermitage de St-Émilion** which is divided into two parts : one contains "St Émilion's Bed", a kind of armchair carved from the limestone, and a spring, now guarded by a 17C balustrade; the other part is said to have served as the recluse's place of worship.
Near the chapel the cliff face opens out into **catacombs** – rock galleries once used as an ancient burial ground, with tombs gouged from the rock. Later, part of this subterranean maze was used as an ossuary : at the top of a central dome is an opening through which bones from a cemetery on top of the cliff were disposed of. At the base of the dome is a primitive representation depicting the resurrection of the dead : three small figures emerging hand in hand from their sarcophagi.

Place du Marché – St-Émilion's main square and market place, in a picturesque setting at the foot of the spur, offers a fine view of the troglodyte church and its belfry. The tree at its centre – a member of the acacia family – was planted in 1848 and originally known as the Tree of Liberty.

Porte de la Cadène – This gateway stands at the end of a street off the main square, with a 15C timber-framed house beside it. The name of the arch derives from the Latin word *Catena,* a chain, and is a reminder that originally, at night, access from here to the town centre was blocked by a chain. It offers an unusual view of the church belfry.

Château du Roi – The King's Castle, founded according to some by Louis VIII and to others by Henri III Plantagenet in the 13C, was used as the town hall until 1720. From the top of the King's Tower (a rectangular keep with latrines on its outer face, standing on an isolated spur of rock) there is a fine view over the huddled rooftops of the town and across to the valleys of the Dordogne and the Isle rivers.

Cloître des Cordeliers ⓥ – The Cordeliers – Franciscans of a strict order distinguished by a knotted cord worn around the waist – built this sanctuary in the 14C. The handsome ruins of their square **cloisters★** include slender twinned columns supporting Romanesque arches. At the far end, on the right, a 15C Gothic archway precedes the stairway which led to the monks' cells.
On the left, the belfry of the old church (15C) is supported by two unusual superimposed arches. Inside, the nave is separated from the apse by a triumphal arch in the Flamboyant Gothic style, which gives access down to a series of caves quarried out 20m – 66ft deep in the bed-rock where red, white and rosé wines made by the Champagne method are left to mature. Of the old **Logis de la Commanderie** (the abbot's lodgings), nothing remains but a covered watchpath and a corner bartizan. There is an interesting view of St-Émilion from the Esplanade (Place du Cap-du-Pont).

Collegiate Church – *Place Pioceau.* This huge collegiate church has an unconventional ground-plan : it is almost 80m – 262ft long and comprises a Romanesque nave barely 9m – 30ft wide with a Gothic chancel reaching 28m – 92ft wide. The entrance is on the north side of the chancel, via a superb 14C porch built at a time when Gaillard de Lamothe, the nephew of Pope Clement V *(qv),* was Dean of the resident canons. The carved tympanum represents *The Last Judgement.* Below, only the lower parts of the statues of the Apostles remain in their niches, the figures having been mutilated during the Wars of Religion and during the Revolution.
Inside, the nave comprises three bays, two of them domed and the third with groined vaulting. Two 12C mural paintings – *The Virgin* and *The Legend of St Catherine* – adorn the far end of the right-hand wall. The 15C choir stalls in the chancel are carved with an entertaining variety of different characters.

Collegiate Church Cloisters ⓥ – *Enter via the tourist information centre.*
The cloisters, which lie to the south of the church, date from the 14C and are still in very good condition; they have much in common with the Cordeliers' Cloisters, particularly in the design of their twinned columns, which are extremely elegant.
Arches reinforce the corners separating the galleries – one of which houses an impressive series of covered niches formerly used as tombs. From another gallery, Romanesque arcades originally led to the chapter-house.
The deanery – comprising the old refectory and the monks' dormitory – has been restored and is occupied today by the tourist information centre. A little further west is the 13C chapter-house chapel.

Logis de Malet de Roquefort – Opposite the Collegiate Church a 15C mansion is incorporated into the ramparts : the old covered watch-path of the fortified town with its corbelled crenellations passes beneath the roof of the house. The building houses the local **Archeological Museum** ⏲.

Ramparts – The ramparts date from the 13C but were reinforced later by the machicolated watch-path. Six gateways allowed access through the ancient walls. The eastern section, which can be driven past by car, is the most impressive.
From Porte Bourgeoise *(north)* the route passes the ruined façade of the Palais Cardinal, so-called because Gaillard de Lamothe *(see above)* lived there after he was elevated to Cardinal. Subsequently the road hugs the old wall, with the vineyards stretching away on the other side. To the right are the Jacobins' monastery and the ivy-covered Cordeliers' cloisters. Finally the road arrives at **Porte Brunet,** from which there are impressive views of the vineyards. It was through this gate, one night in January 1794, that the outlawed Girondins escaped from Robespierre's men after the arrest of their companion Gaudet *(see above).*

Mur des Dominicains (Dominicans' Wall) – Beyond Porte Bourgeoise and to the left stand "Les Grandes Murailles" (the high walls). This stretch of stonework once formed the north wall of a Gothic church which was abandoned when the friars fled to the interior of the town during the Hundred Years War *(qv).*

EXCURSION

St-Émilion Vineyards – *Round tour of 52km – 32 miles. See Vineyards of Bordeaux.*

For information on wine tours around Bordeaux and the Loire – whether on foot or by coach, on horseback or by car – see the chapter on Practical Information (qv).

★★ SAINTES

Pop 25 874

Michelin map 71 fold 4 or 233 fold 27 – Local map p 243.
Town plan in the current Michelin Red Guide France.

To those hurrying through the town via Avenue Gambetta, Cours National and Cours Lemercier (busy shopping streets shaded by plane trees) Saintes offers the straightforward appearance of a prosperous, well laid-out regional capital; for those prepared to visit Saintes, however, there are attractive discoveries in store as the local monuments date from every period since the Romans. From the bridge onwards, visitors can stroll enjoyably beside the River Charente as far as the public gardens and beyond.
The town has given its name to the Saintonge, an old province in the western Charentes.

HISTORICAL NOTES

Origins – *"Mediolanum Santonum",* capital of the Santons during the Roman domination of the Vendée, was built on the hillside sloping up from the west bank of the Charente; the river was spanned by a bridge on which the Arch of Germanicus was erected. The Latin poet Ausonius died in this town, in his Villa Pagus Noverus, at the time St Eutrope was beginning to preach the Gospel. In the Middle Ages, when Saintes was under Plantagenet rule, religious buildings sprang up all over the town; pilgrims on the way to Santiago de Compostela *(qv)* filed continuously across the bridge. They were welcomed and sent on their way to two suburbs which had developed around religious establishments : St-Eutrope and, on the east bank of the Charente, Dames.
Until the Revolution – under which Saintes became the county town of Lower Charente but was deprived of its bishopric – so many luxurious mansions were built by local nobles and lawyers that the town could serve as a lesson in the evolution of Classical architecture.
Town planning had its place in 18C Saintes, laying out the thoroughfares on the perimeter of the old town along the site of the ancient ramparts. In the 19C Cours National (the principal axis of the modern town) was bordered with neo-Classical public buildings; among them, on opposite sides of the avenue, are the law courts and the theatre.

A determined man – In *c*1539 a man called **Bernard Palissy** *(qv)* was working in Saintes as a surveyor. He decided, however, to renounce this profession and devote his time to the art of ceramics, and set up a studio-workshop near the ramparts. Here, in a state of complete privation, he struggled day and night to survive until he discovered the secret of enamelling. "Maistre Bernard, the worker in earth", as he was known, became celebrated for his enamelled terracottas.

A philanthropist – Against his will perhaps, **Joseph Ignace Guillotin** (1738-1814), a doctor living in Saintes, lent his name to France's notorious machine for judicial executions. Until then, decapitation had been reserved for those of noble birth. The doctor believed that all men should be equal at death – and he was anxious to spare the condemned unnecessary suffering. He therefore proposed to the National Assembly in 1789 "a rapid-action beheading machine". Guillotin, himself a Deputy, was gratified when the invention was approved; he was less pleased when the death machine was not unnaturally christened, in 1792 when it was first used, *La Guillotine.*

ABBAYE AUX DAMES *30min.*

This "Ladies' Abbey", which stands on the east bank of the Charente, was consecrated in 1047. The abbey was dedicated to St Mary, and owed its prosperity to Agnès de Bourgogne, whose second husband was Geoffroy Martel, Comte d'Anjou and seigneur of the Saintonge. The Abbey, placed in the hands of Benedictine nuns, was directed by an Abbess – customarily chosen from among the most illustrious families in France – who then bore the title "Madame de Saintes". Charged with the education of young daughters of the nobility, the convent counted among its boarders at one time Athenaïs de Rochechouart, the future Marquise de Montespan and mistress to Louis XIV. After the Revolution and during the Empire period the Abbey fell into decline. It was transformed into a barracks, freed after World War I, but required a great deal of restoration before it could be returned to the Church for religious use.

★ **Abbey Church** – The Abbey Church is in the local Saintonge Romanesque style; it is reached via an 18C porch leading to the Abbey's first courtyard, where it is surrounded by the usual convent buildings. The most remarkable features of the church are the façade and the belltower.

The **façade** presents a richly-ornamented **doorway** at the centre, flanked by blind arcades. The carved coving in the doorway shows, from bottom to top : six angels adoring the Hand of God; the symbols of the Evangelists around the Lamb; the suffering of the martyrs, menaced by a whip, an axe or the Sword of Justice; 54 old men wearing crowns, facing each other two by two as they play music. The coving of the right arcade portrays the Last Supper; that on the left, the presence of a divine Christ, haloed, facing five other figures suffused with light whose significance is uncertain. Note also the historiated capitals (a knight, monsters) and, on the gable, the arms of Françoise I de La Rochefoucauld, Abbess from 1559 to 1605.

The lower level of the **belltower** *(illustration p 000)*, situated above the transept crossing, is square in section and pierced with three arcades on each face. Above this is a shallow octagonal level flanked by pinnacles which is in turn surmounted by a dome pierced by 12 twinned bays separated by small columns. The whole tower is topped by a scaled conical roof, the slopes of which are slightly convex.

Interior – In the first half of the 12C the interior was the subject of alterations, generally thought to have been by the architect Béranger (an inscription carved into the outside of the north wall dates the work as pre-1150). The quadripartite vaulting in the transept arms – and the Gothic chapel in the northern arm – are later (15C) additions. The two-bay nave, lined with six heavy 12C pillars erected in front of the 11C walls, is covered with a timber ceiling which replaced the two original domes on pendentives, destroyed by fire in 1648. On the southern side of the transept entrance, a console supports a 12C head of Christ.

At the intersection of the nave and the transept, before the transept crossing and the belltower above it, four more heavy pillars support a dome on squinches. A gallery for the sick is in the south transept.

Half-barrel vaulting over the Romanesque chancel is prolonged by a slightly recessed, terminal oven vault.

Convent buildings – The façade of the long 17C central block has been restored to its original purity of line : two storeys pierced by narrow windows and surmounted by an attic floor animated by dormers with pediments.

On the left, adjoining three renovated bays of the old 14C cloisters, is a fine 17C doorway, the pilasters of which are adorned with exuberant sculptures that contrast strikingly with the severity of the façade.

SAINTES

Alsace-Lorraine (R.)	AZ	3
Gambetta (Av.)	BZ	
National (Cours)	AZ	
Arc-de-Triomphe (R.)	BZ	4
Bassompierre (Pl.)	BZ	5
Berthonnière (R.)	AZ	7
Blair (Pl.)	AZ	9
Bois-d'Amour (R.)	AZ	10
Brunaud (R. A.)	AZ	13
Clemenceau (R. G.)	AZ	15
Denfert-Rochereau (R.)	BZ	16
Foch (Pl. Mar.)	AZ	20
Jacobins (R. des)	AZ	25
Lemercier (Cours)	AZ	35
Marne (Av. de la)	BZ	37
Mestreau (R. F.)	BZ	38
Monconseil (R.)	AZ	39
République (Quai de la)	AZ	41
St-Eutrope (R.)	AZ	42
St-François (R.)	AZ	43
St-Macoult (R.)	AZ	45
St-Pierre (R.)	AZ	46
St-Vivien (Pl.)	AZ	47
Victor-Hugo (R.)	AZ	49

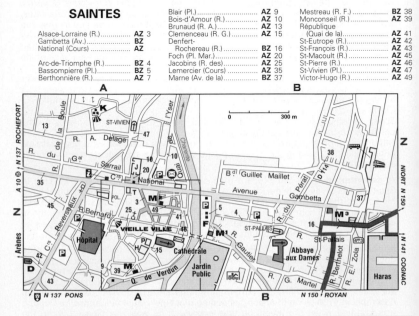

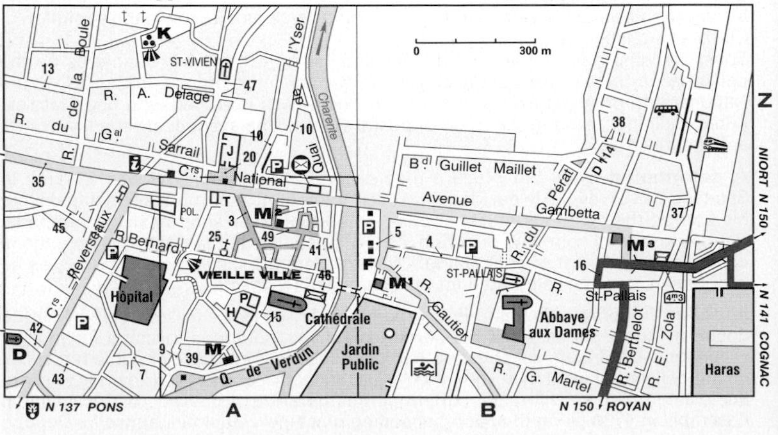

D Église St-Eutrope F Arc de Germanicus K Thermes St-Saloine
M¹ Musée Archéologique M³ Musée éducatif de Préhistoire

SIGHTS

★ **Arc de Germanicus** – *East bank.* This fine Roman arch with its twin arcades stood until 1843 on the bridge that carried the main thoroughfare in Saintes across the River Charente. Threatened with destruction when the bridge, itself Roman, was about to be demolished, the arch was saved by the intervention of the writer Prosper Merimée, who held the post of Inspector of Historic Monuments. It was dismantled and rebuilt on the east bank of the river.
The structure, composed of the local limestone and erected in the year AD 19, was a votive – not a triumphal – arch. Inscriptions still visible dedicate it to Germanicus, to the Emperor Tiberius, and to his son Drusus. The name of the donor, Caius Julius Rufus, also appears. In the centre of the arch the groins of the three pillars supporting the double arcade are emphasized by fluted columns with Corinthian capitals.

Musée Archéologique ⊙ – *East bank.* The building in which this museum is installed was once a slaughterhouse. It lies at the end of a driveway flanked by Doric columns. There is an interesting lapidary collection, deriving mainly from discoveries made when the wall of the ancient Gallo-Roman *castrum* (fort) was demolished. It includes columns, capitals, architraves and remarkably-carved low-reliefs.
Further traces of Roman remains can be seen in the neighbourhood of the museum.

★ **Vieille Ville** – The Old Town district around the cathedral on the west bank of the river preserves the evocative atmosphere of Saintes as it was in the old days.

Cathédrale St-Pierre – St Peter's Cathedral was built on the site of a Romanesque church of which all that remains is a dome above the south transept. Its construction, under the direction of three successive Bishops of Saintes, all members of the Rochechouart family, dates in the main from the 15C. It was severely damaged by the Calvinists in 1568. The massive belltower, made heavier still by enormous buttresses with projecting features, was never completed : a dome with lead panels replaced the spire proposed in the original plans. Angels, saints and prophets adorn the Flamboyant doorway within the porch at the foot of the tower.
Unity and simplicity characterize the architecture of the interior. This impression of coherence is accentuated by rays of light slanting through tall windows, making the stone walls even whiter. Stripped of ornamentation, the large round columns of the nave, like the Gothic pillars in the chancel, support a bare upper wall roofed with visible timbers. Only the side aisles are vaulted in stone.
Both nave and aisles date almost in their entirety from the 16C, the great organ from the 16C and 17C. A door in the south transept opens onto the former canons' cloisters (13C), of which two galleries and the ruins of the chapter-house remain.

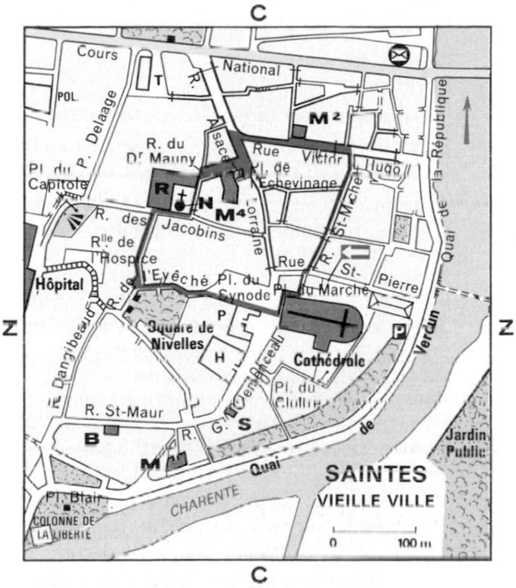

B Hôtel de la Bourse
M Musée Dupuy-Mestreau
M² Présidial - Musée des Beaux-Arts
M⁴ Ancien échevinage - Musée
N Chapelle des Jacobins
R Hôtel Martineau
S Hôtel d'Argenson

The axial chapel, with its niches surmounted by elaborately carved canopies, exemplifies the final effervescence of the Flamboyant Gothic style; the credences were already Renaissance. The **Treasury** ⊙, in an annex chapel, offers a collection of sacred vessels and vestments.

Leave Place du Marché, which is beside the cathedral, and follow the whole length of Rue St-Michel until Rue Victor-Hugo is reached, on the left. Take Rue Victor-Hugo.

A succession of pretty houses, with un-clad stonework in the Saintonge style, can be seen in Rue Victor-Hugo, once known as Grande-Rue, which follows the course of the old road which led via the Germanicus arch to the bridge across the river.

Présidial (M²) – *At No 2 Rue Victor-Hugo, set back at the far end of the garden.* This mansion, a former presidential residence (President Le Berthon, 1605), today houses a fine-arts museum. Architecturally its façade, with wide bays and dormers topped by triangular pediments, marks the beginning of the Classical period.

Continue along Rue Victor-Hugo as far as Rue Alsace-Lorraine. Turn left here and continue to Place de l'Échevinage.

Ancien Échevinage (M⁴) – Beyond the Classical gateway, an 18C façade is attached to a turret dating from the 16C. There is a museum of *Échevinage* (Magistrature).

Return to Place de l'Échevinage and take Rue du Dr-Mauny. Pass through the triple-arcade porch to the Hôtel Martineau courtyard.

Hôtel Martineau (R) – This mansion is now the home of the municipal library.

The Roman Amphitheatre, Saintes.

Chapelle des Jacobins (N) – This chapel has an elegantly designed bay in the Flamboyant style.

Rue des Jacobins. The route passes the rear façade of Hôtel Martineau.

Square des Nivelles – The 17C entrance to a former college leads to this pleasantly laid-out, flower-decked square bordered by fine municipal buildings.

★ **Arènes** – *West of the town centre.* A short distance from the centre, the Roman arena – in reality an amphitheatre – owes part of its sylvan attraction and evocative atmosphere to the fact that grass covers a large proportion of the stepped terracing. This is one of the oldest amphitheatres of the Roman world – it was built in the 1C AD – but is relatively small. Overall dimensions of the ellipse are 125m long × 102m wide (413ft × 335ft), while the actual arena, where performances took place, measures 64m × 39m (210ft × 128ft). The terraces could accommodate 20 000 spectators.
Halfway up the terraced slope, on the southern side, there is a gap in which a small fountain plays. This is dedicated to St Eustelle, a young female disciple of St Eutrope who was beheaded here.

⌚ ►► Église St Eutrope – 11C church, with lower church★; Quai de Verdun; Musée Dupuy-Mestreau (**M**) – Assorted collections in an 18C mansion; Musée des Beaux-Arts★ (**M²**) – Collection of 15C-18C paintings; Musée de l'Échevinage (**M⁴**) – 19C paintings and contemporary works; Thermes St-Saloine (north of the town centre); Musée Éducatif de Préhistoire (east of the town centre) – Includes the giant Grézac tool-polishing stone; Haras (east of the town centre) – Horse Stud.

EXCURSIONS

★ Tour of the Romanesque churches in the Saintonge

75km – 47 miles : allow 4 hours. Leave Saintes heading west (N 150 then D 728).

Corme-Royal – The church, a dependency of Abbaye aux Dames in Saintes, was restored and returned to its original state in 1970. It is noted for its two-storey west front decorated with sculptures.

Abbaye de Sablonceaux – This abbey was founded in 1136 by Guillaume X, the father of Eleanor of Aquitaine *(qv)*. Partially destroyed five times since the 14C, the abbey church with its tall Gothic tower has been restored to something like its original splendour.

St-Romain-de-Benet – In the hamlet of Pirelonge *(south of N 150)*, the **Musée des Alambics** ⌚, installed in a distillery, displays a collection of *alambics* (stills) from the Charente region, of the type still in use for the refinement of cognac *(qv)*. The museum also shows a series of "mobile" stills used by home distillers to make alcohol from wine or fruit. A collection of alcoholmeters is interesting.
In summer the **Alembic Fairs** held in the hamlet revive such local traditions as lace-making, weaving etc. Not far from the distillery *(behind the railway line)* is **Tour de Pirelonge,** a Roman structure still partially roofed with stones carved into scales. It is thought that the tower, which is beside an old Roman road, may have been used as a distance post or some kind of boundary marker.

Meursac – The Gothic church, which is reinforced with powerful buttresses, ends in a Romanesque chancel with half-barrel vaulting. Romanesque capitals in the chancel depict birds pecking lions and a human figure strangling two lions. The altarpiece and tabernacle are of carved and gilded wood. A 5C crypt was discovered beneath the church in 1972; the large chamber was hollowed from the bed-rock and has a domed roof (access via a narrow spiral staircase near the chancel).

Thaims – The modest church was built on the site of a Gallo-Roman villa (remains of the villa walls, up to a height of 2.5m – 8ft, can be seen at the foot of the octagonal church tower, on the north side). In the garden on the southern side of the church are a number of Merovingian sarcophagi. The cornices of the transept crossing inside are Merovingian too, although scenes engraved there, including the Flight of St Peter, are later (Carolingian).
A lapidary museum has been installed between the nave and the chancel. Among other exhibits are the remains of two Gallo-Roman sculptures : a Bacchic scene in marble, and a stone representation of the Celtic divinity Epona.

Rétaud – The 12C church is worth seeing for the extremely decorative frieze of its west front, for its octagonal belltower above the transept crossing, and especially for the richly carved, faceted walls of the apse. The consoles, fashioned into grotesques, are interesting. Noteworthy features inside include the two capitals at the entrance to the apse, the small columns framing its bays, and part of a funerary *litre* (a black band on the church wall decorated with the armorial bearings of the dead).

Rioux – This village contains a simple rural church with a low nave and belfry-porch, known to art enthusiasts for its brilliant sculptured décor.
On the way to Chermignac the road passes within view of the Château de Rioux, which belonged in the Middle Ages to the family of the Seigneurs of Didonne, vassals of the Comtes de Poitou.

Chermignac – Frightening animals and different types of human characters adorn the covings above the church entrance. Near the church is a fine example of a **"Hosanna Cross"** *(qv)*.

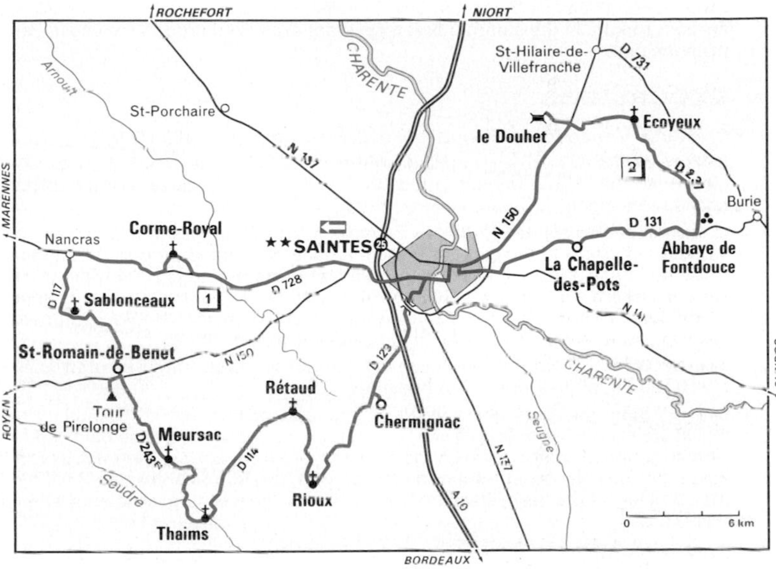

Abbaye de Fontdouce

Tour of 39km – 24 miles : allow 4 hours. Leave Saintes heading east (N 150).

Le Douhet Château ⏲ – The 17C château, with its sober lines, is thought to have been built from plans drawn up by Jules Hardouin-Mansart (1646-1708), the brilliant classicist architect responsible for the Grand Trianon at Versailles and Place Vendôme in Paris. The château and its dependencies, together with the gardens, park and pools, extend over an area of 20ha – 49 acres.
Visitors are recommended to make an exterior tour of the property *(1 hour on foot)* from the Renaissance dove-house to the two mirrored pools of the southern esplanade. These elegant, square, balustraded basins are still fed by the 1C Gallo-Roman aqueduct which once serviced the thermal baths at Saintes. On the way, the hundred-year-old **box wood**★ can be appreciated. Beyond the trees, from the terrace which overlooks the pools, there is a beautiful view across the water to the majestic south face of the château.
Inside the château *(access via the steps below the south front)* – where the period furniture and fittings have only partly been preserved – interest centres mainly on the curious salon named The Lantern, with its 17C woodwork. In the right wing a museum of local traditions has been installed, with the reconstruction of an early 19C bourgeois interior in the Saintonge style, and collections of regional prehistoric, Gallo-Roman and mineralogical items.

Écoyeux – The church here is an imposing 12C building, fortified in the 15C – witness the two turreted watchtowers framing the west front.

Abbaye de Fontdouce ⏲ – This prosperous Benedictine abbey, half hidden in a steep, wooded valley, was sacked by the Huguenots. All that remains today is a small collection of monastic dependencies : a 12C cellar, a heating house with a 15C campanile, the main block dating from the 12C and 13C, and a Charente-style residential hall added to it in the 19C.

Visitors can admire the parlour, the two Romanesque chapels one above the other, and especially the magnificent **chapter-house★**, with its twelve bays in which the ribbed vaulting rests on a forest of pillars. Notable here are the finely carved keystones, among them a curious three-faced head with four eyes, probably symbolizing the Holy Trinity. To evoke the vanished abbey church there remain a few ruined columns and a huge pillar base which would have been at the transept crossing.

La Chapelle-des-Pots – Locally fashioned ceramics, in a tradition dating back to the 13C, are still made today in this village.

ST-GILLES-CROIX-DE-VIE

Pop 6 296

Michelin map 67 fold 12 or 232 folds 38, 39 – Facilities.

The lively fishing port of **Croix-de-Vie** and the town of St-Gilles-sur-Vie, on the south bank of the Vie estuary 30km – $18\frac{1}{2}$ miles northwest of Les Sables-d'Olonne combine to make the single *commune* of St-Gilles-Croix-de-Vie. When St-Hilaire-de-Riez just to the northeast is included, the whole complex is sometimes known as Havre-de-Vie. The fishing boats here supply wholesale fish merchants and factories canning or freezing lobsters, crabs, tunnyfish, sardines etc. A sheltered marina can accommodate up to 600 craft.

The Vie estuary is a geographical curiosity. Approaching the sea, the stream first runs up against a line of sand dunes, the Pointe de la Garenne, and then against the rocky headland known as the Corniche Vendéenne, looping itself as a result into a number of meanders. It finally emerges into the Atlantic between the beaches of Croix-de-Vie (Plage de Boisvinet) and St-Gilles (Grand-Plage) via a bottleneck at the harbour mouth. In the summer **boat trips** ⊙ are organized around the coast, leaving from the port.

EXCURSIONS

★ **Corniche Vendéenne** – *Round tour of 22km – $13\frac{1}{2}$ miles : allow 2 hours.*

St-Hilaire-de-Riez – The town, overlooking the valley of the Vie, has its houses clustered around the church (rebuilt in the 19C), which contains three 17C altarpieces in polychrome stone.

La Bourrine du Bois Juquaud ⊙ *(4km – $2\frac{1}{2}$ miles north via Le Pissot)* is a faithful reconstruction of a turn-of-the-century Breton-Vendée marshland property. A number of small buildings, most of them mud-walled, are grouped together inside an enclosure or "tcheraïe". They include the living quarters or *"bourrine"*, with its adjacent bread oven, a barn, a large outhouse (for the barrow), a small outhouse (for wood), chicken coops, a dairy etc. A vegetable garden is also enclosed.

Sion-sur-l'Océan – This small seaside resort, famous for its shrimps and prawns, lies at the beginning of the Corniche Vendéenne.

Leaving Sion, the route offers views of strange reef formations resembling ruins, which are known as **Les Cinq Pineaux.** Further on, the road follows the bare cliff faces, gashed by small creeks in which the ocean rages. From a rocky platform beyond La Plage des Bussoleries, in front of a turreted villa, the **Trou du Diable** (the Devil's Hole) may be seen : it is a deep, steep hollow into which the sea surges violently when the tide is high.

St-Nicolas-de-Brem – *14km – $8\frac{1}{2}$ miles south.* The church here is curious. It was built in the 11C and partially reconstructed in the 17C. There is a statue of St Nicolas above the entrance. Nearby is a tumulus, an ancient medieval mound probably thrown up to protect the port.

St-Jean-de-Monts – This popular seaside resort boasts numerous facilities : a casino, golf course, salt-water cures...

D'après photo Bras/EXPLORER

La Bourrine du Bois Juquaud.

★★ ST-JEAN-DE-LUZ

Michelin map 85 fold 2 or 234 folds 29, 33 – Local map p 158 – Facilities.

As a smart summer and winter seaside resort, St-Jean-de-Luz dates back only to 1843; as a fishing port, however, the town is ancient, though only one house survives from before the great fire of 1558, when the place was sacked by Spaniards. The sea-front is determinedly modern.
Ste-Barbe headland, which can be reached on foot via Promenade de la Plage and Boulevard Thiers, offers a fine view southwards across the bay to Socoa fort on its rocky promontory.
St-Jean-de-Luz, the most Basque of the towns lying north of the Spanish border, offers all the attractions and amenities of a beach resort together with the picturesque and briny delights of a busy fishing port.

C. Sapra/CEDRI

The harbour, St-Jean-de-Luz.

The town centre – modernized now with many pedestrian precincts (Rue de la République, Rue Gambetta) – has a special charm of its own. The famous "oldest house", its solid dressed-stone construction contrasting with the red-roofed, white-walled Basque buildings nearby, is at 17 Rue de la République, near the port.
The outstanding historical event connected with St-Jean-de-Luz is the marriage of Louis XIV and Maria Theresa.

The Marriage of Louis XIV – The marriage between the King of France and the Infanta of Spain, provided for in the Treaty of the Pyrenees *(qv)*, was delayed because of the monarch's passion for Marie Mancini, the niece of Cardinal Mazarin. The situation was resolved when the Cardinal – successor to Richelieu and Louis XIV's chief minister – eventually sent the young girl into exile and the King yielded for "reasons of State". Louis arrived in St-Jean-de-Luz on 8 May 1660 and was lodged, together with the royal retinue, in an imposing mansion which had been built for the ship-owner Lohobiague; Maria Theresa stayed in an elegant brick and stone house nearby.
On the morning of 9 June the King presented himself at the Infanta's house to claim his bride. The procession moved off towards the church between the Swiss Guards lining the route, and was led by two companies of Gentlemen-at-Arms followed by Cardinal Mazarin dressed in sumptuous robes. Behind him came Louis XIV, in black with lace trimmings, and then the Infanta who wore a dress of spun silver and a cloak of heavy purple velvet, with a gold crown on her head. The King's brother, known in royal circles simply as "Monsieur", was a few paces behind with their mother, the imposing Anne of Austria. They were followed by the rest of the court.
The marriage was solemnized by the Bishop of Bayonne and the service lasted until halfway through the afternoon. The door through which the royal couple left the church was walled up after the ceremony.
The cortège returned to the Infanta's house. From the balcony there the King himself and Mazarin threw commemorative medals to the crowd below. Later the newly-weds dined with the court in Lohobiague's mansion.
Following a strict etiquette they were then led to the nuptial couch, and given the traditional blessing by the Queen Mother as she drew its curtains.

Wedding Gifts – The young Queen was showered with gifts worthy of the Thousand and One Nights. From her husband she received six dazzling sets of jewellery encrusted with diamonds and other precious stones; from Monsieur, twelve jewelled dress ornaments. The present from Mazarin, who was phenomenally wealthy, outshone them all : 1 200 000 *livres*-worth of diamonds and pearls, a great dinner service in solid gold, and two state coaches, one drawn by six Russian horses, the other by six Indian horses, each with trappings and livery to match the colours of the carriages.
Louis XIV found in Maria Theresa a gentle and worthy wife, and when she died the King remarked : "This is the first and only time she has ever made me unhappy."

SIGHTS

Port – As early as the 11C St-Jean-de-Luz, like Biarritz, was a seaport which specialized in whaling. At the beginning of the 17C the Dutch and the English, who had learned the use of the harpoon from the Basques, barred the Arctic fishing grounds to the whalers from St-Jean. A local sea captain nevertheless remedied the situation by developing a more efficient method of whaling : he perfected a method of melting down whale blubber aboard ship. Three tons of blubber produced one ton of oil – which was naturally easier to carry and took up much less space. A single whaler could therefore bring home the product of seven whales; and a ship rendered autonomous in this way – a forerunner of the modern factory ship – could save time and money with fewer voyages to and from the home port.

Loading and unloading in the St-Jean roadstead had always been difficult : there was no question of crossing the bar at the mouth of the Nivelle, nor was it possible to enter the estuary at low tide, when the river lost itself in the marshes (the Basque name for the town, *Donibane-Lohizun,* means St-John-in-the-Marsh).

The Peace of Utrecht in 1713 finally deprived France of Newfoundland, off the shores of which the swarming cod had been fished since the 15C. This was a heavy blow to the fishermen of St-Jean and the shipyards on the banks of the Nivelle, although, as at Bayonne *(qv)*, ships fitted out as privateers were still able to bring home choice catches.

Today local fishermen rely on hauls of sardines, anchovies and especially tuna fish for their livelihood.

The port is at the inner end of the only anchorage to break the long straight line of the Atlantic coast between Arcachon and the Bidasoa River. The estuary, nestling between the Socoa and Ste-Barbe headlands, is further protected from westerly gales by massive dykes and the Artha breakwaters.

From the quays there are picturesque views across the busy harbour of the old town and inland, in the distance, the great pyramid bulk of La Rhune *(qv)*.

★ **Maison Louis-XIV** ⊙ – The house now named after the monarch who stayed here was built by the ship-owner Lohobiague in 1643. It is an imposing building beside the port, with the façade facing the town distinguished by corbelled turrets at the corners.

Inside, the "Old Basque" character of the house is evident in the sturdy, straight-flight staircase which was built by ship's carpenters : like the original floorboards in all the rooms, the treads are kept in place by large, visible, heavy-headed nails which make sanding or planing impossible. From the second-floor landing a passage leads to the apartments where Lohobiague's widow received Louis XIV in 1660; a south-facing, arcaded gallery here offers a splendid view of the Basque Pyrenees.

The huge kitchen boasts an impressive fireplace. The green-panelled dining-room contains a marble Directoire table and – a gift from the royal guest to his hostess – a three-piece service in silver-gilt with inlaid enamelwork.

★ **Maison de l'Infante** – This elegant building in the Louis XIII style, constructed of brick and stone with Italianate galleries overlooking the port, belonged to the rich Haraneder family. The Infanta stayed here with her future mother-in-law, Anne of Austria.

★★ **Église St-Jean-Baptiste** – This is the biggest and most famous of all the Basque churches in France; it was founded in the 15C and was being enlarged at the time of Louis XIV's wedding. The bricked-up doorway through which the royal couple left can be seen just inside the main entrance, on the south side.

Externally the architecture is sober, even severe, with high walls and small windows. A vaulted passageway tunnels beneath the massive tower. A fine wrought-iron stairway leads to the galleries.

Interior – The sumptuous, largely 17C interior presents a striking contrast to the church's exterior.

Three tiers of oak galleries (five on the end wall) surround the broad, single nave; these, traditionally, are reserved for men. The vaulted roof above the nave is lined with remarkable painted panels. The chancel, raised high as in all Basque churches, is separated from the nave by a handsome wrought-iron screen. The dazzling gold **altarpiece**★ dates from *c*1670 (restored 1987). Between the columns and entablatures that divide it into three levels, shallow niches hold statues of the Apostles, angels and local saints. On the top level are a Virgin of the Assumption wearing court costume, and God the Father in Glory.

Among other items of interest are the 17C pulpit supported by sphinxes, the fine churchwarden's pew facing it, the organ case, and – in the embrasure of the walled-up doorway – a statue of Notre-Dame-des-Douleurs (Our Lady of Sorrows). Beside this is a small Virgin of the Rosary in ceremonial dress.

Quartier de la Barre – The Barre district occupies the tongue of land sheltering the harbour from the open sea which evolved from the sand bar shoaling the Nivelle estuary. This was the residential district preferred by the rich ship-owners and shipbuilders of the 17C until a tidal wave in 1749 reduced it by two-thirds and destroyed 200 houses in the town.

Several fine houses remain today, among them St Martin's House at No 13 Rue Mazarin; the best view of its attic and the tower-platform from which the owner could survey the movements of shipping is from the top of the dyke.

The Atlantic Coast of France offers some of the best surfing beaches in the world, with Biarritz the cradle of surfing in Europe. In some resorts surfboards may be hired on a daily basis.

CIBOURE Pop 5 849

Ciboure (in the Basque language, *Zubiburu :* bridge-head) lies opposite St-Jean-de-Luz, on the west bank of the Nivelle; in fact the two towns form a single conurbation, sharing the port between them. One of the local landmarks is No 15 Quai Maurice-Ravel, which is where the composer was born. Rue Pocalette just behind it presents a contrast between half-timbered houses in the Labourd style (corbelled house dating from 1589 on the corner of Rue Agorette) and the more gentrified stone-built mansions, such as that at No 12 by the east end of the church.

Église St-Vincent – *Rue Pocalette.* The church was built in the 16C. It has an unusual belltower terminating in two wooden lantern storeys of decreasing size. The side entrance to the church is across a fine flagstoned square (18C stone cross).

EXCURSIONS

Socoa – *3km – 1¾ miles west via D 912. Park at the port and continue (45min Rtn on foot) towards the jetty.*
The beginning of the dyke offers a good view of the harbour and the town.
Entrance to the anchorage at St-Jean-de-Luz was formerly defended by Socoa fort, which was built under Henri IV and improved by the celebrated military architect Vauban *(qv).*
Turn right, leaving the port, and climb to the lighthouse along Rue du Phare, then follow Rue du Sémaphore to the coastal signal station : to the southwest there is a superb **view★★** of the Basque coastline from Cape Higuer (Cabo Higuer) in Spain all the way to Biarritz. Below, in the foreground, the foliated strata of the cliffs drop steeply down to the crashing waves of the Atlantic.

★★ **La Corniche Basque (The Basque Coast Road)** – *Round tour of 28km – 17½ miles : allow 1 hour. Leave St-Jean-de-Luz west via D 912. Illustration p 155.* The route approaches the cliffs of Socoa, offering superb sea **views★★**. Before snaking down to Hendaye, it passes near **Château d'Abbadia,** the Second Empire home of Antoine Abbadie (1810-97) which the scholar left to the French Academy of Sciences.

★ **Hendaye** – *See Hendaye.*

Leave Hendaye by N 10 east towards Béhobie and St-Jean-de-Luz.

In the distance, beyond Urrugne, the **Château d'Urtubie** can be seen *(left, below the road).* This castle was built in the 14C with the authorization of King Edward III of England; it has evolved and been modified since.

Urrugne – The church at the centre of the town presents an almost military aspect, with high walls and few windows. The face of the adjoining belfry-porch bears a sundial.

From the main square in Urrugne, take the hill leading up to Notre-Dame-de-Socorri.

Notre-Dame-de-Socorri – This pilgrimage chapel dedicated to the Virgin lies in a lovely **setting★** : the shady clearing on the site of the former cemetery offers views of the undulating countryside dominated by the great spur of La Rhune and, on the horizon, the heights of Jaïzkibel and Les Trois Couronnes.

Return to St-Jean-de-Luz by N 10.

★ ST-JEAN-PIED-DE-PORT Pop 1 432

Michelin map 85 fold 3 or 234 fold 38 – Facilities.

This pretty little town, once the capital of Lower Navarre, lies in a mild, picturesque basin watered by the Nive and Petite Nive rivers, its red sandstone houses grouped around a spur crowned by the old citadel. The old or upper town on the north bank of the Nive is encircled by 15C ramparts dating from the time of Navarrese domination; the citadel and fortifications on the south bank, built to defend the road to Spain after the Treaty of the Pyrenees, are part of the 17C military complex designed by Vauban *(qv).*
The name St-Jean-Pied-de-Port is a reminder that the town lies at the foot of a *port* or pass : for travellers heading for Spain it was the last stop before the climb to Puerto Ibañeta, or Port de Roncevaux as it is known on the French side (alt 1 058m – 3 468ft), 16 miles away on Spanish territory. Beyond the crest the monastery of Roncesvalles (Roncevaux to the French) maintained since the 12C a tradition of Christian hospitality – and the memory of the brave hero Roland *(qv),* who fell in the year 778 when the rearguard of Charlemagne's army was overwhelmed by Basque mountain people on the way back from its campaign against the Saracens in Spain (in the epic troubadour's **Song of Roland** – *qv* – the mountain people themselves are transformed into Saracens. In one version of the legend, the cleft in the rock formed when Roland tried to break his magic sword is near the Cirque de Gavarnie; in another it is here at Roncesvalles).

Pilgrims' Way – In the Middle Ages St-Jean was a great rallying centre for *Jacquets,* the pilgrims en route for Santiago de Compostela *(qv),* who journeyed from all over Europe. They wore a heavy grey cloak, a broad-brimmed felt hat turned up at the front and marked with three or four scallop shells (the emblems of the pilgrimage), and carried a bread bag and an eight-foot stave with a water flask attached. Whenever a devout procession of the pious was announced, the town became a hive of activity : church bells pealed, priests intoned prayers, children ran out to escort the pilgrims, and the inhabitants, standing on their doorsteps, offered provisions. Then the pilgrims would move on, chanting the responses; those too tired to continue could stop in Rue de la Citadelle, where the monks from Roncesvalles had organized a refuge for them.

ST-JEAN-PIED-DE-PORT

Citadelle (R. de la) 4
Espagne (R. d') ....
Gaulle (Pl. Ch.-de.) 9

Çaro (Rte de) 2
Église (R. de l') 6
France (R.) 12
Fronton (Av. de) 15
Liberté (R. de la) 17
St-Jacques (Ch. de) 18
St-Michel (Rte de) 21
Trinquet (Pl. du) 24
Uhart (R. d') 27
Zuharpeta (R.) 30

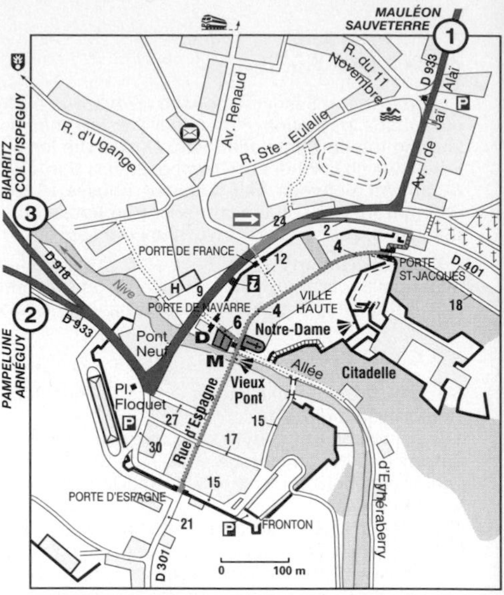

★ FOLLOWING THE PILGRIMS' WAY *1 hour*

Park near Porte de France (one of the old town gates), follow the ramparts and then take the stairway up to Porte de St-Jacques, through which the pilgrims entered the town.

Rue de la Citadelle (**4**) – The street, sloping down towards the river, is bordered by charming 16C and 17C houses with rounded doorways and carved lintels.

Église Notre-Dame – The Gothic church, dedicated to the Virgin, has handsome sandstone pillars.

Rue de l'Église (**6**) – This street leads from the church to Porte de Navarre, passing the former hospital (**M**) which now houses a library and a museum devoted to the game of *Pelota,* and the house of the Jassu family (**D**), paternal ancestors of St François-Xavier (1506-52).

Return to the church, pass through the vaulted passage beneath the belfry and cross the river.

Vieux Pont – From the Old Bridge there is a picturesque view of the church, which is incorporated into the ramparts, and the old riverside houses.

Rue d'Espagne – The street, which climbs uphill to Porte d'Espagne through which the pilgrims left the town, has always been one of the main shopping areas.

ADDITIONAL SIGHT

Citadelle – *Access via the church or from Porte St-Jacques.*
From the bastion facing the entrance to the citadel, the view stretches over the St-Jean basin and the neat little villages within it.

★★ ST-SAVIN Pop 1 089

Michelin map 68 fold 15 or 233 fold 10.

St-Savin rises on the west bank of the River Gartempe; it is famous for its Romanesque abbey church which is decorated with the finest and most complete series of contemporary mural paintings in France.

HISTORICAL NOTES

Part of the legend – Towards the middle of the 5C in Macedonia, two brothers, Savin and Cyprien, were summoned to appear in front of the proconsul Ladicius for having refused to worship certain idols. The brothers were condemned to death, and all pleas for mercy were in vain. They were imprisoned but managed to escape and left for the Gauls, though their executioners caught up with them on the banks of the Gartempe : the brothers were decapitated on the spot. Savin's body was buried by priests on a height known at the time as Three Cypresses Mount, not far from where the town of St-Savin stands today.

The building stages – The first abbey church was erected in the 9C, near the sacred burial site, and placed under the patronage of the martyr Savin. Louis the Debonnaire installed twenty Benedictine monks in the abbey under the tutelage, it is said, of Benoît d'Aniane.
In 878 the abbey was pillaged by the Normans, despite it being protected by a line of fortifications. Reconstruction did not begin until the 11C but was finished in a relatively short space of time. The painted decoration, which completely covered the interior of the church, was added as the building work progressed.

Decline and rebirth – The Hundred Years War brought to an end the period of relative prosperity enjoyed by the monks up to that time : the abbey was caught up in violent battles between soldiers loyal to the King of France and those fighting for the Black Prince *(qv)*. In the 16C the Wars of Religion saw the Catholics and the Huguenots in furious conflict over possession of the abbey : it was devastated in 1562 and 1568 by the Huguenots, who burnt the choir stalls, the organ and the timber roof, and pillaged six years later by the Royal army. Most of the buildings were later demolished as their upkeep was too expensive.
From 1611 to 1635 an adventurer who liked to call himself the Baron of the Francs installed himself in the church as though it were a strongpoint. The arrival, in 1640, of monks from Saint-Maur finally brought an end to the profanities to which the abbey had been subjected for three centuries. However, though the monks saved the buildings from total ruin, the wall paintings suffered from various efforts to restore them.
In 1836 Prosper Mérimée, the writer and Inspector of Historic Monuments, had the church listed as a historic monument and organised important restoration works which continued for almost a century.
It was an engineer from St-Savin, Léon Edoux, who in 1867 invented the hydraulic elevator and perfected it in trials within the bishop's lodgings; he gave it the name "ascenseur".

★★ ABBEY ⏲ *1 hour*

Start the tour in the abbey buildings, where the reception and information desk is situated.

★ **Abbey buildings** – These were rebuilt in the 17C in the extension of the church's transept arm; they have since been restored.
The old **refectory,** to the right of the entrance, houses exhibitions of contemporary mural art organised by CIAM, the International Centre for Mural Art, which is based within the abbey.
To the left, in the **chapter-house,** photographs reveal the appearance of the church crypt *(temporarily closed)*.
From the garden, through which the river runs, there is an attractive view over the elegant rear face of the abbey buildings, from the bishop's lodgings (on the left), which are of medieval origin though remodelled in the 17C and 19C, across to the east end of the church with its apse, apsidal chapels and belfry.

★★ **Abbey Church** – The church, a handsome combination of harmony and sobriety, is also striking for its sheer size : 76m – almost 250ft long with a transept 31m – 101ft across and a spire rising to 77m – 252ft.
The best **view**★ of the church is from the far side of the river. On the left extend the abbey buildings and the elegant belfry-porch – overshadowing the apse, the apsidal chapels and the squat belfry; it is crowned by a crocketed spire surrounded by turrets. On the right stands **Vieux Pont** (the Old Bridge) with pierheads, which dates from the 13C and 14C.
Inside the church, in the nave, there are fine **capitals** deeply-carved with foliage and animals; those by the chancel are decorated with acanthus leaves and lions.

★★★ **Wall Paintings** – Some of the paintings were destroyed during the devastations visited on the abbey, others were damaged by whitewash which the monks applied, still others suffered as a result of the first phases of restoration.
Unlike most frescoes painted from a preliminary sketch, the paintings here were drawn directly onto the wall, using a process halfway between the fresco technique and distemper-painting : the colours were applied to old plaster, thereby penetrating only the top level of this coating and forming only a very thin layer. The few colours used include yellow-ochre, red-ochre and green, mixed with black and white.

Sudres/SCOPE

The Call of Abraham, St-Savin.

The overall effect is one of gentle tones but avoids being insipid through the use of contrast : the different characters are portrayed with great liveliness, their feet suggesting movement, their forms revealed by the moulding of their clothes, their hands often disproportionately long, accentuating the expressive qualities.
This dancing, rhythmic allure is also found in Romanesque sculpture. Faces have large, simple, bold features, with red and white marks describing cheeks, nostrils and chins.
In the **narthex** the various painted scenes recount episodes from the Apocalypse : Christ in Majesty in celestial Jerusalem, combat between the Archangel and the Beast, the New Jerusalem, the Plague of grasshoppers. The predominantly pale tones (green, yellow-ochre, red-ochre) allow the scenes to be clearly read despite the darkness inside the porch.

The nave, however, is the setting for the true masterpiece which is highlighted by the purity of the architecture. The stories told in the carefully-restored paintings on the vaulting unfold at a height of over 16m – 52ft and cover an area of 412m^2 – 1 351 sq feet. The most striking thing initially is the soft tones – beige and pink – of the columns supporting the vaulting. The vaulting itself is covered with famous scenes from the Book of Genesis and the Book of Exodus, ranged in two rows along either side of the centre ridge, which forms a decorative band. A painting behind the main door shows the Triumph of the Virgin.
Two sections are distinguishable in the nave. The first three bays, which make up the first part of the nave, are separated by transverse ribs, while the rest of the vaulting is a continuous barrel which made painting that section of the ceiling easier; the painter nevertheless added a false rib between the 5th and 6th bays.

Stand in the south aisle to see the frescoes on the left-hand side of the nave. The following scenes are recognisable.

NARTHEX

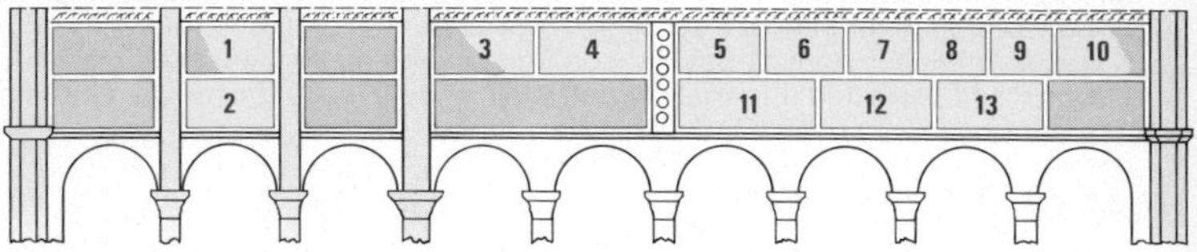

1) Creation of the stars (God adds the Sun and the Moon to the firmament).
2) Creation of Woman - God presents Eve to Adam - Eve and the serpent.
3) Eve, seated, spins.
4) The offerings of Cain and Abel (Abel, God's chosen one, is the only one haloed).
5) Abel's murder - Cain's curse.
6) Enoch, his arms raised to heaven, invokes God - God tells Noah of the forthcoming flood and invites him to build the ark.
7) Noah's Ark during the flood.
8) God blesses Noah's family leaving the ark (showing the famous "Beau Dieu" representation of God).
9) Noah sacrifices a pair of birds and a lamb in thanksgiving.
10) Noah's vineyard.
Before continuing with the story of Noah on the right-hand section, note the scenes on the lower register which tell the end of Exodus and include the life of Moses.
11) Passage through the Red Sea: the waters swallow up the Egyptian cavalry and Pharaoh's chariot.
12) The Angel of God and the column of fire separate the Egyptians and the Hebrews and protect the latter who march in rows, led by Moses.
13) Moses receives the Tables of the Law from God.

Cross the transept crossing and stand at the beginning of the left-hand aisle to view the paintings on the right-hand side of the ceiling.

TRANSEPT

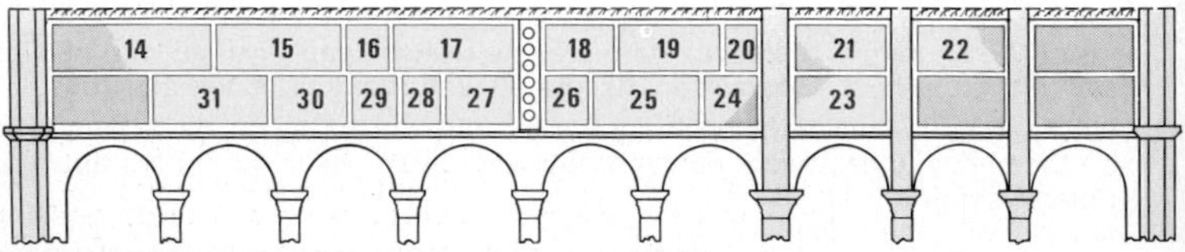

14) Noah drinks and dances, a goblet in hand.
15) Drunken Noah lies asleep, his robes in disarray; Ham mocks his father, while his brothers Shem and Japhet cover him with a blanket.
16) Noah curses Canaan in front of Shem and Japhet.
17) Construction of the Tower of Babel.
18) The call of Abraham *(see illustration).*
19) Abraham and Lot's separation.
20) Announcement of the combat of the kings and call for help from Lot to Abraham.
21) The combat of the Kings *(removed).*
22) Meeting between Abraham and Melchizedeck, King of Salem and priest of the Most High, who brings him bread and wine *(removed).*
23) Death of Abraham.
24) Isaac blesses his son Jacob.
25) Joseph sold by his brothers.
26) Joseph bought by Potiphar, one of Pharaoh's officers.
27) Joseph, Potiphar and his wife (the Temptation of Joseph).
28) Joseph in prison.
29) Joseph explains Pharaoh's dream.
30) Pharaoh puts his ring on Joseph's finger and makes him his administrator.
31) Joseph's Triumph.

Crypt – *Temporarily closed.*

Join us in our constant task of keeping up-to-date.
Please send us your comments and suggestions.

Michelin Tyre PLC
Tourism Department
The Edward Hyde Building
38 Clarendon Road
WATFORD – WD1 1SX
Tel : 0923 415 000
Fax : 0923 415 250

ST-VINCENT-SUR-JARD Pop 658

Michelin map 67 fold 11 or 233 fold 2 – 9km – 5 miles southeast of Talmont-St-Hilaire.

St-Vincent, a seaside village on the Vendée coast, evokes the fighting spirit of the French political leader **Georges Clemenceau** (1841-1929) who spent the last years of his tumultuous life here.

Clemenceau, the son of a bourgeois family in the Vendée, launched himself into politics in 1869 after studying medicine and visiting the United States. He was Mayor of Montmartre by 1870 and a member of the National Assembly (Parliament) a year later. Representing the extreme Left of the time, he earned a reputation as a fighter of duels and a destroyer of Ministers (he earned the nickname "the Tiger" because of the ferocity of his parliamentary attacks).

Bust of Clemenceau.

D'après photo Yan

In 1906 Clemenceau became a Minister (for Home Affairs) and also President of the *Conseil* (Cabinet), and instituted a vigorous policy of reform. Ousted by the Radicals in 1909 after he had harshly repressed a series of strikes in the South, he founded a newspaper which bitterly attacked every government until 1917, when he was recalled to the Presidency of the *Conseil*. It was then that he began to mobilise the enthusiasm of the French, visiting the Western Front, encouraging the troops, sustaining the morale of the civilians : the Tiger had become the Father of Victory. He presided over the 1919 peace conference, resigned his premiership in 1920 and retired to his house in St-Vincent after more than half a century of political life.

MAISON DE CLEMENCEAU ⏲ *30min.*

The house is a short distance from the village, at the end of route D 19^{A}. The site, facing the ocean and the Île de Ré, has a hint of grandeur about it, and is a suitable resting-place for the wild and restless spirit of the old warrior.

The low building, typical of the Vendée, has been preserved exactly as it was when Clemenceau died. The tour includes the salon, Clemenceau's bedroom-cum-study, a kitchen dining room containing a hammered copper watering-can which belonged to Marie-Antoinette, and the thatched summer-house, all of which are filled with souvenirs recalling his political life.

In the garden, which flowers with the roses Clemenceau always loved, there is an expressive portrait bust of the grand old man.

EXCURSIONS

Abbaye Notre-Dame-de-Lieu-Dieu ⏲ – *5km – 3 miles west.* The imposing mass of this ancient abbey, founded in 1190 by Richard the Lionheart, lies between the marshes of Talmont and the coastal pinewoods of Jard. Sacked and pillaged during the Hundred Years War, ruined by the Protestants in the 16C, the abbey was rebuilt by Premonstratensian monks in the 17C, when the storey with octagonal corner bartizans was added. By the end of that century, however, the abbey was again abandoned. Today the fine Plantagenet vaulting can still be admired in the chapter-house, which opens onto a garden laid out on the site of the old cloisters.

Megaliths of Le Talmondais – *22km – $13\frac{1}{2}$ miles northeast.*
The Talmont region (le Talmondais), with its abundance of dolmens and menhirs, is the richest megalithic site in the Vendée.

St-Hilaire-la-Forêt – The Neolithic period, in which these megaliths were erected, is the focus for **CAIRN** (Centre Archéologique d'Initiation et de Recherche sur le Néolithique) ⏲. *Access via D 70.*

Explanatory panels convey information on this ancient civilization and there is a fine display of photographs illustrating the principal sites in western France. A visit to the centre is completed by two slide-and-diorama presentations, one on the Neolithic megaliths of the Talmont *(illuminated map)*, the other on those throughout the world. Outside, in season, there are demonstrations of prehistoric techniques : the building of a dolmen, the use of stone-buffers etc. A number of plants known to have been flourishing in Neolithic times have been cultivated.

Bicycles may be hired for exploring the megalithic sites in the area *(the circuit is indicated by arrows).*

Passing through Longeville, continue to Le Bernard and then take D 91. Turn left at a roadside shrine.

On the way, on the right-hand side of the road, are the three **Savatole Dolmens** *(explanatory panel).*

Dolmen de la Frébouchère – This impressive granite monument, of the type classified as Angevin, comprises a stone portico which leads to a rectangular chamber. The single rock slab (now cracked) covering the chamber weighs 80 tons.

Avrillé – In the municipal park behind the town hall stands the **Caesar's Camp Menhir.** This, the tallest menhir in the Vendée and one of the biggest in France (rising 7m – 23ft above ground), is the sole survivor of a group of stones.

Château de la Guignardière ⊙ – *1km – about ½ mile west of Avrillé.* The château was founded in 1538 by Girard, the *Panetier* (officer charged with the safeguard and distribution of bread) of François I, but was never finished because Girard was murdered.
The original garden façade is in the Renaissance style with granite courses and tall, double-mullioned windows. The high chimney stacks are built of brick. A number of alterations – in the same style – were made in the 18C.
Of particular note inside are the monumental chimneypieces in granite; a fine stairway, also in granite, which is halfway between a spiral staircase and one with half-landings; the attics with their magnificent three-stage rafter-work in chestnut wood; the vaulted cellars.
An arrowed circuit through the grounds leads to a series of ponds fringed by bare, aerial-rooted cypresses, to the castle mill, and – hidden in Fourgon Wood – to three groups of menhirs which were once part of an ancient alignment. The tallest of these megaliths measures about 3m – 10ft.

★ SAUVETERRE-DE-BÉARN Pop 1 366

Michelin map 78 fold 8 or 234 fold 34.

The small town lies on a picturesque **site★** above an escarpment overlooking the Oloron torrent.

The Judgement of God – In the year 1170 Sancie, the widow of Gaston V of Béarn was accused of having killed a child born after her husband's death and was submitted to a trial known as the Judgement of God. On the orders of her own brother, the King of Navarre, she was bound hand and foot and thrown into the river from the top of the town's fortified bridge *(see below)*. However, the strong current cast her up on the bank, safe and sound, further downstream – so Sancie was pronounced innocent and had her rights restored.

A hard bargain – On 12 April 1462 a meeting was held near Sauveterre, at the junction of the territories ruled over by France, Navarre and Béarn, between Louis XI, Jean II of Aragon and Navarre, and Gaston de Foix-Béarn. For a sum of 300 000 *écus* (crowns) in gold, with the *comtés* of Roussillon and Cerdagne as collateral, the King of France agreed to put 700 *lances* (combat units of six cavalrymen with attendant foot soldiers) at the disposal of the King of Aragon to help crush a revolt in Catalonia. A treaty was signed in Bayonne on 9 May 1462. The money was never paid, however, so Louis XI seized the two provinces put up as security, although they did not become an integral part of France until two centuries later.

SIGHTS

Terraces by the Church and the Town Hall – From here there is a wonderful view : the old bridge, the torrent, a tree-covered island, a ruined tower, the Romanesque belfry of the church, the outline of the distant Pyrenees – a most romantic landscape.

Vieux pont ("de la Légende") – One arch of the ancient bridge remains, surmounted by the town's 12C fortified gateway. The legend of Sancie is explained *(in French)* on a panel. From here again there is a magnificent **view★★** of the river, the fortifications, the church and the splendid Montréal Tower.

R.-G. Everts/RAPHO

Vieux Pont, Sauveterre-de-Béarn.

Église St-André – The tympanum above the entrance to St Andrew's Church depicts Christ in Glory surrounded by the four Evangelists. The ribbed vaulting harmonizes perfectly with the Romanesque design of the interior. A pillar on the north side of the chancel is topped by a historiated capital representing Scandal-mongering and Gluttony. The east end, flanked by two apsidal chapels, is surmounted by a quadrangular belltower pierced by twinned windows.

EXCURSION

Château de Laàs ⊙ – *9km – 5 miles southeast via D 27.*
This is an extraordinary château-museum, the contents of which were left to the Touring Club of France by the last owners, Monsieur and Madame Serbat. By collecting together **furniture★**, *objets-d'art* and family paintings from three different homes, the Serbats created a decorative arts museum illustrating also the art of living in the Hainaut region (in the north of France) during the 18C.
Louis XVI panelling adorns the bedchambers and salons. Mme Serbat's room is decorated with illustrations of the *Fables* of La Fontaine. Tapestries and hand-painted fabrics (music room) set off the fine Northern School paintings (Watteau de Lille). Nor is historical anecdote forgotten : a first-floor bedroom recalls the aftermath of Waterloo, for here is the bed Napoleon slept in at Maubert-Fontaine on 19 June 1815.

Musée du Maïs ⊙ – This small, specialized museum in the château outbuildings concerns itself exclusively with the subject of maize.
The cereal, cultivated in central and southern America since 5 000 BC, was introduced into Europe at the end of the 15C immediately after the discovery of America. It filtered into France via Spain and by the 17C had become an essential component of the traditional Béarn agricultural system. Together with the Basque country, the province became the cradle of maize production throughout France.
The museum presents successively the agricultural implements used in the cultivation of maize in the past, traditional methods of harvesting, stripping and shelling; the results of mechanization after World War II; and finally the uses of maize in human and animal feeding, and the revolution brought about by the development of hybrid species with an exceptionally heavy yield.

★ La SOULE

Michelin map 85 folds 4, 5, 14, 15 or 234 folds 34, 38, 39, 42.

The Saison or Mauléon torrent (in Basque *Uhaitz-Handi :* Great Torrent) is one of the largest tributaries of the Oloron. It is also the principal axis of the Soule region, one of the original seven provinces of the Basque country *(qv)*, and the only one on the Atlantic side of the Pyrenees whose upper part was once covered by a glacier. Upstream from Licq-Athérey the valley divides into two branches, gorges in which the Larrau and Uhaitxa torrents run. The mountain tributaries of these streams, slicing through the sedimentary limestone beds which mask the granitic "axial zone" west of Pic d'Anie, have gouged out some impressive channels.
The province, which shares many cultural influences with Béarn – including, for instance, the types of houses – has retained the dances and folk traditions most characteristic of the region.
Economically, as in the neighbouring areas of Cize, Baïgorry and Ostabaret, the collective managing of the land is important, most of the grazing land and mountain forest in the province's 43 *communes* being worked by local co-operatives. The local netting of migratory woodpigeons and ring-doves is considered to be a benefit for farmers.

LA BASSE SOULE (LOWER SOULE)

Round tour starting from Mauléon-Licharre

78km – 49 miles : allow 3 hours.
Map overleaf.

This area is rich in souvenirs of the famous "musketeers" who inspired Alexandre Dumas to write his classic story of d'Artagnan *(qv)* and his three friends.

Mauléon-Licharre – Mauléon is an old strongpoint and the smallest capital in the seven Basque provinces. It rises on the right bank of the River Saison, at the foot of a hill on which stand the ruins of the old castle. Licharre sits on the west bank of the river and contains the Renaissance **Château d'Andurain** ⊙, which was built *c*1600.

Leave Mauléon to the south, along D 918.

Gotein – This Pyrenean village has a church and belfry-calvary typical of the region.

D'après photo Perrin

Belfry-calvary, Gotein.

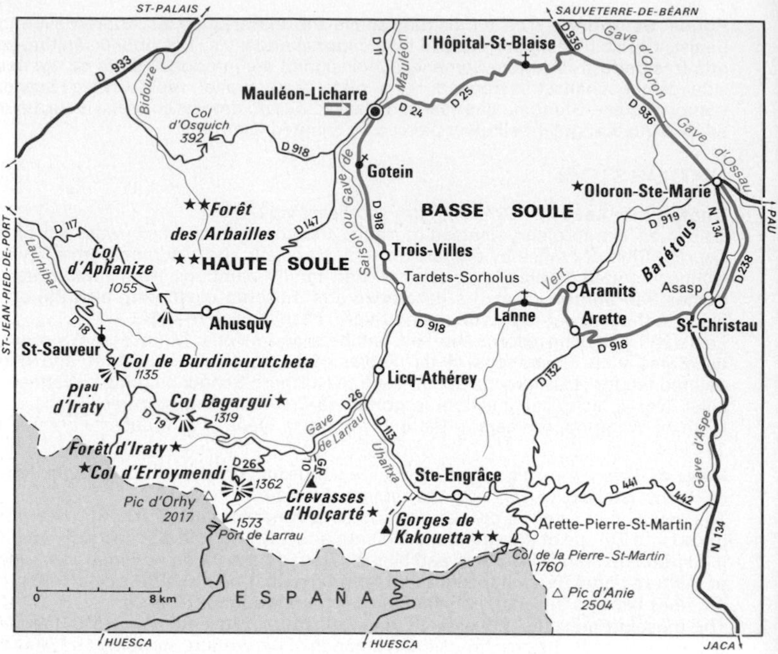

Trois-Villes – The name of the village, more than the château built by François Mansart (1598-1666), the great classicist architect, recalls the military career and the personality of M. de Tréville, Captain of the King's Musketeers under Louis XIII.

The **Barétous,** a transitional region between Béarn and the Basque provinces, offers the visitor a chequerboard of maize fields and magnificent meadows punctuated by thickets of oak trees, with the limestone summits of the mountains in the background.

Lanne – The pretty church, with its double porch, was originally the chapel attached to the château owned by Isaac de Porthau ("Porthos" in Dumas' *The Three Musketeers*).

Aramits – This village was once the capital of the Barétous. "Aramis", another of d'Artagnan's musketeers, was a lay brother at an abbey here which has now disappeared ("Athos", the third musketeer, was named after a village of that name near Sauveterre).

Arette – The small town was rebuilt after an earthquake on 13 August 1967. A mountain road leads to **Arette-Pierre-St-Martin,** a small winter sports resort.

After a pleasant, twisting climb above the Arette basin, the road traverses a slope of the Aspe Valley.

At Asasp, cross the Aspe torrent.

St-Christau – *See St-Christau.*

The road runs down to Oloron along the east bank of the river.

★ **Oloron-Ste-Marie** – *See Oloron-Ste-Marie.*

Take D 936, northwest, for 12km – 7½ miles then turn left into D 25.

L'Hôpital-St-Blaise – A tiny village on the Basque-Béarn border. The church – a rare example of Hispano-Moorish art on the northern side of the Pyrenees – is in the form of a Greek cross, the four arms radiating from a central tower.

Return to Mauléon-Licharre.

★★ LA HAUTE SOULE (UPPER SOULE)

Upper Soule is a magnificent region of forests and pastures, separated from the St-Jean-Pied-de-Port depression by the massifs of Iraty and Arbailles – a difficult barrier because of the rough terrain and the density of the woodland covering it. This is a region particularly suitable for forest rambles, fishing and, in winter, cross-country skiing.

Ahusquy – This was a gathering place for Basque shepherds, whose piercing cries were described by the writer Pierre Loti *(qv)* as "like the call of some redskin tribes in the American forests". There is a (restored) mountain inn still standing on the **panoramic site**★★. Further uphill, clearly visible at the top of a footpath, is a drinking trough from which the excellent Ahusquy spring can be tasted. The water was at one time popular as a cure for kidney and bladder complaints.

Col d'Aphanize – Wild horses can be seen grazing on the slopes around the pass. The pastureland here – "Green, green, magnificently green!" in the words of Loti – is the summer home of many flocks of sheep. East of the pass the **view**★★ opens out wide : from Pic des Escaliers, immediately south, to Pic de Ger on the southeastern horizon, by way of Pic d'Orthy, Pic d'Anie and the Massif de Sesques between Aspe and Ossau.

★★ **Forêt des Arbailles** – This is an upland forest carpeting the higher reaches of a limestone bastion standing clear of the gullies carved by the Saison, the Laurhibar and the Bidouze torrents. The forest rises to a height of 1 265m – 4 150ft at Pic de Behorléguy. The beech groves, hiding slopes strewn with boulders, riddled with hollows, give way in the south to a pastoral zone ending in a sheer drop facing the Spanish frontier.

★ **Col Bagargui** – Eastwards here there is a **view★** of the Upper Soule mountains and the High Pyrenees in the Aspe and Ossau regions. In the foreground, on the right, is the heavy mass of Pic d'Orthy; further away are the elegant limestone summits of the Pic d'Anie chain, and behind them the silhouette of Pic du Midi d'Ossau. Scattered amongst the forest trees below are the buildings of the picturesque village of Iraty.

Col de Burdincurutcheta – Alt 1 135m – 3 724ft. *Park 1km – half a mile below the north side of the pass, where the road approaches a rocky crest. Walk to the edge.* The view extends over the jagged foothills, extensively lacerated, of the frontier massif, gashed by bleak, deserted valleys; in the distance the basin of St-Jean-Pied-de-Port, centre of the Cize region, opens out.

★ **Col d'Erroymendi** – Alt 1 362m – 4 469ft. *7.5km – 4¾ miles from Larrau, by the Port de Larrau road (generally blocked by snow from November to June).* From here there is a vast mountain **panorama★** which highlights the pastoral and woodland activities in the Upper Soule region. A few yards east of the pass there is a different view : the fan of the Upper Saison valleys and, on the horizon, the rocky mass of Pic d'Anie.

★ **Crevasses d'Holçarté** – *1½ hours Rtn on foot, via the footpath signposted GR10, which is visible soon after the café and the Laugibar bridge.* After a steep, stiff climb, the entrance to the "crevasses" is reached : these are in fact very narrow gorges sliced from the limestone to a depth of 200m – 656ft. The path rises to the top of the Olhadubi tributary gorge, which is crossed by a dizzily impressive footbridge slung 171m – 561ft above the torrent in 1920.

★ **Forêt d'Iraty** – This forest of beech groves straddling the frontier supplied wood for masts for the French and Spanish navies from the 18C onwards; it is one of the largest wooded areas in Europe (in France alone 2 310ha – 5 710 acres).

Plateau d'Iraty – Horses and cattle roam here in summer along with the sheep; local sheep's cheese may be bought.

★★ **Gorges de Kakouetta** ⓥ – *It is recommended that this excursion, which is tiring and sometimes almost daunting, should be undertaken when the flow of water is reduced (from early June to late October). Stout footwear is essential as the ground can be slippery. Access is via D 113, the road to Ste-Engrace. Cross the river Uhaïtxa by a footbridge, climb the slope on the far side, and then continue down to the gorges.*
These gorges sunk vertically in the limestone are beautiful as well as impressive, with the beginning of the *"Grand Étroit"* (the Great Narrows) the most grandiose of all : this splendid canyon, more than 200m – 656ft deep, is no more than 3m to 10m – 11ft to 33ft wide at the top of its sheer sides. The torrent roars through the long fissure with its dense clumps of vegetation. The path, frequently difficult, eventually arrives at the water's edge, crossing the stream by a number of footbridges here and there. It ends within sight of a waterfall formed by a resurgence, where a grotto marks the end of this walk.

Licq-Athérey – This village is an excursion centre for the Upper Soule region.

Chapelle St-Sauveur ⓥ – From a distance this chapel looks like a sheepfold. It was once a hostel-chapel on a pilgrimage route followed by the Knights of the Order of Malta on Corpus Christi day. A line of small columns outside marks the Stations of the Cross. A number of naive statuettes are housed inside.

Ste-Engrâce – This is a shepherds' village, surrounded by wooded mountains fissured by steep valleys. The Romanesque **church,** a former 11C abbey church, stands with its asymmetric roof and its heavy masonry on a pastoral **site★** in the upper combe of the Uhaïtxa, marking one of the ancient routes to Santiago de Compostela.
The chancel, closed off by a robust 14C grille, has richly ornamented capitals. These include (left) scenes involving buffoons and jesters; hunting scenes and a Resurrection in the centre; and (right) Solomon and the Queen of Sheba, the royal visitor's elephant bearing on its back a palanquin in the Indian manner.

★ TALMONT

Pop 83

Michelin map 71 folds 15, 16 or 233 fold 25.

Talmont is an enchanting village overlooking the Gironde from a small peninsula 14km – 8½ miles southeast of Royan. Much of the original fortified town, built to supervise navigation in the tidal estuary, collapsed into the sea in Roman times as a result of erosion. What remains today is a protected, classified site, closed to motor traffic, which is famous for its Romanesque church – and for the profusion of hollyhocks which blaze against the white stone or rough-cast walls of the houses lining its narrow, twisting streets.

★ ÉGLISE STE-RADEGONDE

30min.

St Radegund's church, a fine example of the Saintonge Romanesque style, stands on an impressive **site**★ at the tip of the promontory, on the edge of a cliff dropping sheer into the Gironde. It too is continually threatened by the tides which unceasingly attack the horizontal strata of the sedimentary beds on which it rests. The cliff face has more than once been consolidated and the church restored to its original 12C appearance. This stone sentinel standing apart from the village and its tiny port is surrounded by a small cemetery from which there is a fine **view** of the estuary and, off to the right, the white chalk cliffs of Meschers.

M. Garnier/EXPLORER

Église Ste-Radegonde, Talmont.

The building is squat and compact, with a traditional apse and apsidal chapels. A square tower with a shallow pyramid roof surmounts the transept crossing. One bay of the nave was lost to the sea in the 15C.
From the mud flats and seaweed-covered rocks exposed at the foot of the cliff when the tide is out, the spectacular site of the church can be admired to the full, along with the particular elegance of its east end. Rhythmically punctuated by buttress-columns, this is enlivened by a ring of tall, blind arcades which frame windows at first-floor level; a neat row of smaller blind arcades with small columns decorates the second storey.
The fine doorway in the northern arm of the transept has coving adorned with angels adoring the Lamb, acrobats, and men pulling a rope to which are tethered two lions. Note the dome on pendentives, and the capitals around the oven-vaulted apse.

TARBES

Pop 47 566

Michelin map 85 fold 8 or 234 fold 40 – Local map p 30.

Tarbes, the most important town in the Central Pyrenees, is a convenient base for excursions, particularly around Bigorre *(qv)*.
It is a town with a long history. Roman Tarbes experienced the barbarian invasions and saw the Saracens pass by. The Normans destroyed it. Comte Raymond rebuilt it and created it the capital of Bigorre, which it remains today. The Wars of Religion at the end of the 16C were particularly bitter here : Tarbes fell successively into Protestant and Catholic hands and was utterly laid waste. Since the early 19C, however, the place has grown and prospered.
Tarbes has been an industrial centre since 1870 and also flourishes as an agricultural and commercial market, famous for its fairs and horse-breeding; electrical and mechanical engineering, aircraft manufacture, and the production of arms and well-drilling equipment are among other industries installed in the town today. The important growth of tourism and winter sports in the area – stimulated in 1920 by "Monsieur Paul", the head of the southern French railway system – has increased the popularity of Tarbes as a place to visit.

SIGHTS

★ **Jardin Massey** – This pretty public park, brightly-planted with flowers of many different varieties and busy with ducks and peacocks, was created by Placide Massey (1777-1853), the talented naturalist who was director of the Versailles-Trianon and Sèvres-St-Cloud areas near Paris at the beginning of the 19C. Architectural interest is provided by the (partly-restored) Gothic cloister of St-Sever-de-Rustan.

Musée Massey ⌚ – The museum is housed in the former residence of Placide Massey. On the ground floor an archeology section separates two rooms devoted to the history of the Hussars. A series of rooms on the first floor contains a display of French,

Flemish, Italian and Spanish paintings dating from the 15C to the 19C. Notable among these is a 15C triptych by Cock : *The Virgin, The Child, and St John and St Jerome.* From the Italian school of the 16C there is a canvas of *The Holy Family* with well-expressed bliss on their faces; by contrast the ferocity of the pack is gruesomely apparent in the 17C Flemish *Wild Boar Hunt.*
The **International Hussars Museum★** (second floor) holds a retrospective of five centuries of military history through the evolution of the famous light cavalry formation created in Hungary in 1474 and adopted subsequently by 34 countries of Europe and Latin America; the presentation of 100 waxwork figures complete with uniforms, arms and equipment is particularly well staged. Numerous paintings by 18C and 19C masters thematically concerned with the exploits of Hussars underline the prestige of these élite battle corps.

Maison natale du Maréchal Foch ⊙ – Ferdinand Foch (1851-1929), future Marshal of France (and honorifically, of Britain and Poland after the victorious conclusion of the First World War), was born in this house on 2 October 1851. The building is now a museum exhibiting souvenirs and biographical items relating to the Marshal.

Haras (Horse stud) ⊙ – This 9ha – 22 acre park with its low, pale pavilions, shaded by cedars and magnolias, retains a distinguished atmosphere of the First Empire. In the last century the stud produced the best cavalry chargers in Europe, developed from a cross between local strains and Arabs imported soon after the stud farm was founded in 1806. Tarbes, which was then a garrison town, soon became famous among Hussars, Dragoons, Lancers and the men of other select cavalry brigades. Today the horses here are bred more for competition – especially steeplechases – and for show-jumping, dressage, tourist hacking and riding for pleasure.

★ Parc ornithologique du TEICH

Michelin map 78 fold 2 or 234 fold 6. 5km – $3\frac{1}{2}$ miles east of Gujan-Mestras.

Le Teich **nature reserve** ⊙ occupies 120ha – 296 acres of the Eyre delta, 80ha – 198 acres of which are stretches of open water used for breeding fish. The reserve, which is linked to Arcachon Lagoon *(qv)* via a system of locks, is devoted to the preservation of birds threatened with extinction, the broadening of knowledge relating to species unknown in France and the establishment of havens for migrant birds.
The reserve is divided into four separate areas : the Parks of Artigues, La Moulette, Claude Quancard and Causseyre. Visitors have a choice of several different routes, all of them signposted : the short route (Petit Parcours, 2.4km – $1\frac{1}{2}$ miles), the long route (Grand Parcours, 3.6km – $2\frac{1}{4}$ miles), or the entire circuit (Parcours Complet, 6km – $3\frac{1}{2}$ miles). *Bird-watchers are recommended to hire binoculars if they do not have their own.*
Thousands of birds in their elegant feathered finery (widgeon, teal, ducks, wild geese, storks, herons, flamingoes, cranes, gulls etc) live and breed in the water meadows and on the dykes bordering the Eyre or surrounding the fish reservoirs. On each of the walks there are observation posts from which the wildlife can be studied.
There are also observatories which allow visitors to become aware of the extent and scope of the Eyre delta and the Park itself. The rich and varied vegetation here and in the neighbouring marshlands will amaze botany enthusiasts : among the varied plant civilizations are the berried trees (arbutus, brambles, prunus) beloved of the frugivorous birds; water irises, rushes, oaks planted to consolidate the dykes, and both tamarisk and alders used by ducks and moorhens to build their nests.
A special exhibition centre in the Park provides information on nature conservation and the problems facing the environment.

Teal, Le Teich nature reserve.

D'après photo Visage/JACANA

★ THOUARS

Pop 10 905

Michelin map 67 fold 8 or 232 folds 44, 45 – Facilities.

The best view of the **site★** of this old town is from the southern approach (D 39), across the bridge over the River Thouet. From Pont Neuf (New Bridge) there is a fine view of the rocky promontory, cradled by the river on the Poitou-Anjou border, and of the roofs – a mixture of Romanesque tiles and Angevin slates – of the houses clustered below the castle walls.
For many years Thouars remained faithful to the Plantagenets *(qv)* but the town eventually fell to **Bertrand du Guesclin** (1320-80), one of the generals who chased the English from the region, after a memorable siege in 1372. Having purchased Thouars from the Amboise family, Louis XI stayed here several times, and his wife, Margaret of Scotland, expressed a wish to be buried here. Charles VIII gave the town to the House of La Trémoille, and the family remained seigneurs of Thouars until the Revolution. The Protestant faith had been embraced by the inhabitants; after the Revocation of the Edict of Nantes Thouars lost fifty per cent of its population.

OLD TOWN *1 hour.*

★ **Église St-Médard** – The church, standing adjacent to a 15C square tower with overhanging corner turrets, is a Romanesque building despite the Gothic rose window adorning its fine Poitevin **west front★★**. The extensively-decorated entrance is surmounted by a Christ in Glory worshipped by angels. The archivolts – the last of which is interrupted by a resurrected Christ apparently leaving the tomb – spring from historiated capitals depicting the Punishment of the Vices. Splendid effigies of St Peter, St Paul, the Prophets and the Sibyls stand above the lateral arcades. The Romanesque doorway with festooned arches on the north side of the church is of Moorish inspiration. Inside, the three original Romanesque naves were replaced in the 15C by a single nave with lowered vaulting.
Chapelle St-Louis (on the north side) with its lierne-and-tierceron vaulting was built in 1510 by Gabrielle de Bourbon, the wife of Louis II of La Trémoille.

★ **Old houses** – The most interesting of these can be found in Rue St-Médard and Rue du Château, narrow streets leading to the old bridge which were once the principal arteries of medieval Thouars. Near the church is a fine brick and timber building now occupied by the Tourist Information Centre; the Hostellerie St-Médard, flanked by a vaulted passageway, is in the same style. Among the closely-packed houses in Rue du Château are several corbelled façades beneath sharp, steep gables – notably that of the 15C Hôtel des Trois-Rois (Three Kings Mansion) at No 11. It was here that the future Louis XI slept when he was still Dauphin (heir to the throne). A moulded corbel on the façade supports a kind of bartizan from which the street can be watched.

Chapelle Notre-Dame – This chapel, like the château to which it is attached, opens onto an esplanade that was once the seigneurial courtyard. It was built by Gabrielle de Bourbon above a series of crypts, one of which is still the family tomb of the La Trémoilles. The superb Flamboyant Gothic façade is surmounted by a Renaissance gallery with shell decorations. From the esplanade there is a fine view of the town and the broad sweep of river enclosing it.

Château (Collège Marie-de-La-Tour-d'Auvergne) – This imposing edifice dating from 1635, which replaced a medieval fortress, was built by Marie de La Tour d'Auvergne, Duchesse de La Trémoille and elder sister of the Vicomte de Turenne, one of France's most illustrious marshals. A domed pavilion housing a monumental staircase projects from the central block and there are two other pavilions at the extremities. From the gallery promenade there is a fine view of the façade of the château. Through an ancient postern it is possible to go down to the river, where it is crossed by a **Gothic bridge** with a fortified gateway.

Tour du Prince-de-Galles – The Prince of Wales Tower, also known as the Granary Tower because it was used as a grain store when it formed part of the town's defensive perimeter, is round and massive and capped with small bartizans. At one time it served as the town prison.

Porte au Prévôt – This is the gateway forced by Du Guesclin *(see above)* when he penetrated the town in 1372 to end the siege. It is framed by two projecting ravelin towers on octagonal bases.

Ancienne Abbaye St-Laon – This former abbey first staffed by Benedictine monks and then, after 1117, by Augustinians includes a 12C-15C church with a fine, square Romanesque belfry. It was in this church that Margaret of Scotland *(see above)* was buried. The present town hall is installed in the old (17C) monastic buildings.

Chemin du Panorama – Take D 759 northwest of the town and then, on the left, a steep downhill slope leading to a pretty **viewpoint.** From here the valley of the Thouet and the western profile of Thouars can be admired.

EXCURSIONS

⏲ ►► Airvault – 21km – 13 miles south – Église St-Pierre (12C Poitevin and 13C Angevin styles; porch★), Musée des Arts et traditions populaires.
Argenton-Château – 20km – 12½ miles west – This peaceful town sheltering within the remains of its ramparts stands at the confluence of steep valleys.

TIFFAUGES

Pop 1 208

Michelin map 67 fold 5 or 232 fold 41.

Tiffauges is a small town built on a promontory overlooking the confluence of the Sèvre Nantaise and the River Crume, and is known best for the romantic ruins of a castle which once belonged to a man on whom the fictional character of **Bluebeard** is based.

A legendary monster – The French relish their horror stories as much as anyone else, and one of their favourite monsters, about whom innumerable books and articles and psychological treatises have been published, is **Gilles de Rais** (1404-40).
De Rais (or de Retz) was a fine horseman and a cultivated individual before he was out of his teens. In 1420 he married Catherine de Thouars, who brought him as a dowry the seigneurie of Pouzauges *(qv)*. Early on he also demonstrated unusual qualities of leadership and military prowess, acting as a lieutenant to Charles VII in the latter's struggles against the English and fighting beside Joan of Arc during the reconquest of the kingdom. His valour was rewarded with the bestowal of a baton marking him as a Marshal of France at the age of 25.

He was however a vain man, cruel, hot-tempered and arrogant, and the death at the stake of his friend Joan of Arc appeared to trigger his baser instincts. By now proprietor of Tiffauges, Champtocé and Machecoul as well as Pouzauges, the young Marshal began living a profligate and licentious life : a retinue of 200 horsemen and innumerable domestic servants soon depleted a fortune that was already compromised.
In an effort to find some way of making money the dissolute seigneur of Tiffauges turned himself into an alchemist and sought the help of demons.
A necromancer assured him that the Devil would give him all the gold he wanted if he would consent to "offer him as a tribute the hands, heart, eyes and blood" torn from beautiful young children – and this is how Gilles de Rais, companion of Joan of Arc, hero of the siege of Orléans and Marshal of France, became the depraved criminal who terrorised the countryside for 20 leagues around and who was transformed, in one of the fairy tales by Charles Perrault *(qv)*, into the sinister character "Bluebeard".
Retribution was at hand, however, as Gilles de Rais became over-confident, thinking himself immune from the hands of human justice : in 1440 he was arrested by the authorities who had long suspected him. Having confessed to all his heinous crimes, de Rais was hanged and then burned in Nantes, in the presence of an enormous crowd.

CHÂTEAU ⊙ *1 hour.*

The ruins of the castle cover a huge area (3ha – 7½ acres) within a defensive wall. The parts in the best condition are the 12C keep, still protected by a deep ditch, and the 15C Vidame Tower with its enormous machicolations. Guardroom, latrines and an ancient chimneypiece can be seen here, as well as a night-duty room linked to the watch-path around the ramparts (there is a curious acoustic effect from the circular bench on which the watchmen could sit).
The 13C chapel, built over an 11C crypt, has retained its oven-vaulted apse.

★ Château de TOUFFOU

Michelin map 68 fold 14 or 233 fold 9 6km – 3½ miles northwest of Chauvigny.

The warm, ochre coloured stone of this **Château** ⊙ with its terraces overlooking the River Vienne helps to form a unified whole, despite the juxtaposition of four different architectural styles.
The oldest part of Touffou is the massive keep, which was formed during the Renaissance by twinning two older keeps dating from the 11C and 12C. At each of the outer corners the buttresses are crowned by elegant turrets. Four huge round towers were added in the 14C : Tour St-Georges, with finely sculpted openings, Tour St-Jean, Tour de l'Hostellerie, restored in 1938, and Tour de la Chapelle with its prison cells.
The Renaissance wing, linking Tour St-Georges with the keep, was added *c*1560. It is adorned with mullioned windows and dormers, the triangular pediments of which carry a series of 17 different coat of arms, representing the genealogy of the Chasteignier family.
The main sight inside the château is "François I's Room" (also known as the "Four Seasons Room"), which is embellished with fine frescoes illustrating work in the fields throughout the year. A *salle de chasse* is devoted to hunting and the trophies associated with it; a collection of jacket buttons decorated with hunting motifs is on display in Tour de l'Hostellerie.
The attractive grounds include terrraces and a hanging garden.

VILLENEUVE-SUR-LOT Pop 22 782

Michelin map 79 south of fold 5 or 235 fold 13 – Local map p 44.

The town, founded in 1253 on the borders between Périgord and Guyenne by Alphonse de Poitiers, was built to serve as a "support centre" for the strongpoints scattered throughout the upper Agenais region : Villeneuve was one of the largest and most powerful *bastides (qv)* in the southwest.
The town, which has preserved numerous alleys and ancient houses from the Middle Ages (especially around Place La Fayette, a typical old square) is today largely spread around the banks of the River Lot. The fertile alluvial valley, which produces heavy crops of fruit and early vegetables, has made Villeneuve into a busy trading centre and, like Agen *(qv)*, a regional market for plums.

SIGHTS

Town gates – The two town gates – **Porte de Paris** northeast of the old town and **Porte de Pujols** southwest – are the only traces of the old ramparts. The gates are both built of brick and stone, are both crowned with crenellations and machicolations, and both covered by a roof of brown tiles. Porte du Pujols is three storeys high with mullioned windows; Porte de Paris was instrumental in the fierce resistance to Mazarin's troops during the siege of 1653.

Église Ste-Catherine – *North bank of the river.* This brick-built church, in Romanesque-Byzantine style, resting on a granite socle, was consecrated in 1937. Its north-south orientation is extremely unusual. The interior is decorated, apart from the chancel, with a series of restored stained-glass windows; those dating from the

14C and 15C – which came from the old church – have been attributed to the school of **Arnaud de Moles,** the master-enameller and painter who worked on the cathedral in Auch *(qv).* Beautiful 17C and 18C giltwood statues (of Our Lady of the Rosary, St Joseph, Mary Magdalene and St Jerome) adorn the four pillars of the nave above the doorway into the baptistery. The marble font stands bathed in blue-tinged shafts of light. The paintings in the nave show a procession moving towards the chancel.

Pont-Vieux – This old bridge with uneven arches, which was built by the English in the 13C, offers a picturesque view over the banks of the river and over the 16C chapel at the end of the bridge, with its east end jutting over the water.

Musée municipal ⓘ – A large villa near Porte de Pujols, on the corner with Boulevard Voltaire, is now the town museum; the house was bequeathed by Gaston Rapin, one of the old architects of the town. The basement is devoted to local prehistory and to Egyptian and Gallo-Roman antiquities. The ground floor has a room containing religious art (fine polychrome keystone showing God blessing and a Deposition from the Cross) and another housing contemporary drawings and sculpture. The **Piranesi Cabinet** exhibits the entire works (copies) of the Italian architect and engraver (1720-78) who was nicknamed the "visionary of ruins".
The first floor is devoted to 19C and 20C painting and sculpture; one room holds temporary exhibitions. The second floor has displays on local folk arts and traditions, and includes the **Musée de la Prune** which focuses on the special tools etc used in the cultivation and selling of local plums.

EXCURSIONS

Other nearby strongpoints include :

Penne-d'Agenais – *10km – 6 miles east via D 661 :* restored strongpoint, once the fief of the kings of England. **Monflanquin** – *17km – 10 miles north via D 676.* 13C hilltop *bastide* with steep streets lined by houses with round-tiled roofs. **Villeréal** – *30km – 18 miles north via D 767.* 13C *bastide,* which became English during the Hundred Years War, with 13C-14C fortified church and 15C market. **Laparade** – *24.5km – 15 miles west via D 911 and Castelmoron-sur-Lot.* Scenic views over the Lot valley.

★ VOUVANT

Pop 829

Michelin map 67 fold 16 or 233 fold 4 – Local map p 176.

The hedgerows of the *bocage (qv)* and the dense woodland of the forest combine with the rippling waters of the River Mère to confer on this village, perched behind ancient ramparts on a bluff, an atmosphere of silence and safety, redolent of the past – an atmosphere resulting perhaps from the intervention of the Fairy **Mélusine** *(qv),* who is said to have built Vouvant Château in a single night...

SIGHTS

★ **Church** – The church was founded by the monks of Maillezais Abbey *(qv).* The 11C nave was very badly damaged by partisans of the Reformation in 1568 and only the walls of the first three bays remain. The original three apses were rebuilt in the 12C (restored in 1882) along with the crypt below (also restored in the 19C) and the great doorway of the northern transept, which is in the Romanesque style; this doorway, the main **façade★,** flanked by clustered columns and topped by a sharp gable, forms a rich and readable page of sculpture.

Main Doorway – The doorway consists of arched doors twinned beneath a common archivolt, surmounted on the tympanum by two interesting stone carvings in relief. On the right, partly damaged by weather, is the figure of Samson overcoming the lion; on the left is Delilah shearing Samson's hair. A stone shelf separating the two groups once supported a row of statues – probably those discovered in the church crypt. A shield beneath the shelf, supported by two eagles and crowned by a helmet, is thought to have borne the arms of the Lusignan family *(qv),* supposed descendants of Mélusine. The covings above the two doors are decorated with floral motifs and the capitals with animals and fantastic figures.
The first coving of the **archivolt** features a line of supporting atlantes, the second a finely carved succession of characters, Biblical and mythological. On the left above the arch is a haloed Virgin and Child, balanced on the right by an effigy of John the Baptist. Higher still are two friezes on modillions : the Last Supper (below); the Apostles witnessing the Ascension (above).

Château – The old fortress, home of the Lusignans in medieval times, bars the neck of the promontory girdled by a loop of the river. Its defensive walls demarcate Place du Bail, a grassy esplanade planted with chestnut trees now used as a site for country fairs. From the edge there are attractive views over the lazy curve of the River Mere, which widens here upstream from the Pierre-Brune dam.
The former keep, the **Tour Melusine★** ⓘ was built in 1242. The walls, up to 3m – 10ft thick, enclose two chambers, one above the other, with curious pyramid vaulting. The top of the tower can be reached by a stairway of 120 steps. From here, 36m – 118ft above the ground, there is a vast **panorama★** to be admired – from the picturesque site of the village itself to the sombre mass of the forest-covered plateau in the south and the chessboard of *bocage* farmland in the north.

Book well in advance
as vacant hotel rooms are often scarce in high season.

★★ Île d'YEU — Pop 4 941

Michelin map 67 fold 11 or 232 fold 37.

The Isle of Yeu lies in the Atlantic 40km – 25 miles northwest of Les Sables-d'Olonne and 20km – 12½ miles off the Vendée coast, the austere grandeur of its landscape particularly prized by lovers of unspoiled nature. The enjoyment of a visit to the isle – especially to the rocky Côte Sauvage (Wild Coast) on the southwest side – is enhanced by the pleasures of the crossing, even if the sea can be a little choppy when the weather is poor. The principal sights are described below, but it is easy to spend two or three whole days on outings and excursions.

Access ⓥ – From Fromentine or, in the summer season, from Noirmoutier.
The best way of exploring the island is by bicycle; there are many places where these can be hired once the boat has docked at Port-Joinville.

HISTORICAL AND GEOGRAPHICAL NOTES

10km – 6¼ miles long and only 4km – 2½ miles wide, Yeu resembles Brittany much more than the Isle of Noirmoutier, even though the latter is much nearer the Breton coast. In fact, because of its crystalline schist rock formations, because of the wild nature of its Côte Sauvage, facing the open sea, the island is more like Belle-Île than anywhere else. There are even tough Breton-type fishermen, such as may be encountered in Finistère. The eastern and southern coasts nevertheless are pure Vendée : pine trees, holm oaks, dunes and long, wide beaches of fine sand.
The island has been inhabited since prehistoric times (there are a large number of dolmens and menhirs still to be seen) and it is not impossible that this was the island where, according to the Greek geographer Strabo, a religious "college" of Druidesses was established.
A monastery was founded on Yeu in the 6C. The future St Amand, the "Apostle of Flanders", was drawn here at the beginning of the following century. In the 8C the island was given the enigmatic name of "Insula (isle) Oya". In the 16C the entire population of a village in Cornouaille, Southwest Brittany, led by its priest, disembarked on Yeu with the idea of settling here. The prefix "Ker-", attached to certain villages is a distortion of the Lower Poitou dialect word "Querry", meaning a village. Île d'Yeu was ruled by various seigneurs, including Olivier de Clisson, the brilliant warrior who became Constable, before it was sold to the Crown in 1785.
Aside from tourism, the islanders' resources today depend mainly on fishing : the population includes more than 450 fishermen. Between 20 and 30 boats equipped with special note trawl for white tunny off the Portuguese coast in the Azores (the catch in 1991 was 1 530 tonnes, ie 36% of the total production in France).

A Marshal detained – On 16 November 1945 a naval escort vessel landed an old man of 90 on the island. He was to be incarcerated in the citadel at Pierre-Levée. The old man was the "ex-Marshal" **Pétain,** head of Vichy (collaborationist) France from 1940 to 1944. He was assigned a whitewashed cell, damp and sparsely furnished, which he swept out every morning after making his bed and before he was allowed to exercise in a yard with no view apart from a few scrawny chestnut trees. In 1951 he was struck by a double pulmonary congestion and removed to hospital. He died on 23 July. Men who had fought under him at Verdun, in the First World War, carried the coffin to the cemetery at Port-Joinville, where he lies.

TOUR OF THE ISLAND *allow 1 day.*

Cliff paths around the coast offer visitors a succession of splendid views – especially in the south and west – as well as the opportunity to explore the attractive coves and beaches below.

★ **Port-Joinville** – This, the largest town on the island, was originally called Port-Breton; the present name derives from Admiral de Joinville, the third son of Louis-Philippe I, who brought Napoleon's body back to France in 1840. It is one of the

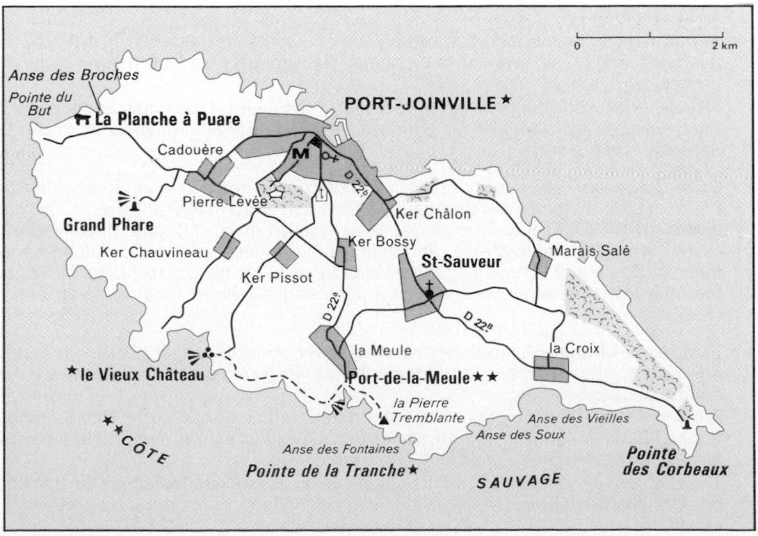

most important tunny-fishing ports in France. Tourists arriving from Fromentine or Noirmoutier can enjoy a picturesque view of the tiny port crammed with tunny boats and small trawlers, their multicoloured pennants, dressed above a series of buoys, fluttering in the breeze. Behind the masts and rigging is a quay bordered by white houses.

With the exception of the outer harbour, the port is left dry at low tide. Beyond the waterfront there is one shopping street and a network of lanes close-packed with fishermen's cottages.

The house where Mme Pétain lived while her husband was imprisoned is now **Le Musée-Historial** (**M**) ⓥ. One room is reserved for the exhibition of Pétain mementoes : in the remainder of the small museum the history of the island is illustrated. The Marshal's tomb, a simple white stone slab in a grove of yews and cypress trees, faces the mainland from the local cemetery.

Port-Joinville.

Dolmen de La Planche à Puare – This megalith stands on a stretch of moorland near the **Anse** (cove) **des Broches,** at the northwestern tip of the island. It is constructed of schistose granite blocks and is unusual in that it has a transeptal corridor – that is to say, a central passage with lateral chambers (two each side of the passage in this case). Ancient bones have been found.

Grand Phare ⓥ – The upper platform *(201 steps)* of the lighthouse is 41m – 135ft above the ground (and 56m – 184ft above sea level). There is a splendid **view★** looking out over the island to the ocean and, in clear weather, to the coast from Noirmoutier to St-Gilles.

★ **Le Vieux Château** – This old castle occupies an imposing site at the seaward end of a moor.

Its ghostly silhouette, almost indistinguishable from the rock on which it is built, is both romantic and spectacular. Its walls rise from a granite spur gashed by a narrow crevasse 17m – 56ft deep, at the bottom of which the ocean waves break with a noise like thunder.

It was built in feudal times (possibly the 11C) and remodelled in the 16C, and this wild pirates' lair now forms a rough trapezoid flanked by defensive bastion-towers.

A foot-bridge, replacing the old drawbridge, leads within the walls. From the top of the keep *(Beware : there is no parapet)* there are marvellous **views★★** of the Côte Sauvage and the sea.

★★ **Côte Sauvage** – The rocky coast, extending in a northwest-southeast line from Pointe de But to Pointe des Corbeaux, is indented in an irregular fashion. The ocean views are magnificent. Two of the best are from a cliff path linking the old castle with Port-de-la-Meule. Perched above sheer rock-faces plunging into the sea *(Beware of vertigo and the possibility of landslips or crumbling cliff edges),* the path leads walkers eventually to a picturesque **view★★** looking down over the creek.

★★ **Port-de-la-Meule** – A long, narrow inlet penetrating the coast. At the inner end is the slipway of the crabbers and lobster boats which sink their pots along the rocky depths of Côte Sauvage.

From the moorland heights above, the small white Chapelle de Notre-Dame-de-Bonne-Nouvelle (Chapel of Our Lady of Good News) watches over the tiny port. The local sailors take part in an annual pilgrimage here.

The cliff path continues beyond the chapel as far as **La Pierre Tremblante,** an enormous boulder perched above the sea which can be made to rock gently by pressing on a certain spot.

★ **Pointe de la Tranche** – A number of rocky creeks surround this headland. There are two named Anse de la Fontaine, one on either side (so-called because each harbours a freshwater spring). Two of the others, particularly calm and sheltered, are suitable for bathing : the Anse (cove) des Soux, where there is a marine grotto, and the **Anse des Vieilles,** the prettiest beach on the island.

Pointe des Corbeaux – This is the southeastern extremity of Île d'Yeu, forming the dividing line from which the astonishing contrast between the island's two different landscapes can best be appreciated – the rocky, storm-tossed, Breton-style coast on the west; a calm, sandy, pine-clad shoreline reminiscent of the Vendée on the east.

St-Sauveur – This is commonly referred to simply as "the Town" as it was once the island capital and residence of the Governor. There is a Romanesque church with a square tower above the transept crossing.

F. Jalain/EXPLORER

Game of pelota.

Practical Information

PHOTOSEGOR

TRAVELLING TO FRANCE

Passport – Visitors entering France must be in possession of a valid national **passport** (or in the case of the British, a Visitor's Passport). In case of loss or theft report to the embassy or consulate and the local police.

Visa – An **entry visa** is required for Canadian and US citizens (for a stay of more than 3 months) and for Australian citizens in accordance with French security measures. Apply to the French Consulate (visa issued same day; delay if submitted by mail).
US citizens should obtain the booklet "Your Trip Abroad" ($1) which provides useful information on visa requirements, customs regulations, medical care etc for international travellers. Apply to the Superintendent of Documents, Government Printing Office, Washington DC 20402-9325.

Customs – Apply to the Customs Office (UK) for a leaflet on customs regulations and the full range of duty-free allowances. The US Treasury Department (☎ 202 566 8195) offers a publication "Know before you go" for US citizens.
There are no customs formalities for holidaymakers bringing their caravans into France for a stay of less than 6 months. No customs document is necessary (although this is currently under review) for pleasure boats and outboard motors for a stay of less than 6 months but the registration certificate should be kept on board.

By air – The various national and other independent airlines operate services to **Paris** (Charles de Gaulle and Orly) and **Bordeaux.** There are also package tour flights with a rail or coach link-up as well as Fly-Drive schemes. Information, brochures and timetables are available from the airlines and from travel agents.
The domestic network operates frequent services : there are regular flights with AIR INTER (☎ 42 89 38 88) between Bordeaux and Lyon, Marseille, Nantes, Nice, Paris, Strasbourg and Toulouse; between Biarritz and Lourdes/Tarbes, Pau and Paris. Flights with AIR LITTORAL (☎ 67 20 67 20) connect Bordeaux with Montpellier, and Biarritz with Lyon, Marseille, Nice and Pau. AIR TRANSPORT PYRÉNÉES (☎ 59 33 16 33) links Pau and Nantes. TAT (☎ 42 79 05 05) operates services between Nantes and Bordeaux, and AIR VENDÉE (☎ 51 62 51 58) links Bordeaux with Clermont-Ferrand.
Transfer buses link up with town terminals and railway stations.

By sea – There are numerous **cross-Channel services** (passenger and car ferries, hovercraft, SeaCat) from the United Kingdom and Eire to the northern coast of France, and a couple of services to the northern coast of Spain (Santander and Bilbao). A service from Portsmouth to Pauillac on the Gironde may also be available. For details apply to travel agencies or to :

P&O European Ferries, Channel House, Channel View Road, Dover CT17 9TJ; ☎ 0304 203388. Ticket collection : Russell St, Dover, Kent CT16 1QB.
The Continental Ferry Port, Mile End, Portsmouth, Hampshire PO2 8QW; ☎ 0705 827677 (to Cherbourg, Le Havre and Bilbao).
Stena Sealink, Charter House, Park Street, Ashford, Kent TN24 8EX; ☎ 0233 647047 (to Cherbourg).
Brittany Ferries, Millbay Docks, Plymouth, Devon PLI 3EW; ☎ 0752 221321.
The Brittany Centre, Wharf Road, Portsmouth, Hampshire PO2 8RU; ☎ 0705 827701 (to Roscoff, St Malo and Santander).
Sally Line, 81 Piccadilly , London WIV 9HF; ☎ 071 409 2240 (to Dunkirk).
Argyle Centre, York St, Ramsgate, Kent CT11 9DS; ☎ 0843 595522.
Hoverspeed, International Hoverport, Marine Parade, Dover, Kent CT17 9TG; ☎ 0304 240241 (to Calais and Boulogne).
Maybrook House, Queen's Gardens, Dover CT17 9UQ; ☎ direct line from London 554 7061, Birmingham 021 236 2190 or Manchester 061 228 1321.

By rail – British Rail offers a range of passenger services to the Channel ports and French Railways (SNCF) operates an extensive network of lines including many high-speed passenger trains and motorail services (to Biarritz and Bordeaux from Calais, and to Nantes, for example) throughout France. There are rail passes (France Vacances Pass) offering unlimited travel and group travel tickets offering savings for parties. Eurorail Pass, Flexipass and Saver Pass are options available in the US for travel in Europe and must be purchased in the US – ☎ 212 308 3103 (information) and 1 800 223 636 (reservations).
Tickets bought in France must be validated *(composter)* by using the orange automatic date-stamping machines at the platform entrance.
Information and bookings from French Railways, 179 Piccadilly, London WIV OBA; ☎ 071 409 3518 and from principal British and American Rail Travel Centres and travel agencies.
Baggage trolleys (10F coin required – refundable) are available at main line stations.

By coach – Regular coach services are operated from London to Paris and to large provincial towns :

Hoverspeed, Maybrook House, Queens Gardens, Dover CT17 9UQ. ☎ 0304 240241.
Euroways/Eurolines, 52 Grosvenor Gardens, Victoria, London SWIW 0AU. ☎ 071 730 8235.

Via the Channel Tunnel – This high-speed undersea rail shuttle link between Folkestone in England and Calais in France is due to begin operating in 1994. Motorists will be able to drive their car onto specially designed double-deck wagons for the 35min trip and drive off at the Calais terminal onto slip-roads feeding directly into the French motorway network. For further information, contact Le Shuttle passenger enquiries (England) : ☎ 0303 271100.

MOTORING IN FRANCE

Documents – Nationals of EC countries require a valid national **driving licence;** nationals of non-EC countries require an **international driving licence** (obtainable in the US from the American Automobile Club).
For the vehicle it is necessary to have the **registration papers** (log-book) and a **nationality plate** of the approved size.

Insurance – Insurance cover is compulsory and although an International Insurance Certificate (Green Card) is no longer a legal requirement in France it is the most effective proof of insurance cover and is internationally recognised by the police and other authorities.
Certain UK motoring organisations (AA, RAC) run accident insurance and breakdown service schemes for members. Europ-Assistance (252 High St, Croydon CR0 1NF) has special policies for motorists. Members of the American Automobile Club should obtain the brochure "Offices to serve you abroad". Affiliated organisation for France : Association Française des Automobile-Clubs, 9 Rue Anatole-de-la-Forge, 75017 Paris; ☏ 42 27 82 00.

Highway Code – There are severe penalties for infringements : fines are high and jail sentences may be imposed. By pleading guilty and paying on the spot (in cash) for minor Highway Code violations, motorists can avoid going to court or having their vehicle confiscated and may be eligible for a reduced fine.
The minimum driving age is 18 years old. Traffic drives on the right. It is compulsory for front-seat and back-seat passengers to wear **seat belts** where they are fitted. Children under the age of ten should be on the back seat.
Full or dipped headlights (which should be correctly adjusted) must be switched on in poor visibility and at night; use sidelights only when the vehicle is stationary.
In the case of a **breakdown** a red warning triangle or hazard warning lights are obligatory.
Drivers should watch out for unfamiliar road signs and take great care on the road. In built-up areas **priority** must be ceded to vehicles joining the road from the right; however, traffic on main roads outside built-up areas and on roundabouts has priority. Vehicles must stop when the lights turn red at road junctions and may filter to the right only where indicated by an amber arrow.
The regulations on **drink-driving** and **speeding** are strictly enforced.

Speed limits – Although liable to modification these are as follows :
- toll motorways 130kph – 80mph (110kph – 68mph when raining);
- dual carriage roads and motorways without tolls 110kph – 68mph (100kph – 62mph when raining);
- other roads 90kph – 56mph (80kph – 50mph when raining) and in towns 50kph 31mph;
- outside lane on motorways during daylight, on level ground and with good visibility – minimum speed limit of 80kph (50mph).

Parking Regulations – In town there are restricted and paying **parking zones** (blue and grey zones); tickets must be obtained from the ticket machines (*horodateurs* – small change necessary) and displayed (inside windscreen on driver's side); failure to display may result in a heavy fine.

Route Planning – For 24-hour road traffic information : dial 48 94 33 33 or consult the 3615 Michelin Minitel Service *(see below)*.
See page 13 for the full range of **Michelin maps** covering France.
The road network is excellent and includes many motorways, mostly toll-roads *(autoroutes à péage)*. The roads are very busy during the holiday period (particularly weekends in July and August) and to avoid traffic congestion it is advisable to follow the recommended secondary routes (Bison Futé – itinéraires bis – with green signposts).
During summer months there are many events and facilities (clowns, swimming, archery, classical concerts, mountain biking, sight and reflex testing etc) laid on – sometimes for free – at motorway service stations and rest areas to encourage long-distance drivers to rest. Look out for the blue signposts showing a javelin thrower which indicate these "sport stops".

Car Rental – There are car rental agencies at airports, air terminals, railway stations and in all large towns throughout France. European cars usually have manual transmission but automatic cars are available on demand. An **international driving licence** is required for non-EC nationals.
Fly-drive schemes are operated by major airlines.

Minitel

Minitel is a French Telecom videotex service offering a wide variety of information. Public terminals are to be found in most post offices, some petrol stations and hotels (over 6 million terminals in France). The cost of consulting Minitel is 1.27F per minute. Foreign subscribers can access French Telecom videotex services (consult own information system).

Michelin Travel Assistance (AMI) is a computerised route-finding system offering integrated information on roads, tourist sights, hotels and restaurants; it covers most European countries and is available on Minitel through the access code **3615 MICHELIN.** This user-friendly travel service is available round the clock.

Route planning : state the point of departure and destination, a preference for motorways or local roads, indicate the sights to see along the way and AMI will do the rest.

Lunchtime or overnight stops : look for that special restaurant, secluded country hotel or pleasant campsite along the chosen route.

Listed below are a selection of other telematic services available :

3614 ED	Electronic service in English
3615 TCAMP	camping information
3615 METEO	weather report
3615 or 3616 HORAV	general airline information and flight schedules
3615 BBC	BBC news
3615 LIBE	USA TODAY

ACCOMMODATION

Places to stay – The map on *p 12* indicates recommended places for overnight stops and may be used in conjunction with the current **Michelin Red Guide France.**

Loisirs Accueil is an officially-backed booking service which has offices in most French *départements.* For information contact Réservation Loisirs Accueil, 2 Rue Linois, 75015 Paris; ☏ 40 59 44 12.

The **"Accueil de France"** Tourist Offices which are open all year make hotel bookings for a small fee for personal callers only. The head office is in Paris (127 Avenue des Champs-Élysées; ☏ 47 23 61 72 for information only) and there are offices in many large towns and resorts.

The brochure "Logis et Auberges de France" is available from the French Government Tourist Office.

Rural accommodation – Apply to **Maison des Gîtes de France,** 35 Rue Godot-de-Mauroy, 75009 Paris (☏ 47 42 20 20) or 178 Piccadilly, London W1V OAL (☏ 071 493 3480) for a list of relevant addresses. The Minitel service – code 3615 Gîtes de France – may also be consulted.

The Fédération Française des Stations Vertes de Vacances et des Villages de Neige publishes an annual list of addresses of rural locations selected for their calm surroundings and the range of outdoor activities they offer. Details from Hôtel du Département de la Côte-d'Or, BP 1601, 21035 Dijon Cedex; ☏ 80 49 94 80.

Gîtes et Refuges, France et Frontières by A and S Mouraret (published by La Cadole, BP 303, 75723 Paris Cedex 25) is a useful handbook in French aimed at ramblers, mountaineers, climbers, skiers, canoeists and cross-country cyclists.

Bed and Breakfast – Gîtes de France *(see above)* publishes a booklet on bed and breakfast accommodation (table d'hôte).

Youth Hostels – There are many youth hostels throughout France. Holders of an International Youth Hostel Federation card should apply for a list from the International Federation or from the French Youth Hostels Association, 38 Boulevard Raspail, 75007 Paris; ☏ 45 48 69 84.

Members of American Youth Hostels should call 202 783 6161 for information on budget accommodation.

Camping – There are numerous officially graded sites with varying standards of facilities throughout the Atlantic Coast region; the **Michelin Guide Camping Caravaning France** lists a selection of the best camping sites. An International Camping Carnet for caravans is useful but not compulsory; it may be obtained from the motoring organisations or the Camping and Caravanning Club (11 Lower Grosvenor Place, London SW1).

Eating out : regional specialities – *See also the chapter on Food and Drink in the Introduction.* In the Charentes, start with the local seafood such as Mouclade Charentaise (mussels cooked *à la crème* or in the *marinière* fashion, with shallots and white wine) or Huîtres à la Charentaise which consists of swallowing a cool oyster followed by a piece of spicy sausage; follow this with a sip of chilled white wine. Chaudrée is a soup of white wine and fish (plaice, sole, conger etc). In Béarn, choose Garbure to start – a traditional ham and lentil soup. In wine-producing areas a typical starter might be *Escargots à la Vigneronne,* a dish of small snails with a wine sauce, onions or shallots, and garlic.

Around Bordeaux it is worth trying lamprey or eel *à la Bordelaise* (the long slender fish is cut into round sections and stewed in a red wine and blood sauce) or *Entrecôte à la Bordelaise* (steak topped by sliced segments of bone marrow, again accompanied by a red wine sauce). In the Basque region try traditional dishes such as sweet peppers stuffed with cod, bass in a hot green-pepper sauce, or hake in cider or parsley sauce.

Among the delicious desserts are *clafoutis* – dark cherries baked in a sweet batter – *tourteau fromager* (a baked cheesecake made from cottage cheese mixed with flour, set in a pastry case) and, in Basque provinces, curdled milk with honey and walnuts, cake made with rum, raisins and egg yolks, and smokey Idiazabal cheese made from ewes milk.

To choose a hotel, a restaurant or a campsite
consult the current edition of the annual Michelin Red Guide France
and the annual Michelin Guide Camping Caravaning France.

GENERAL INFORMATION

Medical treatment – First aid, medical advice and chemists' night service rota are available from chemists (*pharmacie* – green cross sign).
It is advisable to take out comprehensive insurance cover as the recipient of medical treatment in French hospitals or clinics must pay the bill. Nationals of non-EC countries should check with their insurance companies about policy limitations. Reimbursement can then be negotiated with the insurance company according to the policy held.
American Express offers a service, "Global Assist", for any medical, legal or personal emergency – call collect from anywhere ☏ 202 554 2639.
British citizens should apply to the Department of Health and Social Security for **Form E 111,** which entitles the holder to urgent treatment for accident or unexpected illness in EC countries. A refund of part of the costs of treatment can be obtained on application in person or by post to the local Social Security Offices (Caisse Primaire d'Assurance Maladie).

Electricity – The electric current is 220 volts. Circular two-pin plugs are the rule – an electrical adaptor may be necessary.

Currency – There are no restrictions on the amount of currency visitors can take into France. To facilitate the export from France of currency in foreign bank notes in excess of the given allocation visitors are advised to complete a currency declaration form on arrival.

Banks – Banks are open from 0900 to 1200 and 1400 to 1600 and are closed on Monday or Saturday (except if market day); some branches open for limited transactions on Saturday. Banks close early on the day before a bank holiday.
A passport is necessary as identification when cashing cheques in banks. Commission charges vary and hotels usually charge more than banks for cashing cheques for non-residents.
Most banks have cash dispensers which accept international credit cards.

Credit Cards – American Express, Carte Bleue (Visa/Barclaycard), Diners Club and Eurocard (Mastercard/Access) are widely accepted in shops, hotels and restaurants and petrol stations.

Post – Post Offices open Monday to Friday 0800 to 1900, Saturday 0800 to 1200.
Postage via air mail to : UK letter 2.30F; postcard 2.10F; US aerogramme 4.20F; letter (20g) 3.80F; postcard 3.50F. Stamps are also available from newsagents and tobacconists.
Poste Restante mail should be addressed as follows : Name, *Poste Restante, Poste Centrale,* postal code of the *département* followed by town name, *France*. The **Michelin Red Guide France** gives local postal codes.

Telephone – Public phones using pre-paid phone cards *(télécarte)* are in operation in many areas. The cards (50 or 120 units) which are available from post offices, tobacconists and newsagents can be used for inland and international calls. Calls can be received at phone boxes where the blue bell sign is shown.

Internal calls – When calling within either of the two main zones (French provinces and Paris and its region) dial only the 8 digit correspondent's number. From Paris to the provinces dial 16 + 8 digit number. From the provinces to Paris dial 16 + 1 + 8 digit number.

International calls – For Paris dial the country code 33 + 1 + 8 digit number. For the provinces the country code 33 + 8 digit number.
When calling abroad from France dial 19, wait until the continuous tone recurs, then dial the country code and dialling code and number of your correspondent. For international enquiries dial 19 33 12 + country code.
Telephone rates from a public telephone at any time are : Paris-London : about 5.60F for 1 minute; Paris-New York : 10.30F for 1 minute. Cheap rates with 50% extra time are available from private telephones on weekdays between 2230 and 0800, at weekends starting 1400 on Saturdays.

Shopping – The big stores and larger shops are open Monday to Saturday, 0900 to 1830-1930. Smaller, individual shops may close during the lunch hour. Food shops – grocers, wine merchants and bakeries – are open from 0700 to 1830-1930; some open on Sunday mornings. Many food shops close between 1200 and 1400 and on Mondays. Hypermarkets usually open until 2100-2200.

Public holidays – The following are days when museums and other monuments may be closed or may vary their hours of admission :

New Year's Day	France's National Day **(14 July)**
Easter Sunday and Monday	Assumption **(15 August)**
May Day **(1 May)**	All Saints' Day **(1 November)**
V E Day **(8 May)**	Armistice Day **(11 November)**
Ascension Day	Christmas Day
Whit Sunday and Monday	

National museums and art galleries are closed on Tuesdays whereas municipal museums are closed on Mondays.
In addition to the usual school holidays at Christmas and in the spring and summer, there are long mid-term breaks (10 days to a fortnight) in February and early November.

Embassies and Consulates

Australia	Embassy	4 Rue Avenue Jean-Rey, 75015 Paris, ☎ 40 59 33 00.
Canada	Embassy	35 Avenue Montaigne, 75008 Paris, ☎ 47 23 01 01.
Eire	Embassy	4 Rue Rude, 75016 Paris, ☎ 45 00 20 87.
UK	Embassy	35 Rue du Faubourg-St-Honoré, 75008 Paris, ☎ 42 66 91 42.
	Consulate	16 Rue d'Anjou, 75008 Paris, ☎ 42 66 91 42.
		11 Square Dutilleul, 59800 Lille, ☎ 56 42 34 13.
USA	Embassy	2 Avenue Gabriel, 75008 Paris, ☎ 42 96 12 02.
	Consulate	2 Rue St-Florentin, 75001 Paris, ☎ 42 96 14 88.

TOURIST INFORMATION

French Government Tourist Offices – For information, brochures, maps and assistance in planning a trip to France travellers should apply to the official tourist office in their own country *(addresses at the end of this chapter).*

Regional Tourist Offices – These publish information brochures on their own region.
Comité Régional du Tourisme Pays de la Loire (for the Vendée), Rue de la Loire, Île Beaulieu, 44200 Nantes, ☎ 40 48 24 20.
Comité Régional du Tourisme Poitou-Charentes, Rue Ste-Opportune, BP 56, 86002 Poitiers Cedex, ☎ 49 88 38 94.
Comité Régional du Tourisme Aquitaine, Rue René-Cassin, 33049 Bordeaux Cedex, ☎ 56 39 88 88.
Comité Régional du Tourisme Midi-Pyrénées, 54 Boulevard de l'Embouchure, BP 2166, 31022 Toulouse Cedex, ☎ 61 13 55 55.

Departmental Tourist Offices

Charente : Place Bouillaud, 16021 Angoulême, ☎ 45 92 24 43.
Charente-Maritime : 11 bis, Rue des Augustines, BP 1152, 17008 La Rochelle Cedex, ☎ 46 41 43 33.
Loire-Atlantique : Place du Commerce, 44000 Nantes, ☎ 40 89 50 77.
Deux-Sèvres : 6 Rue du Palais, BP 49, 79002 Niort Cedex, ☎ 49 24 76 79.
Vendée : 8 Place Napoléon, 85000 La Roche-sur-Yon, ☎ 51 05 45 28.
Vienne : 15 Rue Carnot, BP 287, 86007 Poitiers Cedex, ☎ 49 41 58 22.
Ariège : Hôtel de Département, BP 143, 09003 Foix Cedex, ☎ 61 02 09 70.
Gers : 7 Rue Diderot, BP 106, 32003 Auch, ☎ 62 05 37 02.
Gironde : 21 Cours de l'Intendance, 33000 Bordeaux, ☎ 56 52 61 40.
Landes : 22 Rue Victor-Hugo, BP 407, 40012 Mont-de-Marsan Cedex, ☎ 58 06 89 89.
Lot-et-Garonne : 4 Rue André-Chénier, BP 158, 47005 Agen Cedex, ☎ 53 66 14 14.
Pyrénées-Atlantiques : 22 *ter* Rue Jean-Jacques-de-Monaix, 64000 Pau, ☎ 59 30 01 30.
Hautes-Pyrénées : Hautes-Pyrénées Tourisme Environnement, 6 Rue Eugène-Tenot BP 450, 65005 Tarbes Cedex, ☎ 62 93 03 30.

Tourist Information Centres – The addresses and telephone numbers of the Touris Information Centres (Syndicats d'Initiative) of most large towns and tourist resorts may be found among the Admission Times and Charges *(qv)* and in the **Michelin Red Guide France.** They can supply large-scale town plans, timetables and information on loca entertainment facilities, sports and sightseeing.

Tourism for the Disabled – Some of the sights described in this guide are accessible to handicapped people. They are listed in the publication *Touristes quand même Promenades en France pour les Voyageurs Handicapés* published by the Comité National Français de Liaison pour la Réadaptation des Handicapés (38 Boulevard Raspail 75007 Paris). This booklet covers nearly 90 towns in France and provides practical information (in French) for people who suffer reduced mobility or visual or aural impairment The **Michelin Red Guide France** and the **Michelin Camping Caravaning France** indicate hotels and camping sites with facilities suitable for physically handicapped people.

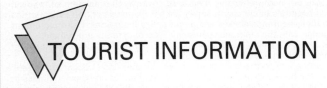

PIX

Mussel posts ("bouchots").

RECREATION and DISCOVERING THE AREA

For visitors who are not pressed for time there are many opportunities to see the countryside from an unusual or different perspective, allowing the best possible appreciation of the local art and architecture, country life and wildlife.

Tourist Routes – *Routes historiques* are signposted local itineraries following an architectural and historical theme, accompanied by an explanatory booklet; contact the Caisse nationale des monuments historiques et des sites (CNMHS), 62 Rue St-Antoine, 75004 Paris, ☎ 44 61 20 00.
There are eight *Routes historiques* within the region described in this guide : Circuit Sud-Vendéen, Trésors de Saintonge, Abbayes et Monuments du Haut-Poitou, Route historique des Plantagenêts, Route des Châteaux de Garonne, Route gasconne d'Henri IV, Route des Cadets de Gascogne and Route des Seigneurs de Béarn.

Horse-drawn Caravans – Why not visit Poitou in a horse-drawn caravan? Caravans, complete with bunk-beds and basic kitchen facilities, may be hired to follow a planned itinerary lasting from 2 to 7 days.
For a tour of the Marais Poitevin (departure from Damvix) contact the Maison du Parc, ☎ 46 27 82 44, otherwise look out for the brochure published by La Maison Poitou-Charentes.

Tourist Trains – Several tourist trains – whether rack and pinion or pulled by steam engines – operate in the region, crossing woods, marshes, mountains and fields; see under Cap Ferret, Coulon, Les Herbiers, Pointe de Gatseau, Pointe de Grave, Lac d'Artouste, La Rhune and Les Sables-d'Olonne *(qv)*.

Rambling – Exploring the region on foot is an enchanting way of discovering the landscape and the life of the countryside. Many long-distance **footpaths** (*Sentiers de Grande Randonnée* – GR) cover the area described in this guide. Short-distance paths (*Sentiers de Petite Randonnée* – PR) and medium distance paths offer walks ranging from a few hours to a couple of days.
GR 4 traverses the Charentes from Angoulême, follows the coast and crosses the forest to Royan; GR 36, from Thouars, crosses Les Deux-Sèvres and a couple of forests before heading towards La Rochefoucault and Angoulême; GR 360 describes a loop among the Romanesque churches of Saintonge; GR 6 links St-Macaire and Monbazillac; its variant the GR 636 crosses Lot-et-Garonne via Monflanquin. GR 65, known as St James' path (le sentier de St-Jacques) links Moissac with St-Jean-Pied-de-Port; GR 10 crosses the Pyrenees from east to west.
A collection of Topo Guides – showing the routes and the time needed, details of access points, accommodation and places of interest en route – for footpaths across France is published jointly by FFRP-CNSGR (the Fédération Française de la Randonnée Pédestre and the Comité National des Sentiers de Grande Randonnée); some of the guides have been translated into English. They are on sale at the information centre, FFRP, 64 Rue de Gergovie, 75014 Paris, ☎ 45 45 31 02, and by mail order from McCarta (from their *Footpaths of Europe* series), 15 Highbury Place, London N5 1QP, ☎ 071 354 1616.
The Association Randonnées Pyrénéennes (BP 742, 65007 Tarbes Cedex, and BP 88, 09200 St-Girons) and local branches of the Club Alpin Français (at Lourdes, Cauterets etc) publish their own detailed guides.

An off-beat idea – How about a walk with a **donkey** for company (and to carry the bags)? Contact the Fédération Nationale Ânes et Randonnées, Ladevèze, 49090 Coux, ☎ 65 31 42 79.

Canoeing – See the region from a watery perspective : canoeists can follow an itinerary through the Marais Poitevin organised by Tonic, 17 Rue de Sully, BP 37, 17410 St-Martin-de-Ré, ☎ 46 09 25 85. Information on other areas in which to canoe from the Fédération française de canoë-kayak, 87 Quai de la Marne, 94340 Joinville-le-Pont, ☎ 48 89 39 89.

Riding and Pony Trekking – The region contains hundreds of kilometres of bridlepaths across *le bocage*, through forests and along the coast; tourist offices can usually provide addresses of local stables.
The Délégation Nationale de Tourisme Équestre (DNTE – Île St-Germain, 170 Quai de Stalingrad, 92130 Issy-les-Moulineaux, ☎ 45 54 29 54) publishes an annual handbook giving details of selected riding stables and equestrian establishments throughout France.
L'Association Les Deux-Sèvres en selle (☎ 49 69 87 71) publishes a leaflet showing suggested tours along local bridlepaths.
Le Poney Club (☎ 51 32 03 07) at Les Sables-d'Olonne organises rides through the countryside and along the coast.
La Ligue Poitou-Charentes des sports équestres (10 Avenue du Point-du-Jour, 17400 St-Jean-d'Angély, ☎ 46 32 12 30) provides a list of the main riding clubs in the Poitou-Charentes region.
The Fédération des Randonneurs Équestres, 169 Rue Blanqui, 33300 Bordeaux, ☎ 56 50 81 46, and the Centre hippique du Lycée Agricole et Forestier, 33430 Bazas, ☎ 56 25 03 21 can provide information on riding in their areas.

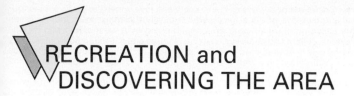

Wine tours – One of the best ways to get to know and love wine is to go on a wine tour – no particular knowledge of wine necessary! Typically these last from four to seven days and are based on one particular area; they are led by a wine expert and include visiting vineyards, cellars and châteaux, hearing lectures and sampling fine wines. They may be tours by coach, horse riding wine tours, walking holidays through the vineyards or fly-drive or cycling holidays with a wine tour itinerary. Gourmet cooking and wine trips are also available in some regions. Contact independent travel agents for details. The École du Vin at Château Loudenne in the Médoc offers a short, three-hour wine course in English on selected mornings (cost about 200F per person; ☏ 56 09 05 03) and individiual châteaux run their own tours (see under Vignoble de Bordeaux, *qv*).

Cycling – Tourist offices should be able to provide lists of local firms which hire out bicycles. Some SNCF stations (Arcachon, Bayonne, Lourdes, La Rochelle, Les Sables-d'Olonne...) offer three types of bicycle for hire; a leaflet giving details is available from railway stations, or consult the Minitel service *(see above)*, access code : 3615 SNCF Services offerts en gare. The Gironde and the Landes Departmental Tourist Offices and the Poitou-Charentes Regional Tourist Office have details of suggested cycle routes and itineraries for tourists on two wheels. Other useful contacts include :
– Fédération française de Cyclotourisme, 8 Rue Jean-Marie-Jégo, 75013 Paris; ☏ 45 80 30 21.
– Bicy-Club de France : 8 Place de la Porte-Champerret, 75017 Paris.

Canal Cruising – The *Guide Vagnon no 7 "Canaux du Midi"* (published by Les Éditions du Plaisancier, BP 27, 69641 Caluire Cedex, ☏ 78 23 31 14), the Tourisme Fluvial year-book (published by L'Office national de la Navigation, 18 Quai d'Austerlitz, 75013 Paris, ☏ 44 23 82 07) and the marine maps *Navicartes* (Éditions Grafocarte, 64 Rue des Meuniers, 92220 Bagneux, ☏ 45 36 04 06) provide general and specific information on canals in the southwest suitable for cruising. Barges may be hired from, among others : Locaboat Plaisance, Quai du Port-du-Bois, 89300 Joigny, ☏ 86 91 72 72; Blue Line, le Grand Bassin, BP 21, 11401 Castelnaudary, ☏ 68 23 17 51; Aquitaine Navigation, Halte Nautique, 47160 Buzet-sur-Baïse, ☏ 53 84 72 50; Gironde Plaisance, 43 *bis* Rue des Salières, 33210 Langon, ☏ 56 63 06 45.

Skiing, Mountain climbing and hiking – Contact the Fédération française de Ski (50 Rue des Maquisards, BP 451, 74009 Annecy Cedex, ☏ 50 51 40 34; the Fédération française de la Montage, 20 bis Rue La Boétie, 75008 Paris, ☏ 47 42 39 80. For information about rambles in the Pyrenees contact Centre d'informations montagne et sentiers, BP 88, 09200 St-Girons, ☏ 61 66 40 10.

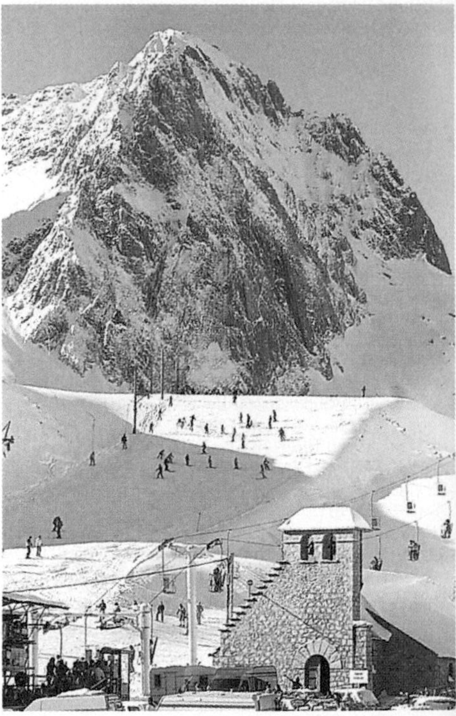
La Mongie.

Freshwater fishing – The abundance of rivers, streams, marshland canals and lakes provides anglers with many and varied opportunities; whatever the site, however, it is necessary to be affiliated to a fishing association and to abide by fishing regulations. Apply to the departmental fishing federations (Angoulême, ☏ 45 92 23 50; Niort, ☏ 49 09 23 33; Poitiers, ☏ 49 58 23 36; La Rochelle, ☏ 46 44 11 18, La Roche-sur-Yon, ☏ 51 37 19 05; Tarbes, ☏ 62 36 62 09) or contact the local tourist office. The folding map *Pêche en France* (Fishing in France) is published and distributed by the Conseil Supérieur de la Pêche, 134 Avenue de Malakoff, 75016 Paris, ☏ 45 01 20 20, and from departmental fishing federations.
A "Gîte de Pêche" category has been created for accommodation which caters for the needs of fishing enthusiasts. Apply to the Maison des Gîtes de France *(qv)*.

Ocean fishing – The extensive coastline, the bays, straits and the wide ocean itself offer almost limitless fishing options, the only restrictions being to adhere to local and national regulations and not to interfere with the business of professional fishermen. For fishing trips out to sea on fully-equipped boats ask at tourist offices.

Surfing – The west coast of France has some of the best surfing beaches in the world, and resorts along the coast here host some of the major surfing competitions (part of the Arena Surfmasters Contest is held in Biarritz; the Quiksilver Lacanau Pro is held at Lacanau-Océan; the Rip Curl Pro is held at Hossegor). Other resorts favoured for the size of their "tubes", "peaks" and "left-handers" include La Sauzaie (just north of La Rochelle), Capbreton, Guéthary and Les Cavaliers (just north of Biarritz).
Surf boards may be hired (about 120F per day) in, among other places, Hossegor where there is also a surf school. Quiksilver, manufacturers of surfing clothes, have a factory in St-Jean-de-Luz which may be visited.

Other watersports : Sailing, landsailing, jet-skiing etc – There are several sailing clubs and landsailing schools along the coast; contact tourist offices, the Fédération française de voile (55 Avenue Kléber, 75784 Paris Cedex 16; ☎ 45 53 68 00) or, for landsailing, the Fédération française de char à voile (Résidence Beaugency, 134 Boulevard de Boulogne, 62600 Berck, ☎ 21 84 27 69).
Windsurfing, which is subject to regulations, is permitted on some lakes and in some sports and leisure centres; apply to sailing clubs. Boards for windsurfing may be hired on all major beaches.
For motor-boating, water-skiing and jet-skiing enquire at the tourist offices of the larger seaside resorts. The use of jet-skis is restricted in France.

Hunting – For all enquiries about hunting and shooting apply to Saint-Hubert Club de France, 10 Rue de Lisbonne, 75008 Paris, ☎ 45 22 38 90.

Hydrotherapy and thalassotherapy – Contact the Fédération thermale et climatique française, 16 Rue de l'Estrapade, 75005 Paris, ☎ 43 25 11 85 or enquire at local tourist offices.

Golf – The **Michelin Golf Map** of France gives comprehensive details of golf courses. An annual guide is published by Éditions Person, 34 Rue de Penthièvre, 75008 Paris. A map showing golf courses and giving the number of holes, addresses and telephone numbers is available from the Fédération Française de Golf, 69 Avenue Victor Hugo, 75016 Paris, ☎ 45 02 13 55.

National Parks and Regional Parks – For all information on the parks, consult the Introduction, see under Parc naturel régional du Marais Poitevin, Parc naturel régional des Landes de Gascogne or Parc national des Pyrénées *(qv)* or contact local tourist offices.

French Government Tourist Offices Addresses

Australia

Sydney – Kindersley House, 33 Bligh St, Sydney, New South Wales 2000.
☎ 612 231 52 44.

Canada

Toronto – 1 Dundas St, West Suite 2405 Box 8, Toronto, Ontario M5G IZ3.
☎ 416 593 47 23.
Montreal – 1981 Ave Mc Gill College, Suite 490, Montréal, Québec H3-A2 W9.
☎ 514 288 42 64.

Eire

Dublin – c/o 38 Lower Abbey St, Dublin. ☎ (01) 300 777.

United Kingdom

London – 178 Piccadilly, London WIV 0AL. ☎ 071 499 6911 (24-hour answering service with recorded message and information) or 071 491 7622 (urgent enquiries only).

United States

Toll-free number : Dial 900 420 2003 for information on hotels, restaurants and transportation.
Middle West : Chicago – 645 North Michigan Avenue, Suite 630, Chicago, Illinois 60611. ☎ 312 337 6301.
East Coast : New York – 610 Fifth Avenue, Suite 222, NY 10020 – 2452.
☎ 212 757 11 25.
West Coast : Los Angeles – 9454 Wilshire Boulevard, Suite 303, Beverly Hills, Cal. 90212. ☎ 213 272 2661.
South : Dallas – 2305 Cedar Spring Road, Suite 205, Dallas, Texas 75201.
☎ 214 720 4010.

J.-B. Lafitte/EXPLORER

Geese from the Gers region.

CALENDAR OF EVENTS

Many Regional Tourist Offices publish brochures listing local fêtes, fairs and festivals Most places celebrate France's National Day (14 July) and, to a lesser extent, the Assumption of the Virgin (15 August).

Last weekend of January

Angoulême .... International Strip Cartoon Fair.

Good Friday to Sunday after Easter Sunday

Lourdes .... Festival of Religious Music; ☎ 62 94 15 64.

April

Cognac .... International festival of detective films.

Around April

La Tranche-sur-Mer .... Flower Festival (Tourist Office ☎ 51 30 33 96).

Early to mid April

Poitiers .... Musical Springtime.

1st May

Mimizan-Plage .... Festival of the Sea.

May

Angoulême .... International festival : mixed music.

Bordeaux .... Musical May (concerts, musicals, recitals, dance). ☎ 56 48 58 54.

2nd Sunday in May

Condom .... Festival des Bandas (folk bands playing in the streets competitions).

Late May to mid June

Melle .... Music Festival.

Weekend before Pentecost and Pentecost

La Rochelle .... International Sailing Week; for details ☎ 46 44 62 44.

Saturday, Sunday and Monday of Pentecost

Pau .... Formula 3000 Grand Prix motor racing.

Vic-Fezensac .... Bullfights. ☎ 62 06 30 08.

June

Auch .... Music festival.

June to September

In the Gironde département "L'été Girondin" : musical and theatrical events inclu ding Jazz in Médoc, the Blaye Theatre Festival etc ☎ 56 52 61 40.

Mid June to late August (Fridays and Saturdays)

Le Puy du Fou .... Cinéscénie : spectacular outdoor show (see under Puy du Fou). For bookings ☎ 51 64 11 11.

Mid June to mid September

Valence-sur-Baïse .... "Pierres Vivantes" *son et lumière* show at Flara Abbey. ☎ 62 28 50 19 or 62 05 77 77.

3rd Sunday in June

St-Émilion .... The Jurade Spring Fête : proclamation on the new wine

3 days around the feast of St John (24 June)

St-Jean-de-Luz .... Feast of St John : Grand Mass; concert; torchlight pro cession; dancing; Basque traditions; *toro de fuego.*

June-July

Pau .... Pau Festival (theatre, music, dance). ☎ 59 27 27 08.

July

Melle .... Goat's Cheese Festival.

Bazas .... Historical Fête in costume. ☎ 56 25 25 84.

1st week in July

St-Jean-de-Luz .... Tuna Festival : procession; games; tastings; dance *toro de fuego.*

Early July

Parthenay and surroundings Jazz concerts.

Mont-de-Marsan .... Festival of Flamenco Arts.

Parthenay .... International Games Festival (tournaments, shows exhibitions etc).

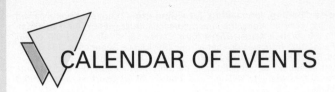

July-August (weekends)

Clisson ... Guided tours of the castle by night (Tourist Office ☏ 40 54 02 95).

Around 14 July

Saintes ... Music Festival. International Folk Festival.

La Rochelle ... Francofolies : festival of French songs. For information ☏ 46 50 56 39.

2nd Sunday of July

Luçon ... Concert and theatre in the Jardin Dumaine.

Mid July to mid August (Fridays and Saturdays)

La Rochefoucauld ... Spectacular historical show at the château with over 500 figures in costume. For details ☏ 45 63 02 33.

Late July to early August

Oloron-Ste-Marie ... International Festival of the Pyrenees.

Anglêt ... International Festival of Humorous Drawings.

August

St-Jean-Croix-de-Vie ... Onion Fair.

Early August

Bayonne ... Traditional fêtes.

Around 15 August

Marciac ... Jazz concerts.

Luçon ... Fair and exhibitions.

Arcachon ... Festival of the Sea : Grand Mass; procession of boats; fireworks; dancing. ☏ 56 83 17 20 poste 51.

Parthenay ... Following the Pilgrims' Way : organised trails on foot or by bicycle with music, stories.

Late August

Parthenay and surroundings De bouche à oreille : festival of traditional and mixed music.

Late August to early September

Biarritz ... Biarritz Surfmasters.

Mid September

Angoulême ... Vintage car race around the ramparts.

Argenton-Château ... Foire des Champs (sheep and cattle competition; secondhand furniture; dog market).

3rd Sunday in September

Ste-Croix-du-Mont ... Festival of the New Wine.

September-October

Cognac ... Celebration of the Grape Harvest/Flower Festival (alternate years). Tourist Office ☏ 85 82 10 71.

2nd week in November

Bordeaux ... SIGMA Festival : theatre, dance ☏ 56 44 28 41.

BOOKS TO READ

Walking in France by Rob Hunter *(Oxford Illustrated Press)*.

A Little Tour in France by Henry James *(Penguin)*.

The Active Traveller in France *(French Government Tourist Office)*.

A Traveller's History of France by R Cole *(Windrush)*.

The Lives of the Kings and Queens of France by the Duc de Castries *(Weidenfeld)*.

A History of Modern France: volume 1 by Alfred Cobban *(Penguin)*.

Henry IV, King of France by David Buisseret *(Routledge)*.

Goose Fat and Garlic by Jeanne Strang *(Kyle Cathie)*.

The Vineyards of France by Don Philpott *(Moorland)*.

Pocket Guide to Wine by Hugh Johnson *(Mitchell Beazley)*.

FICTION

The Three Musketeers by Alexandre Dumas *(Oxford University Press, World's Classics Series)*.

Dominique by Eugène Fromentin *(GF Flammarion)*.

Le Roman d'un enfant by Pierre Loti *(Flammarion)*.

Monsieur des Lourdines by A de Chateaubriand *(Grasset)*.

ADMISSION TIMES AND CHARGES

Every sight for which times and charges are listed is indicated by the symbol ⏱ in the main part of the guide.

Admission times and charges are liable to alteration without prior notice. Due to fluctuations in the cost of living and the constant changes in opening times, the information below is given only as a general indication. Dates given are inclusive. The information was, as far as possible, correct at the time of going to press; information shown in italics indicates that current details were not available.

The admission charges below apply to individual adults; there are usually reduced rates or free entry for children and often reductions for family groups or students; proof of age may be required. In some cases admission is free on certain days eg Wednesdays, Sundays or public holidays. Last admission is often 30-45 minutes before the actual closing time.

Churches and chapels are usually closed during the lunch period from 1200-1400 and do not admit visitors during services; tourists should therefore refrain from visits when services are being held. Visitors to chapels are often accompanied by the person who keeps the key; a donation is welcome.

Many sights close for official holidays (eg 1 January, Ascension, 14 July, 25 December etc), though in some cases sights open especially for the occasion; it is advisable to check in advance.

Most guided tours are conducted by French-speaking guides but in some cases the term "guided tour" may cover group-visiting with recorded commentaries. Some of the more popular sights may offer guided tours in other languages. Enquire at the ticket office or book stall.

Ensure no valuables are left in unattended vehicles.

Enquire at the local tourist office or Tourist Information Centre (Office de Tourisme, Maison de Tourisme or Syndicat d'Initiative) – the address of which is shown following the ℹ below – for local religious holidays, market days, etc.

A

AGEN
ℹ 107 Boulevard Carnot – 47000. ☎ 53 47 36 09

Musée des Beaux-Arts – Open May to September, daily except Tuesdays, 1100-1800 (2000 Thursday); rest of the year, daily except Tuesdays, 1100-1700. 15F. ☎ 53 69 47 23.

Cathédrale St-Caprais – Open Monday to Saturday.

AIX

Access – By ferry from Pointe de la Fumée (25min) : contact Société Fouras-Aix, 14 *bis* Cours des Dames, La Rochelle. ☎ 46 41 76 24. By passenger boat from La Rochelle (1hr), in season : contact Croisières Inter-Iles, 14 *bis* Cours des Dames, La Rochelle. ☎ 46 50 51 88. By passenger boat from Boyardville, Île d'Oléron (30min), in season : contact Croisières Inter-Iles, Boyardville. ☎ 46 47 01 45.

Horse-drawn carriage rides – ☎ *46 84 07 18.*

Musée Napoléonien – Open all year, daily except Tuesdays, 1000-1200 and 1400-1800 (1700 November to March). 17F. ☎ 46 84 66 40.

Musée Africain – Open as for the Musée Napoléonien *(see above)*, daily except Wednesdays. 11F. ☎ 46 84 66 40.

ANGLES-SUR-L'ANGLIN
ℹ Mairie – 86260. ☎ 49 48 61 20

Castle ruins – Guided tour (30min) July to August, daily except Tuesdays, 1000-1200 and 1400-1800. 8F. ☎ 49 48 61 20 (town hall).

ANGLET
ℹ Avenue de la Chambre-d'Amour – 64600. ☎ 59 03 77 01

ANGOULÊME
ℹ 2 Place St-Pierre – 16000. ☎ 45 95 16 84

Hôtel de Ville (Town Hall) – Open all year, Monday to Friday, 0900-1230 and 1400-1800. ☎ 45 38 70 79.

Ancienne chapelle des Cordeliers – For information ☎ 45 38 70 79.

CNBDI – Open all year, Wednesday to Saturday, 1200-1900, Sunday, 1400-1900. 30F. ☎ 45 38 65 65.

Musée municipal des Beaux-Arts – Open all year, daily except Tuesdays, 1000-1200 and 1400-1800. 15F. ☎ 45 95 07 69.

Atelier-musée du Papier – Open all year, daily except Mondays, 1400-1800. No charge. ☏ 45 92 73 43.

Musée de la Société archéologique – Open all year, daily except Tuesdays, 1400-1700. No charge. ☏ 45 94 90 75.

Château de l'Oisellerie : Planetarium – Show at 1600 : during school holidays, daily; rest of the year, Sundays only. Closed 3 weeks in September. 40F. ☏ 45 67 28 28.

Guillard/TOP

Detail of the west front, Angoulême Cathedral.

Moulin de Fleurac : paper mill and museum – Open all year, Monday to Friday (closed Tuesdays), 1030-1200 and 1430-1800, weekends 1100-1500 or later depending on the season. 15F. ☏ 45 91 50 69.

Grottes du Quéroy – Open July to early September, daily, 1100-1900 (1830 Sundays); mid to end June, daily, 1400-1800; April to mid June, Sundays, 1400-1800. 23F. ☏ 45 70 38 14.

ARCACHON

Place F-Roosevelt – 33311 Cedex. ☏ 56 83 01 69

Winter town – *Guided tours July to August, Tuesdays and Fridays.* Contact the Tourist Information Centre.

Aquarium et Musée – Open June to August, daily, 0930-1230 and 1400-2000; late March to May, daily, 1000-1230 and 1400-1900; September to October, daily, 1000-1230 and 1400-1900 (1800 October). 20F. ☏ 56 83 33 32.

Bassin d'ARCACHON

Boat trips – Assorted trips (return to Cap Ferret, tour of the oyster beds, fishing trip, coastal cruise) in high season, ranging from 45F-70F, rest of the year, circumnavigation of Île aux Oiseaux (65F). Embark from Jetée Thiers and Jetée d'Eyrac in Arcachon, or Jetée Bélisaire at Cap Ferret. For details ☏ 56 54 60 32 or 56 54 83 01.

Parc de loisirs de la Hume :
Village Médiéval : Open late June to early September, daily, 1000-1930. 45F. ☏ 56 66 16 76.
Aquacity : Open mid June to mid September, daily, 1000-1900. 80F. ☏ 56 66 15 60.
La Coccinelle : Open late May to early September, daily, 1000-1900. 42F. ☏ 56 66 30 41.
Marinoscope : *Open June to August, daily, 1000-1900; rest of the year, daily, 1400-1800. 26F, child 20F.* ☏ 56 66 59 99.

ARCHIGNY

Acadian Farm – Open July to August, daily except Mondays, 1500-1900; April to June, weekends, 1500-1900; September to October, weekends, 1400-1800. 5F. ☏ 49 85 31 26.

ARGELÈS-GAZOST

Donjon des Aigles – Open April to late September, daily, 1000-1200 and 1430-1830. Eagles in free flight every afternoon. 40F. ☏ 62 97 19 59.

Abbaye d'ARTHOUS

Church and Museum – Open all year, daily except Tuesdays : in season, 0900-1200 and 1400-1800; out of season, 1000-1200 and 1400-1700. 10F. ☏ 58 73 03 89.

AUBETERRE-SUR-DRONNE

Monolithic church – Open in summer, daily, 0900-1200 and 1400-1800; winter, daily except Tuesdays, 0900-1200 and 1400-1800. *13F.* ☏ 45 98 50 33 (town hall).

AUCH

1 Rue Dessoles – 32000. ☏ 62 05 22 89

Cathédrale Ste-Marie : access to stalls – April to September, daily, 0830 to 1200 and 1400 to 1800; rest of the year, 0900-1200 and 1400-1700. 5F.

Musée des Jacobins – Open all year, daily except Mondays, 1000-1200 and 1400-1800 (1700 November to March). 10F. ☏ 62 05 74 79.

Lavardens castle – Open July to August, daily, 1000-1200 and 1400-1900; rest of the year, daily except Monday, 1400-1800 (1700 October to March). 15F. ☏ 62 64 51 20.

Biran church – *To visit, apply to the village grocery shop.*

Château de St-Cricq – Open all year, Monday to Saturday, 0800-1200 and 1330-1700. No charge.

AULNAY

Mairie – 17470. ☏ 46 33 14 44

St-Pierre-de-la-Tour – Open all year, daily, 0800-2000 in summer and 0900-1700 in winter.

AURIGNAC

Musée de Préhistoire – Open July to August, daily, 1000-1200 and 1500-1800; rest of the year, Monday to Friday, 0900-1200 and 1400-1700. 10F. ☏ 61 98 90 08 (town hall).

B

BAGNÈRES-DE-BIGORRE

ℹ 3 Allée Tournefort – 65200. ☏ 62 95 50 71

Musée Salies – Open mid June to mid September, Tuesday to Friday, 1000-1200 and 1500-1800, Saturdays, 1500-1800; rest of the year, Wednesdays and Sundays, 1000-1200 and 1500-1800. 10F combined ticket with the Musée du Vieux-Moulin *(see below)*. ☏ 62 91 07 26.

Musée du Vieux Moulin – Open mid June to mid September, as for the Musée Salies *(see above)*; rest of the year, Thursdays and Fridays, 1000-1200 and 1500-1800. 10F combined ticket with the Musée Salies. ☏ 62 91 07 33.

BASSAC

Abbey buildings – Open all year, Monday to Saturday 1000-1200 and 1430 to 1800, Sundays 1430-1800. No charge. ☏ 45 81 94 22.

BAYONNE

ℹ Place de la Liberté – 64100. ☏ 59 59 31 31

River-boat cruises – Half-day cruise, *c*1400-1800, 58F; full-day cruise, *c*1030-1630, 75F. Embark from Allées Boufflers. For information and bookings, ☏ 59 59 21 93 or 58 72 86 91.

Musée Bonnat – Open mid June to mid September, daily except Tuesdays, 1000-1200 and 1500-1900 (2100 Friday); rest of the year, daily except Tuesdays, 1000-1200 and 1430-1830 (2030 Friday). 15F. ☏ 59 59 08 52.

Musée Basque – Closed for restoration. Apply to the Tourist Information Centre for details.

Cathédrale Ste-Marie : cloisters – Open all year, Monday to Saturday, 0730-1230 and 1500-1930 (1900 Saturday), Sunday, 0800-1230 and 1530-2000. Closed during services.

BAZAS

ℹ 1 Place de la Cathédrale – 33430. ☏ 56 25 25 84

Château de Villandraut – Guided tour (1hr) July to August, daily, 0930-1900; June and September, daily, 0930-1230 and 1500-1900; rest of the year, weekends, 1000-1230 and 1400-1700. 12F. ☏ 56 25 87 57.

Château de Roquetaillade – Guided tour (45min) July to August, daily, 1030-1900; Easter to June and September to mid November, daily, afternoons; rest of the year, Sundays and official holidays, afternoons. 30F. ☏ 56 63 24 16.

Château de Cazeneuve – Guided tour (1hr 15min) July to August, daily, 1000-1200 and 1400-1830; April to June and September to October, weekends, 1400-1800. 30F. ☏ 56 25 48 16.

BÉARN

Arudy : Maison d'Ossau – *Open July to August, daily except Fridays, 1000-1200 and 1500-1800; rest of the year, Mondays, 1000-1200, Tuesdays, Thursdays and Saturdays, 1430-1700, Sundays and official holidays, 1500-1800. 11F.* ☏ *59 05 80 44.*

Notre-Dame-de-Piétat : zoological park – *Same opening times and charges as at Asson (see below). Combined ticket available.* ☏ *59 71 21 90.*

Asson : zoological park – *Open July to August, daily, 0800-1900; rest of the year, Monday to Saturday, 0800-1200 and 1400-1800, Sundays and official holidays, 0800-1800. 30F.* ☏ *59 71 21 90.*

Pène Blanque : cable-way – Operates early July to early September, daily, 0900-1200 and 1330 to 1700. Fares from Gourette : to 1st level (alt 1800m) 19F, 25F Rtn; to 2nd level (alt 2400m) 31F, 36F Rtn. ☏ 59 05 12 17 (Tourist Information Centre).

BÉTHARRAM

Grottoes – Guided tour (1hr) from Palm Sunday to mid October, daily, 0830-1200 and 1330-1730. 48F. ☏ 62 41 80 04.

BIARRITZ

Musée de la Mer – Open July to September, daily, 0930-1900 (2200 mid July to mid August); rest of the year, daily, 0930-1230 and 1400-1800. 42F. ☏ 59 24 02 59.

Pointe St-Martin : lighthouse – Open May to September, daily, 1000-1200 and 1400-1800. No charge. 248 steps up.

BIGORRE

St-Savin : treasury – Open Palm Sunday to mid October, daily, 1000-1200 and 1530-1900. 10F.

Pierrefitte-Nestalas : Marinarium du Haut-Lavedan – *Open all year, daily, 0930 to 1230 and 1400-1900. 25F.* ☏ *62 92 79 56.*

BLAYE

ℹ Allées Marines – 33390. ☏ 57 42 12 09

Pavillon de la Place (Maison de la Duchesse) – Open April to October, daily, 0900-1200 and 1400-1800. 12F. ☏ 57 42 13 70.

ℹ 12 Cours du 30-Juillet - 33080. ☏ 56 44 28 41
ℹ St-Jean railway station (arrivals). ☏ 56 91 64 70
ℹ Bordeaux airport, Mérignac. ☏ 56 34 50 00

Battle-cruiser Colbert – Open April to September, Monday to Friday, 1000-1800, weekends, 1000-1900; rest of the year, Wednesday to Friday, 1000-1800, weekends, 1000-1900. 42F. ☏ 56 44 96 11.

Boat cruises – Embark from Quai Louis-XVIII, by Esplanade des Quinconces : for cruises upriver on the "Aliénor" contact Les Grands Bateaux d'Aquitaine, Hangar 7, Quai Louis-XVIII, ☏ 56 51 27 90; for a tour of the port installations (1hr 30min, 50F) aboard the "Ville de Bordeaux", ☏ 56 52 88 88.

Grand Théâtre – Guided tour (1hr 15min) all year, rehearsals permitting. 25F. ☏ 56 44 28 41.

Musée des Douanes – Open all year, daily except Mondays, 1000-1200 and 1300-1800 (1700 October to March). 10F. ☏ 56 52 45 47.

Porte Cailhau – *Open mid June to mid September, daily, 1000-1300 and 1400-1700; rest of the year, Wednesdays and Saturdays, 1400-1800. 15F. ☏ 56 79 05 39.*

Basilique St-Michel – Closed during services on Sunday mornings.

Tour St-Michel – *Open mid June to mid September, daily, 1000-1300 and 1400-1700; rest of the year, Wednesdays and Saturdays, 1400-1800, Sundays, 1000-1300. 15F. ☏ 56 79 05 39.*

Cathédrale St-André – Closed to visitors Sunday mornings.

Pey-Berland Tower – *Open in summer, daily, 0930-1230 and 1400-1800; in winter, Wednesday to Sunday, 1000-1300 and 1400-1800. 20F. ☏ 56 81 26 25.*

Centre Jean-Moulin – *Open all year, Monday to Friday, 1400-1800. ☏ 56 10 15 80.*

Hôtel de Ville – *Guided tour (1hr) all year, Wednesdays at 1430. Closed 14 July, 15 August and 25 December. ☏ 56 10 15 00.*

Musée des Arts décoratifs – Open all year, daily except Tuesdays, 1400-1800, temporary exhibitions 1000-1800. 18F, no charge Wednesdays. ☏ 56 10 15 62.

Musée des Beaux-Arts – Open all year, daily except Tuesdays, 1000-1245 and 1345-1800. 18F, no charge Wednesdays. ☏ 56 10 16 93. **Galerie des Beaux-Arts** : Open as for the Musée, 1000-1200 and 1300-1900. 20F.

Musée d'Aquitaine – Open all year, daily except Mondays, 1000-1800. 18F, no charge Wednesday. ☏ 56 10 17 58.

Musée des Chartrons – Open all year, Tuesday to Saturday, 1000-1230 and 1400-1730. 20F. ☏ 56 44 27 77.

Musée d'Art Contemporain – Open all year, daily except Mondays, 1200-1900 (2200 Wednesdays). Guided tours available, without advance booking, weekends at 1600. 30F, allowing access to "Arc en Rêve" architecture centre, no charge 1200-1400. ☏ 56 44 16 35.

Musée d'Histoire Naturelle – Open all year, daily except Tuesdays, 1400-1800 (1730 mid September to mid June). 18F, no charge Wednesdays. ☏ 56 48 26 37.

Vignoble de BORDEAUX

Guided tours – Tours through the vineyards are organised by the Tourist Information Centres in Bordeaux *(see above)* from May to October, daily; rest of the year, Saturdays. See also under Recreation *(qv)*.

St-Macaire : Église St-Sauveur – Guided tour in summer, daily, 1400-1900, rest of the year, Sunday afternoons. ☏ 56 63 34 52 in season, 56 63 03 64 (town hall) out of season.

Cadillac : Château – Open July to August, daily, 0900-1230 and 1400-1900; rest of the year, daily, 0930-1200 (1000-1200 mid November to April) and 1400-1800. Last admission one hour before closing. 20F. ☏ 56 62 69 58.

Château de Langoiran – Open July to August, daily, 0900-2000; rest of the year, Saturday, 1400-1800, Sunday, 1000-1200 and 1400-1800. Closed over Christmas. 10F. ☏ 56 67 12 00.

Langoiran : Parc zoologique – *Open all year, daily 0900-dusk. 35F, child 20F. ☏ 56 67 16 54.*

Floirac : Astronomical Observatory – Guided tour (2hrs) by appointment first Saturday of the month excluding during school holidays. Write to Monsieur le Directeur, Observatoire de Bordeaux, BP 89, 33270 Floirac. 10F. ☏ 56 86 43 30.

Sadirac : Maison de la Poterie – Open all year, Tuesday to Saturday, 1400-1800, Sunday, 1500-1800. 10F. ☏ 56 30 60 03.

La Sauve : Old Abbey – Open July to August, daily, 1000-1230 and 1400-1830; rest of the year, daily, 1000-1200 and 1400-1800 (1730 November to March). 20F. ☏ 56 23 01 55.

Rauzan : Château des Duras – Apply to the Mairie (town hall). ☏ 57 84 13 04.

Abbaye de Blasimon – Open all year, daily from 1200.

Château de Malle – Guided tour (30min) July to September, daily, 1000-1830; April to June and October, daily, 1000-1200 and 1400-1830. 35F. ☏ 56 62 36 86.

Montagne : Écomusée du Libournais – Open mid March to mid November, daily, 1000-1200 and 1400-1830; rest of the year, by appointment. 20F. ☏ 57 74 56 89.

Château Siran – Guided tour (30min) all year, daily, 1000-1800. No charge. ☏ 56 88 34 04.

Château Margaux : chais – *Guided tour (45min) from 0930-1200 and 1400-1730. Write or telephone at least two weeks in advance : Château Margaux, 33460 Margaux. ☏ 56 88 70 28.*

Château Maucaillou : Musée des Arts et Métiers de la Vigne et du Vin – *Guided tour (1hr 15min) daily on the hour from 1000-1200 and 1400-1800. 30F. ☎ 56 58 01 23.*

Fort Médoc – Open April to October, daily, 1000-1230 and 1400-1900; rest of the year, daily, 1000-1200 and 1400-1700. 10F. ☎ 56 58 98 40.

Château Lanessan – Guided tour (1hr) mid March to mid November, daily, 0900-1200 and 1400-1800; rest of the year, Monday to Saturday, 0900-1200 and 1400-1800. 20F. ☎ 56 58 94 80.

Château Beychevelle – Guided tour (45min) July to August, Monday to Saturday, 0930-1700; April to June and September, Monday to Friday, 0930-1130 and 1330-1700. No charge. ☎ 56 59 23 00.

Château Mouton-Rothschild : chais and museum – Guided tour (1hr) all year (closed August) : Monday to Friday, 0930-1100 and 1400-1600 (1500 Friday); mid April to October, weekends at 0930, 1100, 1400 and 1530. No charge. ☎ 56 59 22 22.

Château Lafite-Rothschild – Guided tour (30min) all year (closed August), Tuesday to Thursday, 1330-1600. No charge. ☎ 42 56 33 50.

BOUGON

Tumulus – Open May to October, daily except Mondays, 1000-1900 (2100 Friday); March to May and November to December, daily except Mondays, 1000-1730. 25F. ☎ 49 05 12 13.

La BRÈDE

Château – Guided tour (20min) July to September, daily except Tuesdays, 1400-1800; early April to June, weekends and official holidays, 1400-1800; October to mid November, weekends and official holidays, 1400-1730. *26F.*

BRESSUIRE

ℹ Place de l'Hôtel-de-Ville – 79300. ☎ 49 65 10 27

Musée municipal – Open all year, Tuesday to Saturday, 1330-1800, Sunday, 1400-1800. No charge. ☎ 49 65 26 79.

Château – *Open all year. No charge. Guided tour (1hr 30min) available July to August, Tuesday at 1500. ☎ 49 65 26 79.*

Mauléon : Museum – Open mid June to mid September, Monday to Friday 1400-1800, Saturday, 1430-1800, Sundays 1030-1200 and 1430-1800; rest of the year, Saturday, 1430-1800, Sunday, 1030-1200 and 1430-1800. No charge. ☎ 49 81 95 22.

BROUAGE

ℹ Forge Royale – 17320. ☎ 46 85 19 16

Guided tour of the ramparts – Apply to the Tourist Information Centre. ☎ 46 85 19 16.

C

CAMBO-LES-BAINS

ℹ Parc St-Joseph – 64250. ☎ 59 29 70 25

Arnaga – Open May to September, daily, 1000-1200 and 1430-1830; April and October, 1430-1800. 25F. ☎ 59 29 70 57.

CAP FERRET

ℹ 12 Avenue de l'Océan – 33970 Lège Cap Ferret. ☎ 56 60 63 26

Lighthouse – *Guided tour (45min) mid June to mid September and during school holidays, daily, 1030-1230 and 1500-1800; rest of the year, Sundays and official holidays, 1500-1800. ☎ 56 60 62 76.*

Plage de l'océan : access by tourist train – *Trains with turn-of-the-century carriages operate July to August, from 1115; mid to end June and September, during the afternoon. 24F Rtn. ☎ 56 60 60 20.*

CAUTERETS

ℹ Place de l'Hôtel-de-Ville – 65110. ☎ 62 92 50 27

Pont d'Espagne : chairlift to Lac de Gaube – Operates (10min journey) June to October, Monday to Saturday, 0900-1700. 27F Rtn. ☎ 62 92 50 27.

CELLES-SUR-BELLE

Abbaye – For guided tours apply to the Tourist Information Centre, ☎ 49 32 92 28.

Beaussais : temple – *Open May to October, Fridays and weekends, 1430-1900. 15F. ☎ 49 32 83 46.*

La CHALOSSE

St-Sever : archeological museum – *Open July to mid September, daily, 1500-1830. 20F. ☎ 58 76 34 64.*

Laurède : Maison Capcazalière Peyne – Guided tour (45min) July to August, daily at 1500, 1600, 1700 and 1800; mid to end June and September, weekends at 1500, 1600, 1700 and 1800. 15F. ☎ 58 97 95 33.

Montfort-en-Chalosse : Musée de la Chalosse – Open July to August, daily, 1100-2000; mid March to June and September to mid November, daily, 1400-1900. 20F. ☎ 58 98 69 27.

CHARROUX

Abbaye St-Sauveur – Open June to August, daily, 0930-1900; April, May, September and October, daily, 0930-1230 and 1400-1800; rest of the year, daily, 0930-1200 and 1400-1730. 13F. ☏ 49 87 62 43.

CHÂTELLERAULT

🅸 1 Avenue Treuille – 86100. ☏ 49 21 05 47

Musée municipal – Open all year, daily except Tuesdays, 1400-1800. No charge. ☏ 49 21 01 27.

Maison Descartes – Reopening 1995, for details ring the Tourist Information Centre, ☏ 49 21 22 77.

Musée de la Moto, de l'Automobile et du Cycle – Closed for restoration in 1994. Ring for details, ☏ 49 21 03 46.

CHAUVIGNY

🅸 Mairie – 86300. ☏ 49 46 30 21

Upper town – Guided tour July to August, apply to the Tourist Information Centre, ☏ 49 46 39 01.

St-Pierre-les-Églises – Open June to October, daily, 1000-1900. ☏ 49 46 39 01.

CIVAUX

Musée archéologique – Open April to mid November, daily except Tuesdays, 1000-1200 and 1400-1800. 4F. ☏ 49 48 34 61 or 49 48 45 08.

CLISSON

🅸 6 Place de la Trinité – 44190. ☏ 40 54 02 95

Château – Open all year, daily except Tuesdays, 0930-1200 and 1400-1800. 13F. Closed 2 weeks at Christmas. ☏ 40 54 02 22.

La Garenne-Lemot – Open all year, daily, 0900-2000 (1800 October to May). **Maison du Jardinier :** *Open 1000-1300 and 1400-1800 : June to September, daily; rest of the year, daily except Mondays. ☏ 40 03 96 79.*

La Haie-Fouassière : Maison des Vins de Nantes – Open June to September, daily, 0830-1230 (0930-1230 weekends) and 1330-1830; rest of the year, Monday to Friday, 0830-1230 and 1330-1830. No charge. ☏ 40 36 90 10.

Le Pallet : Musée du Vignoble de Nantes – Open mid June to mid September, daily except Mondays, 1430-1830; Easter to mid June and mid September to mid November, weekends, 1430-1830. 15F. ☏ 40 80 40 35.

Château de La Noë de Bel-Air – Open all year, daily, 1000-1200 and 1400-1800. No charge. ☏ 40 33 92 72.

COGNAC

🅸 16 Rue de 14-Juillet. ☏ 45 82 10 71

St-Gobain glassworks – Guided tour (1hr 30min) certain days from mid June to mid September : ring the Tourist Information Centre for details. 37F. No admission for children under 14yrs.

Otard – Guided tour (1hr) July to August, daily, 0930-1730; rest of the year, Mondays to Fridays (and weekends early April to June and September), on the hour from 1000 to 1100 and 1400 to 1700. No charge. ☏ 45 82 40 00.

Hennessy – *Guided tour mid June to mid September, Monday to Saturday, 0900-1730; rest of the year, Monday to Friday, 0830-1100 and 1400-1600. No charge. ☏ 45 82 52 22.*

Camus – Guided tour (1hr 30min) June to September, Monday to Thursday, 1000-1200 and 1430 to 1630, Fridays 1000-1200. No charge. ☏ 45 32 28 28.

Remy Martin – Guided tour (1hr) mid June to mid September, daily; late April to mid June and mid September to October, Monday to Saturday : every 30min July to mid September from 1000-1200 and 1300-1730, otherwise every 45min from 0930-1100 and 1330-1715. 15F. ☏ 45 35 76 66.

Martell – Guided tour (45min) July to August, Monday to Friday, 0930-1700, weekends, 1000-1615; rest of the year, Monday to Thursday, 0930-1100 and 1330-1700 (1400-1700 November to March). No charge. ☏ 45 36 33 33.

Prince Hubert de Polignac – Guided tour (1hr) July to mid September, daily at 1100, 1400, 1500, 1600 and 1700. No charge. ☏ 45 32 13 85.

Musée municipal – Open June to September, daily except Tuesdays, 1000-1200 and 1400-1800. 6F. ☏ 45 32 07 25.

Migron : Écomusée du Cognac – Open April to December, daily, 0900-1230 and 1500-1830. No charge. ☏ 46 94 91 16.

COLLINES VENDÉENNES

St-Michel-Mont-Mercure : tower – Open April to late September, Monday to Friday, 0800-2000, Saturday, 0800-1830, Sunday, 1130-2000; rest of the year, Monday to Friday, 0800-1900, Saturday, 0830-1800, Sunday, 1130-1900. No charge. ☏ 51 57 80 26.

Moulin des Justices – Guided tour (30min) mid June to mid September, daily from 1500; rest of the year, by appointment. 15F. ☏ 51 57 80 84.

Mont des Alouettes : mill – Guided tour (15min) late June to August, Monday to Friday, 1500-2000, weekends and official holidays, 1000-2100; mid February to late June and September to October, weekends and official holidays, 1500-1800. 14F. ☏ 51 65 16 66.

Gare des Épesses : Musée de l'Histoire des Chemins de Fer en Vendée – Open when the tourist train (see below) is operating. 5F, no charge for train passengers. ☏ 51 57 64 64.

Puy du Fou Steam Train – Steam train operates from Mortagne to Les Herbiers (stopping at Les Épesses station) early June to early September, weekends and some Fridays. Ring for details, ☏ 51 64 11 11. 45F single; 55F Rtn.

CONDOM

ℹ Place Bossuet – 32100. ☎ 62 28 00 80

Boat trips – Trips (1hr 15min) on the "Saint-Faust" early July to late August, daily at 1500, 1630 and 1800; late June to early July and late August to early September, daily at 1530; Easter to late June and early to end September, weekends and official holidays at 1530. 35F. ☎ 62 28 46 46.

Musée de l'Armagnac – Open July to August, daily, 1000-1200 and 1430 to 1830; mid to end June and early to mid September, Monday to Saturday, 1000-1200 and 1430 to 1830; rest of the year, by appointment. 10F. ☎ 62 28 00 80.

La Romieu : eastern tower – *Guided tour all year, daily, 1400-1800. Closed during religious festivals and during services. 10F. ☎ 62 28 15 72.*

Montréal : Musée archéologique – *Open mid June to mid September, daily, 1000-1200 and 1500-1900. 2.50F, combined ticket with the Gallo-Roman site at Séviac 12F.*

Séviac : Gallo-Roman Villa – Open March to November, daily, 0900-1800. 15F. ☎ 62 29 48 57.

Phare de CORDOUAN

Access – May to September, weather permitting : from Pointe de Grave (contact M Grass, ☎ 56 09 62 93, or the Tourist Information Centre at Le Verdon-sur-Mer) or from Royan (☎ 46 05 29 91).

Tour of the Lighthouse – Open, weather permitting, July to September, daily, 1030-1200 and 1430-1830; March to June, weekends and official holidays, 1430-1800. No charge. ☎ 56 09 61 78.

CÔTE D'ARGENT

Pointe de Grave : Musée du phare de Cordouan – *Open mid June to September, daily, 1430-1800. ☎ 56 09 61 78.*

Scenic railway – Trips between Pointe de Grave, Soulac and Le Verdon through the forest beside the ocean (1hr 30 min) July to August, daily; May, June and September, weekends. Departure from Pointe de Grave at 1500 and 1700 (and 1000 and 1200 July to August), from Place des Arros, Soulac, at 1530 and 1730 (and 1030 and 1230 July to August). 15F Rtn. ☎ 56 09 86 61 (Tourist Information Centre, Soulac).

Boat trips – Various trips from Le Verdon-sur-Mer offered on "La Bohême II" including coastal cruises, fishing trips and return to Cordouan lighthouse. Apply to M Grass, ☎ 56 09 62 93; to the Tourist Information Centre at Pointe de Grave during July and August; or to Agence Atlantique Avenir, 33 Rue de la Plage, Soulac, ☎ 56 09 94 71.

Soulac-sur-Mer : Archeological Museum – Open May to mid September, daily, 1500-2000. No charge. ☎ 56 09 86 61 (Tourist Information Centre, Soulac).

Soulac-sur-Mer : Fondation Soulac-Médoc – Open June to September, daily, 1700-1930 and 2100-2300. 15F. ☎ 56 09 86 61 (Tourist Information Centre, Soulac).

Moulin de Vensac – Guided tour (30min) 1000-1230 and 1430-1830 : mid July to August, daily; early to mid July, Thursday to Sunday; June and September, weekends; March to May and October to November, Sundays and official holidays, 1430-1830. 15F. ☎ 56 09 45 00.

Maubuisson : Musée des Arts et Traditions populaires – Open May to mid September, Monday to Friday and Sunday, 1500-1900; rest of the year, by appointment. 20F. ☎ 56 03 41 96.

Biscarrosse : Musée historique de l'Hydraviation – Open July to August, daily, 1000-1900; rest of the year, daily, 1500-1900 (1400-1800 in winter). 25F. ☎ 58 78 00 55.

Sanguinet : Archeological museum – Open July to August, daily, 1000-1200 and 1500-1900. 12F. ☎ 58 78 54 20.

Parentis-en-Born : Musée de Pétrole – Open July to early September, daily, 1000-1230 and 1500-1900. 15F. ☎ 58 78 40 02.

Courant d'Huchet : boat trips – Cruises May to mid October, daily at 0900, 1000 and 1430. 45F to Île aux Chênes; 65F to the bridge at Pichelèbe; 80F to the beach at Huchet. Reservation advisable. ☎ 58 48 75 39.

Capbreton : Écomusée de la Pêche et de la Mer – Open June to August, daily, 0930-1200 and 1430-1900; April, May and September, daily, 1400-1800; rest of the year, Sundays, school holidays and official holidays, 1400-1800. 25F. ☎ 58 72 40 50.

COULON

Boat trips – Apply to M Fichet, ☎ 49 35 90 88; M Prada, ☎ 49 35 97 63; La Roselière, ☎ 49 35 90 88; M Thibaudeau, ☎ 49 35 91 71.

Miniature train rides (Le Pibalou) – In season, regular departures (duration of rides : 30min or 1hr 15min) from Place de l'Église. Apply to M Egreteau, 6 Rue de l'Église. ☎ 49 35 02 29.

Minibus tours (Le Grenouillon) – For a two-hour tour with commentary (in French) contact Mme Tingaud, Place de l'Église, 79510 Coulon. ☎ 49 35 08 08.

Aquarium – Open April to October, daily 0900-1900; rest of the year, by appointment. 20F. ☎ 49 35 90 31.

Maison des Marais mouillés – *Open Easter to mid November, daily except Mondays, 1000-1200 and 1400-1900. 15F. ☎ 49 35 81 04.*

D

DAMPIERRE-SUR-BOUTONNE

Château – Guided tour (40min) June to September, daily, 1400-1830; Easter to May and October to early November, Sundays, 1400-1830. 25F. ☏ 46 24 02 24.

Maison de l'Âne de Poitou – *Open all year. 15F. ☏ 46 24 07 72.*

DAX

ℹ Place Thiers, BP 177 – 40100. ☏ 58 90 20 00

Musée de Borda – Open all year, daily except Tuesdays and Sundays, 1430-1830. 10F. ☏ 58 74 12 91.

Crypte Archéologique – Open May to November, daily except Tuesdays and Sundays, 1430-1830; March to April, Monday, Wednesday and Thursday, 1430-1830. 10F. ☏ 58 74 12 91.

F

FLARAN

Abbey – Open July to August, daily, 0930-1900; mid to end June and early to mid September, daily, 1400-1900; rest of the year (closed mid January to mid February), daily, 0930-1200 and 1400-1800. 20F. ☏ 62 28 50 19.

Cassaigne Château – Open all year, daily, 0900-1200 and 1400-1900. No charge. ☏ 62 28 04 02.

Château du Busca-Maniban – Guided tour (1hr) Easter to mid November, daily, 1400-1900 (1800 Monday). 15F. ☏ 62 28 40 38.

FONTENAY-LE-COMTE

ℹ Tour de l'Octroi, Quai Poey-d'Avant – 85200. ☏ 51 69 44 99

Musée Vendéen – Open July to August, Tuesday to Saturday, 1000-1900, Sundays 1500-1900; mid March to June and September to mid November, Tuesday to Saturday, 1000-1200 and 1400-1800, Sundays, 1400-1800 (1500-1900 June and September); over Christmas period, daily except Mondays, 1400-1700. Admission charge. ☏ 51 35 03 84.

Château de Terre-Neuve – Guided tour (45min) June to August, daily 0900-1200 and 1330-1845; May, daily 1400-1830; September, daily 0900-1200 and 1400-1845. 19F. ☏ 51 69 17 75.

Le FUTUROSCOPE

Allow at least one full day to visit. Open daily : July to early September, 0900-2300 (show every evening c2200); April to June and early September to early October, 0900-1900 (2300 Saturdays, April to June); early February to March and early October to mid November, 0900-1800; mid December to early January, 1000-1800. 135F (230F for 2 days), children 100F (170F for 2 days). ☏ 49 49 30 20 (recorded message) or Minitel 3615 access code Futuroscope.

G

Vallée de GAVARNIE

ℹ – 65120. ☏ 62 92 49 10

Centrale de Pragnères – Guided tour (30min) July to September, daily except Tuesdays, 1000-1200 and 1400-1830. No charge. ☏ 62 92 49 82.

Horse and donkey hire – Rides (2hrs Rtn : 10km) available Easter to October, daily, 0900-1800; Easter to mid June 60F, mid June to October 90F. ☏ 62 92 47 16.

GÈDRE

Cirque de Troumouse – Toll-road from Héas : 20.50F per car.

Héas : chapel – Open May to November, daily, 0800-1200 and 1400-1900.

Écomusée de la GRANDE LANDE

Marquèze – Open June to September, daily, 1010-1210 and 1400-1720 (last admission); April to May, Monday to Friday, 1500-1720, Saturday, 1400-1720, Sunday 1010-1210 and 1400-1720; October, Monday to Friday, 1500-1640, Saturday, 1400-1640, Sunday 1010-1210 and 1400-1640. 45F. ☏ 58 07 52 70.

Luxey : J and L Vidal Resinous Products Workshop – Open June to September, daily, 1000-1200 and 1400-1900; April, May and October, Monday to Friday, 1000-1200, Saturday, 1400-1900, Sunday 1000-1200 and 1400-1900. 25F. ☏ 58 07 52 70.

Moustey : Musée de Patrimoine Religieux et des Croyances Populaires – Open June to September, daily, 1000-1200 and 1400-1900; April, May and October, weekends, 1400-1800. 25F. ☏ 58 07 52 70.

Le GRAND-PRESSIGNY

Musée départemental de Préhistoire – Open June to September, daily, 0930-1830; February to May and October to November, daily, 0900-1200 and 1400-1700 (1800 mid March to May). 20F. ☏ 47 94 90 20.

H

HAGETMAU

Brassempouy : La Grotte du Pape – Guided tour (30min) July to August, Monday, Wednesday and Friday, 1700-1800. No charge. ☏ 58 89 02 47 (town hall).

Brassempouy : Musée de la Préhistoire – Open mid June to mid September, daily, 1500-1800; mid September to mid October, weekends, 1500-1800; rest of the year, by appointment. 8F. ☏ 58 89 02 47 (town hall, 1500-1800) or 58 89 04 23 (M René Bayle).

Samadet : Musée des Traditions rurales et Faïences au 18e s – Open June to August, daily, 1000-1800; September to December and February to May, daily except Tuesdays, 1400-1800; January, weekends, 1400-1800. 20F. ☏ 58 79 13 00.

I - J

Grottes d'ISTURITS et d'OXOCELHAYA

Grottoes – Guided tour (40min) July to August, daily, 1000-1800; June and September, daily, 1000-1200 and 1400-1800; mid March to May and October to mid November, daily, 1000-1200 (not Monday and Tuesday) and 1400-1800. 25F. ☏ 59 29 64 72.

JARNAC

Maison Courvoisier : museum – Guided tour (1hr) June to September, Monday to Saturday, 0930-1300 and 1400-1800; early April to May and October, Monday to Friday, 0930-1300 and 1400-1800. Last admission 1hr before closing. No charge. ☏ 45 35 55 55.

L

Le LABOURD

La Rhune : access by railway – Departure from Col de St-Ignace : July to September, daily at 1000 and 1500 and every 35min from 0900 when busy; during spring holidays, daily at 1000 and 1500; May to June and October to mid November, weekends and official holidays at 1000 and 1500. 25F, 36F Rtn. ☏ 59 54 20 26.

Grotte de Sare – Guided tour (35min) mid July to late August, daily, 0930-2030; late August to September, daily 1000-1300 and 1400-1700; Easter to mid July, daily, 1000-1300; Carnaval to Easter and October to December, daily 1400-1700. 25F. ☏ 59 54 21 88.

Larressore : Atelier Ainciart-Bergara – *Open all year, Monday to Saturday, 0900-1200 and 1400-1800. ☏ 59 93 03 05.*

LANDES DE GASCOGNE

Pissos : La Maison des Artisans – Open July to August, daily, 1000-1200 and 1500-1900; April to June and September, daily, 1500-1800. No charge. ☏ 58 08 90 66.

Pissos : Glassblowers' workshop – Open as for La Maison des Artisans. No charge. ☏ 58 08 90 24.

Solférino : museum – Guided tour (45min) mid June to mid September, daily, 1000-1200 and 1500-1800. 15F. ☏ 58 07 24 92 in season or 58 07 21 08 (town hall).

LIGUGÉ

Abbey – Open all year, Monday to Saturday, 0900-1100 and 1500-1730, Sundays, 1115-1200, 1500-1615 and 1715-1830. *Services with Gregorian Chant : Monday to Saturday at 1115, 1800 and 2000, Sundays at 1000, 1630 and 2000.*

LOURDES

Place Peyramale – 65100. ☏ 62 42 77 40

Pavillon Notre-Dame – *Open daily, 0900-1145 and 1400-1800.*

Musée d'Art Sacré du Gemmail – Open Easter to mid October, daily. No charge. ☏ 62 94 13 15.

Cachot – Open Easter to mid November, daily, 0930-1200 and 1400-1900; rest of the year, daily, 1400-1700. No charge. ☏ 62 94 51 30.

Centre Hospitalier – Open April to mid October, daily, 0900-1200 and 1400-1900; rest of the year, daily, 1400-1600. No charge.

Moulin de Boly – *Open daily, 0930-1145 and 1430-1845.*

Bartrès : Maison Lagües – Open all year, Monday to Saturday, 0830-1900. No charge. ☏ 62 94 08 18.

Château Fort – Open April to September, daily, 0900-1200 and 1400-1900; rest of the year, daily except Tuesdays, 0900-1200 and 1400-1800 (1900 Friday). Last admission 1hr before closing. 26F. ☏ 62 94 02 04.

Pic du Jer : funicular – Operates Palm Sunday to October, daily, from 0900 and from 1400, every 15 or 30min depending on demand. 6min journey up to 1 000m alt. 42F. ☎ 62 94 00 41.

Musée Grévin de Lourdes – Open July to August, daily, 0900-1130, 1330-1830, 2030-2200; April to June and September to October, daily, 0900-1130 and 1330-1830. 30F. ☎ 62 94 33 74.

Musée du Petit Lourdes – Open April to October, daily, 0845-1900. 27F. ☎ 62 94 24 36.

Musée du Gemmail – Open Easter to mid October, daily. No charge. ☎ 62 94 13 15.

Musée de Lourdes – Open mid March to mid October, daily, 0900-1200 and 1330-1900. 28F. ☎ 62 94 28 00.

LUCHON

Allées d'Étigny – 31110 Bagnères-de-Luchon. ☎ 61 79 21 21

Thermal cure centre – Open June to September, Tuesday and Thursday, 1400-1500; April, May and October, Thursday, 1400-1500. 25F. ☎ 61 79 03 88 poste (ext) 352.

Musée du Pays de Luchon – Open all year (closed November), daily, 0900-1200 and 1400-1800. 10F. ☎ 61 79 29 87.

St-Aventin : church – To visit, apply to the presbytery (presbytère).

LUZ-ST-SAUVEUR

Place du 8-Mai – 65120. ☎ 62 92 81 60

Fortified church – Open daily on demand. ☎ 62 92 81 75.

M

MAILLEZAIS

85420. ☎ 51 87 23 01

Boat trips – Apply to the Association familiale rurale, ☎ 51 87 21 87, to Aria Loisirs, ☎ 51 52 49 10 or to AFR, ☎ 51 87 21 87.

Abbey – Open July and August, daily, 0900-2000; rest of the year, daily (but closed Thursdays mid November to March), 0900-1200 and 1400-1730 (or as late as 1900). 14F. ☎ 51 00 70 11.

MARAIS POITEVIN

Boat trips – Cruises March to October, departure from Arçais. Contact Nouvelles Croisières, Route de Damvix, Arçais. ☎ 49 35 37 80. See also under Maillezais.

Chaillé-les-Marais : Maison du Petit Poitou – *Open May to September, daily except Mondays and Sunday mornings, 1000-1200 and 1400-1900. 15F. ☎ 51 56 77 30.*

Esnandes : Maison de la Mytiliculture – Open mid June to mid September, daily except Mondays 1100-1900; February to mid June and mid September to October, Tuesday to Friday, 1500-1900, weekends, 1100-1900. 18F. ☎ 46 01 34 64.

La Faute-sur-Mer : Parc de Californie – Open July to September, daily, 1000-2000; April to June, daily, 1000-1900. Birds in free flight July to mid September, daily at 1530 and 1730, otherwise daily at 1530. 38F. ☎ 51 27 10 48.

Nieul-sur-l'Autise : cloisters – Open July to August, daily, 1000-1300 and 1400-1930; mid March to June and September to mid October, 1000-1200 and 1400-1800. 11F. ☎ 51 52 49 03.

Nieul-sur-l'Autise : Maison de la Meunerie – *Open July to August, daily, 1030-1230 and 1500-1900; May to June and September to October, weekends, 1500-1900. 15F. ☎ 51 52 47 43.*

St-Denis-du-Payré : Réserve Naturelle M-Brosselin – Guided tour (2hrs) July to early September, daily, 1000-1200 and 1500-1900; February to June, 1st Sunday of the month and Easter weekend, 1400-1800. 17F. ☎ 51 27 23 92.

St-Michel-en-l'Herm : Benedictine Abbey – Guided tour (20min) July to August, Tuesdays, Thursdays and Fridays, 1000-1200 and 1500-1700. 10F. ☎ 51 30 21 89.

La Tranche-sur-Mer : Les Floralies Tranchaises – Open March to September, daily, 1000-1800. 32F March to April, 12F May to June, 23F July to September. ☎ 51 30 33 96.

La Tranche-sur-Mer : Boat cruises – *Cruises towards Aix, Oléron and Ré operate mid June to mid September; contact Croisières Inter-Îles et Fluviales. ☎ 51 27 43 04.*

MARENNES

Place Chasseloup-Laubat – 17320. ☎ 46 85 04 36

Vidéorama de l'huître – Shown Monday to Saturday : July to August, 0900-1230 and 1330-1930; mid to end June and early to mid September, 0930-1230 and 1500-1830; April to mid June and mid to end September, 1500-1800. 10F. ☎ 46 85 04 36.

Église St-Pierre-de-Sales : tower platform – Open July to August, Monday to Friday, 1000-1230 and 1400-1900; rest of the year, 1400-1800 (apply to 28 Rue Fresneau). 6F.

Château de la Gataudière – Guided tour March to mid November, daily, 1000-1200 and 1400-1800.

Grotte de MÉDOUS

Guided tour (45min-1hr) July to August, daily, 0900-1200 and 1400-1800; April to June and September to mid October, daily, 0830-1130 and 1400-1730. 32F. ☏ 62 91 78 46.

MELLE

Place de la Poste – 79500. ☏ 49 29 15 10

Mines d'Argent des Rois Francs – Guided tour (1hr) mid June to mid September, daily, 1000-1200 and 1430-1930; March to mid June and mid September to mid November, weekends, 1000-1200 and 1430-1930. 25F. ☏ 49 29 19 54.

Forêt de MERVENT-VOUVANT

Parc Zoologique du Gros Roc – Open all year, daily, 0900-1900 (closed for lunch 1200-1400 in winter). 36F. ☏ 51 00 22 54.

Parc Ornithologique-Animalier de Pagnolle – Open mid March to October, daily, 0900 to dusk. 28F. ☏ 51 69 02 55.

La Jamonière : Musée des Amis de la Forêt – Open April to October, Monday to Friday, 1000-1200 and 1400-1800, Sunday, 1400-1800; rest of the year, Monday to Friday, 1400-1730. 10F. ☏ 51 00 27 26.

Pierre-Brune : leisure park – Open June to August, daily, 1000-2000; April to May and September to October, Monday to Saturday, 1400-1900, Sundays 1000-1900. 28F for entrance to La Vallée Enchantée, 17F for mini-golf, 12F for tourist train. ☏ 51 00 20 18.

Pic du MIDI DE BIGORRE

Toll road – Open late June to early October, daily, 0800-1900. 23F per person in a car or 6F per pedestrian. ☏ 62 91 17 17 or 61 73 57 83.

Cable car from Les Laquets – Reopening after extensive works. Ring for details, ☏ 62 95 26 47.

Observatory and Institute of World Physics – Guided tour (45min-1hr) July to mid September, daily, 0800-1800. 12F, no charge for access to the terrace.

MIRANDE

Rue de l'Évêché – 32300. ☏ 62 66 68 10

Musée des Beaux-Arts – Open July to August, Monday to Saturday, 1000-1200 and 1500-1800, Sunday 1500-1800; rest of the year, Monday to Saturday, 1000-1200 and 1500-1800. 9F. ☏ 62 66 68 10.

Bassoues : Keep – Open April to October, daily, 1000-1230 and 1430-1900; rest of the year, daily except Mondays and Tuesdays, 1400-1800. 15F. ☏ 62 70 90 47 (keep) or 62 70 97 34 (town hall).

Château de MONTAIGNE

Library Tower – Guided tour (30min) all year, daily except Monday and Tuesday, 0900-1200 and 1400-1900. 16F. ☏ 53 58 63 93 or 56 24 39 02.

MONT-DE-MARSAN

2 Place du Général-Leclerc, BP 305 – 40011. ☏ 58 75 22 23

Musée municipal – All year, daily except Tuesdays, 1000-1200 and 1400-1800. 20F, no charge Monday. ☏ 58 75 00 45 or 58 75 92 91.

Aire-sur-l'Adour : crypt – All year, daily except Thursday and Sunday, 1500-1830. No charge.

MONTMAURIN

Villa Gallo-Romaine – Open all year, daily (but closed Tuesdays mid October to mid May), 0930-1200 and 1400-1815 (1715 October to March). 20F includes entry to the museum *(see below)*. ☏ 61 88 74 73.

La Hillère : chapel – Apply to a member of staff at the Gallo-Roman villa or the museum in Montmaurin.

Museum – As for the Gallo-Roman villa *(see above)*.

MOUILLERON-EN-PAREDS

National Museums – Guided tour (45min) mid April to mid November, daily except Tuesdays, 0930-1200 and 1400-1800; rest of the year, daily except Tuesdays, 1000-1200 and 1400-1700. 11F for one museum, 16F for both. ☏ 51 00 31 49.

N

Massif de NÉOUVIELLE

Aragnouet : Chapelle des Templiers – Open early July to August, daily, 1530-1800. Rest of the year, by appointment. ☏ 62 39 43 81.

NIORT

Place de la Poste – 79000. ☏ 49 24 18 79

Donjon : museum – Open all year, daily, 0900-1200 and 1400-1800 (1700 mid September to early May). 15F. ☏ 49 32 59 40.

Logis de l'Hercule – Guided tour (minimum 7 people) all year by appointment with the Tourist Information Centre. 25F. ☏ 49 24 18 79.

Coulée Verte – Illumination of the quaysides and monuments, June to mid September.

Musée d'Histoire Naturelle – Open all year, daily, 0900-1200 and 1400-1800 (1700 mid September to early May). 15F. ☏ 49 32 59 40.

Musée des Beaux-Arts – Temporarily closed : collection moving to other premises. Apply to the Museums Service (Conservation des Musées), ☏ 49 32 59 40.

Les Ruralies : Musée de la Machine Agricole – Open mid June to mid September, daily, 1000-1900; mid September to Christmas and mid February to mid June, daily, 1000-1800; January to mid February, daily except Saturdays, 1000-1730. 20F. ☏ 49 75 68 27.

Les Ruralies : Maison des Ruralies – *Open April to mid September, Monday to Friday, 1000-1800, weekends, 1000-2000; rest of the year, Monday to Friday, 1000-1800, weekends, 1000-1900. ☏ 49 75 80 70.*

Beauvoir-sur-Niort : Rimbault windmill – *Guided tour (30min) May to October, Sundays and official holidays, 1500-1800. 12F. ☏ 49 09 73 05.*

Villiers-en-Bois : European Zoorama – Open July to August, daily, 0900-2000; April to June and September, daily, 0900-1900 (2000 Sunday); October to November and February to March, Monday to Saturday, 1000-1200 and 1400 to dusk, Sundays, 1000 to dusk. 38F. ☏ 49 76 79 56.

Château du Coudray-Salbart – *Open daily except Tuesday : May to September, 0900-1900; mid March to April and October, 0900-1200 and 1400-1900. Rest of the year (closed January), 1000-1200 and 1400-1700. 10F. ☏ 49 25 71 07.*

Île de NOIRMOUTIER

Route du Pont, 85630 Barbâtre. ☏ 51 39 80 71

Access – Via the toll bridge, 8F; via Passage du Gois (4.5km), no charge, at certain times (check locally for details of low tide).

Sea cruises – Trips to Le Pilier lighthouse (depart 1100, return 1900) 55F. Cruises (1hr) towards Le Pilier : depart at 1100, 1500 and 1800. Cruises (1hr 15min) towards Bois de la Chaise : depart 1630. 45F. Fishing trips (depart 0700, return 1100) 110F, equipment hire 60F. Tickets available at l'Herbaudière from the boat or at the "Shopping" at the port. Apply to Blanc Moutier, ☏ 51 39 09 62.

Château : museum – Open mid June to mid September, daily, 1030 to 1900; February to mid June and mid September to mid November, daily except Tuesdays, 1000-1230 and 1430-1800. 20F. ☏ 51 39 10 42.

Aquarium-Seeland – Open mid July to mid August, daily, 1000-2400; early to mid July and mid August to mid September, daily, 1000-2000; rest of the year, daily, 1000-1230 and 1400-1800. 38F. ☏ 51 39 08 11.

Musée de la construction navale – Open mid June to mid September, daily, 1000-1900; April to mid June and mid September to mid November, daily except Mondays, 1000-1230 and 1430-1800. 18F. ☏ 51 39 24 00.

La Guérinière : Musée des Arts et Traditions Populaires – Open July to August, daily, 1000-1200 and 1500-1900; mid February to June and September, Monday to Saturday, 1430-1700. 15F. ☏ 51 39 41 39.

O

OIRON

Château – Open July to mid September, daily, 1000-1900; rest of the year, daily, 0930-1200 and 1400-1800. 26F. ☏ 49 96 57 42.

Île d'OLÉRON

Boat trips – Regular trips to Île d'Aix. Cruises, in season, towards Île d'Aix, Île de Ré and on the river Charente : ☏ 46 47 01 45. Mid June to mid September, regular trips between Boyardville and Île d'Aix, and sea cruises from Boyardville-Port : Les Vedettes Oléronaises, ☏ 46 76 09 50.

Musée Oléronais Aliénor-d'Aquitaine – Open over Easter and through the summer, Monday to Saturday. 20F. ☏ 46 47 39 88.

Pointe de Gatseau : tourist train – Operates from Easter school holidays to late September, at regular intervals (1hr 15min Rtn). 50F. ☏ 46 76 01 26.

Le Grand-Village-Plage : Maison Paysanne Oléronaise – *Guided tour (1hr) June to September, daily, 1100-1200 and 1500-1830. ☏ 46 47 51 39.*

Le Marais aux Oiseaux – Open July to August, daily, 1000-2000; April to June and September, daily, 1000-1300 and 1400-1900; rest of the year, Sundays and during school holidays, 1400-1800. 22F. ☏ 46 75 37 54.

Phare de Chassiron – Open, subject to the lighthouse-keeper's discretion, April to September, daily, 1000-1200 and 1400-1900. No charge. ☏ 46 47 86 70.

Parc Ornithologique de Maisonneuve – Open all year, daily, 0900-2000 (1800 mid October to March). 32F. ☏ 46 47 10 32.

La Cotinère : "La Criée" – Market operates all year, Monday to Saturday, 0600-1600. No charge.

OLORON-STE-MARIE

ℹ Place de la Résistance – 64400. ☎ 59 39 98 00

Quartier Ste-Croix : Maison du Patrimoine – Open July to mid September, daily except Monday, 1000-1200 and 1500-1900. 10F. ☎ 59 39 10 63.

Haut-OSSAU

Cable-car to La Sagette and train from La Sagette to Lac d'Artouste – Operate June to September, daily. Combined ticket 74F Rtn. ☎ 59 80 17 28.

P

PARTHENAY

ℹ Palais des Congrès, Square Robert-Bigot – 79200. ☎ 49 64 24 24

Cattle market – Guided tour July to September, Wednesdays, 0730. Apply to the Tourist Information Centre, ☎ 49 64 24 24.

Medieval town – Guided tour July to September, Wednesdays and Sundays at 1600, Saturdays at 2200. Themed tours, Tuesdays, Fridays and Saturdays at 1600. Apply to the Tourist Information Centre, ☎ 49 64 24 24.

Parthenay-le-Vieux : Église St-Pierre – Apply to M Renaudot in the house beside the church.

PASSAY

Maison du Pêcheur – Open all year, daily, 1000-1200 and 1500-1800. 13F. ☎ 40 31 36 46.

PAU

ℹ Place Royale – 64000. ☎ 59 27 27 08

Château : interior – All year, daily, 0930-1145 and 1400-1715. 27F, 18F on Sunday. ☎ 59 82 38 19. **Musée Béarnais** : Open all year, 0930-1230 and 1400-1730. 8F. ☎ 59 27 07 36.

Musée des Beaux-Arts – All year, daily except Tuesdays, 1000-1200 and 1400-1800. 10F. ☎ 59 27 33 02.

Musée Bernadotte – Open all year, daily except Monday, 1000-1200 and 1400-1800. 10F. ☎ 59 27 48 42.

"La Cité des Abeilles" – Open Easter to mid October, daily except Monday, 1400-1800. 25F. ☎ 59 83 10 31.

Lacq : Pavillon d'information du Groupe Elf-Aquitaine – *Guided tour (45min) mid June to mid September, Monday to Friday, 0800-1545. ☎ 59 92 28 99 in season.*

POITIERS

ℹ 8 Rue des Grandes-Écoles – 86000. ☎ 49 21 21 24

Palais de Justice – Open all year, Monday to Friday, 0830-1800.

Baptistère St-Jean – Open April to November, daily except Tuesdays, 1030-1230 and 1500-1800; rest of the year, daily except Tuesdays, 1430-1630. 4F.

Musée Ste-Croix – Open all year, Tuesday to Friday, 1000-1200 and 1300-1700, week-ends, 1000-1200 and 1400-1800. ☎ 49 41 07 53.

Musée de Chièvres – *Same admission times as the Musée Ste-Croix.*

POUZAUGES

ℹ Cour de la Poste – 85700. ☎ 51 91 82 46

Bois de la Folie : Terrier-Marteau windmills – Guided tour July to mid September, Thursday to Sunday, from 1500-1900; mid May to June and mid to end September, week-ends, 1500-1900. 20F. ☎ 51 57 52 83.

Prieuré de Chassay-Grammont – Open mid June to August, daily, 1430-1900; May to mid June and September to mid November, Sundays, 1430-1830. 20F. ☎ 51 66 40 96.

Le Bois-Tiffrais : Musée de la France Protestante de l'Ouest – Guided tour (45min) July to mid September, Tuesday to Saturday, 1100-1900, Sundays, 1300-1900. 15F. ☎ 51 66 41 03.

PUY-DU-FOU

Cinéscénie – Shows Fridays and Saturdays, early June to July at 2230 and mid to end August at 2200. Advance booking essential; foreign language commentary available (English, German, Italian, Japanese) – specify when booking. Strictly no photography. 110F. ☎ 51 64 11 11.

Écomusée de la Vendée – Open May to September, daily except Mondays, 1000-1900; rest of the year (closed January), daily except Mondays, 1000-1200 and 1400-1800. 12F. ☎ 51 57 60 60.

Le Grand Parcours – Open June to mid September, daily except Mondays, 1000-1900; May, Sundays and official holidays, 1000-1900. 75F. ☎ 51 57 66 66.

R

Île de RÉ

The Viaduct – Toll per car : June to September, 110F Rtn; rest of the year, 60F Rtn. No charge for pedestrians.

Réserve Naturelle de Lilleau des Niges – Guided tour (2hrs 30min-3hrs) all year, daily, 0900-1130 and 1600-1830. 30F. ☏ 46 29 45 11 in season, 46 82 12 34 out of season.

Boat trips – *From June to September there are regular trips to Île d'Aix, cruises around the island and towards Île d'Oléron, up the River Charente (embark at St-Savinien) and on the River Sèvre Niortaise. Contact Croisières Inter-Îles et Fluviales, ☏ 49 09 87 27.*

Hôtel de Clerjotte : Musée Ernest-Cognacq – Open July to September, daily except Tuesdays, 1000-1900; October to June but closed one month in January or February, daily except Monday and Tuesday, 1000-1200 and 1400-1700. 21F. ☏ 46 09 21 22.

Ars-en-Ré : Église St-Étienne – Church open all year, daily, 0800-1900. **Belfry** : Guided tour July and August, daily, 1000-1230 and 1530-1800.

St-Clément-des-Baleines : Maison des Marais – *Open mid June to mid September, daily, 1000-1230 and 1500-1900. ☏ 46 99 59 97.*

L'Arche de Noé – Open Easter holidays to last Sunday in September, daily, 1000-1900; February and November school holidays, daily, 1400-1800. 39F. ☏ 46 29 23 23.

Phare des Baleines – Open all year, weather permitting, daily, 1000-1200 and 1400-1800 (1700 in winter). Donation appreciated.

Pays de RETZ

Bourgneuf-en-Retz : Musée du Pays de Retz – Open July to August, daily, 1030-1830; late March to June and September to mid November, daily except Tuesdays, 1000-1200 and 1400-1800.15F. ☏ 40 21 40 83.

Château du Bois-Chevalier – Guided tour (45min) April to September, daily, 0930-1200 and 1400-1900. 15F. ☏ 40 26 62 18.

ROCHE-COURBON

Château – Guided tour (45min) mid June to mid September, daily, 1000-1200 and 1430-1830; rest of the year (but closed mid February to mid March), daily except Thursdays, 1000-1200 and 1430-1830 (1730 December to March). 25F. The gardens and grottoes are open all year, 18F. ☏ 46 95 60 10.

ROCHEFORT

i Avenue Sadi-Carnot – 17300 ☏ 46 99 08 60

Maison de Pierre Loti – Guided tour (1hr) Sundays at 1400, 1500 and 1600, rest of the week at 1000, 1100, 1400, 1500 and 1600 : July to September, daily; mid January to June and October to mid December, daily except Tuesdays. 40F. ☏ 46 99 16 88.

Musée d'Art et d'Histoire – Open July to September, daily, 1330-1900; rest of the year, Tuesday to Saturday, 1330-1730. 10F. ☏ 46 99 83 99.

Hôtel de Cheusses : Musée de la Marine – Open all year (closed mid October to mid November), daily, 1000-1200 and 1400-1800. 25F. ☏ 46 99 86 57.

Corderie Royale : Centre International de la Mer – Open July to August, daily, 0900-2000; rest of the year, daily, 0900-1900 (1800 in winter). 25F. ☏ 46 87 01 90.

Les Métiers de Mercure – Open July to August, daily, 1000-2100; February to June and September to December, daily except Tuesdays, 1000-1200 (not Sundays) and 1400-1900. 30F. ☏ 46 83 91 50.

Conservatoire du Bégonia – Guided tour (30-45min) by appointment, all year, Tuesday and Thursday at 1500 and 1600. 15F. ☏ 46 99 08 26.

ROCHEFOUCAULD

i Halle aux Grains, Place de Gourville – 16110. ☏ 45 63 07 45

Château – Open June to September, daily, 1000-1900; rest of the year, Sundays and official holidays, 1000-1900. 35F. ☏ 45 63 54 94. Explanatory panels in seven different languages.

Ancienne Pharmacie de L'hôpital – Guided tour (30min) all year, daily, 1000-1200 and 1400-1600. No charge. ☏ 45 67 54 00.

La ROCHELLE

i Gabut district : Place de la Petite-Sirène – 17000. ☏ 46 41 14 68

Boat trips – Cruises around the roadstead (50min) depart from Cours des Dames and operate from Palm Sunday to mid November : contact M Guilloteau, ☏ 46 44 01 12. For cruises around the islands (Aix, Oléron, Ré), towards La Tranche-sur-Mer, up the River Sèvre Niortaise, or up the River Charente (depart from St-Savinien), contact Croisières Inter-Îles et Fluviales, 14 *bis* Cours des Dames. ☏ 46 50 55 54. For coach trips to St-Savinien apply to Océcars, ☏ 46 41 93 93.

Tour St-Nicolas – Open June to August, daily, 0930-1900; rest of the year, daily, 0930-1230 and 1400-1830 (1700 October to March). 20F. ☏ 46 41 74 13.

Tour de la Chaîne – Open April to September, daily, 1000-1200 and 1400-1830; February, March and October to December, daily, 1400-1800. 20F. ☏ 46 50 52 36.

Tour de la Lanterne – Open June to August, daily, 0930-1900; rest of the year, daily, 0930-1230 and 1400-1830 (1700 October to March). 20F. ☏ 46 41 56 04.

La ROCHELLE

Maison Henri-II – *Open July to August, Monday to Friday, 1000-1200 and 1400-1800. ☎ 46 34 88 59.*

Cathédrale St-Louis : treasury – Open July to August, Mondays and Wednesday to Saturday, 1000-1200 and 1400-1700. No charge.

Hôtel de Ville – Guided tour (45min), official functions permitting, July to August, daily at 1500 and 1600; June and September, daily at 1500; rest of the year, weekends and school holidays at 1500 and 1600. 16F. ☎ 46 41 14 68 (Tourist Information Centre).

Aquarium – Open July to August, daily, 0900-2300; May to June, daily, 0900-1900; rest of the year, daily, 1000-1200 and 1400-1900. 39F. ☎ 46 44 00 00.

Musée Océanographique – Open June and September, Tuesday to Saturday, 1000-1830, Sundays 1430-1830; rest of the year, Tuesday to Saturday, 1000-1200 and 1400-1730, Sundays, 1430-1730. 16F. ☎ 46 45 17 87. Seal-feeding at 1100 and 1630.

Musée d'Histoire Naturelle – Open all year, Tuesday to Friday, 1000-1230 and 1330-1730, weekends, 1400-1800. 16F. ☎ 46 41 18 25.

Musée du Nouveau Monde – Open all year, Mondays and Wednesday to Saturday, 1030-1230 and 1330-1800, Sundays, 1500-1800. 16F. ☎ 46 41 46 50.

Musée des Beaux-Arts – Open all year, daily except Tuesdays, 1400-1700. 16F. 46 41 64 65.

Musée d'Orbigny-Bernon – Open all year, daily except Tuesdays, 1000-1200 (not Sundays) and 1400-1800. 16F. ☎ 46 41 18 83.

Musée Maritime : Frégate France I – *Open 1000-1900. 33F. ☎ 46 50 58 88.*

Musée Grévin – *Open June to mid September, daily, 0930-2300; rest of the year (closed January), daily, 0930-1900. 25F. ☎ 46 41 08 71.*

Musée des Automates – Open June to August, daily, 0930-1900; February to May and September to October, daily, 1000-1200 and 1400-1800; November to December, daily, 1400-1800. 35F. ☎ 46 41 68 08 or 46 45 31 27.

Musée des Modèles Réduits – Same admission times and charges as the Musée des Automates *(see above)*.

Musée Rochelais de la Dernière Guerre – *Open July to August, Tuesday to Saturday, 1000-1800. 22F. ☎ 46 34 12 92.*

Musée du Flacon à Parfum – Open July to August, Mondays, 1500-1900, Tuesday to Saturday, 1000-1900, Sundays, 1500-1800; rest of the year, Mondays, 1500-1900, Tuesday to Saturday, 1000-1900. 22F. ☎ 46 41 32 40.

Temple Protestant – *Open July to August, Monday to Saturday, 1430-1800, Sundays, 1030-1200 and 1430-1800; rest of the year, by appointment. ☎ 46 41 32 84.*

La ROCHE-SUR-YON — Gallerie Bonaparte, Place Napoléon – 85000. ☎ 51 36 00 85

Museum – Open all year, daily except Tuesdays, 1400-1800. 15F. ☎ 51 47 48 50.

Haras – Guided tour (1hr) July to August, Monday to Saturday, 1000-1700; September to mid February by appointment, Monday to Friday, 1500-1700. 15F. ☎ 51 37 01 85.

ROYAN — Palais de Congrès – 17200. ☎ 46 38 65 11

Boat trips – *To Cordouan lighthouse, ☎ 46 05 29 91.*

Zoo de La Palmyre – Open April to November, daily, 0900-1900; December to March, daily, 0900-1200 and 1400-1700. 55F. ☎ 46 22 46 06.

Forêt de la Coubre – Guided tour (2hrs) available, mid July to mid August : on odd days, tour of the dunes; on even days, tour of the forest. 35F. ☎ 46 22 43 60.

S

Les SABLES-D'OLONNE — Rue du Maréchal-Leclerc – 85100. ☎ 51 32 03 28

Salt-marshes – *For guided tours on foot or on the small tourist train, contact the Tourist Information Centre.*

Boat trips – *Operated by Croisières Inter-Îles et Fluviales. ☎ 51 21 31 43.*

Parc Zoologique de Tranchet – Open May to September, daily, 0930-1900; mid February to April and mid September to October, daily, 1030-1200 and 1400-1800; November to mid February, daily, 1400-1800. 48F. ☎ 51 95 14 10.

Musée de l'Abbaye Ste-Croix – Open mid June to mid September, daily except Mondays, 1000-1200 and 1430-1830; rest of the year, daily except Mondays, 1430-1730. 30F. ☎ 51 32 01 16.

Musée des Guerres de Vendée – *Open April to September, daily, 1000-1230 and 1500-1900. 16F. ☎ 51 95 83 57.*

Tour d'Arundel – *Access to the top all year, 0900-1730 (1900 in summer). If closed, apply to the keeper's house, next door. ☎ 51 32 08 34.*

Château de Pierre-Levée – Tour of the west courtyard only.

Observatoire d'Oiseaux de l'Île d'Olonne – Open July to August, daily, 0930-1200 and 1500-1900. No charge. ☎ 51 33 12 97.

ST-BERTRAND-DE-COMMINGES

Cathédrale Ste-Marie-de-Comminges – Open April to October, Monday to Saturday, 0900-1200 and 1400-1900 (1800 in October), Sunday 0900-1030 and 1400-1900 (1800 in October); rest of the year, Monday to Saturday, 1000-1200 and 1400-1700, Sunday 1400-1700 (1800 in March).

Valcabrère : Basilique St-Just – Open Easter to mid November and school holidays, daily, 1000-1200 and 1400-1900; rest of the year, Sunday, 1000-1200 and 1400-1900.

St-Gaudens : Musée de St-Gaudens et du Comminges – Guided tour (45min-1hr) all year, Monday to Saturday, 0900-1200 and 1400-1830. 15F. ☎ 61 94 78 70.

ST-ÉMILION

🅸 Place des Créneaux – 33330. ☎ 57 24 72 03

Monolithic Church : belfry – Open all year (closed 1 week in January), daily, 0930-1230 and 1345-1830 (1800 November to March). 6F. ☎ 57 24 72 03.

Chapelle de la Trinité – Guided tour (45min) all year (closed January) at 1000, 1045, 1130, 1400, 1445, 1530, 1615 (and 1700 April to October). 33F. ☎ 57 24 72 03.

Cloître des Cordeliers – Guided tour (20min) all year, daily, 0900-1900. No charge. ☎ 56 39 24 05.

Collegiate Church Cloisters – Open as for the Monolithic Church. No charge. ☎ 57 24 72 03.

Logis de Malet de Roquefort : Archeological Museum – Open mid May to mid October, daily except Monday, 1030-1230 and 1430-1830. 5F. ☎ 57 24 72 52.

SAINTES

🅸 Villa Musso, 62 Cours National – 17100. ☎ 46 74 23 82

Musée Archéologique – Open daily except Monday : June to August, 1000-1800; April to May and September, 1000-1200 and 1400-1800; rest of the year, 1400-1730. ☎ 46 74 20 97.

Cathédrale St-Pierre : treasury – *Open July to August and over the Easter period, daily, 1400-1800; rest of the year, apply to the presbytery (presbytère), ☎ 46 93 09 92.*

Musée Dupuy-Mestreau – *Open afternoons. For details ☎ 46 93 36 71.*

Musée des Beaux-Arts – Open April to September, daily except Tuesdays, 1000-1200 and 1400-1800; rest of the year, Mondays and Wednesday to Saturday, 1000-1200 and 1400-1730, Sundays, 1500-1800. 10F, no charge October to March. ☎ 46 93 03 94.

Musée de l'Échevinage – Same admission times as the Musée des Beaux-Arts *(see above).*

Musée Éducatif de Préhistoire – Guided tour (1hr) all year, daily, 1000-1200 and 1500-1800. Donation expected. ☎ 46 93 43 27.

Haras – Open mid July to September, daily, 1500-1700; October to February, daily, 1400-1600. No charge. ☎ 46 74 35 91.

St-Romain-de-Benet : Musée des Alambics – *Guided tour July to August, daily. ☎ 46 02 00 14.*

Le Douhet Château – Open April to October, daily, 1000-1200 and 1400-1900; rest of the year, Sundays and school holidays, 1400-1730. 25F; 35F with museum; 17F grounds only. ☎ 46 97 78 14.

Abbaye de Fontdouce – Guided tour (45min) July to August, daily except Sunday mornings, 1000-1200 and 1430-1830; late May to June and September to October, Sundays, 1430-1830. 18F. ☎ 45 82 76 00.

ST-GILLES-CROIX-DE-VIE

Boat trips – Apply to the Tourist Information Centre.

La Bourrine de Bois Juquaud – Open June to September, Tuesday to Saturday (and Mondays July to August), 1000-1200 and 1430-1830, Sundays 1500-1900; April, May and October, Tuesday to Saturday, 1400-1800. 12F. ☎ 51 49 27 37 in season, 51 54 31 97 (Tourist Information Centre).

ST-JEAN-DE-LUZ

🅸 Place Maréchal-Foch – 64500. ☎ 59 26 03 16

Maison Louis-XIV – Guided tour (30min) June to August, Monday to Saturday, 1030-1200 and 1430-1800 (1730 June); Sundays, June and July, 1030-1200. No charge.

ST-SAVIN

Abbey – Open July to August, daily, 0930-1900; mid May to June and September, daily, 0930-1230 and 1330-1830; rest of the year, weekends (not January and February) by appointment.

ST-VINCENT-SUR-JARD

Maison de Clemenceau – Guided tour (30min) April to September, daily, 0930-1230 and 1400-1800 (1900 July to August); rest of the year, daily except Tuesdays, 0930-1230 and 1400-1700. 20F. ☎ 51 33 40 32.

Abbaye Notre-Dame-de-Lieu-Dieu – Guided tour (45min) July to August, daily, 1000-1200 and 1400-1800. 15F. ☎ 51 33 40 06.

St-Hilaire-la-Forêt : CAIRN – Open early July to early September, daily except Monday mornings, 1000-1230 and 1430-1900; early April to early July and early September to early October, Monday to Friday and Sundays, 1500-1800. Guided tour (1hr 30min) available in high season at 1030; in low season, Sundays and official holidays at 1515. Film show in high season from 1500-1800. 36F. ☎ 51 33 38 38.

Château de la Guignardière – Guided tour (45min-1hr) mid June to September, daily, 1000-1900. 30F, gardens and grounds only 15F. ☎ 51 22 33 06.

SAUVETERRE-DE-BÉARN

ℹ Mairie – 64390. ☎ 59 38 50 17

Château de Laàs – Guided tour (1hr) April to October, daily except Tuesdays, 1000-1900. 20F. ☎ 59 38 91 53. **Maison du Mais :** open same hours as the château.

La SOULE

Mauléon-Licharre : Château d'Andurain – Guided tour July to mid September, Monday to Saturday (closed Thursdays), 1100-1200 and 1500-1800, Sunday, 1500-1800. 25F. ☎ 59 28 00 24.

Gorges de Kakouetta – Open July to October, daily, 0800-1900. 20F. ☎ 59 28 73 44 or 59 28 60 83.

Chapelle St-Sauveur – Apply to the presbytery (presbytère) in Mendive.

T

TARBES

ℹ 3 Cours Gambetta – 65000. ☎ 62 51 30 31

Musée Massey – Open July to August, 1000-1200 and 1400-1830; rest of the year, daily except Monday and Tuesday, 1000-1200 and 1400-1800 (1730 December to January). 20F. ☎ 62 36 31 49.

Maison natale du Maréchal Foch – Guided tour (45min) all year, daily except Tuesdays and Wednesdays, 0900-1200 and 1400-1800 (1700 October to April). 13F. ☎ 62 93 19 02.

Haras – Monday to Friday by prior arrangement (usually two weeks). Contact the Office de Tourisme, 65000 Tarbes, ☎ 62 51 30 31.

Parc Ornithologique du TEICH

Nature reserve – Open all year, daily, 1000-1800. 31F. ☎ 56 22 80 93.

THOUARS

ℹ 17 Place St-Médard – 79100. ☎ 49 66 17 65

Airvault : Musée des Arts et traditions populaires – Open July to mid September, daily, 1430-1800; early April to June, daily, 1400-1700. 15F. ☎ 49 64 70 13.

TIFFAUGES

Château – Open July to August, daily, 1000-1200 and 1400-1900; April to June and September, daily except Wednesday, 1000-1200 and 1400-1800. 30F. ☎ 51 65 70 51.

TOUFFOU

Château – *Guided tour (30min) mid June to August, daily except Mondays, 0900-1200 and 1400-1900. 20F.*

V

VILLENEUVE-SUR-LOT

Musée municipal – Closed for extensive works. Ring for details, ☎ 53 70 01 12.

VOUVANT

Château : Tour Mélusine – *To visit, apply to the Café du Centre, ☎ 51 00 81 34. 2F.*

Y

Île d'YEU

ℹ Place du Marché, Port-Joinville – 85350. ☎ 51 58 32 58

Access – By boat : from Fromentine (35min or 1hr 10min), contact Régie Départementale des Passages d'Eau de la Vendée, BP 16, 85550 La Barre-de-Monts. ☎ 51 68 52 32; from Île de Noirmoutier, late March to early October, contact Navix, ☎ 51 39 00 00; from Barbâtre and St-Gilles-Croix-de-Vie, in season, contact Vedettes Inter-Îles Vendéennes, 85630 Barbâtre, ☎ 51 39 00 00.

Port-Joinville : le Musée-Historial – Open July to late August, daily, 1030-1200 and 1600-1800. 20F. ☎ 51 58 36 88.

Élevage d'anguilles – *Guided tour daily except Sundays, 1130-1200 and 1730-1800. 20F. ☎ 51 58 32 72.*

Grand Phare – Open Easter to September, daily, 0930-1200 and 1400-1700. Donation appreciated. ☎ 51 58 30 61.

INDEX

Fontenay-le-Comte .... Towns, sights and tourist regions. Isolated sights (dams, castles, dolmens, points...) are listed under their proper name.

La Rochejaquelein .... People, historical events and subjects.

The Département is given in brackets after the town, see abbreviations below:

Char.-Mar.: Charente-Maritime H.-Gar.: Haute-Garonne L.-et-G.: Lot-et-Garonne
H.-Pyr.: Hautes-Pyrénées Pyr.-Atl.: Pyrénées-Atlantiques
Tarn-et-Gar. : Tarn-et-Garonne

G

H - I

J - K

L

M

S

T

U - V - W - Y - Z

MANUFACTURE FRANÇAISE DES PNEUMATIQUES MICHELIN
Société en commandite par actions au capital de 2 000 000 000 de francs
Place des Carmes-Déchaux - 63 Clermont-Ferrand (France)
R.C.S. Clermont-Fd B 855 200 507

Dépôt légal novembre 1994 - ISBN 2-06-138001-B - ISSN 0763-1383

Printed in the EC 10-94-20
Photocomposition : A.P.S., Tours - Impression : I.M.E., Baume-les-Dames - N° 9589
Brochage : S.I.R.C., Marigny-le-Châtel